THE AMERICAN JOURNEY
OF ERIC SEVAREID

THE AMERICAN JOURNEY
OF ERIC SEVAREID

RAYMOND A. SCHROTH

STEERFORTH PRESS

SOUTH ROYALTON, VERMONT

Library of Congress Cataloging-in-Publication Data
Schroth, Raymond A.
The American Journey of Eric Sevareid / Raymond A. Schroth.
Includes bibliographical references and index.
p.   cm.
ISBN 1–883642–12–4
1. Sevareid, Eric, 1912–   . 2. Television journalists —
United States — Biography.
I. Title.
PN4874.S43S37   1995
070'.92—dc20   94–44441

First Edition

For Mary Gibbons-Holl
1952–1993

CONTENTS

Preface   ix
Introduction   xiii

 1 Velva   1
 2 Canoe Trip   21
 3 West by Rail   43
 4 University Years   53
 5 Marriage   83
 6 Fired   97
 7 Paris   109
 8 Flight   129
 9 London   161
10 Home   181
11 Burma   205
12 Climax   235
13 The Dream   267
14 Valley Lane   281
15 Finding His Voice   291
16 Adlai   305
17 Divorce   329
18 Vietnam   351
19 Nixon   383
20 Belen   391
21 Peace   401

Acknowledgments   429
Notes and Sources   433
Selected Bibliography   447
Index   451

PREFACE

WHY ERIC SEVAREID?
It began when I was a seventeen-year-old freshman at Fordham University in New York in 1951. Like all Jesuit colleges in those days, Fordham made some effort, which we naturally resisted, to instill some order and discipline into our daily lives; so we were supposed to be in bed with our lights out at 11 P.M. I may have had my lights out, but I was not asleep. My ear was glued to the CBS news emanating from the little radio by the side of my bed, waiting for the distinctive, thoughtful voice of the man with an unusual name who came on for the last few minutes with his little essay. One that stuck was a piece on Harold Stassen, whose only sport, Sevareid said, was rifle marksmanship, which is cool competition with oneself. I had been pretty good at rifle marksmanship myself, and I knew that he was right. Another was about the governor of Illinois, of whom I had never heard before and who might make a good president of the United States. Adlai Stevenson became my second hero in American politics. FDR, of course, was the first.

From then on, indeed for the rest of my life, Eric Sevareid remained one on a short list of journalists—the others are James Reston, Anthony Lewis, I. F. Stone, Tom Wicker, and Jim Dwyer—whose thoughts and words really mattered to me, who either spoke my thoughts better than I could myself or made me rethink my own position.

So when I saw a sabbatical ahead, I knew it was time to write another book; and when Jack Deedy, a friend from my days at *Commonweal,* said, "Do Eric Sevareid," I knew he was right.

I never met Eric Sevareid while he was alive. Once in the mid 1960s I wrote inviting him to speak to us at Woodstock College, the Jesuits theology school outside Baltimore, and he politely declined. After a year reading through his papers in the Library of Congress and interviewing over eighty men and women who knew him from his first years in Velva to his last in Georgetown, I sometimes think I can sense his presence, or imagine how the atmosphere in a room might change if he were to enter. And I have a fairly clear idea of what he would say today about Haiti, Somalia, Bill Clinton, health care reform, or multiculturalism. But he remains an elusive figure in death as he was in life—which is probably the way he would want it.

The highpoints of my research were climbing the hills overlooking his birthplace in Velva, North Dakota, looking out over the wheat fields and the Mouse River; visiting Eric's old friend and canoeing companion, Walter Port, in Minneapolis just a few months before his death; discovering in the archives of the University of Minnesota Eric's application to be editor of the *Minnesota Daily*; and climbing another hill in Virginia to find his beloved cabin retreat.

But the greatest satisfaction has been the privilege of reading so many pages and paragraphs where Sevareid's words reinforced my own ideals. Recently Eric's sister-in-law, Celia Brokaw Sevareid, sent me a few of Eric's lines which she had copied from a book called *Minnesota Writers* in 1945:

> Early, I came to the conclusion that the deciding, the important planes of human thought and action in my generation are the political, the social. I had to move and think in that dimension. The world was rolling itself toward possible destruction too rapidly for me to sit in an ivory tower, and coddle my precious imagination and cherish my precious words and phrases. Unless the world was saved pretty quickly there wouldn't be any ivory towers, nor any ivory to build them, and there wouldn't be any literature of any kind.
>
> If the world . . . has saved itself, I'll feel I had something to do with it, not much, but something . . . So if my artistic sense doesn't feel well-fed, my conscience, my social conscience does.

When he wrote those lines, the world had just been saved, so it seemed, from fascism; and the saviors were able to succeed, he believed, because they were committed to human brotherhood.

If this book stirs in the heart of one reader even a fleeting sense of human solidarity and our responsibilities toward one another, my conscience too will be well-fed.

I dedicate this book to Mary Gibbons-Holl. When I taught journalism at Fordham in the 1970s, two of my best friends were John Holl and Mary Gibbons. John was editor of the *Fordham Ram,* and Mary was also a student leader. Occasionally, late on Saturday night, we would sit talking journalism over a few drinks in a wonderful old bar under the Third Avenue El called the El-Dorado, "the El-D"; and John and Mary were kind enough to laugh when I slipped into my spontaneous imitations of Eric Sevareid and Winston Burdette . . . "in *Rome,*" which Winston delivered with a dramatic tremolo in his diaphram. I celebrated their wedding in the Fordham chapel, and we spent New Year's Eve together for many years. John became an assistant attorney general in the Department of Law and Public Safety of the State of New Jersey, and Mary, the mother of two sons, John Gibbons and Thomas Francis, got a master's degree and taught religion.

The last week in September, 1993, we had dinner together, and I was full of Eric and they were full of encouragement and fun. Two days later, Mary died of a cerebral hemorrhage, her third, while I was on my way to Boston to interview Janet Murrow. She already lives on in many lives, but I am privileged to have her live in these pages too.

Raymond A. Schroth, S.J.
Loyola University,
New Orleans,
Thanksgiving Day, 1994

INTRODUCTION

IT IS WEDNESDAY evening, October 21, 1970.

"This is the CBS Evening News with Walter Cronkite. With Eric Sevareid in Washington, Mike Stanley in Washington, David Culhane in Montreal, Murray Fromson in Wichita, and Mike Wallace in New York."

Cronkite sits in profile at the managing editor's desk, shuffles papers. Glasses on desk.

"Good evening."

Those viewers who read the *New York Times* and the *Washington Post* every day already have a head full of events and some of the images that go with them. In Fort Hood, Texas, an army court martial has heard testimony of how screaming Vietnamese women, children, and old men were shoved into a ditch and shot by Lieutenant William L. Calley, Jr. In Mexico City, Lazaro Cardenas, the president of Mexico since 1934, is dead. At Ohio's Kent State University, where national guardsmen shot and killed four student demonstrators the previous May, police arrested a student leader and a teacher in a roundup of twenty-five persons indicted for their role in the demonstrations. The controversial professor, a socialist who also ran an antipoverty program in Akron, had once described the manufacture of a Molotov cocktail to his class. Kent State student leaders called for nonviolent protests across the country the coming weekend.

In excerpts from her diary published in *McCall's* magazine, Lady Bird Johnson revealed that exactly one month after ordering the bombing of North Vietnam in 1965, President Johnson said to her, "I can't get out. I can't finish it with what I've got. So what the hell can I do?"

In New York, in a case which the defendants called politically motivated, thirteen members of the Black Panther party went on trial on charges of plotting to kill policemen and blow up buildings. President Nixon swung through the Middle West telling the American heartland that "a rising tide of terrorism and crime" could be stemmed only by voting for Republicans in November. In New York, Republican mayor John Lindsay endorsed the Democratic candidate, former Supreme Court Justice Arthur Goldberg, for governor over Nelson Rockefeller.

In Montreal, labor minister Pierre Laporte, kidnapped and slain by terrorists, was buried. On the *New York Times* op-ed page, Yale law professor Charles Reich said that, thanks to the young—"the generation of Consciousness III"—"Faces are gentler and more beautiful. People are better with each other. There are more smiles, more love. There is new hope, for young people have discovered the future, where until recently no future could even be imagined." In California, Dr. Victor Ohta, a wealthy eye doctor considered one of the "beautiful people," was found —along with his wife, secretary, and two sons—strangled and shot and floating in the blood-tinted waters of his swimming pool.

Meanwhile, Vice President Spiro T. Agnew, who since 1969 had been leading what he himself called, "the politics of polarization," the Nixon administration's strategy for isolating its critics by vigorously attacking them, charged in Chicago that he was the victim of a "hate" campaign abetted by the national press. On a talk show he also proposed that some kind of panel of public figures be set up to quiz TV commentators, specifically CBS's Eric Sevareid and ABC's Howard K. Smith, about what their opinions were. "The people who are watching that tube have a right to know what your opinions are, if you happen to be a man who is telling the news every night because you can select what parts of the news you want to emphasize and by your language you can convey a point of view that is not an editorial and yet is colored by your viewpoints."

No one was more conscious of the fact that TV must select what it covers than Walter Cronkite. On an average day the *New York Times* put twelve stories on page one, the *Washington Post*, nine. But the reader could study the in-depth coverage in the *Times* and *Post* for hours. The evening news is mostly a headline service, cramming at most, as it did this night, sixteen items—treating only five in any depth, of two minutes or a little more—into a twenty-two-minute "news hole."

The lead story: inflation rises as cost of living goes up one-half of one percent. Presidential economic adviser Paul McCracken says the economy is making real progress. Representative Wilbur Mills is deeply concerned about the future of the country because of the rising deficit— the amount by which federal expenditures exceed tax revenues. The stock market falls slightly. Geritol is one of the nice things you can do for yourself. Lectric Shave makes electric shaving smoother than a barber's shave. Pierre LaPorte was not shot but strangled by a religious medal chain around his neck. Three barefoot hippies are being sought for killing Dr. Ohta and family. Chief Justice Earl Warren says that injustice to minorities remains the nation's biggest problem. Klear Floor Wax never yellows. Two generals die in a plane crash in Turkey. No cease fire announcement in Saigon. In New York, Nixon backs James Buckley for senator rather than Republican Vietnam War critic Charles Goodell. Nelson Rockefeller puts on a hard hat and rides a bulldozer. Arthur Goldberg admits he's a bit aloof and dull. An Iowa agronomist working in Mexico gets the Nobel Peace Prize for developing "miracle wheat." Forty of sixty-four rats fed enriched white bread for ninety days starve to death. A little girl on horseback who uses Crest has no cavities. In Northern Ireland, Bernadette Devlin is released after serving four months of a six-month sentence. In Algiers, Black Panther leader Eldridge Cleaver says escaped radical Bernadine Dorn, along with escapee Timothy Leary, is in Algiers.

Then, a few seconds ahead of time, Agnew's face appears on the screen behind Cronkite's head.

Then Eric Sevareid's.

It is a long, craggy Nordic head, with a wide brow topped by a full head of gray hair streaked with dark brown. The high, prominent, cheek bones emphasize the dark depth of his eyes. It is a handsome head—so handsome that when it first appeared on Edward R. Murrow's pioneer documentary *See It Now* in 1951, Murrow joked about taking him off the air because he didn't want anyone on the program whom the ladies found more striking than himself.

But it is an unsmiling, solemn visage. Probably because he grew up in semipoverty in the 1920s and 1930s and, throughout his life, knew little about diet and nutrition, his teeth are bad; and though his frame is large, his shoulders seem stooped, and his body emanates a certain fragility. He has been broadcasting for more than thirty years, but he is clearly uncomfortable, and in the two or so minutes he speaks he will gulp or pause to swallow six times.

Twenty million people watch him every night. In the first weeks of World War II, as his sometimes quavering voice brought the radio news of the first bombing of Paris into American living rooms, he became an instant celebrity. A 1974 Roper survey found that 66 percent of those polled recognized Sevareid.

Yet few viewers guess that the brooding face of this principled but very private man masks a personal life suffused with sadness and even scandal.

He has spent the whole day thinking, talking, listening, then finally typing out what he is about to say. He has scoured the papers and passed over the New York political race, the Black Panthers, the murdered Canadian minister and California family, and focused on Spiro Agnew for many reasons. In Chicago, Agnew scrapped with the Democratic senatorial candidate Adlai Stevenson, III—son of Eric's late friend—and Stevenson called him a "peddler of hate." The next day in Baltimore, Agnew labeled Senator Joseph Tydings a "radical liberal." In that morning's *Times*, Eric's friend James "Scotty" Reston, in a column modeled on Poor Richard's Almanac, twitted Agnew with an instant aphorism, "Vice Presidents rush in where Presidents fear to tread"; and in the *Post*, Marquis Childs pointed out that Agnew's campaign resembled Vice President Nixon's in 1958, slamming the opposition and building political strength for himself.

But, most important, Agnew had attacked Sevareid personally; not an attack on his character or patriotism this time, but a misrepresentation of what he does—and thus who he is.

Sevareid had been writing and speaking all his life, but Agnew was saying that a panel should find out Sevareid's opinions, as if he had been hiding his true beliefs and pressing a secret and sinister agenda. The real point was that the government in power did not like what Sevareid said and was trying, by this blunt intimidation, to shut him up. So, in this "analysis"—one of several thousand he did for CBS during his career—Sevareid would have to say what it was that he did and, without editorializing, say why Agnew was dangerous.

> Mr. Agnew wants to know where we stand. We stand, or rather, sit, right here, in full glare, at a disadvantage as against politicians. We can't cast one vote in committee, an opposite vote on the floor.

We can't say one thing in the North, an opposite thing in the South. We hold no tenure, four years or otherwise, and can be voted out with a twist of the dial.

We cannot use invective and epithets, cannot even dream of impugning the patriotism of leading citizens, cannot reduce every complicated issue to yes or no, black or white, and would rather go to jail than do bodily injury to the English language.

We can't come down on this side or that side of each disputed public issue because we're trying to explain far more than to advocate, and because some issues don't have two sides; some have three, four or half a dozen, and in these matters we're damned if we know the right answer. This may be why most of us look a bit frazzled, while Mr. Agnew looks so serene.

Another reason may be that we have to think our own thoughts and write our own phrases. Unlike the Vice President, we don't possess a stable of ghost writers. Come to think of it, if there are mysteries around, unseen spirits motivating the public dialogue, maybe that's the place that could use the glare of public scrutiny— that stable of anonymity.

Finally, at the risk of sounding a bit stuffy, we might say two things. One, that nobody in this business expects for a moment that the full truth of anything will be contained in any one account or commentary, but that through free reporting and discussion, as Mr. Walter Lippmann put it, the truth will emerge.

And second, that the central point about the free press is not that it be accurate, though it must try to be, not that it even be fair, though it must try to be that, but that it be free. And that means, in the first instance, freedom from any and all attempts by any power of government to coerce it or intimidate it in any way.

Now it is Wednesday afternoon, September 16, 1992.

"I can't believe he's gone," Richard Salant said to Emerson Stone, as they had made their way from New Canaan, Connecticut, to the National Press Building in Washington, D.C. Yet Salant—president of CBS News for sixteen years and guardian of its values during the Vietnam War and Watergate years—knew too well that Eric Sevareid was gone.

For weeks he had been working over two speeches he had to give about his old friend who had died July 9: one that afternoon at the memorial service; the other a talk four days later at the New Canaan Public Library, establishing, with his personal gift, an Eric Sevareid News Center to encourage "news literacy." Except for explaining how Eric himself was "like a library," the texts would be much the same, but the audiences would be very different.

Like members of a huge family, many of whom are estranged from or strangers to one another and who gather in the attorney's office for the reading of a will, not all of the seven scheduled speakers and almost three hundred guests who filed into the grand ballroom at the National Press Club were fond of one another.

In Peter J. Boyer's book *Who Killed CBS?* (1989), Salant had said of Howard Stringer, president of the CBS Broadcast Group, who like Salant was scheduled to speak, "He's a dishonest son of a bitch. He's so ambitious that he's manipulative." Stringer was widely despised by CBS's older generation of newsmen—"Murrow's Boys," and those trained and nurtured by the founders like William Paley, Frank Stanton, and Salant—as one of those who had sold out the tradition of news excellence for ratings and profits. The massive budget cuts and two hundred firings of 1987, carried out by Stringer, had been the executioner's bullet in the head to a news organization that had once been the best in the world. Dan Rather's *New York Times* op-ed protest the next day was headlined, "From Murrow to Mediocrity." Boyer quotes Stringer: "If I hear the words *public trust* one more time, I think I'll shoot someone."

To many of the bright and ambitious young men and women who came along in the 1980s, who developed the term "sound bite," and who were wizards with the new graphics and satellite technology, the older generation were nostalgic whiners devoted to dead formats like plodding documentaries and lacking in marketing smarts. In short, a good number of those in the room felt that the institution that had once set the standards for broadcast journalism had lost its identity, its moorings, and much of its prestige. But for Eric Sevareid, dead of stomach cancer after fifteen years in retirement—the CBS news analyst and writer who dwelled with Walter Lippmann and Edward R. Murrow in a pantheon of twentieth-century journalists—they shared a solid respect, even love.

On the status of his legacy, which was spiritual rather than material, they might disagree. His legacy was an attitude toward journalism that he had picked up in North Dakota at the age of six hanging out in the office of the Velva *Journal,* that he had adapted to covering the fall of France and his survival in a Burma jungle during World War II, and that he honed into an oral literature during more than thirty years of radio and television commentary. The essence of that legacy was a respect for his readers' and listeners' intelligence and for the primacy of the word.

The National Press Club, on the twelfth floor of the National Press Building, is a network of restaurants, watering holes, meeting rooms, and a journalists' Hall of Fame. Sevareid once said of the ballroom, with its dark wood decor and its ceiling of wooden strips laid in, for acoustical effect, like undulating ocean waves: "This room is the sanctum sanctorum of American journalism, it's the Westminster Hall, its Delphi, the Mecca, the Wailing Wall [to] everybody in this country having anything to do with the news business, the only hallowed place I know of that's absolutely bursting with irreverence . . ." and he added later, in an irreverent quip about the ceiling, "Somehow I get the feeling I'm talking into a rolltop desk."

The mood of the guests, most of whom were there by invitation, was, for the most part, relaxed. The family—three children, a widow, her family, relatives from the extended family of Eric's mother—sat toward the front. CBS people—of whom Walter Cronkite was the best known, but who had not been invited to speak—were scattered throughout the room.

Larry LeSueur, one of the last survivors of the original Murrow team, who had covered the London Blitz with Sevareid and known him longer than anyone in the room not related by blood or marriage, had not been invited. But he came anyway, and sat quietly with former NBC newscaster and scholar, Ray Scherer. He scanned the room for familiar faces. There were few.

Some couldn't help remarking that they had been to quite a few funerals and memorial services recently. Still fresh in their memories was the 1985 service for the brilliant and dashing Charles Collingwood, whom Murrow had also hired at the outbreak of World War II. More than twelve hundred people had crammed into Saint Bartholomew's Church on Park Avenue in New York; and even then the generational split was evident. While Dan Rather praised Collingwood from the pulpit for his loyalty to CBS, Bill Moyers, angry that CBS had abandoned the Murrow-Collingwood style of reporting and replaced it with "fluff," stood up and left the church, muttering on the way out, "Hypocrites! If he was so great, why didn't they put him on the air?"

Then Douglas Edwards, the first to do the TV evening news, died; then CBS founder William Paley in 1990. At Paley's service, like this one organized by CBS, two thousand guests—including Richard Nixon and John Lindsay—filled New York's Temple Emmanu-El. He was eulogized by Henry Kissinger, David Rockefeller, Cronkite, and Frank Stanton, who had to walk the delicate line between praising him as a "master builder" and telling the fuller truth. Then Harry Reasoner, who, when CBS failed to use his talents, had moved to ABC.

William L. Shirer, one of original "band of brothers," was still alive and writing his last book in Connecticut. But he was alienated from the brotherhood. Howard K. Smith was writing his memoirs. Larry LeSueur sat unrecognized in the room. To nearly everyone there, Sevareid was the last link with the tradition. And now he was gone.

Dan Rather rose to speak.

He began with an anecdote about rooming with Eric when they covered Nixon's 1971 trip to China. But whatever lighthearted anecdotes this day would elicit, the only way to recapture Eric Sevareid's power to speak to the American people was to imagine that those who had watched *CBS Evening News* in the 1960s and 1970s had stored the tapes of those programs in their heads and now could call up his finest moments.

There was his October 4, 1965, commentary on Pope Paul VI's visit to the United Nations, a fine display of both Eric's sense of history and his own religious awareness:

> Essentially, the United Nations now struggles to impose its authority on a nationalistic world. The Catholic church now struggles to retain its authority in a revolutionary world. Pope John opened the windows of the church. Modern ideas flow in. And the new Pope flies out, to see the world, to be seen, to inspire and to warn. Today he seemed to liken himself in missionary function, to his namesake

Paul, and the U. N. to the Aereopagus where Paul spoke of the Unknown God to the wondering Athenians.

There was January 31, 1967, when the three astronauts killed when their capsule caught fire were buried:

> Grissom and White and Chaffee—mortals who aspired to the moon and eternal space—were returned to the earth today from which they came and to which we all belong.
>
> They had lived more intensely in a very few years than most of us do in our lifetimes and they shall be remembered far longer.
>
> They were among the men who wield the cutting edge of history and by this sword they died.

There was December 23, 1968, when three other astronauts "floated through the blue blackness of space in the neighborhood of the moon":

> Through the television camera in the streaking capsule we can see our whole world, and it appears a small thing, ourselves smaller than crawling ants in the lens of our natural eyes. This is a humbling experience to many, but there is another way of considering man's dimensions which is not so humbling, a sense in which man is enormous. His physical body is, so scientists have said, just about halfway in size between the smallest entity we know, the particle, and the largest entity we know, the galaxy. As for the mind of man, it seems immeasurable, exalting and terrifying in its capabilities. It is, after all, a symbolic coincidence that man imagined and then found the way to put human life on the moon in the same period in which he imagined and then found the way to put an end to all life on his own earth.

There was April 2, 1973, when he paid tribute to the retiring Frank Stanton, the CBS president who, perhaps more than anyone, protected the independence and integrity of CBS News and should have succeeded Paley as chief executive officer if only Paley had had the grace to relinquish control:

> Stanton was always the backstop and in a crisis, the front line.
>
> Sometimes you didn't even know who had silenced the enemy's guns till the fight was long over. Once, in the hysterical Joe Mc-

Carthy days, a powerful senatorial committee chairman proposed a deal to Stanton—he would leave CBS alone provided it got rid of two people, Ed Murrow and that fellow Sevareid. Stanton not only didn't accept it, he didn't even mention it, to Murrow or me.

But certainly few of his analyses matched the power of his words on Wednesday, April 19, 1972, when the futility of the Vietnam War became overpoweringly evident as the level of violence, on the battlefield and at home, exploded. On April 15, while fighting intensified around Hue and a fierce tank and infantry battle was waged for Anloc, sixty miles north of Saigon, Nixon ordered heavy B-52 raids on North Vietnam, including Hanoi and the port of Haiphong. The Soviet Union protested that bombs had hit four of their ships. At Harvard about two hundred students stormed the Center for International Affairs, smashed windows and ransacked offices, and protests erupted at campuses all over the country. On the nineteenth, for the first time, North Vietnamese MIGS strafed and bombed U.S. ships which had been shelling the coast. That afternoon, twenty-eight senators, for over an hour, debated Vietnam policy. Senator Harold Hughes said, "We have bled enough."

In his analysis, Eric Sevareid agreed. To the Nixon-Kissinger argument that these issues are too complex to share with Congress and the people, he responded:

> . . . the trouble is that democracy can't operate in accordance with secret complexities, it can respond only to great simplicities.
>
> One great simplicity is that whatever our obligation to South Vietnam it was paid, long ago; they now possess a million-man army, a forty-thousand man air force with a thousand planes and five hundred helicopters, completely controlling their skies . . .
>
> It is a great simplicity that should the north take the south by force and quickly—rather than through coalition and compromise—a great many southerners would be executed, imprisoned and exiled. But here we are asked to play God, because this is balanced by another great simplicity—every week the shelling and bombing go on, a great many people are being executed, maimed, and exiled from their homes, including the women, the children, the elderly.
>
> If we have reached the dreadful point where the honor of the state and the conscience of the people collide, then what does honor mean, anymore? We are asked to believe it is dishonorable

to depart and risk the safety of Vietnamese political and military leaders, but honorable to go on contributing to the certain death and misery of the wholly innocent.

We are asked to believe that better arrangements with Russia are worth the loss of our own sense of moral identity. There does come a time when the heart must rule the head. That time is when the heart is about to break.

Dan Rather's anecdote was about the night he and Eric shared a room in China. In the middle of the night they were awakened by Chinese employees bringing gifts before their guests departed. Eric sat up suddenly and asked, in his best voice, "Who *are* these men?" The anecdote was more confusing than funny, and revealed little about Eric, except that he had chosen Rather as a roommate.

Robert Craig stepped to the podium as a representative of one of Eric's "other lives"—off camera, the commentator was a roving lecturer, intellectual consultant, and above all, a fly fisherman. Craig had first met Eric in 1957 when he invited him and "Scotty" Reston to the Colorado Aspen Institute, a foundation-sponsored seminar for business leaders concerned about ethics and social issues. Sevareid referred to Aspen occasionally in his essays, and he and Craig began a friendship, based partly on their mutual love of trout fishing and partly on their shared political philosophy—at a time when Eric was becoming more conservative—which lasted till Eric's death.

One time in the early 1970s when they fished "Sixteen Mile Creek, which runs out of the Crazy Mountains north of Bozeman down into the Missouri watershed," Craig could hear Eric struggling with a big fish and calling out, partly in his arthritic pain, "Oh my!" When Craig caught up with him ten minutes later, Eric was on his knees in his waders in shallow water, clutching an enormous, writhing, brown trout —so big his large hands could barely grasp it. With tears in his eyes, he said, "I can't kill this fish, and we have no camera and no one will ever believe me. If it weren't for the snakes, I'd stay with him here for the summer."

Trout fishing for Eric was a metaphysical experience—it abstracted him completely from that worldly data which, because of his temperament, made him very serious. And a return from a fishing vacation, often with Craig, usually left him pining for that simpler rural life into which he had been born and into which he retreated for spiritual renewal as often as he could. On July 17, 1971, he began his commentary, "This reporter has returned to sea level Washington from an eight-thousand-foot elevation among the pines, aspens, elk and the trout streams of Colorado, and, judging by the current state of the Capitols' quarrels, 'descent' is the appropriate verb, spiritually as well as topographically."

Bill Leonard first met Eric when Leonard was starting out with a CBS radio show called *This Is New York;* later Leonard was Eric's boss when Bill took charge of elections, conventions, and documentaries; and they became particularly good friends during Eric's retirement years in Washington. In his tribute he simply let Eric speak for himself, and read the text of his last commentary, which concluded: "Tens of thousands have written their thoughts to me. I will always feel that I stand in their midst."

Erik Bye, of the Norwegian Broadcasting Corporation, explained that *sevareid* meant a low, narrow strip of land connected, usually, with a wilder territory, jutting out into the sea; ancient Viking mariners would save time by hauling their boats, using timber rollers, over this strip of land rather than risking the fury of the North Sea. *Eric* meant chief, king ruler; but, he said, Eric Sevareid always retained the prairie peasant's skepticism of men of power.

Salant began with warm memories—Eric's interviews with the brilliant British dramatic actor, Peter Ustinov, who was playing the parts in a CBS documentary of England's eighteenth-century prime minister Lord North and King George III; and the interview at the Parthenon with the king and queen of Greece, where Eric communed with the oracle at the temple of Delphi—but he also did what he knew Eric would have done had he been materially present: he delivered a short lecture on the ethics of journalism. It was Salant's last chance to stick up for the values he had protected when CBS was his.

> A great reporter must have the keenest of eyes with which to see the world as it is. He must have the warmest of hearts to understand the world and the people in it. He must have the head and the mind to put it all into precisely the right words.

He said there was no substitute for having a "thoughtful journalist on staff with a regular slot and whose last sentence of his piece cannot be predicted from his first sentence." He said this knowing that no network had that person, that the art of the broadcast analysis—that is a regular, thoughtful, independent essay—had died when Sevareid retired in 1977. He tried to tell them that, borrowing the first line from the Gospel of John, "television in the beginning is the word," and that a "talking head" with something to say can be more gripping than irrelevant and distracting pictures.

He said this to people who, when Eric came out of retirement in 1985 to do a commentary on the fortieth anniversary of V-E Day, ran irrelevant file footage of combat with only Eric's voice behind it. Eric had flown to Europe happy to be back in harness after seven years of retirement, ready to reenact the commentary he had delivered forty years before. But the staff members seemed oblivious to who he was or what he represented. The simple shot of Sevareid overlooking the battle scene would have been "too dull."

Michael, one of Eric and Lois's twin sons born in Paris as the German army drove toward the city in 1940, spoke last and longest. To a few it may have seemed that the son who had inherited his father's handsome head, and who had been an actor and now taught drama, had made the lectern a stage. Yet, more than anyone, he brought his father's flesh and blood into the room, recalling stories of Eric's childhood escapades—the time a Velva, North Dakota, farm boy pal of Eric's built a soapbox airplane and tried to fly it out of the hayloft of a barn—and reading from a diary his father had kept when he was sixteen:

> January 4, 1929: Helped Mother with the housework. I don't like it, but poor Mother is all worn out. Mother says her heart aches for poor dad. So does mine. He has it pretty tough. Same old grind, day after day. The long streetcar ride to the bank just about does for him. He is not used to it. Maybe we'll have to move nearer to St. Paul. I hope to God I can finish Central first, though. Dad wants to send Paul, who is out of work, to the U., but he doesn't just know what to do. Oh, I wish I could help some way.

Then Michael recounted his father's toughness, his self-questioning, his willpower—fighting to climb stairs in the agony of his final illness—his temper, his lyricism, his integrity.

When it was over the family and those invited moved across the street for a reception in the Crystal Room of the Willard Hotel.

And Larry LeSueur went home. A year before Eric died, Larry had seen him for the last time at a dinner at the Washington home of Mrs. Jefferson Patterson, who, when she was Mary Marvin Breckinridge, had covered the German invasion of Belgium and France with Larry and Eric for CBS. After Eric's operation for stomach cancer, Eric and Larry had made several dates to see one another again, but Eric's wife would call and cancel, saying he wasn't up to it.

Larry had to admit to himself that the Eric Sevareid described during the memorial service was not really the man he had known. The speakers were not from his generation. But then, few from his generation were still alive. Larry had first known Eric when Eric was in his twenties, still impressionable, still in love with Lois. People become different persons as their careers develop. And the final Eric Sevareid—the "pundit" accustomed to the deference famous pundits receive—was not the man he had been in the beginning.

1

VELVA

IT IS A BRIGHT, gently brisk, mid-October weekend afternoon, and the leaves—vermilion, orange, red, yellow—have just begun to turn, and some have begun to fall. You have brought sweaters to ward off the dread Dakota cold; but in the late afternoon Velva, the little town of about nine-hundred citizens—none of whom are in sight—seems to exude not just tranquility, but warmth. You stroll over toward the bridge that spans the river into the little city park and eight teenagers in sweats—all white and cheerful and clean-cut—are making their way, laughing and talking, from the football field on the far side of the park toward their homes—low, plain frame houses with huge, orange jack-o'-lantern trash bags stuffed with autumn leaves in front of their porches. Later, five teenagers—four boys and a girl—play touch football in the center of an empty street. The streets are free of trash, of plastic containers and broken bottles; and no graffiti defile the Main Street shop-fronts or walls.

You feel you might have seen this town before—not in life, but in Willa Cather, Sinclair Lewis, or in the opening pages of Larry Woiwode's *Beyond the Bedroom Wall,* where, each night when he cannot sleep, the author retraces his steps through the streets of the town where he grew up, Hyatt, North Dakota, "a village so small it can be seen through from both sides." Woiwode says he lived there until he was six, returned once when he was eight, and never went back again. Yet, obviously, he never escaped. To grow up in a North Dakota town, it seems, is an experience so radical—in the original meaning of that word, "root"—that it is more than a clue to the character of anyone who has survived.

Velva's streets, perhaps to accommodate cattle drives in the nineteenth century, are very wide and absolutely flat; and, though there is a Park Avenue nowhere near the park and a Riverside Drive which drives only a few yards, most streets are numbered rather than named: six blocks from the railroad to the river; thirteen from west to east. No town heroes to memorialize? No planners or developers to root the town's identity in western history or feed townfolks' fantasies with street names from Camelot?

You hear an occasional whirr as a car passes on Route 52 on the other side of the railroad tracks which—with the towering grain elevators—mark the southern border of the town; or you hear the slow rumble of a pickup truck or tractor on Route 41, which is also Main Street, as the truck moves through the center of town, to the bridge over the Mouse River (also called the Souris River), and slowly north up the hill, into the vast golden wheat fields—without which this town would cease to be.

Wheat was "the sole source of meaning of our lives," a Velva native wrote later. These lives that "were given in continuing hostage to the vagaries of this pewter-colored ocean that lapped to the thistle-covered roadbed of the Soo Line and receded to perpetually undulating billows as far as a child could see from the highest point, even from the top of the water tank. We were never its masters, but too frequently its victims."

You walk down Second Street and stand on the railroad tracks and try to imagine the roar of the old steam locomotives seventy years ago as they belched great clouds of smoke and pulled their grain cars into town and stopped by the elevators to load up, then coughed and chugged, and clanked and roared out into the infinity of the larger world.

You remember the story of a boy who lived down this very street seventy years ago and ran away at the age of four, crossed these tracks, trudged up the hills on the other side and suddenly found himself lost, alone in an "eternity of nothingness." At five he wandered off again to visit friends on a farm five miles away. His mother knew nothing of the trip until a neighbor told her she had seen the boy entering the farmyard. You imagine that same boy as a tall, gangly ten-year-old listening to those trains, watching an occasional vagabond hop a freight and make his way to Minot and beyond, and getting his first practical concept of the possibilities that lay on the other side of the hills that seemed to smother him in their embrace.

Further southeast on the railroad line are even smaller towns with names like Voltaire (pop. 630), Bergen (pop. 12), and Balfour (pop. 33); and scattered around to the northeast sit little patches of blue with names like Stink Lake, Poison Lake, Smokey Lake, Flat Lake, and Round Lake—which suggest the no-nonsense, don't-waste-any-words attitude of the original settlers, mostly Norwegian, who put their stamp on the landscape.

Velva sits in a valley just at that bend where the Mouse River (did the first settlers see mice swarming around its banks?), which has meandered down in its squiggly course from Canada, through Lake Darling, meeting the railroad tracks above Minot, suddenly turns north and makes its way back to Canada again, all the way to Hudson Bay.

Indeed it is the river—though, like the Jordan or Rio Grande, its actual breadth would tempt a good athlete to try to jump across it—that has given the town its character. As the stream flows down into Velva's northwest corner in a little loop it creates a quasi-island the town fathers turned into a charming, though rudimentary park. Periodically, as if it did not love the folk who had embraced it with their settlement, when heavy rains swelled its course—as they did in 1904, 1969 and 1974—it has flooded the town.

In recent years, the Army Corps of Engineers has built a levee that turns the river's course and eliminates the loop that ducks down into the town. This has "rescued" Velva from its floods; but, by altering the river's character, it has also undermined the impact of the first sentence of *Not So Wild a Dream,* the book that made Velva a central image in twentieth-century American literature: "The small brown river curved around the edge of our town. The farmers plowed close to its muddy banks and left their water jugs in the shade of the willows."

For, as you descend Route 52 and turn left at the light under the trestle onto 41, you are greeted by a gigantic gray, blue, and white sign: "Welcome to Velva, North Dakota, Home of 1300 Friendly People. Birthplace of Eric Sevareid."

Eric's father, Alfred Eric Sevareid, who was born in Kenyon, Minnesota, in 1882, moved due north fifteen miles up to Velva from Ruso—now a town with a population of eight—in 1909. In Ruso, where he had lived for two years after graduating from college, he had been a homesteader, but also worked in a bank and in real estate.

He had come to Ruso by way of Luther College in Decorah, Iowa, where he had been a star athlete. In fact, as a posthumous 1976 Luther College Hall of Fame citation testifies, he was one of the best athletes Luther College had ever seen. He played basketball for two years, and in baseball, with a "blazing fastball and sharp breaking curve," he pitched nearly all the games for five years. There Al was a hero, and fellow students long remembered the sight of him on the way home from games in his resplendent red uniform.

Later, in a 1965 address at Luther College, his son described Decorah as "a corner of America where the spring is lovely beyond belief, the land rolling and intensely green like the center of France, the rivers small between oak-covered bluffs and crossed by bridges where boys still sit with pole and line, hook and worm."

Although he had never been there before, Decorah reminded him of his own childhood. It was a place, he said, which the young may leave for the crowded cities, but to which their hearts more and more drift back in their older years, "trying—I hope not vainly—to find the magic talisman of peace." And Luther College, one of those small denominational and liberal arts colleges that have traditionally moved rural talent into the American mainstream, was, said the son, one where Latin and Greek remain honored for what they are—"keys to the past and the proper tools for honing the mind in the discipline of exactitude."

It was in Decorah that Al met and married Clara Pauline Elizabeth Hougen. She was the daughter of an itinerant Lutheran minister of the Norwegian Lutheran Synod, Johan Olai Jensen Hougen (1857–1927) and the first of his three wives, Thrine Kristine Johnson, described in a family chronicle as "the belle of Clinton County," Iowa. John Hougen married Thrine in 1882 while he was a pastor in Fargo, North Dakota. In Fargo, Eric Sevareid's mother, Clara, was born.

The Reverend Hougen, who had also been educated at Luther College and seminary, was one of the pillars of the Norwegian-American community. He had come to America from a farm in Norway in 1857 when he was six years old. He was known as one of the founders of Concordia College, a scholar, traveler, and journalist, with, according to the family history, a "sunny disposition and tolerant spirit" that brought peace to strife-torn parishes—in spite of personal poverty and a painful nervous disease that gave his life a note of continual suffering. Yet, he kept his sufferings to himself.

In his move to Velva, where he was to take a job as cashier, and then become a vice president of the Merchants State Bank, Alfred was following his Ruso friend Bill Francis, who the year before had moved up to Velva to take over the weekly newspaper, the *Velva Journal.*

When the young Sevareids arrived, the town too was still young.

August Peterson, an emigrant from Sweden, had filed the first claim there in 1882 or 1883, early in the period known as the Dakota Boom, during which the flood of pioneers took up land under the Homestead Act and established the giant wheat farms that made Minneapolis the milling center of the nation. A short thin man with a quick step, Peterson was also the town blacksmith. His original cabin, the town's first dwelling, is today painted red and relocated in the city park, which is itself land Peterson sold to the city for $300.

The first settlers had probably chosen the site because it was beautiful, sheltered beneath 100- to 150-foot-high hills on both sides of the valley, with an abundance of oak and elm trees, and fed by an inexhaustible supply of pure spring water. Originally the locality was called Scriptown because the McHenry County courthouse was nearby; but, when in 1886 the Great Northern Railroad made Towner, to the north, the county seat, they loaded the log courthouse on skids and dragged it to its new site.

So when the Soo Line came through in 1893 the former Scriptown needed a new name. No one knows how the name Velva was chosen. The story that the founders were inspired by the alleged "velvety" texture of the countryside sounds like one of those forced explanation stories that come along generations later. It is more likely, since the early settlers included many Norwegians, Canadians, and Germans whose families had previously migrated to Russia, that they named it for the Velva River in northeastern Siberia, which some of the immigrants might have seen. If Velva resembled the rest of North Dakota, most of the townsfolk were foreign born. By the census of 1920, when settlement was completed, only one-third of the North Dakota white population had native-born American parents.

In the first decade of the twentieth century, Velva was just getting its roots in the soil. It had recovered from its first great flood in April of 1904, a devastating event in which the town was inundated and hundreds of cattle were swept away and drowned, their rotting corpses left dangling in the trees.

In 1909, although the farmers were suffering their first real crop failure and a two-year drought—when one June day the temperature had hit 113 degrees in the shade—Velva was nevertheless a relatively prosperous community. The population was 800; the residents worshiped at Catholic, Congregational, Lutheran, and Methodist churches, sent their children to a graded school with two classrooms, and patronized an "opera house"—a three-story, cement-block building on Main Street, which featured traveling shows and local talent, a dance floor, a large stage with scenery, wings, and curtains, and seats for three to four hundred people. There were three hotels, a livery stable, a blacksmith, six grain elevators, two feed mills, and a creamery; plus coal mines and stone quarries in the vicinity. The railroads shipped out wheat, flax, cattle, coal, and stone. Land was worth ten to fifteen dollars an acre unimproved and twice as much plowed. Mail came daily and telephones were just being installed. A power plant and electric lighting were in the works—and then, inevitably, motion picture shows.

But more important, the town's historian Oscar Anderson recalls, Velva citizens entertained one another. They built a pavilion and bandstand in the city park. Under the direction of Gustave Livdahl, Velva's first mayor, president of the Merchants State Bank, and cornet player, the men formed the Velva Cornet Band. Other "talented" citizens specialized in practical jokes: like G. W. McKnight, the pharmacist and mimic, who used the new telephone system to phone customers in the front of his store from a second phone in the back, pretending to be someone's wife or mother, pleading with him to bring home another pound of sausage or loaf of bread. Or J. L. Lee, the attorney and ventriloquist, who, the story goes, would "throw his voice" to the top of a tree and convince a passerby that some poor chap was trapped in the tree and had to be rescued. The would-be hero would run, get a ladder, and climb the tree, only to find it empty. And it was the "journalist" Lee who sent the story to the *Chicago Blade*, a sensational tabloid, about a "wild man" captured by a posse in the "wild woods" west of Velva and now chained to the wall in McKnight's drugstore basement!

Growing up in Velva, Arnold Eric Sevareid hated the sound of the Norwegian tongue. He and his brothers were bored when visitors in the parlor talked about the old country. But in 1975 at Carnegie Hall, addressing the sesquicentennial celebration of Norweigan immigration to America, Al and Clara's son, the ten-year-old boy whom you imagined staring down the railroad tracks when Velva was young, tried to reach back to 1854 in a "Letter to a Grandfather I Never Knew." He imagined his father's father, Erik Erikson Sevareid, in Norway, deciding to leave "the solitude of the mountains for the solitude of the prairie where the soil was rich, and a hundred and sixty acres was kingdom for a man." And his mother's family in Fjellhaugen, "a croft of unpainted boards and logs, just across that narrow fjord you looked upon each day, high up in the naked rock and the wind."

He based this imagery on the text and old photographs in his mother's family history, "Emigration Centennial of Jens Johannessen and Christine Olsdatter Hougen, 1857–1957, Compiled by their Grandchildren, Celebration at Story City, Iowa, Sunday, June 30, 1957." For the book his mother had written a lovely essay about Ana Johanna Hougen. Aunt Ana never married but, devoted to "duty," spent most of her life caring for her Uncle John, until she died at 94.

Duty became a theme of Eric Sevareid's remarks; but, clearly, Eric was selecting American values which he held in esteem and projecting them back onto his Norwegian forebears.

He tells his grandfather to rest easily in his grave beneath the Minnesota prairie, because his grandfather had done what was right:

> You believed that hard work was what a man and woman did, in order to matter. Some speak of this now as the "work ethic," as if it were some curious, irrelevant quirk or cult.
>
> You were at ease with the word "duty," you knew there could be no rights and privileges without responsibility. You found it natural to teach probity to your children, and self-denial, so that others too, could have elbow room in which to live. You blamed yourself for misfortune, not others, not the government, not society itself.
>
> You knew what was known by ancient philosophers you never read—that civilized life cannot hold together without these values. Now, some speak of them as the "puritan ethic," as a curious outmoded, illusion. But you were not wrong.

Arnold Eric Sevareid was born on November 26, 1912, in a little house across the street from the Oak Valley Lutheran Church, which had been established in 1900, where the family worshiped regularly and where Arnold was baptized a year later on November 11. (He would change his name to Eric in Paris in 1939.) His older brother Paul had been born two years before, his brother John in 1915, and finally his sister Jeanne in 1922. Shortly after Arnold was born, the family moved a few blocks away to a new brown-and-white shingled bungalow, built by his father in 1913, at 405 Second Street, the second house from the corner.

Across the street stood the one distinguished residence in town: a three-story, white, seventeen-room Victorian mansion, with broad, wrap-around porch, three-story turret, fireplace, and imposing staircase. Al Sevareid's boss, the cornetist-banker Livdahl, had recently built it for his wife and seven children. The Sevareids lived in a house less than half its neighbor's size; and, as young Arnold grew tall, he must have hit his head often on the sloping ceiling of his cramped, upstairs room.

To the handful of people who remember daily life in Velva seventy years ago, it sometimes seemed as if the Garden of Eden had been transplanted into northern North Dakota—though a compromised Eden where a little discipline was needed to keep the good people good.

As Margaret Loberg, who was in Paul's class at school, recalls, "Life was very happy in Velva in those days. Everybody knew everybody, and that's what kept people in line." But even a town that small had its pecking order: if you were Norwegian—store proprietors often spoke Norwegian with their customers—and had a good job, you were all right. By these criteria, the Sevareids were town gentry. The Sevareid boys had bikes before the other boys did, and Arnold had the first erector set in town. But, when a friend told Arnold that his father was the richest man in town, Arnie hurried home close to tears and was relieved to learn that "possessing great wealth was a false accusation."

Meanwhile, there were lots of things to do—like hiking in the country to the neighboring lakes, especially Strawberry Lake. Or even getting a ride north to the big city in Minot. Margaret's father ran the movie house called the Iris, where children watched silent films for fifteen cents, and in the evenings paid twenty-five cents to come in and dance to the music of the player piano.

All the children played together—kick the can and red rover come over. They stole watermelons and threw tomatoes at one another and, good Scandanavian Lutherans that they were, felt guilty about it for years. One ten-year-old made himself a soapbox airplane, a crate with wings on it, and had Arnold and another pal push him out the second story of the barn. In the winter they skated on the rink, where the new city hall stands now. There a nice policeman would watch over them and send them all home at nine in the evening.

Yet while the other children played together, Arnie, whom they all called "Buddy," would often hang back, aloof, sitting off on the side on his bike, his long legs dangling. Although he had been laid low by the 1918 flu epidemic, which had almost killed his mother, and had missed six weeks of first grade, Arnold was already, in the estimation of his peers, a very handsome boy. He had a lean, rugged face that in photographs made him look several years older.

Buddy's two sports, other than the duck hunting, pheasant shooting, and fly-fishing, which every male mastered in the rituals of growing up, were baseball, in imitation of his father, and swimming. The boys crossed the foot bridge into the park and swam naked in the swimming-hole section of the Mouse River, where there was a nice sandy beach, down by the ball field. When the men came up from Voltaire, which had neither river nor lake, to play baseball, they would join in, and slide down the muddy banks into the pool, the pale, white skin of their bodies a dramatic contrast to their arms and faces burnt brown and rough by farm labor and sun. Then a lookout would cry, "The girls are coming!" Indeed, the girls deliberately signaled their coming with their laughter and animated talk; and the boys scampered to pull on some clothes.

But Arnold had another life, for the most part invisible to his playmates; a life of his imagination nurtured by two sources: books and periodicals. The love of books may be attributed to his mother. Clara Sevareid was a tall, elegant, forceful woman, who knew how to dress beautifully, to give the impression she was a "Victorian princess," who might have had servants but was actually a hard-working middle-class housewife. Her temperament could also make her difficult to deal with. She constantly complained about her illnesses, though she lived to the age of eighty-four, dying in 1969. Clara was also a talkative woman, perhaps to fill the long silences left by her big, stern Norwegian husband's reluctance to communicate; and she had her own ideas about educating her children.

Rather than introduce them to the standard children's nursery rhymes, like "Little Miss Muffet" and "Hickory Dickory Dock," she started them out on Shakespeare and classical music.

Furthermore, the old stone bank building on Main Street where Alfred Sevareid worked also housed upstairs, forty-two steps up, the town library established by the Velva Women's Club. Arnold would slip in among the bookshelves on days when the library was closed to everyone else and read everything he could get his hands on. One of his favorites, which he later had read to him when he was dying, was *Brighton Fair*, the diary of an irrepressible twelve-year-old who was always getting into trouble. He studied picture books of seaside places, mountains, and crowded cities, traced the rectangle of North Dakota on the map and asked himself, What am I doing here?

In school Arnold was only an average student, with particularly bad handwriting; but left to himself he would read with the ravenous hunger that Richard Wright describes in *Black Boy,* where books broke the chains of a world, however defined, which was too small for the boy who realized early he wanted to write.

At the *Velva Journal*—a full-sized, four-page weekly—editor Bill Francis, who had no children of his own, seemed to adopt the children who hung around his shop. He would print out their names in linotype and give them the slugs as souvenirs; and Arnold he made a sort of apprentice, taught him how to set type and instilled in him perhaps the earliest strong conviction in Sevareid's life: that above all he wanted to be a newspaper man. There was nothing else.

Arnold also had his dreams. During World War I, after his father had lifted him to the window of the troop train passing through Velva to shake hands with his Uncle Ephraim who was on his way "over there," Arnold dreamed that a column of "Huns" was marching down Main Street, past the McKnight drugstore, and that he, perched on the roof of the bank with his father's Winchester .22, mowed them all down.

And often, as a child, and for almost thirty years after, he had the nightmare where "immense, fat, tan-colored clouds" rolled remorselessly over him "straining and crushing." And he always awoke from this dream sick and sweating. He did not escape from this terror until he realized, thirty years later, that the great hills which had both "protected and imprisoned" his childhood were not majestic mountains but merely low, rolling, pleasant windbreaks.

Later his most vivid memories were of individuals who personified the town's spirit: like "Duff" Aaker, the country doctor who played the piano, cello, and violin—who saved his mother during the flu epidemic, who "understood my mother's longing for the green and leafy places, and to him alone she could talk"—and who died painfully of internal injuries suffered when he tripped coming out of church where he had played the organ for the funeral of a friend. That night the Sevareid children could hear their otherwise silent father's bed shake as he sobbed.

The intermittent drought years of the 1920s did not take their full toll until the Dust Bowl, *Grapes-of-Wrath* years of the 1930s; but the occasional bad years were enough to ruin a string of North Dakota banks, including Alfred Sevareid's. In 1925 he moved his family for a while up to Minot, where thirteen-year-old Arnold attended seventh grade and, though he lacked the aggressiveness to do it well, tried to sell newspapers on the street.

After a year the family moved again, this time to Minneapolis, where they finally settled into a big frame house, larger than their Velva bungalow, in a middle-class neighborhood on south Portland Avenue.

In his 1946 autobiography, *Not So Wild a Dream*, Sevareid offers very little explanation of exactly why the family left Velva. He tells us his mother—"who came from a green and pleasant city in the distant, mystical East," in Iowa—feared and hated the fact that wheat so absolutely controlled their lives as "our solace and our challenge." It is easy to imagine that, though she was incensed by Sinclair Lewis's portrayal of small town life in *Main Street*, as a cultivated woman from an intellectual family, she knew the ways in which he was right.

Meanwhile Alfred Sevareid, who kept his feelings bottled up, simply met the challenge without emotion, the father confessor as well as the banker for the men whose livelihoods fell apart in a swarm of locusts or a "reaper which broke its axle on a rock." In time, "years of drought ruined his wheatlands and broke his bank." Years later the sons learned that the father, true to those Norwegian principles of self-reliance and the Protestant work ethic, had blamed himself rather than fate for the bank's failure and tried to make up some of the farmers' losses from his own savings.

By the time he wrote *Not So Wild a Dream*, the thirty-three-year-old Sevareid was already the author of *Canoeing with the Cree,* a book on his 2,250-mile canoe trip to the Hudson Bay, which he made at the age of seventeen. He had been a student rebel and graduate of the University of Minnesota, a world-famous CBS News correspondent who had covered the fall of France and the battles to take it back. He had survived a parachute jump and a month among headhunters in the Burma jungle, and was now a newscaster and analyst. But, for all this experience, in *Not So Wild a Dream*, he interprets Velva as the paradigm of true democracy, where wheat made all men equal. When he read in college of the great struggle for a classless society and witnessed this struggle around the world, it occurred to him "that what men wanted was Velva, on a national, on a world scale."

But he often asked himself the same questions that Velva citizens ask to this day. "North Dakota. Why have I not returned for so many years? Why have so few from the prairies ever returned?"

Velva prospered for a while and its population grew to fourteen hundred in the 1970s. But, after the lumber yard, power plant and other enterprises closed, the town slipped back to nine hundred in the 1980s. After the terrible droughts and Depression of the 1930s, North Dakota's population declined in every decade except the 1950s, and by the 1960s nearly half the persons born in North Dakota were living in other states.

Helen Kramer has kept track of Arnold's returns. Still beautiful at eighty, of medium height and with only a very slight stoop, she retains a vivid memory. When she occasionally forgets the names of townspeople whom she knows well, she simply asks them their names. She lives in a large white house on Second Avenue just a few yards from the new steel bridge that crosses the Mouse River into the city park. The interior of the house is immaculate, decorated with pictures of her children, grandchildren, and great-grandchildren, and her late husband John, who died of a heart condition after years of treatment at the Mayo Clinic. He was a big, heavy man, a fisherman and hunter, with a clouded right lens on his eyeglasses, the result of a cataract operation.

She is one of a handful of folk in Velva with clear memories of the Sevareids, the only one in town with Eric's Washington, D.C., address and phone number, and the only one with whom Eric kept in contact up to his death in 1992. With his help, in references to her in his radio broadcasts and articles and in a conversation on the *Jack Paar Show,* Helen Kramer, then Helen Bloomquist, had become known as "Eric Sevareid's childhood sweetheart." She is clearly the self-designated keeper of the flame, the official living link between the lanky sixth-grader on his Woolworth's bike and the man who at the time of his retirement, a year after America's Bicentennial, was perhaps the primary interpreter of what it meant to be an American.

She is also—though more in the visitor's mind than in her own—a "what-if" woman in a "great" man's life. In one sense, he clung to her friendship, writing to her and calling her several times a year until a few weeks before he died, as the last link to that Edenic childhood frontier life that first formed his character. She was the ever faithful—and faraway—woman who gave him loyalty and affection while the first two of his three marriages fell apart. Yet, any woman who was content to spend all her days in a town like Velva could never have been the right wife for the man who became Eric Sevareid. She wrote to Eric, December 12, 1955, "It only takes average intelligence to live here, anyone with more couldn't—and doesn't stay here. We do have a nice life, tho." Although she has always said she loved John Kramer, she sometimes allows herself to wonder what would life have been like if things had been different, and she concludes, "I just don't know."

"I was the girl that all the boys fought over," she says, with some satisfaction, as she shows the visitor her grade-school portrait—blond, vivacious, pert, smiling, captivating. "Who would have thought that that man could keep this little girl in mind all these years?"

Sevareid came home to Velva three times. The first return was at the age of twenty in the summer of 1933. Armed with an invitation to work in a northern California gold mine, he had hopped a freight train to Minot and hitched a ride down to Velva for a few days in the last week of June. When he left Velva at the age of twelve, he wrote later in the July 13, 1933, *Velva Journal,* he had dreamed that he would return wearing a Panama white suit and roll into town in a white chauffeured limousine in a cloud of dust. The limo, at his command, would pull up in front of McKnight's pharmacy, and, a twenty-five-cent cigar jutting from his "handsome, world-weary mouth," he would step into the store, "calmly order three hundred ice cream cones, and distribute them to the crowd of gaping little boys and girls." He would smile politely as the crowd whispered, "I always knew that Sevareid boy would make good."

In reality he was a sunburned, blistered, college boy limping down Main Street with a soiled backpack sagging from his shoulders, who says he heard a bystander ask: "My gosh, who is that funny looking oaf?"

It was the Saturday of the annual high school homecoming reunion dinner and dance, and the young traveler thought this might be his chance to reconnect with Helen Bloomquist. They had written to one another for a while, but when she told him she had a steady boyfriend, his letters dropped off.

Arnold who was staying with Bill Francis and skipped the dinner, then came down to the dance at the pavilion in the park. He did not go in, but hung around at a distance looking in. Through a friend, he sent word in to Helen that "Bud" was outside. Then, just as the band began to play the last dance before midnight, he broke in, grabbed her for the dance, and whisked her outside to talk. It was then she told him she had married John Kramer and that they had a baby boy.

Arnold retreated for a few days to Strawberry Lake, then made notes on changes in the town for his *Journal* report. He found a new "intellectual center" in town, not the library but a "rustically furnished room in a tumbledown house back in the woods, near the 'rapids,' where, with their books stacked against the four walls, a group of unemployed college men hold forth." There was a beautiful new school, filling stations had replaced the livery barn and blacksmith's shop. Velva's "loveliest home," he said, was still the one where his family used to live.

In September 1953, Mrs. Clarence Miller, chairman of the Velva Clinic Activities Committee, wrote to Eric Sevareid for help. She described changes in Velva and the benefit dances, auctions, chicken dinner in the Lutheran church basement, carnival, concerts and outright donations that had enabled them to build the much needed new medical clinic that summer. But his Velva, she assured him, was still there: "Still the tree-clustered surprise of the prairies, Velva is the home of the same openhearted people who lived here in your youth whose differences in life's position seem leveled by the friendly tenor of living up and down

Main Street." Since he had "well near immortalized" Velva in *Not So Wild a Dream,* and since his nightly commentaries were heard over KCJB-radio from Minot, would he please support the drive by "mentioning Velva's fund-raising problems on your CBS program." The image of Eric Sevareid as the Man from Velva was taking hold in the public imagination. He responded with a letter to the committee supporting the project.

Two years after this letter, Eric returned to Velva for the second time, on assignment for *Collier's* magazine, to write "You Can Go Home Again," (published May 11, 1956) one of his most powerful essays, an ambiguous work that could be read either as an indictment or endorsement of American small-town life in the mid 1950s.

This time he took the Great Northern Railroad from Minneapolis to Minot and rented a Studebaker for the drive to Velva. It was North Dakota at its best, a mid-October Indian summer day. He knew that for his family Velva memories were painful. It was probably his mother who had said, "I can never go back. I cannot go a mile west of the Red River anymore. I glimpse those prairies and I get sick."

Eric had read psychologists and consulted a psychiatrist about his boyhood memories and understood that we "tend to remember the sweet and forget the harsh," and that his profound emotional attraction to the Mouse River was an "oceanic feeling," a deep yearning for our ultimate origins. The golden threads of the past, in vivid images, dominated his memories: ". . . the creak of saddles and the smell of horses, the nectar of cactus berries and the stain of plums, the secret, devilish gang-thrill on Halloween, the cold, dripping joy of the ice wagon in the hot summer night . . ."

The moment he arrives on Main Street he spies Bill Francis, who has sold the *Journal* and married "Aunt Jessey" Beebe: "Daggone, Bud, you haven't changed." Both Bill's and Jessey's spouses had died and each had realized the other needed to take care of someone or be cared for. He goes hunting with John Kramer, the man who "stole" his sweetheart. In Helen's twelve-year-old son Mike he sees himself. In his essay, "Once More to the Lake," E. B. White takes his young son to a vacation camp he himself had gone to as a child and, contemplating his son, loses the distinction between his son and himself. Apparently, in Mike (the same name as one of Sevareid's twin sons) Eric sees the son he might have had if his family had not moved away when he was twelve and he had stayed home and fought for Helen and won. The boy haunted the town library and had read a book a day that summer. Eric struggles within himself over whether to advise the boy to leave town when he gets older, but concludes that, as a result of this visit, his own "certainties number less than ever."

At lunch at Aunt Jessey's, Helen and John come into the kitchen. Her "peace and serenity had not abated. She had stayed and she was happy, as she had been fashioned from childhood always to be. Place never had anything to do with it." That night in bed, he listened to the night country noises, and "tears came in a silent flood."

Exploring the town alone, he knocks on the door of his own home, but there is no answer. At the old schoolhouse (though he doesn't mention it in his article) Margaret Loberg, now a teacher, helped him find his old desk. The *Journal* office still has the linotype that had printed out their names, but the player piano at the Iris theater has been replaced by Cinemascope. On Main Street a drunken farmer paws at Eric's shoulder and starts quoting passages from his books, "whole passages of the love and loneliness of a prairie boy." A constable leads him away.

The sights and sounds have changed: the diesel locomotive has replaced the steam; Sunday morning world news broadcasts have replaced the Norwegian Lutheran hymns. At the sight of Swedlund's barn on the hill he remembers the time a runaway horse galloped right into the barn with him crouching over his mane and the time a hired hand coldly picked up Fanny, a beloved mongrel dog who had chased some chickens, and put a bullet through her head.

Back home in Washington, Eric wrote to Bill Francis: "It was all pretty wonderful for me and I want to get back there again before I get too much older and 'sot' in my eastern ways." He was struggling to finish the article in the "small snatches of time I seem to have for contemplative writing these days."

In the article Eric concludes that modern technology, the consolidation of resources, and the mass media's ability to bring the world into the small town's kitchens have changed the character of town life but liberated it from its stifling narrowness. Velva's population has grown to thirteen hundred because the residents can commute to their farms and mines. "In this generation my Velva friends have rejoined the general American society that their pioneering fathers left behind when they first made the barren trek in the days of the wheat rush."

If small-town folk no longer know one another as well as they used to, that's all to the good. "For personal and social neuroses festered under the hard scab of conformity. . . The world was not 'too much with us'; the world was too little with us and we were too much with one another." There is no real freedom without privacy. Young people must leave, he decides—unless perhaps there are opportunities for those who stay. Finally, he concludes: small towns "are not stagnant plants at all, but seedbeds, ceaselessly renewing themselves, their seed constantly renewing the nation."

Velva readers snapped up the 450 extra copies their stores had ordered and called for more. Bill Francis read the story twice to Aunt Jessey, whose eyesight was failing; he particularly liked the "seedbed" conclusion. In June, Harold Anderson, who ran the drugstore, reported that everyone was still talking about the article. Unfortunately, there was that one percent who didn't like it; they were people who had gone to school with Eric and were jealous of his success or who "misinterpreted" the piece as anti-Velva. Eric responded that he was startled by the negative reaction to an article "written out of affection for the place and its people." Response from around the country had been overwhelmingly favorable, particularly from former Velva people.

One resident wrote a "not-for-publication" letter to *Colliers* charging that Sevareid had deeply offended the school teacher, the eighty-year-old Miss West, by calling her "indestructible." Thus implying, says the correspondent, that Eric wants her dead! Eric, says the writer, had a "subconscious wish" to hurt the town because it had treated his father unfairly when his bank failed. Eric, young at the time, had unconsciously absorbed his father's resentment. Eric's response to the attack was to write a warm note to Miss West telling her that several readers were happy to learn she was "still going strong."

A few years later the wife of one of Eric's college friends mentioned to him that she was from Minot, the "Magic City," the "distant and splendid Baghdad" of his writings. He replied with a chilly brusqueness, which some who knew him for years interpreted as shyness and others as rudeness, "I really don't have anything to do with Minot or Velva anymore. We moved to Minnesota when I was very young. I've never been back except for special occasions."

If somehow he resented being seen as still intimately linked to a world he had left, his public would not allow him that combination of freedom and privacy that allows one to control one's own public image. When he retired from CBS in 1977, a North Dakota native who was his contemporary wrote to him that his last broadcast sounded like a requiem mass. He felt strongly that Eric Sevareid had to "go on forever." Because they were both from North Dakota. He still yearned for "massive acres of ripe wheat, coyotes crying in the night, wind whining through the screens and, in the winter, eight-foot snowbanks over barnyard fences and snow so hard that boots left no imprint." All reasons someone else might have for leaving a place behind.

In *Dakota: A Spiritual Geography* (1993), Kathleen Norris, who lives in Lemmon, South Dakota, writes that by the time a town is seventy-five to one hundred years old, it may be filled with those who have come to idealize their isolation, people who never left at all or have fled the demands of a more complex society, who have come to exaggerate their own importance. A librarian, for example, might see an interlibrary loan request as an insult to her own collection. They see a national honor to a local citizen as demeaning to the rest of them. In idealizing their changlessness they lose the town's true history. (The bound volumes of the *Velva Journal,* for example, were almost discarded and today are crumbling without adequate maintenance in the school library, which doubles as the town library.) They see themselves as belonging not to other people but to the changeless land.

One of the consequences of this is that anyone from a small town who wants to be a writer—like Willa Cather, Sinclair Lewis, or Larry Woiwode—must first flee the town; otherwise, he or she risks self-censorship to avoid offending relatives, or the local history syndrome that romanticizes the past. The truth is not seen as something that makes one free but that causes pain. It would follow from this that, even though Eric might have "affection" for his hometown and its people, there is no way in which he, as an artist, could embrace its values totally or allow himself to see Velva as Velva saw itself.

He returned for the third and last time in 1987, just five years before his death, with his sister Jeanne and a PBS television crew to produce an

American Experience documentary on the early chapters of *Not So Wild a Dream.* The project took three days, and this time they didn't even stay in Velva but in a big hotel in Minot, from which they commuted to work. Eric had changed a lot. For the shooting he looked dapper in his old off-white correspondent's jacket with all the pockets, but he was not feeling well, arthritis had claimed him, and he moved around slowly with a cane. The visuals featured brief shots of wheat fields and the muddy Mouse River, which, because the engineers' flood-control levee cut off the park loop from the main current, is now a stagnant pond. The script, lifted largely from the text of the book, began: "Why have I not returned for so many years?"

Today Velva, as one citizen described it, is a town of four bars and three churches. Its practical center is the Bee Bop Cafe and Bowling Alley where folks come for brunch after church and where the Association of Commerce meets for a meat-loaf-sandwich lunch every Monday in the back room. The Sevareid house, now painted red, is the home of Jerry and Lisa Stewart and their two children. They welcome visitors— including Eric's daughter Christine in October 1993—and are restoring the house to its original interior and planning to put a plaque out front.

The Oak Valley Evangelical Lutheran Church is still looking for a minister.

After mass, attended by about 140 parishoners at Saint Cecilia's Roman Catholic Church, a high school boy told the visiting priest that he might not leave town. There are new businesses coming in, he said, like the two antique stores—one of which used to be the Iris Theater and now has a player piano for sale. Not only that, he said, but they're thinking of establishing a Heritage Center, in honor of "some anchorman who used to live here."

Forty-seven-year-old Jack Jackson, a big, heavy man who has been a logger, a radio broadcaster, a starving entrepreneur, a sign painter, and a prize-winning editor of other small weeklies, has bought the weekly paper that had descended from the *Velva Journal* but lost touch with its roots and renamed it the Velva *Valley Star.* He moved to town a year ago because he wanted to live and work in the place that gave the world Eric Sevareid. He sits in on city council and Association of Commerce meetings and promotes his vision of the community: sell lots on Prospect Heights—the hill overlooking the railroad, grain elevators, and town— at a fraction of the Minot real estate costs, and make Velva a "suburb with a soul," a place where people who work in Minot—like the mayor and Jerry Stewart—can enjoy a higher standard of living, with more security and less cost. The planners want the town to grow, but not much, maybe to fifteen hundred. They don't want to sacrifice identity to size.

In the January 4, 1918, *Velva Journal*, Bill Francis wrote an editorial that argued that every successful community is known for the one product it makes and exports. For example, Le Perche in France breeds the famous Percheron horses; New Salem, North Dakota, breeds Holstein cattle. So, the farmers of Velva should get together, cooperate, and make one product that will advertise the town.

As history unfolded, that "one product" turned out to be the little six-year-old boy in his print shop who was watching him set the type.

2

CANOE TRIP

THE MINNEAPOLIS in which Arnold Sevareid grew into manhood was one of the most beautiful cities in America. An unsigned editorial, "Utopia? Well, Almost," in the February 26, 1930, *Central High News*, of which Arnold was the editor, exclaims: "What a wonderful thing it is to reside in a clime where we have such a variety of climate, where the weather is always interesting!" It lists the city's virtues: It's clean, well laid-out; most citizens have their own private homes; not much crime; schools, "the country's best." "We could find no better place to live."

Hedley Donovan, later Arnold's colleague at the University of Minnesota and Henry Luce's successor as editor of *Time* magazine, recalls in his 1989 autobiography, *Right Places, Right Times*, that the Minneapolis of the 1920s was "a privileged time and place to be growing up." The city was and always has been particularly proud of its seasons. He learned in school that Minneapolis stood precisely halfway between the equator and the North Pole. Thus the arctic winters and scorching summers— including a record 35 degrees below zero in January of both 1936 and 1970, and 108 degrees in 1936. Hedley Donovan loved the smells of fresh mud in March and April, of blossoming lilacs in May, and above all the "glorious smoke of burning leaves" in October.

The narrow Mississippi River dropped down through the city from the north, wound through the center of the town to where the Minnesota River branched off to the southwest, then turned up beneath the towering bluffs of adjacent St. Paul, and dropped down into Spring Lake on the southeast. From a plane, as one observer described it, a summer visitor would look down upon "what seems to be a forest dotted with houses, threaded with the blue of lakes that loop the town from the Mississippi to the Minnesota River like a chain of beads each in a green velvet setting, and crossed by dozens of straight white lines which lead with scarcely a curve or an angle into the city's business heart." The seven lakes within the city limits offered beaches, rowboats, canoes, sailing, iceboating, and hockey rinks.

Railroad tracks converged from the east and west upon the grain elevators and flour mills that, since the city's rapid expansion in the 1870s and 1880s, had been the basis of its prosperity and its identity. But the founders, not content with prosperity, also wanted sophistication. From the start, they sought to balance rapid growth with a preservation of those sites that gave the city its character—like the internal lakes and parks and the sixteen-foot St. Anthony's Falls, named by their discoverer Father Hennepin in 1680. They also determined that the city would have high standards in education.

Though still a young city, its population had risen to more than 464,000; its two industries had increased to over one hundred; its school system compared well with any in the nation, its literacy rate was high, its university had the third highest enrollment in the country. It had an orchestra and art museums. Though its theater was nothing—except for university performances of *The Desert Song* and *The Vagabond King*, and concert performances by Lily Pons and Lawrence Tibbett—there were nine first-run movie theaters and everyone went to the movies. Indeed, an invitation to dinner at a middle-class home usually included an excursion to the movies after dinner.

The streets were laid out in a traditional grid, with both streets and avenues numbered. In the 1930s, an estimated 50 percent of the citizens had their own homes, nearly all with tree-shaded lawns and shrubs, scattered over the fifty-eight square miles of gently rolling land. Most families had their own barn—later a garage—in the back, plus space for vegetables or flowers.

Although ethnic distinctions were inevitably breaking down, descendants of the New England entrepreneurs, who arrived as early as the 1850s and made the primitive outpost into the "Paris of the Plains," controlled "society" and set the tone. The Scandanavians who swept into Minneapolis after the Civil War and kept coming through the Dust Bowl migrations quickly entered the city's professional life and middle class as storekeepers, doctors, lawyers, tailors, and bankers. Though most were Lutherans, the quasi-absolute authority their pastors had exercised on the frontier had been tempered by urban reality. The inevitable secularization that goes with urbanization and education was under way.

The Sevareid home, a large three-story wooden house at 3648 Portland Avenue, was in a quiet middle-class, single-home neighborhood, six blocks west of Powderhorn Lake in Powderhorn Park, and thirty-odd blocks south of the center of town, the Mississippi River and St. Anthony's Falls, and the University of Minnesota.

One can easily imagine a continuity with the spirit of Velva—flat, broad streets; children who all knew one another skating on the pond until the policeman told them to go home; large portions of the population who still spoke Norwegian; the still strong presence of the Lutheran church, specifically Our Saviour's Lutheran Church on Chicago Avenue where Arnold was confirmed. Yet in no way could Velva compare with the new levels of intellect and imagination.

Not that Arnold was immediately recognized as a precocious intellectual. A diary he kept when he was sixteen shows him to have been like most sixteen-year-olds: preoccupied with many things—his own good looks, how girls reacted to him, and also other peoples' problems and how he might help them. He was one of those students who knew the answers but never raised his hand.

Hedley Donovan, writing in the late 1980s, remembers the public schools as excellent. He recalls, with a hint of irony, the dedication of teachers and their "untroubled confidence that they were doing exactly what the city of Minneapolis, the state of Minnesota, and the United States of America had entrusted them to do, in behalf of the civic future, gave them easy control over a large roomful of children who essentially believed the same things."

Young Sevareid sat silent in the face of much of this "dedication."

For one thing, he wasn't thinking about the classroom material as much as he was dreaming about journalism. He was convinced that the American press was awaiting another Richard Harding Davis—and that he was squirming in a seat too small for him at Central High School. One day when ex-heavyweight boxing champion Jack Dempsey came to town, young Sevareid stuck a cigarette between his lips and announced to his high school journalist chums that he was going to breeze down to the Niccollet Hotel and snag the Manassa Mauler for an interview. Arnie and a pal cornered the champ in the elevator and followed him to the street. When Arnie stammered a half-request, Dempsey said, "You want an interview? OK. Work hard. Live clean. Get lots of exercise." And he was gone.

No teacher really knows what is going through the head of a bright but closemouthed adolescent; but perhaps this one was saving what he had to say for *Not So Wild A Dream,* where he excoriates a system that allowed them to read the life of Herbert Hoover but never told them about Norman Thomas; to study George Washington, but not Simon Bolivar. "We were not taught these things, because our teachers, with few exceptions, did not know them." He concedes that the virtues of the system, which had nothing to do with the intellect, were real. Boys learned to relate to girls as friends, not only as sexual objects; sports taught teamwork, which won World War II.

He concludes: "I finished Minneapolis Central High School in the summer of 1930, pale and skinny, having learned nothing except how to put the school paper to press, believing that the ability to write a two-column 'A' headline was of a higher order than the ability to write a sonnet, believing that Herbert Hoover was a great man, that America was superior to all other countries in all possible ways, that labor strikes were caused by unkempt foreigners, that men saved their souls inside wooden or brick Protestant churches, that if men had no jobs it was due to personal laziness and vice—meaning liquor—and that sanity governed the affairs of mankind." Within three years he stopped believing all of these things. Exactly what changed his mind is not completely clear; but between high school and graduation from college he would undergo a series of trials, adventures and disappointments that would mark him for the rest of his life.

To a degree which both Arnold and Hedley Donovan were too young to understand, Minneapolis was not quite the Utopia they imagined. The visitor who arrived by Union Station would see the flophouses, employment agencies, bars, and other signs of urban decay. The city had been declining since the end of World War I. The lumber industry, having stripped the north woods, was moving west. The opening of the Panama Canal in 1914 had made it cheaper to ship goods by sea than by land. A labor war was brewing between the unions and a group of businessmen who called themselves the Citizens' Alliance, a conflict that would add the word "fascism" to Sevareid's vocabulary. But as a high school student, fascism was less pertinent to him than romantic poetry.

Now the Young Men's hearts are troubled for the whisper of the Trues;
Now the Red Gods make their medicine again . . .

We must go, go, go away from here.
On the other side of the world we're overdue. . .

A seventeen-year-old senior broods over Kipling in English class on a warm May afternoon. The sunshine streams into the room on the light hair of the student sitting in front of him and falls in funny speckles on the pages of his textbook. "As the spot of light shifted back and forth over the type, it seemed as though the letters were alive and crawling in bewilderment, trying to get away."

Get away! It is the same boy who tried to run away from Velva at four and who watched the freight trains with the open boxcars rumble by when he was ten.

The teacher snaps him out of his revery: "Tomorrow it will be *Paradise Lost.*" *Paradise Lost,* indeed! As long as he remains in that room, he tells himself, he is lost. "Paradise was outdoors, out on the greening hills and along the lazy river."

So begins *Canoeing with the Cree,* Eric Sevareid's first book, written when he was eighteen, about a 2,250-mile canoe trip with his friend Walter Port from Minneapolis to the icy waters of Hudson Bay.

When he was older he tended to downplay the trip and the book, referring to it as a work for young people. As late as 1980, he referred to it as an "awkward triviality." His correspondence when he wrote it makes it clear that it was, in a sense, a "boys'" book. He was a Boy Scout with the rank of First Class, a reader of *Boys' Life,* the popular Scouts' magazine. But although he wrote it for contemporaries, its reception made clear that, for some reviewers, it transcended young peoples' literature. When the Minnesota Historical Society reprinted the 1935 book in 1968, the *Minnesota History* reviewer, the noted conservationist Ernest C. Oberholtzer, who had paddled the same waters in 1912, found the story "exhilarating," proof that, in the words of George H. Adams, editor of the *Minneapolis Star,* the "frontiers of courage and romance . . . beyond which only the exceptional soul will venture" still beckon.

In *Not So Wild a Dream,* Sevareid, fifteen years removed from the event, approaches it with the ironic ambivalence of a sophisticated young man. "I then proceeded to an adventureous enterprise so heroic in its scope that I am staggered to this day when I recall it. It is practically devoid of meaning and implication. In any case, I am going to relate it."

The adventure was far from "devoid of meaning," as he himself makes clear in his analysis. It was a defining moment of his life.

Furthermore, in a way he might not have foreseen, the canoe trip entered into the history and folklore of famous American wilderness adventures. It became one of those mythical frontier experiences that inspired other Americans either to repeat the adventure literally in their own canoes or to repeat it spiritually, by imitating the virtues of self-reliance, cooperation, imagination, courage, and perseverance that these two boys displayed. It was no accident that the young author imagined the rivers and woods of the north which he had never seen as paradise. That is how Americans, even those from North Dakota, were accustomed to imagine the frontier.

In *North American Canoe Country* (1964) Calvin Rutstrum lists the Port-Sevareid expedition as one of the four contemporary canoe journeys worthy of particular study. What happened on the other three trips will help put what became known as the Port-Sevareid trip in its proper context.

First was the journey Ernest C. Oberholtzer made in 1912 with his Indian companion, Billy Magie, from The Pas, Manitoba, up to Lake Nueltin, out to Hudson Bay, down the Hayes River to Lake Winnipeg, and down the lake shore to the town of Gimli. Ernest was just a few years out of college, Magie was fifty. To fully appreciate their—and later the Port-Sevareid—ordeal, one must examine a detailed map of Manitoba. Except for the southern portion, the province is less a land mass than a confusing network of large lakes, small lakes, swamps, and rivers. The canoeist may paddle for days not knowing whether he is in a lake or a river or whether the island before him corresponds in any way to what appears as a land mass on his map. This is the heart of the area known historically in the eighteenth and nineteenth centuries as the north woods; through it ran the Voyagers' Highway from Grand Portage on Lake Superior to Fort Chipewyan on Lake Athabasca in northeast Alberta; it was the route of the fur trade controlled by the Hudson's Bay Company.

Early in the twentieth century, portage trails were few—and often barely distinguishable from paths trampled by local caribou. Many of the rivers are swift and rough, with rocks that could easily tear a hole in the vulnerable canvas canoes of those days. Summers are short and the winter comes quickly and is slow to depart. In October and the first week of November, on the last leg of their trip, Oberholtzer and Magie had to paddle through sleet storms on Lake Winnipeg far out into the heavy breakers because, if they had hit a reef and overturned, they would surely have frozen to death.

The second, in 1903, was the expedition undertaken by Leonidas Hubbard and Dillon Wallace, accompanied by George Elson, a half-breed Cree Indian, to explore the interior of Labrador by paddling from Hamilton Inlet, up the Naskaupi River, to Lake Michikamau, which stretched over ninety miles of uncharted wilderness. Because of a mistake, missing the mouth of the Naskaupi and stumbling into the dreadful Susan River, they were caught in the Labrador winter and never reached Michikamau. Hubbard died of exposure and starvation.

Third, in 1936 two young New York office workers in their twenties, Sheldon P. Taylor and Geoffrey W. Pope, set out to paddle from the Forty-second Street Dock, up the Hudson River to Lake Champlain, to the St. Lawrence River, to Montreal. By the time they reached Montreal, their trip, with newspaper publicity from gossip columnist Walter Winchell, had so captured the public imagination that they decided to continue on across Canada through the Yukon, taking the Yukon River to the Bering Sea and on to Nome, Alaska.

They saw quickly that their principal obstacle was their own "bushiness," a backwoods psychosis wherein the clash of personalities in confined circumstances turns friends who must depend on one another into enemies. They drew up ten "commandments," guidelines to help them resolve their conflicts rationally; but eventually, after they reached Fort Smith, on the southern border of the Northwest Territories, they had to separate for the winter, each one attaching himself to a different local trapper, and resume the voyage in the spring.

As Arnold read his Kipling and dreamed, he knew nothing of Oberholtzer, Hubbard, Wallace, or Taylor and Pope and the scores who would follow them. He knew only that he wanted to break out.

And of course when Walter Port came over to Arnold's desk, slumped down in the next seat, screwed up his fountain pen and said, "Bud, why in the world don't we get out of here this summer—go somewhere? I'd be partial to the North Pole or South Africa, myself," neither knew that canoeing in the north woods could mean starvation, psychological breakdown, death. Looking at the map, they were struck by the "fact" that one could go by water from the Red River area to the Atlantic

Ocean in the north—and that, therefore, since the Mississippi flowed into the Gulf of Mexico, one could travel from ocean to ocean, right through the heart of the continent, by canoe!

They were also gulled by that odd bit of Minnesota folklore, the yarn about the Kensington Rune Stone, an alleged fourteenth century tablet—now regarded as a fraud—"discovered" by a Minnesota farmer in 1898. The stone purported to demonstrate that Norwegian explorers had penetrated the Middle West—apparently coming from Hudson Bay, through Lake Winnipeg, and the Red River of the North—more than a century before Columbus.

By the usual standards of American high schools, Walter Port was the superior lad; and Arnold seems to have recognized it. Sevareid says in *Not So Wild a Dream* that he was "the slavishly devoted comrade" of this boy who was the confidant of everyone from the principal to the janitors. . . . "The girls liked him, and to me he was a knight without fear, without reproach."

As senior class president and yearbook business manager, Walt was apparently one of those natural leaders who both knows how to plan difficult enterprises and involve others in the planning. His classmates did not know his real age; as far as they knew, at fifteen he had hopped a boxcar and ridden alone to North Dakota with only fifty cents in his pocket. A gymnast and swimmer, he had once swum a six-mile race in the choppy waves of Lake Minnetonka with cramps in both legs. Growing up in northern Minnesota, he worked in lumber camps, in harvest fields, and as a summer fishing guide in Bemidji. With his favorite sports being swimming, diving, and boxing his ideal was Teddy Roosevelt, and for him the perfect man would be a cross between Roosevelt and Mark Twain. Meanwhile he worked from late afternoon till ten at night at a soda fountain in a drugstore to put himself through high school. Finally, unlike his pal Arnold, Walt was an honor student—and a photographer.

On June 16, 1930, Walt brought his gear over to Arnold's house, where the boys sat up late talking in front of the fireplace until Arnold's father chased them up to bed. At 5 A.M. they rolled out of bed, and two hours later they shoved off into the Mississippi under the Mendota bridge in their secondhand, eighteen-foot Old Town canvas canoe, with the center thwart missing. They had christened it the *Sans Souci* and had painted on the bow, "Minneapolis to Hudson Bay." They rode the current down to where the Mississippi meets the Minnesota River at historic Fort Snelling.

Planes flew overhead, in the background guns fired, and a bugle played at Fort Snelling. Their parents stood waving on the dock. In a chorus that would continue all the way to York Factory on Hudson Bay, friends and teachers—including the football coach who had argued for hours that they should save their money for college in the fall—had warned them that they would never make it. But their parents had let them go.

Suddenly, the Mississippi met the Minnesota, the canoe turned southward, and the boys were alone.

Arnold, who considered hmself at the time as "a second Robert Louis Stevenson," had badgered W. C. Robertson, managing editor of the *Minneapolis Star,* an afternoon paper, into financing the trip by paying them one hundred dollars for the articles he and Walt would write and send back en route. In all, Sevareid would write about the same trip about six times: in the daily journals in which both Walt and Arnold would briefly record the day's events; in the eleven pieces they jointly wrote for in the *Star;* in several free-lance articles in boys' magazines; in *Canoeing with the Cree* (1935); in *Not So Wild a Dream* (1946); and again, when *Audubon* magazine (1980) reunited Eric and Walt, now two old men, and flew them over their boyhood route.

A June 14 *Star* article planted to promote their series explained that they expected to do thirty miles a day for ten weeks and arrive at their goal around September 1. Then they would sell their boat and either hitch home or work in Canadian sawmills and logging camps.

They emphasized that since they couldn't afford the fee for a hunting license in Canada, they would not bring a rifle. But, as the daily journal, later articles, and the book make clear, they brought along a .22-caliber rifle, single shot, and used it to kill, or try to kill, the local wildlife for their meals. Their list of equipment, published in *Canoeing with the Cree,* included sixty-one items—like two sponges for canoe cleaning, a bottle of boot oil, "closely cropped hair" and "carefully examined teeth," a rod and reel, two knives, and a hatchet; but altogether their packs were about one hundred pounds. Their food supply was basic: a side of bacon, peanut butter, cans of beans and soup, and a pound of flour for frying fish. Their hope was to scrounge food along the way, catch fish, buy a good meal on shore on Sunday, or live off the hospitality of those along the way who were either inspired by their courage, moved to pity, or charmed by their personalities—like the waitress in Morton, Minnesota, who gave them each a free piece of pie.

They shared the work of keeping the daily journal, and it is hard to tell whether Walt or Arnold was the recorder on any one day, since they refer to themselves in the third person, as Bud and Walt in each account. For example, June 19, their third day out:

> Tent fell down. Took picture of blue heron. Sunburn hurt. Current was very strong. Faces like beets. Many bends and turns to make river longer. Went swimming at noon to refresh ourselves. Haven't much appetites [sic] and stomachs are in bad shape. Made camp on high bluff in soft grass of pasture. Sore but stronger muscles. Belle Plaine.

The bad stomachs can be explained. The heat was intense and the boys couldn't cook. Those who knew Eric Sevareid in later life observed that he had never learned "to boil an egg," that is, to take care of himself at home. On the trip he cooked the pancakes for their first breakfast and recorded for history that "but for the fact that they were burned on the outside and doughy inside, they were good."

For the first six days the river dragged them south to Mankato before turning north to New Ulm, and eventually to Ortonville, its source, on Big Stone Lake. In Fargo, North Dakota, this stream would become the Red River of the North, which moves straight up to Canada. The Red River, one of the few rivers in the world that runs from south to north (the Nile is another) forms the border between Minnesota and North Dakota before it passes into Manitoba for the remainder of its course into Lake Winnipeg. For ten thousand years, much of this area was a vast inland lake.

In their full expedition regalia, the boys wore breeches; well-oiled, knee-high leather boots that laced up the front, wool or cotton shirts, and bandanas around their heads. But most of the time they wore very little. They began taking off their shirts systematically, for five, ten, or fifteen minutes, to get used to the sun. Eventually, by the time they reached Lake Winnipeg, they were down to white shorts, and once frightened children along the way who mistook them—bronzed, bare, and ragged—for Indians.

Their encounters with wildlife in the first weeks ranged from the odd sighting of a four-week-old swimming rabbit to the turtle, which they captured, named Alice, kept as a pet in the boat, then shot it (twice) for dinner.

Meanwhile, along the way the boys received little encouragement. Two truck drivers yelled from a bridge: "Are you the two —— fools from Minneapolis?" and Arnold reacts in *Canoeing with the Cree*: "It was queer that so many of the people can see only the hardships and discomfort of our trip. No one seemed to realize what great sport it was."

On July 8, the *Star* published their third story, with the lead, "We have licked the Minnesota River upstream." With their arrival at Big Stone Lake, right below the border of North and South Dakota, they had traversed five hundred miles in three weeks, almost one fourth of their planned journey. From there on they would not have to paddle upstream. This was Walt's home territory. He had grown up in nearby Ortonville, which he had left ten years before; and as a little boy he had several times run away from home for days at a time to ride a yacht around the lake.

Here, when the strong winds billowed up the surface of the lake into whitecaps, it gave the boys their first "glorious" thrill of rough water. "Bare from the waist up, with the cool air rushing over us," Arnold wrote, "it was thrilling to shoot along on the big rollers . . . it was hard to keep from yelling from pure delight."

On Lake Traverse to the north, the waves grew bigger, but the boys learned that the light *Sans Souci* could "ride the rollers like cork." Mud Lake, well named, was a different ordeal. For a day, eaten by mosquitoes in the smelly swamp, they had to get out and drag their boat though mud and water up to their hips. Finally, after several days of intermittently dragging the canoe along the shallow river bank, wading, and poling around rocks, in North Dakota where the Bois de Sioux and Otter Tail Rivers joined, they came into the Red River of the North.

For a while the current carried them along, but then grew, and remained, sluggish. It was a miserable river. The carcasses of dead cows, pigs, and dogs who had died mired in the muck dotted the banks, and their dreadful stench filled the air. Herds of cattle seeking relief from the flies waded into the stream and caught the little boat in a storm of horns and hoofs.

On July 17, one month on the trail, with seven hundred miles behind them, they paddled into Fargo in a downpour. They stayed with Arnold's relatives, got barber-college haircuts, and ate twenty pancakes each for breakfast. The day after, they resumed their journey, however, laden with cookies and jam ("everything a canoeist is not supposed to eat") but they were forced to return to see a doctor about Walt's thumb, which had been bitten by a fly and, as a result of the blood poisoning, was swollen as big as the thumb on a boxing glove. The otherwise rugged Walt was now overcome with pain.

The doctor was Frederick Gronvold, who, they discovered, had grown up on a farm next to Arnold's grandfather in southeastern Minnesota. This lovable man refused payment, made the boys his guests for eleven days, gave them gifts and theater tickets, and sat and chatted with them for hours about the outdoors. There were tears in all their eyes when they had to part. A half mile away the boys looked back and the doctor still stood on the river's edge watching them disappear. His last words had been: "Don't let anyone, no matter who he is, convince you your trip can't be completed." Years later, when Eric Sevareid was a famous broadcast journalist, he still exchanged letters with Doctor Gronvold.

When the boys reached Crookstown, Arnold's father telephoned to assure them that if they wanted to turn back it would be all right. They wouldn't think of it. They were seeing too many wonderful sights. And doing some good. Again and again along the riverbank, they stopped to rescue stranded sheep from the mud—plus a trapped cow whose owner considered her useless and would have just as well let her die. Further evidence that not all men cared as much for their animal friends as they did: they saw the corpse of a dog who had been drowned with a rock tied around its neck.

North of Grand Forks they saw their first Indians, women and children washing their clothes in the stream. The journal entry: "all very good looking for Indians." In *Canoeing with the Cree*, Arnold called on his high school English course to help catch the image: "Tall and straight, with long black hair and fine facial features, they were characters of

Hiawatha come to life." The next day they spied two girls swimming—one naked. They told their *Star* readers (August 11) that, bashful boys that they were, they turned their heads away; but Arnold, or his editor, with their young audience in mind, omitted the episode from the book. Perhaps an earlier incident was still smarting in Arnold's psyche. Once he had, by chance, observed his mother and younger sister dancing naked at home; and his father, catching him, had reproved him with a powerful slap.

He also left out two vices that the diaries included—smoking and drinking. Arnold puffed regularly at his pipe, and, once they passed into Canada, they often enjoyed the local beer.

The first crucial moment of the voyage came on August 8, at Drayton, North Dakota, not far from the Canadian border. Walt received a letter from a teacher at Central High School informing him that he had been awarded a two-year scholarship at the University of Chicago, but that he would have to be in Chicago by the last week in September in order to take advantage of it.

It was one of those "what-if" turning points in a person's life. If Walter Port, with all his talent, had gone to the University of Chicago, it could have been the first step in an extraordinary career. But they were already two weeks behind schedule, there was almost no chance of their making Hudson Bay and returning in time. Arnold remained silent, ready to turn back if Walt wished. They walked wordless down to the riverbank and picked up their paddles. Then Walt said, "If we don't get back in time, we just don't, that's all. But we can't quit now."

In *Not So Wild a Dream*, Sevareid omits the story of Walt's scholarship and concentrates on the Canada half of the ordeal, which he remembers as almost uninterrupted "emotional weariness, anxiety, and downright fear. . . . For years afterwards a visit to the woods produced a moment of nausea."

But in Canada he saw his first wild deer and and quaint Frenchmen, one of whom might have "stepped out of the pages of Victor Hugo." At night they sat bolt upright and stared at each other at the first thrilling sound of the solitary whippoorwill. The members of the Winnipeg Canoe Club welcomed them warmly, but with equal warmth, for their own good and safety, tried to talk them out of their foolish adventure. But the boys accepted instead the judgment of one old prospector who thought it possible. For both it was a lifetime lesson in epistemology, the ability to distinguish between hearsay and fact. Local people, they decided, tended to exaggerate the dangers of their own neighborhoods; furthermore, although they had moved confidently in these streams and woods all their lives, the locals actually knew very little in the way of precise details about their habitat.

Soon the Red River spilled them out into the overwhelming immensity of Lake Winnepeg. Although it might seem prudent for them to make their way north by paddling along the shore, that route was longer and, because of the reefs—just visible in the whitecaps breaking over the rocks, more dangerous. Rather, they paddled out in the deep water, learning to take the breakers just right by rolling the boat with their hips away from the waves. One morning when they did follow the shore-line, Arnold misjudged the location of a rock and they would have crashed and drowned, weighed down by their heavy boots, if another wave had not literally lifted them over the reef. But they made the Berens River settlement, halfway up Winnipeg, in a week, half the time predicted by the nay-sayers at the club.

Berens River also marked their first encouner with the Cree. With Willie Everett, a pure Cree who nevertheless looked like a white man as their host, they made the rounds of the settlement, watched the Indian boys swim "in the raw," observed how the store-bought clothing obscured the natural grace of the girls, met the chief—a "fiery old reprobate," a fast talker who had been in office for fifteen years, and who received visitors reclining in a dirty hammock in his front yard. The boys liked the chief and were offended when white men and women, who arrived by steamer, offered him candy as if he were a bear in the zoo.

But their biggest thrill was meeting Private Alfred Jones, their first "Mountie," a muscular, shirtless young man who gave the *Sans Souci* a "try" and dazzled the boys, who had developed a good opinion of their own canoemanship, by seemingly transforming their old tub into a racing boat. When Arnold shook his hand it was the greatest honor he had had since he had shaken hands with Jack Dempsey himself.

On their next to last night at Berens River they typed out their ninth story for the *Star* by candlelight. The next day they met Betty Kemp, the daughter of the owner of the Log Cabin Inn, who wanted them to join her for a midnight swim. Earlier the boys had developed a plan to "beat the cold" by conditioning themselves with daily cold swims in Lake Winnipeg. By this time Arnold had lost confidence in the plan, but Walt went along.

It was a one-minute splash of a swim, but the date was long enough to delay their planned late-night departure. A Mountie had suggested paddling at night when the lake surface was calm; but now, suddenly, what had been the small sound of a sighing wind grew into a stunning storm, a howling northwestern gale with thunder that shook their cabin and lightning that illuminated the white billows far out on the lake. If they had left earlier they might have perished.

A few hours of staring into the wind also convinced Arnold that this time their nay-sayers were at least partly right. It would be foolish to try to paddle the next hundred and fifty miles north to Norway House at the top end of the lake against the murderous gale. Walt argued against him, but they flipped a coin, waited two days, and boarded the steamer *Wolverine* for the last overnight leg.

After dinner they watched the square dancing on the upper deck and tried to sleep. Arnold climbed alone to the deck at sunset. He did not record what he saw in the diary, but recalled it a year later in this way: "The dying sun, a huge blood-red disk, tinted deeply the low-hanging western clouds; and on the heavy waves the blood of the sun seemed to be sprayed, enchanting each white billow which leaped and rolled with its brothers in a crimson sea. . . . I felt something of the urge which turns sailors' faces always toward the water. I felt a sense of power over the strong, crafty lake that I had never known before."

That sense of power would soon desert him.

On August 31 they left a request with the Norway House Royal Canadian Air Force wireless operator to contact the *Minneapolis Star* if he did not hear from them by September 20. At daybreak they pushed away from the wharf in a cold, drizzling rain. Arnold was scared and he knew it. By the time he wrote *Not So Wild a Dream,* he had survived the fall of Paris, the London blitz, and the Italian campaign; but this last, grim leg of his adolescent adventure had become not just an adventure tale but a

moral grounding for every future crisis. "What I was entering upon at
Norway House was a contest with myself. I knew instinctively that if I
gave up now, no matter what the justification, it would become easier
forever afterwards to justify compromise with any achievement."

Today, anyone who looks at a standard map, for example, the *Encyclo-
pedia Brittanica Atlas* map of Manitoba, would first of all be astounded
that anyone could set out from Norway House, cross the territory that
no one had both navigated and recorded, and arrive five hundred miles
away within twenty days. Conventional map wisdom would argue for
the more-or-less straight Hayes River route—the Nelson River to the
Hayes and there you are. But, trusting their instincts and a local trapper,
Karl Sherman, the boys picked the Gods Lake and River route, which
took them on a loop to the east, through territory where they would
have to carry their canoe, and where no white man had been before.
But where, the argument went, they could finally link into the Hayes
and zip down to York Factory.

On the first day out they met a priest coming in the opposite direction. He had been in the wilderness for five years and was returning to
civilization. By the look in his face—gray hair, weak blue eyes, missing
teeth—the wilderness had beaten him and it might do the same to
them. He was thirty-five and looked twenty years older. How would
Arnold and Walt look at the end?

Soon, they were lost. And soon they met a white man, Ralph Butchart, traveling with two Crees, who led them deeper into the lakes over
a series of portages. Ralph, who was Scotch, told them their trip was the
"greatest thing he had ever heard of," and his party taught them about
making a sail for their canoe that would whisk them along like "sailor-
men in grand style." Soon they lost Ralph and continued alone. As
Arnold and Walt rode the rapids into Gods Lake and dogs barked to announce their arrival, Arnold could not "imagine how a lake could be
more thrillingly beautiful than Gods Lake. No wonder that name—
God's country indeed. Such sights as these are reserved for those who
will suffer to behold them."

But Gods Lake contained over five thousand spruce-covered islands
that looked exactly alike. Eventually, on a sunny day, they found the
current that sucked them into Gods River at its source. It was the last
time they saw the sun. What followed was eleven days of uninterrupted

misery—constant rain, portages, rapids, sleeping and working in wet clothes; scraping to kill fish so they would not starve. On September 13, the diary records, Walt cut his hand badly skinning a fish. "Hands were so numb, Walt had to skin his fish with his teeth."

But two days later the diary shows that, whatever their pain, they have not lost their awe of the wilderness:

> We are getting more daring and skillful in rapids. Met a lot of shallow stretches that did a lot of damage to the bottom of the boat. Sun came out a few minutes. Walt saw a small wolf in the woods. Woods very beauiful with dark green of the spruce mixed with the yellow of the birch and poplars and the purple of the cranberry bushes close to the water. . . .

September 16 is more typical:

> Another miserable day. Raining again. Late start. . . Ate a cold lunch out of the wind and driving rain, Water in our clothes nearly freezing . . . Grub getting very low. Sugar low. Both very wet and cold and miserable. . . .

They had nothing but rain till the end. The diary does not record the event, but sometime in mid September the psychological pressure mounted to the point of the "bush fever" that had almost destroyed the Pope-Taylor expedition. They began to accuse one another of offenses they would have ignored the week before. *Canoeing with the Cree* and *Not So Wild a Dream* remember the clash in different ways. The older Eric recalls Walt's very words that brought them to blows: "Why don't you wash that goddam pot the way it ought to be washed?"

This was an important event, not only on the trip, but in Sevareid's life, and he twice described it in print, with different emphases. They fought. In 1931 Arnold wrote, "Something in our minds snapped, our moral strength broke down." They rolled over and over until they struck a tree trunk. Eventually they realized that separation in the wilderness would mean death to both of them. In 1945, he wrote that they rolled "through the ashes of the campfire," that though Walt's deep chest and heavy arms gave him an advantage, Arnold was "taller and broader," and neither could defeat the other. Just as well, "since the loser would very probably have been killed."

What does this mean? Was Arnold Sevareid going to murder his pal Walter Port in the north woods? Did the older man, who had survived World War II, rediscover in his soul and admit to darker urges that he could not have acknowledged as a boy? He records in *Not So Wild a Dream*, but not in *Canoeing with the Cree*, that he thought about his mother, started to cry inside, and said over and over to himself, "I'm too young to die."

On September 17 they met a party of Cree and two Hudson Bay men who put them up in their cabin. Their first hot water in a week. At sixty miles a day they would make York Factory in two days. The next day they ran their swiftest rapids and that night watched the glorious northern lights flash their pastel hues across the sky. Another day of cold and rain. Then, on the twentieth, the tremendous Hayes rushed them along its course between limestone cliffs a hundred feet high. Suddenly they were there. Arnold was overwhelmed by a dreamy calm. He intellectualized the event: "This is what all the rivers come to. All those rivers. This is the sea, where everything ends."

Walt shouted: "Bud! Bud! The ocean! The ocean! Wake up, man, wake up! We've done it, we've done it and they said we couldn't."

Two days later, as they rested at York Factory, the captain of a schooner asked them how old they were. He had presumed that Walt was twenty-three and Arnold twenty-five. The hardships, Arnold concluded, had done something to their faces.

They did not arrive home, by train, boat, and hitchhking, until October 10. That fall the Central High School newspaper, in an editorial, drew a moral from their experience. The first point was that the boys had planned out every step of the expedition, they had studied, tried to foresee every possible problem—thus: preparedness. Second, no matter what the odds, they had persevered.

It was of course too late for Walt to accept his scholarship to the University of Chicago, but the high school faculty had found him another one, to Shurtleff College in Alton, Illinois. He stayed there just a year, learning, he said later, "how to write a letter." These were Depression years and young Walt's life had a period of struggling for security and direction. He first attempted to get a job as an apprentice seaman on a ship bound from Seattle to China. When that failed, he stayed in Seattle awhile selling fruit and sundries. He made his way back to Minneapolis, where he decided to return to the talents that had distinguished him in high school. In 1934 he moved north to Bemidji, a town of eleven thousand in the lake district of northern Minnesota, where he guided fishing parties out of Birchmont Lodge, worked as a circulation manager for Minneapolis newspapers, and married Emma Kupka in 1936. They had four children and ten grandchildren.

But Walt did not settle down. In 1941 he drove a truck for a naval base on Kodiak Island, Alaska. In 1943 he worked on the Alcan Highway, the then hazardous road across Canada from British Columbia to Alaska, constructing a telephone line. The next year he was drafted into the service as a seaman. After the war he returned to Bemidji, where he set up a photography department in Johnson's Corner Drug Store. Though the friendship was real, he and Eric Sevareid now lived in different worlds. Walt dropped Eric a very short note in 1950 commenting on one of his broadcasts, and remarking on his "new" name said, "You'll always be Bud to me."

In June 1980, three years after he retired from CBS News but still anxious to keep writing, Eric Sevareid said yes to an invitation from the editor of *Audubon* magazine to rejoin Walter Port for a "Return to God's Country," this time, with photographer Richard Frank, flying over the route in a little Cessna 402. Fishing had since become Eric's one semi-athletic passion, and he brought along his gear. Together, they got as far as Norway House, but bad weather kept them from continuing on to York Factory, though Sevareid and Frank returned in August to finish the assignment.

The article is in many ways a replay of his 1955 return to Velva: the older man, now 67, reevaluating his youth and its meaning; the struggle of the seemingly aloof but psychologically sensitive writer to comprehend the dark forces that have moved him; the lament of the journalist-historian faced with the evidence, in the age of progress, of civilization's decline.

He relates Gods River to the Mouse. He retells the mystical, "oceanic" experience when, at the age of forty, he found his feelings "slipping down the staircase of his emotional existence," until they stopped at the river's bank. While he has repressed the bad memories of

Velva, he says, he remembers only the pain of those last eleven days between Lake Winnipeg and Hudson Bay. But he is still willing to confront the river and try to conquer it—this time emotionally. Besides, he knows that his "awkward triviality" of a book has created the annual phenomenon of Minnesota canoeists—now with featherweight tents, freeze-dried rations, tubes of fire-starter goo, radios, strobe lights, precise maps, metal and plastic canoes and lightweight paddles—repeating his feat.

So, on June 15, at the Minneapolis Sheraton-Ritz Hotel, he is re-united with Walter Port for the first time in forty-five years. Walt seems shorter, a bit bent, his hair as grey as Eric's own. He discovers now for first the first time that Walt is in his early seventies, that he was not nineteen in 1930, as he thought, but quite a bit older! He finds too that Walt speaks so softly that he can sometimes hardly hear him—a trait that his CBS colleagues often attributed to Sevareid himself.

As they fly over the old terrain, the town of Mankato reminds him of the Indian uprisings and the thirty-eight Sioux killers whom President Lincoln had hanged in 1862; Walt spots the bridge where the two truckers had shouted, "Are you the two damn fools from Minneapolis?" At the sight of the Red River, Eric remembers how the scene in the great film *African Queen,* where Humphrey Bogart, devoured by insects and leeches, dragged the boat through swamps, made him sweat in the movie theater years after he had done the same in the Red River mud. He recalls the excruciating pains in his arms and legs brought on by the cold winds and recognizes them now as the first signs of the rheumatoid arthritis that broke out in his system in his early fifties, but seems in remission now. They meet Ralph Butchart, now seventy-four, who saved them when they were lost, and the sons of old Chief Berens, who are still annoyed that in *Canoeing with the Cree* he labeled them as Cree Indians when they were really Saultreaux, a branch of the Ojibways; and they learn that Betty Kemp, whom Walt "romanced with midnight swims," is alive and living in New England.

But God's country is also, in many ways, God-forsaken. Eric weeps when he sees a little camping spot where they had slept littered with beer cans and broken glass. Norway House is now all planes, snowmobiles, and four-door sedans. Now you can drive from Winnipeg to Norway House and overland to Hudson Bay. Indians who have no sense of mechanical maintenance have wasted their savings and welfare payments on cars and abandoned them "if the starter didn't work."

The old settlements have died and been replaced by Indians living in prefab houses. "Life in them has no meaning; it is mere existence, rather brutish existence, I am sorry to say." Here the garbage, the excrement, the stink, the obscene graffiti "are worse than in any city slum I know of." Indian youth are being destroyed by drunkenness, violence, and drugs. The Mounties have changed. Mounties may marry. Since force is officially discouraged, women and small men can be Mounties, too. "One despairs," he writes, and concludes that the Indians, like the citizens of Velva, must be integrated more swiftly into modern life; he repeats the line from Wordsworth about the world being too much with us, and concludes again that the world is too little with these isolated people, and they with it.

But surely the most memorable episode of the trip is Sevareid's account in *Audubon* magazine of the layover at Elk Island where the aging Sevareid and aging Port bunk together, fish for pike, and talk for four days, as they wait for the fog to lift on Hudson Bay. Eric lies on his bed staring at the naked lightbulb and knows that Walt in the next bed is remembering what he is remembering—their fight.

Eric had been "startled," he writes, to reread *Not So Wild a Dream* and discover that he had spoken of him and Walt actually on the verge of killing one another. Somehow, remembered in 1945, the fight had "swollen beyond its real dimensions." But it also meant that their friendship was never truly close again. Yet, he knows that "a characteristic of mine persisted: anyone I have once loved I cannot entirely stop loving, no matter what." He suspects Walt is the same. Walt continually calls him "Bud." And, "One night, as I dozed, I felt him arranging the fallen blanket over my exposed feet. That is the second time on this return journey of rediscovery that I felt the sting of tears."

3

WEST BY RAIL

IN THE 1930s when Arnold Eric Sevareid was a student, the University of Minnesota was counted—depending on who was counting—as among the best half dozen or dozen universities in the United States. It was, he wrote later, a city in itself—the state's fourth great city after Minneapolis, St. Paul, and Duluth; it was, like the Minneapolis public school system, a "miniature of American life, faithfully accomodating the taxpayers of the state in all their ideas of what their children and their civilization should grow up to be." Years later the university would boast that during that decade it turned loose into American life Hubert H. Humphrey, Harold E. Stassen, Hedley Donovan, and Eric Sevareid. And according to the testimony of those who were there, those years really were one of those special historic times when, though on a relatively small stage, great events and great men came together.

To Hedley Donovan of the class of 1934, a brilliant young man who nevertheless could not afford Harvard, his first choice, or Columbia, his father's school, it was the fullest expression of Minnesota's devotion to education as the secular religion, the "pinnacle of the faith." It was also his introduction to serious politics when, in the depths of the Depression, students and faculty, seized with the urgency of the national and international crises, brought controversies into the classroom and turned those years into a "kind of Hard Times Golden Age." Furthermore, it was his gateway into a journalism career, which he began as editorial writer for the *Minnesota Daily;* and his window into world affairs—a Rhodes scholarship, which took him to Oxford in September 1934, then on travels through western Europe on the edge of war.

Donovan and Sevareid just missed crossing paths with Hubert Humphrey, who had driven with his father from Doland, South Dakota, to register in the fall of 1929. Hubert's father dropped him in a rooming house just off the campus in a room ten feet by twelve, and told him,

"From here on, it's on you," and left him to fend for himself. His first year did not go smoothly. He joined the freshman debate team, but the *Daily* turned him down. After Christmas, when his father had to cut off his ten-dollars-a-week allowance, he washed dishes in Swoboda's campus drugstore for twenty cents an hour.

In the fall of 1930, when his father said Hubert would have to come home and work so his brother Ralph could have a shot at college, Hubert complied; but his uncle Harry gave him fifty dollars to get through the winter quarter. Financial crises overwhelmed the family. The older Humphrey moved his store to Huron, South Dakota, and both sons soon dropped out of college. Hubert could not return to the University of Minnesota until the semester after Sevareid left, and this time as a married man—and into a city and an institution still hurting from the terrible political and social confrontations of the preceding years.

Both followed on the heels of Harold Stassen, who had recently graduated from the college and law school, and was on his way to being elected Minnesota's youngest governor in 1938.

The university's academic standards blended egalitarianism and elitism. Operating on a quarter system—the fall term began in October, then winter and spring and two summer sessions—it admitted anyone from Minnesota with a high school diploma in the fall and flunked out a third of them by Christmas. It even went through the motions of monitoring fraternity and sorority grades, with the *Daily* publishing their standings in each year's first issue.

Meanwhile, the university as a whole was bucking the impact of the Depression. Under the leadership of Lotus D. Coffman, who had taken charge in 1921, it met enrollment dips with budget cuts, jacked registration to a peak of twelve thousand in 1934, and, whatever the constant struggles of its local students to scrimp and toil to pay their bills, it maintained at least the surface of that carefree way of life which movie musicals and popular fiction put forth as "college." Donovan spent almost as much money on fraternity dues and parties as he did on tuition and books. Not sated by the pervasive football madness—so bad that even Coffman, according to Sevareid, prayed that the team would occasionally lose—the students fielded a polo team, subsidized by ROTC, as well; they crowded in to hear visiting celebrities like Christopher Morley, Dorothy Thompson (just expelled from Hitler's Germany), and

Alexander Woollcott; and some men followed a tradition of wearing their white tie and tails to class the morning after the prom.

The 1935 yearbook, the *Gopher*, lyrically spells out the moments of the typical day. At 5 A.M., long before dawn, the weary, ink-stained editors of the *Minnesota Daily* survey their newborn edition "freshly released from the jaws of the press, then stagger home for a few hours sleep before class." The other students rise at seven, shave meticulously. They ride the Minneapolis streetcar to class or, if they don't have morning class, hang around the post office, read the *Daily*, and chat. During lectures they nod over or scribble in their notes. At lunch they split: fraternity brothers and sorority sisters to their ceremonious repasts at houses along University Avenue, all the others, who have carried their lunches to school, to the union, the common cafeteria. In the afternoon, boys play pool. Coeds rest up, preserve their "pep" for the night's parties. "Curled up on a davenport, comfortably propped with pillows, the coed finds pleasure in reading a romantic tale, munching chocolates as she reads." When the athletes get to the locker rooms, "the musty odor of liniment and sweaty bodies mingle to give a pungent aroma that becomes a vital force . . ." By eight o'clock, the boy with no date may be stuck in the library; the others fuss with ties, as they dress for the symphony, the movies, the theater, or the sorority dances where they will waltz and fox-trot till 3 A.M.

But this typical college life, except for the all-consuming schedule of the student journalists, was a far cry from the college life of Arnold Sevareid. To begin with, he had not planned to go directly to college. Since he had hung around Bill Francis's *Velva Journal,* he had known exactly what he wanted to be—a newspaper man. For him, as he recounts in *Not So Wild a Dream,* there was no sensual pleasure more satisfying than the warmth and smells of the city room, and the "warmer, noisier, greasier composing room upstairs"—all leading to the "ordered cacophony of improvised symphony to the thundering finale by the great presses below the street. . . ."

After he returned from the great canoe trip, Arnold worked till December in the shipping room of the Minneapolis Honeywell Company; then, on the basis of his *Minneapolis Star* stories on the canoe trip, the *Journal* hired him as a copy boy, and, within six weeks (passing over older, unemployed men who had been waiting months for a job, but would demand higher salaries) moved him up to reporter at fifteen dollars a week. As it happened, the young man's first stint with the *Journal*, which lasted from 1930 to the summer of 1933, was one long series of disillusionments.

Of the three papers in the city—the *Minnesapolis Star,* which had been founded as the *Minnesota Daily Star* in 1920 as a champion of farmers and workers; the *Tribune*, the survivor of a series of mergers and ownership changes that went back to the Civil War; and the *Journal*, which had been founded in 1878—the *Journal* was tied closest to the establishment.

According to University of Minnesota journalism historian George S. Hage, who got his start as a *Minnesota Daily* student writer in the early 1930s, the *Journal* had followed a conservative, pro-Republican editorial position since its founding. Its most notable publisher, Herschel V. Jones, a New Yorker, bought it in 1908 and when he died in 1928, passed it on to his son, Carl W. Jones. As Sevareid wrote, "It spoke with authority in the land, if not with wisdom, and it was an interconnecting cog in the social machinery of a widely scattered civilization." He was unaware, as an eighteen-year-old idealist, of the paper's "true function"—that its owners and publishers were more concerned with maintaining the power and privileges of the potentates of the timber, railroad, and milling industries than with printing the truth or protecting the welfare of the common reader.

The cub reporter learned some fundamentals about life—that preachers are obnoxious in their pursuit of publicity, and that the poor are more vulnerable than the rich to prying reporters who come scrounging for photographs of murdered husbands. But he went to college because he was driven partly by fear—fear that without an education he would end up like the older men on the staff, exploited and abused for most of their careers, living in fear of their editors, or anyone above them who could send them jobless onto the street. Like the charming old essayist, who had given his life to the newspaper, but still grovelled lest an editor be "rough" on him if he were late with his copy. Like the financial editor, who told Arnold, as he cleared out his locker after eighteen years, "I've been fired by a guy I used to teach where to put commas."

Because Arnold had to keep working he began college by attending night classes. On the way to class he passed the fraternity houses where the boys lolled in their sweatshirts and sent their laughter and phonograph music drifting into the classroom, as a reminder of the gulf between the world of affluent and working students.

After one term his editor gave him a schedule that allowed him to work mornings and attend regular classes in the afternoon. In his freshman year, fall 1931 through spring 1932, he took a light schedule: each quarter one introductory English course, one economics course for two quarters, and one French course. In night school he had taken English, French, and one-credit courses in Latin, geometry, and physics. Like everyone in the land grant university, he had to suffer through compulsory drill (earning two A's and a D), and physical education. He took up boxing and did well, qualifying for the welterweight championship finals, when he was knocked out. In the spring, following in his father's footsteps, he pitched baseball, but not well. After four good innings he went to pieces and walked everyone, until the coach sent him to the showers.

He took this as a sign that the grind of a full-time reporting job and schoolwork had become too much for him. One of the paradoxes of Sevareid's life is that the man who endured the 2,250-mile canoe trip was constantly sick. In this way he seemed to resemble his mother, a woman who constantly complained about her illnesses. Most of the illnesses—like the arthritis that plagued him for years and the cancer that finally killed him—were genuine; but over the years many of his professional colleagues came to see his less specific complaints as psychologically based, as a manifestation of the tensions between what he had to do and what he either wanted to do or felt he should do.

He had not enrolled for the fall 1932 quarter, but he held a B average for the winter and spring, and, at the end of his sophomore year, was inducted into the Delta Phi Lambda, the honorary society for creative writing and literary arts. But in June 1933 young Sevareid saw himself as pale and ill. If he wanted to continue with journalism and college, he had to act decisively—he had to do something about his health. If he consulted a doctor, he does not say; but his solution to the problem is more in the spirit of Walt's idol, Teddy Roosevelt, a sickly young Harvard man who rebuilt his strength on the frontier. That summer Arnold decided to go work in a gold mine in California's High Sierras.

He traveled alone. "It is the right and only way," he wrote later, echoing that earlier democratic individualist Henry David Thoreau. "You do not have to talk if you would rather be silent; you can stop where you will, doze when you wish, and think your own thoughts. All that the eye sees, the mind registers, and the heart envelops is filtered by the screen of yourself, untreated, unmodified by the conditioning presence of another being."

Strong words from a man who had it not been for helpful friends on his travels might have been killed. He might not have articulated his reasons that way when he was twenty; but they are consistent with the young man his contemporaries describe: the aloof, reserved, standoffish observer, sizing up a person or situation, not just through rational analysis of experience but on the basis of a part visceral, part aesthetic instinct. He was entering the second great adventure of his life—one, considering the nation's social and economic crisis, as hazardous as his expedition to Hudson Bay. This time he would hitchhike and ride the rails.

William Manchester describes the Depression well in *The Glory and the Dream*. About two million Americans were on the road in 1933. Like Arnold, more than a quarter of a million were young people between sixteen and twenty-one. Some of the two million were experienced "knights of the road," men who for years had developed survival skills and who knew the safe, hospitable towns like East St. Louis with its welcoming Salvation Army station, and those to skirt—like Cheyenne, Wyoming, which would greet you with clubs and gunshots, and California, which had posted guards at the borders to turn back the poor. But most of the travelers during those years were homeless, penniless victims of economic calamities: bankers, farmers, civil engineers, college students and professors, and ministers. They included, says Manchester, a dipomat, and a former chef.

As Cabell Phillips wrote in the *New York Times,* the man who knocked on your door at night "might be the same fellow who a few months ago or a year ago had cheerfully O.K.'d your loan at the bank or had written the editorials in your newspapers or had been the vice president of a leading real estate company." Thomas Wolfe described the nomads who quarreled over the stools in the public latrines outside New York's city hall as "hungry, defeated, empty, hopeless, restless, driven by they knew not what, always on the move, looking everywhere for work, for the bare crumbs to support their miserable lives, and finding neither work nor crumbs."

For a young man concerned about his health, Arnold was plunging into a hazardous way of life. In Congressional testimony, an agent for the Missouri Pacific Railway reported that of 387,313 Depression nomads of whom he had taken "official notice," 335 had become casualties. There were other risks as well: many of the travelers were drug addicts, thieves, and male and female prostitutes. Henry Ford said, with unintended irony, "Why it's the best education in the world for those boys, that traveling around! They get more experience in a few months than they would in years at school."

The *Velva Journal* (June 29, 1933), reporting on Arnold's passing through town, said that the young man, now a student, is "fitting himself for further work in the field of journalism." Journalism had already taught him that "life was a relentless, never-ending struggle; one never 'arrived'"; that big institutions, motivated by greed, can crush the men and women who depend on them. This trip introduced him to what he called, ironically, "this world of private enterprise and individual initiative," a "jungle," a great underground world where men, women, and children fight to survive, "steal one day, beg with cap in hand the next, fight with fists and often razors . . . happy only when the wheels are clicking under them, the telephone poles slipping by."

In mid June he hopped a freight from Minneapolis to Minot, where he hitched a ride down to Velva, which, he wrote twelve years later, had grown younger, while he had grown older. Parking signs had replaced hitching posts, Buicks had replaced dusty buggies. After a few days with Bill Francis and at Strawberry Lake, an old boyhood friend drove him back to Minot, where he slept in what he thought was a park, only to discover at dawn that he was next to an animal cage in the Roosevelt Park and Zoo.

A telephone lineman drove him forty miles in a Ford half-truck and a young traveling salesman seven hundred miles into Montana. From Helena, a chubby man named Smith drove him to his uncle's home in Seattle. From there, for five dollars, a double-decker bus took him to northern California, where he bathed in the "brown and thick waters of the Sacramento River," and made his way on foot and by hitchhiking to the mountain mining camp of the man he calls "a certain Fitzgerald." His host was actually the brother of Alice Fitzgerald Dreschler, Arnold's high school French teacher, who had arranged the summer job, and who remained one of Arnold's most devoted friends and fans for the rest of his life.

On the way out, the journalist-in-training came to see his occasional traveling companions, as he analyzed them later, as American types, as various incarnations of the American character. The traveling salesman, with the dark sunglasses, starched collar, and pressed suit, who bragged that he knew how to impress the local yokels, was the "wise guy incarnate," symbolic of all the slick operators in the world who, in countries where honest people starved or stole that their families might eat, never missed a meal. (Had Arnold read in 1932 that President Herbert Hoover, refusing to economize in the White House kitchen, sat down each night in a tuxedo to a seven-course meal—for the sake of the country's morale?) The "honest" whore who sat next to him on the bus from Seattle became a symbol of all whores working "the Ritz hotels of the world." The unlettered men of the mining camp he saw as natural artisans, who never studied physics or chemistry but knew with their hands how to turn a motorcycle engine into a power saw or create a plumbing system out of a creek and a few pipes—they were that half of America he could never enter but which produced the sergeants and corporals who (like the team players in the Minneapolis high school system) won World War II.

But first he had to learn to get along with them, to communicate in their language. Fitz baited him with the same semi-affectionate abuse every college boy gets from day laborers who half envy, half resent his education. What do they teach you in that college anyway if you don't know how to hold a shovel or stick dynamite in a hole? They called him "Slim" and "Tenderfoot" and pulled pranks on him; though when they heard he had been a reporter they began to lay off. He joined their beer parties and competed with them swinging the shovel and sawing the trees.

And, as he had in the north woods, when he was alone he contemplated the wilderness and his own ordeal with awe and made notes he would later turn into transcendental prose. "The day sounds would begin: the shrill chippering of a squirrel overhead, the dull smacking of a woodpecker, and down in the valley the tinkle of a cowbell . . . the taste of salt was sharp in the corner of the mouth, and the wooden shovel had a good, grainy feel in the hand. In these moments the power of life exploded slowly through the veins, and one worked in a savage orgasm until exhaustion came."

At the end of the month, he rode a truck to Reno and climbed into an empty boxcar on a Union Pacific freight that took him across the Great American Desert to Salt Lake, and on to Minneapolis. Among his traveling companions were a sixteen-year-old homosexual hustler who amazed Arnold, who knew little about homosexuality, by bragging about his sexual exploits as casually as if he were talking about baseball; a big, threatening Negro homosexual who tried to seduce him; and thugs who plotted to steal his last four dollars. But the trip, like all American road sagas, had its idyllic, Edenic interludes, when Arnold and his friends sunbathed nude on a flatcar and "swam naked in deep mountain pools of cool, clear water."

He arrived home miraculously in better health than when he left, with a deeper chest and heavier shoulders; and he had reason to look forward to the fall semester. *Canoeing with the Cree*, which he had been working on steadily, showing drafts to teachers in class assignments, was almost ready for publication, and the *Daily* had announced on May 13 that their new "anonymous" columnist was a rather tall young man who worked on the *Minneapolis Journal*, last year pitched freshman baseball, and was a friend of the editor.

Financially he was no better off. He had paid Fitz for board and taken no pay for his work, except the souvenir phial of gold dust, worth eighty cents, which his mother mistook for dirt and washed down the sink.

4

UNIVERSITY YEARS

THE UNIVERSITY OF MINNESOTA in the fall of 1933 was in a state of intellectual and political upheaval. Just as the students of the 1960s poured out of the campus to march in civil rights demonstrations, headed south with the Student Nonviolent Coordinating Committee (SNCC) for the "Mississippi Summer" to assist in black voter registration, joined the fall 1967 Pentagon march against the Vietnam War, and shook their fists into the night outside the Chicago Hilton in their antiwar demonstration at the 1968 Democratic Convention, Sevareid's generation joined the picket lines during the famous Minneapolis truckers' strike in the summer of 1934, fought for the elimination of compulsory military drill on campus, and sharing the disillusionment of their parents who saw the aftermath of World War I as a betrayal of the ideals for which the war had been fought, they turned their backs to the conflict again coming to a boil in Europe.

Presiding over this tumult was Lotus Delta Coffman (1875–1938), university president from 1920 till he died in office of a heart attack, who is probably best known today as the university adminstrator who unfairly thwarted the just ambitions of the future CBS-TV News commentator. But as president he was an innovator with a national reputation. With a Ph.D. in education from Columbia University Teachers' College, Coffman was above all an "educationist": a professional dedicated to teaching as a profession and training teachers in teachers' colleges rather than a research scholar in a liberal arts discipline like philosophy or history. He instituted special programs for both gifted students and those who would never make it through, and short courses for businessmen to advance them in their fields. He created a fine arts department and art gallery, erected more than forty buildings, including a music buiding, brought the Minneapolis Symphony Orchestra to campus, and added a school of journalism.

He saw the university as a public service corporation, bound to serve the people of the state. Deeply disturbed by the impact of the Depression on students who had to struggle to pay their way, he won a grant from the Federal Emergency Relief Adminstration in 1933 to fund university jobs—research assistants, typists, cafeteria workers, buildings and grounds laborers, even art models—for carefully selected students who showed signs they would use the money well. The so-called federal students, forerunners of today's work-study programs, were enormously successful, with better grades and higher morale than their peers. Both Sevareid and Humphrey were among those who benefitted from Coffman's program.

Coffman had firm and clear opinions on just about everything, including international affairs. He said often that he deplored "all forms of excessive emotion and super-patriotism that lead to war," and he regretted that his own country's isolationism had done nothing to promote real peace.

Student publications, by nature reluctant to recognize the humanity of university presidents, nevertheless treated him with reserved affection. A brief *Daily* profile (February 2, 1933) tells us that he reads the *Atlantic Monthly, Country Gentleman,* and *Outdoor America* and books on the Depression, that he hunts and fishes, golfs at 80, eats steak and onions, listens to *Amos an' Andy,* fools with change in his pocket when he talks, and follows the philosophy of Émile Coué: "Every day in every way, I'm getting more and more out of life."

Hedley Donovan estimated that perhaps one student in ten was intensely interested in politics—up from the 5 percent of the 1920s. In 1933–34, Donovan's senior year, attendance at student forums, weekly speeches by political leaders—for example, pro-and-con talks on Hitler—was up 30 percent. And, as a look through the yearbook and newspaper will verify, within the activist 10 percent there was considerable overlap among the various groups who organized the forum, ran for the student government offices, demonstrated against ROTC, and wrote for the *Daily,* the *Ski-U-Mah* humor magazine, and other publications.

Donovan used his post as editorial writer for the *Daily* to make some admittedly confident and ponderous pronouncements on campus and national affairs. When the student editor spiked a Donovan 1932 editorial tweaking New York governor Franklin D. Roosevelt for refusing to admit he was running for president, Donovan's father passed it along to *Journal* publisher Carl Jones, whom he had met on the streetcar. Jones published it as the lead editorial in the *Journal*.

Also, editorials on the 1930s peace movement—the American response to the "Oxford Resolution" in which the members of the Oxford Union took its famous 1933 "oath" that they would "in no circumstanes fight for king and country"—ran regularly.

This reflected the mood of campuses across America. Students were reading John Dos Passos' *Three Soldiers* and Hemingway's *A Farewell to Arms,* stories of young people whose lives were ruined by a war that made no sense. The university movie theater, newly equipped for sound film, showed *All Quiet on the Western Front,* with its scene where a nationalistic professor seduces his students with a false dream of battlefield glory. Many nodded in agreement with North Dakota's senator Gerald P. Nye, chairman of the Senate Munitions Investigating Subcommittee, who focused blame on a conspiracy between Wall Street financiers and European warmongers: "We didn't win a thing we set out for in the last war. We merely succeeded, with tremendous loss of life, to make secure the loans of private bankers to the Allies."

In one national poll, 39 percent of undergraduates said they would not participate in any war, and another 33 percent said they would do so only if the United States were invaded. In 1935, over 150,000 students demonstrated in a nationwide student strike for peace. Donovan, who was not swept along by the pacifist enthusiasm, recalls that the national pacifist mood was all the more intense at Minnesota because of the traditional isolationism of the Middle West and its provincial Protestant millenarianism. He recalls that after the Japanese had taken over Manchuria, former secretary of state Frank Kellogg, author of the Kellogg Pact that outlawed war, was asked by a student during a 1934 visit to the campus if there was danger of war. He replied, "There is no more chance of war with Japan than a war with Timbuktu."

At the center of this whirl at Minnesota was a little band of brothers to which Donovan, having already pledged himself to one of the "academic" fraternities, could never belong; they called themselves the Jacobin

Club. They had named themselves for the most notorious political group of the French Revolution, called Jacobins because they held their regular meetings at the former convent of the Dominicans, who were known as Jacobins. Organized as "friends of liberty and equality," the original Jacobins, who eventually had thousands of club branches all over France under the leadership of Robespierre, became a symbol of dictatorship, violence, and terror; but surely the Minnesota 1930s branch must have taken the name in fun. One participant recalls them having a charter at one time with a phrase like "in the midst of chaos we will be organized and seize control . . ." They didn't really mean it.

On the other hand, while they did not see themselves as precursors of a reign of terror, they did not allow their clever wits to prevent them from taking themselves, as bright young men, quite seriously. They were conscious of being smarter than the other students: at one time their collective scholastic average was 2.2 on a scale of zero to 3, (compared to 1.5 for the fraternities) and, by pulling the usual strings of student politics, they infiltrated their men into many campus leadership positions. While built around the French Revolution's ideal of *fraternité*, they made a point of not being the usual college frat. Most of them, with their Depression-stricken families and part-time jobs, could never afford fraternity dues. They had no house, no formal rules, and—though a handful of them had more clout than the others—it is hard to imagine their egos allowing them to be easily led. The group varied in size from a dozen to about fifteen, and their one obligation was to show up for the monthly or weekly lunchtime meeting at a cafeteria table in the union, where they held their highly animated conversations about international politics, the new science, the failures of institutional religion, the American Newspaper Guild, and the stupidities of their archenemy, Dean of Students E. E. Nicholson.

From time to time they would give the administration grief by inviting controversial public figures like the Trotskyite teamster labor leaders, the Dunne brothers, and progressive, Farmer-Labor Party, iconoclastic Minnesota governor, Floyd B. Olson, to come on campus and speak. Philosophically, they were mostly socialists; in state politics, Farmer-Labor, and nationally, Roosevelt New-Dealers. And of course Marxists, Trotskyites, and other communists dealt with them, although they scorned communists as ineffective. In campus politics, they belonged to different parties and often ran against one another for office.

Although individual Jacobins might hold a variety of political opinions, collectively they were rebels. Like their successors of the 1960s, they wanted to redistribute power—from the university administrators to student committees, from the industrial capitalists who hoarded their wealth to the families of workingmen stifled by the economic system which, in its failure, had brought on the Great Depression.

Sevareid all his life was described as reserved, aloof, and self-contained, yet he still had an apparent need to belong to and be intimately identified with small groups and larger institutions. His association with the *Minneapolis Journal,* until he perceived its corrupt core, filled him with a sense of well-being, and more than half his life he would derive much of his public identity from CBS; in these very formative years, he was strongly attached to the Jacobins and the *Daily.* He needed to "belong."

The Jacobins included a remarkable roster of talented young men, many of whom went on to prominent political and journalism careers. One of the "founders" was Richard Scammon '34, an enormous (six foot four, 260 pounds) young man with a Rabelaisian wit and a booming voice. The son of the dean of medical sciences at the University of Minnesota, he struck at least one contemporary as a young man rebelling against his father. When he graduated, he headed right for the London School of Economics to study political science under the famous Harold Laski, then returned to go to law school at the University of Michigan. But after four weeks, he switched to political science. With Ben Wattenberg he later wrote *The Real Majority* (1970) and became a prominent Washington political analyst.

Another "founder," Lee Loevinger, Arts and Letters, '33, Law School '36, was perhaps the most politically wired of the group. As editor of *Ski-U-Mah,* he had once portrayed the univeristy board of publications, the official overseer of the campus newspaper and magazines, with a picture of horses' behinds. Rumor reached him that the faculty, angry over some outrage or other, had met to consider expelling him, but concluded that he already had enough credits to graduate. Later he became a prominent Minneapolis and Washington attorney, a judge on the Minnesota Supreme Court, an adviser to Hubert Humphrey, and member of the Federal Communications Commission.

Also among the early Jacobins was Earl Larson, law student, president of the all-university council, who agitated for increasing student membership on various student-faculty committees, particularly the student affairs committee and the senate committee on intercollegiate athletics. He is now a Minneapolis judge. Martin Quigley '38, another *Daily* reporter, humor columnist, and *Ski-U-Mah* editor, became a successful novelist and baseball writer—among his writings is *The Crooked Pitch* (1984), a book on the history of the curve ball. Other Jacobins were Bill Costello, one of Sevareid's best friends, who also became a CBS reporter and foreign correspondent; Sherman Dryer, *Daily* drama critic, campus radio newsman, and later host of a radio political roundtable in Chicago; Phil Potter, *Daily* editor, later White House correspondent for the *Baltimore Sun*; and Al Kosek, *Daily* editor, now an Edina, Minnesota, lawyer who split with the group and would be held responsible for the most bitter and painful memory of Sevareid's life.

The Jacobins' guru was a young, debonair, and brilliant political science professor, Benjamin E. Lippincott, who was a disciple of Harold Laski. It could well be argued that Laski, through Lippincott, was the Jacobins' true teacher once removed. Laski had, as historian Arthur Schlesinger, Jr., describes him, "burst on the United States in 1916, a twenty-three-year-old prodigy out of Oxford who joined the Harvard faculty and proceeded to dazzle everyone of importance." On this and later visits to America, he built a network of influential friends; the political, literary, and journalism eminences dazzled by Laski included Justices Holmes and Brandeis, Herbert Croly of *The New Republic,* Walter Lippmann, Edmund Wilson, Max Lerner, and Edward R. Murrow.

Back in England Laski was a Labour Party activist, a political and intellectual gadfly, a prolific author, and, like Lippincott, a great teacher who molded the minds of future leaders. Unlike Laski, the disciple handled classroom "problems" with humor. When Hubert Humphrey returned to the university in 1937, he naturally made his way to Lippincott's classroom; but, taking advantage of Lippincott's Socratic method, he tended to talk too much. Finally, the professor had to shut him up: "Humphrey, if there are going to be any five-minute speeches made in this class, I'm going to make them." Laski, like his pupil Lippincott, is remembered more today for whom he taught than for what he wrote, a reputation with which many good teachers would feel satisfied. Scammon went abroad to study with him, and Sevareid sought him out in London during the 1940 blitz.

When the Jacobins sat at Lippincott's feet he was just getting started, a thirty-year-old assistant professor. After graduating from Yale in 1925, he studied for two years at Oxford, then completed his Ph.D. for the University of London in 1930, after he had begun teaching at Minnesota as an instructor in 1929. Like many professors who pour their energies into their students, he was not to produce a great body of scholarship, but he did publish a few works that remain on library shelves.

Like other very good teachers, Lippincott was not popular with everybody. Sevareid recalls: "Lippincott would survey us with darting eyes, a tinge of sardonic humor in his soft, mobile face." Some students found his unfamiliar Socratic method—rigorous, open-ended questioning, playing one student against another—unsettling, and some quickly dropped his course. But for those who remained, it was a wonderful trip—from Genesis, the Greeks, Romans, churchmen of the Middle Ages, through Locke, Hume, Roger Williams, Jefferson, Paine, Adam Smith, Rousseau, Voltaire, Burke, Marx, Hegel, Spencer, Lenin, and Trotsky.

Clearly, it was one of those survey courses that touch a lot of bases, and it is difficult to know how much of these authors the students really read. But the broad exposure had its intended effect. Sevareid writes: "Like all average brains, mine required the impulse that cannot be planned—a stray book, a disturbing remark, or the challenge of a great teacher who deliberately kicks at the self-starter with which every mental engine is presumably equipped." Lippicott's broad introduction gave him those thousand references he would drop into his commentaries for the rest of his life; from political science and economics he acquired the philosophical depth and practical focus that would give those commentaries authority.

The influence of Lippincott also sanctioned Arnold's rebel streak. Though that streak would soon subside, the example of this American Laski reinforced the impression that, yes, it was right to be at odds with the authorities. At one stage, according to Lippincott, President Coffman, who was a Republican and a Baptist and therefore a "pretty tough hombre," had been blue-penciling Lippincott's proposed two- and three-thousand-dollar raises because he was a Socialist. Coffman finally called him in and said, "Rumor has it that you're a Communist. Is that true?" Lippincott answered no, he was a "Democratic Socialist," then, since Coffman had no ashtray on his desk, bent down and flicked his cigarette ashes into a wastebasket under Coffman's desk between his legs. Growing grimmer, Coffman asked him to sign an affadavit to that effect. Lippincott agreed, "on one condition, that this doesn't interfere with my academic freedom."

Meanwhile, the professor did not limit his contact with students to his classroom or office. For those in his large classes, which would be fifty to sixty students, he ran an additional voluntary seminar on Saturday morning. Occasionally he would come to a Jacobin meeting; and, with his wife Gertrude, a dancer and one of his students, whom he married in 1934, he loved to entertain; the novelist Frederick Manfred recalls, "when those two put on a party it was something to write home about."

But perhaps an even stronger influence on the imaginations of these young men was Floyd B. Olson, governor of Minnesota from 1930 to 1936, leader of the Farmer-Labor Party, and the spiritual successor, says Sevareid, of two now-forgotten, turn-of-the-century Minnesota heroes, Ignatius Donnelly and Charles Augustus Lindbergh, father of the pilot who would define America's modern undersanding of the words hero and celebrity. Donnelly (1831–1901), a Minnesota Republican congressman of the 1860s, left the party when he saw that in the coming struggle "between the few who seek to grasp all power and wealth, and the many who seek to preserve their rights as American citizens and freemen," the Republicans were on the side of the few. He ran repeatedly for office as a Greenback-Democrat and a Populist; and he gained wide influence through his great oratory and popular writing, including the utopian novel, *Caesar's Column: A Story of the Twentieth Century* (1891).

The elder Lindbergh (1859–1924) a Swedish immigrant, was also a Republican congressman (1907–17) and Roosevelt "reformer," until defeated by Frank B. Kellogg for the Senate in 1916. When he published a critique of American participation in World War I, and tried to speak against national policy, the St. Paul and Minneapolis press vilified him, mobs broke up his meetings and threw stones at him. A biographer describes him as a champion of common people, but friendless; the kind of man "to whom statues are erected only after the lapse of many years."

Son of a not-very-ambitious Norwegian father and an authoritarian Swedish mother whose nagging probably turned him against conservative values, Olson was a colorful, fun-loving, county attorney, a master of charm and sarcasm from Minneapolis's tough North Side. He had worked as a farmhand and railroad laborer, and in his neighborhood, which was almost a Jewish ghetto, he learned Yiddish and earned spending money doing sabbath tasks—turning lights on and off, keeping furnaces going—for Orthodox familes.

He swept into the governor's mansion in 1930 as a candidate of the Farmer-Labor Party, backed by the the Non-Partisan League. A Humphrey biographer describes Olson as a kind of Humphrey predecessor; with his Scandanavian background, sharp tongue, and streetwise tactics, he became Minnesota's first truly modern urban politician, and the first Minnesotan to become a truly national figure. Before the Minnesota contingent of the Bonus Marchers left for Washington in 1932, Olson told them that if capitalism wasn't able to deal with the nation's problems, "I hope the present system of government goes right to hell where it belongs."

What attracted students like Sevareid and the Jacobins to Olson must have been his rare combination of idealism and *joi de vivre*. Part of his combative class consciousness came from the wounds of an impoverished childhood, but he was neither petty nor vindictive. He hated stuffed shirts, but he could deal with them respectfully. He never carried a watch, so he fell behind on his official obligations, and he loved to sing, swim, fish, dance, drink, and tell dialect jokes. When he died of a lingering stomach cancer in 1936 at the age of forty-five, Sevareid was crushed. For him and his friends it was also the death of their hopes for a more humane and progressive era. Later in life, Sevareid would write with equal feeling about only one other person—Edward R. Murrow. For him, at least, Olson seems to have been a mythical father figure at a time when his own father—a reticent, conservative banker who saw labor strikes as akin to revolutions—was far from comprehending the transformation his Arnold was passing through.

Although the Minnesota campus was in constant ferment, protest against military training was not the only activity that absorbed students during the 1933–34 academic year. Insofar as any campus newspaper is a mirror of student life, the *Daily* reflected a day-to-day culture that was simultaneously significant and trivial—a year rich in the political drama and silliness that characterized the larger society: The fraternities and sororities compete with one another and the impact of the Depression to survive. In a student body that typically declines from 11,000 to 9,000 total enrollment in the course of a year, 1,000 belong to thirty fraternities and 600 to sororities; supporting this way of life costs each one about $500 a year in room, board, and fees. Meanwhile their grades continually slip and administrators huff and puff about suspending any house with a collective average below C.

To protest the construction of new dormitories, two hundred unruly Greeks form a torchlight parade, troop over to Coffman's home and, to the consternation of both the president and his wife, tramp on their lawn. Eugene Ormandy, director of the Minneapolis Symphony, performs regularly on campus. John Charles Thomas appears with him. In an editorial, a downtown newspaper criticizes the university's production of Sigmund Romberg's *The Desert Song* for its misguided effort to "make dancing houris out of nice coeds." The forum sponsors a discussion, "Resolved: That the U.S. Needs A Dictator." The traditional Pajama Parade gets out of hand; three hundred pajama-clad students invade the nurses' dorm and, besides pilfering stockings and underwear, steal expensive books, dishes, and clothing, and drive girls naked from their showers through the halls.

But the engine driving the *Daily* is editor-Jacobin Phil Potter, who judiciously orchestrates his coverage so as to addrerss the controversial issues fairly, while winning the coveted Collegiate Press Association award, the Pacemaker—a sort of college journalism Pulitzer—and producing the news stories and editorials, written by Hedley Donovan, that will eventually undermine the legitimacy of mandatory drill on campus. In his autobiography, Donovan downplays his role in the peace movement, says he was not a conscientious objector and, on the Oxford oath, argued in an editorial that "thinking persons . . . would be loath to surrender the right to fight in any strictly non-aggressive war for self-defense." But in fact, the editorial, published on April 19, 1933, just three months after Hitler's rise to power in Germany, neutrally presents three possibly valid responses to the oath. In an article for the Cornell University *Areopagus* (November, 1934) Sevareid credits Donovan's series of editorials with creating the climate to defeat the military.

Meanwhile, as a journalist, Sevareid operated on two levels: as an activist, the image he adopts in his autobiography, and as a "humor" columnist, a role he never mentions. On one level, the *Daily* was his whole life; but a contemporary describes him as aloof, not one of the boys, "not a team player," a "specialty writer." Although he wrote three important articles on the drill issue, he was, from May 1933 to June 1935, primarily a columnist, often a very private, introspective occupation.

And an odd column it was. It appeared irregularly—sometimes weekly, sometimes two or three times a week. Called in its first year "Bubbles Off the Beaker" (as in a chemical reaction), and in its second, "The Beaker," it was, for the most part, a random collection of snippits, tidbits, jokes, doggerel, anecdotes, inside jibes directed at fellow staffers, professors, frat boys and sorority girls, and lists of people and things that irritate. There are continual self-conscious references to the trials of writing a column, including the shopworn columnist's device of "here I am with a deadline. What do I write about today?" His contemporaries read it religiously and remember it fondly. Martin Quigley recalls a Sevareid quote to this day, an exchange of letters (perhaps imaginary) with Coffman in which Coffman uses the expression, "in the final analysis" and Sevareid replies, "In the final analysis, there is no final analysis."

One Sevareid column relates an anecdote about an English professor shooting holes in Hedley Donovan's sonnet and a sheepish Hedley replying, "Well, ah—at least you will have to admit it has fourteen lines." In another he quotes a letter from a student reader who observed him during dinner at the junior ball and writes to make fun of the columnist's appearance: "You resemble Ichabod Crane trying out as a flagpole sitter. And the way you went after that chicken . . ." One makes light of a *Minneapolis Star* (November 22, 1934) news item about himself: he and his friend Sherman Dryer prevented a train wreck when they discovered that, in a washout, a wooden pole had fallen across the tracks; they ran a quarter of a mile, notified the signalman, and saved the day. On another day, his typewriter, Elsie Smith, talks back, with a note on his writing methods, which did not change much over the years: "Sometimes you sit and just stare at me for hours, which is unnerving to say the least. And then you suddenly lash out with those fishhook claws of yours with the tender touch of a bear sweeping up trout."

A few of the better ones are stylistically experimental, stream-of-con-
sciousness stringing-togethers of vivid, concrete, sensuous images from
student life, bursting with a young writer's love of words and a delight in
his own powers of observation: "red-haired girls with orange rouge and
orange fingernails . . . dark men, blue jowled . . . ting of a waiter's bell . . .
coed limping over lost heel . . . jacketed freshman in yellow corduroy
carrying lunch in brown wrapping paper . . . well-brushed fraternity
head slumped with sleep on arm of green leather divan . . . blackboard
chalk screeches and pimpled face whitens . . . bare branches run shadow-
less against rough-cut building stone . . . dormitory men, near nudeness,
studying by green, goose-necked study lamps . . ."

Only occasionally does he touch on issues, and then in a noncon-
frontational style. In January 1934 he celebrates the completion of his six
quarters of required drill. He raises no moral issues. The army officers
were gentlemen, he says; it's the senseless repetition of useless exercises—
order arms, present arms—that has frustrated him. He says in *Not So
Wild a Dream:* ". . . we knew that in their hearts the professional fighters
wanted war, enjoyed war. We hated them for it." If so, in his college writing, he never allowed the intensity of that "hate" to show.

Only occasionally is there a sustained piece of prose where one might
spot the seeds of the later incisive and whimsical *CBS Evening News*
commentaries. One, April 17, 1934, and reprinted a year later, which a
faculty member told him was one of the best pieces of journalism he
had seen anywhere, begins: "In the Yukon, when the ice suddenly lets go
with a surprised roar, they know spring is just around the first bend upstream. North Dakota, without grass or trees or rivers, has to rely upon
some inexperienced robin in his first mistaken flight for a herald. But it's
so much more complicated at the University of Minnesota." Sevareid
goes on to describe President Coffman observing a green patch of grass
outside his window and deciding therefore that the golf season has
begun—and to smile.

To a degree, Sevareid's behavior pattern at the *Daily* foreshadows his
work pattern years later at CBS News: the daily, isolated chore of concentrating his energies on a two-minute commentary that will usually
be taped before the broadcast, where he is not really part of the team
putting together the news "package"; but then there were the special projects, documentaries, conventions, and elections. Despite his prodigious

accomplishments, he would always be a man of limited emotional, psychological, and physical energies. There were only so many things he could do at once. At college, while other students were sleeping off last night's party, Arnold would rise at five, take the streetcar halfway across town to the campus, report for his job at the university post office, his bones shivering in the icy wind, distribute bundles of the *Daily* hot off the presses, and then drag himself to morning class.

He says he remembers his college years as a "struggle," not so much the struggle of working his way through, but the struggle over ideas, and the emotional exhaustion of public debate. He remembers "exhilarating triumphs and the most acute bitterness of my life." The triumph would be the abolition of obligatory drill, the bitterness was what fellow student and lifelong friend Arthur Burck would decribe years later, still with emotion in his voice, as "the terrible thing that happened to him."

The campaign against compulsory military drill first took on momentum on November 15, 1932, when George P. Conger, associate professor of philosophy, told a crowd of four hundred students at the forum in the union that the world wanted peace, that it was absurd to think that France, Germany, or Russia would attack us, and that this "useless" compulsory drilling of students must be brought to an end. The next day the *Daily* endorsed his idea in a front-page editorial, calling drill a "waste of time." It is interesting that the *Daily*'s arguments, then and throughout the campaign, were not based so much on moral principles, like the value of human life, but on a revisionist historical analysis of the First World War.

In fact, as George W. Garlid shows in *Minnesota History* (winter 1967), "by the middle of the 1930s the revisionist view had become the quasi-official position of the Minnesota state department of education." Pamphlets issued by the department stressed the economic roots of the conflict, that the Allies wanted to destroy Germany's industrial competition; American bankers, manufacturers and merchants wanted to get fat on the arms trade; the press condemned submarine warfare because it threatened our rich foreign trade; and the "common people in all countries [were] naturally peace-loving." Republicans joined the Farmer-Laborites in accepting this revisionist thesis. Thus, the peace-movement university students were not only parroting the opinions of their professors, but also voicing ideas they had inhaled from the Minnesota's social and cultural atmosphere.

Student editorial writers exhaled these concepts as: the "uselessness" of World War I; the political theory that "preparedness," another word for militarism, instigates rather than prevents war; and that military drill, as an exercise, is an impractical training for battle. The *Daily* editorial concludes: "Let the men get practical training in burrowing through mud, vermin, poison gas and germs of consumption and dysentery; let them learn how to take their part in modern warfare."

Within a week, Dick Scammon called together the committee for optional drill and Conger addressed their meeting. By January, another more militant group, the antiwar committee, demanded an end to all ROTC programs. When the American Legion auxiliary, representing twenty thousand Minnesota women, responded with a survey "proving" that the bulk of students who had taken drill did not find it "degrading," the *Daily* replied by refuting their arguments and by quoting John Dewey that military training is "undemocratic, barbaric and educationally wholly unwise" (February 2, 1933).

In March, the state legislature held hearings on the drill issue but failed to take action, setting the stage for the spring quarter's highest drama: on April 26, the forum sponsored a debate on the Oxford oath. Throughout the country college papers were polling their readers on whether they would refuse to bear arms. They worded their questions in a variety of ways. The Brown *Daily Herald*, for example, added "except in case of invasion." But many, such as those at Columbia and Northwestern, were finding overwhelming sentiment against war. At Columbia, 42 percent of the faculty pledged that "under no circumstances" would they don the uniform.

The *Daily* editorialized: "The Oxford movement is giving normally apathetic students a subject to get roused up about." In a room crowded with three hundred students, Lee Loevinger fired up the meeting with a speech that accused politicians of inciting the people to fight for reasons they themselves did not understand. Others asserted that Hitler and Mussolini were the result of Wilson's attempt to "make the world safe for democracy" or called for a revolution of the working class. A cadet officer declared that "a country good enough to live in is good enough to fight for"—but he was not heard. Fifty cadets, in their shined boots and Sam Brown belts, stormed out in protest. The meeting broke up in disarray. Although a vote had not been scheduled, the chair called for a poll of those who remained. The resolution backing the oath carried 92 to 3. Loevinger, Scammon, and Sevareid voted for; Donovan against.

On June 5 the *Daily* reported on the nationwide poll that showed that of 22,627 students who voted, 39 percent would under no circumstances fight "for flag or country," 33 percent would fight under certain circumstances, and 28 percent adhered to "traditional patriotism." At their June 5 meeting the university board of regents postponed indefinitely any decision on drill. In his testimony to the board, Dean E. E. Nicholson perhaps revealed more than he intended about the real function of drill on campus and why the student body, with the instinct the young often have for real human motivation, could abstract themselves from the threat of Hitler and see "militarism" in a purely local and personal context. "I am impressed by the growing tendency among students to disobey," the dean said. "Military drill is the last bulwark of any semblance of discipline or respect for law."

The first breakthrough came the following October 26, when Arnold Sevareid broke the story of twenty-two-year-old Minneapolis freshman, Ray W. Ohlson, who had come to hate militarism as a high school student, refused to drill, faced expulsion, took his case to president Coffman, and won. Ohlson, who had saved his money for three years so he might have a liberal education, decided after two weeks of drill that he was compromising his own integrity. Inspired by a *Daily* editorial, he wrote up his ideas in an English term paper and offered the paper to the admistration to support his position. At the April meeting he took the Oxford oath. Coffman interviewed him three times, could not shake his resolve, was convinced he was sincere, did not want to lose him, and allowed him to substitute physical education for drill. It was the first time, Sevareid wrote, "that a student has been excused from military drill on the grounds of conscientious objection."

On March 1, 1934, Sevareid published a lengthy front-page analytical article, unusual for a student newspaper, on the status of the drill debate at Minnesota and around the country. Individual conscience, he says, has become the focal point of the fight. He says that the educational debate over militarism goes back a century, but became more pointed since World War I, now that the "youth crusade" is challenging the fundamental assumption that war is inevitable. Drill opponents took encouragement from the fact that DePauw University regents voted to abolish ROTC in January. He traces the history of drill to the Morrill Land Grant Act signed by Lincoln in 1862, but makes clear that the law, while it requires that military science be taught, does not require that it be compulsory.

As journalism, the piece is a model of that genre in which a writer analyzes, does not editorialize, does not make the reader's judgments for him, but leads him to the conclusion the writer has in mind. Yet, considering what was to happen to this writer a year later, one strange sentence stands out as prophetic. Unfortunately, he says, controversy has become more bitter. It is dividing campuses. "Student editors have been chosen or rejected on this one point."

On March 16, Sheldon Kaplan, an honors student in philosophy, was suspended from the college for excessive absences from drill. Kaplan was not a conscientious objector; he missed some classes because of various illnesses, and for two others he maintained that he had been present at the lectures but that the officer, who confused him with another student of the same name, had marked him absent. Tested on the material taught during those disputed classes, he failed—later explaining that, with the teacher's consent, he had always used military class time to do his other work. With Scammon as his advocate, Kaplan defended himself before a military tribunal and was found guilty, only to be reinstated by Coffman the next day. Sevareid speculates in the *Areopagus* that Coffman, knowing that Kaplan planned to take his case to the courts, simply wanted to keep things as quiet as possible till the regents could settle the matter in June. The other possibility is that Coffman, though he believed profoundly in the value of drill, was too clever to hand the movement a martyr at this time.

Smarting from the *Daily*'s coverage, ROTC fought back with a petition to cut the *Daily*'s subsidy, that subscriptions be optional rather than supported by a student fee. The *Daily* is "biased and unfair" they charged, and "not representative of the student body." The *Daily* knew this was simply a ploy to intimidate them, but they did back off from the issue for a few weeks. Until the paper discovered in mid May that the drill issue had become the hidden equation in the election for the all-university council. The military and the fraternities joined forces to block the election of Richard Scammon as president. Scammon, candidate of the Pnyx party, had characterized his opponents, the Gophers, as the party that had been in power too long. "Intellectually they have stagnated; morally, their conscience has grown dull." But the medical and nursing students—whose dean was Scammon's own father—had allied themselves with the militarists and kept the Gophers in power by a slim margin of one hundred votes.

Beaten but unbowed, within a day Scammon began organizing a massive antimilitary demonstration to be held on "Jingo Day," May 23, to coincide with the annual military review. Governor Olson, invited to speak at a rousing all-university peace conference, appeared on campus and cheered the rebels on. He implied to his audience of a thousand that he had been forced out of the university's law school because he had "declined to take drill," when, according to the university's centennial history, actually he had been dropped for nonpayment of fees. Compulsory drill, he said, was an invasion of one's constituional rights: "I hope you students make your demonstration more picturesque and more interesting than the military review itself." In fact, offstage, he was deeply involved in the controversy. The Farmer-Labor Party opposed drill, and that year Olson appointed four new members to the board of regents.

As the demonstration day approached, tension rose. The demonstration leaders secretly reshuffled their plans as rumors flew that they would be attacked or expelled. Nicholson backed off from a refusal to allow the parade but tried to impose a special censorship committee to supervise the *Daily;* so the *Daily* dropped editorials for a day and published a boxed notice under the masthead to the effect that the policy of the *Daily* "no longer represents the opinions of the editors or the editorial staff, but those of the censorship committee appointed by the Board in Control of Student Publications." The day of the review, Phil Potter, obviously reacting to adminstration criticism and pressure, tried to make some fine distinctions for his readers. He explained in a page-one box that, while the *Daily* backed the idea of holding the conference and the demonstration, the *Daily* was not the sponsor of these events and had in no way tried to influence their deliberations and planning.

The day after the review and counterdemonstration, the *Daily* began: "In the shadow of the battlements of the University's ancient Armory, the scene of countless military reviews, some 2,200 members of the ROTC cadet corps marched in review yesterday on Northrop Field while 5,000 spectators looked on." Meanwhile, not far away, in front of the union, and within earshot of the military band and bugle calls, another crowd of 1,500, some of whom hustled back and forth between the military parade and the peace rally, struggled to hear the speakers who stood on an improvised platform in a first-floor window. Across the street a gang of cadets in drill uniforms tried to hoot them down. The thousand cheered as Ray Ohlson proclaimed, "It is a thousand times better to die or go to jail in protest than to go to war." When a cadet officer tried to take handbills away from a pacifist demonstrator, the pacifist socked him in the jaw.

Two days later, the censorship committee was replaced by a three-person editorial committee of the university board of communications. On June 6, in its final editorial, the *Daily* deplored the tense, semihysterical atmosphere that had surrounded the controversy for years and wondered how a "comparatively liberal" adminstration, which had instituted so many educational reforms, could resist this one for so long.

They did not have long to wait. On June 18, university commencement day, at the meeting of the board of regents in the administration building, Anna Determan, one of Olson's new appointments and the only woman on the board, made a surprise motion to drop compulsory drill. Because one pro-drill member was in Washington and another switched his position from the previous year, the resolution carried six to five. Together, an exultant Al Kosek, who had been named editor for the next year, and Arnie Sevareid put together a special one-page issue headlined, "EXTRA! COMPULSORY DRILL KILLED BY REGENTS," that included a Sevareid story beginning on a note of simple triumph: "Compulsory military drill at the University of Minnesota is dead."   ·

When America entered World War II, Sheldon Kaplan enlisted in the army in June 1942 and served four years. Richard Scammon joined the army in 1941 and served in England, France, and Germany till he was discharged as a captain in 1946. Lee Loevinger served as lieutenant commander in the U.S. Naval Reserve from 1942 to 1945. Sevareid performed heroically as a war correspondent and agonized for years over whether he should enlist.

In 1965 Loevinger, then on the Federal Communications Commission, returned to the university to speak on "The Temper of the Times." He remembers his college years as dominated by three themes: the Depression, labor's drive to organize, and concern about "the continuing threat of war." In an assessment hard to share by anyone who had read *Not So Wild a Dream* or the *Daily* from 1932 to 1936, Loevinger says that "Liberals dominated campus demonstrations and expression and demanded U.S. intervention in foreign trouble spots and international cooperation to deter aggression." While there were mass meetings, he says, they were disorganized, and most students were simply interested in enjoying themselves for four years, getting a degree and a job. Most of his speech surveys student protests around the country, a comparison between the 1960s and the 1930s, and a final weighing of the evidence. Ultimately he concludes that contemporary rebels are "seeking nothing less than a society which treats each man with all the respect due to any man." But some of their behavior is ominous. The 1960s demonstrators, he observes, are more violently aggressive, intense, bitter, shrill. Their revolt "is not so much against social injustice as against society itself, and against the university as a representative of society."

Loevinger ties in other manifestations of violence, like Hell's Angels and teen-age suicides; and he quotes his friend Sevareid, who by then had a reputation for being a bit of a grump about student demonstrators, though he was clear to say he deplored their violence, not their goals: "There is some common thread binding together the racial demonstrations, police savagery, juvenile delinquency, adult crime, pornography and the often senseless milling and marching of college students . . . Somehow we must learn new strategies and tactics for the containing and controlling of disorder, as we are obliged to learn new ways to confront guerrilla warfare overseas. All the ties that bind this society together seem to have gone loose and slack" (*Washington Evening Star,* March 23, 1965).

Young Sevareid's first sense of the slackness of society's ties was his realization that the *Minneapolis Journal* exploited its employees. His second came in the spring and summer of 1934, right on top of his exhilarating success in political journalism, as he and some fellow students were drawn into a bloody truckers' strike.

Humphrey's biographer, Carl Solberg, describes the atmosphere of those days: "Violence was in the air. In St. Paul, where John Dillinger, Al Karpis, and Babyface Nelson were resident gunslingers, gangs kidnapped bankers and brewers and held them for ransom. In Minneapolis, where down-and-outers fought over bread crusts in riverside Hoovervilles, the Citizens' Alliance mustered goons, spies, stool pigeons, Burns detectives, and grand-jury fixers to keep the unions down." Eleanor Roosevelt's journalist friend Lorena Hickock wrote to Harry Hopkins in December 1933 warning that business and labor were heading for a showdown.

That showdown, which took on aspects of a civil war, was between the Citizens' Alliance, which represented the old families and eight hundred businesses, and had succeeded in keeping Minneapolis an open-shop town, and the Dunne brothers.

As Lois Quam and Peter J. Rachieff demonstrate in *Minnesota History* (fall 1986), the Citizens' Alliance was in many ways the most powerful and well-organized employers' group in the country. A combine of class-conscious industrialists, merchants, and lawyers, they had begun to work together during the 1917–18 trolley strikes. By the 1930s they were a national case study of how to keep an open-shop town.

Their two ideological drums were the constitution and religion. Since a union shop, they argued, violated the Constitution, all alliance members had to sign a statement swearing they would not hire any person who believed otherwise. Alliance leaders invoked religious authority to support their policies and thus convince their members that their motives were not selfish and profit-oriented. It would be a mistake to imagine the alliance as a small group of plutocrats. Membership was open to all employers in Hennepin County who could pay the ten dollars dues and were approved by two men on the membership committee. It would also be a mistake to imagine them as governed by the proprieties that allegedly governed upper-class behavior. A *St. Paul Daily News* story (October 8, 1936) describes them as just as ruthless in cracking down on moderate businessmen as laborites might be in disciplining their stray sheep. It used "terroristic methods as freely as Local 574."

The six Dunne brothers had grown up in Charles A. Lindbergh's hometown of Little Falls, where, the story goes, the oldest brother, Bill, had been alienated from the Catholic Church when their priest caught him reading a Victor Hugo novel and tore it up. Most became communists of the Trotskyite faction.

The Dunne brothers, because they were colorful rebels, because Minneapolis working men really were exploited, and because the brothers were very expert at their craft—organizing the logistics of a citywide strike with the precision and imagination one normally associates with military genius—enjoyed campus popularity.

The National Recovery Act of 1933 permitted workers to unionize, Minneapolis teamsters were quick to use it. Ray Dunne, who had experience plotting strikes in the West, struck the coal yards and won union recognition. The strike demonstrated that Minneapolis, as a regional distribution center, was so dependent on trucks that the city's four thousand drivers had more power than anyone had realized.

Emboldened by their first victory, they determined to organize all the city's drivers. On May 12, after employers refused to negotiate and collective bargaining broke down, the workers voted to strike. On May 19 union pickets were attacked and beaten. Beginning on May 21, violence escalated, and for two days strikers, marching in columns of six hundred and wielding clubs and lead pipes, battled with the Citizens' Alliance army of deputies and police in Minneapolis's Central Market. The alliance's soldiers included the socially prominent willing to take some personal risk to protect their power—among them a young man from Yale who went into battle wearing jodphurs and a polo helmet. For two days the strikers outnumbered their foes and dubbed the fracas the "Battle of Deputies Run." But, on May 22, two "special deputies" of the Citizens' Alliance, one their vice president, were killed. Governor Olson imposed a truce.

At the university, the strike first impinged as a minor inconvenience. Construction on the new dormitory halted when building supplies stopped coming in. Strikers did not impede the university trucks which brought milk from the university farm to the cafeteria and hospital. So that *The Student Prince*, with guest star Metropolitan Opera tenor Clifford

Menz, could go on as scheduled, the crew brought the scenery in their private cars. In *Not So Wild a Dream,* Sevareid remembers fraternity boys showing up downtown with clubs, eager to give the strikers a drubbing; but Donovan and a *Daily* editorial (May 24) say that when a delegation of businessmen appeared at the Intrafraternity Council to urge the Greeks to join the forces of "law and order" and "get out and fight" to preserve civic peace, the fraternity men rejected them and rebuked their leadership for dabbling in the strike.

The antagonists maintained the governor's truce till the strike resumed on July 16. On "Bloody Friday," July 20, in 102-degree heat, a truck filled with fifty police ambushed a group of strikers. Up to this day the police had not used their guns, but now they fired away. While strikers tried to retreat with their wounded the police raked them with buckshot. They killed two and wounded sixty-seven.

Olson declared martial law, arrested the Dunnes, raided the alliance headquarters, and got Roosevelt to threaten secretly to withhold all Reconstruction Finance Corporation funds from Minneapolis unless the employers recognized the union.

That summer Sevareid had taken a job at the *Star,* the paper most likely to give the strikers fair coverage; and on the night of Bloody Friday he made his way to the hospital, where the nurse led him among the wounded strikers and demonstrated that "nearly all of them had wounds in the backs of their heads, arms, legs and shoulders." They had been shot while trying to run away. "Suddenly I knew. I understood deep in my bones and blood what Fascism was." It was a radicalizing moment, a revelation akin to the one experienced by many liberals at the Democratic National Convention in Chicago in 1968 when they saw the bleeding heads of student demonstrators who had been gassed and clubbed by Chicago police. It is the central insight of Norman Mailer's novels and Jack London's *The Iron Heel,* that power will use violence to sustain itself in any society—whether socialist, communist, or democratic and capitalist—whether in Europe or the American Middle West.

Alfred Sevareid, gray-haired and pale, was sitting on the screened porch of the Portland Avenue home, clutching the newspaper. "This—this—is *revolution!*" he said to his son.

"Well," the son recklessly replied, "if it is, maybe we'd better make the most of it."

Crushed, the father let the paper slip from his fingers and held his head in his hands: "I did not ever think that one of my sons would become a revolutionary." The son—who never did become a revolutionary —only then began to understand how, for people like his father, civic order and public institutions held a religious significance.

During the 1934–35 academic year, the *Daily*, under editor Al Kosek, maintained its level of excellence—its neat, gray, traditional format, good writing, balanced tone—though it might have lost some of its political fire. To the editorial page Kosek added a new column of national and international news briefs by William Plymat and a regular letter by Rhodes scholar Hedley Donovan on his adventures in Oxford—where his British chums had invited him to join the Oxford Military Training Corps! In his final columns (May 17 and 18), Donovan describes Europe on the brink of war. He is shocked that the airplane, which is a potential guardian of peace has, in the bomber, brought war closer. Perhaps the realization that ten days of modern warfare could reduce the capitals of Europe to smouldering ruins, he says, may still be an impetus for peace.

A *Daily* policy gave half its news and editorial space to off-campus political and cultural issues, so a typical front page (January 23, 1935) includes: a report of a talk on Hitler's occupation of the Saar; an item on the skull of General Custer's dog, who had died of old age in Minneapolis, gathering dust on campus in the zoology building; a lead story on the *Literary Digest* nationwide student poll on the war issue; and record enrollment of 2,950 on the farm campus.

That year, Earl Larson, varsity golfer, Gopher party mainstay, and outspoken critic of the fraternity system, ran against and beat his fellow Jacobin, Richard Scammon, for president of the all-university council; and Lee Loevinger, the man credited with stampeding the student audience into voting for the Oxford resolution, and who had proposed the abolition of the communications board the year before, became its head and strove to pull it away from the administration's sway.

In a November 7 campus visit, Senator Nye, his voice hoarse from campaigning in the North Dakota election, called munitions manufacturing the "rottenest international racket of all time; and the next day the American League Against Fascism and War staged another campus demonstration, with talks by journalism chairman Ralph Casey and Ben Lippincott, choosing November 9 to offset the nationalistic feelings usually associated with Armistice Day. On November 21, Arnold Sevareid interviewed Christopher Morley, who used the occasion to run down Gertrude Stein. If the conservative columnist Westbrook Pegler were ever to go to work on Gertrude, he said, "well, you would hear a very distinct thud as she hit the floor."

One story that deserved coverage but got only two inches all year: Loevinger raised the issue of racial segregation in the dorms. Finally a committee proposed that one black male be allowed to live in a dorm as an experiment.

Editorials, the *Daily* announced, would now reflect a greater diversity of opinion rather than a consistent view. They also took a more on-the-one-hand-and-on-the-other tone. When the peace controversy heated up again in the spring, as the campus prepared for a climactic participation in the nationwide April 13 strike for peace, Kosek withheld enthusiastic endorsement. In boxed editorials on page one, signed with his initials (an indication that he may have lacked staff support) he argued that outside organizers—the National Student League, the League for Industrial Democracy, the National Council of Methodist Youth, the Inter-Seminary movement, and the American Youth Congress—had come to campus, threatened to cripple the university, and endangered its academic freedom (April 10). That same day Coffman told the *Daily* that if the state legislature, fed stories of "subversive activities" on the campus, wished to investigate it was welcome to do so. On the day of the strike, the *Daily* editorial regretted that a protest against war could become an attack against the university. "Cool, directed reason and not general, amorphous emotion will find the way to peace." That day, across the country, 150,000 students demontrated, while at Minnesota Olson told 2,500: "Train a hundred men in boxing and they will soon want to go out and try their skill on the citizenry. The same is true of military organizations."

While all this was going on, another struggle—for some of greater emotional import—ensued. April 10 was the deadline for filing applications for the editorships of the yearbook, the *Ski-U-Mah,* the *Literary Review,* and the *Daily*. Arnold Sevareid was busy collecting statements of eligibility from Mary P. Skinner, assistant to Dean Nicholson and Ralph Casey, chairman of the communication board's editorial committee, and typing up his ten-page application, a statement of his qualifications and his platform.

He has also been doing a little politicking. Early in the year, Sevareid apparently wrote to Hedley Donovan in Oxford, seeking help in the coming contest. Bill Plymat had suddenly surfaced as a possible rival candidate, and Sevareid wanted a statement from Donovan that, because Bill had not had enough time on the paper, he should not be eligible. Donovan replied, on February 14, that he didn't want to get involved. Since the petition was coming from one who was himself a candidate, it wouldn't look right. Better for Arnold to take his evidence to Loevinger and the board.

Perhaps only someone who has been a student newspaper editor or faculty adviser can appreciate how totally consuming, how tied to an ambitious student's ego, how expressive of one's deepest identity the editor's position can be. The rituals of the selection process, whatever the differences of time or place, have been remarkably constant: the editor emerges, through toil and talent and the consent of his and her peers. At Minnesota the candidates submitted applications in mid April, the selections were made by the board of communications, consisting in 1935 of Dean Nicholson, journalism professor Ralph D. Casey, Professor T. E. Steward, law student and chairman Lee Loevinger, and six other students, elected from the student body but none of whom were on the *Daily* staff. Sevareid writes in his memoir that he expected to follow Kosek "by right of seniority and general agreement, as editor in my senior year." The "agreement" of course was among his friends, not among the members of the board.

What Sevareid omits from his memoir is that he had already run for the editorship the year before and lost to Kosek then. In April 1934, officially classified as in the class of '35, he describes himself in his application as twenty-one years old, unmarried, a junior, expecting to graduate next year, with a major in political science and a minor in history. He says he intends to spend a year in graduate work in journalism. It is an impressive document, which begins: "I have been working with newspapers since I was fifteen years old." He lists his many high school journalism awards, his after-school jobs, the canoe trip, and the manuscript he is trying to publish, his two years at the *Journal,* his participation in "every activity" of the *Daily.* He tells how the president of Luther College offered him a scholarship to come there and establish a news bureau, but he passed it up for Minnesota. He even throws in his experience at the *Velva Journal,* without mentioning how young he was at the time.

Above all, he makes every effort to anticipate the charge that he is too controversial. "I have written a column three times a week and I consider it something of an achievement to have been able to write about personalities and controversial subjects without arousing the serious enmity of any person—at least so far as I know," he says. His policies section begins: "My interest has never been in anything but newspaper editorial work. It is to be my life occupation, very likely in this vicinity, and I do not intend to jeopardize my future, nor lose caste with my present associates in the profession by making a mess of running the *Daily.* Nor do I intend to willfully make a body of enemies of the men and women who run the university. The days of traditional undergraduate opposition to the administration I hope, are dead and buried as far as Minnesota is concerned, and I will do my part to keep them buried." He goes on to say that the *Daily* should not dedicate an inordinate amount of space to "pet causes" unless student opinion favors its view.

For six pages he critiques the work of his colleagues, deplores "high-school girlish" material that gets into print, promises to seek advice from the journalism faculty (although in three years he has taken only one journalism course), advocates more interviews of the famous men and women who come to campus, an improved sports page, and better "esprit de corps." Morale is low, he says. Staff members don't even know one another's names. They need more praise and encouragement to get their work done. The document portrays a person quite different from the rebel image that he imagined dwelled in the minds of the administration and the board, and milder than the Jacobin he suggests in his own autobiography. But it is, ironically, quite consistent with the image of the *CBS Evening News* commentator of the 1960s and 1970s who, fans and critics agreed, addressed controversial subjects without arousing serious enmity, who had little wish to make foes of the men and women who ran either the nation or CBS News.

Perhaps he felt, a year later, that, having made an "early run" and lost graciously to fellow Jacobin Kosek the year before, his 1935 election was assured. In any case, he barely bothered to update his application. This time, though, he describes himself as a junior again, twenty-two years old, expecting to graduate "next year" with a major in political science and a minor in economics. His grade point average is 1.9. Ms. Skinner classifies him as in the class of '36. This is a puzzle. In fact, he graduated in December 1935, a quarter behind what would have been his class, probably because of his missed quarter in the fall 1933, and he stayed on after graduation to take journalism courses in the winter and spring of 1936. This projected schedule would make him eligible to be editor for the 1935–36 academic year.

To read many of the same paragraphs in light of his previous year's try is to sense someone making a little less effort to prove himself, perhaps because he thinks his record speaks for itself. He suggests more articles written by campus authorities, and he takes issue with the editorial page which, he feels, has reverted to running many editorials on "petty subjects of restricted interest." He prefers that "more space be given to topics of wider importance. . . . We have undergraduates on this campus with the ability to handle these topics on a par with most daily newspapers, but they cannot be attracted to the *Daily* without first instituting such a policy. I do not like assertive methods of editorial writing, which tend to lead into the fatal path of the doctrinaire. We have gone too far this year from the empirical approach." Here again we hear the voice of the later commentator, who presumed that the way to engage an audience in intelligent discourse was to talk to it intelligently.

His mistake was to assume that, approached rationally, people would respond the same way. Rather, he maintains in his memoir, his enemies joined forces to block him out—beginning with the Greeks who, anxious to break the power of the Jacobins, spread the rumor that he had got his girlfriend pregnant and needed the editor's salary so he could marry. The conspiracy extended to Coffman himself, who "turned the head" of Kosek with flattery and convinced him to stay on in law school in order to be editor again. Furthermore, Sevareid says, Coffman ordered his own faculty representative to vote against Sevareid or lose his job.

Almost sixty years later, the transaction between Coffman and that unnamed faculty member is difficult to reconstruct. That Coffman would prefer Kosek more is easy to believe: Kosek echoed Coffman's refusal to allow the university to become, as James Gray quotes him in the university's centennial history (1951), "a sounding board of propaganda." But Coffman wanted a school that was open and tolerant as well. That he would pass the word to squash a would-be student editor casts him in the fascist mold.

At any rate, all the contemporary witnesses alive today—Loevinger, Larson, and Arthur Burck, who was chairman of the publications board the following year—agree that Sevareid was robbed and that Coffman was directly responsible. Burck attributes the irrational fear of Sevareid to a red scare among the faculty, who were proposing that students who attended radical meetings would have to sign their names at the door. Arnold was not a red, but simply someone who spoke his mind. Many on campus could not tell the difference.

Without naming him in his autobiography, Sevareid heaps scorn on Kosek, and today his ex-fellow Jacobins refer to him as a mediocrity and a nonentity—although a dispassionate reading of the *Daily* during his two years as editor reveals a competent editor. Kosek today remembers the incident just a little differently. He verifies that the administration opposed Sevareid, partly because his editorship might interfere with fund raising. He describes Sevareid, without bitterness, as a strong-minded intellectual, a leader who had actually shown little interest in management positions at the paper, preferring to "do his own thing." Although the yearbook lists Sevareid as feature editor, there is no such title on the masthead, which remained remarkably free of Sevareid's name during his three years on the paper. In Kosek's version, the board first decided the editor would never be Sevareid, then prevailed upon Kosek, although he had no desire to be editor a second year, to stay on. Sevareid's friends say the tradition of a one-year term was so strong that Kosek should still have said no. Burck, however, agrees that, although Sevareid may have seen himself as entitled to the job, he had really not had the editing and leadership experience to prepare him for it.

The meeting was a short one with little discussion. Arnold lost by one vote. Loevinger forced a second secret meeting and tried to reverse the decision, but failed, and called again for a restructuring of the procedure so that the staff, rather than student politicians, would have more say. When Loevinger broke the news of his defeat to Sevareid, he was stunned. Somehow, he concluded, the same naiveté that allowed him to think that the truth would defeat Hitler made him think that he would get a position he had earned. Sherman Dryer caught up with him and put his arm over Arnold's shoulder and said, "this changes my whole philosophy."

The Jacobins met and expelled Kosek into outer darkness.

In 1937 Coffman told the *Journal* (February 16) that he was thinking of retiring when he reached sixty-five in 1940, unless he was "kicked out sooner." He knew that liberals in the legislature felt that he had repressed liberal student organizations under the guise of preventing "exploitation" of students, presumably by outside liberal influences.

Readers of *Not So Wild a Dream* ask how a mature man with so much fame and experience could still bleed, after so many years, over not becoming editor of a college paper. In Scammon's view, "It's the old story. The fall you take when you're a kid you remember all your life." There are two additional possibilities. First, all his life Sevareid had a profound sense of fairness. Perhaps it was the blood of those Lutheran ministers in his veins. Perhaps it was a sensitivity or insecurity that made him strike back immediately when he felt his personal integrity was being questioned. Later, on the basis of a hearsay report that an army instructor had referred to him as a communist, he fired a letter to the secretary of defense threatening legal action. Second, like student editors today, he saw the editorship as the necessary door to his newspaper journalism career.

Arthur Burck, who knew Sevareid in Europe during World War II and who welcomed him as a guest to his Palm Beach home in the 1970s and 1980s, believes this college trauma made Severeid more cautious, less willing to stick his neck out, for the rest of his life. This would give critics who called him "Eric Severalsides" some explanation for the phenomenon they feel they observed.

In April 1950 the *Daily* asked the chief CBS Washington correspondent to write a piece for their fiftieth anniversary issue. In the article, which is an adaptation of a commentary he had already broadcast on the Korean War, he remembers his *Daily* as a "portentous journal, written in words of silver fire, responsible each morning for the hope or doom of mankind," and he gripes about their having gone from a full-spread paper to a tabloid format in 1940. Then he gets serious. American youth, he says is "wrong only in the rather appalling degree to which it confuses opinions with facts; it is practically never wrong in its instincts." He writes as the cold war is warming up, when it is argued that security is more precious than freedom. In one of the most moving essays he ever wrote, he answers: "The surest way to make war inevitable would be to yield to our phobias and imitate the Russian half of the equation by checking our freedom and our individual will. War comes from fear; men fear the unknown, and however much we fear the Russian un-kown, I see no reason to encourage them to fear us. They really don't, yet, despite their propaganda."

He concludes, perhaps recalling what he typed out in April 1934 and 1935, with a list of what he would do if he were editor of the *Minnesota Daily* today. He would say five things every day of the week. Adjust our personal ambitions. Lower our standard of living, pay more taxes, serve the community. Resist every attempt to suppress our thoughts. The police and military are our servants, not masters. Countenance no religious, racial, or class discrimination: "Discrimination among corpses is unknown." The fate of the world is the fate of America, and vice versa. Yield our national sovereignty, whenever the practice looks sound.

But in April 1935 Arnold Sevareid knew only that his life plan of becoming a newspaperman in Minneapolis had been thwarted. Though he almost certainly dreamed that he would rise to the top of his profession, he never foresaw the circumstances that would enable him to play editor of the *Minnesota Daily* at last.

And that spring he had a third reason to be angry about not getting that job. He did need the money. On May 19 he was getting married.

5

MARRIAGE

IN MAY 1935 Sherman "Sherm" Finger, in his eleventh year at the
University of Minnesota, had a lot on his mind. He had mellowed
into one of those campus figures who are respected or admired not just
for their competence but because their identity is somehow woven into
the spirit of the institution. His title was associate professor in the department of physical education and his role was the track and field
coach; and though football was the university's all-absorbing passion, all
sports—much more than political activism, pacifism, or even Greek
life—were so much at the center of the campus consciousness that a
colorful and successful track coach has a head start on the road to becoming a campus legend.

Even poised behind his desk in the athletic office in the old armory,
Sherm Finger was an imposing presence, with an air that struck the visitor as "professional" rather than athletic, as if, with those gold-rimmed
spectacles and his gray business suit, he were a surgeon or even a Methodist minister. But it was in the fieldhouse and out on the track where
the full personality of this lively, talkative, enthusiastic coach burst forth.

Finger, the son of a German Congregationalist minister and his second wife, had begun his athletic career in 1904 at Yankton College in
Yankton, South Dakota, where he played football for coach Major Griffith, who later became commissioner of athletics for the Big Ten conference. When the coach moved to another college and took some of the
best players with him, Finger decided to move to Chicago with his parents, where he played fullback for the University of Chicago's Alonzo
Stagg for the 1905–06 season. One of his memorable games was their 4
to 2 loss to the University of Minnesota Gophers when an all-night
downpour had turned the Northrop field into a big slimy puddle, and
near-freezing temperatures and the wet ball made the Maroons' forward-
pass strategy impossible. The defeat ruined Sherm's and his teammates'

dreams of an undefeated season; but by then Sherm had already decided that his life was going to be dedicated to sports.

After graduation he took a job as head football, basketball, and track coach at Cornell College in Mount Vernon, Iowa, and moved their sports program from obscurity to a high rank in Iowa athletics. And there he met and in 1910 married Lois Martin, a student, the year after her graduation.

In doing so, Sherman Finger had married into one of the more prominent families in the history of Cornell College and the recent history of the Northwest. His bride's father was Eben Wever Martin, who had graduated from Cornell College in 1879, where he met and married Jessie Miner, whose father had run a flour mill in Cedar Rapids, Iowa. Martin got his law degree at the University of Michigan, Ann Arbor, moved himself and his bride by wagon to Deadwood, Dakota Territory (now South Dakota), where Lois was born, and served as a Republican United States Congressman from 1908 till 1915. He then practiced law in Hot Springs, South Dakota, till his death in 1932.

It was in Mount Vernon that Sherman and Lois Finger's four children—Lois (b. 1911), Lydia (b. 1912), Sherman (b. 1915), and Eben (b. 1918)—were born and raised, until, in 1924 he moved the family to Minneapolis with his new job as freshman football and track coach at Minnesota. There he really prospered. He bought a big, beautiful, modern house perched on a steep hill, with an estimated seventy-nine brick steps leading up to the porch, at 29 Barton Avenue, a tree-lined enclave at the foot of Tower Hill Park, just a few minutes southeast of the university. (A neighbor remembers a picture story in *Life* magazine about someone taking all day to shovel the snow off those steps—only to have another snowstorm cover them again that afternoon.) As a coach he had developed one of the best shot-putters and some of the best hurdlers and sprinters to compete in the Big Ten.

What Sherman Finger didn't know in May 1935 was that he had less than two years to live. Those chest pains that went insufficiently diagnosed were symptoms of the heart disease which would take his life in March 1937. That May day, however, the second most important thing on his mind was that within a few weeks he and his wife would leave for a fifteen-month tour of Europe to observe preparations for the Olympic Games. In 1932 he had driven the family from Minneapolis to Los Angeles to witness the Olympics there and had brought along some Minnesota track stars to compete in the trials. Now he was off to England, Scotland, Norway, Sweden, Finland, Czechoslovakia, and Germany. Their plan was to study European methods of training and conditioning, sail from Genoa on a month's cruise of the Mediterranean, see the games in Berlin in August, and return for the fall quarter in 1936.

But the main thing on the coach's mind was his family. The boys, Sherman and Eben, were in college and high school now, had a place to stay and could take care of themselves. Lydia was a special case, a retarded girl with a birthmark on her face. Other families would have institutionalized her perhaps. But the Fingers insisted she should participate in the family's social life and live as fully as possible. Eventually Lydia would spend the last part of her life in an institution.

But the star of the family was Lois. Those who knew Lois Finger fifty and sixty years ago describe her first of all as brilliant. As daughter of the track coach, she was known as a "child of the campus." She was a beautiful, striking woman, tall, slender, big-boned, around five-feet ten inches tall, with dark hair usually pulled back in a bun or swept up. Her brother Sherman jokes that, "She inherited all the good qualities of our parents and didn't leave much for the rest of us." She was an athlete who inherited her father's enthusiasm for track and could even outrun her brothers.

At the university, she was a social and intellectual leader: an active sorority woman, president of the Pan-Hellenic council, a delegate to their national meeting in St. Louis, and an outspoken student leader. When the April 1932 student elections degenerated into fistfights over stolen ballot boxes, she told a Minneapolis newspaper that the fracas was "not very bright." Reform of the student government system, she said, should come not from the faculty but from the students themselves. "We are all grown-up men and women and should be perfectly able to govern ourselves." Reform would come, she said, "But it will never be accomplished by childish methods such as the stealing of ballot boxes and fist fights. However I do not think the demonstration was the fault of any one individual or individuals. I think it was the fault of the system as a whole." Her choice of words—"not very bright," "childish," and "govern ourselves"—hint at a strong confidence in her own intelligence and strength of personality. With good reason. She would receive her law degree, with honors, in June. Of the 128 graduates who took the bar exam, she would be the one woman among the 63 new lawyers admitted to the Minnesota bar in September. She was the rare phenomenon in the 1930s of the independent woman, trained for and capable of charting her own career.

But it didn't happen.

On Saturday afternoon, May 18, 1935, she donned the same wedding dress, with a high neckline, lace collar and sleeves, full skirt and long train that her mother had worn twenty-five years before. At five o'clock in the living room of her home, with no attendants and only the immediate families present, before the Reverend Herman A. Preus, she married Arnold Eric Sevareid. A buffet supper followed.

Then the young Sevareids retreated to spend the summer at a cabin in northern Minnesota.

Exactly when Arnold and Lois first met is not clear. He tells us virtually nothing about her or their relationship in *Not So Wild a Dream*— reflecting either the profound desire for privacy that characterized his whole life or perhaps his understanding of her role in his public career. We do know that women found him, with his tall, rugged handsomeness, enormously attractive. Nan Scallon, a student actress a few years behind Sevareid, recalls that he would come up behind her and run his fingers through her thick curly hair. Lee Loevinger, who was short and scholarly, recalls that whenever he himself was in the company of attractive women he would usually lose them when Sevareid showed up. Newbold Noyes, who covered World War II for the *Washington Star* in southern France with Sevareid, remembers that the most beautiful and sophisticated women flocked to Sevareid whenever he appeared. But clearly he was drawn to Lois as a woman who appeared to be at least his equal in every way.

From time to time Sherm Finger's name popped up in an anecdote in the "Beaker" column; and one can imagine the columnist making his way on foot from the *Daily* offices in the basement of Pillsbury Hall, down University Avenue to Barton Avenue, and climbing those steep steps to visit his girlfriend. Judging from a comparison of their homes and their neighborhoods, Sevareid was marrying into a family more prominent and wealthier than his own, and marrying, moreover, a woman more accomplished than he and with a more promising future

than his own. In fact, though the public ceremony was in May 1935, Sevareid wrote in May 1954 to the editor of *North Dakota Teacher,* who
had asked for a four-hundred-word autobiography, that he and Lois had
"eloped" to Hudson, Wisconsin, in the fall of 1934 and had considered
themselves "married" since that time.

When the couple returned from their summer trip they settled in for a
new life in a cramped apartment at 1000 University Avenue. This was
right outside the campus gate, across the street from a long row of fraternity houses, where the dance music, boisterous songs, and drunken
laughter that had first alerted Eric to a way of life that had shut him out
could now taunt him on his very doorstep. But their home was also on
the edge of an old "Bohemian" neighborhood called Dinkytown.

Frederick Manfred, who lived there on 14th Avenue in 1937 while
he worked on the *Journal* and wrote his first novel, would walk down to
the corner of 4th Street on Thursday afternoons and watch the swarm
of students, professors, and housewives mill in and out of the bookstores,
theater, restaurants, and shops; and he describes it in his monograph,
Dinkytown: "Times were very tough then, yet most students wore good
conventional clothes, sober colors for the men, gray and blue, somewhat
more lively colors for the ladies, yellow and green, with the housewives
almost always wearing a shawl pulled tight over their hair with only
their faces showing. Quips and laughter could be heard all afternoon
long. Since everyone was just about in the same plight, almost broke,
everyone bore up with a tough-titty smile. We were all in the same
foundering boat so we might just as well smile as curse."

Life was also tough but cheerful at 1000—which Eric's father Alfred
Sevareid, in a reference to the current Ethiopian war, had christened
Addis Abbaba. Indeed, though colleagues and the public inevitably describe the mature Sevareid as serious or even gloomy, the young couple
radiated joy. Arnold was full of fun and Lois laughed a lot. Though
Arnold's wit was a little quirky: once, having agreed to meet his friends
at church, he arrived early, plunked himself down in the back pew, and
announced audibly, "Well, I'm here. Where's God?"

Arnold still had to finish college, and Lois got a job—not in a law
firm but a clerical job that would, for the time being, support the two of

them. "The only thing the law degree prepared me for," she quipped later, "was how to read a contract. And those I sign anyway." She also had to take care of—"mother"—her brothers, Sherman and Eben, who had moved in with the newlyweds while their parents were in Europe. Meanwhile, Arnold's younger brother John, following his older brothers Paul and Arnold, had enrolled and was commuting to school; the next year he would become circulation manager of the *Daily*.

As the Finger boys remember the year, the married couple tolerated them very generously, even when the boys had to cut through Arnold and Lois's bedroom to move from one part of the house to the other. Since Arnold had not improved on his housekeeping skills since the canoe trip, Lois did all the cooking. On Sunday she would make a big pot of soup, which the four of them would "keep going" during the week, adding leftovers after every meal, until they finally tossed out what was left on Friday night. Sherman, a student at the university and a bit more conservative than his brother-in-law, was content to go along with ROTC drill. Eben, a high school senior, found Arnold, who loaned him $100 to buy an old Ford, and shared with and finally gave him his old canoe on Lake Calhoun, to be kind and generous. Often the two of them would sit at the table in the evenings and have long and serious conversations about the state of the world. Arnold solemnly assured the younger man that, yes, war in Europe would come. "But," Eben asked, "who will fight whom?"

"Ah," Sevareid replied, "that is always decided at the last minute."

Back on the campus, the *Minnesota Daily*, once again under the hand of Al Kosek, opened the fall quarter with the traditional stories on registration (up 10 percent) and grades (the general student average up to 1.25, a ten-year high). A new press that could turn out twenty-four thousand copies an hour and installed by their printer, the Liberty Poster Company, meant that the staff might now get home before dawn. Bill Plymat took over Sevareid's column space on the editorial page and named it "The Barrister." Arnold's friend Arthur Burck took over the board of publications with a determination to save it from faculty control. Professor Lippincott announced plans to leave for Europe where he would spend his sabbatical. After two months in Cambridge, Massachusetts, finishing *Critics of Democracy,* he would sail to Paris, to work on a new edition of de Tocqueville's *Democracy in America.*

In June 1936 Dean Nicholson's senate committee on student affairs denied the application of the student communists to form their own club, on the grounds that not enough students were interested in the teachings of communism outside the classroom. Meanwhile, the most interesting "exclusive" story in the *Daily* for the year was its March 4, 1936, page-one interview with Nelson Eddy, who had arrived secretly in the Twin Cities for a concert, wearing dark goggles and his hat pulled down over his eyes to avoid the press. Eddy was a miserable grouch, ranting that he wanted to be treated like a serious concert artist, not chased around like a celebrity.

For his last quarter as an undergraduate, Arnold took two political science courses, economics, and journalism, earning respectively, B, C, B, and A. For his whole college career he had cared very little about grades. His whole life had been in Pillsbury Hall. Now the *Daily* went through the year without his byline. But he had to keep his name in print. In the *Literary Review* (fall 1935), a new publication he had a hand in starting up, in a review of Sinclair Lewis's new novel, *It Can't Happen Here,* Arnold gives evidence of how his own thinking was developing, and of his skills in political and literary analysis so evident in later years.

Lewis's novel, a warning that America is ripe for fascism, he concludes, is sociology, not literature; and that is its strength—a judgment of the novel that would be echoed by later critics and biographers. If it teaches the American middle class to read fascism's advance signs, Sevareid says, Lewis will be entitled to more credit than the editors of the *Nation* and the *New Masses.*

The novel's central character is Doremus Jessup, who sees creeping fascism as "revolution in terms of Rotary"—racism, red-baiting, civic righteousness, American Legionism, "drawing-room liberalism and the silk shirts of Wall Street turned to priestly robes in the cult of wealth worship." Torn as to how to oppose this threat to democracy, Doremus can join neither the communists nor the "Yankees"; he decides to remain a "liberal," "scorned by all the noisier prophets for refusing to be a willing cat for the busy monkeys of either side"—an ideological position that resembles that of the later CBS commentator. The novel's emerging dictator, based on Huey P. Long, is Senator Berzelius Windrip.

Sevareid concludes that the improving economy will probably forestall an American embrace of fascism: "But when we do ripen for a Windrip, one will arise, never fear. Heaven always provides a leader when one is needed." By "heaven" we can presume he means the religious right, as in the popular radio priest Father Charles Coughlin, of Royal Oaks, Michigan, as a prime source for homegrown fascism.

On Thursday, December 5, the Sevareid name erupts one more time onto the *Daily's* page in a flurry of controversy. At a Tuesday forum meeting investigating student government, Sevareid publicly challenged his nemisis E. E. Nicholson, dean of student affairs, to a public debate, charging that student government did not actually exist, because all real power rested in a senate committee appointed by the administration. Students don't care about student government, he argued, because it has no real power.

Nicholson bluntly refused.

One can't help thinking there is something unusual about the challenge to debate a dean from a student who plans to graduate in two weeks. Certainly the resentment over the denied editorship was still festering. Yet, one of the driving ideas of Sevareid's philosophy was and would remain his confidence in democracy, in the ability of people of any age or station to govern themselves; and he could not pass up a chance to strike a blow for it, even in his last days as an undergraduate.

On Thursday, December 19, in Northrup Memorial Auditorium, at 11:15 A.M., the band played Mendelssohn's "March from Athalie," and the December graduating class processed to their places. W. Hamilton Fyre, LL.D. gave the commencement address, "Idols and Ideals in Education," the organist played "A Christmas Carologue," and university president Lotus Coffman conferred the degrees. Sevareid was one of forty-eight graduates in the College of Science, Literature and the Arts; his total college average of 1.904 and political science major average of 2.302 did not entitle him to honors, but that did not seem to disturb him. In ways in which he did not foresee, honors in plenty would come later.

In any case, he was far from finished with the University of Minnesota. During the winter and spring quarters, he took six graduate courses in journalism and three in economics. Years later, in 1956, he wrote to a Mississippi high school student, Bill Silver, son of a friend, who had asked for advice that taking journalism courses is not really necessary if you have natural talents. "If you are preparing to reach high in this general field and not just get a job, I think you ought to concentrate on history, literature, languages, with whatever political science and economics you can crowd in." Clearly the older commentator was using his life experience rather than his own college education as the basis for his guidance. The subjects he would have young Miller "crowd in" are the ones he concentrated on.

Over six years, Sevareid took fourteen courses in political science, nine in journalism, and six in economics. Of his five courses in English, only two in Shakespeare were above the introductory level; of his five in history, three were American and two, European surveys. His three French courses, on top of his high school French, brought him to the intermediate level. Anyone listening to his commentaries from the 1950s on would conclude that here was a man steeped in history and philosophy. In so far as that was true, it was history and philosophy absorbed either through his own reading or through the back door of political science. Indeed, when his CBS secretary, Rita Stearns, visited his Alexandria home in the late 1940s, what struck her was the library bursting with history books. He was making up for lost time.

April had delivered another blow: a letter from Carl J. Friedrich, chairman of the government department at Harvard, informing him that, because the number of good applicants far exceeded the openings, etc., there would be no fellowship for him in "public service." Obviously, although he does not refer to this in his autobiography, Sevareid must have decided that a Harvard graduate degree in government was the best training for a journalist like himself. He must have realized too that his grades did not offer much hope for a fellowship; but he gave it a try.

Sevareid's university contemporaries remember two things about his university career—the battle against compulsory drill and a strange final episode which he himself calls "one last fling."

In May, as the school year moved into its final weeks, the rest of the nation was in the early stages of the 1936 presidential campaign. The *Daily* had been paying less attention to the growing international crisis, and the off-campus world was gearing up for a referendum on the first four years of the New Deal. The university's tradition, every four years, called for a mock political convention; this year, it would be on Wednesday night, May 20, in the fieldhouse, with three local radio stations plus Sherman Dryer's campus station on hand to broadcast the proceedings live throughout the area.

Four political parties—Democrat, Republican, Socialist, and United Front (Governor Floyd Olson's backers)—prepared candidates and platforms. To the Democrats, Roosevelt represented liberalism, Olson, radicalism. For the United Front, the alternative to Olson was "the inferno of a new world war and a fascist dictatorship." For them, in a literary allusion that implies that every Minnesota student would have read Dickens, FDR was a Micawber, "waiting for something to turn up."

As the hour approached, the 450 delegates and visiting observers were taking the contest fairly seriously; rumors swept the campus that the Democrats and Republicans would unite to head off a liberal coalition of Socialists and the United Front. But the *Daily* editorial gave a hint that surprises were in store: "The unpredictability of the outcome lends further entertainment to the affair. It is possible that Hoover may be elected on a Socialist platform or that Bernarr MacFadden will strongarm his way to victory." The well-muscled MacFadden (1868–1955), a physical culturist and publisher of *Liberty* magazine, had staged the first American physique contest in New York City in 1903 and in 1936 was actively promoting himself for the Republican nomination.

The night of the convention did not go smoothly. The temporary chairman, in his opening remarks, tried to strike a note of order by asking that no cigarette butts or bottles be left on the floor. The keynoter, a long-winded Minneapolis KSTP commentator, told the delegates that this night should develop an interest in politics that would "carry over into your post graduate days." Then Lee Loevinger took up the gavel and tried to steer the hundreds of cheering, yelling, snake-dancing, booing college students through the night. As Sherman Dryer, piling cliché upon mixed metaphor—"the Republicans' stiff collars keep their noses out of the grindstone"—approached the climax of his Olson nominating speech, his opponents dropped an effigy of Olson with a noose around its neck from the rafters. The enormous Scammon prowled the convention floor as a "delegate at large." Someone nominated Dean Nicholson. Other nominees: Alf Landon, Roosevelt, William T. Borah, and Norman Thomas. The trumpeter blared away with "The Battle Hymn of the Republic" and "Solidarity Forever." At one point, Loevinger, exasperated, pounded his gavel: "Apparently the convention doesn't care whether or not the United States has a president."

But the highpoint was when the delegate from the Canal Zone asked for the floor. Arnold Sevareid, wearing a sombrero, a baggy coat and red kerchief, and sporting a big cigar, approached the rostrum brandishing a huge placard proclaiming Bernarr MacFadden.

"Fellow Americans," he began. "Are we men or mice?"

"You, Mr. Chairman, are you a mouse or a man?" Looking other delegates in the face: "And you—and you—and you —?"

"I pray God we are all Men."

The jeering stopped. The crowd pressed forward to hear.

What this country—like Germany and Italy—needed, he said, was a "STRONG MAN." Elect MacFadden and he would give America the "BODY BEAUTIFUL." At that, he introduced a muscular football player and a girl acrobatic dancer who threw off their robes, flexed their muscles and jumped through their calisthentics.

Most of the five-hundred-word oration is a string of puns and one-liners that kept a receptive late-night crowd in hysterics. "My candidate, ladies and gentlemen, is the only nominee who can tear up a New York telephone book with his bare hands. Nor is that all—he has been known to dash out of his home and tear up the street!" He takes a crack at Minnesota's athletic obsession: "We promise an education for every young man in any college of his choosing, which college must be in good standing with the Amerian Amateur Athletic Association. Our motto: 'Every student an athlete and every athlete an athlete.'"

His political target is the government's preparedness program. Forget the Japanese navy, he says. Remember that the Japanese won the championship in long distance swimming at the Olympic Games. Let the people of California beware lest they "are suddenly confronted by a horde of Japanese invading this country in bathing suits!

"Therefore—the MacFadden platform calls for Compulsory Military Swimming courses in all American colleges."

Olson beat Roosevelt 204 to 153. MacFadden got one vote. Sevareid got the laughs and the press coverage. His nominating speech was broadcast—the first time the Sevareid voice had been heard on the radio—

and was rebroadcast by the campus radio station the next night. Both the *Daily* and the *Journal* put his picture on page one and declared his speech the convention's "high."

"With this speech, with this message to my fellow students, I ended my university career," he wrote later with a note of embarrassment. "It was one year before the battle of Shanghai, two years before the *Anschluss*."

It was an odd blip on the screen of his life: the humor is not surprising; his radio and TV commentaries snap and crackle with wit. But it's the only recorded instance of his playing the clown, of the shy man who will be terrified of microphones and cameras reveling in the approval of the crowd. In Scammon's recollection, Arnie thought the convention was getting too serious and he wanted to "throw in a little firecracker of merriment." CBS colleague Roger Mudd commented later that he was "sometimes inpenetrable and sometimes frivolous." That night he was both.

Part of the charm of university campuses is their ability to defy time. They are by definition conservative; professors, by trade and nature, "own" the past—as if in a box—and dispense it selectively according to their own concept of the public good. The campus, like the teaching profession, can almost pose as a bulwark against death—a sacred haven where one's youth remains bottled like an elixir, and where the alumnus, prominent or plain, can repair for a periodic swig. Writers keep notebooks to remind themselves of who they were, to better understand who they have become. For the same reasons, writers return to their old campuses. Just as Sevareid never stopped writing about Velva, he never stopped writing about Minnesota. When names like Stassen, Humphrey, and Loevinger appeared in his columns and commentaries, it was always with the knowledge that they shared the same roots, the same education. And every time he wrote about youth, his own very public youthful judgments haunted him. In that sense, every return to campus becomes a test of what a writer has gained and lost.

Perhaps it was the embarrassment too—over his youthful idealism and isolationism—as well as pride in his roots, that kept Sevareid so close to the university for the rest of his life. He corresponded with journalism professors Ralph D. Casey and Mitchell Charnley. In the 1930s the Jacobins had turned up their noses at fraternities. In 1950 the dean of students brought him back to speak at the Intrafraternity Greek Week banquet, and informed him in a letter that "without realizing it, you were upholding and reinforcing principles and positions taken by the very progressive and open-minded leaders of both sororities and fraternities." In 1953 he returned to give the memorial address sponsored by the Twin Cities Newspaper Guild. Meanwhile, the university chose him to receive its Outstanding Achievement Award. Later that year Bill Plymat, out of contact since graduation, wrote a "Dear Arnold" letter from DesMoines to ask if he remembered his "fellow columnist" from the *Daily*. In those days, he says, he was an extremely reactionary Republican and Arnold was extremely liberal. Now Bill says, "I have come over to your position almost entirely." When Sevareid received the Dupont Award, the most prestigious broadcast-journalism award, in 1955, he handed it over, according to Dupont custom, to Casey at Minnesota for a journalism scholarship—with the caveat that it should go to a man, not a woman, "given the existing conditions of opportunity for real usefulness in this business."

After his retirement he returned to lecture in 1980 and in 1987. In 1985, the University of Minnesota magazine, echoing the yearbook of fifty years before, caught the spirit of the campus by following it through the day of October 10, 1984. For the university as a whole, it says, the days are literally without end. "Though the classroom doors close, work goes on—in hospitals, research labs, libraries." The sun rises on students milking cows on the St. Paul agriculture campus. At 6:00 A.M. the disk jockey on the campus radio, WMMR, announces, "My name is Ralph Simpson, kamikaze D. J. Let's get down and get funky." By 8:00 A.M., students gather in old Al's Breakfast in Dinkytown, for pancakes swimming in syrup, while they read their textbooks and newspapers. The mall is filled with students whose clothes are "more colorful than the leaves." At noon the University Democratic-Farmer Labor Party has spent the morning draping banners on Northop Auditorium for a rally for U.S. Senate candidate Joan Growe. Meanwhile in the gym, forty employees are puffing their way through an aerobics workout. Says one: "What you get from this exercise is mental euphoria and mental strength, and you need that at a univeristy of this size." At the 3:00 P.M. editorial board meeting of the *Daily*, the editors decide to "bump down" the next day's paper from twenty to sixteen pages. "There's no way we could fill this sucker," the editor says. That night—the New York City Ballet in Northrop Auditorium. Not a word about primping for a sorority dance.

6

FIRED

I N OCTOBER 1935, fellow Jacobin Richard Scammon, traveling in England and studying with Harold Laski, wrote to his newly married friend to twit him solicitously about his future. Did Arne have a job lined up? he asked. "You spoke of the difficulty of a young and, we hope, rising journalist to locate a position which does not require him to sell his soul. The truth of this fact is axiomatic, but never forget that one must eat, and that two can generally be counted on to eat twice as much as one."

The worldly Scammon knew his colleague well. On one level, the *Minneapolis Journal* was one of the better papers in the country; but five years before it had taught a wide-eyed copyboy the gap between what used to be called the "romance" of the newspaper "game" and what newsmen's memoirs of that era refer to as slave labor. But when Sevareid returned to the *Minneapolis Journal* newsroom in the summer of 1936, he found it in several ways a transformed, much better place. The oppressive, sweatshop, exploitive atmosphere that characterized newspaper offices everywhere had, in this place, been replaced by a spirit of healthy tension and defiance.

On August 7, 1933, Heywood Broun, the feisty, liberal, syndicated columnist of the *New York World-Telegram,* threw out a challenge to his fellow journalists across the country who had feared that the "romance of the newspaper game" would be compromised if reporters organized into a union: "I think I could die happy on the opening day of the general strike if I had the privilege of watching Walter Lippmann heave a brick through a *Tribune* window at a nonunion operative who had been called in to write the current 'Today and Tomorrow' column on the gold standard." Lippmann could not picture himself heaving the brick; but newspaper writers across the country responded. Cleveland was first, and Minneapolis and St. Paul were second in signing up members for the Newspaper Guild. By 1938, seventy-five newspapers were guild shops.

As a student, Sevareid had complained to the national headquarters of Sigma Delta Chi, the professional journalism fraternity, that they didn't discuss guild issues at their annual convention. Now he was on the front line of the battle to organize journalists, much as the teamsters had organized the truckers the year before. Certainly the *Journal* publishers had played ball with the Citizens' Alliance, and now, he says in *Not So Wild A Dream,* "began in this period to reap the painful reward of having subverted their precious public trust to private, selfish purposes." Yet he did not sense when he came aboard again that the *Journal* had less than three years to live: in 1939 they would sell out to the *Minneapolis Star* and become the *Star-Journal,* and in 1941 even a remnant of the name would disappear as it merged into the *Minneapolis Star* and *Minneapolis Morning Tribune.*

But on a fat day that fall, the *Journal* was a thirty-six-page package with eighteen pages of news and ads, three pages of social news and features, four pages of sports, a strongly political editorial page, columns by Walter Lippmann and Westbrook Pegler, five pages of business and classified, and two pages of comics including "Dick Tracy" and Zane Grey's "King of the Royal Mounted." The crowded, eight-column front page held fifteen to twenty stories, focusing on the presidential campaign, the exploits of aviator Beryl Markham, 4-H competitions, sports, hunting, the Prince of Wales' affair with Mrs Simpson, and above all, the Spanish civil war. A particularly harrowing dispatch (August 30) by Jay Allen, correspondent for the *Journal* and the *Chicago Tribune,* describes how Generalissimo Francisco Franco's rebel forces slaughtered four thousand men and women in Badajose: they marched young peasants into a bull ring and mowed them down with machine guns. In short, Minnesota may have been "isolationist," but Minneapolis readers were well informed on the threat of fascism—at least in Spain.

As his review of *It Can't Happen Here* made clear, Sevareid was particularly absorbed with the growing ideological split that threatened to tear the country apart. Then some communist friends tipped him off to a semisecret group of fascists organizing in Minneapolis, and he saw his chance for his first big story.

Perhaps Sevareid remembered that Sinclair Lewis had woven the "Silver Shirts" into *It Can't Happen Here.* The Huey Long-like would-be dictator,

Berzelius Windrip, showing off his literacy, boasts his acquaintance with the "grand literature produced by Bruce Barton, Edgar Guest, Arthur Brisbane, Elizabeth Diling, Walter Pitkin, and William Dudley Pelley." Pelley, he lauds for his "self-sacrificing work in founding the Silver Shirts. These true knights, even if they did not attain quite all the success they deserved, were one of our most noble and Galahad-like attempts to combat the sneaking, snaky, sinister, surreptitious, seditious plots of the Red radicals and other sour brands of Bolsheviks that incessantly threaten the American standards of Liberty, High Wages, and Universal Security."

Lewis's wife, the journalist Dorothy Thompson, had just returned from Germany and made a powerful impact on University of Minnesota students in her campus lecture. To Lewis, her picture of a political and social system in Germany paralleled the fascist movements welling up in the United States. So he poured the headlines of 1935 and 1936 into a tract and labeled it fiction.

As Leo P. Ribuffo depicts the period in *The Old Christian Right: The Protestant Far Right from the Great Depression to the Cold War* (1983), there were usually four sometimes overlapping and contradictory categories of American fascists: German nationals or "untrustworthy" German Americans, like those who formed the German-American Bund; outraged members of the middle-class, far-right activists who preached anti-Semitism or cooperated with the Bund—including Pelley, Father Coughlin, Louisiana governor and then senator, Huey P. Long, and Gerald L. K. Smith; in the minds of some critics, like Herbert Hoover and Norman Thomas, the New Deal mimicked the Rome or Berlin "corporate state"; to the Communist Party line, FDR would be considered a fascist, because he would fall in step with Long and Coughlin and solidify a reactionary capitalist dictatorship.

The Silver Shirts, the national network of Klan-like clubs, which Sevareid was about to discover, had been founded by Pelley in 1933. According to Ribuffo's scholarship, their claims of 300,000 members nationwide and 6,000 in Minnesota were wild exaggerations. Actually, they started with about 400 members, grew to a peak of 15,000 the following year, declined to 5,000 in 1938, and disbanded in 1941. Concentrated in the Midwest and West Coast, their members were an even mix of working and middle class, including teachers, clergymen, physicians, and corporate executives; most were of British extraction, followed by

Germans, and a few Scandinavians. To join, they swore allegiance to Christian principles, submitted a photograph, and listed their "racial extraction," baptismal faith, lodge affiliations, and income. Membership entitled them to wear blue corduroy trousers, leggings, a tie, and a silver shirt emblazened with a big scarlet "L," which stood for Love, Loyalty, and Liberation.

Their founder, William Dudley Pelley (1890–1965), was a five-foot-seven-inch, 130-pound, one-time journalist, YMCA worker, and Hollywood screenwriter with "demonic" eyes, a goatee and pince-nez, who claimed his life had been mystically transformed by a seven-minute vision, when he "died and went to heaven" in 1928. This and subsequent visions tutored him on the superiority of Hitler's state and the various conspiracies by which the Jews—including Roosevelt—would take over the world.

For Sevareid, to discover a movement like this not just in a novel but on his own doorstep was "an unbelievably weird experience; it was like Alice going down the rabbit hole into the world of the Mad Hatter." After his initial research his city editor refused to believe his report, then attended a meeting for himself and came back to the office distraught. "Get me a drink, quick," he cried. "God, I feel I've been through the most fantastic nightmare of my life."

Sevareid prepared a series of articles, then discovered—in another one of those life lessons that city rooms teach best—that often the public, even those groups that might be expected to gain by the exposé, doesn't want the truth. The communists wanted the story held till it documented the ties between the fascists and the Twin Cities' big capitalists; the Jews feared the story would stir up more anti-Semitism. But the city editor was willing to go ahead—yet only after editing the stories, to Sevareid's lament, in a way that altered their tone and diluted their impact.

The first big story burst out of the top of page one in a two-column spread on September 11, right next to a story of Franco's fascist rebels killing two thousand government troops on Majorca and pressing their air, land, and sea assault on San Sebastian. The headline read: "NEW SILVER SHIRT CLAN WITH INCREDIBLE CREDO SECRETLY ORGANIZED HERE. WEIRD ORDER, BESET BY UNBELIEVABLE FEARS AND HATREDS, CLAIMS SIX THOUSAND MEMBERS IN MINNESOTA." Following a long editor's note preparing the readers for the series, and under a prominent Arnold Sevareid byline, it begins: "You probably won't believe this story."

The six stories were timed to coincide with Pelley's prediction and his followers' belief, based on interpretation of symbols on the walls of the Pyramids of Giza, that on September 16, the Jewish holiday of Rosh Hashanah, the Jews and communists would rise up and take over the world. Thus providing *Journal* readers with the last laugh when the prediction didn't come true and the editorial page a chance to sum up the series' revelations.

The young reporter had read Pelley's magazine, *Pelley's Weekly*, and news reports on their organization in the state of Washington, had attended meetings, and interviewed several members, including one businessman in his home, where the cupboards were stocked with canned goods he had accumulated for the apocalyptic day. Arnold discloses that some members believe that Roosevelt is a Jew, that Maurice Rose, Governor Olson's chauffeur, is an international banker in disguise, and that treasury secretary Henry Morgenthau is flooding the market with Russian-made quarters bought for a nickel. The *Journal* wrap-up editorial declares that however ridiculous and pitiful these deluded citizens may be, "this is a serious matter." Fanaticism is inescapable in a democracy, the paper says, but fortunately the *Journal's* exposé "should prove sufficient to dissipate it in this region."

But the *Journal* overestimated its power. Two years later, in August 1938, the *Journal, Star,* and *Tribune* had to point out that the Silver Shirts were back again. Eventually, in 1942, Pelley, long a target of the House Un-American Activities Committee and an irritant to the Roosevelt administration, was indicted for violating the Espionage Act of 1917 by undermining the war effort with his propaganda. A jury agreed, and he was sentenced to fifteen years in the federal penitentiary.

In *Not So Wild a Dream,* Sevareid recounts that the success of the series helped make his personal life a torment. Friend Sherman Dryer deplored the articles' frivolous tone, but the public was not amused. Arnold received so many threatening letters and calls that his brothers, John and Paul, wanted to sleep armed in his apartment to protect him. Irate readers who stormed into the *Journal* office got the sympathetic ear of the publisher when the reporter dared to argue back at them. One Sunday he and Lois sat in the balcony of the biggest Baptist church in

Minneapolis and heard the pastor denounce him as a "Red" and, worst of all, a "cub reporter." At which Lois turned to him and said, "After all, darling, you *are* a cub reporter, really."

Read today, the articles are thin stuff. Though the reporter is skeptical of their membership claims, he gives his readers no realistic estimate of the party's strength. The articles identify not one single member of the organization and give no hint of what strata of Twin Cities' society they represent; nor do the articles allude to the larger national and international contexts—like the alienation or desperation engendered by economic crisis, Hitler's persecution of the Jews, and the string of Franco victories in Spain—which encourage paranoid societies to fester. Modeled obviously on Hitler's Brownshirts, organizations with names like Black Shirts, White Shirts, Khaki Shirts, the Minute Men, American Nationalists, and Silver Shirts had been proliferating in the 1930s.

William Manchester records that Huey Long quipped to his fellow senators in the cloakroom, "Men, it will not be long until there will be a mob assembling here to hang Senators from the rafters of the Senate. I have to determine whether I will stay and be hung with you, or go out and lead the mob." And Roosevelt wrote to his ambassador in Italy that Americans "are going through a bad case of Huey Long and Father Coughlin influenza—the whole country is aching in every body." Meanwhile, Manchester explains, in the early days of the New Deal, America's ruling elite—men like Columbia University president Nicholas Murray Butler, Congressman Hamilton Fish, Jr., and 1928 presidential candidate Al Smith—talked readily about the advantages of a virtual dictatorship to snap the country out of the chaos of the Depression. Lippmann wrote: "The danger is not that we shall lose our liberties, but that we shall not be able to act with the necessary speed and comprehensiveness." Without realizing it, America was hesitating between the threat of fascism and the use of fascist methods to repress it.

Sevareid would understand this more fully twenty years later when the same atmosphere that mothered the Silver Shirts would bring forth Senator Joseph R. McCarthy of Wisconsin; but for now, they were mainly "unbelievable."

For a while, the Silver Shirts furor subsided and the Minneapolis newspapers turned to other crises—like Katharine Hepburn. If she remembered

Minneapolis as a crisis she neglected to deal with it in her 1991 memoir, *Me;* she had other things on her mind when her train pulled into the station on a freezing mid-February day in 1937. She had finished a film with George Cukor, *Sylvia Scarlet*, and had returned to the stage with a touring company of a Theater Guild production of *Jane Eyre*, booked to stay on the road from December 1936 through April 1937.

A smitten Howard Hughes had been pursuing her for months, landing his plane on a golf course while she played, checking in at her hotels as she moved across the country from Boston to Detroit, Cleveland, and Chicago. The relationship would ripen into an affair; but now she was fleeing the press. The fact that they had rooms on the same floor in the Ambassador Hotel emboldened the Chicago papers to headline: "HUGHES AND HEPBURN WILL MARRY TODAY." Small wonder that in Minneapolis she slipped secretly off her special train into the big sedan that her chauffeur had driven over from Illinois and was spirited off to the Curtis Hotel, where, at 1:00 P.M., she went right to bed.

Sevareid, in *Not So Wild a Dream* and in a *Saturday Evening Post*, May 10, 1959, article, remembers their encounter as one of his eighteen-year-old cub reporter exploits; but other evidence, like the dates of her tour, would make him a twenty-four-year-old married young man. "I'll fix her," he recalls saying to his colleagues shivering in the cold at the train station. "I've got a plan." It was a plan worthy of any young man who had spent his adolescence watching movie comedies: he disguised himself as a waiter to gain entrance to her hotel suite.

Though Arne had early on modeled himself on that gallant turn-of-the-century war correspondent and ideal gentleman Richard Harding Davis, his style this time was closer to Danny Kaye. "I was transfixed by this intimate proximity with glamour. She spoke to me and I stammered. She requested a dish and I dropped it. She smiled sweetly and wasn't fooled for a minute. By the time I was escaping through the lobby, she had already bawled out the hotel manager . . ." Yet he had made enough mental notes to pass on to the gossip columnist and give scorned journalists their revenge: Kate's breakfast in bed—shared with her forty-year-old blond female traveling companion and handsome long-haired secretary named Stephen—was omelet, waffles, grapefruit, juice, and coffee, and cost $2.95. "La Hepburn had two white pillows propped behind her and a tiny, black, silk one of her own that was right next to her deep red hair. Her pajamas were of cotton print, with small blue and gray checks. She ate with lips that were lip-sticked a flaming red."

Frederick Manfred (who grew up as Feike Feikema) was an Iowa farm boy who prepared himself as a writer by reading all of Jack London and James Fenimore Cooper and Shakespeare, and when he got to Calvin College in Michigan, the *New York Times* and the *New Republic*. In April 1937 he moved to Minneapolis mainly to give some moral support to his younger brother Floyd, a University of Minnesota basketball recruit whose homesickness was interfering with his game. Part of Manfred's reward for bucking up his brother was a job at the *Minneapolis Journal*.

He had been there only a few days when he spotted a tall, very hand-some man with dark hair and sharp, piercing eyes taking a drink at the water fountain from a paper cup. This was a man, he told himself, who knew who he was and what he wanted to do. Fascinated, he thought of approaching him; but they just looked at one another and sized one an-other up and didn't exchange a word. This was a man who was usually off by himself, "the kind of man who didn't feel he had to say Hi to people all the time to see if they would like him."

Then one day soon, while Manfred was eating alone at Kirk's Place, the hangout for newspapermen with a pool hall in the back, Sevareid came over and sat down at his table. They hit it off immediately; they talked for about half an hour about books, what each of them was read-ing. Manfred was reading Marx and leftist economists, and they were both reading the Greeks along with their opinion magazines. Man-fred was on Sophocles, plus the *New Masses,* and Sevareid was working through Aristophanes, while keeping up with the *Nation* and the *New Republic*. The *New Masses,* Manfred confessed, reminded him of the evangelical Christian magazines he used to read back at Calvin College which were always "dead right." The two of them laughed and glowed a bit with this shared conviction: they hated the "dead righters," those guys who were always absolutely sure of where they stood. Though Se-vareid studied very little science in college (two courses, both zoology), Manfred remembers that he loved to talk about science—about Ein-stein, Bohr's quantum mechanics, and nuclear physics. Paradoxically, his new friend did not strike him in conversation as being "deep." Rather, his elevated language gave the appearance of depth. He had "a very wide-ranging mind, a very measured way of looking at everything," always a "reacher," listening to everyone in order to find something out.

Although Sevareid had been out of the university a year, like many students who have had love-hate relationships with their schools, he seemed to remain a campus presence; and soon Manfred was moving in Sevareid's university circle. He recalls seeing the whole Sevareid family one night at dinner in Charlie's Cafe: the father, "a strict, protective man; these small town bankers are kings," and their beautiful daughter Jeanne, whom the father seemed to want to shield from her surroundings. He mixed with the Jacobins and met Lois, who struck him as a "good looking, bright girl, whose mind was always racing ahead. It was as if she was trying to show how bright she was, although her train of thought never seemed to come to the point." Once she struck him as flirtatious, when their knees met under the table; yet this could easily be due to the fact that Manfred was six-feet-nine inches tall and any knees under the table would be crowded while his were there. He had an intimation that Sevareid's marriage might not last.

At the *Journal*, the creative tension of a year before turned uglier. An atmosphere of fear hung over the office, as otherwise fearless newshounds scuttled for cover rather than be seen talking in the hallways when management walked by. Officially, the last-hired-first-fired rule prevailed; but management was capable of ignoring it to fit their purposes. It began to dawn on Sevareid that his successful stories and scoops, which he thought would assure him a strong future on the paper, counted for little. Manfred recalls that the Jones family—four brothers and a sister who had inherited the paper—were unable to agree among themselves who should run it, and brought in a banker, who knew nothing about journalism, under the assumption that a banker could run anything. Sevareid, at that time the kind of man who would walk away from a group telling dirty stories and who hardly ever used rough language, bluntly referred to the new boss as a "prick."

When an editor sent Sevareid out to do an upbeat story on a benevolent banker and his businessmen friends who were subsidizing a suburban camp for elderly panhandlers, he came back with the story that this was not a purely benevolent gesture but, in the words of the banker, a ploy to get these "filthy bums" out of sight lest they tarnish the downtown image and drive down real estate values. When he resisted writing the kind of story the editor wanted he was told to "conform or resign from the paper." Young journalists run into these moral dilemmas again and again on their way "up," and few—all aware of Scammon's rule about eating—resign. The crux is always: the split between the way the institution wants the news reported—and interpreted—and the way you see it yourself. At CBS he would have at least one more chance to make the same decision. He did not resign.

There are at least three explanations of how and why Arnold Eric Sevareid was fired from the *Minneapolis Journal*. The flimsiest appeared in a nostalgia column in the *Minneapolis News*, August 29, 1952: "Something about a difference of opinion between the board of regents of the University of Minnesota and himself concerning what he'd written about the board for the paper, wasn't it?" Sevareid's own explanation is that, thanks to the guild contract, he was due for a hefty raise, but the management seized on one mistake—he confused the American Legion and Veterans of Foreign Wars in a single paragraph squib—to put him out on the street. Manfred adds an interesting twist. Sevareid had a story on a bankers' conspiracy to break the Dunne brothers' teamsters union and, when the *Journal* refused to use it, tried to sell it to the competition, the *Star*, which, unknown to Sevareid, was already in the process of buying the *Journal*. The *Star* "snitched" on Sevareid to the *Journal*. Meanwhile, both Manfred and Sevareid joined the picket lines for the guild in their strike against the radio station, WCTN. That Sevareid would try to sell a story elsewhere rings true. When he got an idea, he wanted it to appear. Later, at CBS, he slipped a rejected radio script into the *Congressional Record* and a rejected TV commentary onto CBS radio.

However it happened, it was the consequence of his trying to say what he wanted to say. And whatever the circumstances, firing is one of those traumatic moments that leave a man devastated, often emotionally wounded for life. Most likely, his career plan matched that of all his ambitious contemporaries in journalism: to move from the *Journal* up the line to better papers in Chicago, Philadelphia, Washington, and finally New York.

By fall of 1937, he and Lois—they had moved to St. Paul to be closer to Lois's job—decided to make a more radical break from the Minneapolis cultural and political situation that seemed to jell with neither of their ambitions. They would go live in Europe. They booked passage on the *Black Eagle*, a freighter loaded with Virginia apples and about a dozen passengers, sailing from New York to Antwerp. Yes, Europe was slipping toward war. But maybe somewhere in that crisis was a new life, a new opportunity. Nan Scallon remembers a great party the night before the Sevareids took the train east to New York: about fifteen Jacobins and mutual friends in an apartment, lots of exotic sausages, sauerkraut, plenty of beer and toasts, and jokes—and above all the feeling that what these two young people were doing was very brave.

7

PARIS

IT WAS AN ENORMOUS, handsome piece of furniture, like an old
Victrola, a floor model of polished wood built around a small, six-inch
glowing tube, greenish and shimmering in the darkened apartment on
London's Queen Ann's Street. On the screen: a dark, underground dugout illuminated by a glimmer of moonlight shining down the steps to
the door and two candles stuck in two bottles on the table. A soldier, a
captain in a World War I uniform, tries to dry his sock over the candle
flame.

Until a few months before, the apartment had been the two-floor
home of Cesar Saerchinger, who had been in Europe since 1918 working for the *Philadelphia Public Ledger*, the *New York Post,* and for the last
seven years, arranging talks and special broadcasts—like those by Leon
Trotsky, H. G. Wells, and George Bernard Shaw—for the Columbia
Broadcasting System. His greatest scoop came in 1936 when, right before the prime minister could read the announcement that Edward VIII
had resigned, Saerchinger blurted into the CBS microphone, "The king
has abdicated . . ." and beat every medium in the world.

Now CBS had replaced him with a younger man. He had handed
over his apartment to Edward R. Murrow, who had sailed for England
the previous April. This was Murrow's third trip to England and, like his
two guests that night, he had developed his own ideas about his host
country: an uncomfortable combination of the respect that American
Anglophiles have for the political traditions that were the theoretical
basis for American democracy, and the abhorrence of the British class
structure where part of society enjoyed unearned hereditary privilege
and the rest, to put it mildly, did not.

The guests of Murrow and his wife Janet had just arrived in Europe.
They had crossed America from Minneapolis to New York on a bus and
were still absorbing what they had seen. From a train, Sevareid wrote in

Not So Wild a Dream, you don't really enter into the countryside and its communities—those small-town banks, schoolhouses, and hotels you can peek into from your bus window. Or the Wisconsin German farm boys with their hair slicked back standing outside their white churches as the bus rumbles by on Sunday. In New York—"terrifying" in its directness—they had enjoyed a reunion with Lee Loevinger, then working as a lawyer for the labor board; and they had escaped that frightening metropolis, Arnold determined that this was "a city I would have to circumvent the rest of my life."

For Sevareid, Europe was a continent which, as a third generation Norwegian-American, he had known all his life. He was struck, above all, by its smells: "the odor of fresh bread, of people, of roasted coffee, of old leather, and of urine. It is an interior smell; it is like the smell inside a general store in a country town."

And here they were in London, after dinner, watching television.

The picture was surprisingly sharp, but as far as most of the world knew, TV had not even been born. General Electric in Schenectady had done the first experimental broadcast of a dramatic production, *The Queen's Messenger*, in 1928; the first commercial NBC-TV broadcast would be FDR's opening of the 1938 New York World's Fair the following year. But the BBC had recently started broadcasting an hour of TV programming every Monday through Friday night—newsreels, sports, and drama—to fifteen hundred London sets, with a signal reaching up to seventy miles, and had given the Murrows one of the fifteen hundred. For a while they watched it every night, but after a few weeks, Ed got bored and they turned it off.

Tonight however, there was a "good" show, a filed version of R. C. Sheriff's 1928 antiwar drama *Journey's End*, a sad play about the death of youth in battle, which one critic had said the peace societies should put on tour around the country. Considering England's mood at the moment, the BBC's scheduling was ironic. On November 5, while England's fifteen hundred watched a pacifist play, half a continent away, Adolf Hitler, in a four-hour meeting, spelled out for the first time his scenario for war to the six men who would lead it. Germany needed space (Lebensraum); two "hate-inspired" countries, Britain and France, stood in its way; but Britain was bogged down with its troubles in Ireland and India, and France was internally divided; he would prolong the

Spanish civil war to keep Britain and France embroiled with Italy; then he would strike at Czechoslovakia and Austria with lightning speed.

The Murrows' guests, Arnold and Lois, had come with a letter of introduction from Jay Allen of the *Chicago Daily News*, and were bubbling with their impressions of the Belgians and the French and the British; he was convinced that the English "were afraid of one another, afraid of nothing on earth except one another," and he was appalled at their "mental and spiritual isolationism," which surpassed anything he had known at home.

And they were also planning to see Europe by bike!

On the screen, the mortally wounded second Lieutenant Raleigh, a boy who had come fresh from high school to the Western front, asks, "Could I have a light? It's—it's so frightfully dark and cold." Dawn is breaking. A faint sound, something between a sob and a moan, comes from the bunk where he lies. Captain Stanhope, a man hardly older than he, comes over and gently takes his hand. Raleigh is dead. Stanhope lightly runs his hand through the dead boy's tousled hair. Outside the shelling rises to a fury. A shell bursts on the dugout roof, the roof caves in and all falls into darkness.

Murrow got up, flicked off the set, and said, in one of those recorded quotes that historians relish but can never fully reconstruct, "That's television. That's the wave of the future right there." He could have meant it ironically, or ruefully. In fact, television was the "future" for those two young men—one twenty-nine, the other twenty-four—but neither had any idea of the degree to which that would be true. Sevareid didn't even know much about radio; to him it was just something to listen to music on. That would change.

Murrow and Sevareid had met briefly before that evening when Sevareid was making his London explorations, taking notes for some of the six dispatches between November and April he was to sell to the *Minnesota Daily* at a rate of one cent a word—like the humorous account of his attempts to communicate in college French, and observations on the soapbox orators in Hyde Park. He stopped in on a communist rally, encountered the British fascist Sir Oswald Mosley, strolled through the gray buildings of Oxford, and witnessed the opening of Parliament.

After reading British history in college, Sevareid had come as a pilgrim to a shrine, but he found himself resenting what he saw as British culpable ignorance of the outside world—Oxford, he discovered, had only one or two chairs in American history!—a narrowness more dangerous than the Minnesota isolationism he had left behind.

The January 5, 1938, *Minnesota Daily* published an ambivalent piece that probably captures his state of mind immediately after his English sojourn. The people are getting scrawnier and army recruiting officers are turning down 68 percent of the applicants for "'insufficient nutrition' says officialdom . . . 'a polite word for starvation,' says the honest man." He describes the Woolwich district, the world's greatest arsenal, where seventy-five thousand men and women toil at piecework, girls at ten dollars a week, making cartridges, bayonets, tanks, to buy an extra beer or a new table fork. "Prosperity at Woolwich . . . merchants beam, landlords smile, the doctors like it too."

Here again are the establishment, the capitalists, the war profiteers exploiting the poor. "We love peace, the ruling class says. But London's streets are cluttered with statues of soldiers. Pistols and swords poke at you from every corner if you kneel in Saint Paul's. There is a cannon in Westminster Abbey." One might wonder whether Sevareid who, though confirmed a Lutheran in adolescence had, according to his contemporaries, distanced himself from religious faith early on, actually "knelt" in Saint Paul's; but he is not softening on militarism as war draws near.

Meanwhile, nothing in England had impressed Sevareid more than this young American, less than five years older than he, "a tall, thin man with a boyish grin, extraordinary dark eyes that were alight and intense one moment and somber and lost the next. He seemed to possess that rare thing, an instinctive, intuitive recognition of the truth." They talked about England through half the night, and Sevareid found himself wanting to write down what his brilliant new soulmate had said. "I know I wanted to listen to this man again, and I had a strong feeling many others ought to know him."

Surely as they talked each saw the other's life reflected in his own. Murrow, born in 1908 as the youngest of three sons of a North Carolina farmer father and a pious Quaker mother, moved with his family to the state of Washington when he was five. "We both came from kind of middle-class families in a way, we had come through the Depression . . . a lot of poverty in our families. We both had to work like dogs . . ." Sevareid said later. Murrow labored as a logger and worked his way through college at Washington State, where he pitched into debating, theater, student politics, and—unlike his dinner guest—ROTC. Like Sevareid, he was profoundly touched by one teacher—for him, Ida Lou Anderson, a young, crippled speech instructor who taught him how to time his delivery for emphasis, how to say, "*This* . . . is London." Like Sevareid, he married a brilliant and beautiful college woman, Janet Huntington Brewster, from Middletown, Connecticut, and Mount Holyoke College, and who, like him, was active in the national student movement—and who came from a family more prominent than his own. Sevareid had seen Hudson Bay, a California mining camp, and the West through a boxcar door, but nothing else outside Minnesota until the last few weeks. He probably seemed gangling, aloof, and unsophisticated, compared with his worldly, handsome, new pal, but both, within a remarkably few years, would develop an aura that drew both men and women to them.

Both were shy and both could be distant, standoffish, in personal relationships. And both were nervous—Murrow would sweat and Sevareid would gulp and tremble—in front of a microphone. Though Murrow remarked later, "Yes, both Eric and I are shy, but I hide it better."

Most important, in their dislike of the British class system, which Sevareid angrily referred to as a "racket" worse than that of American political racketeers, both shared a common understanding of democracy. This meant a respect for "little people," ordinary citizens, whose inherent wisdom, if tapped, would provide fodder for an infinite number of exciting radio programs, and if well-informed, could legitimately guide a nation's future. "I thought of Velva," he wrote, "of the thousand Velvas scattered over America. Yes, it was better, it was a step in advance of this."

Not all of these shared experiences and assumptions would hold up. Television would be the "future" for both, in ways which neither foresaw; but Murrow would come to see TV's dual nature—as an educational and entertainment medium—put an overwhelming tension in his career and eventually defeat his high-minded vision. Sevareid would see the TV image overpower the words he had spent a lifetime learning to craft.

Murrow's marriage, though strained and tried by the "no-rules" moral atmosphere that infests any close-knit group in the midst of a war, would last—leaving a valiant widow who would spend the rest of her days preserving and promoting his legacy. Sevareid's marriage—marriages—would not fare as well.

And the clear, simple notion of democracy, which in the 1940s saw Depression-era gold miners, farmers, factory workers, and loggers joining hands against fascism—and later, in a different way, against communism—would in the 1980s and 1990s disperse into a "multicultural" America that seemed to lack a common soul. American society, for a number of reasons—including a more open sexual freedom and the breakdown of the family, the failure of the economy to expand enough to fulfill each generation's version of American dream, new immigrants and a new ethnocentricity that resisted their assimilation, the shrinking of organized labor unions while the multitude of clerical and white collar workers grows—would be more divided at the end of the twentieth century than during the great immigrant waves at its beginning. National identity would be not only more elusive than ever but, in some circles, scorned as a cloak for nationalism, an insidious myth that disguises prejudice and injustice.

Whatever the virtues of a Velva-inspired national identity, in Paris the Sevareids felt they found something they had never known in England or in America—the freedom to be themselves, liberated from a thousand taboos with the confidence that "nobody really cared a damn what you did, how you dressed, or what you said." So they forgot about the bike trip they had planned and settled down to stay at the Hotel Select, number One, Place de la Sorbonne, where a room and breakfast cost fifty cents a day, and registered for French classes at the Alliance Francaise, to which they trekked early every morning through the Luxembourg Gardens, past the big round pool and fountain where little boys sailed their boats and old men hid their faces in their newspapers.

When Arnold walked into the offices of the old Paris *Herald*, known formally as the *New York Herald Tribune* Paris edition, he saw it as "the absurd little house organ for the diminishing American colony" abroad—a colony made up of journalists, embassy people, American Legionaires who had married "Mademoiselle from Armentiers," and Harlem trumpet players who had come over in the jazz era and gone native in Montmartre. But the *Herald* had once been much more.

When James Gordon Bennett, Jr., inherited the *New York Herald* in 1872 at the age of twenty-six from his father, who had founded it in 1835, he brought to New York's best news-gathering paper the combination of imagination, high, nervous intelligence and an unstable personality. He sent Henry Morton Stanley to Africa to find Dr. Livingstone, who did not know he was lost, in 1872; the notorious antimonarchist Mark Twain to "welcome" the Shah of Persia in London the following year; and the great war reporter Richard Harding Davis, without whose presence no conflict was permitted to commence, to cover the Boer War in 1900.

But, raised as a spoiled brat, Bennett could not censor his own behavior. At a New Year's Eve party in 1876 at the home of his fiancée's parents, he was foolish enough to relieve himself in a grand piano (some say a fireplace) in mixed company, and was punished with a horsewhipping outside the Union Club by his now ex-fiancée's brother till the snow was dappled red with his blood. No longer welcome in polite society, Bennett retreated to Paris for the next forty years, where he lived royally, continued to run his newspaper very successfully by cable, and in 1887, founded the *Herald*'s Paris edition. Its circulation fluctuated between 10,000 and 15,000 for its first thirty years as must reading for tourists, expatriates, and European high society; but it soared to 350,000 with the arrival of the American expeditionary forces in 1918. Bennett had long argued for American intervention; and when his French staff went to defend France, the owner rolled up his sleeves and helped put out the paper himself, running the back page in French to make up for the Paris journals that had closed. Its war coverage was excellent, filling inside pages with superb maps and often all of page one with war and diplomatic news.

But standards plummetted when Frank Munsey, owner of the *New York Sun*, bought the New York and Paris *Heralds* in 1920, following Bennett's death in 1918. William Allen White said Munsey had "the talent of a meatpacker, the morals of a money changer, and the manners of an undertaker." He installed Laurence Hills, Paris correspondent for the *Sun,* with only one directive: keep costs down.

Hills was quite unsuited for the job. As Richard Kluger describes him in *The Paper,* his history of the *New York Herald Tribune:* "Owlish in his horn-rimmed glasses, he suffered from a somewhat irascible nature that made it difficult to tell from his expression whether he was smiling or his teeth pained him." He sacrificed good journalism to economy: he cut the staff to a few deskmen to rewrite wire copy and press releases, plus a few feature writers and stringers. When the Ogden Reid family bought the *Herald* and merged it with the *Tribune* in 1924, they poured profits into new presses and a new building on rue de Berri, a block from the Champs-Elysées, but made the mistake of not only leaving Hills in charge but expanding his authority over all the *Herald Tribune's* foreign correspondents. For a while the new administration tried to make its deteriorating staff a little more productive with a rule against getting drunk while on the job. (Arriving drunk was another problem.) Nevertheless, the old "newspaper game" culture, in which drunks were somehow laughable and an "old pro" could pound out his story drunk or sober, was too strong to crack.

Most significant, influenced strongly by the tourist advertising revenue from Germany and Italy, Hills was a fascist sympathizer and made his sympathies show. As Kluger writes, "In his fear of economic collapse and encroaching anarchy, Hills sought new political gods and thought he found their embodiment in the strongmen seizing or contending for power in Italy, Germany, Poland, Portugal, and Rumania." During the Spanish civil war, he sometimes made sure *Herald* stories referred to the Loyalist troops as "reds," and as late as July 1938 he had his assistant kill a Walter Lippmann column on the coming war on the grounds that it would frighten tourists and thus harm their advertising revenues.

Finally, at the end of 1938, Dorothy Thompson wrote to Helen Reid that her friends in Paris tell her that "the Paris Herald Tribune is playing the Fascist game from start to finish. Inasmuch as this is certainly not the policy of the Herald Tribune, I feel that you ought to do something about it." Hills, who was now slowly dying of cancer, was told to stop writing editorials on political topics; but the Reids had tolerated him too long to remove him now. Too late, in 1939, Hills realized what a fool he had been. Saturday, May 11, 1940, the day after Germany invaded Holland, Belgium, and Luxemburg, Hills repudiated his past positions in a page-one, boxed editorial, "Hitler's Latest Victims," signed with his own initials. "It is useless to blind one's self to the deadly dramatic import of yesterday's developments. The 'guerre totale' has commenced." As Bennett had done over twenty years before, he called for American intervention to rescue democracy in Europe.

Sevareid got a job in his first week in Paris by walking into the *Herald* office on a December night, in 1937, skinny and bewildered, just as another employee was walking out for good. Sevareid's day city editor was a vicious, ill-tempered Hitler-lover named Kospoth, who bullied the new boy until the new boy, who had done a little boxing as a college freshman, threatened to hit him. The editorial writer was a socialist pro-fascist Maltese, with an Oxford degree, who took the new boy to a nudist colony on an island in the Seine, where he plunged nude into the freezing, dirty water. His name, which Sevareid's memoir does not record, was Vincent Bugeja; he had studied on Malta to be a Jesuit, but left rather than sign a statement saying that the theory of evolution was false.

Francelia McWilliams Butler had, like the Sevareids, sailed to Europe for a new start after losing her job at Washington's Raleigh Hotel by helping to stage an integrated Oberlin College alumni dinner there. Like Arnold Sevareid, she had gotten her job at the *Herald* as a "drama critic" because the job had just opened up. The previous drama critic, Bradish Johnson, had been killed covering the Spanish civil war. At the *Herald* she met and married the copy editor, Jerome Butler, whose roommate, Jimmy Lardner, son of writer Ring Lardner, had just died in Spain fighting with the Abraham Lincoln Brigade. She recalls the *Herald* staff giving young Sevareid a hard time, mocking his pretensions as a writer, his attempts to make a name as a free-lance writer, beyond the daily leisurely grind of mediocre *Herald* journalism. The Butlers' best friend at the *Herald*, whom Sevareid does not mention in *Not So Wild a Dream*, was Robert Sage, a cripple, a brilliant friend of James Joyce, and an editor of a magazine called *transition*, in which Sage published parts of *Finnegan's Wake*.

But the *Herald*'s most memorable character was its "sports editor," the elderly (his age was estimated at between seventy and eighty) William Robertson, called "Sparrow" because, small and gray with prominent nose and glittering eyes, he looked like one. Robertson had come to Paris with a YMCA athletics group after World War I and had not set foot outside the city since.

This endearing little old fellow, whom Westbrook Pegler called "the man who poured Paris to bed," spent his days and nights making the rounds of the American hangouts—the *Herald's* office, Harry's New York Bar, Fred Payne's Bar in Montmartre, and Luigi's, off the Champs-Elysées—gathering material from "old pals" for his daily column. Then, relying on the only two words of French he had learned, "à droit" and "à gauche," he guided the taxi driver to the Hotel Lotti where he lived. After the Germans occupied Paris and the paper closed, Sparrow, oblivious to their presence and curfews, kept making his rounds and filing his copy as if the Germans didn't exist. "These swine don't bother me, he told young reporter Walter Kerr as he cleared out his desk for the last time. "I go anywhere, anytime." One day his friends found him, crumpled up like the dead sparrow he was.

As a feature writer, and then as city editor, Sevareid was free to do stories on whatever amused him. "Le New York," as the French called the *Herald,* was basically a "village paper," so the comings and goings of Americans were its prime material: the busty dowager, a member of "Americans of Royal Descent," who promoted her own tea concerts and once broke into song in the office; U.S. ambassador William Bullitt, who regarded the *Herald* as his personal house organ, who gave a speech in the pouring rain without an umbrella at Lafayette's grave, and reduced to tears a young woman reporter who dared to ask about his buying up most of the fresh caviar in Moscow to be shipped in for an embassy party; the adjutant general of the Montana National Guard, who insisted the *Herald* describe him as "conferrin'" with military authorities at the embassy, in order to justify his trip; the traveling Fordham University football team, who put on an exhibition game in the December mud before twenty thousand fans who knew not the rules but cheered wildly at every player and play—from the water boy to the "Statue of Liberty" play, which, since it pleased the crowd, was used again and again. One of his favorite topics was the "Vagabond Coed," a University of Wisconsin self-promoter on a world "good-will" tour, whose nightclub act consisted of blowing "smoke bombs," floating bubbles, like those from a bubble pipe, but of smoke and saliva, which would float over her audiences' heads, land at random, and pop.

In the midst of these stories, something else changed: Arnold Sevareid became Eric. In later interviews he made little of the switch: children have no say about their names, he preferred Eric. But any name change, particularly of a public person and a writer—Mark Twain, George Orwell, Malcolm X—is significant. Arnold, which sometimes came out as Arne, Arnie, or Buddy, lent itself too easily to the diminutive. Eric is the Norwegian, the traveler. With the change he further distances himself from the small-town childhood, the university that didn't appreciate him, the newspaper that fired him.

Soon the name Eric Sevareid, one of the few writers to get regular bylines, rolled off the tongues of the American colony in Europe. He reviews, very favorably, a Maurice Chevalier show at the Casino de Paris, but includes what today would be called a John Simonesque negative judgment on the "faces" of a "distressingly high percentage" of the women in the chorus line, whose figures and curves otherwise pass inspection. He reports, with obvious relish, on American novelist Louis Bromfield's new pamphlet, *England, A Dying Oligarchy,* causing a stir in London. "England," writes Bromfield, "is not a democracy and never was a democracy." Bromfield, a friend, told Sevareid personally, "Oh, the secret of Britain is when you walk into a drawing room, don't ever ape their clothes or their accent or anything. Just be as goddam American as you know how to be. That's the only way that they'll respect you."

In Gertrude Stein's apartment, Sevareid sits and listens to the finest flow of talk he has ever heard. In his report she reads him excerpts from her new version of the opera *Faust,* laughing aloud at her own favorite lines. And her new children's book called *The World Is Round,* which begins, "The world is round and you can go on it round and round." And her next project, a novel about persons like Lindbergh, whom she calls —anticipating the distinction Daniel Boorstin will draw between the hero and the celebrity in *The Image*—"publicity saints."

"He is a saint with a certain mystical something about him which keeps him a saint; he does nothing and says nothing, and nobody is affected by him in any way whatsoever." The reporter is either wise or kind enough to omit from his story Stein's inane political opinions. "Hitler will never go to war. He is not the dangerous one. You see, he is a German romanticist. He wants the illusion of victory and power, the glory and glamour of it, but he could not stand the blood and fighting involved in getting it."

In April 1938, reverting to his Arnold byline, Sevareid sent his last article to the *Daily*, this one a little more somber than the others in its picture of the apparent French resignation to the coming of war. He quotes one: "A lot of poor people are going to die, aren't they?" Refugees from Vienna are beginning to flood into Paris, which absorbs them without a whimper, he says. Then he recounts the arrival of Claudette Colbert from Vienna, too. Most of his attention in this article for the folks back home focuses on Minnesota alumnus Will Rogers, Jr., whom he met ambling unsteadily away from the Dôme cafe, full of beer and political opinions, and on his way to Barcelona. "When I asked young Rogers what he thought of Paris, he exclaimed, 'This is the most aphrodisiac town I ever saw!' which I thought was pretty good."

At the same time, that flood of refugees from Austria and Spain, coupled with the bizarre hatreds that fragmented the French people, had done much to deepen Sevareid's understanding and abhorrence of fascism. Still thinking in the model of the Minneapolis truckers' strike, he saw the fascist of Europe, like the Minneapolis police, as preparing a gigantic ambush.

Lois, meanwhile, had not been content to be just a reporter's wife. Francelia Butler recalls Lois applying for a job in the visa section of the U.S. Embassy, but not getting it because something cold in her personality worked against her. She did get a position in the reference room at the American Library, but did not rest with that. Determined to use her law training for some public good, she joined a delegation of women lawyers in Geneva to argue for women's rights.

In one of his *Daily* columns (February 9, 1938) her husband wrote that "I have time to write this column only because my wife is an Idealist. She believes in Progress. So she has gone to Geneva to help convince the League in matters concerning the Legal Status of Women or something. That is why I get no dinner and have some time." According to the *Women's Law Journal* (spring 1938), she went to represent the National Association of Women's Lawyers, and to present to the League of Nations Assembly the NAWL's resolutions on equality for women. She remained in Geneva afterward to meet with the International Labor Organization. It does not seem to have occurred to Eric that he could learn to make his own dinner. That he felt free to make light of her Geneva mission to his Minnesota University readers may represent his whimsical streak. More likely, it may suggest that he resented Lois's aspirations.

Working with Frederick Thompson, a wealthy conservative Catholic from San Francisco dedicated to leftist causes, Lois turned their apartment into a way station for refugees. Though there was little in Eric's background to equip him to understand Catholic activists, he makes clear in *Not So Wild a Dream* that he admired Thompson enormously.

Indeed, it is a measure of Eric and Lois's combined generosity that their little apartment in Paris was constantly open to family and other visitors alike. Lois's brother Sherman and his bride stayed with them in Paris on their honeymoon. They invited Eric's younger sister Jeanne over to live with them and go to school in Paris. A Czech refugee lived with them for months. Ernst Adam, a socialist professor from Germany who helped organize the defenses of Madrid, Hertha Pauli, a pacifist novelist from Vienna, and "Karli" Frucht, a gentle German boy, fleeing the Gestapo, would all make extended visits; and even after Sevareid returned to America in 1940, he would not abandon them.

When in 1940 he asked Mrs. Roosevelt to intervene to get Adam a visa, surprising word came back from Undersecretary of State Sumner Welles that Adam (pen name Mikulas Bedam) was a communist. Hertha and Karl eventually made it to America; but Karl was first rounded up by the French police and herded into a camp for German nationals. There Eric, visiting the camp as a correspondent, met him and was reduced to tears of shame over his inability to help him. Ten years later, when Karl applied for an electronics job with Sylvania, Sevareid would be asked to testify to his loyalty, and he gladly did so.

It was partly this refugee traffic that convinced Eric and Lois that they ought to see the Third Reich up close before it unleashed its power against the rest of Europe.

In the third-class compartment of the train that carried them across the Rhine in December 1938, they stared at the handsome, sensitive face of the eighteen-year-old blond boy across from them. His parents had been Polish, but he had been raised in Marseilles; though he knew nothing of Poland he had been called back to serve in the army. He was crying. Again turning a chance encounter into a symbol, Sevareid wrote in *Not So Wild a Dream,* "In him was all the unutterable tragedy of the

European night; he was all the innocent hearts and clean bodies of the guiltless youth of Europe, unwilling but unable to protest, pulled and shoved to the unfamiliar sentry posts and barricades along the unreal frontiers everywhere upon this forever unhappy, eternal continent of Europe."

The Sevareids felt they knew Germany because they knew the Nordic civilization of the American Northwest—the same faces, clothes, bathrooms, kitchens, and food. But Germany had been poisoned. In Munich's Hofbrau Haus the people no longer sang nor carelessly clinked their mugs but sat fearful and silently drank their beer under the burning eyes of Der Führer's portrait on the wall. On New Year's Eve the two other guests in their Munich pension leaped to their feet and saluted at the sound of Joseph Goebbels' voice from the radio. At their Alpine ski resort at Kreutzighaus, Deputy Führer Rudolph Hess sat next to their table, and on the slopes the last day, Eric took a fall and wrenched an ankle rather than collide with him. On the little intercity ski bus they watched with excruciating pain as a Jewish man got on and stalled looking for a seat, obviously trying to avoid the humiliation of some boy or girl next to him cringing from his presence. Even in Oberammergau, in the theater where the Passion Play was performed, there were signs saying Jews were excluded.

As the train took them back toward Paris they stared again at the fresh clean faces of German boys in field-gray uniforms, the same faces they had seen outside churches in Wisconsin, and Eric concluded: "The German people were sick, neurotically sick, their nerves on edge. They hated the world, and they hated themselves."

That spring of 1939 the German-French-American relationship played itself out in another kind of drama—though a sideshow, one of those sensational international murder trials that can capture the world's attention and give a young reporter his greatest opportunity since his first big fire.

It began with the disappearance of Miss Jean DeKoven, an attractive young American from Brooklyn who had taught dancing in New York and come to Paris with her aunt for the great International Exhibition of 1937. She had been seen from time to time at parties with a handsome, well-dressed youngish man who spoke English with a Canadian accent, but whom nobody seemed to know. Within the next five months five more people—four men and one woman—were kidnapped, robbed (often of small sums), and murdered, five of them with a bullet in the back of the neck. An investigation led police to an isolated villa in the forest of St. Cloud and a man living under the name of Karrer who, confronted, pulled a gun and tried to shoot his way out, only to be overpowered. His real name was Eugen Weidmann, a thirty-year-old German Catholic from a law-abiding family who had spent prison time for petty crimes in both Canada and Germany, and who confessed that he and three accomplices had killed all six merely for their money. Jean deKoven he had taken to tea, strangled, and buried under the front doorstep. He emphasized that there had been nothing improper in their relationship.

It was a great trial not because of a mystery about who committed these crimes but for three other reasons. First, because of superficial but titillating parallels with the 1928 trial of "Bluebeard" Henri Désiré Landru, the Parisian who claimed to have made love to 283 women, killed and chopped up 10 of them, and been sentenced to the guillotine in the same Versailles courtroom seventeen years before. Landru's trial had attracted the cream of the world's journalists, like the legendary William Bolitho, author of *Twelve Against the Gods*. Weidmann was even given "Bluebeard's" cell. And one of his four attorneys, a little Corsican-born orator, M. de Moro-Giafferi, had tried—and failed—to save Landru from the guillotine as well.

A second feature of the trial was Weidmann's magnetism, his "charming eyes" and "gracious smile." On one level, the defense would attempt to show that he was insane, even though the state's "alienists" had established his sanity before the trial. On another level, the mystery of his motivation and attractiveness for women remained. Though he had killed two women in a cold and brutal fashion, women in the galleries were enraptured by him and cheered him on. Finally, Weidmann's defense raised fundamental questions about human freedom and responsibility, and even touched symbolically on the relationship between two countries that were gearing up for war.

For his whole professional career Sevareid would be fascinated by psychology, character analysis, and human motivation; he was also quick to generalize about national traits, as if countries had character, like individuals. This was his first opportunity to write sustained commentary—and

Paris *Herald Tribune* style gave him enough flexibility to mix "objective" reporting with his own interpretation.

On the trial's opening day, March 11, streetcars rattled over the cobblestone pavement outside the courtroom, where the guillotine would be set up. The manacled German, freshly shaven and wearing a well-fitting blue serge suit, was led from cell no. 3 before the red-robed judge, the twelve elderly men who would decide his fate, and the ten lawyers, one hundred spectators, eighty-five newspapermen, and sixty soldiers maintaining order in and outside the court. Sevareid's portrait of Colette Tricot, the fourth defendant and shared mistress of Weidmann's other two accomplices, is scathing: "there was little to suggest the girl-friend for whose favors Blanc and Million contested. She had gathered fat in jail, she wore no make-up, her brown coat with a thin collar that lent sobriety if not sex-appeal. She frowned and bit her lip on first entering but remained impassive thereafter."

That week, in the larger world, Pius XII was crowned Pope as five hundred thousand cheered in St. Peter's Square. Hitler took Czechoslovakia. Joseph Barnes wrote from Berlin on March 13: "With German troops pouring steadily across the frontiers since dawn and with Chancellor Hitler in Prague to see with his own eyes his new addition to Greater Germany, the Third Reich's first conquest of an alien people became an accomplished fact." The *Herald Tribune's* lead editorial was beginning to wonder about Germany's motives.

In the courtroom at Versailles, Weidmann, who had infuriated both the emotional judge and his own attorneys for days by murmuring yes or no answers and insisting on his own guilt when his attorneys tried to shift the blame to an unnamed party, suddenly brought tears to the eyes of even the hard-bitten gendarmes as, in an emotional speech he named his accomplice Roger Million, not himself, as the murderer of Roger LeBlond, their fourth victim.

Our reporter writes caustically that in his speech Weidmann has probably claimed his "seventh victim" in a carefully rehearsed and staged piece of dramatic acting. "If he is a good enough actor to lure six people to their deaths, he's good enough to fool this courtroom."

Weidmann dropped his head and paused to allow a hush to fall over the courtroom. For months, he said, he had tried to rediscover the God, the faith, of his childhood. He would never accuse an innocent man. But the truth was that Million killed Leblond. "His voice broke and he collapsed in his seat. The rest of the afternoon he sat red-eyed and silent. Weidmann might have made a great dramatic actor," says Sevareid, "if he had preferred working to killing." Without anticipating the word "image," which will not join the vocabulary of media analysis for another twenty years, he analyzes the details of Weidmann's courtroom presentation—offering his left profile, never his dark, heavy, full face, to the jury; declining to speak in German, lest his words lose impact in translation; covering his face with his hands as he sits in silence—as a strategy calculated to shift the jury's animus toward his accomplice.

When two psychologists testified that Weidmann had an undeveloped moral sense, but was nevertheless sane, the defense led one to admit that the violent political atmosphere in Germany and Austria could possibly have pushed the defendant from being merely a "small-time crook" to a serial killer. When the second psychologist granted that Weidmann's case was one of *"anomalie constitutionnelle instinctive,"* the defense determined to base its whole case on that term. When a juror asked a third expert, a psychoanalyst, whether a man with instinctive moral perversities was "normal," the expert gave a reply which, in Sevareid's judgment, was "as enlightening to the general audience as most of what had gone before." His science was a newly developed one, the witness said, but: from the point of view *"psychiatric classique," "oui,"* from the point of view *"psychologie affective," "non."*

On the last day of the trial, March 23, there was "absolute silence in the courtroom as the murderer leaned forward looking straight at the presiding judge, swallowing after each halting sentence and wetting his lips." Before the court, said Weidmann, was a man ready to "accept the sacrifice of reparation."

"I ask you once more to try to understand me. I am guilty, terribly guilty. I offer everything that I can—my life. But after that there is punishment. There is also pardon. I . . I . . . have need of it." Then he sank into his chair and wept.

Weidmann's first lawyer, Madame Renée Jardin, whom the reporter refers to continually as "his red-haired woman attorney," portrayed him as a mystic, torn by the conflicting impulses of his split personality. It was not possible, she cried, that the man whose moral transformation they had witnessed remains a bad man. The courtroom burst into applause.

Sevareid's picture of the Corsican's plea gives us an idea of what daily newspapers lost when he went into radio:

> For more than three hours Mr. de Moro-Giafferi thundered and pleaded. He preached and he implored. He quoted police records and German philosophers. He stretched his bulky body far over his wooden stand and thrust out his massive jaw at the jurymen. He rocked on his heels and softly begged. He stamped and he raged and banged his fist and caressed his grey moustache. He bellowed at the State Prosecutor and made him blush. Verbally he caressed the bent-over form of Weidmann and made him weep.

He warned the jury that in previous cases psychologists had found defendants sane who later turned out to be insane—like the Papin sisters who had destroyed their victims in a tub of acid and now howled away in an asylum—and quoted a pile of psychology texts to prove that though "sane," Weidmann was an "instinctive pervert who could never be cured."

Then came his climax. Weidmann's principal crime was that he had been born. His crimes came from the "climate" of his childhood. They were "German crimes." "I love Germany," he said. "I love the nobility of German courage. But I have the right to say that every people has its genius. Ours is made of softness. The German genius is made of brutality." The German's race had made him a killer; France's "grandeur," which the jury must demonstrate, is its "pity." Sevareid does not comment on this extraordinary line of argument.

Outside Versailles: In Spain, ending 989 days of conflict that brought one million dead, following the example of Madrid, the last remaining provincial capitals surrendered to Franco's troops. In Paris, French premier Edouard Daladier, in a speech broadcast to the nation, declared that France will fight for its liberty rather than accept dishonor.

When the jury found Weidmann guilty of homicide on all six counts, his only reaction was a wan smile of resignation.

The night before his execution, June 17, he read passages from Goethe to Madame Jardin and consoled himself with Thomas à Kempis's *Imitation of Christ*. In response to a telegraphed plea from deKoven's Brooklyn parents, who had for a while insisted she was still alive, he wrote them a solemn affirmation of their daughter's virtue. Sevareid's

Sunday, June 18, page-one description of the execution, which begins
with a one-sentence paragraph, "Eugen Weidmann died yesterday with
his eyes tightly closed," beautifully, almost elegiaclly, evokes a mood of
sympathetic sadness as he ticks off hours from midnight till the knife
falls in the bare light of dawn at 4:30 A.M.

The crowd, six hundred people, fill the local cafes, cheer, whistle, and
down sausages. Police and troops clear the cafes and move them back.
Spectators appear on the rooftops. "As the light intensified, the shafts of
the guillotine appeared to grow taller and taller by imperceptible degrees until they dominated the scene." The Abbé arrives. Weidmann
attends mass. Milk carts roll over the stones of adjacent streets. Weidmann appears, eyes shut at the sight of the blade, his shirt pulled down,
his bare "shoulders startlingly white against the dark polished wood of
the machine upon which he was pushed."

Sevareid withheld from his *Herald* readers what he confided a few
years later in *Not So Wild a Dream:* his revulsion at the mob of French
men, women, and children who booed and chanted and, as the knife
fell, "sent up a savage, blood-curdling scream like an animal pack's." He
discovered in this civilized nation a strain of sadism he had known in
neither England nor America. The French themselves were so appalled
by the crowd's behavior that this was France's last public execution.

In the *Herald,* Sevareid gave the news analyst's most valuable space, his
last sentence, to Moro-Giafferi: "This man lived like a monster, but he
died like a saint."

An ocean away, the *New York Times* restricted its coverage of the execution to a Friday, June 16, story that Weidmann would die at dawn.
Sunday's paper was too full of the New York World's Fair to make room
for a French execution, but it did find space for a story on two young
New Yorkers, Robert Fuller and Richard Slobodin, who had just finished their six-thousand-mile, year-long trip from Manhattan to Fair-
banks, Alaska, mostly by canoe. And for an editorial on "Television's
Worries," casting doubt on whether the industry could ever come up
with the money and resources to produce, as the British experience indicated was necessary, an hour-long play every day.

Meanwhile, in London, Edward R. Murrow was reading about Weidmann's death in his copy of the Paris *New York Herald Tribune.* That
Sevareid can write, he said to himself. And I like his ideas.

8

FLIGHT

IN THE FACE of what Winston Churchill called the "gathering storm" in mid 1939, William Paley decided that the time had come to expand CBS's European coverage. His decision came at a moment when all four of the elements essential for a historic communications breakthrough were in place—a broad new audience anxious to read or listen; new technology that enabled communicators to reach this audience; a political crisis to intensify the appetite for news; and personal genius.

The American public had been hungry for entertainment, particularly for the constant stimulation that the new mass media made possible, since the popular, often sensational, "penny" press made its debut in the 1830s. The Depression of the 1930s had heightened the country's craving for diversion, for some release from what novelist Tillie Olson recalls as the "degrading misery, the aloneness, the ravening hunger, despair," of that period. Along with the film industry the radio pioneers, NBC's founder David Sarnoff and his new competitor Paley, who bought CBS in 1929, were poised to satisfy that hunger.

The technology was ready. Wireless transmission between Europe and America had been possible since 1907. Since the early 1930s, both NBC and CBS had been broadcasting "talks," rather than interviews, by renowned writers, politicians, even kings, from Europe to American audiences. And both networks had experimented with war reporting.

NBC's frontline agent was Floyd Gibbons, the World War I *Chicago Tribune* reporter who had deliberately sailed on the *Laconia* in 1917 with the expectation that it would be torpedoed and give him a big story. During the war, he was the one who reported the immortal words of the marine sergeant who led his troops over the top yelling, "Come on, you sons o' bitches, do you want to live forever?" He also lost an eye at Belleau Wood, and made a white eye patch a part of his public persona. In 1932, in the first news broadcast from Asia, Gibbons reported Japan's conquest of Manchuria, and in 1935 both NBC and CBS covered Italy's invasion of Ethiopia.

By 1938, nine of ten urban American homes had radios, and thanks to the New Deal's program of rural electrification, seven of ten farm-family homes had them as well. Since 1930 the number of sets doubled, so that more homes had radios than had telephones.

When Sevareid remarked that radio at that time was for listening to music, he could have had in mind Paul Whiteman, Bing Crosby, Kate Smith, Nelson Eddy, or *Your Hit Parade* in mind. During the thirties, at times three-quarters of broadcasting time each week was unsponsored, and networks filled the air with popular music, mostly tea-dance tunes, and around twenty to thirty hours of classical music.

But, thanks to both CBS and NBC, news of Europe's march toward war was breaking through. It had become a journalistic rule that wars—as in the Civil War, the Spanish-American War, and World War I—have four effects on the newspaper business: they boost circulation; they stimulate the media to develop new technology to cover combat in a timely way; in the tension between freedom and censorship, they spark the struggle between the media and the government over control of information; and they give birth to a unique breed of individuals—those seemingly mad "great correspondents," entrepreneurs who risk all to record history under pressure. World War II would make that axiom true for radio as well.

Throughout journalism history, individual genius harnesses these forces. His vision and leadership move an institution to a point where it can influence history. Paley's leadership at the key moment was the catalyst that led to the development of the broadcast news industry that Murrow and Sevareid came to symbolize; but his contribution is best understood in two broader ways. Broadcasting, more than print journalism, is a collaborative enterprise; so CBS News took on the ambience of a "team" or "club." Because he was at bottom a businessman, not an idealist, from the beginning Paley pursued the appearance, the image, of news excellence and responsibility more religiously than he pursued excellence as a value in itself. This trait would create a tension between CBS as an institution and the Murrow team—a tension that would gradually alienate many of them from the network that had "made" them.

In the late 1920s, American radio listeners received only one daily news broadcast, read off the wires at 217 words a minute by NBC's irrepressible Floyd Gibbons. Sensing that Gibbons's "Chicago School," of abrasive journalism may have had its day, Paley came up with golden-voiced Lowell Thomas. He had made a reputation by "discovering," during World War I, T. E. Lawrence, whose exploits he vastly exaggerated in his book, *With Lawrence in Arabia*, and on lecture tours. In his first network broadcast, on September 29, 1930, Thomas called Hitler another Mussolini and warned him that if he wants to conquer Russia, as he said in *Mein Kampf*, he should consult Napoleon. Thomas's program ran till 1976.

But the first journalist to bring authority to international news was Hans Von Kaltenborn, an associate editor of the *Brooklyn Eagle*, who joined CBS in 1930, and whose clipped, precise, theatrical delivery, working from notes rather than from a script, convinced listeners that here was a man who knew what he was talking about.

Von Kaltenborn, already known as radio's first news analyst, boosted his reputation on September 3, 1936, during the Spanish Civil War, when he made the first actual battlefield broadcast in history. From a haystack between the lines on the French-Spanish border, his words were carried by telephone line to Bordeaux, Paris, London, and Rugby, then by short-wave to New York. He became the prime example of the man whose extremely broad experience—his knowledge of German that allowed him to translate Hitler and his travels, adventures, Spanish-American War service, and Harvard education—equipped him to keep talking, talking, talking. Because, during the Spanish civil war, neither CBS nor NBC had yet formulated standards of "objectivity," he was free to let his sympathies for the "Loyalists" over the "Fascists" shine through. Nevertheless, his didactic style and overbearing ego set him off against the low-key intellectuals like Sevareid whom Murrow was beginning to recruit.

If the legendary era of CBS News begins with the sound of Edward R. Murrow's voice broadcasting from a rooftop during the London Blitz, and ends with Eric Sevareid's retirement, the foundation that made the legend possible began during the 1930s when Paley collected a team of men whose talents would complement his own—particularly Frank Stanton, Edward Klauber, and Paul White.

Young Bill Paley backed into radio in 1927, when his father, Sam, a Russian Jewish Philadelphia cigar magnate, asked the twenty-six-year-old Bill to supervise a half-hour program, "The La Palina Smoker," he had bought on the Columbia network. Paley redesigned the program, introduced a sultry-voiced "Miss La Palina," who wisecracked and sang with a comedian as master of ceremonies. Thanks to the success of the jazzed-up version of the radio show, the Paley family's sales of Congress Cigars grew from four hundred thousand to one million a day. The network prospered, the Paleys bought it from its other investors, and Bill moved into a plush paneled office in Times Square's Paramount Building as president in 1928.

Self-conscious about his youthful appearance—NBC president David Sarnoff referred to him as "the kid"—Paley compensated for his youth by quickly mastering the details of the operation. He soon demonstrated his marketing genius, his analytical skills, his ability to listen—or appear to listen—to others' ideas and, above all, his instinct for spotting talent. He knew that what he liked, everyone would like.

A radio program, he told a 1934 interviewer, "must appeal to either the emotion or the self-interest" of the listener. Broadcasters could not "calmly broadcast programs we think people ought to listen to if they know what is good for them." He quickly established the national network's benevolent dominance over its far-flung affiliates. While NBC, then the leading network, required its subsidiaries to pay ninety dollars for each hour of network broadcasting, CBS supplied its stations with fifteen hours a week of free nonsponsored time to fill their schedules, in exchange for the right to preempt any part of the local affiliate's schedule to play a network-sponsored program. This meant that CBS could guarantee a sponsor that its programs would be heard at a particular time all across the country.

Then he began his talent hunt. He heard Fats Waller playing the piano at a socialite's party and snapped him up. Next the Mills Brothers and Kate Smith. In 1931 Paley heard Bing Crosby on a shipboard phonograph and wired his executives to hire him, assigning guards to Bing all day to make sure he showed up sober. In 1936, in the first of his many talent raids, he snatched Al Jolson, Nelson Eddy, and the Major Bowes Amateur Hour away from NBC.

From the start, CBS took much of its creativity from America's preeminent public relations expert, Sigmund Freud's nephew, Edward

Bernays, who defined public relations as "the engineering of consent." It was Bernays who choreographed Woodrow Wilson's entrance into Paris after World War I, and whose cigarette promotional campaigns turned smoking into a symbol of a smart woman's independence.

In the long run, however, Paley's most significant new arrival was Frank Stanton. The twenty-seven-year-old Stanton and his pretty, brunette wife Ruth drove their model-T Ford from Columbus, Ohio, to Manhattan and CBS in 1935. A Ph.D. in Industrial Psychology from Ohio State, Stanton was convinced that radio's impact was more profound than that of print and had focused his research on how networks measured the size of their audience. He invented a small black box which, plugged into a radio, recorded which stations were tuned in at different times during the day. As he worked his way up in the corporation—like Paley he mastered every aspect of the business—he continued to develop the science of schedule and audience analysis; and he convinced his bosses to reverse the conventional wisdom of spreading news throughout the day and instead group similar programs back-to-back. As a result, 6:00 P.M. to 7:00 P.M. became the daily time for news and analysis.

Stanton became vice president in 1942, took on the role of second founder of CBS, and came to represent the network in the public mind as much as Paley did. As Sally Bedell Smith says in her biography of Paley, *In All His Glory:* "Stanton was everything Paley was not. Paley was long on creative spark but short on follow-through. Paley, in effect, provided the architectural drawings; Stanton turned them into steel and concrete."

CBS's initial commitment to news and public affairs, however, stemmed not from Paley's zeal to serve the public but, in a scenario scripted by Bernays, a strategy to ward off congressional regulation.

In 1930 the Senate Committee on Interstate Commerce was considering requiring that 15 percent of all channels be reserved for educational use. Paley, however, did not naturally think of CBS as an educational instrument; it was his property, his investment, and also an extension of his personality. Like his fabulous modern art collection, it was his public presentation of his better self. So when the words "public service broadcasting" struck his ears, what he heard was: beating NBC, personally beating Sarnoff, creating an identity that would soft-soap Congress, distinguishing CBS from NBC and Paley from the other Russian Jew.

When CBS signed Arturo Toscanini and the New York Philharmonic for Saturday afternoons, NBC began broadcasting the Metropolitain Opera and then hired Toscanini to conduct the new NBC Symphony Orchestra. Paley reached for another attention-getting high road. With fanfare, he announced that CBS would restrict commercials to 10-to-15 percent of broadcast time, that CBS would accept no more ads for laxatives, deodorants, and other "bodily function" products, and would reduce violence in children's programs. NBC had already followed those policies for years, but had neglected to publicize the fact.

Once Bernays taught Paley the long-range commercial advantage of the high road, that CBS should become known for more than merely entertainment, Ed Klauber, Paley's right-hand man since 1930, brought news to the fore. "Ed Klauber was an intolerant man," Murrow said later, "intolerant of deceit, deception, distortion, and double talk . . . If there be standards of integrity, responsibility and restraint in American radio news, Ed Klauber, more than any other man, is responsible for them." A stocky, growling taskmaster, Klauber was also Paley's hatchet man. He came to CBS, through Bernays's sponsorship, after stints at the *New York World* and *New York Times,* whose standards he adapted for broadcasting. He put order in the often-absent Paley's schedule, controlled access to his office, and came to be loathed by his staff for both his perfectionism and the chewing-outs he delivered as he sat behind his massive desk, peered over his pince-nez, and flicked ashes from the cigarette at the end of his long holder. Paley said later: "He had the highest standards of any man I ever met. He'd drive you crazy but he was right."

What became CBS's guidelines for fairness and balance—some of which anticipated the Fairness Doctrine codified by the Federal Communications Commission in 1949—actually developed by trial and error, and in response to government warnings. To get rid of the rabid Father Charles Coughlin, who was anti-Jew and anti-FDR, CBS began the *Church of the Air,* which rotated religious speakers. Up through the 1936 presidential election CBS tolerated the generally liberal partisanship of its two commentators, H. V. Kaltenborn and Boake Carter, both of whom endorsed FDR, partly because Paley's wife Dorothy was a liberal supporter of the Loyalists in Spain. Paley himself, though in his heart a conservative businessman, also knew it was to his advantage to ingratiate himself to the Roosevelt administration. The government had regulatory power over CBS, and FDR, who knew that newspaper publishers opposed him, had mastered the new medium of radio to get directly to the American people.

Within a year, however, Paley and Klauber realized that too much controversy upsets advertisers and affiliates, that CBS's future depended on a reputation for fairness, neutrality, objectivity—goals that the profession would never adequately define, but by which it would strive to operate. In an address to the National Conference on Educational Broadcasting, on November 29, 1937, Paley put down principles that would be codified and tested over the coming decades: CBS "must never have an editorial page . . . and discussion must never be one-sided as long as there can be found anyone to take the other side." But in the early days of developing its guidelines, CBS failed to build in adequate protection for the commentator's freedom. One mistake was the policy that allowed a single advertiser to sponsor a particular news program, rather than buy one of several sixty-second time slots. This meant that a journalist would have to keep a single sponsor happy and trim his script accordingly. It was a practice Murrow objected to from the beginning. And wisely. For, in varying degrees, it would come back to haunt two of his protégés, William L. Shirer and Eric Sevareid, and ultimately Murrow himself.

The principal impetus toward developing a real CBS news organization was the 1932–33 battle between the newspapers and the news broadcasters where radio began scooping the papers, and the papers pressured the wire services—Associated Press, United Press, and International News Service—to cut off their services to their radio competitors. At first, CBS decided to fight back and unleashed Paul White, a boisterous, hard-drinking Kansan who had joined the CBS publicity department in 1930, to develop an independent national and international staff of reporters, mostly part-time, that would let CBS do without the wire services. With six hundred reporters, CBS produced three news programs a day, while NBC resigned itself to feeding bulletins to Lowell Thomas, whom they had bought from CBS, and now Walter Winchell, the Hearst sensational gossip columnist who blurted out his rat-a-tat-tat "exclusives" to twenty million listeners every Sunday night.

The broadcasters backed off from their defiance in the 1933 Biltmore Agreement and, for a while, allowed newspapers the upper hand; but the agreement fell apart within a year, and White had shown that CBS was ready to cover the world on its own.

White's 1938 trip to Europe convinced him that war was on the way and that CBS had to be ready to cover it. Their main weapon, for a while, was a little round-faced, dull-voiced fellow whom Murrow had hired the year before, William L. Shirer.

The Chicago-born Shirer, determined to go "where a man could drink a glass of wine or a stein of beer without breaking the law," had come to Europe on a cattle boat after graduating from Coe College in Cedar Rapids in 1925. In Paris he signed on with the *Herald's* rival, the Paris edition of the *Chicago Tribune*, spent time with Hemingway and Gertrude Stein, covered Lindbergh's landing in 1927, the 1928 Olympics, and Mahatma Gandhi's India resistance. When the *Tribune's* arch-conservative publisher, Colonel Robert R. McCormick, fired him in 1932, he joined the *Herald* for a while, then became the German correspondent for Hearst's International News Service.

Murrow brought Shirer on board not so much as a correspondent but to help him arrange those "talks," educational broadcasts, which both Shirer and Murrow considered inadequate—because they were not *news* —to the rapidly changing political situation, as the growing war cried out to be reported. Through the winter of 1938, Paley and Klauber resisted using Murrow and Shirer as reporters lest they violate the new CBS neutrality guidelines; but on March 11, 1938, when the German Army entered Austria, Shirer was in Vienna, the only American broadcaster to witness the invasion. But, the Nazis had driven him out of the broadcast building at bayonet point, and he had no way to get the story out.

Finally, CBS decided to bring the full resources of radio to the story. Shirer flew to London, where, using BBC facilities he broadcast the first uncensored eyewitness report. In New York on Sunday, March 13, Paul White tacked blankets on an office wall to turn it into a broadcasting studio and, with Paley's enthusiastic support (because NBC had returned to Vienna and was broadcasting exclusives), ordered Shirer and Murrow to prepare a special program of live reports from European capitals for broadcast that night. Shirer lined up stringers in Paris, London, and Rome, while Murrow himself flew to Vienna. Robert Trout anchored

from New York. Miraculously, it worked. At 1:00 A.M. London time—
8:00 P.M. in New York—the deep, steady voice of Murrow entered
American homes: "I arrived by air from Warsaw and Berlin only a few
hours ago . . . From the air, Vienna didn't look much different than it has
before, but nevertheless it has changed."

Though not the first multiple pickup from Europe, it was the first live
news roundup from overseas. It opened a new age in American broadcast journalism, established the primacy of radio over newspapers at least
in its immediacy, identified CBS with news in the public mind, and
began a process that would eventually bring the Vietnam War and the
Persian Gulf war into American living rooms.

During the Munich crisis in September 1938, as Hitler partitioned
Czechoslovakia, White brought his team together again in an extraordinary display of both ingenuity and endurance. Over eighteen days, the
sixty-year-old Kaltenborn, anchoring and analyzing from New York, set
up a cot in the studio and did eighty-five broadcasts. Shirer and Murrow
became household names. Although NBC scooped CBS several times,
CBS made a stronger impact because its staff, which now also included
the Indiana born Rhodes scholar Elmer Davis, not only reported but
explained what the news meant. Indeed, Kaltenborn explained too much:
he analyzed the archbishop of Canterbury's prayer and irked Murrow
by even analyzing Murrow's analysis. Nevertheless, the stage was set for
White to tell Murrow to start building his staff. And Hans Von Kaltenborn decided the time had come to change his name to H.V.

By the summer of 1939 Eric Sevareid was working at the *Herald* during
the day and moonlighting as a United Press reporter at night. Pre-guild
salaries being what they were, it was common for a newspaperman in
the 1930s to try to juggle two jobs; and Sevareid, though often a generous man and not greedy or materialistic, was developing what would be
a lifelong anxiety about money: he never had enough. Lois had an income from her job in the reference room at the American Library, and
that helped. But they liked to travel and needed to make some decisions
about the future. He had his family on his mind. The newly married
young Sherman Finger had come through on their honeymoon and
stayed with them. And Lois's mother had visited in July and taken Lois

touring for ten days through the Riviera, Carcassone, Avignon, and Rheims. Eric and Lois had also invited his sister Jeanne to come over and live with them in their apartment and go to school in Paris. This offer was declined; and the way things were developing politically, it might be just as well.

Lois was pregnant. Scammon's Rule—that one must eat and two eat more than one—was all the more true for three.

The Paris *Herald* was not the sort of paper where an ambitious journalist spends his whole career. By temperament Sevareid was never really happy with the nature of the United Press big-news-agency work, with its pressure for scoops, "exclusives," and the constant orders from New York to rewrite and update leads on fast-breaking stories. One hot mid-August night the United Press's president and general manager, Hugh Baillie, an administrator who retained his reputation for being a reporter "first, last, and always," arrived from New York and offered Sevareid a promotion. He saw this as the chance he had been looking for to report on the war to an American audience, but again he dreaded the pressure for scoops. As he sat alone in the office thinking it over, Murrow phoned from London with a counteroffer. "There's only Shirer and Grandin [Thomas Grandin, hired during the Munich crisis] and myself now, but I think this thing may develop into something." There would be no pressure for scoops—just honest news.

Flattered, Sevareid agreed for a test, and prepared a short talk on the Weidmann execution, which he thought would be broadcast over a closed circuit to CBS executives. Informed two hours before air time that he would be carried over the entire CBS network, Sevareid rewrote his piece and delivered it into the microphone "with my hands shaking so violently that listeners must have heard the paper rattling." New York replied that Sevareid's material was good but his manner of speaking was poor. Murrow answered, as he had about Shirer, that he didn't care about his reporter's voice. He wanted a staff who could think and write.

Meanwhile, Sevareid learned that his old University of Minnesota mentor Mitchell Charnley was in Paris. Sevareid phoned his hotel. He needed advice. Could they meet? That night, at midnight, the two sat for hours in a small cafe as Sevareid poured out his doubts about his abilities to his old professor. All his experience had been in print journalism and, worse, he did not speak well. What should he do?

Charnley fired right back: "Grab it!"

But Sevareid couldn't make his mind up on the spot, and the professor departed without knowing his former pupil's decision. Then several weeks later, when back in the United States, Charnley turned on his radio and heard, "This is Eric Sevareid in Paris."

On August 16 Murrow wrote to his new recruit, confirmed the previous day's phone conversation and Sevareid's new salary of $250 a month, and told him to start learning the ropes from Grandin. He had a lot to learn in a short time. Some things were technical and practical, like voice modulation and tone, and how to commandeer and adapt to broadcast facilties in a crisis, that is, find transmitters that will beam CBS stories across the Atlantic in the middle of the night when German troops are but a few miles away. And how, without scarcely a moment's notice, to squeeze material from a seven-hundred-word text into a precious minute of airtime.

When Murrow brought Sevareid over to London for a few days he put him on the air with H. V. Kaltenborn, who gave him fatherly advice. When they got on the air, Kaltenborn began to ad-lib and kept talking, and talking into the young rookie's allotted time. The novice had to slur and stumble his way through his meticulously prepared script, trying to shorten it as he went along. The broadcast was a disaster, and Murrow stood by growing dark with smothered rage. When it was over, the three of them walked toward the elevator in silence, Murrow in front of them, not saying a word. Then Murrow took his pencil and broke it in two. That was all. It was Sevareid's first glimpse of the other side of this strange man whom he had given up a newspaper future to follow. Like himself, Murrow had powerful feelings which he had trained himself to keep in check.

Although Sevareid had accepted Murrow's offer partly because he was caught up in the aura of this man, he also thought he was escaping the pressure of deadlines and the demand for scoops. This was true in the sense that he might go several days without pressure to produce a story; but he also discovered that, unlike print journalism where scoops move from event to print in a matter of hours, in radio a scoop means beating the competition by a matter of minutes or seconds. On September 1,

1939, Sevareid and a little bunch of his fellow journalists were sitting around a big table in a little sidewalk cafe on the Champs-Elysées when word came over the phone that Hitler had just invaded Poland. Like nineteenth-century fire horses galloping out of the firehouse at the sound of the alarm, Sevareid's fellow journalists yelled and scrambled for the phones. Sevareid sat alone quietly, finished his drink, thought about what all this meant, and strolled back to the office. This scholarly—his critics called it leisurely—disposition toward his material never left him, but the coming months and year would push him to produce under pressure in a way that was at once contrary to his personality yet consistent with his seemingly contradictory drive to dominate, to excel.

In his first weeks on the job, Sevareid also had to digest a series of directives from Klauber and White about the journalist's ethical obligations in wartime, particularly the professional neutrality of a reporter speaking to—and, in a sense, for—a country that was then professedly neutral. In a September 5 four-page memorandum, Klauber reminded his staff: "Columbia, as an organization, has no editorial opinions about the war ... Those, therefore, who are its voice in presenting or analyzing the news must not express their own feelings. This does not preclude informed appraisals of the meaning of facts."

The seventh paragraph stated the principles on commentary that remain to the present day:

> What news analysts are entitled to do and should do so [is] to elucidate and illuminate the news out of common knowledge or special knowledge possessed by them or made available to them by this organization through its news sources. They should point out the facts on both sides, show contradictions with the known record, and so on. They should bear in mind that in a democracy it is important that people not only should know but should understand, and their function is to help the listener to understand, to weigh, and to judge, but not to do the judging for him.

Within these guidelines, CBS gave its reporters considerable freedom to use their own judgment. It recognized that fairness could not be determined by a mathematical formula. If reporters could not state their own opinions, they could report the opinions of others.

Both CBS and NBC agreed that war was sensational enough without the added thrill of excited newscasters bellowing into their microphones.

They also reminded their listeners that information was censored, incomplete, and sometimes wrong. In many ways, the CBS version of objectivity fit Sevareid's temperament well; he knew that the first casualties of war are usually truth and the language and, since college, he had been giving himself the kind of education wherein the more one learns the less he is confident he knows.

But Sevareid did have strong feelings and convictions, a hierarchy of truths and values, planted in his mother's first instructions, shaken at the *Minneapolis Journal,* and redefined at the university and on Paris's Left Bank. The image of a widow wiping her husband's blood off her front steps with a shower curtain after Germany's first bombing raid of Paris, the sight of Frenchmen gathering up the bloody "red meat" morcels of the British pilot whose plane had been shot down over their village, and his own fear and exhaustion as he flees France and the nation implodes will further clarify that hierarchy. Its dominant principle will become: fascism must not be allowed to overcome democracy. Its corollary: in some way, without sacrificing fairness and honesty, the media should promote preparedness, the war effort. When he crosses the invisible line that, at least in theory, separates neutrality from advocacy, White will let him know.

During these weeks Eric also developed his new ways of seeing. The radio reporter, like the nineteenth-century print journalist before the development of the tabloid and the wide use of photographs by newspapers, had to be the eyes and ears of an audience a continent away. He had to make the listener present by talking in pictures—for Murrow, against the live background whistle and distant *crump* of a falling bomb or the *boom-boom-boom* of the ack-ack gun. Sevareid's descriptive powers, which he began to develop in *Canoeing with the Cree,* would serve him well.

Great Britain and then France declared war on Germany on September 3, and within a week the British landed an expeditionary force of 158,000 on European soil to head off the German onslaught, now rolling across Poland, wherever it turned west. On the third, between Britain's and France's declarations, Sevareid fought and griped with his studio engineer trying, by cable and phone, to get word of his scoop on France's decision first to America and then, when he could not reach the

New York studio, to England. Finally the engineer, who had been doing his best, broke down and yelled at him to get out. A family man who had been wounded in the last war and been imprisoned in a German camp for a year, he had just been called back into active service that morning. Sevareid felt ashamed—with his useless script and precious neutrality—like the *Journal* reporter he had once been, asking the family of a murder victim for a photograph of their lost loved one.

In New York, CBS enhanced its shortwave reception center so it could monitor four European signals at once, and added a tower to the top of its studio.

As the crisis grew, he and Grandin broadcast steadily for two or three days—up at 2 A.M., repeating their reports again and again, and falling fully clothed into bed at the end. Once Sevareid's voice cracked with fatigue; once the windows blew open and Americans heard the eerie wail of the air-raid sirens in the background. But even that realism was too close to "sensationalism" to be allowed.

If the past came to be a continuing presence in Sevareid's worldview, it is because he witnessed the perpetual presence of World War I in the French absurdly denying the reality of another war building up on their frontiers. He often employed the old reporter's shortcut of talking to his cab driver,-the always available common man who, the theory goes, absorbs the wisdom of the streets and stores it until the journalist comes along. As Sevareid hung outside the Gare de l'Est watching veterans from the last war arrive in their old uniforms, still tired from 1918, he listened to his driver pour out his pain, his memories of Verdun, and his anxieties about his son on his way to the front. On July 14, Bastille Day, Sevareid had escorted his mother-in-law to the train station as she hustled to get the boat train out of Paris just a half hour before the parade began, a parade he described in his *Herald* report as France's "most impressive demonstration since the victory parade of 1918."

> The people of Paris, the pundits say, "go down to the streets" for two different reasons—when they mean political business and when they mean to play. Both purposes were fused yesterday. The military parade was a spectacular show, but it was meant to impress, and every Parisian was aware of the fact. And so, in a sense, it was not just the military on parade, but the whole of France as a community and a power.

The empire was on display. The Foreign Legion swung deliberately past, making its first Paris appearance. Then Algerians and Moroccans, cantering their white-and-gray horses, their long white robes flowing behind. Three hundred and fifty planes roared overhead. Tanks and artillery rumbled by. This was France ready to fight, they seemed to say. Let the enemy beware.

But that glorious display was an illusion. France was neither a community nor a power. The French war plan, British military historian J.F.C. Fuller wrote in 1948, was "one of the most suicidal ever devised." The Maginot line, an "impregnable" string of underground fortifications, reached along the French-German border from Switzerland to Belgium, where it stopped, leaving the northern Belgium-Netherlands corridor vulnerable to attack. Furthermore, says Fuller, the French strategy assumed that the "entrenched stalemate" of World War I would repeat itself. In short, France's reaction to the German advance, which Hitler temporarily halted once Poland fell, was simply to sit and wait for something to happen. The *Blitzkrieg* became a *Sitzkrieg* or the "phony war." Ultimately, historians would attribute France's collapse to its political and moral corruption, its political divisions, and its lack of will to fight. Writing on September 2, 1939, Fuller suggested that when war came the French army would "sit in the Maginot line, snip up *La Lie parisienne*, decorate their dug-outs with very unsatisfying young ladies, and then want to go home." Sevareid would have to decide to what degree he shared that judgment.

On September 10 he and his friend Geoffrey Cox, a New Zealander and correspondent for the London *Daily Express*, drove up to Cherbourg on the English Channel to watch the first troops of the British Expeditionary Force arrive. In one of the best sentences he ever wrote about himself, Sevareid remarked in *Not So Wild a Dream,* "I am conscious of the eyes and faces of men, their voices and their hands." An observer of faces, he could see in the ruddy complexions and vigor of these young men that, unlike the French, they did not know the experience of their parents who had landed in this same port twenty-five years before.

He was also very conscious in these days of the good company of Geoffrey Cox. Their working relationship grew quickly into one of those special friendships that last a lifetime. Athough they grew up on different sides of the world, they came from similar backgrounds. Born in country districts, remote from the centers of power, both yearned from the beginning to see the world. "The small town boy," Cox said later, "brings an innocent eye to events, a wonder for what is beyond the horizon. He takes a magical delight in events."When they first met, both shared the liberals' distaste for the reigning powers of the 1930s; and both moved from a position of seeing war as unthinkable to war as necessary. Though they became friends quickly, perhaps like many men in their situation, they did not—or could not—talk about intimate topics, like family. "We were so caught up in great events," said Cox, "that families didn't seem important."

A week later, with Walter Kerr, of the *New York Herald Tribune*, and Charles Findley, a film-company newsreel executive, he made his way by car unimpeded through Chateau-Thierry, Rheims, Verdun, and Metz—all the scenes of the First War the boy in Velva had studied in the library's picture books—to the Luxembourg border, just a few miles beyond the low hills from what was once again the western front. Their story, when they wrote it, was that there was no "story." Just an eerie waiting for something to happen. With his friend Cox, Sevareid toured the still "neutral" Netherlands and Belgium and found Belgian border guards drunk and 50 percent of one regiment AWOL. In Amsterdam he astonished the American consul, who conceived of radio as purely an entertainment medium, by broadcasting about the news of the day rather than about tulips and windmills. In the little town of Hilversum, he became "suddenly, overpoweringly, homesick," at the sight of clean, tree-lined streets, and boys and girls with white shirts and "open, understandable faces" strolling arm-in-arm.

To watch the war from the Grand Duchy of Luxembourg was literally to watch—as if their cafe-table wicker chairs were orchestra seats in a theater. The little group of reporters would sip their yellow wine on the veranda of a cafe at Remisch on the vineyard slopes and listen to the dull boom of the big guns or watch an airplane twist crazily along the Moselle River as puffs of smoke from antiaircraft fire mushroomed around it. They lived in a hotel where German General Ludendorff and his staff had stayed in 1914 and they drank a great deal of the excellent wine served by the American consul, the gracious George Platt Waller of Alabama. The official censor for Sevareid's broadcasts was the Luxembourg foreign minister himself, the courtly "Ruritanian" Dr. Joseph Bech, who never changed a word, and would chuckle aloud to himself as he read the script and pat Sevareid's arm and say: "Excellent, my boy, excellent! The Nazis won't like it but, after all, we are still masters of our own house, you know."

At the end of November, Russia invaded Finland.

In December, in two days which were to shake him profoundly, Sevareid donned his correspondent's regalia, an adaptation of a French army uniform, his warm coat and gloves, and toured French detention camps, which rumors had described as comparable to the Gestapo camps inside the Reich. In a camp for German nationals, whom the French had decided could not be allowed to be seen sitting leisurely in cafes by returning soldiers, he saw dark barracks packed with men as young as sixteen and as old as seventy, "their eyes fixed upon my face, their eyes peering out of their long, matted hair from dead faces white as chalk." The next day, at the camp for politial refugees, the French lieutenant irritated him by prattling on and on about how wretched this bare, muddy place had been before he and his men had fixed it up. Pulling up an image from his boxcar days, he wrote later: "He had the pious, ingratiating tones of a professional benefactor. He sounded like the Salvation Army official in a stinking flophouse in an Idaho town."

Sevareid was the first man these poor souls had seen from the outside in months. They clung to his coat and pressed messages into his hands. An Austrian journalist, another journalist who had covered the Weidmann trial for the *Chicago Tribune,* a novelist, a tenor from the Vienna Opera, students—they were the collected civilization of Europe reduced to an animal state. Suddenly his young refugee friend Karli was beside him, his face now Christlike with a new beard which made his eyes even more soft and gentle than before. Oddly, their talk was formal, stilted. Sevareid was in a hurry; the French officers were waiting to take him to the best little restaurant in the village for a dinner of duck à l'orange. Karli slipped his arm around his shoulder, and the older man turned away, filled with self-loathing and, the French officers looking on, began to sob into his handkerchief.

Later that month, at Christmas, he traveled along the Maginot line and came to his first tentative conclusions about the relationship between the French character and the crushing defeat they were about to face. The French troops, he felt, were as sick of the chauvinist's use of *"la gloire"* for national motivation as he and his fellow Jacobins had been sick of "patriotism" when they heard it from Minnesota militarists. These young people did think their country was worth fighting for, it was just that they had no wish to face the agony of a war. "Their tragedy was that they had reached a high point of human progress too soon," he wrote later, "they were living before their time. They were the last people on earth who should have had Germany for a neighbor." When one French soldier in a fortification on the Rhine was killed by a sniper while Sevareid was visiting, the lieutenant and his troops were virtually paralyzed with grief. How would they bear the millions of deaths to follow?

As the reporter worked his way through the vast underground cities supporting the giant guns covering the valley between France and Germany above, the awful vulnerability of these fortresses dawned on him. True, a regiment could not storm these walls. But one brave man could render them useless. A single paratrooper could land on top and drop a hand grenade or gas bomb in the turret, and the battle would be over. Meanwhile the officers served two-hour lunches for the correspondents, where it was forbidden to talk about the war, and staged drills and inspections for distinguished visitors like Britain's Neville Chamberlain and King George. Sevareid declined to refer to the Maginot line as "impregnable" in his broadcasts, but he and most of his fellow correspondents failed to make clear to their listeners how poorly prepared the French were for war. Meanwhile Ambassador Bullitt convinced Roosevelt that the French would put up a magnificent fight.

In January, Murrow came over to meet William L. Shirer in Holland and replace him with new recruit Mary Marvin Breckinridge in Berlin so Shirer could see his wife and daughter in Switzerland. Then Murrow joined Sevareid and Grandin for a brief meeting in Paris. Paris was bitter cold however, and Murrow stood coughing and hacking in the snow at the airport unable to get out. After several days, Sevareid and NBC's Fred Bate, worried about Murrow's illness, had him checked into the American Hospital at Neuilly, and told London to cable Janet, who was in Switzerland visiting Shirer's wife. Janet hurried to Paris, furious to find that Ed had a severe strep infection and pneumonia, while London had assured her it was a just a little flu, a little fatigue. In fact, he was "frightfully ill." She stayed with the Sevareids on rue Casimir-Perrier, waiting for the medications to knock out the germs, arguing that they should go away to the mountains and rest, while Ed made light of it all, determined to go right back to work. In Murrow's world, Ann Sperber remarks in her biography, real men didn't get sick. He won, of course, and they returned to London's winter smoke and fog.

In Paris, since there was no "real" war to report, CBS filled the silence with feature stories. A good one, which Sevareid wrote about in *Not So Wild a Dream* and again in *American Heritage* in August 1963, was his encounter with Philippe Bunau-Varilla, the extraordinary engineer who, after the French attempt to build the Panama Canal failed in 1889, convinced the United States Senate in 1902 to take up the Panama project rather than start fresh in Nicaragua. After campaigning tirelessly for years, he finally swung their vote after a volcanic explosion in the West Indies killed several thousand people and he reminded the senators of Nicaragua's history of volcanic eruptions.

Bunau-Varilla was the man who, after receiving an implicit assurance from Theodore Roosevelt that the United States would support him, fomented the Panamanian revolt against Colombia when Colombia reneged on giving the United States the right-of-way. He was also the man who helped clear the imprisoned Captain Alfred Dreyfus of treason by publishing a photostat of a letter from Dreyfus to himself alongside a photostat of Dreyfus's alleged "treason" letter, to demonstrate that they could not have been written by the same man. At Verdun, during the First War, he lost his leg; but all he remembered about the battle was the fact that he developed a system of water purification there that is now used all over the world.

New York cabled Sevareid to find out if Bunau-Varilla was still alive and, if so, to have him do a five-minute live broadcast for the Ripley's *Believe It or Not* program about his role in the Panama Canal. Sevareid found him, and together they worked for days discussing his life and condensing it into a five-minute chunk of airtime. Then New York cabled and twice reduced his time, leaving the proud old man no more than three minutes! The eighty-year-old colonel cried, "No, no, impossible!" and, furious, hopped up and down on his wooden leg. But of course his pride, and reluctance to offend young Eric, won out. He agreed to have a midnight dinner at the Sevareid apartment, which was right across the street from the French studios, before the broadcast, which was set for 4 A.M.

That night, February 16, 1940, a blizzard hit Paris; but Bunau-Varilla dragged himself up the stairs to the Sevareid apartment. They ate and drank and talked by the fire, the old man frail and delicate, yet filled with force and drive. They fell asleep and Sevareid's watch stopped, and they almost missed their broadcast, bursting into the studio with only four minutes to go. The old man spoke his words firmly and proudly. The next day he sent a box of candy to Lois. Lois wrote a note to herself on the back of his calling card and stored it with her mementos: "This came with the beautiful box of candy the next day after he called on us from midnight to 4 A.M. He's an awfully nice old man, very entertaining and has a wooden leg and lots of money and memories."

On May 18 he died, four days after Hitler crashed across the border into France. Eighteen years later, when Sevareid was CBS's Washington correspondent, he accepted an invitation from the French ambassador to meet the ambassador's new wife. It was her second marriage, and, Sevareid discovered, she had been the daughter-in-law of Bunau-Varilla. With her were her two children, a beautiful daughter and her son who was twenty. In him Sevareid saw the grandfather—slim, small, slight, the same widely spaced, grave, steady eyes—then went home to Virginia and searched through Lois's things and found the card.

Meanwhile, brave little Finland, with white-clad "invisible" guerrilla ski-troops who could swoop out of the woods and shadows, raise havoc with the invading army and slip away, had convinced some French politicians that the way to weaken Germany was to help Finland defeat Germany's then-ally, Russia. Reading between the lines of an editorial in *Le Temps*, a semi-official paper, Sevareid the analyst became convinced that France had decided to send troops to Finland. He carefully constructed a highly nuanced three-minute broadcast built around that insight. But it happened again; the previous reporter, Bill White in Holland, ran over his time, leaving Paris with ninety seconds or nothing. In great distress, Sevareid plunged into the script, reading just the bald prediction, cutting the qualifiers as he went along. The "fact" of France's plan was reprinted and broadcast all over the world, Russia replied with a violent *Pravda* editorial and Paul White warned Sevareid he had gotten himself "the furtherest limbward." He might be in trouble. Finally the French confessed that he had been right and abandoned the project.

The French, however, had worse problems than that. Daladier's government fell, and he was replaced as premier by Paul Reynaud, an intelligent man but not a strong one. Sevareid's heart sank as he stood in the galleries and heard Reynaud's weak acceptance speech. France, which needed a moral hero, had come up with a compromise candidate.

Meanwhile, Lois's pregnancy had become very difficult. Most French doctors had been called into the army, so Dr. Vigne, one of France's foremost obstetricians, an elderly colonel who also ran a large military hospital, stopped by the apartment every Sunday to check on her progress. X-rays showed that Lois was pregnant with twins. But the chance that she might lose them was strong. This meant that for the last three months of her pregnancy Lois had to remain in bed, to take every precaution to prepare for a safe delivery. During that time Eric often had to leave town on assignment and sometimes he would arrange for a friend, like CBS correspondent Larry LeSueur, whose main beat was London with Murrow, to sit in the apartment with Lois over the weekend. On the morning of April 25, just when Eric had a broadcast due, Lois went into labor. Suddenly, William White, the same broadcaster who had run overtime on Eric a few months before, arrived from Holland and filled in for him while the Sevareids raced to the Clinique St. Pierre in Neuilly, a suburb to the west of the city.

During the delivery, Dr. Vigne twice, exhausted, came out of the operating room—once to look at Eric, say nothing, and return; then to light a cigarette and say, "I think it will go. For a time I was not so sure." A few minutes later, the nurse burst in and exclaimed: *"Deux beaux garçons!"*

They named them Peter and Michael. They were fraternal, rather than identical, twins; and their lives would follow very different paths.

At 3 A.M., Eric drove Dr. Vigne home and watched him move slowly, bent and incongruous in his uniform, toward his apartment. Again the metaphorical mind jumped from the individual to his cosmic role: "He was France, weary with the unceasing struggle for humanity and life, revealing in an unguarded moment that she did not fit and did not wish to fit the trappings of rationalized evil and justified death."

Now, however, whatever his domestic situation, Sevareid had professional obligations to fulfill. Italy might enter the war, so he had to travel to southern France and Algiers and Tunis to line up CBS stringers to cover a widened conflict. Of course he had to go. Of course. But it would be one more of many separations to strain a marriage that seemed ideal in Minneapolis but was headed for difficult times.

On May 9, as he climbed aboard his train for the south at Gare de Lyon, Sevareid ran into Karli again; the British had taken charge of the refugees and given them paid labor. The next day Germany invaded Holland, Belgium, and Luxembourg and rumors spread that they had bombed Paris. From Valence, Sevareid turned around and grabbed the train back to the French capital, arrived at the clinic at midnight and rushed up the stairs to Lois's room. She lay there looking at the door with wide eyes as he hurried in. She had lain alone helpless, unable to walk, for hours as everyone else seemed to be fleeing the building, perhaps abandoning her and her twin sons.

Eric had two things to do. Because she had had twins, the doctors thought Lois should stay in bed for a month, but he had decided to get an ambulance and drive his family to a safe place outside Paris; and he had to cover the war, join the correspondents who were leaving for Cambrai on the Belgian border. He got the family, with a Danish nurse, to a little inn between Versailles and Chartres, in Ponchartrain. Lois never learned her nurse's name—she just kept calling her "Hello." Somehow, because word spread that she was writing letters in German, the neighbors became convinced that Lois's nurse was a spy, and she later fled in fear. But by midnight of that day Eric was in the railroad station hotel in Cambrai.

From her window, Lois watched the solemn procession of humanity in flight trek by her little roadside inn, remembered it well, and wrote about it later from New York for the *Minneapolis Star Journal:*

> They came on foot, they rode bicycles, crowded into farm wagons
> ...Young people pushed carts in which old folks were riding. Others rode horseback. Mothers pushed their babies in perambulators.
>
> There wasn't much moaning or complaining. The people were either stunned by what was happening to them or else they had long since cried their eyes out.
>
> They just seemed to move forward with strange unseeing eyes and set faces. They dragged bedding or odd possessions. They limped. They helped their less agile fellows—but always there was just that grim expression—to get away, far away.
>
> Sometimes a face would turn back.

I often wondered whether they were looking for someone or taking a last glimpse of a place they wanted always to remember before the Germans came.

At Cambrai, Eric was finally face-to-face with real war. The building shook with the roar of airplane motors and explosions. A German and a British plane shot one another down in a dogfight. Alongside the smouldering pit where the British plane crashed one of the pilot's black boots stood upright, the only remnant of its wearer who had been blown to bits. But the authorities had no intention of letting the correspondents know how the war was going, for it was going badly. They boarded the train back to Paris; an hour later dive bombers demolished the station and killed fifty people waiting for the next train. What should have been a four-hour trip took eighteen. By counting the seconds between the flashes on the horizon and the sounds of the big guns in the distance, the correspondents calculated that the battle was well inside the French frontier. The Germans were already closing in on Sedan!

In Paris Sevareid wrote out a one-line telegram, which was actually a prearranged code, and sent it to New York. Whoever received it didn't know it was a coded message and left it on his desk for hours, until Paul White dug it out, deciphered it, and had Elmer Davis announce that, "according to a usually well-informed source," the Germans had broken through.

However real the war was now, the people of Paris, as if oblivious to the hoards of refugees who swarmed in from the north and east, carried on as if the barbarians were nowhere near the gates. Mary Marvin Breckinridge, a well-traveled former student activist and photojournalist, whom Murrow had added to the team as CBS's first woman correspondent, remembers New York chiding her when she betrayed too much emotion describing the plight of the refugees. Yet her average day-to-day activities—punctuated by the news of Holland's capitulation or air raid alerts—now seem astonishingly routine: lunch or drinks with Grandin and Sevareid at the hotel Crillon; an appointment to get her hair done; a visit to Lois and the twins at the clinic; fifty broadcasts from various cities; her efforts to find shelter for the refugees; buying a gas mask at the big department store, the Galleries Lafayette; most important, her fitting for her bridal gown—white with red and blue embroidery, a subtle affront to the Nazis. She was engaged to Jefferson Patterson, the Dayton-born American diplomat stationed in Berlin. On May 25 she bought a bike and a knapsack. She didn't know exactly when the Germans would enter Paris, but she wanted to be sure she had some means to escape.

On May 28 she reported that the surrender of Belgium left the British Expeditionary Force trapped at Dunkirk. Thus began the eight-day epic evacuation of three hundred thousand Allied troops.

Shocked by the evidence that the French seemed to have no plan to defend Paris, Sevareid sought out the poet-pilot Antoine de Saint-Exupéry, whom he found writing in a ledger at a cafe table on Boulevard Saint Germain. Surely he had the vision to make sense of this. He had expected to find a poet's face, but this man's was tough and scarred, with hard, cold eyes. The pilot had just returned from an observation flight, what had he seen? The author of *The Little Prince* and *Wind, Sand and Stars* had little to say: "From the air, the war is a frieze. You see the black dots which are the tanks and the trucks and the veil of dust. There is no movement when you see it from 20,000 feet. It is a still life."

Walter Kerr forced Sevareid to face reality, to admit that there was no way the French could stop the coming defeat. To a degree the corrrespondents had hidden the truth from themselves because if they knew it they might feel ethically obliged to tell the world. Sevareid had always believed that the truth was its own justification, but he was not sure he believed it now. To tell the truth would play into the hands of Nazi propaganda. As long as there was any chance of a survival—a miracle perhaps?—perhaps he should hold back. Or should he?

He was sure of one thing. He had to get Lois and the twins out of the country. He brought them back to Paris for a week together before another parting. The liner *Manhattan,* the same ship that had brought the Murrows and Breckenridge to Europe, was about to sail from Genoa on June 1. With a special plea to the manager of the United States Line office, he booked her a cabin. At the Gare de Lyon the French clustered around Lois to admire the babies, each one wrapped tightly in a basket. Byron Price, the Associated Press executive who would join the Roosevelt administration after Pearl Harbor, was on the train and promised to keep an eye on the family. French authorities gave Lois canned milk, and the adorable *enfants,* in effect, served as their passport from Paris to New York, as conductors and customs officials melted at the sight of them.

Aboard ship, Lois and the twins shared a room with Mrs. Charles Findley, who was going home because she was pregnant. The *Manhattan* was crammed beyond capacity, with 1,907 adults and 194 children, with the men sleeping in dormitories and many more on cots in the public areas. Laundry took two days, and Lois boiled milk for the boys over a canned-heat stove in her cabin. In the next cabin a sick baby cried incessantly and Peter and Michael listened to their unseen comrade, wondering perhaps what he had to be afraid of. None of the passengers were the least bit afraid of submarine attacks, Lois wrote, because "we just didn't have time to think about it."

They were lucky. When the thick cloud of smoke settled over Paris in early June, Paris *Herald* writer Jerome Butler told his wife Francelia that he had seen the same phenomenon in World War I. It was the dust stirred up by the advancing German army.

On June 10, on behalf of CBS, Mrs. Dorothy Paley, splendidy dressed and in a limousine—plus a swarm of photographers—greeted Lois and the twins when the *Manhattan* docked in New York. As she descended the gangplank, carrying one twin in each arm, her friend Joan Younger met her and reached to help with one. "No," said Lois. "You'll unbalance me." In the Ambassador Hotel, where CBS had booked her a suite, she painstakingly unraveled the twins' swaddling clothes as their grandmother picked them up and, cooing, insisted that they were trying to talk to her. The ordeal over, Lois confessed to one desire: she had worn the same dress through France and Italy and across the ocean. She was going to buy a new one. Then she would take the children to Minneapolis and get them settled with their grandmother.

Then she would rejoin Eric in Paris.

The situation in Paris, however, had changed radically since Lois had left. On June 3, the Germans bombed the city for the first time. Parisians had become accustomed to all-night antiaircraft fire over the past month as their guns popped away not at bombers but at reconnaisance planes. When the real attack came it was a big one, the largest of the war to date—250 planes at twenty thousand feet. Their main target was the

Citroen factory, where they scored good hits. To listen today to a recording of Eric Sevareid's broadcast that night is to agree with the New York judgment that as an announcer he was not good. The pace is uneven and the voice almost singsongy.

The prose, however, is polished and picturesque. First the details: a thousand bombs fell, mostly outside the city; two hundred casualties, forty deaths. Then he talks in scenes. Two bombs landed on the Air Ministry building where Ambassador Bullitt was standing around at a buffet. One bomb remained on the roof, the other came through and landed in the room six feet from the ambassador. It didn't go off. The ambassador departed, leaving his hat and gloves behind. Later that night the bomb exploded and the hat and gloves were destroyed. The reporter had been having lunch that hot, still, sultry day at a Left Bank cafe; near him sat an American student, Robert Moore, cramming for exams in international law and German philosophy. Then they heard the planes coming. Their sounds "melted and mingled together like an approaching thunderstorm." The reporter hurried through the streets and along the Seine to survey the damage. Because the buildings were old and well constructed, their facades held. "No rooms were laid bare with the walls peeled off." Rather, the impact of the explosions, "like an invisible hand, reached into the bedrooms and plucked things out." One tree had simply been uprooted by a blast and now stood alone upright in the middle of a street.

By now CBS had established a schedule: a daily fifteen-minute news roundup from London, Paris, and Berlin at 8:00 A.M. and 6:30 P.M.; a Kaltenborn or Davis analysis every morning and evening; with 2:45 and 9 P.M. time slots held open if needed.

That night in New York, on the same broadcast, CBS World News Today, H. V. Kaltenborn speculated that there might be a peace party within the German government. Elmer Davis reported on the British fleeing for their lives at the port of Dunkirk; and William L. Shirer in Berlin reported German charges that the British Secret Service was trying to provoke unfriendly feelings against Germany in the United States.

On June 8, Mary Marvin Breckinridge left Paris, not on her new bike, but by train to Genoa, and then to Berlin for her June 20 wedding.

The smoke grew darker in the Paris skies, sometimes blocking out the sun. On June 10 at Walter Kerr's desk in the *Herald* office, Sevareid, knowing that the Paris radio station would be shut down that night, typed out his last Paris broadcast, phrasing it in a way that would let America know Paris had been abandoned to the Germans and still get through the censors. The minister of information, he wrote, was optimistic, but could not say why. His text exemplifies a life-long trait: he was more often than not slow to judge, to condemn. He would rather praise courage than curse cowardice.

> I do not think there was any deliberate attempt to hide the real state of affairs from the people of Paris. They are a fatalistic people. There is this quality which makes Frenchmen stand half-naked in this wilting heat, feeding their red-hot guns until literally crushed out by German tanks.

Sevareid returned to his apartment for the last time, gathered what he could of his belongings, said goodbye to the Bulgarian maidservant, and with Edmond Taylor, Grandin's replacement, got into their little Citroen. Beside the silent masses of Parisians, they began to follow the government in its flight south. "Paris lay inert," he wrote later, "her breathing scarcely audible, her limbs relaxed, the blood flowed remorselessly from her manifold veins. Paris lay dying, like a beautiful woman in a coma, not knowing or asking why." They passed through Chartres, and the spectacular spires of its cathedral sank into the horizon behind them. Overturned cars, dead horses, sleeping families lay strewn in the ditches beside the road.

At Tours, in the Loire valley of the grand chateaux, the government and the press paused while Reynaud broadcast, by recording, a sad plea to the world, for America to send a fleet of airplanes that would blot the Germans from the skies. As if America was the land of instant miracles. Then the caravan picked up and moved to Bordeaux, leaving Tours just an hour before German planes bombed the city center.

In Paris a skeleton staff put together the final, June 12, one-page, censored edition of the Paris *Herald Tribune*. The war was spreading. Italy joined the fight by bombing Malta. The army was fighting valiantly along the Marne. The government was "somewhere in France." The German army goose-stepped into Paris on June 14. Hitler himself arrived on June 21. At the Invalides, he peered arrogantly down at the tomb of Napoleon and, we might imagine, assured himself that he would soon accomplish what those Corsican bones had not. He told his photograh-per, "It was the greatest and finest moment of my life."

From Lisbon, on his way home, Walter Kerr sent brilliant dispatches to the New York office:

> It is not easy to explain why all this happened. Many factors are in-volved: eight months of idleness after September [when the war had begun in Poland]; German propaganda that England was the real enemy, not France; a censored press that was not allowed to hint that anything was wrong; the unwillingness to defend the city and thereby cause its destruction; no training to withstand air and tank warfare; not enough radio equipment and so easily severed communications; not enough planes; too little mobile artillery; and ineffective 25-mm anti-tank guns; the average French soldier's be-lief that he was to fight in the Maginot line and not away from it; the rude awakening.
>
> And the result was a feeling among the men that they had been betrayed. They still think so.

The government and its entourage settled in the wine country at Bordeaux, the economic and cultural center of southwest France. There ocean-going ships slipped up the Gironde River from the Atlantic and made port.

And there, the CBS team finally had some luck. While most of the foreign press was dependent on the Press Wireless news service transmit-ter, an hour's drive outside Bordeaux Sevareid discovered another trans-mitter in the center of France, not yet overrun by the Nazis, used by the Bordeaux Radio studios right on the edge of the city. Privately he made his way to the studio offices and arranged for access to a microphone on demand to beam the transmission to New York where CBS, listening around the clock, would pick him up. Unfortunately his NBC competi-tor, an English-speaking Frenchman, followed him to the office, and, when the angry Sevareid asked him to leave, simply smiled.

Late one night, as he sat on the floor of the labor exchange with a bunch of fellow journalists, a tipster ran in with the news that Reynaud had resigned and that the eighty-four-year-old Marshall Pétain, the cau-tious hero of Verdun, had been named president of the council, and had appointed a new cabinet. Sevareid and Meyer Handler, the United Press reporter, ran down the cabinet list—conservative military men like the German sympathizer Admiral Francois Darlan and civilian partisans of Pierre Laval, a champion of Franco-German cooperation who had proposed appeasing Mussolini by giving him much of Ethiopia. The correspondents realized at once that this meant surrender. They raced through the streets to the "secret" studio, only to meet the NBC man coming down the stairs with the same smug smile on his face.

"What did you say on the air?" Sevareid demanded.

"Why, I said this means continued resistance. Look at all the generals and admirals in the cabinet," he replied.

Elated that they still had their scoop, Sevareid rushed to the microphone and blurted out that France would capitulate.

The next day, the doddering old Pétain climbed those same stairs and called upon France to lay down its arms. *"Il faut cesser la guerre."*

As Pétain finished his speech a brief but violent thunderstorm broke out, as if registering Heaven's anger at his pathetic abandonment of his country and its people. Sevareid made his way toward the town square, ashamed that his mind dwelt now not on suffering individuals but on historical currents; this was a shift in the European balance of military power as dramatic as the defeat of the Spanish Armada. The town square had fallen silent. Then the stillness was shattered by the roar of a bomber plane, and eyes turned toward the sky. A single French plane dived toward the square, pulled up and dived again, then did circles over the rooftops. Strange. But the crowd chose to interpret the wild stunt as a last poetic act of defiance. "It is Saint-Exupéry," someone said. The French imagination, at least, was still alive.

Depressed, exhausted, and beaten, Sevareid thought of joining the mass of neutrals making their way over the Spanish border to Lisbon, and from there to America; but he chose rather to try to stay with the war a little longer, to get to England and, he hoped, report to Murrow, although Murrow had never actually given him permission to leave France. With the help of friends, Sevareid and Taylor found the young Norwegian-American captain of the *Ville de Liege* drinking a beer in a waterfront bar. He was headed for Liverpool, and yes, he would take them aboard.

The ship, clogged with over three hundred refugees, with very little food and lifeboats for no more than a third of the passengers, made its way down the Gironde, out through sub-infested waters into the Atlantic, in a wide circle that would bring them back toward Belfast. Sevareid lay for hours every day in his bunk, skipping meals, internalizing the defeat of France as if it were his own. He wrote later, "Everything was cut adrift; I no longer had a home, my family was scattered, all my books and possessions were gone, and I did not even know whether I had a job."

Worse, he was afraid. As a teenager he had identified with Richard Harding Davis, whose battle stories had the unfortunate effect not only of making war look romantic but of suggesting that war correspondents —in the Spanish-American War and the Boer War—were somehow invulnerable, that bullets passed over their heads or hit only combatants on either side of the intrepid reporter. Davis himself had realized in his frustrated attempts to cover World War I that the old gentleman's rules of war no longer applied. With the machine gun and bombing from the air, everyone was vulnerable. In World War I Floyd Gibbons lost an eye. In World War II many correspondents would lose their lives. Eric Sevareid didn't want to be one of them. Yet, though he feared death, he feared something else more.

> It was, I think, because I was just beginning to understand that there are forms of life that are worse than death, that there are causes in whose behalf it is worthwhile to die, almost a privilege to die. And for me, the idea seemed a little easier to confront because of the children. I suppose most men feel that way when their first children are born—that death is not the complete end for them.

He pondered the fate of France and could not buy into the thesis that its "decadence" had done it in. His friends were not decadent. France had simply been overwhelmed. There just happened to be twice as many Germans as Frenchmen.

Yet anyone who wonders why the later public image of Eric Sevareid seemed so severe should read the chapter in *Not So Wild a Dream* on his flight from France as the nation fell apart. What stands out in his imagery—particularly in his descriptions of the leadership, like Reynaud, who set the stage for the Vichy government, and Pétain, who, in effect, handed his country over to fascism—is his emotional identification with the city that gave this North Dakota and Minnesota boy a new life. He wrote to a Paris friend's widow in 1986, "We were, indeed, two excited young men loosed on Paris before the world went crazy in war and the joy went out of Paris." He never forgot how—and by whom—the city had been robbed of its joy.

It is significant that when Sevareid retired in 1977 and his staff put together a collection of news clippings by which his grandchildren might learn who their grandfather had been, among the half-dozen pieces that Sevareid himself selected for the collection was his April 6, 1947, front-page *New York Times Book Review* critique of William L. Langer's *Our Vichy Gamble,* a state-department-approved book that was basically a defense of America's wartime cooperation with the Pétain-Darlan government which, in Sevareid's view, had sold out the French people. It is hard to know what the grandchildren would make of the review. They would have to know that, by the Sevareid-American code, temporizers like the Vichy admirals and generals, with whom the American policy-makers made deals, were basically traitors, while the true France lived on in the exiled leader of the Free French, General Charles de Gaulle—in grandad's judgment, "the greatest single French figure since Clemenceau." He concludes the review:

> Langer quotes an interview of the wretched Darlan in which the Admiral says, "One makes politics with realities, not with sentiment." Langer himself asserts the same thing in his defense of our attitude toward de Gaulle and the Free French. And this is the basic mistake of politicians like Darlan, manipulators like some of the State Department people, and historians like Professor Langer. They will not understand that the sentiment of common men is the basic stuff of politics, the most solid reality of all.

So as the *Ville de Liege* pulled into Liverpool it bore not just hundreds of refugees but an emotionally broken journalist, who was nevertheless, without realizing it, ready to commit himself to an experience even more harrowing than the one he had just escaped.

9

LONDON

IN LAURENCE OLIVIER'S classic 1945 film of Shakespeare's *Henry V*, filmed in Ireland when World War II's outcome was still not clear, the young king rallying his badly outnumbered forces for the battle of Agincourt calls them "We few, we happy few, we band of brothers." In the minds of his movie theater audiences he was not talking about the fifteenth century.

When Henry's cousin Westmoreland wished aloud that a few of those men still back in England were with them now, the king declared that years from now, "gentlemen in England, now a-bed, shall think themselves accurs'd they were not here." At that, Olivier's British and American audiences thought immediately of the Battle of Britain, the London blitz, which they had survived together—some in London, some over their living room radios in Kansas City, Trenton, and Chicago.

As Agincourt was a turning point in the War of the Roses, so too, in popular memory on both sides of the Atlantic, was the Battle of Britain—the air war between the hardpressed RAF and the hundreds of German planes that began their attacks on July 10, 1940, then filled the sky over London every night from September 7 to November 3, 1940. It was the turning point in the battle to preserve Western civilization.

Over one hundred and twenty American correspondents covered the blitz; and America's understanding of Britain's crisis was built on a number of feature films, newsreels, and newspaper and magazine articles; but the pictures that stuck were those that radio invoked. Americans, still politically neutral and isolationist, sat around their radio sets with maps, as FDR had urged them to do in a fireside chat, measured Hitler's advance across Europe to the English Channel, and listened to reports of his troops massing for the inevitable invasion. In the minds of American journalists, it had become their job to make Americans see how England's fate was also theirs.

For a few dozen men and women—a half-dozen or so known as "Murrow's boys"—who would constitute the firm backbone of post-World War II broadcast journalism, their Henry V—their Olivier, their "little touch of Harry in the night" was Edward R. Murrow.

He was boss, mentor, and friend. He was also, in his own way, a teacher and role model. They were his "boys" not just in the metaphorical sense that a baseball coach's players are his boys, but to a degree, in the psychological sense in which the father and son must decide where one's identity begins and the other's leaves off.

Eric Sevareid's father, he tells us, was a big, stern, quiet man not given to displays of feeling or emotion. The son was a tall, quiet man who looked sterner than he was, and was also reluctant to open his heart. Yet, in *Not So Wild a Dream,* in interviews and documentaries, he talked more intimately and passionately about Murrow than about any other person in his life, including his father and his wife. He did not shrink from saying that he "loved" and "adored" the man. On one level, Sevareid owed him his job. He knew that, because of his technical inadequacies as a broadcaster, any other administrator would have fired him; but Murrow kept him on because Murrow saw something in him—partly his writing style, partly his lucky string of scoops—worth holding onto.

But on a deeper level it seems clear, for the twenty-eight-year-old Sevareid, still unformed, Ed Murrow, more than his father or his professors, was the man he wanted to be like. Faced with the choice in Bordeaux of returning to Minneapolis and his wife and children or, though uninvited, joining Murrow in London, he chose London. In one sense, going to London was simply a career move: it was a way of keeping his job, and wars make journalists' careers. But at the same time, it was a way of going back to school, of learning to master this new medium, perhaps of learning to conquer his fear.

On the horrible boat trip from Bordeaux to Liverpool his melancholy deepened as, on June 21, he sat by the captain's radio and heard the voice of Bill Shirer broadcasting France's surrender from Compiegne, forty-five miles from Paris.

> Here, a few feet from where we're standing, in the very same old railroad coach where the Armistice was signed on that chilly morning of November 11, 1918, negotiations for another armistice—

the one to end the present war between France and Germany—began at 3:30 P.M., German summer time, this afternoon. What a turning back of the clock, what a reversing of history we've been watching in this beautiful Compiegne Forest this afternoon!

When Sevareid called the CBS London office from Liverpool, Murrow welcomed him and put him right to work. By now Murrow was establishing himself as a special American presence in London, indeed, in some circles, more important than that of the American ambassador. Winston Churchill knew well how to use the press to his purposes, so Murrow was a frequent dinner guest at 10 Downing Street. His working relationship with BBC included CBS use of BBC's faciltities, meaning a small, sweltering, underground studio in Broadcasting House on Portland Place, and a series of broadcasts Murrow made to the British people—talks on American literature, including an ill-informed analysis of *Uncle Tom's Cabin* (he said that slavery had been dying out anyway), and discussions of American and British higher education with Murrow's socialist political scientist friend Harold Laski. In one program, Murrow proposed a postwar faculty exchange program, much like the Fulbright Scholarships, that, he hoped, would bring Laski back to America.

American journalists, because of their influence at home, were welcome in British society; but upper-class hostesses considered the suave, moody, handsome Murrow, who had begun to dress elegantly in Saville Row togs, a special catch. The Murrows were frequent guests at Ditchley, the four-thousand-acre Oxfordshire country home of Ronald Tree, son of American heirs of the Marshall Field fortune. There the antifascist set chatted with Anthony Eden, the Duff Coopers, and Churchill himself about England's fate. Meanwhile, the appeasement set, which then included United States ambassador Joseph P. Kennedy, met at the Astors' estate called Cliveden.

On many evenings Murrow and Sevareid joined other journalists and scholars for soirees at Laski's home, where they would rail against the inequalities in England's social system. Caught in the mystique of the man who had been the mentor of Lippincott, his own mentor at Minnesota, Sevareid began sitting in on Laski's lectures at the London School of Economics and found himself stimulated, thrilled by the experience. Sadly, however, within a few years the Murrow-Laski friendship deteriorated. As Murrow became more famous, Laski became more possessive, resenting Ed's apparent defection to the upper classes and the disciple's failure to pay court with his old regularity. Laski had made the mistake of confusing Ed's natural humanism, his democratic egalitarianism, with Laski's own socialism. Intellectually, Murrow was not Laski's kindred spirit. William L. Shirer, struck by the apparent inconsistency of Murrow's two-tier friendships, accused Murrow of becoming a snob, but Murrow simply replied that, "these people are valuable to me."

Sevareid's other educational soiree was in the little world of central London. If we imagine the BBC's Broadcasting House—which was a short walk from both Murrow's apartment at 84 Hallam Street and Sevareid's place nearby—as the center of a circle, moving counterclockwise, Hyde Park was a mile to the southwest; Buckingham Palace, just a mile to the south; Trafalgar Square and the Thames, about a mile to the southeast; and the Bloomsbury neighborhood, where Leonard and Virginia Woolf lived at Mecklenburg Square when not at her country home, was a half-mile east. Westminster Abbey, the houses of Parliament, and the Foreign Office were just south of Trafalgar Square, on the banks of the Thames, where the river bends from north to east under Waterloo Bridge.

So, even more than Paris, London was reporter-friendly, its big stories usually within walking distance from one's doorstep.

Among the regulars at the Murrow dinner table was Larry LeSueur, the reporter on the team whom, Sevareid said, Murrow really loved. With his warm, easygoing disposition, unlike Eric, he helped Murrow to relax.

Holding forth in a loud voice late into the night was the most famous member of the band, the author-journalist Vincent "Jimmy" Sheean, whose romantic autobiography, *Personal History*, helped set the standard for a generation on how a "great journalist" ought to talk about himself. Like Laski, Sheean was a socialist, and like Murrow, he wanted to see social privilege abolished, but he drank champagne with dukes, he said, because dukes were people too. With other correspondents, Sheean liked to drive out to the first cliff west of Dover called Shakespeare Cliff, because Shakespeare was said to have written *King Lear* with this cliff in mind. There, on a clear day, they could see evidence of German movement twenty-five miles across the water, and Sheean would watch the German-RAF dogfights overhead—the "terrible beauty" of air combat, which to him, was like the clash of knights in armor. He wrote soon after in his memoir of these times, *Between the Thunder and the Sun:*

> You could read of casualties by the thousands in a battle on land and calculate their results, the territory gained or lost, the consequences to the enemy; you could not see a duel in the air without thinking of two hawklike youths in armor, brief falcon lives launched one against one in the briefest, purest combat ever known.

In the last pages of his book, Sheean took the logical moral step he felt the story he had just told and the crisis of the time required: he enlisted in the Air Force. He did not present his decision as a challenge to his journalist contemporaries. But they would have been blind to not read it as the challenge it was.

In these critical months of the war, when Britain stood alone, the journalists working with Murrow established the principles of a new kind of journalism. Although Murrow never spelled out rules for his "boys" to paste inside their reporter's notebooks, here are five of them. They come from his biographers—Alexander Kendrick, A. M. Sperber, and Joseph Persico—and the research of University of Western Michigan scholar R. Franklin (Bob) Smith, who, in the early 1970s, interviewed Murrow's American and British colleagues about his London years.

Radio is different. The quality of the first generation of radio and television reporters, many of whom covered World War II, is often attributed to the first generation's previous experience in print journalism. Yet, Murrow himself had no journalism experience and, except for some time on the Washington State radio station, little radio training. He concentrated on speech, debate, and theater in college. And when he hired Rhodes scholar Charles Collingwood in 1941, he said he wanted someone uncontaminated by print, although Collingwood, in fact, like Sevareid, had come up through the United Press.

Murrow meant that the new medium called for a differently structured prose. Sevareid recalled that when he would read one of Murrow's scripts before the broadcast it would not seem to hold together by the usual rules of good-writing. But when Murrow read it, it clearly worked. Murrow believed that one should write for the ear. When he saw BBC reporters dictating rather than typing out their own scripts, he adopted their method. Conscious of time limitations, he learned how to rewrite in his head as he read along, when he had to suddenly reduce a three-minute broadcast into one minute without time for a rewrite. A. M. Sperber describes the evening when war correspondent Ernie Pyle sat in on a Murrow broadcast from studio B-4 to write it up for his syndicated column. The British censor stood by with his hand on a switch. A square microphone sat in the center of a green felt-covered table, by a glass of water, and an ashtray (the BBC's no smoking rule had been unofficially waved for Murrow).

> The newspaperman found himself fascinated as he watched the broadcaster pace himself, one eye on the clock, timing the manuscript in his head as he talked. That night, as it happened, Murrow's timing sense told him that the piece was going to be too long, that he had overwritten. As a nervous censor and thirty million Americans listened, he rewrote in his head, wound up the prepared copy and ad-libbed through the remaining minutes, walking a fine line between dead air and uncensored material.
>
> His voice betrayed no hint of effort. But when it was over, he sagged back, beads of sweat on his forehead and upper lip.
>
> By now, however, even a routine broadcast on any night would produce rivulets of nervous sweating—the result of tension, awareness of responsibility, and above all, of mike fright.

Revising a script in mid-broadcast was hard enough. Worse were the moments when the radio reporter had no script at all, but was forced to ad-lib with just the event itself before his eyes. Consider Murrow's famous broadcast from the roof of the unnamed (BBC) building during the bombing raid of September 20, 1940. It was the first live, eyewitness broadcast of a raid. BBC had feared that rooftop broadcasts would be picked up by German radios and compromise security. To get permission, Murrow had to ask Churchill to intervene.

> I'm standing again tonight on a rooftop looking out over London, feeling rather large and lonesome. In the course of the last fifteen or twenty minutes there's been considerable action up here, but at

the moment there's an ominous silence that has a great deal of dignity. Just straightway in front of me the searchlights are working. I can see one or two bursts of antiaircraft fire far in the distance.

What stands out today as we listen to recordings of those nights is the deft, spontaneous interaction of sound and verbal description. We hear something. Murrow, with no emotion is his voice, no reference to his own danger, tells us the meaning of the sound. A bomb burst. Ack-ack fire. This night, the danger has passed, the bombers are not overhead, and the reporter is stuck with a relatively tame evening, which he must present with sufficient drama to hold his listeners but not sensationalize or distort the event.

This is a skill Eric Sevareid never really acquired. In the 1930s and 1940s he wrote radio reporting that fed pictures to the brain through the ear. In the 1950s he virtually invented a hybrid literary form that we might call the five-minute radio essay, often aimed directly at the intellect, and which he carried over into the two-and-a-half-minute commentaries he delivered on the *CBS Evening News with Walter Cronkite*. But he did not ad-lib well. Much of his off-the-cuff commentary at political conventions, on election nights, and after presidential press conferences was obviously weaker, less pointed, than his prepared material. When Nixon's vice president Spiro T. Agnew, in a calculated assault intended to neutralize press criticism of the Nixon administration, condemned "instant analysis" by TV commentators, Sevareid was quick to recommend an end to the practice. He simply wanted more time to prepare.

Realism. The best medium, like the best teacher, Murrow might say, calls no attention to itself, that is, it eliminates rather than manipulates the distance between the event and the audience. The reporter's job is to make the listener present at the event. The reporter, therefore, selects those devices that bring the listener in; but Murrow did his best to let the sounds speak for themselves. Paley, for a number of reasons, refused to let CBS News record programs to broadcast later. Somehow he feared that if programs could be recorded he would lose control over the affiliates, whom he wanted to keep dependent on CBS in New York to broadcast network programs at a given time. Murrow argued that this restriction put him at a great disadvantage; but Paley was adamant.

A classic example of how Murrow achieved realism, even given Paley's restrictions, was heard on Saturday night, August 24, 1940, when CBS stationed reporters with microphones all over London to broadcast live, at 11:30 London time (dinnertime evening news in New York) Londoners' reactions to the raid CBS knew would come. Murrow stood in Trafalgar Square, Sevareid in a dance palace, Sheean in Piccadilly, and, a special addition, British author J. B. Priestley at Whitehall for a wrap-up commentary. When the sirens started, Murrow let the sirens—and the antiaircraft guns—speak for themselves; but he lowered his microphone to the pavement to catch the *unhurried* sound of Londoners' footsteps as they *calmly* made for the shelters.

When microphones cannot be there, the reporter's task is to recapture the essence of an event by a rich detail that sums up its meaning. If he did not ad-lib well, Sevareid could, on short notice, write a report that brought listeners as close to the scene as he was. On the first night of the blitz, September 7, Eric was on duty while Murrow, Sheean, and Ben Robertson, a likable young correspondent from the liberal tabloid *PM* enjoyed a two-day ride in the country. The bombs that afternoon hit not central London but the slums, and Eric rushed to the scene in a cab.

> A warden stuck his sweat-stained face in the cab. I asked him how many bombs had fallen. He said, "Good Lord, they just rained from heaven. I'm glad to be alive." . . . Store fronts for blocks had fallen out and the mass of broken glass was literally being shoveled into the gutter. I could see several brick flats without roofs, and the back end of a small church was torn away. From a window, two wardens were carefully lifting out a man's body. Hundreds of women were pushing baby buggies and carrying their worldly goods in their arms, getting out of the area. Thousands will have to find new homes. They looked nervously at the sky as they walked.

Jefferson-Jacksonian Democracy. A difficult concept to express, this is meant to encompass two of Murrow's intimately connected beliefs. The first is the principle inherent in the First Amendment, that a democratic society, unlike an authoritarian or totalitarian society, absolutely depends on a free press if citizens are to be well enough informed to participate in their own governance. The second is Murrow's conviction, fundamental to Jefferson and Jackson, that the common man, given information, has the intelligence to judge well for the public good.

When he arrived in England in 1937, Murrow surprised the British with his ideas for joint BBC-CBS broadcasts that would bring together ordinary working people in England and America for conversations about common problems. His weekends at Ditchley did not weaken his conviction that ordinary people, in crisis, often showed more mettle than their so-called betters.

His most-cited advice to his staff, often retold, sums up his basic rule that one must speak in a way that both respects the audience's intelligence and excludes no one who wants to listen: "Imagine you are dining at the home of a judge or political leader who has asked you to explain a controversial event, and you see that the maidservant is listening at the kitchen door."

In practice, this meant that reporters would choose images that would be *common* to the survivor of Dunkirk and the wheat farmer in Kansas. Thus, in a description of the "unbeaten men" coming back from Dunkirk he focused on a platoon who had brought with them a quivering, shell-shocked mongrel dog. He knew that the dog itself was not news; but he also knew, like every tabloid city editor, that Americans can't resist a suffering dog.

Maybe he knew, or didn't know, that one of the most heartrending tales of World War I was Alexander Woollcott's story in the *Stars and Stripes* (June 14, 1918) about Verdun Belle, the shabby mongrel setter who adopted a marine around Chateau-Thierry and, when the marine was wounded, followed him to the hospital and licked his face as he came out of shell shock.

As to whether Sevareid fulfilled Murrow's concept of radio's interaction with the common man, the answer would be yes and no. One of the fascinating aspects of Sevareid's life-long appeal is that, in spite of his image as an "intellectual," "common," or less-educated people did not complain that he was over their heads. The anecdotal lore and his office correspondence are packed with testimony from ordinary working people who respected him for exactly what he was, a smart man who, like Murrow, did not degrade his material. And in his commentaries he was quick to tell stories of dogs, children, and birds because these experiences he shared with all his listeners.

But he did not agree with Murrow's idealistic conviction that people all over the world shared the same aspirations, the same values. He did not buy what became known in the Eisenhower years as "people-to-people friendship," the idea that if only the people of Africa, Asia, Europe, and the Americas could talk, differences would be resolved. Sevareid's travels in Africa, Asia, and Latin America in the early 1960s convinced him that these alien cultures often wanted power, to be on the winning side, not the righteous side. In a controversial 1961 newspaper column about Latin America, Sevareid wrote that there was no such thing as "world opinion." Murrow told him angrily, "I'm sorry to see you abandon your principles so easily." Yet perhaps it was Murrow's principles Sevareid was abandoning, not his own.

Action. There are other terms to express this idea—like courage, or the cult of experience. But the concept of the journalist being, whatever the risk, in the center of the action is the most fundamental expression of the more complicated personal question about Murrow's own seemingly reckless disregard for his own safety.

Any journalist with a lust for the work will rush to do things from which other people shrink: look at a mangled corpse, enter a burning building, describe the blitz from a London rooftop, walk down Main Street taking notes in the middle of a race riot, chase the U.S. Army into Kuwait City in the last hours of the Iraq war. But Murrow consistently courted death. He drove his car at crazy speeds. He flew on so many bombing raids over Germany—during which other journalists perished—that his friends couldn't help asking what demons drove him. A Pawling, New York, Quaker Hill neighbor of Murrow's in his last years told me that he felt Murrow kept smoking, although cancer was killing him, because surviving the London blitz had made him think he was invulnerable.

Was there a deep-seated death wish? Was it a psychological need unrelated to his war job? Was it the guilt that all correspondents feel because they themselves are not fighting? Or was it physical and emotional exhaustion? If his plane went down, at least it would mean the end of his toil. He told one friend that it was his attempt to share the experience of those who were actually fighting the war. In that sense, without reading, as far as we know, Sartre, Camus, or Malraux, he shared the existentialist's conviction that accepting death—or, in their case, atheism—frees one from fear.

Murrow was, by common consent, braver than other reporters. Three of Murrow's offices—at the Langham Hotel, on Portland Place, and Duchess Street—were hit by bombs. Murrow got used to the idea. He even developed, it seemed, an instinct for danger. Once when Murrow, LeSueur, and Sevareid were walking down Portland Place during a raid, Murrow suddenly pulled them into a doorway just as a shell casing fell where they had stood a second before. For a while Sevareid responded to every explosion by moving—from sitting to standing, from standing to lying down; eventually he concluded that whether one was to be hit or spared had nothing to do with one's behavior—it was all luck. Murrow, he thought, found that a relief. The same realization threw Eric into depression.

Sevareid told R. Franklin Smith that Murrow was the truly brave man, that is, one who feared death but fought his fear. Yet, he shared some of what Sevareid called Hemingway's "fixation with physical bravery." Sevareid spent many hours in air-raid shelters. Murrow refused to go near them, not out of bravado but because he feared that once he tried one he would run to them all the time. "He was afraid of himself," Sevareid said. "And therefore he did things that I thought foolish. But somehow, they gave him confidence."

They also gave confidence to his fellow reporters. Sevareid knew the limitations of his own physical courage. He remained ever conscious of his frazzled nerves and rebellious stomach. Yet, two years later, when he could have stayed safe in Washington, he felt compelled to get back into the war. The *Washington Star's* Newbold Noyes, a correspondent who covered the war in southern France with Sevareid and cartoonist Bill Mauldin, remembered Sevareid fifty years later as basically brave. Like all of them, he was afraid; but he conquered his fear.

Commitment. Living the tension required for honest journalism, Murrow was committed to both Truth and truth as he saw it. Perhaps the most misused word in debate on media ethics is "objectivity." In theory the term presupposes an epistemology that separates absolutely the judgment of the subjective perceiver from objective reality he or she perceives. As if one's life experiences, backgroud, training, value system could have nothing to do with what one sees or how one sees it.

In practice, we all like to consider ourselves "objective," that is, not moved by prejudice or ignorance when we form our opinions. Often, however, to say that someone else's judgment is not "objective" means that the judgment disagrees with ours. To avoid this terminology, editors substitute terms like fairness, balance, and "both sides," sometimes encouraging the misconception that truth consists in matching up a pro-and-con debate or a roundtable discussion in which a variety of opinions are as likely to cancel one another out as lead to deeper understanding.

Murrow tried to avoid that epistemological trap. In September 1947 he began the first of a series of daily radio programs with a quotation from his contract:

> News programs are broadcast solely for the purpose of enabling the listeners to know facts—so far as they are ascertainable—and so to elucidate, illuminate and explain facts and situations as fairly as possible to enable the listener to weigh and judge for himself.

Murrow told his listeners that this was lawyers' language. He assured them he would resist the temptation to use the microphone as a privileged platform; but he added: "It is not, I think, humanly possible for any reporter to be completely objective, for we are all to some degree prisoners of our education, travel, reading—the sum total of our experience."

He believed, says R. Franklin Smith, in the "reflective mirror" theory of mass communication. Thus if the honest mirror held up to conditions in America or Europe reflected "bad" news, at least bad news was better than propaganda, and the problems could be faced. He saw radio, and later television, as foremost a medium of information and enlightenment. The message must emerge from the content, not the medium. That is one reason the correspondent's voice didn't matter. It was his information, what he said. That is why his "boys" had to be well educated and reflective, so that when the message came through it would not be propaganda but the credible basis for an informed decision.

Ultimately, however, Sevareid told Smith that Murrow just didn't have the capacity to "draw back" from issues. "Wasn't in his training. Maybe that was one of his great strengths." There was, he said, "A lot of preacher in Ed." In Murrow's famous April 12, 1944, broadcast on what he saw at Buchenwald, for example—the day that was also the day of Roosevelt's death—he poured out his anger at the Germans responsible. Anger against Nazism was not a failure of objectivity, it was a commitment to the truth.

Charles Collingwood put it this way:

> But besides the truth, which to him was a constant object of pursuit, there are things that sound awfully big and windy, but things

like honor—very important to him—his personal honor, his country's honor, and concepts like that made his heart beat faster.

Sevareid adds:

> He was a great moralist, you know. He expected individuals, and his government, to live up to high moral standards. He believed in a kind of foreign policy based, I think, on that, on moral principles, which few people really believe in anymore.

On the institutional level, Murrow eventually left CBS frustrated by television's failure to be a truly educational force. As Collingwood put it: "I think he realized the structural nature of the problem. It is built in. Here you have a medium which is not fundamentally, as a newspaper is, a news disseminating medium."

It is a great paradox that Sevareid, whose talents were not really suited for television, defended the medium from criticism to the end of his life, while Murrow, who gave TV news its first reputation of dignity and integrity, left disillusioned.

Sevareid's conclusion that people didn't much believe in a foreign policy based on moral principles may reflect his mood in the early 1970s when he gave Smith the interview. He rejected both the political rightness of the Vietnam War and the moral righteousness of some of those who protested it. In his personal morality, he faced some unresolved problems. Yet all his life he retained a powerful sense of his own integrity as a journalist. In 1958, when the prominent Republican spokeswoman India Edwards criticized his October 12 program as "so biased it made me really angry," Sevareid shot back an indignant reply:

> I am returning your letter of October 13. It impugns my integrity as a reporter and is therefore unacceptable to me.
>
> I think that upon further reflection you may agree that "bias" was intended neither by me nor by Mr. Lubell; if for no other reason, because bias in such a program would be purposeless, would indeed harm only ourselves.

Finally, Sevareid caught the ultimate difference between Murrow and other correspondents in a powerful paragraph in *Not So Wild a Dream*.

> It was not his perfect poise, his magnetic face, or even his compelling voice that made him the first great literary artist of a new

medium of communication. No practice, training, or artifice made him the greatest broadcaster by far in the English tongue. He was simply born to the new art.

In Murrow the personality and the product were the same. He was "mixed up irretrievably in its essence." It meant that the speaker had to be the person he appeared to be.

The implications of that idea for Sevareid in later years, as he assumed the role and image of sage, are considerable. The implications are staggering for a later generation of television newsmen and women, untrained in real journalism—and often barely touched by the broad reading, hardships, and heroic personal influences that form character.

Thus, in 1940, as Hitler massed his forces across from Dover, Murrow's staff prepared to enter the laboratory where Murrow's principles were formed, tried, and adapted.

On July 16, 1940, Hitler wrote to Field Marshall Wilhelm Keitel and Chief of Staff General Alfred Jodl that "Since England, in spite of her militarily helpless situation, shows no signs of willingness to come to terms, I have decided to prepare a landing operation against England and, if necessary, to carry it out." He wanted the operation ready by mid-August. His plan, which went through many changes all summer, was to land two armies of twenty-five divisions between Dover and Portsmouth. He would prepare for the fall landing by bombing attacks in three phases, beginning August 8 with attacks on convoys and coastal objectives, designed to draw British fighters into combat; then attacks on airfields; and finally on cities, particularly London, to break the people's will. In mid and late August the fat Luftwaffe commander Hermann Goering sent aloft as many as a thousand planes a day—their main object, to destroy the RAF. Thanks partly to the new invention of radar and air control centers that deployed Spitfire and Hurricane fighter planes over southern England, the RAF survived. But another reason for the RAF's survival was Hitler's decision to shift the focus of his attacks to London on September 7.

In the first week in September it became clear to the British and the broadcasters that something ominous would soon occur. Over the past two weeks the RAF had lost over four hundred fighters and over one hundred pilots; the Ministry of Information was finally ready to grant Murrow permission to broadcast air raids live, with the hope of persuading Americans to send more aid. But on Saturday morning, September 7, when the CBS engineers in New York were setting up the feed for the morning news roundup, they failed to get Berlin. Although they did not realize it at the time, it was a sign that a new German offensive was under way.

When the big attack came, Murrow, Sheean, and Ben Robertson were on an afternoon drive through the country. They had planned to pick apples, have dinner, and stay at an inn on an estuary of the Thames. Then they heard the terrible roar: huge waves of German bombers in V formation, twenty to twenty-five in each—in all there were three hundred bombers and six hundred fighters—on their way to London.

RAF fighters rose to meet them, antiaircraft batteries fired away and shell fragments rained down in a murderous hail over the countryside. Murrow and his friends took refuge first in a haystack, then in a ditch. The attack wore on for twelve hours and left four hundred dead and whole sections of London, mostly factories, warehouses, and slums, were turned into blazing infernos.

When the raid began Sevareid himself was far out in a western suburb. Larry LeSueur remembers that he and Eric had taken a bus to an outdoor swimming pool at Roehampton, where Eric, who had retained his swimmer's build, could work out.

They were due for a rest. The day before Larry had delivered a long, charming broadcast in which he spelled out for his listeners the average day of the average London correspondent—himself. It was a dawn-to-dusk-to-dawn cycle of sirens, meals, more sirens, mundane routine, and brushes with death. The previous, pre-blitz night had been a long one, with the buzzing of German planes, like so many angry mosquitoes, droning through the night, dropping their fire bombs over a wide area till the all-clear sounded just before daybreak.

For breakfast: oatmeal, tea and toast with jam and an eighth of a pound of butter. At the office, sirens interrupted the morning routine, but half the staff ignored them and continued their work. At midday the restaurants were too crowded to let Larry in, so he sauntered over to Broadcasting House, showed his pass to get by the guards, and descended the two flights of stairs, through gas-proof doors, to the studio.

By the time the all-clear sounded he was able to get a lunch of steak and kidney pie. In the afternoon he stopped by the air ministry and the Ministry of Information. That evening, Eric, returning tired from a night in an air-raid shelter on the Thames estuary, joined him for dinner. Eric had a large steak, Larry a mixed grill of kidneys, sausage, mushrooms, and tomatoes. Together they taxied to the studio, as the sirens sounded again. Then they groped their way through the blackened-out streets to Murrow's home for a drink. There, when the sirens wailed and the anti-aircraft guns began, they put on their tin hats and climbed to the roof and watched the blue flashes of the guns, the sharp orange flares of bursting bombs, and searchlights scanning the sky. Finally, Larry went home to bed, where the guns kept him from sleep most of the night, and sirens woke him for breakfast.

Now he and his friend Eric were finally relaxing in the sun.

Eric, who was in the water when they heard the ominous rumble overhead and looked up to see the German planes, leaped out of the pool. LeSueur remembers that Eric warned him that "water is noncompressive"—meaning that the shock waves from the bombs could injure someone in the pool. A quaint resort, LeSueur thought, to arcane scientific vocabulary in a moment of life and death.

Sevareid was the sole passenger on the bus that carried him east toward town, along virtually deserted rush-hour streets where little family groups stood in every doorway, their hands shading their eyes as they scanned the sky.

The next wave that evening cut off his dinner.

In his radio report, Sevareid struggled to combine incomplete official reports, his on-the-scene observations, and the accounts Murrow phoned from the inn on the RAF's combat against the first waves.

He concluded: "The blitzkrieg has reached London on the eve of the Day of National Prayer. Tomorrow morning, in all the churches of England, the people will pray for the safety and victory of Britain."

An atmosphere of crisis gripped the city. On September 11, Churchill told his radio audience that this week "ranks with the days when the Spanish Armada was approaching the Channel, and Drake was finishing his game of bowls; or when Nelson stood between us and Napoleon's Grand Army at Boulogne." Virginia Woolf wrote in her diary: "Churchill has just spoken. A chear, measured, robust speech. Says the invasion is being prepared . . . Our majestic city —&c. which touches me, for I feel London majestic. Our courage &c. Another raid last night on London. Time bomb struck the Palace . . . Meck. Sqre evacuated. A plane shot down before our eyes just before tea: over the race course; a scuffle; a swerve; then a plunge; & a burst of thick black smoke."

While England prayed, Murrow and *New York Times* correspondent Scotty Reston and Sevareid and others, unable to sleep, sat around together in one another's homes and speculated about what this experience was—or might be—doing to the England they had known a few years ago. They were coming to see the Blitz as a social leveler: "Some kind of a moral revolution was underway," Sevareid wrote later. Every class, group, profession, trade realized it needed the other. Technicians, firemen, chemists became as valuable to the nation as its traditional ruling elite. It seemed as if Hitler was accomplishing in weeks what the working class in a century of struggle could not: force England to see the latent genius of the lower classes.

On September 15, after the Germans bombed Buckingham Palace, Murrow explained to his American listeners that Londoners had not really needed that symbolic raid to convince them that royalty and commoners were in this thing together. Some of the wealthy neighborhoods had built superior shelters for themselves, now citizens were coming from other parts of the city and gaining entrance. "You must understand," Murrow said, "that a world is dying, that old values, the old prejudices, and the old bases of power and prestige are going." On October 1, he was a little more critical. He reported that the British people were asking serious questions about the country's war aims. But he emphasized that "all are equal under the bomb."

Today it would seem that Murrow and Sevareid, anxious to extract a positive meaning from their daily agony, were premature at the least in their discovery of an emerging classless society. Phillip Knightley, in his history of war reporting, *The First Casualty*, demythologizes the blitz and portrays it as a time that brought out the worst as well as the noblest aspects of the British spirit. The RAF and Luftwaffe were comparable in size, says Knightley. RAF pilots scorned the glamorous vocabulary that transformed them into "knights." The air ministry exaggerated, sometimes doubled, the number of German planes shot down. Wealthy families, like the Duff Coopers, sent their children—among the six thousand in 1940—to America and throughout the Commonwealth. Richer neighborhoods did have better shelters, and the subway stations used as shelters became stinking slums. When Coventry was bombed, its citizens rioted in panic. In 1970, looking back on the "heroic" legends of those days, Malcolm Muggeridge wrote in *Esquire* that some Churchillian rhetoric was as "empty as Laurence Olivier pounding out Henry V's peroration before Agincourt."

Certainly Murrow and Sevareid were correct in their admiration for British grit; but, in their hopes for a changed class system, perhaps they were reading the American experience—egalitarian democracy nurtured in the shared hardship of the frontier—into a much older culture too set in its structures for even a blitz to transform them.

Whatever the positive note, however, Sevareid sensed that he had had enough. There had been days when he could barely find enough energy for the most trivial tasks, when he felt he was wandering in a trance. One morning when he could hardly make it to the bathroom, the doctor told him he had been sick for weeks. He had probably been sick since Bordeaux.

He asked to be sent home.

In his last broadcast, delivered three years to the day after he had sailed out of New York harbor, he spoke of France, about Paris dying in her coma, about cities that had broken in spirit and about London, which had not. Perhaps recognizing the echoes of Henry V's Agincourt exhortation, he quoted "someone" who had written: "When this day is all over, in the days to come, men will speak of this war, and they will say: I was a soldier, or I was a sailor, or I was a pilot; and others will say with equal pride: I was a citizen of London." Sevareid's voice broke and he was ashamed of his own mawkishness. But when he returned home to America he met a businessman and an English professor who had heard him and wept.

Ed drove him to Waterloo Station. The cabin of his plane to Lisbon smelled sweetish of vomit. Perhaps this foreshadowed of another kind of sickness he was to encounter when his plane landed in neutral Portugal and he made his way to the Palace Hotel in Estoril, the resort oasis fifteen miles down the beach from Lisbon.

Portugal's neutrality was, at the moment, its only strength. Estoril was lovely with palm trees, but the rest of the country was dry and poor. Pockmarks pitted the faces of its inhabitants, half of whom were illiterate. Dictator Salazar leaned toward the Axis, yet his country had become the escape hatch of Europe—and the international crossroads of both diplomats and spies. Twenty thousand French, German, and Belgian refugees had formed a restless colony there as they waited—or rather, hoped—for their visas to America.

In the lobby and softly lit dining room of the Palace, the exhausted Sevareid listened to the string quartet and scanned the faces of his fellow guests—recognizing some as those he loved, others whom he loathed.

There was the pianist Paderewski, once Poland's premier, now on his way to exile in America. And there, Ambassador Joseph Kennedy, who took Sevareid walking on the beach, picked his brain for what he had learned in a few days in Lisbon about Germany, the Balkans, and Russia and, astonished, exclaimed that American diplomacy needed more men with newspaper training!

There was the wise old Joseph Bech, from Luxembourg, who pointed out to him a man known as Biefurn, Himmler's sinister assistant. Biefurn was in deep conversation with Friedrich Sieburg, the Hitler agent who had weakened Belgium by convincing its rich families that Hitler would never take their land.

One night, in the corner of the casino, he ran into a young German wearing an ill-fitting pair of trousers that had once been Sevareid's; it was the socialist writer, Ernst Adam. They left the smoky room and sat on the rocks and talked of freedom while the surf pounded around them. In the morning, there again was Karli, who spied him from the far end of the opulent lobby and came bounding toward him. As they sat on the beach together Eric saw lines in Karli's face that had not been there before; they both knew that Eric could leave this place and Karli could not.

At long last, Sevareid was getting some distance, some focus on the last three years, a sense of how he was no longer the person he had been. First, he had a new sense of belonging to the world, analogous to the feeling of home he had had with the Jacobins; though now he was part of an international fraternity of "men of goodwill," and this would be his only club, his only home thereafter.

Second, what happened to Paris and was happening to London had taught him that he had a duty to fight with every means available to save the world from fascism. Otherwise, "the Silver Shirts and all men of darkness like them would move out of the dim parlors and into the city halls."

Finally, months ago he had given Adam his trousers and Karli his coat. Those were parts of him, gestures. Not enough. He would try to do something more about the refugees.

10

HOME

IF ANY YOUNG college student who has gone away to Europe for his junior year returns, under the spell of Soho and Montparnasse, alienated from his homeland, we can imagine how Eric Sevareid felt when, after three years away, a year as witness to the fall of a civilization, he came home to find few Americans with much understanding of what he had been through.

He was, by his own account, an innocent, a novice broadcaster with no confidence in his own skills, and nevertheless a celebrity. In New York one day, blaring from a car radio, he heard the familiar voice of his friend Larry LeSueur, and suddenly realized that much of America had heard his own voice in the same way. At a CBS reception in Washington one day he found himself at the fringe of a group clustered around Bill Paley who, unaware of his presence, boasted to the chairman of the FCC, "We've got a young fellow, Sevareid. Speaks like Ed Murrow."

He turned to Paley and introduced himself, "I am Sevareid." Now Paley could tell them apart. Murrow had always emphasized to his "boys" that they not imitate him, that they simply be themselves; but his personaity was too strong for an impressionable young man not to absorb some of it. And this was the pupil's first realization how much he had become like his mentor, that he had taken on Murrow's mannerisms, that their identities as well as their fates were intertwined.

Among the first messages to greet Eric on October 29, right after his arrival in New York, was a welcome-home telegram from H. V. Kaltenborn, inviting him and Lois for dinner at his Brooklyn home or for a few days' rest at their country place. Kaltenborn, who had achieved cult hero status symbolized by his role playing himself in Frank Capra's *Mr. Smith Goes to Washington,* had jumped—or, rather, had been shoved—to NBC the previous April. His lack of "neutrality" with regard to the war had made Paley nervous; and, fearing government regulation, CBS had told Kaltenborn's sponsor, the Pure Oil Company, that it no longer had an evening quarter-hour spot available. Determined, over the next several years, that commentators retain some control over their new, and thus not clearly defined profession, Kaltenborn got to work setting up an Association of News Analysts, a sort of mutual protection society of commentators, and signed up Eric as a member of the club.

Barely back a day, Eric was swept along into New York night life. A fast-talking publicity man—who said "Hi-yah" a lot—set up an evening with the sensationalist *New York Mirror* Broadway gossip columnist Walter Winchell, for whom Eric was to write a "guest" column. He and Lois endured a midnight session at a crowded nightclub, "watching the confident men with glistening hair who smiled brief measured smiles at one another in passing, and the amazing girls, no more than twenty, with chalk-white faces and scarlet, weary mouths, who sat with their thin elbows on the tables, the white petals of their fingers drooping under the burden of a cigarette."

Next to him, a small man with whitish hair and soft, white flesh, clearly bored with Sevareid's accounts of the fall of France, rolled his eyes around the room. Only after the man abruptly left did Sevareid learn that he had been talking to the great Winchell. The next day, Winchell sent a note, "nice meeting you and your wife."

On October 29, using Lois's Barton Avenue home address in Minneapolis, Eric registered for the draft. At six-foot-two, he now weighed only 165 pounds.

Emotionally, he felt that he had come home but did not feel at home. On his return to Minneapolis, Eric lay in his old bed in his parents' house and listened to the "soft thudding of the snow clumps as they fell from the familiar lilac trees beneath the window," and realized that he had probably offended his family by his silence as they chatted on about children and relatives.

He had laughed at his father's concern about the government debt. When old friends and reporters had met him at the airport he had had little to say. His aloofness had come across as vanity. When he returned to the university for a football game, the hulking Finns and Swedes on the field reminded him of Nazi storm troopers crushing Poland and France. His mind and emotions were in Paris, London, and Lisbon. How could American public opinion be so blind to the depth of the evil that was sweeping across Europe? Part of his fervor was the enthusiasm—and intolerance—of the convert. How could he have failed, six years before, to realize the full implications of his stand against ROTC?

One of his tasks was to rediscover America, to get a new sense of its strengths, but this time in a culture stranger to him than Europe: the New York City that had appalled him only a few years before. For a November 5 Election Day broadcast he explored New York neighborhood by neighborhood, developing a democracy-ethnic diversity angle for his report. New York's "diversity" has become a journalistic cliche, and the word now has political meanings it did not have in 1940; but that fall the theme did capture the spirit of a populace that, thirteen months later, would have to unify itself for war.

Sevareid walked around the city for hours, stopping at an Italian barber shop and an Armenian cafe, just watching people waiting to vote. The last time he had watched the faces of men standing in line, they had stood with tears in their eyes and packs on their shoulders, boarding a train for the front; the women had stood waiting for a piece of bread and a week's ration of meat. Here people talked and joked civilly, yet conscious that for them voting was a solemn moment. His Jewish taxi driver confessed that he had been thinking over his vote for a month: "I can't decide, and I've only got till nine o'clock. It's torture."

That night Harry Romer, the Jewish taxi driver from Brooklyn, turned on the radio, heard about his dilemma on the evening news, and wrote to the newsman. He couldn't hear the newsman's name right, he said, because of the static; but he wanted to tell him he voted for Roosevelt.

Once established as a celebrity, Sevareid took the natural next step; he hit the lecture circuit—a lucrative function he would perform, sometimes well and sometimes poorly, for the rest of his life. Indeed, of all the Sevareid papers deposited in the Library of Congress, almost a third consist of lecture scripts and invitations to speak. His texts would be well crafted; and, like most journalist-lecturers, he would repeat or recycle the same material again and again. Exhausted by the travel and sometimes irritated by the obligation to socialize with his society lady sponsors—"a little supper, just a few of us"—he nevertheless crisscrossed the country, alerting his fellow citizens to the war, growing in his own sense of self-importance, and gaining new insights into the American character—including, to his disappointment, its fundamental suspicion, a Yankee trait, its resistance to being "taken in" by what the media were telling them about the war.

His speaking engagements brought him moments of deep consolation and also of revulsion. In 1941, after war had been declared, reporter Sevareid spent some days with shipyard workers—like his boyhood exposure to California gold miners and hoboes—who "slept in trailers, in filthy tenements, four and five to a room, under conditions more Spartan that any we imposed on our soldiers outside of battle." He found there "proud men who were responding to incentives that had nothing to do with the 'profit motive.'" He found "the construction officer who launched a modern destroyer sixty days after the keel was laid. He was a hero, not to a board of directors, but to his men—and that was reward enough."

In the evening a thousand of these men who had already worked ten hours that day gathered to hear him talk about the war in other lands. He "felt a communion with them he had never known with any other audience," he spontaneously discarded his notes and poured out his heart about the spirit which had made America. He feared they would reject him because of his "soft hands." "But they came to their feet in one rippling motion, cheered at the top of their powerful lungs, and crowded to the platform to shake hands with me." He was close to tears. He recalled in *Not So Wild a Dream:* "I began to see America as a composite picture, in its paradoxical complexities, its frivolity, and its dignity, its generosity and its meanness, and to realize that it is almost impossible to generalize about this country, harder than with any other I had known." But it was his job to generalize about this country.

His job was complicated even more by what he saw in the Deep South, which he termed a "spiritual wasteland—the soiled, airless basement of the house." The auditorium in which he was to speak was connected to a police station; and as his hosts ushered him through the station into the hall, he watched the police drag in a good-looking Negro woman, rummage over her body to search her, open her blouse, feel her breasts, and thrust their hands into her skirt. It "was not inhuman but unhuman," and therein lay its "immeasurable brutality." But he didn't really know how to react, other than to express his revulsion later.

For the next forty years he would be called upon to sit at his typewriter with a four-o'clock deadline and write two-to-five-minutes of wisdom every day, and many of those days would be ones in which black people had been beaten, arrested, or killed. And we can be sure that every day he saw that unnamed young woman with southern white men "rummaging" over her body.

A big display in the *Dayton Daily News* (June 3, 1941) gives another perspective on his lecture tours. There he enjoyed a reunion with his old Paris friend Mary Marvin Breckinridge, now Mrs. Jefferson Patterson. Patterson came from an old Dayton family. And the paper there printed a ten-picture spread of his handsome, mobile face before an audience of three hundred at the Biltmore hotel. According to the *Daily News*, "The good-looking man smiled, frowned, scowled, drank water and pleaded with his eyes as he related the events of the German sweep across France." He also fingered his bow tie, stroked his upper lip with his forefinger, scratched his brow, and generally got the point across that here was a very smart guy who was to be reckoned with.

In the first week of December, CBS sent Sevareid to Mexico to cover the inauguration of President Avila Camacho. Since the young reporter had no experience in and knew little about Latin America, it would seem an assignment meant to train the correspondent, or perhaps bring a fresh perspective to press coverage of a place which, in the imaginations of some Americans, could have been as far away as Tibet.

Yet American interest in its neighors to the south had recently picked up for two reasons. First, in his 1933 inaugural address, FDR, aided by the leadership and talents of Cordell Hull and Sumner Welles, had proclaimed his Good Neighbor policy, an attempt to replace the nineteenth century, Monroe Doctrine image of Yankee imperialism with another idea—the ideal of Pan-American friendship and cooperation. A series of almost yearly Pan-American conferences had strengthened the ideal, and another conference was scheduled for 1942—which Sevareid would cover as well.

But, on a more pragmatic level, as John Gunther spells out in *Inside Latin America* (1941), with the coming of the war, Latin America, the producer of fourteen strategic materials that the United States totally lacked, with its unstable governments, with American investments of almost $4.5 billion, had suddenly become "our exposed southern frontier."

Americans, it seems, have always feared that the primitive development of Latin America's "democracies" has made it vulnerable to communist and/or fascist subversion. Gunther writes, "'Democracy' to a Latin American state means, as a rule, not a formal system of government but a desire to be let alone to work out its own destiny. It means, as a rule, not personal liberty for the citizen but political liberty for the state." In 1940 Latin America was home to well over a million first- and second-generation Germans, who kept their German nationality, formed political parties, published local newspapers, and through what was called the Fifth Column, supported German propaganda and, in some instances, espionage.

Hitler had told an interviewer: "We shall create a new Germany in Latin America . . . Mexico is a country that cries for a capable master." If Germany won the war, American strategists fully expected it to move into the Caribbean to gain control of the Panama Canal; invade Brazil by way of Vichy-controlled Dakar in Senegal—which a glance at the map will demonstrate is only sixteen hundred miles from Brazil's Natal; and, through a local fascist party, seize a key country like Uruguay or Colombia in a domestic Nazi putsch.

Camacho, successor to President General Lazaro Cardenas—a veteran of the 1911 Mexican revolution who was president from 1934 to 1940 and who had nationalized the oil fields in 1938—had "won" what was supposed to be the first freely contested election in Mexican history, but which had degenerated into chaos and bloodshed once the opponent, General Juan Andreu Almazan, charged fraud. The idealistic Cardenas, in an attempt to demonstrate to the world that the election was truly free, had left security lax, and both sides had fought over stolen ballot boxes. But FDR's decision to send Vice President Henry Wallace to Camacho's inauguration was a signal that the neighbor to the north approved of this quiet, stolid, Catholic former secretary of defense, who was humorously known as the "Unknown Soldier."

Right before Wallace arrived, Almazan's supporters rioted in front of the American embassy, and Sevareid was caught for a moment between the tear-gas pistols of the police and the stones of the demonstrators. Scribbling telegrams about the fighting in an alley, he was sure he had a scoop; but the Mexican censors held them up. Later at the Senate, a bunch of tough-looking generals descending the stairs and crammed around Camacho inadvertently knocked over Sevareid's microphone and jammed him against the railing, almost cracking his ribs. The next day, December 2, his 4:30 broadcast emphasized Camacho's character, in so far as it could be discerned from his appearance. He found "that Camacho is rather a typical army man. He appears to be more vigorous than graceful; more honest than subtle, more capable of strong emotion than imagination. He gives the impression of courage and solidity, but did not appear to have developed the instinct of dramatization, such as Cardenas shows. Camacho was nervous as he read his speech, in a monotone."

But Sevareid the traveler had developed a particularly cold eye for what he considered the sometimes ugly sight of Americans abroad. In *Not So Wild a Dream,* he depicts the "well-fed Americans of the business colony" who "sat in their exclusive tearooms, sipped cool drinks, and sneered at the Mexican people whom they had been milking for so long that they had come to believe they were there by some divine right of economics." His trip made him reflect on the relationship between the Mexican revolution, still struggling to succeed, and the larger international struggle against fascism. A Hitler victory would strengthen Latin American fascism which would, in turn, overwhelm Mexico. It became all the more obvious to him that the world was one, "that no barricades of water or desert or mountain range could fence away ideas."

When in January 1941 CBS sent Sevareid to his new assignment at the news desk in Washington, D.C., the nation's capital still retained some of the character of the southern town it had been early in the nineteenth century when it centered around Lafayette Square across from the White House. The Mall reached out to the Capitol on the east; and to the west, on the other side of Rock Creek Park, lying along the northern shore of the Potomac, the old neighborhood of Georgetown, with the influx of New-Dealers, was undergoing the transformation that would transform it from a Negro slum into the most fashionable urban neighborhood in the country.

It was also the neighborhood where Eric Sevareid would die.

What would stand out on a map, or a view of the whole area from a plane or the top of the Washington Monument, would be the vast patches of green—Potomac Park below the Capitol Mall, created from dredged swamplands, the rolling hills encircling the city from the north, the tree-lined avenues reaching out into the wooded suburbs and countryside.

Before the New Deal, Washington had appeared to be a mere satellite of New York City; but New Deal spending, particularly on construction—much of it on new monuments and public buildings like the National Gallery of Art and the Jefferson Memorial, and landscaping, like the redesign of Dupont Circle—transformed it into a boomtown. By 1939 the number of federal workers had increased to 160,000; with the completion of the George Washington Memorial Parkway along the Virginia side of the Potomac, Arlington, Virginia, became the fastest growing county in the nation. Pearl Harbor would only accelerate this process; construction began on the Pentagon on August 11, 1941, and its first tenants, three hundred employees from the Ordnance Department, moved in on April 29, 1942. Below the Pentagon, Alexandria, Virginia, an old Civil War town surrounded by woods and hills, would soon swell into a populous suburb. It would also be the Sevareid's home for the emotionally most tumultuous years of his life.

But Washington, for those who looked, also provided a glimpse of the shabby underside of American urban life and a foreshadowing of where other American cities were going. An article in *Harper's* (December 1941) drew the picture:

> Washington the Capital is a symbol of democracy and America. Washington the city is a symbol of almost everything that sincere and thoughtful men know is wrong with democracy and America. Washington the Capital is the hope of world freedom; Washington the city is overcrowded, badly housed, expensive, crime-ridden, intolerant, with inadequate transportation, schools, and health facilities. It staggers under a dilapidated and hopeless governmental organizataion, and its problems are rapidly getting worse.

Sevareid was first struck by the city's college-campus-like unreality, its suburban separateness from the sweat and noise of the nation it led—"a strange and disarming place. A quiet collection of lofty stone museums, a leafy, dreamy park." But Eric Sevareid loved—or came to love—Washington very much. If New York made too many demands on his nervous system, Washington allowed him to both reside at the center of the political world, enjoy lunch at the best French restaurants and, in his homes over the years in Chevy Chase and Virginia, escape to a semirural sanctuary not too far in spirit from the place where he had grown up.

Above all, he told an interviewer in his last years, Washington was *the center,* the greatest center of world news since ancient Rome. CBS News' 1980s gimmick of sending its top correspondents into the American heartland, as if real news was in some remote town, was the equivalent, he felt, of interviewing a room full of cab drivers. The world's front page was Washington, D.C. "That's why I've stayed here," he said.

Besides, it reminded him of Paris. With one difference. In April 1942, a Frenchman, a friend from Paris, came to visit; and, having seen the statues and galleries, asked to see Washington's nightlife, "its Montmartre and Montparnasse." So Eric took him on a tour, not to find D.C.'s Hotel Crillon and Maxim's but to prove that they didn't exist. The American people, with their high moral standards, he said, would not tolerate a decadent capital. Finally he drove his confused friend out Connecticut Avenue to Chevy Chase and showed him the rows of homes with soft yellow lights in family living rooms and a high school couple saying goodnight under a street lamp; and they listened to the sounds of clinking glasses and the snapping of a deck of cards emanating from the homes. Outside New York, he told his friend, "This is America after dark . . . And personally, I don't think it's so bad."

As CBS Washington correspondent, with his office at WTOP in the Earle Building, Sevareid's job was to do a daily capital news roundup at various times during the day, often at 7:00 A.M., 5:45 P.M., or 11:00 P.M. Working several items into each broadcast, he concentrated on the war— preparedness, lend-lease, submarines off the American coast, FDR's comings and goings, the imposition of price and wage controls, Admiral Darlan and Vichy France. But his recent past was always with him and occasionally it burst out into his scripts. In a movie theater, during the newsreel, he suddenly spotted the face of the old Paris *Herald* copy boy in a refugee camp! One day, May 9, 1941, he told again the story of how the *Ville de Liege* rescued him from Bordeaux: the *Ville de Liege* had just been sunk. Occasionally, as if preparing for the next stage of his career, he would do a five-minute personal essay, as on March 21, 1941, when he described again the fall of France and bombing of London, then told of America girding for war—the "real work" in the fields and factories

outside Washington; and here, the "mental girding," the "purely intellectual change—in men's minds—and thus in our policy." In this "ger-
minating movement of thought in Washington lies the secret of our
country's destiny."

Meanwhile, Sevareid had been reliving his France-London-Lisbon
experiences on still another level—in his creative imagination. If every
newspaperman is a novelist at heart, with that hot manuscript smolder-
ing in his desk drawer, Eric Sevareid, whose friends like Frederick Manfred and James Reston said he should be a novelist, had been working
on both a Broadway play and a film script. Since the main characters are
expatriates or refugees, the scripts represent his attempt to both do something for refugees whom he felt powerless to help during his flight, and
to deal, on an imaginative level, with the philosophical and moral problems that disturbed him greatly: the apparent failure of his countrymen
to realize that the survival of democracy was in doubt, and his own failure, so far, to act radically on his convictions—to enlist.

He was also fascinated with Hollywood and with actresses—all his
life he wanted to turn his experiences into films and TV documentaries,
and during his 1950s radio commentaries he often dropped gratuitous
references to actresses into his scripts—and he wanted to make big
money.

In a February 19, 1941, long letter to playwright Robert E. Sherwood, author of *Lincoln in Illinois* and FDR speechwriter, whom he
wanted to actually write the play based on his story idea, Sevareid spelled
out his inspiration for a play-to-become-a-movie about the democratiz-
ing influence of life in air-raid shelters during the blitz. Enduring this
crisis, he argues, has meant a "release in the soul of the ordinary garden
variety of Englishman. He doesn't want to hold up during this siege and
then just fall back into his old mold again. This thing has brought out
the deep instincts of manhood in the hearts of a lot of miserable, kicked-
about men who've never had a chance to show it before, nor did their
fathers or grandfathers."

He has based his story on his experiences during the blitz when he
sat through the raids in the basement restaurant of his middle-class
apartment building. There the apartment dwellers—the retired trawler
captain, the beautiful girl who does the hair of the duchess of Kent, the
shy spinster house manager, the lovely sculptress from Montparnasse

who is also the air-raid warden, and the deaf garage mechanic—move from being strangers to being friends. Into this group comes the central character: a bitter, cynical, young, French ex-pilot, despondent over the moral rot in his own country. It is this young man who flew the defiant swoop over Bordeaux when "old man Pétain" capitulated, whom the Countess de Vogue imagined to be Saint-Exupéry! This is the story of the "*moral regeneration*" of this young man, who is saved from cynicism by these people, who falls in love with the sculptress and "helps her pull bleeding old men out of ruins."

"Do you think there is a play somewhere in this stuff?" he asks. "It seems to me that somebody," he tells Sherwood, "has got to demonstrate in a graphic manner to Americans that this war as the British are fighting it, *is* a people's war, that rare kind of war that doesn't degrade people but enobles them."

Sherwood decided there was not a play for him in all that stuff. So Sevareid turned to Robert Ardrey, author of the play *Thunder Rock*, who would later gain another level of fame with his *African Genesis* and his controversial theories on the origins of human violence. Ardrey, at work on projects of his own and uncomfortable about developing another person's idea, turned him down as well. "I'm pulling my guts out like macaroni on the current play," he answered. "I wouldn't have enough left for you." But he added, "A guy who produces material like this is someone I'd like to know." Ardrey became one of Sevareid's best friends and remained so till his death. In June, Carl Zuckerman, a famous German playwright living in Vermont, also turned him down.

Eric's enthusiasm for Hollywood had been whetted by an invitation to do a publicity trailer for a Warner Brothers' war picture, *Underground,* starring Jeffrey Lynn as a German soldier who has lost his arm at Dunkirk and returns home, not knowing that his brother is secretly working against Hitler, operating an illegal radio station in the underground. When Lynn's character accidently reveals his brother's treason and sees his father and brother beaten by the Gestapo, he joins the radio movement himself, taking his brother's place.

The publicity for the trailer urges theaters to display Sevareid's photo and poster in the lobby, with the banner line, "Eric Sevareid, Nationally Famous Commentator, Came Back to America to Tell This Amazing, Uncensored Story!" On screen, Sevareid intones: "Hello America! This is Eric Sevareid broadcasting for the first time in five years without any restrictions. . . ." Indulging in some PR hyperbole he would avoid the rest of his life, he tells the theater audience that he has watched the undergound movement gather momentum and that "this is the most amazing story to reach the eyes and ears of the American public."

Perhaps seeing *Underground* and advertising it emboldened him to write a spy story of his own. In a letter to Helen Meinardi, his Hollywood collaborator, he spells out the plot of *Lisbon Clipper*. Its basic elements: love, fear of the Gestapo, and a yearning for the good life, represented by the consuming desire to reach America.

The Girl is a beautiful actress, a refugee from Prague, in a French concentration camp. The Man is the young American vice consul, who visits the camp on an inspection tour and later falls in love with the Girl. The Other Man is a young Czech refugee who worships the girl. Goebbels himself wants the Girl, to use her acting talent for the Reich. Secretly, the Gestapo help the Czech flee with the Girl to Lisbon, with the understanding that he will betray her to them there. Meanwhile the vice consul has been transferred to Lisbon, where he has the power to grant visas.

In the film's turning point, when the vice consul's superior denies a visa to the actress because she has been traveling with the Czech while not married to him, which immigration law calls "moral turpitude," the vice consul rebels against the letter of the law—"henceforth he is concerned only with the spirit of the human soul and its struggle for freedom and decency." Next he wins the Czech away from the Gestapo by telling him he has quit his job to join the army: "No man has the right to call himself a man if he fails now to fight against what his generation is destined to fight." Assisted by the Czech, the Man and the Girl fly off to America.

The early concentration camp scene is a reenactment of Sevareid's emotionally wrenching camp visit in France, and the Man seems a combination of himself and Jefferson Patterson, whose responsibility it was to visit interns in prewar German camps. The story reflects his only partly successful attempts to get visas for Karli, who with the help of the underground, made it to America, and Adam who, because he had been a communist, not even Eleanor Roosevelt could save. Indeed, while he was working on the screenplay, Karli wrote him from Indiana; he had lost his research job in New York because of his bad English and was going to try something else. The shifting loyalties of the Czech may well reflect a story one of Eric's Paris friends has told, that Eric was once deceived, and emotionally hurt, by a refugee he was trying to help. His defense of the unmarried couple who travel together is interesting in light of how Eric will travel eighteen years later. But most significant is the vice consul's resolving his moral quandary by two steps Eric Sevareid was never able to take: quitting his job and joining the army.

While he would certainly never admit to being a propagandist, Sevareid clearly believed the media—radio and film—should bolster the national purpose.

For months he had been reporting what isolationists Charles Lindbergh, Senator Burton Wheeler and Senator Gerald P. Nye said every time FDR tried to wake America up. On July 5, 1941 he wondered in his morning report whether, in this grave emergency, the "reactions" to "men responsible for averting catastrophe" should get the attention they got.

Paul White was down on him within forty-eight hours:

> It seems to me that, although you may be disgusted by the process, it is essential in a democracy that anyone and everyone should have his say at all times. Thus, I cannot agree with you that there is any journalistic problem at all. I grant you that you said you were not certain of the answers to the questions you raised, but it seems to me that your very raising of the questions was a sort of answer in itself.
>
> Briefly, it seems to me that you ventured into a dangerous line of territory.

This was a fine example of White's acting definition of free speech, and also an insight into the seeds of an emerging Sevareid rhetoric. Perhaps more than any commentator, throughout his life, Sevareid will say that what this means he does not know.

Eric replied with a six-page memo saying that frankly he has not changed his mind. Every editor, he argues, exercises judgment. There are just so many column inches in a newspaper and minutes in a broadcast day. But it is completely irresponsible for a paper like the *New York Times* to give the same space to London and German communiqués when Berlin habitually lies. To give Senator Wheeler—an "irresponsible man"—time to answer FDR seems to make Wheeler a sort of opposition president.

On September 17, 1942, almost a year after Pearl Harbor, Sevareid returned to these themes in a "Town Meeting of the Air" which began: "America is not all out for war . . ." America was still suffering from "twenty years of corrosive materialism. Twenty years in which we tried to forget that we were members of the human race." Borrowing from Thomas Paine's *The Crisis*, he said these were "times that try men's souls," in which America needed not the "silky tones" of advertisers selling them "hair oil and liver pills" but simple, honest speech. Commercials, he suggested, should be censored, because ads for laxatives, breath sweeteners, and chewing gum did not bring the day of victory closer.

Perhaps smarting over the rejection of his two scripts, he says that motion pictures have also failed to come to grips with the reality of the war. His friend Walter Wanger had made the excuse that the public would not buy reality; but the media cannot accept that excuse; they must educate—guide people "into reality and understanding." The media must resist the tyranny of the box office—today that would translate as "ignore ratings"—and, in that way, be in *real* touch with the people.

In October 1954 the issue of art as a force for social good would come up again. When a bad review in the *Herald Tribune* helped kill his friend Ardrey's anti-McCarthyism play, *Sing Me A Lullaby,* Sevareid wrote the *Tribune* an angry protest. Later he tried unsuccessfully to get his friend Robert Hutchins at the Fund for the Republic to underwrite the play, either to keep it on Broadway or to get it on television. America needed this play, he was convinced, because it dealt with "the present political-moral sickness in the country," which was "thought control." The *Tribune* reviewer, Walter F. Kerr, replied to Sevareid that, as much as he agreed with its politics, the play was disastrously clumsy, verbose, and pompous, more likely to hurt Ardrey's causes than help them.

In the fall of 1941 Sevareid got another chance to wear his military correspondent's regalia, including his favorite boots, which had laces up to the knees. He seemed to enjoy the uniform, which he had, in Richard Harding Davis tradition, fashioned for himself since he had covered the fall of France. Accompanied by *Time* correspondent Robert

Sherrod, who would soon become a noted military historian and later editor of the *Saturday Evening Post,* he traveled by train to Louisiana in September to cover the largest peacetime army maneuvers in history.

Beginning in Louisiana swamps in September the war games continued in November into the Carolinas. It was like a camping trip, though unlike the standard camping trip, Sevareid got a ride in a dive bomber. "It was glorious to ride a lead dive bomber through the splendid world of blue and white, to look to the right and the left and see the wing planes steadily there, so close one could amost touch them, the brown faces of the pilots turned at the same precision angle, arrowing in toward me." But, also unlike camping trips, men died. And he made a point of reporting the real, accidental, dead—four in the first two days—in an unreal "war."

For a man who made his first "national" reputation based on his opposition to compulsory military drill, he entered readily into the military *esprit.* "You see," he broadcast on November 26, "the whole aim of these maneuvers, the thing which must be achieved, is to make these men, no matter what their unit, fight instinctively, fight as an automatic reaction . . . that is being developed . . . you see far more of it than you did two months ago in those maneuvers. . . ."

In one of those marvelous minor ironies of human life, one of the commanders of the maneuvers was General Hester, who had commanded the University of Minnesota ROTC when Eric Sevareid the student rebel had broken its hold. Sheepishly, the reporter confessed to Hester that he had just received a postcard from an unnamed Minnesota alumnus who had sponsored the Oxford oath and who recently had spent his spare time drilling at night with "home Guards," and had joined the army as a volunteer.

Hester's response was that "people *do* change their ideas"; but Sevareid's reply in his broadcast, November 28, was that *events* change people's ideas. The Oxford oath, a rejection of militarism, sprung from a conviction that the propaganda of militarism had dragged us needlessly into the First World War. His friend's goal remained the same—peace and security—but, since Hitler, the means to achieve them had changed.

While Hester and Sevareid talked, General Mark Clark and the Third Army chief of staff, then Colonel Dwight D. Eisenhower walked in. Eric's friend Sherrod had urged him to get to know Eisenhower in

September, but Eric had failed to follow up. In fact these maneuvers were credited with making Eisenhower's reputation; and within a few months General George Marshall promoted him to major general and sent him to England to command American forces in Europe.

Ed and Janet Murrow returned to America at the end of November to be honored at a Paley-sponsored dinner for one thousand guests in white tie and tails in the grand ballroom of the Waldorf Astoria. Murrow had been told that he was famous, but like Sevareid, he had had no comprehension of the extent of his fame. At the dinner, Archibald MacLeish said, "You have laid the dead of London at our doors and we knew the dead were our dead—were all men's dead—were mankind's dead—and ours. Without rhetoric, without dramatics, without more emotion that needed be, you destroyed the superstition of distance and time."

The next week, Sunday, December 7, Eric was sitting at home, in his living room, talking with his old friend Phil Potter, former *Minnesota Daily* editor and now news editor of the *Baltimore Sun*. He had a dinner date later in the day with the Greggs, a Canadian family he had recently gotten to know. A neighbor, hatless and in a hurry, tapped on his window and told him to turn on his radio, and dashed to the next house on the street.

His first response was to call the Greggs and apologize: he could not come to dinner because the Japanese had just bombed Pearl Harbor.

At eight that night he broadcast in the midst of the chaos of the press room at the White House. He had driven in from his house to see tourists oblivious to the fact that their nation was now at war. But word had spread. He had argued over a cab with a recently discharged marine who had heard the news and was on his way to reenlist. He contrasted Americans to the French, who had gone to war with deep regret. "Of that, I see nothing here."

Murrow, meanwhile, was with Roosevelt. He and Janet had been invited to supper at the White House and Eleanor, remarking that, "We still have to eat," insisted that they still come. FDR worked in a study next to his bedroom, receiving a parade of cabinet members, congressional leaders, and military men, while Eleanor served the Murrows scrambled eggs, milk, and pudding. When Ed and Janet started leave at 10:30, FDR sent word for Ed to wait.

At 1 A.M., an ashen, but calm and steady FDR had Murrow join him for a beer and sandwich, then, after asking how the British were holding up, poured out the shocking, top-secret details of the Pearl Harbor losses. Later, with Janet, Ed paced up and down in their bedroom, pounded his fist, and said, "I've got the greatest story of my life and I don't know if I should go with it or forget it." He did neither.

Roger Burlingame's biography of Elmer Davis, *Don't Let Them Scare You* (1961), catches CBS's professional response to the disastrous news. The immediate public reaction was that "it would all be over in a month, six months at most . . . Everyone was confident that the great United States was invincible."

> Then the calm, rather sad voice of Eric Sevareid shattered all illusion. Sevareid and Davis consistently refused to sugar-coat bad news if they believed it to be true. It was this that built the confidence of the American people in wartime radio news; that turned them away from bombast and oratory and dramatics and pontifical statement . . . But it was the broadcast of Eric Sevareid in the evening that really set the wheels turning in American factories. For the first time, he told the grim truth about Pearl Harbor: that the damage to the American fleet had been disastrous, that it would be impossile to exaggerate it—that indeed the very core of naval defense in the Pacific had been wiped out . . . For the first time since the early Civil War, the United States had been badly licked in combat.

The Third Pan American Conference in Rio in the last two weeks of January 1942 was yet another step in the Europe-centered Sevareid's quick newsman's education in the "lower half" of the world. In its vast mountain ranges and jungles viewed from his plane window he saw the irony of Brazil's history. A few generations ago a civilization had flourished there and quickly faded. Pavlova had danced in an Amazon opera house now drowning in jungle growth. At the turn of the century an Engishman had smuggled rubber plant seeds out of the jungle and planted them in the Malay Straits; and so Brazil's rubber industry died. Now war was bringing Brazil back into the world's mainstream.

In his January 16 broadcast, he spelled out the United States' goals for the conference: get unanimity on the resolution to break all relations with the Axis powers; settle the Peru-Ecuador boundary dispute; prove to the Latin American nations that the United States can help support their economies and get them weapons.

For Sevareid personally, the sight of a so-called benevolent dictator, President Getulio Vargas, seemed a challenge to much of what he had believed about the superiority of democracy. "This midget, kewpie doll of a man," as he called him, had seized power in 1930, crushed three revolts, including both communists and fascists, and now ruled so as to convince even American embassy officials that stability was worth more than some discarded civil liberties. When the young reporter dared to tell his embassy companions that he thought he preferred even Mexican democracy to Vargas-style rule they snorted in derision. To them, tranquility and order were the prime social goals. For him, it was freedom. The freedom of the individual to develop his own personality to the fullest.

"You mean that black man carrying the hod at the corner must be guaranteed the opportunity to find out whether he is another Tolstoy or Picasso?"

Yes, he replied. And they smiled. But in the evenings Brazilian students came secretly to Sevareid's room and spilled out their stories of friends and teachers imprisoned in the hills or on barren islands, of intellectual and artistic life snuffed out in the name of "order."

This was Ruritania, Sevareid concluded—one of those mythical, mid-European countries that exist only in Romberg or Lehar operettas. (John Gunther, whom Sevareid undoubtedly read, says Paraguay is Ruritania.) It was a country where he could do a broadcast from the presidential summer palace with Vargas playing with his grandchild in the room, but which, months later, confiscated all the copies of the *Saturday Evening Post* in Brazil because of an implied criticism of the government in Sevareid's report on the conference.

As in much of Sevareid's reporting and in his remembering, strong personalities loom large; and their physical presence and demeanor evoke his feelings about their characters. In *Not So Wild a Dream*, he depicts the Argentine ambassador, Ruiz Guinazu, as "an insufferable, pompous man with a pince-nez and haughty abdomen," who would cancel press conferences, reschedule them, and keep reporters waiting for hours.

The formal, "old school tie," Harvard accent diplomat Sumner Welles he saw as a man rigid in manner and in integrity, with a Jacksonian sense of duty—a characteristic fatally lacking among the leaders of the French. Mexico's foreign minister, Dr. Ezequiel Padilla, with his soft, curling black hair, bronzed Indian countenance, and "tender serenity in his big, dark eyes," was the handsomest man he had ever seen in public life. He "spoke in a low, compelling voice of the brotherhood of men and the dreams of freedom and liberty which had lived in the breasts of those who came to settle this new world and to struggle for its survival." Even though Sevareid knew little Spanish he understood him clearly.

The January 24 broadcast reported the successful completion of the conference: eighteen republics had broken with the Axis powers in action, and two—Argentina and Chile—in words. The Nazi residents of Rio were out buying the silk stockings and other luxuries they would soon be unable to buy when they got back to their own countries.

Meanwhile Eric had found time to enjoy the city, which was not Paris, but had its pleasures. He had found old friends from his Paris days. One, Katri Blake, then married to the Dutch journalist and photographer Jurgen Kirchner, had escaped from France, through Spain, to Portugal at the same time as Eric, and they had met again in Lisbon. Katri had known only a few Americans, and Eric came to symbolize for her all she had imagined an American would be like. Tall, slim, and handsome, with a Western appearance, he always had, she thought, a little ironical and always amused expression on his face. She has always remembered him sitting in the Copacabana Palace in a group of celebrating European expatriates and his journalism colleagues, dressed in a white tuxedo and black tie, very elegant—yet still slightly aloof, watching the merrymaking.

His much-remarked aloofness was not necessarily snobbishness; rather it was usually an indication that he was simply thinking about something else, always thinking. One of the things he had to think about on the Copacabana beach one morning as the sun warmed his drowsing body was the lead story in the newspaper a friend dropped beside him. The first American division had just been sent overseas—a National Guard division composed of Scandinavians, Germans, and Irish from Minnesota, Iowa, and the Dakotas.

At the beginning, all the war news was bad. At Pearl Harbor, America had lost 2,403 men and most of its Pacific Fleet, including all eight battleships, three cruisers, and many destroyers. Fortunately, the aircraft carriers were at sea.

Germany joined Japan and declared war on the United States three days later. In imitation of the Nazi blitzkrieg, the Japanese army, with perhaps the most underrated infantry in history, swept through Southeast Asia in a matter of months. Indochina, under Vichy French control, offered no resistance, and Thailand fought no more than four hours. Hong Kong capitulated on Christmas Day. Japan then surged into Malaya, headed for the British stronghold of Singapore, which—realizing too late that its big guns trained toward the sea could not be turned around to defend it against an enemy from the land—fell on February 17. In May they took Burma, and General Joseph Stillwell dragged himself out confessing, "We got a hell of a beating. We got run out of Burma and it is as humiliating as hell."

Following the Pearl Harbor attack, the Japanese immediately bombed the Philippines, destroying half the American air force on the ground, and then landed forces on Luzon. On February 22, FDR told General Douglas MacArthur to escape to Australia. The islands resisted until April, and the tiny island fortress of Corregidor—a fleeting symbol of lonely courage—held out till May 5th.

Since the American people knew even less about the Far East than they did about Latin America, their anxiety was all the more intense. In the public imagination, soldiers and sailors lost in the Pacific became victims of malaria, sharks, cannibals, and headhunters as well as of the Japanese.

Now, except for the south Solomon Islands, the Japanese controlled the Pacific west of Midway and north of the Coral Sea. Australia and New Zealand saw themselves as ripe for invasion.

During 1942, German U-boats sank 1,160 ships, about three a day, including one right off the old Victorian summer resort of Cape May, New Jersey, and a Japanese sub was bold enough to shell the Oregon coast.

In Europe, Germany, in a foolish act of hubris, turned from England to Russia in June 1941 and was laying siege to Stalingrad. In North Africa, Field Marshall Irwin Rommel, the "Desert Fox," who had taken Tobruk in the summer of 1942, was threatening to move on Egypt, Cairo, and the Suez Canal.

For the Allies, there had been a few bright moments. On April 18, General Jimmy Doolittle made a carrier-based, American morale-boosting air attack on Tokyo. In May, the U.S. Navy took a draw in the battle of the Coral Sea; and in June, at the decisive battle of Midway, which was an air battle more than a fight between surface ships, the United States crippled Japan's air power by sinking four carriers and around twenty other ships.

Convinced they must soon go on the offensive, the Allies decided that North Africa—in spite of the danger of angering Spain and the ambiguity of dealing with the Vichy French who controlled Tunisia, Algeria, French Morocco, and French West Africa—was the right place for the first initiative of the land war. On November 8, 1942, U.S. and British troops landed in French Morocco and Algiers. Some Vichy French resisted the Allies; but by November 10, Admiral Darlan, acting in the name of Pétain, issued orders for the Vichy French to give in.

Whatever the political and moral compromises, Roosevelt was elated with the invasion's success. It was eleven months after Pearl Harbor. When he received the news at his Shangri-La hideaway (now known as Camp David), he turned to his friends and said, "We have landed in North Africa. We are fighting back."

Throughout the first year of the war Sevareid gained a strong reputation as a reporter-commentator who stayed just inside the censor's line but still got the stark facts—often bad news—of the war across. Meanwhile much of the color in his broadcasts came from his personal reflections and the little details he selected to imply another dimension to the story. On April 4, 1942, he reported the arrest of William Dudley Pelley, leader of the Silver Shirts, for sedition, and followed on July 23 with news of the indictment of twenty-eight men and one woman—including some Silver Shirt followers—for sending seditious pamphlets to members of the armed forces. This time, more than he had been able to do in 1937, Sevareid paused to analyze the origins of American fascism—as spawned in an era of economic troubles, ignorant of economics, victims of what psychologists call stranger hatred. "Crabbed old men and neurotic women with a weakness for tea leaves and mystic symbols . . . in colonial days they would have been hunted as witches."

In May of '42, reporting a German submarine attack in the Gulf of Mexico, he says, "a sunburned crew of adolescent Germans enthusiastically poured shells into the vessel even though seamen were descending the ladders to their life boat . . . four were killed on the ladders. . . ." The listener is invited to imagine the German boys sunbathing on the deck before battle, then enjoying their killing as if it were a game.

When the Allies landed in Algiers in November 1942, Sevareid was thrilled. But when the Allies then appointed Admiral Darlan, a fascist sympathizer, as high commissioner in Algiers—although Eisenhower and General Mark Clark had previously negotiated with the antifascist General Henri Giraud—Sevareid thought the ideals for which the war was being fought had been betrayed. The military pragmatists were interested only in saving lives; he, on the other hand, saw the war as a chance to spread as well as save democracy.

When Larry LeSueur returned from Russia the two of them attended a Roosevelt press conference, which in those days was a handful of about fifteen reporters sitting around the president's desk, then lingered afterward for a private talk. To Eric, Franklin D. Roosevelt was simply a very great man. FDR had a sense of the invisible course of history, he understood the country and the workings of democracy in a way ordinary men did not; and Sevareid found himself absorbed in the man, as if he was sitting with a friend. FDR went through the motions of asking Larry about Russia; but it became clear that he was not really interested in the answers, he was simply using two congenial reporters for a few moments of relaxation. To Sevareid this meant that the burden of the war was becoming too much for the president, he was no longer the confident master of himself.

Larry had brought the president a souvenir, a German medal, the Iron Cross. FDR flinched; he did not want it if it had been taken from a dead body. A few days later, in an uncharacteristically petty gesture, he took the Iron Cross out of his desk drawer during a press conference and awarded it, *in absentia*, to the bitterly anti-Roosevelt *New York Daily News* columnist John O'Donnell, who had recenty offended him.

Meanwhile, the war was about halfway through its course, and Eric had still not resolved his personal moral dilemma. His contemporaries, including the Jacobins, were in uniform and he was not. When he had registered for the draft in October 1941, his Minneapolis board had classified him as 3-A, which, according to Selective Service, was the original classification for men with dependents. When in December of that year he changed his official address to an apartment at 307 East 44th Street in New York City, he was reclassified as 3-B, a category giving greater protection to men who were in an essential industry or in "activities essential in the support of the war effort." Although journalism is not listed as an "essential activity," it is easy to see how a draft board could consider Sevareid's newscasts "essential." Indeed, when he discussed joining the army with the army chief of public relations, he was told to just go on with what he was doing.

Certainly it was not a lack of physical courage that had made him reluctant to enlist; he had demonstrated his bravery when he was seventeen. There is no evidence that reluctance to leave his wife and children was a factor. Nor was it moral unwillingness to kill. His objections to compulsory drill had been more practical than ethical.

Rather, he shied away from the psychological strain of barracks life, from being surrounded by boisterous, back-slapping, hard-drinking men, most of them ten years younger than he. Intellectually he believed in teamwork, but he also knew he was no good at it. He was a very private person who needed time to think and the social freedom to express himself on his own terms.

Then what drove him to consider enlisting? Partly patriotism. Partly the common belief that the great event of any generation is its war, and not to fight in it is not to have lived. But it is reasonable to surmise that there was an even stronger motive—ambition. Sevareid was a driven man, with a sense that he was meant to achieve something special. He knew enough history to conclude that, for a journalist, the "center" in 1943 was not Washington but North Africa, or wherever the army landed next.

In June 1942 CBS made Eric head of the Washington bureau. His family was enjoying its little house on Oakridge Avenue in Chevy Chase where there was plenty of yard space for his two-year-old boys to roam around. But he was very restless.

For a lot of reasons, he wanted to go abroad. On July 20 he wrote to Murrow, half threatening that if the only way he could see the war was as a soldier he would have to quit and join the army. On August 26 Murrow replied: "You have improved tremendously as a broadcaster and your work so far as I have heard, does not reveal any messianic tendencies." He asks him to not be too hasty in joining the army and half promises to send him abroad later. Throughout the year he and Murrow sparred over his desire to return to the war; Eric threatened to join the *New York Times*. In January 1943, Murrow suggested that maybe he can send him to Africa.

When word of Eric's intentions to go abroad and cover the war reached the sponsors of his evening news program, the J. Walter Thompson Advertising Agency and Eric's sponsor, the Parker Pen Company, protested. They didn't like being dropped in mid-contract. Parker suggested that perhaps they should make the break early, to allow time to develop a replacement, but graciously backed off, acknowledging that, yes, going to war is important for Sevareid's career.

By summer 1943 it was decided that he would return to Europe as a war correspondent. But a lot would happen before Sevareid would see Europe again. Within a few weeks he would leap into the most terrifying adventure of his life.

11

BURMA

THE LEFT ENGINE went out. A shock, if not a surprise. The plane was a C-46, a new, large transport, one of forty or so, which had recently been shipped—unfortunately, before they were really ready for operation—to the American air force base in Chabua, Assam, in India's northeast corner, to fly men and supplies over the Burma "Hump"—hundreds of miles of Himalayas and jungles—to Kunming, in free China. They had arrived with some 196 alterations still to be made—their deployment moved up because the imperious and prickly Madame Chiang Kai-shek, during a prolonged goodwill tour and shopping spree, had goaded Roosevelt by manipulating public opinion, to hurry-up aid to the Nationalist Chinese. And now their pilots were referring to these planes as "flying coffins."

Suddenly the plane turned; perhaps the pilot was heading back to Chabua. The plane was losing altitude. Jagged mountain tops and trees rose closer. A blast of light and noise filled the plane as a sergeant pulled the door from its hinges and threw out a suitcase.

The order came to throw all passenger baggage out! Eric Sevareid had spent weeks in Washington gathering the "perfect" correspondent's outfit, and now he was supposed to throw it away? He felt sick. His stomach was rebelling again. When a soldier tried to snatch his bag, he pulled it back; then he tossed it out himself. Then he jammed his briefcase, filled with his notes on the first weeks of the trip, under a seat. How could he sacrifice his notes? A few minutes later he threw the briefcase out too.

The baggage gone, the plane circled. They were lost. It was 9:15 A.M. The men donned their parachutes. Diplomat John Paton Davies, political adviser to China-Burma-India commander General Stilwell, crouched in the opening, then threw himself into the void. One by one the others followed. For a second Eric thought the plane might stay up, but then it pitched to the left. It was in a dive. Now the plane was only five hundred feet above the ground. Sevareid closed his eyes and leapt head first into space.

Five seconds later the plane crashed into the mountainside and exploded in an orange, fiery ball.

What had been discussed as a CBS assignment to the European or North African theater was changed to a trip to China at the initiative of the Roosevelt administration. Japan had already conquered Manchuria, Northern China, and the Chinese coast, as much of the Chinese mainland as it could effectively control, and Chiang Kai-shek's forces had settled into a defensive position, with headquarters at Chungking, as a blockade against Mao Tse-tung's Chinese Communists, whom they had been fighting, except for a brief truce to oppose Japan, for almost a decade. While demanding more military and economic aid, which he used to pay off his corrupt warlord generals, Chiang had even threatened to establish a separate peace; and Japanese-occupied and free China had opened up a lucrative trade relationship. Apparently the Chungking government was more interested in making money than in making war.

Washington foresaw, however, that if Chungking and the Chinese Communists did not join forces again against the Japanese, the Japanese could eventually overwhelm Chungking and deprive the Allies of their bases on Chinese soil, and thus inevitably make the final Allied assault on Japan—which would presumably be a land invasion—all the more costly.

A major obstacle to forcing Chiang into an alliance with Mao was the poorly informed American public, who had been charmed by the American-educated, Methodist Madame Chiang, taken in by the propaganda of the "old China hands"—both Chiangs appeared on the covers of Henry Luce's *Time* and *Life* magazines—and deprived of the facts by Chinese censorship to imagine Chiang as one more Allied icon—like Churchill and de Gaulle. The American public was emotionally committed to China not because it understood the current complex political situation, but because it had read Pearl Buck's novel, *The Good Earth,* and news stories about the colorful American commanders in that theater of war, like Colonel (later Major General) Claire L. Chennault, the army air corps officer retired in 1937 for defective hearing who commanded, from Kunming, the "Flying Tigers," an American volunteer group who flew planes—like the P-40 fighters with tigers' teeth painted on the nose—for the Chinese. Who would argue with Chennault after seeing the 1942 film, *Flying Tigers,* starring John Wayne, with a personal introduction by Chiang himself?

Stilwell. Major General Joseph "Vinegar Joe" Stilwell, who was both commander of the China-Burma-India theater and adviser to Generalissimo Chiang, having been driven out of Burma by the Japanese, was now determined to return. Most Americans did not know that Stilwell despised the corrupt Chiang, whom he code-named "Peanut," and that Chennault and Stilwell vied with one another, pushing rival strategic plans. Stilwell, backed by chief of staff General George C. Marshall, wanted a land attack across Burma; Chennault, backed by Chiang and FDR aide Harry Hopkins, wanted an air attack on Japan.

This was the national climate when an unnamed man described as a friend of Roosevelt's asked Sevareid, with no strings attached, to go to China and come back and write and broadcast what he saw. What moved the "president's friend" to seek out the broadcaster? Most likely, FDR had not really delegated him to approach Sevareid on his behalf; rather, FDR had probably made an offhand remark like, "Too bad our friend Sevareid isn't over there," and someone present had imagined himself sent on a confidential mission. Eric had referred to Madame Chiang in a broadcast as "a great woman," but he was far from under her spell. Like most American liberals of his generation, he had read Vincent Sheean's description in *Personal History* (1934), based on his long visit in 1927, of the divided and foundering Chinese revolution and knew Sheean's conclusion that the Communists, rather than Chiang, seemed better guardian's of the revolution's ideals.

Most likely the invitation had been prompted by Sevareid's February 19, 1943, broadcast, the day on which Madame Chiang, at a press conference sitting next to FDR, who had just said he would increase our aid to China "as fast as the Lord would let us," quipped that "the Lord helps those who help themselves." Although he did not call it that on the air, Sevareid considered her remark an arrogant affront to the president, and he added that "there are people here who feel the Chinese could do more, now, to help themselves." Remarking on "China's hold on the emotions of the American public," he speculated—wrongly—that just as the invasion of North Africa proved to doubters that American will was firm, so perhaps "recent history in the West will be repeated in the East."

The Roosevelt circle's gamble in promoting a Sevareid mission was that a dose of Sevareid-delivered truth—even bad news—would either soften the greater shock of a later Chinese collapse or strengthen the president's hand by making public opinion demand more of the generalissimo. It is easy to see why Sevareid accepted. The assignment got him back into the action; he revered Roosevelt; and he did believe that a hard dose of the truth is often the best medicine for an ailing democracy.

He could not have foreseen the many levels on which the mission was doomed to fail—above all that for the next decade Chiang's fall to the Communists would be blamed on the handful of diplomats and journalists who had tried to tell the truth in the first place.

In July he got his war correspondent's uniform, passport, dogtags and portable typewriter and began the long, arduous flight across the South Atlantic to Ascension Island, to the Gold Coast of Africa, to Khartoum, to Eritrea, over the Red Sea to Aden, to New Delhi, then Ramgargh, and finally Chabua, the vital corner of Northeast India facing Burma and Tibet, at the foot of the Himalayas, and the jumping-off point of the lifeline to China.

For three months, all day he would scribble notes to himself on pads in tiny, indecipherable handwriting; much of the evening he would sit at his typewriter for hours and tap out, in minute detail, his observations and reflections. A small fraction of his notes would make it into broadcasts; but most of them would emerge in a variety of magazine articles and eventually be among the richest chapters of *Not So Wild a Dream*.

Two themes stand out in Sevareid's reflections on his long journey through the military bases and, for him, strange civilizations between Washington and Chungking: America's boys, the young military men as representatives of American culture, as both the embarrassment and the pride of their native land; and the decay of an older European culture, Britain's, in the context of its corrupt and withering colonial empire. Like the Mark Twain innocent abroad—though now a very worldly innocent—he is always making comparisons: this or that institution is like or unlike American democracy. And vividly etched individuals, a GI or a colonial official, become representative of a whole system of values. In a typical insight, he quotes the saying: "The British walk the earth as if they owned it; the Americans walk the earth as if they don't give a damn who owned it."

Those thousands of marvelous young men—twelve years his junior, they make him feel old—from Des Moines and Peoria filled him one minute with mild pique, as they ignorantly disparaged or insulted the cultures through which they swept; but most moments they filled him with awe, pushing his prose to rhapsodic heights. On the youngsters in the Air Transport Command:

> They measured the far horizons and calculated the heavens with their stubby schoolroom pencils. They peered through the majestic avenues of castellated cloud and wiped their dime-store colored spectacles. Their young eyes looked into the depths of mysterious seas and regarded the unfolding of the vast continents which showed on their faces the laboring of God's time and the hands of men, while they munched a wad of Wrigley's Spearmint, fingered the newly sprouted mustache, and wondered about its effect in Lauterbach's drugstore back in Des Moines. They knew the lines and corrugations of the ancient earth as they knew the palm of their hands, and took them equally for granted.

On Ascension Island they built an airstrip on a precipitous crag of pumice stone where British engineers said it couldn't be done. "Our men did it because they were the children of men who had tamed and settled the mountains, deserts, and forests of North America, after which nothing was impossible."

Delayed for a week in the Gold Coast, he worries about the sex lives of the soldiers. The boy canoeist who once claimed to have averted his eyes from girls swimming nude in the Red River now sees masculine sexuality as an energy that must be periodically expended, or else. Perhaps men in some other countries can, but American men, he says in *Not So Wild a Dream*, simply cannot do their work for hours without having women. The Red Cross girls are no solution; most are adventuresses who smile at enlisted men during the day and give their nights to the officers. The intelligent procedure, he suggests, would be to supply the troops with large numbers of "carefully regulated" prostitutes. Although he does not develop this suggestion fully, one might ask whether this basic need or right to satisfy one's sexual appetite belonged to married men separated from their wives as well.

Sevareid's discovery of the evils of colonialism echoes George Orwell's classic essays, "Shooting the Elephant" and "Marrakech." It is a system that both exploits the brown and yellow people and morally ruins the exploiter. In the Gold Coast he toured a hospital and viewed with horror the Negroes ravaged by venereal disease, tropical ulcers, and elephantiasis. Since the labor supply was abundant, the mine owners were content to let thousands of workers die of malaria each month rather than invest in prevention.

In New Delhi, where the British imperial rulers had imprisoned Gandhi and Nehru, imperialism had taken the form of fascism; the moral climate was poisoned and neurotic. The British administrators, he observed, were second-rate men who in London would be middle-class bureaucrats, but here constituted a ruling class consumed with a love for status and an irrational hatred for Gandhi. At a charming dinner party at a British official's home, a young Oxford man, the government whip in the legislature, explained why he hated Indian leaders. "Turn India over to them? My dear boy, you don't know what that means. Why—why, these villains would stab us in the back before we could get our families to the boat."

One of the most devastating passages Eric Sevareid ever wrote, one still bristling with anger over the class system he had endured at home, is his description of a party in the gardens of a wealthy Hindu industrialist, who had just given a large donation to the poorhouse and had gathered the local elite—who worshipped wealth "as abjectly as it ever was worshipped in America"—to celebrate his generosity. The event took place on October 31, on his way home from the East; but he describes it in *Not So Wild a Dream* as if it were part of his journey to China.

> Officials who were capable of casting the Christlike Nehru into jail fawned upon this man and murmured: "Hear, Hear!" to the humorous speech of the Jam Saheb of Nawanager, a kind of super-wealthy Irvin Cobb, who jested with our host about his money in the traditional banter of rich men anywhere, while the pure emerald buttons twinkled on his enormous, shaking belly. A few

withered bodies, stupefied by hunger and disease, had been shoved out of sight into the poorhouse and, with this as an excuse, fat and powerful men gathered to congratulate one another upon their fat and their power. I had seen essentially the same thing in Minneapolis; it was no less indecent here.

The British had to go, Sevareid concluded; but meanwhile the Americans had not blended in smoothly. Americans and British officers competed for the few available white women. The influx of American dollars disrupted the order of the social structure. Paradoxically—and tragically—the arrival of Americans brightened the hopes of the subject masses who thought that American freedom and democracy would follow; but soon the Americans, worn down by heat and native inefficiency, and softened by easy living, became as arrogant and selfish as the British, and American freedom became one more myth. It also became clear that just as Chiang was saving the Chinese army to fight the Communists later, England, rather than commit the two-million-man Indian army to the proposed attack on Burma and China, was saving it to keep the Indian masses under the British heel.

Once out of New Delhi, however, Sevareid could be thrilled by the brave men actually fighting the war. At Ramgargh, Stilwell was retraining Chiang's starved and spiritless army into a real force. In Chabua in Assam, however, the listless British planters lacked the togetherness of North Dakota farmers, while the Americans and natives slaved in heat and rain to get supplies to China.

Here he heard the inspiring—and terrifying—stories about the struggle to cut the Ledo Road through the mountains and jungle to link up with the Burma Road, and of the pilots who, sometimes twice a day, flew scores of three-hour trips through ice-capped Himalaya peaks, over Japanese- and headhunter-infested jungles to China. He listened to tales about men whose planes went down, who were rescued, who hiked out, or who disappeared forever.

Sevareid's flight on August 2 consisted of twenty-one men—military men and a handful of high officials, including John Paton Davies; Captain Duncan Lee, a Rhodes scholar OSS man; and William Stanton, of the Board of Economic Welfare.

Eric's first reaction to the fact that the plane was going to crash had been, "Oh, no, no! Oh, no! This can't happen to me, not to *me!*" But even as the crew bailed out he found himself still furiously writing down notes, through sheer force of habit. Davies, who had provided some moral leadership by being the first to jump, had kept his calm through the general panic. While Eric shouted that it was useless to continue on to China without their baggage, Davies stoically remarked, "Just kids, just kids running this thing," and jumped.

As Eric's parachute opened and the shock jolted his eyes open, he heard his own voice shouting in the silence, "My God, I'm going to live!" As the wind pulled him toward the site of the burning plane, he prayed again, "Dear God, don't let the fire get me. Please!" Eric had not prayed in a long while, but his prayers were heard. He plunged through the trees and landed unhurt.

Then suddenly realizing his predicament—lost and alone with no food or weapons—he went hysterical, plunging through the underbrush, trying to scream for help but with no sound emanating from his throat. He accepted the fact that he might die. Then he thought of Lois and Peter and Michael, forgot himself, and began calculating his savings and insurance. Would he leave them enough to be cared for?

Within minutes some of the other survivors, for the time being eleven, some bleeding, began to appear, including the pilot Lieutenant Harry Neveu, who had a map, and the radio operator, Sergeant Walter Oswalt, who had radioed their position at the last minute, and whose leg was broken. Near the wreck they failed to find the copilot, Lieutenant Charles Felix, who had gone down with the plane, but they did find Eric's typewriter—melted. Thanks to Oswalt's persistence, within an hour of the crash a rescue plane zoomed overhead and dropped survival tools, two rifles, a radio, and a note: *Stay where you are until a rescue party reaches you.*

These orders became moot when fifteen or twenty short, brown, naked men with deep chests and straight black hair, and spears, came singing and marching through the bush. Sevareid, realizing that he was uninjured and that his mind worked faster than the others, had instinctively assumed leadership of the crew. As a soldier survivor, William Schrandt, remembers him fifty years later, "Eric Sevareid was in my estimation a very well educated mid-westerner who was not a leader, but by his presence, evoked some leadership. He was a big man and older than most of us, but he did his walking up and down mountains with the best of us." He greeted the natives with a "How!" as if they were in a western movie. It worked; the natives smiled and transported them to their village. As Schrandt recalls, "They took control of our lives immediately." In the village, a tall, dark warrior with a magnificent physique brought them a message from John and Duncan who had landed on the other side of the mountain; Eric sent an answer asking them to join their group.

The next message from the airdrop emphasized: *Do not go to the native village, as they probably are not friendly.* Too late. The natives, who turned out to be the fierce headhunters, the Nagas, had already made them at home. That evening, just as the crew was settling down, a plane came by again and three men dropped down. As he rushed to meet them, Eric was moved to tears at the thought that his countrymen would voluntarily plunge into this danger to share their fate. Their leader was thirty-seven-year-old Lt. Col. Don D. Flickinger, a doctor who knew they needed medical help. Sevareid the uncomfortable leader of men quickly let the colonel take charge.

That night, by the light of torches and the village fire, as a hundred pair of native eyes stared through the cracks of the bamboo hut, Flickinger set Oswalt's leg, treated leech wounds, and taught an old native man, whose child had an abscessed ear, how to chew the medicine for the child and spit it down the child's throat.

Exhausted, Eric lay in his wet clothes and listened to the pouring rain—only to be awakened at midnight by distant yelling and torches. In a second, John Davies, with Duncan and three others, stood before him beaming, "Doctor Sevareid, I presume." They had survived not only the seven-mile hike in the dark but their village's hospitality, which had required them to drink the warm blood from the body of a freshly decapitated goat.

The next day they found the body of Charles Felix and buried it on the hillside. Flickinger had taken charge and appointed Eric chaplain.

At one time, as a boy, Eric had considered a vocation to the Lutheran ministry. It made sense: there was a prominent minister in his family history, and he had always been idealistic. To be a minister would give him both the freedom and the status to speak publicly on what was right and wrong. But now, as a self-described "back-slidden Lutheran," he re-sisted—but, on orders, played the role nonetheless.

Unlike many other autobiographers, this very private person did not record the process of his religious disaffection. But in a 1954 introduction he wrote for Daniel Lang's book on social impact of atomic power, *The Man in the Thick Lead Suit*, Sevareid says that Lang's conversations with Wernher Von Braun recreated an almost mystic experience of his youth.

Once when dozing through a freshman lecture at the university, Eric had seen in a flash of intuition that man would never discover the secret of the universe or the origin of life. As he lost this insight in later years, he realized that this loss was due to the waning of his religious instinct. Man can only label his mysteries—as energy or matter—he cannot un-derstand them. This, says Von Braun, is because "any real scientist ends up a religious man." Sevareid, accepting Von Braun's observation, seems to imply that where scientific knowledge ends religious imagination begins.

This is not merely a variation of the God-of-the-gaps theology, wherein the idea of God "answers" the universe's unanswerable mys-teries—a theology common in the nineteenth century, but not held by modern theologians. Rather, it seems to be an acknowldgment that one's religious instinct is an avenue toward a deeper understanding of the universe. Eric does not explain how or why his own religious in-stinct waned; one can surmise that, although he was confirmed, his Lutheranism was inherited rather than fully chosen, or that, as he be-came centered on his career and his advancement, what he had learned in confirmation class no longer seemed to apply.

Commenting on Sevareid's character more than fifty years later, Davies observed that the deepest element of Eric's personality was his sense of himself as a professional newsman, his drive to get the story and then to consider its meaning. In that sense, his quest for news had be-come his quest for transcendent truth. But now, in a foreshadowing of his later role as America's TV conscience, he found himself playing a role which, in the public's mind, seemed to fit him, whether it truly matched his character or not.

So, at 11 A.M., the time he remembered going to church at home, on Sunday, August 8, 1943, chaplain Sevareid constructed a large cross and conducted a memorial service for Felix. They read two psalms: the 107th—"the Lord brings us home from foreign countries"—and 23rd —"the Lord is my shepherd." Then they recited the Lord's Prayer, and he led the men in singing "Holy, Holy, Holy, Lord God Almighty," which he remembered from his youth. He sensed that the men had been feeling the drama of their salvation and needed a way to express it. He felt uncomfortable, in that his clerical role had separated him more from the men, but he felt better when the colonel told him the men had been consoled and when Davies said he was really moved. That night Eric and Duncan sat together by the fire and agreed they were glad this stupid accident had happened to them; it had helped narrow the gap between them and the fighting men. A few days later some visiting tribesmen wanted to use the cross as a target in their spear-throwing contest; but they were dissuaded.

For two weeks the twenty survivors, now joined by Corporal Lemmon, whom the natives delivered on a stretcher on the fourth day, settled into the routine of village life. They encamped on the edge of the native compound, called Pangsha, encircled their turf with a bamboo barrier, stood guard around the clock, watched for Japanese planes, picked up the bales of provisions the American planes, storming in at no more than fifty feet off the ground, dropped off almost daily—a radio receiver (the transmitter broke), rice, tea, socks, shoes, guns, books, magazines, undershirts, canned goods, an excellent waterproofed map, plus precious rock salt as a gift to pacify their hosts. When the ATC airdrop dumped a bundle of carbines for them, to protect themselves from the headhunters, the bundle missed, tumbled down a hill a half-mile away, and landed by the river. The headhunters fetched it.

When the men ran out of toilet paper they used a mimeographed monograph on world organization for peace from Davies' briefcase, which the natives had found and returned intact. They bartered with the natives with tin cans and silk cloth from their parachutes; and although some of the enlisted men rudely treated the natives like children, the colonel's leadership and Davies' unflagging diplomacy smoothed what could have been a difficult—even fatal—relationship between the troops and their hosts. When the natives festively slaughtered a bull—one boy repeatedly stuck his bare toe in the dying bull's eye—the colonel took off his shirt and expertly skinned the beast himself; and, as the village listened solemnly, the Americans sang "I Been Working on the Rail-road" and the "Star-Spangled Banner."

All day and much of the evening they hovered around Oswalt's radio receiver and listened to Benny Goodman's music coming from San Francisco, Bob Hope, Glen Miller and, nearly every day, a distress call from another plane going down somewhere in the jungle.

Eric, scribbling each day's events into the diary, with pens and ink he has scrounged from everyone, caustically remarks: "Suppose the Wash-ington columnists still bleeding into their typewriters about our not trying to get supplies to Chinese." On August 10 he records: "Long dis-cussions around fire at night. Talk about kinds of women we have known (no names), how different movie stars look in the flesh, Winston Churchill, Clare Luce, restaurants and dishes and drinks, socialized med-icine, democracy. Flick [colonel] thinks democracy expensive luxury, I think it basic necessity. Typical locker-room talk. Passes the time." On August 11, "Stars, full moon at night. We sang for hours. At such mo-ments I love it here, wouldn't be elsewhere."

But the colonel was training them, with daily calisthenics and tactical drills on how to combat Japanese paratroopers, for the trek out. Then one Saturday afternoon, just as the survivors' spirits were at their lowest, out of the fog came the low chanting of many voices, which grew louder and louder. A hundred dark, glistening, naked bodies emerged from the ravine and engulfed their camp. Before them stood, like a blond god, the tall, slender, dashing form of a white man, with firm bronzed legs, with soft blue eyes, wearing a blue polo shirt and shorts and low walking shoes. A long cigarette holder dangled from his hand-some face. He spoke in an Oxford accent and looked like Leslie Howard. He was twenty-nine-year old Philip Adams, the British Sahib of Mokokchung, the "king" of these savage hills, leading a hundred-man rescue party of coolies and sixty Nagas armed with shotguns.

They had pressed on at double time, eighty-five miles in five days, be-cause, unknown to Eric and the others, Pangsha and the neighboring village of Ponyo, where Davies had landed, had been quarreling over the fate of their guests. The previous year the Ponyos had taken a hundred and six heads from neighboring villages. Some of their young hotheads were urging an attack. Several years before, the British, under Adams, had burned down the Pangsha village to punish them for their raids.

They had made peace six months before, but it was not clear how long the truce would hold.

In long conversations with Adams, Eric learned about the Nagas and analyzed them, comparing them to "civilized" races, according to his own categories. They wage their wars for the same reasons as civilized nations, but they keep their treaties and do not torture their prisoners. They have maintained relative peace not because of "education" or "spiritual regeneration" but because of the rule of law backed by force. They have a highly developed sense of personal honor and integrity. Stealing is almost unknown among them. When sentenced to jail, they are simply given a slip and they report on their own. A Naga is very reluctant to insult another man, lest it "make his mind hurt." They are "instinctively democratic." They convince Eric that equality and tolerance are deeply rooted human instincts, and he suspects that the accumulation of capital goods would split them into conflicting social classes, concentrate political power, and kill their true democracy.

Adams had acquired a deep love and respect for these "savages"; and Sevareid, who was characteristically drawn to powerful men who also possessed some spiritual qualities, quickly acquired a profound respect for Adams. He says in *Not So Wild a Dream*, "For me, he takes a place among the few rare men I have known, of limitless courage, unfettered mind, and controlled compassion for others—the great, lonely men, some in the spotlight, others in obscurity, who are everywhere and always the same, devoted co-workers in the difficult and dangerous conspiracy of goodwill."

Compassion, apparently, had to be controlled, lest it render the hero soft. Adams had to be willing occasionally to burn native villages to keep order; and when the Ponyos asked him for permission to massacre a distant village who had slandered them, Adams, knowing the other village was out of his jurisdiction, left it up to the Ponyos. When a fight almost broke out on the last day over food and cloth the party was leaving behind, Adams single-handedly thrashed the instigators and distributed the spoils among the chiefs.

On August 18, their column stretching almost two miles through the twisting trails, the expedition began its 140-mile, ten-day march out. For days, from first light till last, they climbed steep hills and slid down the other side, forded streams and cataracts, wilted under the broiling sun, got sick from drinking too much water, each wondering whether he would be the next to collapse by the side of the road. The natives carried the weak in litters. Eric endured huge, painful blisters on the soles of both feet. For him endurance became a moral test as much as a physical one. "It is the Manitoba canoe thing all over again," he wrote to himself. "Damn this phony Norwegian pride and dignity complex, causes me great suffering." The colonel treated their cuts and flea bites and Davies kept rousing their spirits with jokes and songs.

The second day out, they cut their way, carbines ready, through a jungle pass known for headhunter ambushes. At the home of Sangbah, one of Adams's Naga colleagues, they all got drunk on a native liquor, *zu*; and Eric slept little that night as pigs rooted under his cot and rats ran across his chest. The next day he could tell he was losing control: he began to see specks and babble about why does ice cream taste better in a cone than in a dish. The colonel caught him as he fell and dragged him to the side of the road. As William Schrandt recalls the moment, "I do remember one time he turned green from exhaustion."

Why did some men endure better than others? Eric asked himself. What extra something made a man superior? Was it that one, a Mormon, has religious faith? Or Stanton's country club, polo-playing lifestyle?

On August 22, grinding a hand-cranked wireless set that was dropped from a plane, correspondent Sevareid sent out the first story on the ordeal, four hundred words to the United Press. Its lead sentence summed up both the drama and paradox of their adventure: "Burmese jungle headhunters, every one a primitive killer, saved our lives. . . ." On the final days, as they trekked through villages, they realized that the danger was over. The Chinese colonel, Kwoh Li, who himself had inspired the others by refusing to be carried despite injuries to his feet, through Davies, sent Sevareid a compliment: it was remarkable that a literary man should be such a good soldier. Davies replied that in America literary men are not content with literature, but try to emulate soldiers, explorers, and bullfighters.

At Mokokchung a few of them dined at Adams's home, listened to Frank Sinatra on the radio, sipped brandy and talked of London, New York, and the Nagas. How far should civilization be allowed to bring its so-called benefits to these happy people? So far, they said, "civilization" had been represented by Baptist missionaries, who had taught them that their seminudity was shameful and replaced their stirring chants with dull hymns. The natives lost their roots, stole, told lies, and fell into debauchery. Adams had only one fear about returning India to Indian rule: what would Hindu politicians and traders do to innocent Nagas?

A few days later, as the party tramped deeper into India, a delegation of fellow journalists marched out to meet them—Frank Martin of the Associated Press, Albert Ravenholt of United Press, James Shepley of *Time,* and finally the *New Yorker* writer, St. Clair McKelway, whose joking messages had helped keep Eric's spirits a little lighter during the ordeal. It was the party's first realization that their story had been followed by the world.

The next morning a fleet of jeeps and trucks and a battery of cameras confronted them. Eric Sevareid was pulled before a microphone and asked to speak. Somehow now, in front of the basic instrument of his profession, he felt more sick and exhausted than on any day during the whole hike. He had lost fifteen pounds. As he summed up the experience in a nineteen-page summary cable to CBS, their accident and rescue had meant weeks of work for hundreds of Americans, the disruption of thousands of natives' lives. They remembered their hosts in the hills with affection. The Nagas could have followed their normal procedure and killed them, but they helped them to live.

Back at Chabua, Sevareid, according to his notes, seemed depressed to be back to "this is where I came in," to be fighting with censors already on how much of his story he could get out, and too tired to collect his thoughts and write. Into this glum atmosphere walked a group of touring United States senators, including Henry Cabot Lodge, whom Eric knew, and "Happy" Chandler from Kentucky, whom he had never met in his life but who insisted on grabbing his hands in his "fat, moist fingers" and blurting, with a politician's obvious insincerity, that he had prayed for Eric every night.

Inevitably, local enthusiasm for the group's reported heroism had its limits. Troops and fellow journalists griped that Eric and the others had had it easy out there, with those daily supply drops, and that the government had poured more resources into their rescue because of the "famous people," like Davies and Sevareid, in their party.

With Flick—whom he considered "the most normal man I ever knew," a lover of horses, guns, and dogs, who had decided long ago that he could not solve the deeper issues of life and now exudes supreme self-confidence—he retreated to Calcutta, to rest, treat his wounds, and write—Eric pounded out a six-thousand-word story in twelve hours while Flick kept a party going in their room. And then he had to try once more to fly into China without crashing.

By the second week in September Sevareid was in the air and over the Hump again; this time over the northern route in the company of a general and the same pilots who had brought in Wendell Willkie the year before on his celebrated visit to Chiang Kai-shek—a visit likely inspired by an FDR gesture to flatter someone with a "mission." But even the best pilots couldn't control the weather, and they had to endure two hours in the fog, stacked up with twenty-two other planes, over Kunming at seventeen thousand feet, while one of the planes above them ran out of fuel and had to be ditched. Again, Eric got sick and took to bed with a fever.

His fellow correspondents, the absentminded St. Clair McKelway and the corpulent little playwright Charles MacArthur, who had often kept him up all night drinking and laughing in Calcutta, arrived the next day, followed by the top generals, including Stilwell, from the whole China-Burma-India theater of war for a conference with Chennault. That evening the reporters dined with the brass in Chennault's austere house, while the military men told airplane stories and listened to news commentators from San Francisco discuss the collapse of Italy.

As was his custom, Sevareid hung back making mental notes; he checked out the general's library and noted his tennis equipment and oil portrait on the wall. He sized up the character and intelligence of the men in the room. The "intellectuals," MacArthur and McKelway—whom he particularly admired for having actually joined the army rather than remain civilians—with their hesitant speech and deference in the presence of rank, though in many ways superior, seemed inferior to the "men of action." He, on the other hand, unhindered by military rank, felt he could talk with generals on even terms.

The next morning, September 11, Sevareid delivered the first of four broadcasts from Chungking. China, he found, did correspond to his childhood images, inspired by picture books in the Velva and Minneapolis libraries, of this mythical land, with its round, red, and finished soil.

But Chungking did not. After six years of war, it was ugly beyond words, a battered, impoverished, war-worn city, where all the colors were gray and black—painted black as a camouflage to confuse Japanese bombers.

Millions swarmed through the gray dust of the streets, where, except for the privileged few with cars and a few others who rode rickshaws, everyone walked. Rather than horses, three or four men with rigid muscles in their legs pulled heavy wagons as their sweat mingled in the dust at their feet. Thousands still lived in cliff-side caves where they had fled to escape the bombs. Because, when the Japanese captured all the great cities on the coast, China had had to move its capital so far inland, he told his listeners, it was as if St. Paul had taken the place of Washington, D.C. With John Davies he stood on a terrace over the Yangtze River: "As we watched the immense panorama of this pulsating hive of people, you could not escape this sensation: that for the uncounted Chinese, this was only an episode in their ancient story, a brief distraction in their unquenchable life."

There was really no way in which he could like or be comfortable in Chungking. His aesthetic instincts shrank from ugliness. Since he was always quick to spot a handsome male face or a beautiful woman, a beautiful boulevard or city bridge, there was little in this forsaken city of starving soldiers, garbage-strewn alleys, and air heavy with the stench of exhaust from alcohol-driven busses, to please his sense, except the sunset—when, he told his listeners, "the two great rivers which enfold the city flow red and golden with a million tiny flames dancing on their rushing currents, and then the bare mountain peaks nearby soften and purple as the day grows misty with night. . . ."

But privately, he was miserable. For days, like other members of his party, he was in bed with dysentery, aggravated by every Chinese meal; and he was losing weight steadily. On Sunday night, October 3, after finishing E. M. Forster's *A Passage to India*, he told his notes: "I should be beside myself with loneliness and despair after six months here . . . it is the loneliness of this room that bothers me . . . you yearn for a brightly lighted, warm, cheerful room . . . it is hard for me to take solace in my work; I just snatch at it as I do at a cigarette and the relief is only passing. . . ."

Part of his problem was that the reporter-intellectual had to deal with an intellectual problem with emotional overtones. From what point of view, both politically and morally, was he to evaluate what he was learning in the six weeks of interviews, press conferences, broadcasts, real and staged news events (the huge, tumultuous welcome afforded Wendell Willkie, he learned, had been staged), bull sessions with servicemen and fellow journalists, and just plain exploring the streets?

Among the foreign observers, the scholarly community—and Sevareid the self-taught historian could share their thought patterns—viewed the corruption, hypocrisy, despotism, and passivity within the context of centuries. What Westerners called graft and duplicity were really cultural differences, tradition, face-saving. The tyranny of the Kuomintang government was stability, the closest a country with a history of tyrants could come to democracy. Their failure to fight the Japanese was their way of enduring just another wave of invaders who, like the others, would fade away in time.

But Sevareid quickly opted for the correspondent's mentality: trust one's own judgment to evaluate the evidence in front of one's eyes. He had seen that not all the Chinese were lazy and corrupt. Since China claimed membership in the modern world, he would judge it by modern democratic standards; and he found it evil.

To make things worse, like the fascists in Brazil, government authorities took all criticisms as personal attacks. In August, the *New York Times* military writer Hanson Baldwin had written a piece on the China situation for *Readers' Digest,* which had been planted there to prepare public opinion for what Sevareid might discover in the fall; but Chinese reaction to it had shown that they had no idea of "objective" journalism, that a writer might say something simply because he believed it. To the Chinese, everything had subjective implications.

Generalissimo Chiang, Sevareid concluded, was a great historical figure, a symbol of unity; but, as he prepared his October 10 broadcast report on Chiang's inauguration as president of the republic, he concluded, but of course could not say, that the Kuomintang government was fundamentally fascist. The small, slim, neat man read his colorless speech in a high singsong voice and went through the motions of allowing a member of the People's Political Council to "answer" him. He was like Hitler in his talk of "one leader, one party, one nation," and like Pétain in his desire to return to an outdated, feudal society. If Chiang was the man *of* the hour, he decided, he was not the man *for* the hour.

As the young Vincent Sheean had done in 1927, he sought out Madame Sun Yat-sen, widow of, as Sevareid referred to him, the "Chinese George Washington." Between 1911 and his death in 1925, the

Western-educated Sun Yat-sen, based on the principles of nationalism, democracy, and socialism, founded the Kuomintang Party, and, in an alliance with the Communists, became the founder of modern China. Madame Sun Yet-sen was a member of the Soong family, one of three daughters of T. V. Soong, a Harvard-educated Chinese statesman and businessman devoted to the Kuomintang. Of his three sisters, one, a graduate of Wellesley College, in 1927 married Chiang Kai-shek, who established himself as Sun Yat-sen's successor. Another, educated at Wesleyan, married Sun Yat-sen in Japan, and after his death in 1925, stayed with the Kuomintang until they expelled the Communists in 1927. She became reconciled in 1939, and was living in an uncomfortable truce with Chiang when Sevareid visited her in October.

Eric was struck by the sight of a "famous name and gallant heart" living in a fake-modern house, "within a dusty, ramshakle courtyard littered with broken-down, rusting trucks, squawking chickens, and naked neighborhood children." He saw her as a hostage to fascism and a rallying point of democracy. Though her beauty had faded (born in 1890, she was only fifty-three!), in conversation—as often occurred in a conversation with Eleanor Roosevelt—her countenance took on an inexpressible sweetness. She spoke of the thousands of peasants dying from a famine the authorities denied and of the liberal professors and students dying of malnutrition while businessmen and generals got rich on the profits of wartime inflation. After several days of negotiations, Sevareid got her to agree to broadcast her ideas to the world; but, the day before, she pulled out. Whatever her intellectual freedom, she was still physically in jail. Eventually she split with the Kuomintang; in 1949, after Chiang Kai-shek retreated to Formosa, she became a non-Communist member of the Central Committee of the Peoples' Republic of China, received the Stalin Peace Prize in 1951, and lived into the 1980s.

One day, with Brooks Atkinson of the *New York Times*, Sevareid made his way to the Chungking Communist headquarters, and there he was dazzled by an encounter with a tall, willowy woman with glossy black hair, named Kung Peng, dressed in a simple gray cotton gown, so overpowering in her presence that what would have been sexual attraction was replaced by awe and admiration. Her Communist husband had been captured by the Japanese and had died; and now any number of foreign correspondents and diplomats imagined that they were in love with her. To Eric, she was a "woman of soul and exalted vision," and he and his colleagues debated ways to rescue her, perhaps get her to the United States on a scholarship. On one of their last evenings together she said, "If only I could be for a little while in a place where there is freedom, just to see what it is like again for a little while." Her words gave Eric that old feeling of uselessness; once again he was the ineffectual liberal, the writer, while others were making real sacrifices for the ideals about which he wrote.

Finally, he left with strong impressions of Stilwell, whom he interviewed early, in mid September, and whom he had been turning over daily in his mind and in discussions with fellow correspondents. He saw Stilwell at home in the evening. The general, with his close-cropped hair and thin shoulders, crouched over his desk in an almost bare room, save for the enlarged photographs on the wall of his Chinese troops being trained at Ramgarh. They talked for hours as the general pulled on cigarettes and popped peanuts into his mouth, and Eric had that sense that he occasionally got with "great men," like General Marshall, that here was a man with a "white flame," and one with an "impossible ideal of what a true soldier ought to be." He was the general who had led his troops out of Burma on foot and who remained contemptuous of the younger officers who could not keep up with him. Clearly, Sevaried sympathized with Stilwell's position; but he seemed to sense that Stilwell's refusal or inability to use diplomacy or persuasion doomed his mission to failure.

Meanwhile Sevareid's biggest frustration was his inability to get his story to the American people. Broadcasting facilities in Chungking and throughout China were so primitive that Chungking broadcasts reached perhaps only a few thousand people, and any number of Sevareid's broadcasts to the United States were never received. In mid October Theodore H. "Teddy" White of *Time-Life*, who later became one of Eric's most trusted friends, returned from two months in Chinese Turkestan with a story on how the Russians were pulling out of there, determined to eliminate any points of friction with the Chinese; but White was told that the generalissimo himself would have to examine his story before he could send it out. The generalissimo had been too busy to give Eric even the customary fifteen minutes he usually concedes to foreign correspondents; but he had time to pore over a *Time* reporter's stuff!

On his last night in Chungking, as Eric made his way through the rain to his billet, he listened to a woman coughing and a man trying to vomit, and despaired of understanding this land where he was not meant to be. Then, he says in *Not So Wild a Dream*, he spied a child, an orphan standing motionless in a dark corner and, reaching once more for a symbol to sum up a larger concept, decided that this child *was* China, "of mysterious origin and incomprehensible destination, timeless, old and young, suffering and saying nothing, patient in the rain, with straw and the sky between him and eternity." And he muttered a prayer, "Oh Christ, this land of China!," though it was not clear to him what God could ease this pain.

On October 12 he flew back to Kunming, where he enjoyed his first hot shower and shampoo in six weeks, to learn that the day before the Japanese had started fighter attacks on the unescorted transports flying across the Hump. Lord Admiral Louis Mountbatten, the Earl of Burma, and great-grandson of Queen Victoria, the new commander of Allied forces in the Far East, had just arrived on his way to charm Chiang Kai-shek, and at the sight of Sevareid and Brooks Atkinson, jumped out of his car and bounced over to Eric demanding to hear about his "jungle jump" in August. Clearly here was not a representative of the old British colonialism that had so appalled Eric throughout his trip. They sat up together in the evening and drank cocktails and talked grand strategy. It was obvious, said Eric, that the next Allied invasion would be into Sicily.

"Quite," replied Mountbatten. "But you know—we *almost* went to Sardinia."

And in Kunming Eric sat back again and made his notes on American boys—the fliers with their firm faces and clear skin, white teeth and steady eyes, who insulted one another casually with the grossest obscenities, but with a steady smile. Was their nonchalance an American cult? American boys, he wrote in his notes, cannot dissimulate, they have no "front" or pose that carries them unchanged through all conditions; "their only pose is complete naturalness."

At Kunming the Americans ran a Chinese infantry training school to which boys of fourteen or fifteen had marched five hundred miles, their feet wrapped in rags, to try to learn the simplest routines—don't close your eyes when you aim your rifle—which the average American Boy Scout knows at an earlier age. In one instance an American colonel interrupted his class to send officers who had been sleeping at their desks back to their barracks. Later he learned that, in punishment for snoozing, they had been shot.

In the crowded streets of the town, coolies picked up the bodies of the dead poor, covered them with burlap, and carted them away, their feet sticking out from the makeshift shrouds.

On October 18, the correspondents flew to the airbase at Kweilin, far down in southeastern China near the Japanese-occupied coast—an old walled city renowned for its exotic mountain formations, like green, separate, Gothic spires jutting up from the plain. It was both the "spy capital" and the "sex capital" of free China, with a nightclub and brothel —enlisted men one night, officers the next—right near the base. But on the flight down the weather forced them to stay over at a fighter field at Lingling, where they enjoyed a raucous dinner party with a bunch of young pilots and their twenty-three-year-old commander Captain Elsner.

The boys drank raw wine and ate burned steaks and spouted playful obscenities in one anothers' faces like a bunch of college freshmen; and again the reserved, senior Sevareid felt himself at the emotional edge of the group. At their earlier bull session in Elsner's room, the floor covered with cigarette butts, they had talked about their losses—recently six planes had gone out and only one returned—and complained about not knowing when, if ever, they might get home. One rosy-cheeked boy had turned to Eric and asked, "Can you go home any time you wish to?" He had dreaded that question. They just couldn't understand why he did not want to go back to the states.

Clearly the men worshipped their captain; and the correspondent, too, as he tended to do with strong men, held him in a kind of awe: these men were a brotherhood, he told himself—it is a thing to see and never to be forgotten, more evidence in his emerging interpretation of something grand that was happening to America in its war years. But in the face of these high jinks a melancholy thought struck him as well: some of these men were going to die. Two weeks later word would reach him in New Delhi that Elsner had been killed.

And what did these boys think of the tall, dark correspondent who drank in their every word and gesture, yet was clearly not one of them? According to Davies, they were delighted to have him there. He was a celebrity, and he was genuinely interested in them and flattered them by his attention. Furthermore, he was very amiable, good company.

On his last day in Kunming, Sevareid settled down for a private hour with Chennault and found the legend more impressive than the man. He was less inspiring than Stilwell, a narrow tactician rather than an imaginative strategist, a man respected by his subordinates but not loved.

Aside from those few exhilarating moments when he had admired either the courage of American fighting men, or the endurance of Lieutenant Colonel Kwoh Li, for whom he wrote a letter of recommendation as soon as he got home, or the primitive nobility of the Nagas, Sevareid ended his Burma-China adventure with few positive reflections, and with his Jeffersonian liberalism, which he thought had served him well in debates with decadent Americans in Rio, shaken to its roots. Personal contact with crooked Chinese had taught the American troops to despise their Oriental "brothers." And the young man who had learned political science from Lippincott and Laski was no longer confident that the wisdom of the Enlightenment could apply to a culture so impoverished that it could think of nothing but trying to put something in its belly lest it die. He sensed that perhaps the West's slow medicine of education and tolerance could not compete with Russian Communism's promise of a more drastic surgical cure.

On the flight back to Chabua he fought his fear of crashing again, worried out loud when one of the engines didn't sound right, and took his turn watching for Japanese Zeros. In New Delhi, sick and tired, and thirty pounds lighter than in August, he checked into the hospital and started working on a series of articles that he hoped would achieve the original purpose of his trip.

For nine days, beginning on November 4, 1943, Eric lived in the tail section of an old Liberator, the *Rangoon Rambler*, which—with stops at Cairo, Tripoli, Marrakech, Dakar (where the Frenchmen looked shabby but the women attractive), and Natal—flew him home. As they passed over the Holy Land, the Bible places—the Dead Sea, Galilee, and Jerusalem—looked just as they had on the colored cards he had studied in Sunday school in Velva. For several days he and his fellow passengers were sick with diarrhea. Over Africa he read Churchill's *Early Life* and Stendhal's *The Red and the Black*. On November 13, at the end of a bitterly cold flight from Miami, over the purpling foliage of the Carolinas, the plane delivered Sevareid, terribly sick to his stomach, home to Washington. Coming into Bolling Air Force Base, the plane almost crashed.

Now his job was to write. In the *New Republic* he analyzed the Chinese economy, its skyrocketing inflation, where an American dollar would buy only a half-pack of cigarettes or six sheets of typing paper; and he exposed the scandalous but thriving trade between Free China and the Japanese. A long feature article on the Hump stressed the gallantry of the flyers, but also made its political points: don't complain about our not doing enough to get aid to China. He had sold his Burma adventure to *Vogue* for five hundred dollars until *Reader's Digest* called and offered him ten thousand! He sheepishly called *Vogue* and said it could hold him to his agreement if it wished, but . . .

But the crushing blow was the fate of the thirty-five-hundred word essay in which he did what he had been sent to do: he courageously but fairly spelled out his negative assessment of the Chinese army and the Chiang Kai-shek regime. He explained that it was not true that millions of Chinese were holding back millions of Japanese; rather the Japanese had taken as much of China as they could conveniently administer. China was not a unified country and its revolution for democracy had been forgotten. The Communists, not the Chungking government, had given Chinese people civil rights. China's young men resist military service; no one with education or a job is conscripted. The generalissimo does not really lead all of China, he is more a "balance wheel." Japanese spies have radio transmitters in all the major cities. More Chinese soldiers die from malnutrition than from enemy bullets. Because of the controlled press, the Chinese people "see nothing, they read nothing which is real and vital about their own terrible problems of living." If the Chinese and American people are to remain friends, we must end the "polite lying, the false propaganda and the concealing of fault."

The War Department censors killed his exposé outright. He cut offending passages and tried again, got approval, only to have the piece killed again by the State Department. Angry and frustrated, Sevareid negotiated for months into 1944 and in March left for Europe hoping, wrongly, that it would appear.

It is hard to say today what the piece's impact would have been. There was so much resistance to what he had to say in both the public mind and in various reaches of the administration that it might have been but one more shout in the storm. Davies does not think the essay would have had much impact at the time. When Teddy White in 1945 declined to write a soft article on Chiang for *Time*, he was called home and split with Luce—partly over China policy. A year later, White's book, *Thunder Out of China*, written with Annalee Jacoby, stirred great controversy because of their criticisms of Chiang. But in 1944 the political climate was not right.

We do know what happened. Roosevelt, concentrating on Europe, moved back and forth in his China policy. He had backed Chennault's air strategy; but after the Cairo Conference in 1943, the Joint Chiefs of Staff, convinced that the route to Japan lay through the Pacific, no longer believed the Chinese army was essential for victory.

In January 1944, Allied forces, including Stilwell's Chinese-American Army, invaded Burma. Progress was slow but, by August 1944, Stilwell's troops had taken Myitkyina, where there were three airfields. This meant planes previously sent over the Hump could be rerouted, avoiding the Himalayas and shortening the route. Under the overall leadership of Mountbatten, the rest of Burma was retaken by May 1945, a remarkable campaign that called for a half-million men, the special jungle training of Chinese and American troops, close coordination of ground and air forces that dropped in supplies and flew out casualties, and considerable feats of engineering—all things which Sevareid, in his few weeks there, had seen and experienced firsthand.

At Chiang's request, Roosevelt sent Major General Patrick J. Hurley to try to reconcile Stilwell and Chiang. This proved impossible, and in October 1944 Roosevelt replaced Stilwell with Major General Albert C. Wedemeyer. On October 29, Sevareid, who was then broadcasting from London, marked Stilwell's departure with an analysis: Stilwell, he said whatever his diplomatic problems, believed two things passionately: "That Japan must be defeated on the soil of China and that the Chinese army, despite its unbelievable state of inefficiency, could be hammered into an effective fighting force. That was his mission and his dream."

But Chiang's political victory was short-lived. His reputation in the United States suffered; Wedemeyer continued Stilwell's criticisms of Chinese passivity; inflation got worse; Chennault was eased out by Spring 1945; and the Communists strengthened their position in the north. With the fall of Japan, full-scale civil war erupted; the very factors that Sevareid had tried to point out—the Nationalists' corruption and alienation from the masses of the Chinese people—led to total Communist victory in 1950 when Chiang's Nationalist government fled to Formosa.

As Barbara W. Tuchman describes that period in *Stilwell and the American Experience in China, 1911–1945* (1970), "No sooner was Fascism defeated than Communism loomed as the new enemy."

Even before the Communist victory, Republican politicians and opinion leaders, desperate for a return to power after five consecutive Democratic victories in presidential elections, had begun to blame General Marshall, President Truman, and a whole list of State Department advisers for China's collapse. When Hurley was named ambassador in 1945 he dismissed John Davies and John Stewart Service, who had briefed Sevareid in Chungking, and other young men who had had the misfortune of giving advice which later turned out to be unpopular. Davies, who had been born in China of missionary parents, was a strong anti-Communist, but facts did not matter to Senator Joe McCarthy and others who were determined to make a domestic political issue out of China's collapse. In October 1947, William C. Bullitt, whom Sevareid had considered a bit of a fool in Paris, published a "Report on China" in Henry Luce's *Life* magazine, charging that Washington was shackling Chiang by withholding arms. Democrats were said to have "lost China," and denounced as the "party of treason." This China episode helped fuel one of the strangest and most destructive eras of American history—the decade-long hunt for Communist sympathizers in government, the arts, churches, and universities—which split American society as deeply as a racial or religious war.

The crises of this period brought out several of Eric Sevareid's character traits, one of which was fidelity to his friends. When John Service's loyalty was questioned in 1950, Eric wrote a long letter to the State Department Loyalty Board concerning their September 1943 meeting. Service was held in the "highest esteem" by everyone in China and India, he said. If there had been any question as to his loyalty, he would have known it. On November 8, 1954, Sevareid delivered one of the most powerful and widely reprinted of his late-night radio analyses. He began by retelling the story of his weeks lost in the Burma jungle and of an unnamed diplomat who again and again had proven his superior

Eric Sevareid at 17 during the 2,000-mile canoe trip he made from
Minneapolis to Hudson Bay the summer after he graduated from high school.
He is standing on a diving board of the Winnepeg (Canada) Canoe Club.
(Photo courtesy of the Minnesota Historical Society.)

Visitors to Velva, North Dakota are greeted by a sign honoring the town's most famous son. Since the sign was erected the population has dropped below one thousand. (Photo by Raymond A. Schroth.)

Sevareid's childhood home in Velva has changed little since he described it in his first book, *Not So Wild a Dream*. (Photo by Jerry and Lisa Stewart.)

EXTRA!

The Minnesota Daily

The World's Largest College Newspaper

MONDAY, JUNE 18, 1934.　　　　Al Kosek, Arne Sevareid, Editors

COMPULSORY DRILL KILLED BY REGENTS

By Arnold Sevareid

Compulsory military drill at the University of Minnesota is dead. It died this morning.

The board of regents killed it with a vote of 6 to 5.

The resolution to abolish compulsory drill and to continue it as an optional feature of the school's curricula was made by Anna Determan, the only woman member of the board.

Mrs. Determan was appointed to the board by Governor Floyd Olson last winter.

The resolution came as a surprise move. There apparently had been no knowledge of it among the many outsiders interested in the highly controversial question.

The resolution, it is taken for granted, becomes effective next October when school convenes again full time.

No reporters from city papers were at today's meeting to hear the vote. Gradually, however, the news leaked out. It got into the hands of the many students and faculty members interested in the problem of drill and rapidly went around the city by telephone.

Since the news go around so late, editors of THE DAILY could not get in touch with President Coffman, nor board members, all of whom were attending the commencement exercises tonight when the news broke.

No afternoon papers carried the story, but it will appear tomorrow.

Apparently there are two reasons for the outcome of today's vote.

One is that Regent Butler from Mankato, staunch opponent of the optional forces, was in Washington today, working on the newspaper code.

The other reason is that somebody switched his vote. Who it was could not be ascertained for certain, but the rumor is that the man was Mr. Hagen.

Last fall a similar vote was taken on the question and the board voted to retain the compulsory feature by seven to five.

So that matter stood during the school year. A new commandant at the armory came in, Colonel Fredendall and the school's military forces continue their work as in former years. But the agitation went on—by faculty members, by church and peace organizations, by individual students, and by the Minnesota Daily, which has waged a fight against drill for the last decade.

Today's line-up on the vote could not be determined, but on the action last fall, the sides were as follows:

In favor of compulsory drill:
Butler
Coller
Hagen
Mayo
Rand
Snyder
Williams

In favor of optional drill:
Determan
Lawson
Murphy
A. E .Olson
A. J. Olson

A group of deans, named by the board, has been giving the drill question study this year and for many weeks word has been expected from them as to their decision. None came and apparently there was no report from them at the meeting today. It was a simple resolution, uninfluenced by any outside group, apparently.

Today's action represents the most significant change in the policy of the college since its history began, as far as thousands of students are concerned.

Compulsory drill is 65 years old —as old as the University itself— and until today there has never been a crack in its hoary armor.

That is—except for one or two minor cracks which occurred this year, which may have had something to do with today's decision. Last fall, a young freshman, Ray Ohlson of Minneapolis, was excused from compulsory drill by President Coffman because he was a conscientious objector. The president, however, insisted that that move did not represent a "precedent" in his policy on drill.

Several other cases of conscientious objection have been hanging fire this year but none of them have received action by the administration who ostensibly were waiting for the deans' report.

Another young man won a moral victory in a controversy in which he was charged with being absent from drill on two days after signing an agreement to attend. He fought the decision of the administration to suspend him from school and although a "military court" gave a decision against him, he was reinstated by the president, who has since refused to discuss that particular case. The boys' name is Sheldon Kaplan. He is one of the highest ranking scholars in the Arts college.

In the many years of its existence, the military department at the school has turned out thousands upon thousands of cadets. That the number of graduates from the two-year basic course will drop next year very drastically is a foregone conclusion. About 2,500 are now enrolled in the basic corps.

The advanced course will continue, of course, and should remain about the same size since it has been only those interested in drill who have gone on into the advanced course.

However, if the number of basic students drops too much, some of the officers on the present staff no doubt will be transferred to active duty by the war department or to some other schools.

Minnesota is the second "land grant" college to abolish compulsory drill. Wisconsin did several years ago and the basic enrollment there has dropped very much.

De Pauw University made their course optional about five years ago and since that time the basic enrollment fell so low that the regents of the school this year asked the War department to completely remove the military unit from the campus.

And such a possibility for Minnesota is likel yto become the next objective of the group of students and others who have fought against drill for so many years. However, nothing can be predicted now.

The fight against drill this year resulted in a flaring up of sentiment on both sides to new heights, a big rally against drill on the day of the annual military review and a temporary censorship over the Minnesota Daily.

Petitions were circulated among students by cadet officers, asking that the Daily be made an optional paper. With that and the pressure backing the petition from the administration the Daily was forced to say nothing about drill for some time.

Sevareid's greatest triumph at the University of Minnesota was his role in defeating compulsory drill; his greatest disappointment was his failure to become editor of the student paper—the result largely of official anger at his role in opposing drill. (Photo courtesy of the University of Minnesota archives.)

Sevareid (left) and Thomas Grandin report the imminent collapse of French resistance to Hitler in June 1940 from a CBS studio in Paris. (CBS photo, Broadcast Pioneers Library.)

In 1943 Sevareid's plane crashed behind Japanese lines in the jungles of Burma. He is wearing a white hat in the back row, fourth from the left, with other survivors who trekked out to safety.

Bearded and half-starved, Sevareid emerged from the Burmese jungle carrying a native staff. (Library of Congress photos.)

CBS released this publicity photo of Eric Sevareid's first wife Lois meeting him at a New York airport in 1941. Sevareid was returning to the United States after covering the fall of France and the Battle of Britain. (Library of Congress photo.)

Sevareid (right) and Edward R. Murrow in 1958. Sevareid was always proud to be known as one of "Murrow's boys"—the small group of CBS news broadcasters who shared the values of the man who invented modern broadcast journalism. (Photo courtesy of Edward Bliss, Jr.)

Eric Sevareid as millions saw him when he was commentator on the *CBS Evening News with Walter Cronkite.* (Photo from the author's collection.)

courage and character. He had met, he said, many men around the world:

> I have known none who seemed more the whole man, none more finished a civilized product in all that a man should be—in modesty and thoughtfulness, in resourcefulness and steady strength of character.

The name of this man is John Paton Davies. He is the man Secretary of State Dulles, on the recommendation of a five-man board, has just broken on the wheel of official disgrace. The Foreign Service officer has been dismissed three years short of retirement and pension, after giving twenty-three years of his life—an almost life itself—in the arduous service of his government. Eight times he was investigated; eight times he was cleared. One by one the politically inspired charges of communism or disloyalty or perjury were dropped; the ninth board came up with something new called defects of character. Mr. Davies is not, concluded the board and Mr. Dulles, of sufficient judgment, discretion, and reliability.

Sufficient, one might ask, unto what? Their test can only have been on supernatural design. I saw their victim measured against the most severe tests that mortal man can design. Those he passed. At the head of the class.

The broadcast was widely reprinted, and Herbert Bayard Swope, the legendary editor of the old *New York World,* fired off a note the next morning: "It was good stuff, and you showed courage and understanding . . ." To Davies, who felt honored to have such an effective champion, it did take courage in that the words "went against the general hysterical frame of mind in the country"; but in another sense it did not take courage. Sevareid, said Davies, "really believed what he said, and it was his business to say what he believed."

And what of the Nagas? Their social organization was more complex than Sevareid had earlier observed; it included egalitarian democracy, dictatorship, hereditary chiefs, and councils of elders. And the influence of the missionaries was more varied than their puritanical restrictions on drinking and dress. The American missionaries brought books and magazines and the American story of a diverse but unified nation formed on

the principles of human freedom and a war of independence against
Great Britain. British rule itself had brought the seeds of nationalism,
along with education, good medicine, and improved communications.
World War II, during which most but not all Nagas supported the Allies,
brought a higher standard of living, rapid communications with the rest
of Burma through new roads and railways, new images of the outside
world through regular jungle encounters with downed pilots and celebrated visitors like Sevareid and Davies, and finally, large numbers of
guns and ammunition that they would use in their own fight for independence.

When India became independent in 1947, a nationalist movement
among the Naga tribes claimed that Nagaland was a separate sovereign
state. After years of disputes among themselves, in July 1960 Nagaland
became a state within the Indian Union. But this did not resolve tribal
differences, which continued through the 1970s, with Naga dissidents
receiving training and arms in China.

Eric however had other reasons to care about the Nagas. Hollywood
wanted to make a major feature film about his Burma adventure, and he
had long seen his experiences as the basis of a good movie or play.
Through 1952 and 1953 he corresponded with Twentieth Century Fox
about the project, which seemed a sure thing for a while. Unfortunately,
the political situation made it impossible to film on location in the Naga
hills. The producer went up to India with Philip Adams, but the Indian
government refused cooperation; they didn't want to give credit for the
rescue to the British, who were no longer there; and now the Nagas were
out of hand.

In 1954 the Ponyos went wild and took a few hundred heads and the
Pangshas took fifty-seven. Unlike Philip Adams, Nehru didn't know
how to cope with misbehaving tribes. The next proposal was to film in
New Guinea, or maybe Africa, with the renowned C. S. Forester, author
of the popular Captain Hornblower novels, as scriptwriter, and building
the story around not Eric but the glamorous Philip Adams, who had
moved on to a new post in Malaya and visited Eric in Washington in the
early 1950s.

But these were ephemeral considerations compared to the other
emotional responsibilities—some minor, some grave—that Eric Sevareid
assumed once he had told the story of his Burma ordeal. Since he

recounted the story several times on different levels—in newspaper and magazine articles, in a fifteen-minute CBS Radio drama "Dateline . . . Burma" on November 26, and again in *Not So Wild a Dream* in 1946— each telling reached a wider audience. The son of one of the Nagas who had helped rescue the crew, now a Nagaland diplomat, complained in 1967 that Eric's accounts had not mentioned his father's name, only mentioned his "barrel chest." More important, families who had lost sons when their planes crashed over Burma asked for his help in finding their sons' remains or in dealing with their loss.

To his credit, as far as I could tell, Sevareid never shrunk from this moral obligation. He hated the annoyances that went with being a celebrity; but he seemed to sense that once a journalist turns on the public emotions, he must deal with the consequences of this in his personal life. Typically he would have to write, as in late 1954, "I am terribly sorry I have no information about your boy."

At Christmas time in 1943, as he sat writing in his father's house in Minneapolis, he received a call from the father of Lieutenant Felix, the pilot of Eric's crashed plane. The father was in Minneapolis; he had not received the long letter Eric had written from Chungking, but now had tracked him down at home and wanted to talk about his son. Mr. Felix dragged himself trembling through the cold to the Sevareid house.

He had a wooden leg, to replace the one he lost in World War I. Sevareid had never seen the boy's face, just the back of his head; but he tried to convince the father that the boy had died instantly and had not suffered. The father had no resentment about the C-46s; he had seen the same thing in World War I. He pressed Sevareid's hand and said he felt much better now and clumped down the stairs coughing into his handkerchief. But October 29, 1946, Mr. Felix's employer, at a radio station in Cedar Rapids, Iowa, wrote to Sevareid that now Mr. Felix was distraught that his son's body had been moved from its jungle resting place to a cemetery in Calcutta. Could Sevareid explain this or offer some further consolation? Eric responded that Mr. Felix should see his pastor, and that he should take comfort from the fact that other soldiers had at personal risk gone into the jungle to move his son's remains to a well-tended grave.

But Eric's most important personal discovery, as he sat over his typewriter on December 22, tapping in whatever came to his mind, was that he was not the same person who three years ago had come home flaming with indignation against the complacency of American life. There were still some things that annoyed him: like the way advertisers exploited the suffering of troops in the Solomon Islands by somehow linking the troops' dedication to the advertisers' products; and the movies that showed Errol Flynn bayoneting fifteen Japs without mussing his hair; and the fact that the whole country, as if on a cycle, was moving to the right. But he was less irritated than he had been three years ago by the middle-class culture of his own family—the doilies, the floor lamps. This was, after all, the good life.

As he typed he heard the sound of tremulous girls' voices from the street below singing "Oh Little Town of Bethlehem." He heard the door open and neighbors say "Hi, Lorraine, Hi, Nancy." He was touched. He told himself he would do something he had not done for a long time. He would go to church this Christmas. Even if this was superstition and even if a personal God could never allow to happen the things that he had witnessed these last years, he would go to church this Christmas. For religion was a "*personal* affair."

12

CLIMAX

TO SOMEONE who has seen the Mississippi, or the Amazon, or the Congo, the Rhine, as a river, is not imposing. Rising in Switzerland, for about 865 miles it flows generally north and west, forming the border between France and Germany until it cuts up toward Speyer. Then, with Luxembourg, Belgium and Holland off to the west, it slips through Germany, past the cities of Mannheim, Mainz, and Coblenz, and enters Holland near Arnheim, where it continues through channels to the North Sea. If the Hudson has been called America's Rhine, it is not so much because they look alike—although both flow between high cliffs and through their nation's industrial heartland—or because both, since the early nineteenth century, have been the heart of an inland waterway system that has forged some economic and political unity, but because each, through history and folklore, come as close as any other landmark to summing up its region's identity, to capturing its soul.

But as Eric Sevareid stood shivering on the banks of the Rhine on March 24, 1945, his boots sinking into the soft earth, he found himself impressed by neither its might nor its history. For him it was listless and colorless, though perhaps possessed of a certain "torpid dignity." He could think only of the significance of two leaders, in their very different imaginations, had imposed upon it. To the Kansas mind of Eisenhower at Allied Supreme Headquarters in Europe, it was just another river, an obstacle to be crossed, with the West Point historian's reassurance that there had never been a successful river defense in military history. To Adolf Hitler it was the Reich's ultimate shield against invaders—the last of his many illusions. To Sevareid, who more and more used France's recent history as a metaphor, it was Germany's Pétain, "their old Marechal; and they take the calm facade for omniscience and strength."

Eric peered across the river at German troops occupying the tiny village of Wesel with its small spires reaching through the haze, and he revelled in the realization that he knew something the enemy did not know: that this night would begin the last battle of the war in Europe. The end, the climax, was but hours away. And the reporter projected himself into the role of representative for the whole human race; the enemy was Caesar and the reporter was one of the emperor's intended slaves, innocent of Caesar's crimes—he had never burned a book or kicked a Jew—and he was about to triumph.

After the German defeat in the Ardennes, Eisenhower's plan, conceived as a methodical military conquest of Germany rather than a political race against the Russians to occupy Berlin, was to cross the Rhine along its entire length in three phases, then proceed eastward in a broad front to link up with Russian forces at the Elbe River. The campaign had begun in February, Allied forces had captured the Remagen bridge in a surprise attack on March 8, the campaign was going well. At Wesel, a prolonged artillery and air bombardment would soften up the target, combined American and British forces would make the amphibious attack, and paratroopers would seize the airhead. For Eric, who found himself with a battalion of British commandos, the crossing was momentous for a personal reason: it was probably the last fighting he would see in his lifetime, and he wondered if perhaps he should leave the British to be with his own people, to observe American boys. But hadn't the whole thrust of his war experience to date taught him that these *were* his people, that distinctions among Americans, French, and British were being wiped away? He would stay with the British. As the sun set, the first American bombers appeared out of the dusk.

A lot had happened to Eric Sevareid between Christmas in Minneapolis and the eve of the climactic "last battle" on the banks of the Rhine. He had arrived in Germany by way of the Italian campaign—Naples, the volcanic eruption of Mount Vesuvius, the bloody landing on Anzio beach, and the fall of Rome—then the invasion of southern France. Some of the certainties about democracy and Western civilization that had braced him in political debates in Rio and had been severely tested in China were much less certain now.

But other assurances were taking their place. One was this almost compulsive drive, in the once shaken young man who had fled the blitz, to be in the center of things. If he did not recklessly court death and tease fate like some correspondents, he heard and saw enough bombs, bullets, and corpses to know that his life could end in a second. Three ideas seemed to impel him: the need to identify as fully as humanly possible with the soldiers who were actually fighting the war; the desire to gain a clue to the future of European civilization, whose meaning he had just begun to grasp; and, though he does not state this, the wish to fix his own place in the flow of events, as if one might somehow freeze the river of history, as one stops a film, and spot his lone canoe, small but clearly focused, on the screen of time.

Eric's family had scattered. In September 1943, Lois sent the twins to Minneapolis to live with her mother for the duration of the war. While Eric was in China, she decided to work for the government, to get some kind of a war job; and, one woman working with two men, she became part of the original planning group that was to become the United Nations Relief and Rehabilitation Administration (UNRRA). Officially founded in November 1943, UNRRA began formal recruiting in Washington in January 1944 and set up the Balkan Mission, which was to open in Cairo in May.

Ten days after Eric returned from China, Lois set out for Cairo, arriving on Thanksgiving Day. There, one of the first women to undertake this kind of work, she would organize relief for the Balkans. It was an extremely difficult task, since these countries were already in the midst of the political struggles that would come to a head at war's end, and UNRRA's job was to distribute food, clothing, and medicine to suffering people and stay out of politics while doing so. Like Eric, Lois was just not the kind of person to be left out of the action when there was a war on.

Was this heading off in different directions the natural consequence of the war that temporarily separated millions of families, or did it signal other, more personal, disruptive forces at work? To Geoffrey Cox and his wife, who spent a holiday with Eric and Lois and the twins at Martha's Vineyard in the summer of 1943, Lois' decision to leave the children for UNRRA was the first sign that she was "a bit odd." Mrs. Cox became convinced that Lois was "mad," determined to inflict her will on other people.

Meanwhile, war reporting and CBS in particular had developed considerably since Murrow, Shirer, Sevareid, and LeSueur had formed the first brotherhood in London and Paris. On the professional level, war correspondents, of which there were more than a thousand in the European theater alone, now considered part of the military's public relations apparatus, had been gradually absorbed into the massive military machine in the crusade to defeat Hitler. And generals, always conscious of their own military and political ambitions, adopted a variety of attitudes toward the press, at once flattering, manipulating, or intimidating reporters into polishing the brass's images.

Press historian Phillip Knightley argues that for the most part during World War II the correspondents, rather than trying to be truly independent journalists, functioned as an arm of the government. He cites Eisenhower's comment that he always considered correspondents as "quasi-staff officers," and Drew Middleton's opinion that censorship was helpful because it made generals feel free to discuss top secret material with reporters—whereas in Vietnam, where there was no censorship, he found everyone more wary of the press. When operations flopped, when troops murdered prisoners, panicked and went AWOL by the thousands, or when officers fled the battle, reporters could either fight censors or simply look the other way. This left the reporter with three choices: opt out, stay comfortable in Paris or Brussels and print press releases; write reflective, atmospheric essays, like those of A. J. Liebling and Rebecca West in the *New Yorker;* go the Ernie Pyle route, ignore grand strategy, concentrate on human interest stories with lots of names and hometowns, about the otherwise anonymous enlisted men—until the emotional drain of looking into too many young faces and taking notes makes the journalist a casualty too. Pyle said at the end of his European stint, "If I heard one more shot or saw one more dead man I'd go off my nut." At various times, Sevareid wrote all these types of stories and sometimes he fought censors as well.

On the individual level, Murrow, as an escape some said from other pressures, had begun riding the bomber raids over Germany, including his spectacular December 2–3, 1943, flight on a British Lancaster over Berlin—"a kind of orchestrated hell, a terrible symphony of light and flame . . . The job isn't pleasant; it's terribly tiring. Men die in the sky while others are roasted alive in their cellars . . . This is a calculated, remorseless campaign of destruction."

Meanwhile, he had expanded his team. Larry LeSueur had been CBS's Russian correspondent from October 1941 to October 1942. In March 1941 Murrow hired the man who, with his glamorous appearance and mellifluous voice, many would see as Murrow's natural successor—the handsome, twenty-three-year-old Rhodes scholar from Three Rivers, Michigan, Charles Collingwood. Collingwood played tennis and baseball and swam at Cornell University, and worked for the U.S. Forestry Service during his summer vacations. At Oxford, he worked part time for the United Press. When the Rhodes committee told him to give up one or the other, he replied, in a letter to his family, that he was finding it harder and harder to care about medieval law with the war coming closer and closer. "I have never wanted knowledge for its own sake," he wrote. "I have always wanted it for a purpose." When Murrow took Collingwood on he said that he had picked him because he wanted someone "who had not been contaminated by print," meaning that he had not been at UP long enough to be spoiled by the conventions of printed journalism, with its standard lead-and-pyramid structure of a story.

Murrow soon added another Rhodes scholar, Louisiana-born and Tulane-educated Howard K. Smith, another tall and strikingly handsome young man who, after graduation in 1936 had made two trips abroad, working his way across on a freighter, traveling through Germany and taking notes, making a study of the Nazi system. After two years at Oxford he joined the UP, which sent him to Berlin, where CBS grabbed him in 1941.

The Harvard *summa cum laude* graduate Winston Burdett, the foreign correspondent whose deep, breathless tones held American listeners rapt for thirty-seven years, came to Murrow first as a free-lancer in neutral Stockholm during the fall of Norway. Murrow caught up with him at the end of 1942 when, in his first real experience as a front-line war correspondent, Murrow followed the Allied invasion of North Africa. Furious at what he considered Eisenhower's naive deal with Admiral Darlan, an anti-Semite who had handed over hostages and refugees to the Germans, Murrow had attacked Allied policy in his broadcasts. In Algiers he saw his first Nazi corpse. He also found in Burdett a kindred spirit—although he did not know him as well as he thought. Murrow auditioned the Harvard man, signed him, and later gave him advice: "Sit down with your script more," revealing to Burdett for the first time how tight and self-conscious his broadcasts had been.

Yet there was another Winston Burdett, unknown to CBS. A former film and book reviewer for the *Brooklyn Eagle,* where he had joined the guild, he was a secret member of the Communist Party and a spy for Russia in Finland and Yugoslavia until 1942. He quit the party that year after Soviet agents shot to death his first wife, Leah, an Italian journalist.

In 1942 Murrow hired the twenty-seven-year-old son of a railroad engineer, Bill Downs, also from UP, whom Sevareid later described as "no great intellect, but no fool."

Later it would be Downs who would prod Murrow to take on Senator Joseph R. McCarthy. Already in the UP Berlin bureau when Smith arrived was the New Yorker, Richard C. Hottelet, whom the Nazi's had confined for four months and charged with espionage because he had investigated British bomb damage in March. Murrow brought him on the CBS team in January 1944.

Thus, by the time of the Allied offensive in western Europe, CBS had in place a squad of superbly talented young men who—along with a handful of others, including Quentin Reynolds who described the retreat from Paris in *The Wounded Don't Cry*; columnist Ernie Pyle, "the G.I.'s friend"; *Stars and Stripes* cartoonist Bill Mauldin; the New York *Herald Tribune's* Homer Bigart; *Life* photographers Carl Mydans and Margaret Bourke-White; the *Chicago Sun's* H. R. Knickerbocker; UP's Walter Cronkite, whom Murrrow, building his staff for D-day, tried unsuccessfully to hire—would collectively define the war to Americans. For some, the war would also define them. Not only would the war give new meaning to their lives; without the war they would seem empty, unfulfilled.

Sevareid's January return to the battlefields of Europe began badly—with a mutiny, a gun-wielding quarrel between the young skipper and his ensign which went on for days, on the Liberty ship *Thomas B. Reed,* which Eric boarded in Brooklyn. In time, they got under way, followed the convoy to the Mediterranean, pushed on through a gale and the Gulf Stream. Eric studied Italian in his cabin and listened with his earphones to the BBC and the voices of the Free French calling *courage, confiance.* At the thought of his beloved France's plight, tears came to his eyes.

When he arrived at Algiers, what had been a prosperous resort, a nest of spies, and Vichy headquarters, was now an Allied command center far behind the lines. There he mixed with the determined young men planning the future French republic, though without assurance that the Allies—who had finally allowed Charles de Gaulle to take over from the assassinated Darlan and his successor, General Henri Giraud, who had briefly shared the presidency with the overpowering de Gaulle in 1943—would eventually allow them to run their own country.

From Algiers Eric made his way to Cairo to spend some days with Lois. There are hints between the lines in Eric's *Not So Wild a Dream* one-paragraph account of the visit that Lois, in the vanguard of the UNRRA project, was having a difficult time. For one thing, since funding did not start until March, the staff had been paying its own way. The UNRRA official history by George Woodbridge refers cryptically to personnel problems in the Cairo office. In spite of every effort to recruit only the best people at the beginning, the historian writes, "Unfortunately, some of the unsuitable individuals employed in the first rush of the early days were sent abroad, and especially in Cairo, where the UNRRA Balkan Mission, the Administration's first—and possibly most unhappy—overseas venture, was taking shape." A small number of unfit recruits spoiled the agency's early image. Certainly there is no reason to conclude that Lois, with her exceptional qualifications, was one of these troublesome few; but one can guess that, whoever they were, they made her life and work more difficult. Eventually the job broke her health and she had to be hospitalized.

A year later, back in Washington, on November 14, 1945, without mentioning his personal connection to UNRRA, Eric built one of his 11:10 P.M. news analyses around its problems. The growing debate about UNRRA, he said, was not about its principles but its efficiency. He had seen the UNRRA operation abroad, he said, and many UNRRA officials agreed with some of the criticisms. But they took issue with the congressman who had called UNRRA the "laughing stock of Europe." Then Eric quoted a letter from an UNRRA worker handling displaced persons: " . . .old people, poor, in shawls, young men with sunken eyes who have lived through years in concentration camps . . ." who kiss the worker's hand and say, "God bless you."

During Eric's visit to Cairo, he and Lois stayed in a little villa on the Mena road near the Pyramids. From the back door they looked out over ancient Egypt, a little mud village where men and women squatted working in the field and barefoot boys tugged at their donkeys. Along the road in front, army trucks and limousines rumbled by. Eric viewed the scenes from the front and back of his house and saw himself caught between two worlds. If all men are brothers and if we must move toward world government, he thought, these worlds would have to meet.

The Italian campaign, conceived at the Casablanca Conference of January 1943 as an alternative to the immediate invasion of southern France or the invasion of Greece and the Balkans, began with the conquest of Sicily in the summer of 1943. At the end of July, Mussolini was forced to resign and was jailed, while the king handed the government to Marshal Pietro Bagdolio, who opened negotiations for surrender to the Allies.

Under the command of British Field Marshall Viscount Alexander, in September the Allies landed in Italy itself—General Bernard L. Montgomery's Eighth Army at Reggio on the toe, and General Mark Clark's Fifth Army at Salerno, just south of Naples. But north of Naples the Germans held firm all that fall at the Gustav Line, which reached from coast to coast, halfway between Naples and Rome, through Cassino, site of the ancient Benedictine monastery.

On January 22, 1944, in a surprise end run, the Allies landed 50,000 troops and 5,000 vehicles on Anzio beachhead, only thirty-three miles south of Rome. But rather than moving swiftly into the Alban Hills, they paused long enough to allow Hitler to pull in 70,000 troops from France and Yugoslavia and pin the Allies down for five months in what became one of the most frustrating blunders of the war. General Clark aggravated a bad situation by unneccessarily calling in the air force to pound Monte Cassino Monastery into a rock pile—thus raising serious questions worldwide about the ethics and wisdom of the campaign and, incidentally, giving the Germans, who had not occupied the site in the first place, a more effective line of defense.

From the beginning, the Italian campaign was exceptionally difficult and, some critics would say, fruitless. Strategically, the main purpose of establishing what came to be a secondary front in Italy was to maintain pressure on Hitler's armies, to tie them up in southern Europe during the winter and spring in order to drain off forces that otherwise would have been free to counter the coming cross-channel invasion of Normandy in June. The basic tactic was to force a slow, painful advance over difficult terrain, using heavy air and artillery bombardment to pummel mountain towns—often leveling everything in sight with the false hope that one could crush the enemy from afar rather than shoot him face-to-face.

Thus, Sevareid arrived to find Allied forces disillusioned and cynical. He learned, but could not report, that in November two hundred men from the Thirty-fourth Division, men from his native region whom he had also observed on maneuvers in Louisiana, had refused to advance into certain death in a minefield, that had watched in horror as their comrades died screaming while the Germans poured artillery fire into the field. Sentenced or threatened with execution for "cowardice," they had been saved only by the intervention of his own uncle and personal hero, his mother's brother, Lieutenant Colonel John Hougen, the brilliant Minnesota lawyer. "Uncle John," a reserve officer, had turned down a federal judgeship and a university professorship; here he used his persuasive manner to save these frightened boys from what Eric called, "irreparable injustice at the hands of various little Napoleons."

Naples itself was known as a "pigsty in paradise," where even the children looked old, where its weary citizens offered fish and venereal disease to one occupying army after the other. One day, climbing the stairs in the press building, Sevareid glanced through the open door of an apartment and his eyes fell on a shirtless, unshaven, Italian soldier, beneath the portrait of a bemedalled military ancestor, playing his violin. This, thought Eric, symbolized the current generation of Italian manhood.

From Naples, from March through May, with regular forays up to the front and on other side expeditions, he made almost daily broadcasts. Some were routine reports on the bombing raids from Naples over the Balkans; many were the kind of Ernie-Pyle upbeat reports that bolster homefront confidence in the troops; some, like the one on May 11, were laced with the cosmic generalizations—sometimes slipping into blather —which anticipate his commentaries thirty years later:

> . . . so one waits . . . two months and more have gone by and no changes in the lines have occurred which you could mark on any map of Italy your library atlas might contain . . . but do not call this a deadlock; that implies inability to move on . . . but for weeks now we have not tried to move on . . . it is a natural law of warfare in such a condition that armies rest, and gather their strength . . .

On the dark hills a few miles north of here our soldiers stand in their foxholes . . . they come from many lands—America, Canada, India, England, New Zealand, France, Africa, Poland; like the massed battalions in Britain, they face toward the heart of Europe . . . the source of their respective and mutual trouble and tragedy . . . the voices on the radio speak of a tenseness gripping the continent . . . Italy is part of the continent. We return you to General Electric in New York.

On March 20, when Mount Vesuvius—some said in response to the bombing of Cassino—erupted, with a power an awestruck Sevareid later called second only to the Hiroshima explosion, he accompanied a truck-load of signal corps officers and men to the summit in an attempt to record the "deep coughing" of the world's most famous volcano. As hundreds of people watched from their roofs, a thirty-foot-high river of fire rolled down from the summit. It was like the beginning of the end of the world.

In the same broadcast, in an aside that irritated the authorities, he told his listeners that Naples was "becoming the Cairo of this campaign"— meaning that the army personnel, with no battles to fight, had settled into the nine-to-five good life. They broke out the liquor and competed for the best invitations to Italian homes. "The suave tail-coated waiters who served the Fascists and Germans are just as suave and elegant now for us." To his disgust, the same social class distinctions that had separated Americans at home continued in the military. Social climbers from New York tried to ingratiate themselves with Italian nobility; poor boys sat on the doorsteps of poor families. He would witness selflessness and the admirable "team spirit" at the front, then wince at the pompous, self-serving generals in the rear who flaunted their swagger sticks and bickered among themselves.

Sevareid had a particular antipathy for General Mark Clark, perhaps because of his role in the Darlan deal the year before, but mostly because Clark thought always in terms of the Fifth Army, *his* Fifth Army, with its membership cards and its Fifth Army song beginning, "Stand up, stand up for General Clark." In his judgment, if generals like Mark Clark treated correspondents with respect it was simply to gull them into giving generals personal publicity. Once he encountered Clark driving to the edge of a battle with his photographers. At the edge of the danger zone, Clark went over a map and pointed to a distant hill while the photographer snapped away, always at the General's left profile. Although a soldier could be fined for not wearing his helmet, Clark wore only his little overseas cap, lest the helmet obstruct the profile. Once the picture session was done, the jeep turned around and drove the general back to where it was safe, now with the steel helmet on his head.

Clark felt the same way about Sevareid. Martin Blumenson, who had access to Clark's wartime diaries for his consistently sympathetic biography, *Mark Clark* (1984), records that Sevareid interviewed Clark in April, early in his Italy assignment, for about forty-five minutes. The chemistry was bad from the start. "Sevareid's lack of understanding of the problems astonished Clark. Sevareid saw Clark as a self-important figure motivated by personal ambition." Blumenson acknowledges Clark's thirst for publicity, but defends it on the grounds that "the profession of war is the most competitive of all occupations."

In telling contrast to the corruption and bureaucracy at Allied headquarters, a visit to a group of Yugoslav partisans recuperating in a little hospital near the Italian coastal town of Bari moved Sevareid so profoundly that he cabled Paul White that "I shall try to write this without emotion but I am not sure I will succeed . . . it is an experience of the heart. You will pardon me if I say that I have the feeling of having been in the presence of a great spiritual force." He had led most of his recent life with complicated people, so was not ready for the simplicity of these determined youths: young Colonel Didier, confidant of Tito, with the neck of a bull and the heart of a poet; Ante, a black-eyed boy of twenty who had already killed at least three hundred Germans, Italians, and Chetniks; a breathtakingly beauiful eighteen-year-old girl, whose chestnut hair rippled to her shoulders, who had killed forty herself; a beautiful girl named Boja, lying paralyzed by a bullet in her spine, who felt ashamed that she had killed only one; the hero Djuro, a farmer, still alive with twenty-five machine-gun bullet holes in his body. The visit left him both inspired and shaken.

Sevareid, perhaps still ambivalent about his correspondent's role when so many men and women both older and younger than he were in combat, seems to have taken these stories at face value. And perhaps he has allowed his admiration to smother the journalist's critical intelligence. How does one man kill three hundred men? How did the girl kill forty? It may be that they were exaggerating, or that they killed their victims not in combat but in mass executions.

Later in London one of Churchill's associates pointed out to him that, among the Nazis, Hitler youth manifest the same zeal. Eric was taken aback, he realized that he would be appalled to see his own children become like the boys and girls he had seen that day. And yet, something in him allowed him to see glory in it. Although he knew well the shattered voices that spoke for much of his generation in *All Quiet on the Western Front* and *A Farewell to Arms,* and although he would soon grow sick at the stench of corpses, the word "glory," in war, would stay in his vocabulary. And nothing seemed to renew its meaning more than intimate contact with fighting men.

Ernie Pyle came ashore at Anzio at the end of March and, with a side trip to Tunisia, stayed for a month. "When you get to Anzio you waste no time getting off the boat," he wrote, "for you have been feeling pretty much like a clay pigeon in a shooting gallery. But after a few hours in Anzio you wish you were back on the boat, for you could hardly describe being ashore as any haven of peacefulness . . . In our first day ashore, a bomb exploded so close to the place where I was sitting that it almost knocked us down with fright. It smacked into the trees a short distance away."

On Saturday, April 20, during the final week of Pyle's stay, an army plane, circling out to sea to avoid German shore guns, skimmed in over the waves to deliver Eric Sevareid and his colleagues to the same Anzio beachhead. Two shells passed over their jeep and landed forty yards away—providing Sevareid with a single terrible line in a broadcast the following day.

On the next day, from an improvised broadcast station in an Italian banker's bomb-damaged summer villa, with a Hallicrafter 299 transmitter named Jig Jig, Eric delivered the first direct broadcast from Fifth Army positions on the Anzio battleground. The moment was a culmination of two months of tests, conducted by RCA in Italy, to establish what Eric termed, in a cable to White, one of the most complicated setups in radio history: his voice set out from Anzio, to an RCA receiver in south Italy, to Naples, back to south Italy, to Long Island, and thence to hundreds of individual stations in America.

The Anzio scene he portrayed was both grizzly and ambiguous. They were "living on a bull's-eye," he said. Struck by yesterday's shells, "A Negro truck driver a hundred yards from this house disintegrated into a thousand anonymous particles." An odd, isolated sentence. No attempt to explain, cushion the impact, or personalize the unnamed Negro, now as "anonymous" as his thousand particles. All that night their quarters had trembled under the bombardment. Sunday, as he spoke, men sunbathed on the roofs and rowed into the surf. "They are not exactly fatalists; they are not unafraid, but they have learned poise in the face of danger, yet very often they wonder just what this is all about."

During Eric's visit, Pyle wrote a series of pieces about the work of the Quartermaster Corps, the last on April 25, on their care of the military cemetery.

> Even the dead are not safe on the beachhead, nor the living who care for the dead. Many times German shells have landed in the cemetery. Men have been wounded as they dug graves. Once a body was uprooted and had to be reburied.
>
> The inevitable pet dog barks and scampers around the area, not realizing where he is. The soldiers say at times he has kept them from going nuts.

The Sevareid who found some sort of emotional and moral reassurance in the front lines consistently found a deeper comfort in the men of ideas whom he would seek out and whose minds and souls he would milk. Although Sevareid has usually been categorized as an "intellectual" reporter, the journalist's mind is not intellectual in the narrow concept of that word—one who through persistent research in a narrow field brings forth new material. Rather, he is an intellectual in the sense that ideas matter to him, and he questions and probes looking for insights to be quickly shared. Thus, he is often best in repose, sitting in leisurely fashion with another intelligent person.

So one day Eric fled Naples to Sorrento in search of the seventy-eight-year-old philosopher, historian, and literary critic Benedetto Croce, long a foe of Nazism and fascism, now living his last years in a villa once owned by John Jacob Astor. The old man regretted that the king had "retired," not abdicated, and he hissed at the mention of Mussolini, who had once bragged that he had never read a word of Croce—though Mussolini had plagiarized a quote from one of Croce's books. Croce briefly joined the Italian cabinet later that year and lived till 1952, but Sevareid, in his compulsive search for living metaphors, saw Croce, as if he were on the brink of death, as "Italy itself." (What happened to the shirtless violinist?) Croce, in his old villa, looking out at the unchanging sea, was surrounded by the past, "guessing wistfully at the future and incapable of present action. The men of the old Italy were dying; where were the men of the new?"

With the fall of Cassino in mid May, the Allied advance on Rome moved inexorably, and Sevareid had the good luck of scooping the competition on the story of the May 25 linkup of Allied armies near Anzio, because his regularly scheduled 2 P. M. broadcast coincided with the official release time of the news. But he resented the Fifth Army publicity machine claiming that this belated success justified the Anzio strategy all along. On May 26, after the battle at Cisterna, rather than pursue and capture the retreating German forces, Clark shifted his strategy and pointed his Fifth Army toward Rome. He had convinced himself that *his* Fifth Army had earned the right to be the liberators of the Eternal City. When Sevareid attempted obliquely to question this move in a broadcast, the censors cut the line out; but Clark, who had apparently read the uncensored script, attacked the undelivered broadcast in front of the other correspondents. No "amateur," he said, could question his decisions.

After the ceremonies on Memorial Day, at what was probably the largest cemetery of the war, Eric came upon six unburied bodies stretched in the sun. The burial sergeant begged him not to write a story about what he was doing during the war. He didn't want his family to know. When his assistant remarked, "You get used to it after a while," the sergeant replied, "It isn't true—I never get used to it. With a thousand, it would be just a problem of sanitation. With six, it seems like a tragedy." Now Eric realized that he himself was becoming obsessed with the deaths of these youngsters, that he was writing about death more and more.

As he remembered the experience later:

> Sometimes in the long, lovely evenings when we sat by the sea, the old feelings about death of youth which I had experienced as a college boy began to steal back, unnerving and frightening me. It

would not do; one had to shake off these moods. But it was becoming harder and harder to escape them. I realized now with a start that the sight of a dead German boy did not affect me, while the sight of a dead American did. Did this reaction come from the deep-seated national feelings which go back to childhood, or was it due simply to propinquity? I was unsure.

On June 4, the morning after his last broadcast from Anzio, when it was clear that Allied forces would be in Rome within hours, Eric was suddenly overwhelmed by the stench of rotting corpses. The bodies were out of sight, perhaps dragged into the brush just off the road, baking in the hot sun; but he could not escape the sweet, sharp, gaseous stench of death. He began to cough and choke and gasp and weep as he ran blindly up the road, the vomit high in his throat. He almost fainted before he reached his jeep and he was still sick hours later.

A few days earlier, behind the lines at Anzio, Sevareid had taken time to formally work out some details about his future and his career. By one of those wartime coincidences that bring old comrades together, his old *Minnesota Daily* friend, Arthur Burck, was serving as the military censor. Eric, who was scheduled to make the rounds with *Life* photographer Carl Mydans, was coming down with sinus trouble, so he proposed a deal: Arthur, in Eric's place, would accompany Mydans to the front, and Eric would stay home and serve as censor for a day. With time on his hands, he typed out a letter to Paul White.

He said he was happy at CBS and couldn't imagine himself leaving, but he thought he needed more money. He had compared his own salary with what the other correspondents were getting, particularly those writing for magazines, and had determined that he should like a "regular sustaining salary of $200 a week," plus complete freedom to write whatever he wished for publication. This was perhaps a sign that deep down he saw himself fundamentally as a writer more than a broadcaster. White replied a month later (July 3): a three-year contract at $150 a week the first year, $175 the second, and $200 the third. On outside writing, if he was to earn $300 a week on other projects, his CBS salary would be reduced to $100.

On their trip to the front, Burck and Mydans had a close call. In a search for photo material, they spied, on the ground in an archway, the picturesque configuration of a wine jug covered by a German helmet.

But it wasn't in the proper light. Carefully, Burck moved it a few inches into the sun, and Mydans clicked away, catching with his usual skill a striking still life of the helmet in the lower right foreground in the sunlight, framed by the arch, and Burck visible in the background. Burck thought of taking the helmet home, but decided to just leave it where it was. A few hours later another GI was tempted by the helmet and blown to bits; it was a booby trap. Perhaps if Eric had gone out that day he would have been tempted as well.

Rome fell on June 4, but Eric was too physically and emotionally exhausted to summon up his usual eloquence. He stood in a field overlooking the city at 8 P.M. and told his listeners that American troops had just crossed the city boundary line, then, back at his quarters, he fell into a deep sleep, undisturbed even when German planes strafed his house. At 6 A.M. he was shaken awake by Winston Burdett, haggard and red-eyed, but bursting with his story: at midnight he had gotten into the center of Rome, almost alone, and driven through the ancient ruins by moonlight.

That day Eric exulted with everyone else at the grand entry of the Allied forces into the city; he felt good, important, a representative of those ideals for which he believed the war was being fought. But he squirmed as Clark, in his press conference, called it a "great day for the Fifth Army," while he saw it as a great day for the world, for all those who had suffered to bring this day about. He also exulted in getting the jump on his press rivals, who tended to see him as a "commentator" rather than a hard-boiled reporter—by broadcasting his Rome story to Naples from a military transmitter on a half-track rather than driving it back to Anzio. That afternoon he also saw the pope. Though he had never had any religious feelings for the Vatican, which, it seemed to him, had inclined toward fascism, Sevareid found himself stirred by Pius XII's showmanship and political genius as he seemed to flow out onto the balcony overlooking St. Peter's Square in his shimmering white cassock and raised his arms over the throng in prayer.

That night, near midnight, Sevareid discovered two paratroopers on the street with nowhere to stay, and brought them back to his room in the Luxurious Grand Hotel. After they had chatted for a while, the scene suddenly turned strange. One of the men pulled out a German pistol and said that he had killed a man—not a combatant but a prisoner—that morning to get it. "You know, it kind of scares me," he said.

"It's so easy to kill. It solves all your problems, and there's no questions asked. I think I'm getting the habit."

Finally, on June 6, word came that Eisenhower's armies had landed at Normandy. The final phase of Europe's liberation was under way, Eric told his listeners, and the Italian campaign had succeeded: it had captured the first fascist capital and drained off Hitler's forces from northern Europe.

For the first part of the summer Eric enjoyed the relative peace. He swam off the rocks in the warm blue water of Capri, hung around Naples and Sorrento, returned to Cairo for a few days, then retraced his steps to Rome where he took notes and did feature reports on the soldiers' daily lives in the Eternal City, which was becoming as unholy as any city in Europe.

And the more he saw and the more he thought about it, the more heartsick he became about the whole meaning of the Italian campaign. As if a symptom of Italy's deeper malaise, the once-smart Hotel Excelsior had become a twenty-four-hour brothel. He could not blame the young American officers who used it, but the Italian women, he thought, unable to find satisfaction with Italian men, threw themselves at their conquerors, the Fascists one day, the Americans the next. And as he trekked through the countryside it became all the more clear that neither logic nor decency had guided many of our decisions. An artilleryman would say, "I'm getting tired of seeing that big white building there. Knock the goddam thing down." And now, in a widely questioned strategy, General Alexander had continued the Italian campaign north of Rome into the Po Valley, and the operation had bogged down. Restricted by censors, mostly British, it was not until the first week in November, after he had moved to the CBS London bureau, that Sevareid could fully express himself on the whole experience.

In response to a November 1 press conference in which Alexander had defended his decision, Sevareid offered a long critical analysis, published in the British magazine, the *New Statesman*. Since we had apparently devoted more men and supplies to the effort than the Germans, rather than pin down the German army, it seemed, we had allowed the German army to pin down us. We had wasted men and resources to take Rome, which was a political but not a strategic objective. We had helped lay waste and impoverish for many years a major part of Italy. We had erased "ancient Roman towns and art works which belonged not to

Fascism but to all time, not to the Italians but to all civilized peoples."
We had left three thousand Americans buried in Anzio cemetery.

If Sevareid's months in Italy were to leave a bitter taste, his return to
France, where he had dreamed of reentering Paris on the day of its liberation, would be, if not sweet, at least satisfying. The fall of France had
been not just a national capitulation but, for Sevareid, a paradigm of the
interplay between personal and national weakness. The impression lingered that a weakness in the national character, which had brought this
beautiful civilization to ruin; but now France had a chance to redeem itself, to save its own soul.

Under Allied plans approved in 1943, an Allied army of four hundred
thousand officers and men, including the French First Army, were to
land on the southern coast between Toulon and Cannes, where they
would be joined by twenty-five thousand Maquis, partisans. The French
were to liberate Toulon, Nice, and Marseilles, while the Americans
chased the Germans up the Rhône valley toward Germany. At the same
time, in the north of France, Allied forces in Normany would push toward Paris. Eventually, all the armies would form a continuous front
from Switzerland to the North Sea. The proponents of the Italian campaign, like Churchill and Alexander, opposed the invasion of southern
France, called Operation Anvil, but Eisenhower insisted that he wanted a
port in the Mediterranean, so resources were moved from Italy for the
undertaking.

In a drawing, Eric won one of the two places reserved for radio correspondents on the landing crafts for the initial assault. For a while he
was "as happy as a child told he could go on a picnic," but when town
gossip let him know that the invasion plan was was far from secret, he
was tempted to pull out. Geoffrey Cox, his New Zealand army-journal-
ist friend who had survived almost as many misadventures as he, arrived
in Italy and helped him laugh off his fears. Yet, the driving force for
sticking with the expedition was his recollection of that night in Norway House at the turning point of his canoe trip, when he realized that
if he backed away from this challenge it would cripple him for the rest
of his life.

On the night of August 14 he huddled with hundreds of men in the
LST and sucked in what strength he could from the silent comrades

around him. His description of that night, as recollected in *Not So Wild a Dream*, is almost mystical, transcendental, a Thoreau-inspired sense of his spirit blending with the expedition. He meditates on his natural surroundings, then concludes:

> I was happy to be where I was; I would not have been elsewhere for anything in the world. The others perhaps felt differently about our destination, but for me, to come back to France in this manner with my own countrymen was the reforging of an old, broken link; it was a justification, a reaffirmation of personality, a victory.

Perhaps because the Allies had dropped 12,500 tons of bombs on southern France since the end of April, the landing went well. Too well, it seemed. The Germans did not resist. Eric came ashore with the Forty-fifth Division at Saint-Maxime to find the inhabitants stunned by the shock of battle—and disappointed that the troops come to liberate their little town were not French.

Eric the reporter, who had told Hugh Baillie and Murrow in Paris in 1937 that he didn't like the pressure for scoops, was once again driving himself to get the news out first. He broadcast three times that day, first from the landing craft in the early morning as they waited to land. Next, with a transmitter they had brought ashore, and with the cooperation of the censors, he flashed the news to Rome before the official noon release time, gloating to himself that the old die-hard journalists who considered radio not real journalism had been left behind again. And finally that night, when Sevareid told America the names of the five soldiers who had helped him cut red tape, he pointed out that this was the same area in which Napoleon had landed when he returned from Elba.

To follow Eric's account of his expedition's reconquest of France, imagine him in his jeep—often in the congenial company of Bill Mauldin, Homer Bigart, and young Newbold Noyes—and the American army, moving east along the Riviera from St. Tropez, to St. Raphael, to Cannes, then northwest, with the Alps of Italy to the East, to Crest on the Drome River, which flows into the Rhône. Next north to Grenoble, northwest to Lyon on the Rhône, and finally northeast to Besançon by September 8, approaching the Swiss and German borders. The French Division linked up with General George C. Patton's Third Army in that area on September 11.

But the most emotional event had happened two weeks before, when Paris was liberated on August 25, and the next day Charles de Gaulle arrived and led a military parade down the Champs-Elysées, and said of himself, which Eric, had he been there, would have assented to: "Since each of all these here had chosen Charles de Gaulle in his heart as the refuge against his agony and the symbol of his hopes, we must permit the man to be seen, familiar and fraternal, in order that at this sight the national unity should shine forth."

The next day Eisenhower and General Omar Bradley tried to slip quietly into the city but were quickly recognized and embraced by the crowds. As a show of solidarity and force, de Gaulle requested a combined parade; Bradley agreed, and on August 29 marched his men down the Champs-Elysées and past the reviewing stand, but in full battle gear. They were literally on their way back to combat. This time on the way to the Rhine.

Meanwhile, the Anvil forces were actually enjoying the war; even the men who once had detested soldiering were crying "On to Berlin." The cheering French, as they greeted their rescuers, reminded Eric of a young boy who "long ill, leaves the sickroom and walks for the first time in the garden and the sun."

But if the southern campaign was a success, it was still a real battle. Outside Cannes Sevareid's party was caught in a cave, held down by shell fire directed right at them. In a weird crisis at Crest, the Thirty-sixth Division suddenly found itself accidently almost completely surrounded by German divisions that were supposed to be running away from them! So informed, Eric found the situation mad, preposterous, and demanded to speak to the commanding general—only to discover, to his alarm, that the general, disheveled, dressed only in trousers and an undershirt, was losing his nerve. The general wanted to arm the correspondents for the fight; but cooler officers told them that they should escape right away while they still could. For twenty minutes, among the most distressing of his life, Eric and the others debated whether they should get out or stay and fight, die, or be captured with the men. They finally realized that if they stayed the men would not admire their courage but rather regard them as idiots.

Outside Grenoble, in La Chapelle, Eric listened to the grizzly story of how the Germans, taking reprisals against the Maquis, had lined up twenty-two noncombatants against the wall, shot them, and dumped them in a mass grave; and in Grenoble itself evidence mounted not just of German atrocities but of the hidden savagery in the French heart he had witnessed not long ago when Weidmann went to the guillotine. In several towns he had seen German prisoners summarily shot and women collaborators caught, shaved, stripped, and humiliated by mobs.

While some of his journalistic colleagues were shocked by the frontier justice of the Maquis, Eric, who thought he knew what the French Resistance had suffered, tended to sympathize. On a dismal rainy day he was present to hear thousands of Grenoble citizens let out a terrible savage scream of satisfaction as a firing squad executed six young men in their teens and twenties. The dead boys slid slowly to their knees, their heads falling to one side, and an officer jumped from one to another adminsitering the coup de grace with his pistol. One of the victims moved his mouth as if to try to say something to his executioner at the last second.

Back at the press camp Eric argued against two colleagues who criticized the French for their drumhead justice. A few minutes later a friend took him aside and told him what he had missed. Right before the shooting a loud speaker had announced that since the people had expressed dissatisfaction with light sentences given others on trial, the courts would henceforth revise their rules. It dawned on Eric that he was most likely witnessing mob rule—but he was still not ready to condemn it.

Sevareid's tolerance of this extralegal, or rather impromptu French Resistance system of justice—which was quite capable of being a system of injustice—is not consistent with standard principles of liberal democracy, which normally would rather allow a guilty person to escape retribution than, by violating procedures that protect individuals from the state's abuse of power, risk punishing someone who is innocent. Sevareid's defense of the French, which he repeated often in the months ahead, even if well thought out, does not seem morally or philosophically persuasive. He simply stated that the French had suffered a great deal for four years, implying that their suffering justified—not merely explained—their illegal behavior. His moral system sometimes seemed based on instinct rather than a consistent set of principles. Thirty years later, when Eric Sevareid was established as a sort of gray-haired, remote, Olympian wizard in the corridors of the CBS Washington office, a group of younger reporters invited him to lunch, to get to know the liberal patriarch they had admired from a distance. As the talk heated up, they were shocked to hear Eric propose that the way to handle neighborhood drug dealers was for the neighborhood men to get baseball bats and take the offenders aside and beat them up. They concluded, as others had, that he was getting more conservative as he got older, not knowing he had held similar ideas, in a different context, when he was thirty-two.

Before France fell, Gertrude Stein made clear in her Paris interview with Sevareid for the *Herald* that she had never fully understood the seriousness of the Nazi threat. As Americans, she and her companion Alice B. Toklas were advised to leave immediately for the United States; and as Jews they should have sensed the possible consequences of their staying in Nazi-occupied France. But they were artists, not political analysts. Their *raison d'être* came from their salon, from being the center of what their biographer James Mellow called a "charmed circle," with painters like Picasso and Matisse and novelists like F. Scott Fitzgerald and Ernest Hemingway—who, the story goes, was taught to write by Stein crossing out his adjectives at a Montparnasse cafe, the Dôme.

Stein was, perhaps, too distracted by art to sense how art would suffer if fascism, in even its subtlest forms, was to prevail. She was even supportive of Pétain, who she thought had restored order after World War I. Living in Belley, in Vichy, however, they grew weary of the petty Vichy bureaucracy and began to tell their neighbors openly that they expected, wanted, the British and Americans to win the war. In February 1943, when, after a quarrel with their landlord, they were planning to move to nearby Culos, eighty kilometers from Grenoble, they were warned to flee to Switzerland lest they be put in a concentration camp. But they finally decided that here they were and here they were going to stay.

So they moved to Culos where the mayor and the servants and the townspeople shielded them from the Nazis, who occupied the town and one day in July 1944 even stayed overnight in their house. Gertrude worked on a manuscript called *Wars I Have Seen*, recording the exploits of the brave young Maquis who escaped from Nazi prisons and slipped off to the mountains to fight again; and she and Toklas followed the war news day-by-day—the rescues of Rome and Paris—and waited impatiently for the moment when the Americans would come back—for the day they referred to as "the liberation of Gertrude Stein." They fattened up a rooster and weighed it daily, ready to serve the honored bird to the first American general who came their way.

In August the Maquis took the town and soon some Americans joined them. On September 1, walking along the street, Gertrude met an American officer, Lieutenant Colonel William Perry, and his jeep driver, Private John Schmaltz, introduced herself, and invited them both home for dinner and to spend the night in the beds in which the German soldiers had slept.

The next day, worn out by the feast but jubilant at their liberation, Gertrude and Alice chatted away at lunch when the cook came running in. There were more Americans at the door! Gertrude rushed down and threw her arms around Eric Sevareid and Frank Gerasi from *Colliers*. Eric had asked Paul White to help track her down for him, had looked in the wrong town, then happened to meet Colonel Perry on his way home. The women served their guests another magnificent meal, decent coffee with real sugar. Eric gave Gertrude a cigarette and they talked and gossiped for hours. When Eric mentioned that they had just seen her old friend Hemingway's wife, Martha Gelhorn, also a war correspondent, Gertrude tsk-tsked her disapproval, "That makes his third wife."

When the correspondents finally drove away, their hardheaded driver from Boston asked, "Who'n hell is that old battle-ax?"

Told it was Gertrude Stein, he replied, "That beats the —— out of me."

Two days later Eric drove Stein forty miles to Voiron where he had set up a CBS broadcast to the United States. Her fabled flow of talk poured out unimpeded by the rules of syntax which hobbled lesser poets.

> What a day is today that is what a day it was day before yesterday, what a day! I can tell everybody that none of you know what this native land business is until you have been cut off from that same native land completely for years. This native land business gets you all right. Day before yesterday was a wonderful day. First we saw three Americans in a military car and we said are you Americans and they said yes and we choked and we talked . . .
>
> . . . I can tell you that liberty is the most important thing in the world more important than food and clothes more important than anything on this mortal earth, I who spent four years with the French under the German yoke tell you so. I am so happy to be talking to America today so happy.

There can hardly be two personalities more distant in style than the serious, "dark" Norwegian, who would never dream of writing an un-punctuated sentence, and whose intellectual approach to fascism in any form was like that of a hound dog smelling a fox, and this seventy-year-old Bohemian, who had given up premedical studies at Johns Hopkins in 1902 to live abroad, to be the mother and namer of the "lost generation." Yet it was important for Eric to identify himself with Gertrude Stein. For one thing, he had read about her and about Hemingway in one of the books that had the most impact on him as a college student, *The Autobiography of Lincoln Steffens.* Furthermore, both he and she had done the same thing: they had left home after college to find themselves in Paris. And both, whatever their differences in politics or deportment, slaved in order to give words their maximum impact, through sense, sound, and rhythm as well as syntax. And she was also, whether Eric would articulate this or not, his channel to a generation of writers with whom, as Hemingway would say, he had to compete. When Gertrude died in 1946, Eric sent Alice one of his typically brief and beautifully stated condolence notes, recalling their visit and the broadcast at Voiron, and concluding, "God bless you."

On September 8 at Besançon, the Allies broke into the German-occupied northern zone and linked up with the armies that had come down from Normandy. Immediately, Eric sensed the difference between the people of the two occupation zones—the Vichy collaborators of the south and the citizens of the north who, embittered and made hard by four years of humiliation, were vigorously—sometimes violently—bursting into life. One night he observed that the sweaty, reckless fighters who had not bowed to the Nazi yoke took over the middle-class cafes and dined and drank with their pistols in their belts. For Eric this was a symbol of "moral renewal and regeneration through armed rebellion." After all, he had insisted in 1941, in his play that never made it to the stage, that this was a war of moral regeneration, so it follows that he would see intimations of the London air-raid shelters in Besançon.

Later, after the armies had pushed toward Germany, Eric doubled back to be in Besançon to stand with most of the population of the city as they waited for two hours in the cold autumn rain to see de Gaulle. He had seen the general in London four years before and found him stiff; but now he watched the faces of the Frenchmen as their leader spoke. Their sourness and cynicism melted away, replaced by an almost fanatical reverence and awe. De Gaulle had mastered the gestures as well as the fact of leadership. He told the crowd they must earn the respect and help of other nations by their own political and moral reform. He asked them to sing the "Marseillaise" and walked slowly down the narrow street reaching out and touching them by the hundreds. Now, thought Eric, the French had a Roosevelt of their own.

If four years before, France had been apparently unembroiled in what journalists and politicans called a "phony war," in October 1944, in the euphoria of the Allied armies' advance toward the German border, the American public seemed excessively caught up in an anticipatory victory. *Time* magazine, published a premature story on local plans for "Victory Day," with its parades, speeches, and booze. Soldiers were beginning to shrink from combat. Why die when it's almost over? Ernie Pyle wrote the famous last column from Europe in which he confessed that he could no longer stand the sight of a dead young body. Eric, in what would be one of several tiffs with *Time*, felt obliged to offset the impact of Luce's journalism. He cabled a dispatch to CBS in which he tried to explain that plans for victory celebrations were fundamentally irrelevant to the daily sufferings of men who still struggled to do a nasty job.

> Your map tells you that the going has been rapid, but you seem to have forgotten that war is still war, that feet still swell in wet boots, that one can still shiver and ache on the ground all night, that the stomach still contracts when a shell bursts near by, and that a dead boy with punctured lungs, with the little rivulet of blood dried on his chin, remains a sight that does not bring thoughts of gaiety, organized or otherwise. Nobody really wants to reproach the people at home. They cannot see what the soldier sees nor feel what he feels. It is only to repeat that the imagination, no matter how it tries, cannot bridge the gulf between those who are living more miserably than ever in their lives before and those who, for the same cause, are living better. We shall see the difference, no doubt, on that Victory Day. The civilians will want to make noise for once, and the soldiers will want to be quiet for once. They are so very, very, tired of noise.

Those were his last words from France for America; but he was also bold enough to speak to the French in a September essay for *La Liberté*, in Lyon. As an attempt to both summarize his own seven-year love affair with France and tell the French what is going on in the minds of American servicemen, it is a remarkable document, summing up in much simpler language than his extended ruminations in *Not So Wild a Dream*, his honest, but critical, affection for both France and the troops who were noisily blustering their way through once quiet small towns, drinking too much, and chasing French girls.

First he reassures his audience that the French so-called decadence did not bring on the country's defeat and that the German occupation did not poison France's soul. As Gertrude Stein said, "The German presence was like the presence of a fog; you just walked through it without thinking about it." He praised the French contribution to victory in Italy, where French mountaineers had helped clear the path from Cassino to Rome. But he reports—without necessarily siding with the critics—that Americans were shocked by what he calls "little things"—the sight of women who had fraternized with Germans shaved and paraded nude through the streets and alleged collaborators beaten and executed without a legal trial. "Remember," he says—in a sentence whose ambiguity or squishy logic could be used to justify or excuse any number of summary executions in "revolutionary" situations for generations and wars to come—"that the American soldier has never experienced the terrorism of the Gestapo; and so he does not hate the Germans, nor their accomplices, quite as you do." He goes on to point out to the French that their wartime standard of living, compared to the United States, China, and Russia, has not suffered badly, then pleads for patience with the misbehaving GIs: "It is their way and they mean no harm. At heart, they are decent and generous boys. They are, after all, just boys."

Read today, in the context of Sevareid's whole life, his forgiving the French and forgiving the GIs may suggest that he wanted to see himself as forgiven as well.

On his flight to London, he passed over Paris and realized for the first time that, for him, the mystique of the city had been lost. It could be Pittsburgh or Kansas City—or even London. This did not mean that he had lost a love of these places or their individuality, but that now he thought of cities not in terms of nostalgia for their past but in terms of their future; he took this as the signal that at long last he had become a citizen of the world.

Sevareid's London, toward which his feelings had so long been ambiguous, had not stood still since he had left. If the old blitz had ended, a new threat had replaced it. Six days after D-day, the first V-1 flying bomb—heralded only by a mysterious buzzing sound followed by a high-pitched whine and then silence—destroyed two hundred houses in a working-class borough. Three months later the V-1s gave way to the V-2s, launched from two hundred miles away in Holland. It was a new level of terror: no warning buzz, only a terrible blast. The two weapons left 8,700 dead before Allied troops captured their launching sites. Murrow grasped the full, long-range strategic import of this new technology: although he could not have foreseen the intercontinental ballistic missile armed with a nuclear warhead, he saw that in a future war it would not be necessary to send bombers over the enemy's land.

Now Allied headquarters had been moved from London to Paris, and London had become, like Naples and Rome, a rear area.

> London was like the grimy anteroom of a great factory, where people have been working overtime on rush orders too long. London was like a famous hotel, gone seamy and threadbare after an interminable business convention which gave no chance for decoration, where the formal politeness of the overcrowded staff had worn away, and they had become direct, abrupt, and a little testy. London was tired and bored.

Eric strolled the empty space behind St. Paul's cathedral, which had once been blocks and blocks of narrow, winding streets. Sitting for a while in the churchyead of Saint Dunstan's-in-the-East, where only the front of the church remained, he met the gaunt rector, who joined him for a walk down to the Tower of London; the rector chatted easily not about what had happened during the bombing but about the continuity of English history, as if his faith in the city was like his faith in God. Eric found himself humbled by the man's belief in the future as an integral part of the past, and left him a contribution to help rebuild his ruined church.

If London was showing its sores, so was Murrow. He had the satisfaction of being elected president of the Association of American Correspondents in London, four years after radio broadcasters had not been considered serious journalists; but he was so worn out that he talked of getting out of broadcasting and accepting the presidency of Washington

State University. His personal life was also at the crisis point. He had fallen in love with Pamela Churchill, the then-wife of Winston Churchill's son Randolph, a woman notorious for her skillful pursuit of rich and powerful men, including Murrow's boss William Paley. Janet Murrow had gone home in September to see her family, and Ed had decided to soon follow her. So Sevareid was as welcome as he had been in 1940: he would take Murrow's place.

But before Murrow left, he gathered his correspondents for two roundtable discussions, precursors of the annual roundups CBS would air on radio and television with its star foreign correspondents, allowed each to state his opinions as well as simply report. The October 7 discussion, which brought together Shirer, Downs, LeSueur, and Sevareid, focused on whether the war would be over by Christmas. LeSueur, who had just returned from the American First Army attacking the Siegfried line, reported that the boys at the front, though ready for winter warfare, thought constantly of their families and needed more letters from home. Eric said that the boys who had been so jubilant with victory in France had, once they were fighting in the woods of the Vosges mountains, grown homesick again. He added that in both Italy and France the Communists looked like the most organized and purposeful postwar, political groups. And once again he stuck up for the French system of extemporized justice: "I would like to make one thing clear—this is not civil war in France. At the worst, a few murderers have been murdered, without trial—except a four-years' trial by their neighbors." Finally, he urged people at home to be patient, as soldiers have to be patient. "Do not make it any harder for your sons. Americans here still die with every dawn; do not celebrate the victory until it comes."

The following week, October 13, five years after Britain landed troops in France in response to Hitler's invasion of Poland, Murrow, Shirer, and Sevareid talked for fifteen minutes about their already fading hope that somehow a new economic and political order would be born out of the conflagration. Collectively they were disappointed that the Allied powers, having urged the people of France, Italy, Greece, and Yugoslavia to throw off their oppressors, now gave scant support to the liberation movements, for example, in Italy, by leaving Field Marshall Pietro Bagdolio in place. Ironically, although fascism was being defeated, said Murrow, the war had increased the power of the state over the individual, fulfilling Hitler's observation that the strength of National Socialism was that it would force those who fear it to imitate it.

In October Sevareid began a series of regular broadcasts, three-hundred-word combinations of news and analysis similar to what he had done in Washington. On November 22 he took his listeners behind the comfortable facade of London to the skeleton houses in poor sections where whole families lived day and night in tiny tin-roofed shelters, into the subway stations where the homeless still lived four years after the blitz. After a bombing incident, an ancient, decayed woman came up to Eric and the other reporters, all her belongings in a market bag, and whispered that she had no kin to take her in; she remembered the address of a woman she had met casually in a food shop. Eric took her there and the woman, though really a stranger, took her in at once. He left them chatting and making tea. She would probably stay there till she died.

For December 17, he wrote but could not deliver because of a technical failure, a hundred-word meditation on the awesome responsibiiy of taking Murrow's place for a while: "To be asked to speak in his place is about like being handed an unfinished copy of *War and Peace* and told, "dash off a chapter—old man Tolstoy is on vacation." The remark is a clue not just to his admiration of his mentor, but to how he viewed the writing process—even a daily three-minute broadcast; it was an ordeal tied to an obligation to produce art that would last.

Murrow was not just on vacation. In New York he met with CBS executives and in Washington he had another dinner at the White House. The dinner, rather than raising his spirits, reinforced his conviction that the Allies had compromised the moral crusade that he and his fellow correspondents had imagined the war to be. At the same time, Murrow was also struggling with his marriage. In December, refusing to tell CBS where he could be reached, he and Janet dropped out of sight together, retreated to a dude ranch in Texas to sleep, eat, and ride horseback until he was ready to return to England in March.

For three months Eric lived at Hallam Street, doing regular commentaries, including a witty piece about his difficulties buying a good suit in a London that was no longer the male fashion capital of the world. But, while Britain prepared for a crucial election that would test his theories about the direction of postwar Europe, Sevareid moved about the countryside and worried about England. In Sussex he sat in a local pub and watched the men in their Home Guard outfits down their Sunday predinner pints. On Brighton Road he rediscovered a ditch and a pillbox dug and built in 1940 as a line of defense against the Germans then expected to invade across the Channel. It reminded him of the summer day in 1932 when he had returned to Velva, wandered in the woods by the river, and rediscovered a fort he and his gang, the Terrible Five, had built to defend themselves against the imaginary Sioux.

Meanwhile, he became convinced that England had lost its self-confidence, that it was neurotically obsessed with comparing itself to America—interpreting every Allied victory as a British victory, as if the American army was a collection of thick-skinned football players and theirs a regiment of Rupert Brookes. Where would the next generation of Britain's leaders come from? And America, where would America get its new leaders? How many would-be leaders matched the character of men like John Paton Davies and Edward R. Murrow? Eric grew depressed at the thought of passionless, apolitical, young operators, like those represented by *Time* and *Fortune,* with their gray suits and gold-tipped fountain pens, setting the national tone and agenda.

One night at a small dinner with journalists and government officials, an American correspondent, with a curl in his lip, said, "I remember how you and Scotty Reston and others used to write about the 'New England.' When are you going to learn that your naive ideals just play into the hands of the realists? Democracy in England! You were fooled by what you saw in the blitz." This grim assessment had seemed confirmed in December when British bayonets supported martial law in Greece, backing a regime in power against the very Greek partisans who had taken the Allied side during the war. Churchill, the heroic wartime leader, had revealed his other, deeper, authoritarian self. He had lost touch with his country and even the conscience of the British people.

More and more, Sevareid wanted to get away from this, to return to the front lest the war end without him there to watch. Yet he finally realized that he had failed in his attempt to fully identify with the men he covered. It was not just his age; it was something basically incommunicable in individual human experience. In the end of a late-March Sunday broadcast, he poured this confession out in what became one of his most touching and memorable pieces:

That is what the war is like, this Sunday afternoon. That is, that's what all those called correspondents or commenators, analysts or observers, will be saying it's like. They believe it, the listeners and readers understand it, and what we say is true enough—but only within our terms of reference, in the unreal language of standard signs and symbols that you and I must use. To the soldier, that isn't what the war was like at all. . . .

Only the soldier really lives the war. The journalist does not. He may share the soldier's outward life and dangers, but he cannot share his inner life because the same moral compulsion does not bear upon him. The observer knows that he has alternatives to action; the soldier knows he has none. It is the mere knowing that makes the difference. Their worlds are very far apart, for one is free, the other a slave.

War happens inside a man. It happens to one man alone. It can never be communicated. That is the tragedy—and perhaps the blessing. A thousand ghastly wounds are really only one. A million martyred lives leave an empty place at only one family table. That is why, at bottom, people can let wars happen, and that is why nations survive them and carry on. And, I am sorry to say, that is also why in a certain sense you and your sons from the war will be forever strangers.

If, by the miracles of art and genius, in later years two or three among them can open their hearts and the right words come, then perhaps we shall all know a little of what it was like. And we shall know, then, that all the present speakers and writers hardly touched the story.

So, along the banks of the Rhine, on the day of the "last battle," Eric Sevareid sat on his helmet behind a brick house to avoid the enemy mortars now being lobbed in as close as fifty yards away, waiting for the night's precrossing bombardment to open up.

A Cockney sentryman leaned against the wall. "I say there, correspondent," he said, "ye wouldn't be Mister Vincent Sheean by off chance, would ye?" The soldier had read Eric's friend and rival's book. One can easily imagine that this was a reminder to the correspondent that he soon ought to produce a book of his own.

At seven o'clock the barrage began—a ceaseless, maddening racket, which made the blood beat in his head and frayed his nerves. For a while Eric climbed a church steeple for a better view, then watched a commando unit of assault troops, their faces black with soot, file out of the woods, singing softly in cadence as they marched toward their landing craft. His attention became fixed on a major nearby who, as each soldier filed by, silently reached out and touched him. The major had only one eye. He had lost the first during a commando raid in Norway, and now he had been given two weeks leave from his post in Wales and had chosen to spend those two weeks here. Eric watched him, as he moved back and forth from the men, transfixed. Suddenly he realized why. He was looking into this man's heart and seeing himself. He remembers in *Not So Wild a Dream:*

> The war had become his very life; these men were all his world. Here with them under the dark moon, in the middle of the hellish noise, in this moment when his comrades prepared to challenge the unknown, he was intensely alive. Elsewhere, he was half-dead. And, I thought, there will be many like this man, many who will remain but half-alive when all this is ended.

Wesel was the "last battle" in only the broadest sense. The Germans resisted for a few more weeks. Hitler shot himself on April 30, a cease-fire sounded along the front on May 5, and the surrender was signed two days later at the French cathedral town of Rheims. Europe was free. And Eric Sevareid was free to go home—though feeling only half alive.

13

THE DREAM

Y OUR FATHER is coming home," Lois told the twins, now five years old. For most of their lives, they had hardly seen their father at all. Delighted to have a father at last, they ran around telling their friends, "Our father is coming home! Our father is coming home!"

Then one day there was a knock at the door, and this big, tall, thin man loomed over them. "Our father is coming home! Our father is coming home!" they cried, thinking this stranger would like to know.

The stranger sat down and wept.

The father was home, but he was home with work to do. And he would have to go away to do it. This time however, he would take them with him. So with Lois and the boys around him, he took a leave from CBS and withdrew to a house on a cliff at Carmel, overlooking the California coast, and tried to explain what it meant to be an American in 1945.

In the first chapters of *Trees, Why Do You Wait?* (1991), his analysis of the alarming disappearance of rural culture, Richard Critchfield, who knew Eric Sevareid and himself grew up in a small North Dakota town, suggests that the idealism and optimism Eric Sevareid voiced for his generation in the late 1940s sound outdated today.

Sevareid ends *Not So Wild a Dream* with "little Velvas" all over the world, the democracy he had known as a child now taking root where America's muscle, voice, and will had traveled during the war. Today, says Critchfield, after forty-five years of postwar involvement in the world, we have a more complex, sophisticated understanding of peasant villages within ancient civilizations. And the way of life, the moral code that Sevareid extolled, with the small town's sense of community, fell victim to the social and economic forces unleashed by the war.

Yet, *Not So Wild a Dream,* although categorized as a journalist's auto-biography, has been rich and varied enough to enjoy two lives: one as a best-seller in 1946, and another, when it was reprinted with a new introduction, in 1976. What was read one year as a World War II memoir returned thirty years later for the Bicentennial as an American anthem, a restatement of the values almost lost during McCarthyism of the 1950s, and the wave of disillusionment and distrust that followed Watergate and Vietnam. When he retired in 1977, hundreds of people wrote to him about the book's influence, and dozens wrote to this writer in 1993, several saying that Sevareid's life story had changed their own lives.

The book that enjoyed two lives also had a brief resurrection. After his retirement, two groups talked about turning *Not So Wild a Dream* into a TV series—one a Los Angeles group who would do a docudrama, the other, the Public Broadcasting System. Both projects died, and Eric wrote to Irving Lazar in Beverly Hills (January 18, 1979) for advice. "If the book had intrinsic merits for a TV production a year ago, it still does. It looks like it will remain in the literature of the war period as a permanent fixture." It is interesting that he described it as a "permanent fixture" of the "war period," when his intention was clearly to create something that transcended its time and place. Finally, PBS's *The American Experience* did an hour on the Velva-1940 chapters in 1988. Hollywood's failure to follow up could be due to a number of factors: production costs and so on, or a sense that there was no longer an audience, or a market, for what Eric Sevareid had to say.

In 1946 the Minneapolis *Sunday Tribune* (October 13) reviewer, Hjalmar Bjornson chided Sevareid for giving as much space to losing his *Minnesota Daily* editorship as he did to the fall of France, and for linking the "fascism" of the local Citizens' Alliance during the trucking strike with Hitler and Mussolini; but he agreed that Sevareid spoke for his generation as it wondered how liberalism will survive the postwar struggles and the consequences of Hiroshima. In the *Saturday Review* (October 12) Elmer Davis, who had lived through much of it, was most impressed by the "appallingly vivid recreation of the terrible year 1940—the hour when heaven was falling, the day the earth's foundation fled." When the popular radio program, *Author Meets the Critic,* sponsored a letter contest about the book, one of the winners, Samuel W. Stein, who was about Eric's age, wrote that he too felt that a moral depression seemed to have gripped the world, but "I too have been crying for that 'dream' as I believe Mr. Sevareid has. I too have been saying to those I know, that fraternity and peace and goodwill among men are possible."

While nearly all the critics compared it to Sheean's *Personal History,* Eric's favorite reaction must have been in the personal letter from Feike Feikema (Fred Manfred): "I am all the more confirmed in my opinion that it backs Mr. Sheean off the map. He was a bit affeminate [*sic*] for me; but you, you have the rare thing of sounding like a he-man and a poet."

To achieve both the best-seller status and that he-man poet tone, Eric had to make a number of decisions about both where his life and career were in 1945 and about how his book should be like and unlike the many similar books—for example those by Lincoln Steffens, Richard Harding Davis, Richard Halliburton, Vincent "Jimmy" Sheean, William L. Shirer, Howard K. Smith, and Larry LeSueur.

"The autobiographer," writes William Gass (*Harper's,* May 1994), "will think of himself as having led a life so important it needs celebration, and of himself as sufficiently skilled at rendering as to render it rightly. Certainly he will not begin his task believing he has led a botched life and will now botch the both." Meanwhile a variety of motivations are at work. Eisenhower's *Crusade in Europe* both put his version of the war on the record and made him financially secure. *The Autobiography of Malcolm X* both preached Malcolm's interpretation of the Black Muslim movement and, as a classic religious conversion story, gave testimony to God's grace. Jane Addams's *Twenty Years at Hull House,* an attempt to explain the sources of her inspiration, traces the success of the settlement house movement to the childhood influence of Lincoln. Finally, one writes to create a work of art. In that sense, autobiography is a self-portrait, an artifact that symbolizes the writer. It is as subjective as any painting, no more intended to represent the whole of reality than is a van Gogh or a Matisse.

In that sense, the writing is a process of deciding what to put in—usually what makes the author unique—and what to leave out. The journalist will center on those episodes when identity and profession converge. The best journalists, like Mark Twain and Richard Harding Davis, became national barometers of what it meant to be an American and, in some instances, what it meant to be a man. The roving correspondents among them become instant historians, interpreters of their time, the modern replacement for Henry Adams, who warned about the "acceleration" of history, about the danger of being overwhelmed by the pace of change. And they provide the real life stories that a young nation still needs to help explain what it means to be an American.

When the Cockney soldier told Eric Sevareid on the banks of the Rhine on the eve of the battle of Wesel that he had "read Vincent Sheean's book," he was saying more than he realized. By then Sheean had written a dozen books; but the one that "everyone," including Winston Churchill, had read was his 1935 memoir, *Personal History,* the volume which in many ways sums up all the ingredients of its type.

Maybe Eric could "beat" Davis. Sheean, maybe later. As a high school boy, Sevareid identified with Davis who, until his death in 1916, was America's idea of the journalist as hero. Peter Finley Dunne said that Davis probably knew more "waiters, generals, actors, and princes" than any man who ever lived. The power of his image was so pervasive that when the North American Newspaper Alliance sent Sheean to cover the Chinese revolution in 1927 the editors grew impatient because, they said, Sheean had been sent not to analyze the politics but to have adventures "in the Richard Harding Davis tradition"; and, in later generations, the on-the-scene presence of a particular correspondent, the writer with the public persona, rather than the event itself, bestowed meaning to the news.

Thus Hemingway, trailing the aura of *A Farewell to Arms,* returned to cover World War II, carried a weapon, landed at Normandy, and personally "liberated" Paris. And Norman Mailer, author of the best World War II novel, *The Naked and the Dead,* in *Armies of the Night,* made his participation in the 1967 march against the Pentagon a political and literary event. And Sevareid's friend and fellow China correspondent Theodore H. White, who developed a new journalistic genre in his *Making of the President* books, called his 1980 memoir *In Search of History,* joining the tradition of Sheean and Sevareid.

The classic young journalist's first book does not usually start out as an autobiography. While the older journalist, usually in retirement—as in C. L. Sulzberger's *Seven Continents and Forty Years* (1977) and James Reston's *Deadline: A Memoir* (1991)—looks back with satisfaction over a lifetime of big stories and interviews with famous personages, the younger writer tends to come fresh from a story with which he has been identified. The book will be the "full" story, a chance to tell what censors or the enemy tried to kill. It is also, as David T. Bazelon, who reviewed *Not So Wild a Dream* for the *Nation* (November 2, 1946) said, "the kind of book that most sincere journalists write or want to write—have to write in order to maintain their sincerity and their balance."

Unless the format is a diary, like William L. Shirer's *Berlin Diary* (1941) and Larry LeSueur's *Twelve Months That Changed the World* (1943), the genre seems to require two tacked-on chapters about the writer's early life: childhood, college, first job, disappointment, before the story itself. Thus, though the college chapters have interest, Sheean's pace picks up when, at the age of twenty-three for the Paris edition of the *Chicago Tribune,* he is sent to interview Clemenceau on the death of his friend Sarah Bernhardt. Indeed, Howard K. Smith was aware of the hybrid quality of his memoir. In his preface to *Last Train from Berlin* (1942), which contains "what American correspondents in Berlin tried to tell the world between the lines of their dispatches last autumn," he told the readers that, if they wish, they may skip the first two chapters about his student travels and personal convictions.

This tension between early life and adult adventure was one of the creative tensions Sevareid would have to resolve. His work so far, like Murrow's, had been an unusual blend of the objective and subjective, rational observer and committed liberal. People who had known him professionally for many years scarcely knew him, yet some of his writing could be courageously personal.

As Gass writes:" I know of nothing more difficult than knowing who you are, and then having the courage to share the reasons for the catastrophe of your character with the world. Anyone honestly happy with himself is a fool. (It is not a good idea to be terminally miserable about yourself either.)"

So on July 4, 1945, on leave from CBS, he sat alone at his typewriter in his Monterey, California coastal retreat to write his book. The day before he had received a challenging cable from his best friend. Scotty Reston, sweltering in Washington's ninety-nine-degree heat, sent him some advice:

> Well, I am pleased about the progress on the book. There is not another of my colleagues who has more to say. I am absolutely sure of that. Moreover, you have got away and gathered your family round you: and every time you look at your two boys you must get a sense of time-past and time-future which will lead to that

reflective quality you mention. Don't hesitate to be reflective and personal, and philosophic about it. The essence of this crisis of man is moral and therefore personal and if one can see it in terms of one's own experience, perhaps it can be put down with more meaning than in any other way. I am delighted you are doing it and it will be printed and widely read and appreciated, and as you say, if this prophecy proves to be wrong, why you shall have gained by the task anyway. We all need to get away and reflect and define and we do not do it often enough.

Eric's typing table was situated under the stairway, and Michael, the more rambunctious of the twins, loved to run and jump down the stairs, landing with a heavy thump on every third step. His father would grab him and swat him playfully. Then they would take a break, stroll along the beach, climb the cliffs and watch the fins and backs of whales crest out in the ocean as they migrated north.

Roosevelt died on April 12, the day Eric flew from London to Washington, and he arrived in time to stand tearful on Pennsylvania Avenue and watch the coffin go by, and think back to Floyd Olson's funeral, when he had been astonished to see how *small* the casket was—that all his youthful hopes for a more just America could now fit into a box and be buried in the ground.

Sent to cover the April–May San Francisco conference on the establishment of the United Nations, Eric watched his war adventures parade before him in the hotel lobbies and on the podium: Bech from Luxenbourg, whose hair was now gray, and Didier from Yugoslavia, who stared into his glass and mourned his martyred wife. In the lobby of the St. Francis Hotel he found a Maquis whom he had last seen in Besançon bragging about the bridges he had blown up—now a diplomat from France. In his May 1 broadcast, Eric assured his listeners that the men who fought the war were making the peace.

Back in New York, CBS was going through a drastic postwar change. In 1943 Paley had convinced Robert E. Sherwood to bring him into the war effort as a consultant to the Psychological Warfare Branch of the Office of War Information and, with the rank of first an honorary colonel and then a commission, he was stationed in Algiers, Italy,

London, and Paris. It was, writes Sally Bedell Smith, a turning point in his career, "He yearned to escape both his marriage and his network." Paley's contributions to wartime propaganda were considerable, but for him it was largely a chance to associate with people like Eisenhower, Churchill, British press lords, and especially Murrow and his "boys." His fondest memory was of a drunken stag party at Collingwood's London flat: "It was that everyone loved each other," he said, "and it was just a brawl. A great big lousy brawl, but it was one of those nights in my life that was very outstanding."

He also pursued, among others, Lady Edwina Mountbatten, whose husband was in Burma, and Pamela Churchill, who was deeply involved with Murrow. But, driven by both his social ambition and the excitement of the power that went with his work, Paley collapsed from nervous exhaustion. He returned to New York and to CBS a different person—feeling ennobled by his association with British aristocracy, primed to build CBS into a more powerful commercial entity by raiding the stars—like Jack Benny—from NBC, having decided to make Frank Stanton president and himself chairman and to bring Murrow home in a new role as an executive. And he was ready to get rid of his wife Dorothy.

Murrow meanwhile had saved his marriage. Janet became pregnant during their vacation, and Murrow's deeper principles of family loyalty and commitment won out. The status of Eric's marriage was another question. Lois's life had been, in some ways, as turbulent as his own. It is possible that her real reason for going to Cairo was to be near him, to try to protect their marriage. Because UNRRA was working with refugees in Greece, she had flown to Greece on Thanksgiving Day in 1944 for ten days, getting out just the day before the Greek revolution erupted. She returned to the United States in time to join Eric at the San Francisco conference; but, while they were in New York staying at "Jimmy" Sheean's apartment, Eric had seen the first frightening sign of the problem that would transform the rest of his life and test his moral fiber as severely as had the north woods or the Naga hills. One day he found Lois curled up in a fetal position, in a virtual catatonic state. The episode passed, but Reston's reference in his cable to Lois "getting rest" is an indication of both the love their friends had for Lois and the first of many letters that will refer to her health.

Unfortunately, as both Sevareid's memoir and Paley's later reminiscences attest, the atmosphere of wartime capitals did not support marital fidelity. A woman journalist who knew Sevareid's circle during the 1940s said: "I don't know anyone who didn't have an affair during the war." Paley said of London, "It was sort of like the normal, conventional morals of the time were just turned on their ear because of the urgency . . ." In Paris, Eric had gotten to know a young Hungarian girl, Gitta Sereny, stepdaughter of the conservative economist Ludwig Von Mises; and the friendship, which continued back in the United States, ripened into a "close relationship." Eric spent time with her when he returned from China while Lois was in Cairo. At the time Gitta was very much in love with him, but engaged to another man in Europe, and Eric was "a little bit" in love with her, but the husband of a wife of ten years who was developing some problems, and the father of two five-year-old boys whom he had barely seen. But Gitta creeps into his book: he devotes over two pages to her beauty, her zeal, her work for refugees, her analysis of her own generation—almost as much space as he gives to Lois.

That was his present situation. Now he had to put that out of his mind. What other books might creep into his own? Had the spirit of Richard Halliburton invaded his story? In the late 1920s Halliburton wrote, and young men like Eric read, his purple-prosed real-life travel adventures like *The Royal Road to Romance* and *The Glorious Adventure,* where he tracked the footsteps of Ulysses, climbed Mount Olympus, paid homage at the grave of Rupert Brooke, swam the Hellespont, and, though Vesuvius was dormant, watched Stromboli explode. Troops in Italy told Sevareid they were disappointed when various scenes were not as glorious as Halliburton's books had depicted them.

If Richard Harding Davis was the ideal war correspondent, Lincoln Steffens fixed in the public mind the image of journalist as world citizen and reformer, muckraking Cincinnati and Europe in turn, hobnobbing with revolutionaries in Mexico and Russia, and returning to advise the president of the United States. In 1910 he "discovered" Walter Lippmann by asking Harvard professors for "the ablest mind that could express itself in writing." In Montparnasse, he gossiped with Hemingway and Gertrude Stein. At fifty-six, living in Europe, he moved in with a twenty-one-year-old woman, and married her when she became pregnant, then returned to California as a lecturer and guru of the left.

Read today, Steffens' windbaggy sense of self-importance may alienate a later generation of readers; and it is possible that modern readers might take Sheean's *Personal History* as a 1930s artifact rather than enduring literature; but with his book Sheean is credited with introducing a new form of writing that came to full flower in Mailer's *Armies of the Night*, semi-autobiographical political journalism where the committed observer interprets a moment of history while he strides—sometimes swaggers—across the stage

Sheean starts with the armistice of 1918, when he was eighteen, rushes through the student paper and fraternity life at the University of Chicago, works as "a professional observer of the peep show of misery" at the *New York Daily News*, and is off to Paris to work for the *Chicago Tribune*, in 1922. He covers peace conferences and minor wars, but makes his reputation by his expedition into Morocco's Rif mountains to cover the rebellion that inspired Sigmund Romberg's *The Desert Song*. Four-fifths of the book treat his coverage of the Rifs, the Chinese Revolution, and the Holy Land, where he was shocked by attempts by militant Zionists to provoke confrontations with the Palestinians. He also meets Hemingway getting off the Paris-Moscow Express in Berlin, and declares him ". . . of all the writers or artists of this approximate age, the man who had most amply developed and exactly applied the gifts he possessed."

Clearly a young person's book, written when he was thirty-two, *Personal History* bursts with energy, tragedy—the death of a woman he reveres —and hope. When the 1969 edition appeared, William McWhirter said: "With the exception of Norman Mailer's *Armies of the Night*, there has never been a better book about what journalism is really like and what it should be when it is very, very good. And, naturally, like Mailer's book, it is not about journalism at all . . . Sheean instead shows a good many of us not only how to report but how to live—to dare to be involved, vulnerable and exposed."

So, in the company of Sheean, LeSueur, Shirer, Smith, and even Hemingway, Sevareid set out to be the writer who "most amply developed and exactly applied the gifts he possessed." In many ways there is a striking similarity in structure in the books written by all three men: childhood, college, first job, Paris, the big story of World War II taking up about four-fifths of the book. Yet, Sevareid's early years, Velva, are not a tacked on childhood, but the spiritual center from which the rest of the narrative flows, the symbolic basis for his later judgments on the nature of democracy, and the framing device by which he returns the reader to the beginning on the last page. While the books of his contemporaries were about the story, the war, Sevareid's is really about America, about the feelings and experiences of the whole generation who fought the war and wondered what kind of a future would emerge from it.

Sometimes long passages from Sevareid's notes, diaries, articles and broadcasts made their way, occasionally with only a few changes, into the text of *Not So Wild a Dream*. Very often though, the book's version—as in the canoe trip—reflects years of meditation, or a change in perspective. For example, on his return home from China he describes in his notes his desire to go to church at Christmas. In the book version, he concludes, "I had a deep desire to let go, to sink back to childhood beginnings, to recapture, if I could, something I had lost. But one can never do it; there is no going back. One can only go on with those of his own generation, living in his own time." Church, apparently seen as "going back," is dropped. Later, to the London broadcast story of the old bombed-out woman whom he leaves having tea, he adds: "I did not experience the old rush of blood to the head over another barbarous act of Fascism. There had been too much, too long. The old woman did not represent an innocent victim of modern barbarism; she represented an entry in a ledger in some government bureau."

But if Eric has been personal about his feelings of fear and disillusionment, he has virtually hidden, except for the dramatic birth and escape of the twins, his family. He doesn't even tell us Lois's family name! Although he twice makes very oblique references to seeing his "brother" in Germany; he does not tell us he has two brothers and a sister. We know the father through the impact of his bank's failure and his Minneapolis conservatism, and the mother only through her ambiguous feelings about life on the frontier. Perhaps he is protecting their privacy as well as his own; perhaps they are simply not central to his theme.

Or rather the several themes that a number of these authors, on similar journeys through history, have come to cherish.

The land, the river, as sources of life and challenge. Lincoln Steffens was born a street away from the yellow Sacramento River, which occasionally would get a boy in its grip and drown him and "then let his body come up all white and small, miles and miles away." Sevareid remembers that when the men on the baseball team from the neighboring town stripped off their overalls to swim in the Velva River, their bodies were white and only their forearms and faces and necks were tan.

The loss of innocence. Steffens as an adolescent working at a racetrack learned that races were fixed! Sevareid was stunned when, as a young reporter on the *Journal,* he saw a veteran financial editor fired by the "guy" he "used to teach where to put commas."

The discovery of evil as an overwhelming, unfathomable force. For Steffens it was the shame of the cities, the bribery, which in time failed to shock him. Sheean discovered fascism in Italy in 1924 and "murderous and hypocritical" imperialism in the Rif mountains of Morocco where he lived for months among Arab tribes.

Howard K. Smith, in a beer hall in Worms, watching fine-looking, young officers drink, shout, and sing, began, for the first time, to think about Germany:

> not as an academic subject to gather facts about for discussion at home, but as a real, direct and imminent threat to the existence of a civilization which gathers facts and discusses. A schism deeper than the Grand Canyon separated my world from that of the young man across from me, whose face bore fencing scars and carried a monocle over one glassy eye. The fetishes of my world, the values it worshipped, if it did not always attain them, were contained in words like "Reason," "Think," "Truth." His fetishes and his values were "Feel," "Obey," "Fight."

For Sevareid the evil was always fascism in its many shifting faces; but as the war progressed human cruelty took more complex forms. He saw, but could not report, that American soliders often, apparently out of whim or for convenience, murdered their German prisoners. Yet, after he crossed the Rhine and moved deeper into German territory, he saw that he himself had lost the ability to feel pity for the Germans. He came to see the German people, as a people, as morally inferior.

Hope in the future. Smith thought the German people could still be converted by the other nations practicing "Total Democracy" and to

explain how, Smith, who all his life would be concerned about his freedom to say what he thought, ends his book as a reporter-turned-
commentator, in his "first editorial." LeSueur warns in his last line, "We
cannot afford to lose Soviet Russia as a friend if we are to avoid a third
World War."

Sheean concluded in 1929 that even if he could not be a revolutionary, he could at least give himself as a writer to explain life as the
"coherent struggle toward the reasoned control" of the materials of existence. His inner voice, attributed to the spirit of the young woman, an
American romantic idealist, whom he loved as a friend and who died in
Moscow, tells him at the end:

> Your work, if you ever do anything that amounts to a damn, will
> have to be some kind of writing, I suppose; I don't know much
> about that, but it might be a good idea to try to learn how to
> write. And if you ever do learn how, the obligation upon you will
> be just this: to see things as straight as you can and put them into
> words that won't falsify them. That's programme enough for one
> life, and if you can ever do it, you'll have acquired the relationship
> between the one life you've got and the many of which it's a part.

Sevareid, having survived his canoe trip to Hudson Bay, the bombing
of London, a plane crash in the Burma jungle and most of the battlefields of Europe, puts his faith in the American character, in the
"teamwork" that harvested North Dakota crops, built planes and tanks,
and whipped Hitler. But he is not merely nostalgic or nationalistic, he
internationalizes the Velva spirit—as if, in the theological sense, it was
the Holy Spirit, the Creator breathing life into the brotherhood of
mankind.

This brotherhood was also the theme of the hour-long radio drama
CBS commissioned in 1944 to hail the Allied victory in Europe. They
turned to Norman Corwin, a thirty-four-year-old Boston-born newspaper man who switched to radio in the mid-1930s and experimented
with various forms of radio drama that tried to use verse in a way that
made poetry palatable to the ear. He joined CBS in 1938 and for years
produced verse dramas, like *Words without Music,* and radio adaptations
of Carl Sandburg, Walt Whitman, and other poets. One of his greatest
successes was *Ballad for Americans,* which combined the talents of com-
poser Earl Robinson and singer Paul Robeson. His 1945 verse drama,

On A Note of Triumph, draws heavily on news accounts of the rise and fall of fascism, including Shirer's account of France's capitulation at Compiegne, and bursts with place names, ship names, popular war songs, and the horrors of the blitz and the Holocaust. A 1946 reviewer of *Not So Wild a Dream* called both the book title and Corwin's masterpiece "mawkish." Yet both spoke for much of America that year, and both open a window into their authors' concept of the American civil religion—that amalgam of values from the religious tradition that takes the public place of religion in a secular state. Some excerpts:

> *And the kid with the bright blonde hair and the turned-up nose, moans all night among the rubble because his left leg hangs in blackened tatters, and he cries to his mother, who is dead.*
>
> What we have learned from the war . . .
>
> WE'VE LEARNED THAT THOSE MOST CONCERNED WITH SAVING THE WORLD FROM COMMUNISM USUALLY TURN UP MAKING IT SAFE FOR FASCISM . . .
>
> WE'VE LEARNED THAT WOMEN CAN WORK AND FIGHT, AS WELL AS LOOK PRETTY AND COOK . . .
>
> WE'VE LEARNED THAT SOME MEN WILL FIGHT FOR POWER, BUT THAT MOST MEN WILL FIGHT TO BE FREE.

Corwin's text ends in prayer:

> Lord God of test-tube and blueprint
> Who jointed molecules of dust and shook them till their name was
> Adam,
> Who taught worms and stars how they could live together,
> Appear now among the parliaments of conquerors and give instruction to their schemes:
> Measure out new liberties so none shall suffer for his father's color or the credo of his choice:
> Post proofs that brotherhood is not so wild a dream as those who profit by postponing it pretend:
> Sit at the treaty table and convey the hopes of little peoples through expected straits,
> And press into the final seal a sign that peace will come for longer than posterities can see ahead,
> That man unto his fellow shall be a friend forever.

14

VALLEY LANE

T HE FIRST IMPRESSION today's visitor gets as he peers up from
the street at the almost fifty-year-old modern house barely visible
through the trees is that whoever lives here wants to be left alone. Old
or former neighbors, who talk about what has happened to Alexandria,
Virginia's, Seminary Hill in the last half-century, say yes, the corner of
Pegram Street and Polk Street, which fifty years ago were dirt roads,
now seems in some ways as cut off from its larger suburban context as it
was when Eric and Lois Sevareid drove by in 1946 and saw horses graz-
ing below by the road and the lush meadow spreading out through the
valley, reaching up a steep slope to a modernistic house on the top of the
ridge. Here, they decided, was where they wanted to live.

Fifty years ago, before the woods grew up to their present wild domi-
nation, the excitement of the place must have been, along with the
house's modern design, the height, the combination of distance and en-
gagement: the freedom to sit on the veranda and gaze upon the world
below.

From that perch, you could think about the world and commiserate
with its intractable problems from on high, and next morning make the
twenty-five-minute drive to the office, face a typewriter, and ponder
formally what you pondered formally the night before.

Today, Seminary Hill, named for the Episcopal seminary that has
given an identity to this area for most of this century, is a populous suburban neighborhood in Alexandria, reached by turning off Interstate 395
south at Seminary Road, which leads you, for the most part, through
congested, teeming, commercial streets. East off Seminary Road, what
is now called Pegram Street drops down a steep hill to its conjunction
with Polk Street into a little valley that fifty years ago was a rural enclave
for a handful of families working at the heart of the New Deal and planning for the new nation being shaped out of the World War.

Today, an elementary school, with its broad playing fields and out-door gym apparatus, reaches out toward some white-columned houses at the far end of Polk. Leaping up from the Polk-Pegram corner is a steep hill, wrapped in a dense woods, sheltering on the hilltop a red-wood-and-glass one-floor modern home, one of three designed in the mid-1940s by the well-known architect Robert Goodman. Here the Sevareids lived for thirteen years.

Across the street a private tennis court is sheltered in the woods. A hundred yards from the corner, a sharp, now-paved path, sided by split-rail fences, leads up through the woods another hundred yards to the home. A blooming red azalea bush welcomes the visitor at the foot of the hill, but the ascent into the dark woods of oak, maple, and spruce, to the summit, where sunlight fights to break through, seals off the neigh-borhood below. The only immediate sounds are the birds. Robins and a cardinal flit through the branches. A squirrel rustles the dried leaves that have lain since last autumn on the woods floor. But another sound in-trudes: the constant hum of afternoon rush-hour traffic grinding by on 395, out of sight but only three minutes away.

Yet, what struck Eric Sevareid about his new home was not so much the isolation as the long, sloping meadow—which the last thirty years have reclaimed as a woods—leading up to the house. That's where he could keep the horses; he was going to teach the twins to ride.

He must have also known that he was moving into a neighborhood of kindred spirits. Virginia Foster Durr, the civil rights activist from Montgomery, Alabama, recalls in her autobiography *Outside the Magic Circle* how she and her husband, the lawyer Clifford Durr, moved to Washington in 1933 to work for the New Deal. He was with the Re-construction Finance Corporation, exhausting himself every day trying to save the banks, and she told her real estate agent she wanted to live somewhere in the country where the people were "poor and genteel."

That was Seminary Hill. It was a "beautiful place with the old brick buildings of the seminary and the brick buildings of the Virginia Episco-pal High School. This was where the gentility of Virginia had gone for generations. They would refer to 'the High school,' 'the Seminary,' and 'the University,' which meant Virginia Episcopal High School, the Vir-ginia Theological Seminary, and the University of Virginia."

Among their neighbors was a man who talked to the trees, a family who didn't believe in eating cooked food, an old Englishman who was convinced that the invention of the automobile had put the world on the road to hell, Thurmond Arnold, Supreme Court Justice William O. Douglas, a congressman from Massachusetts, the BBC's Washington correspondent, and John Kenneth Galbraith; and good Virginia manners presumed that they visited one another in the afternoon and everyone was supposed to have tea and cookies ready. On the periphery of that elite circle, where people lived in older, larger homes, were the Sevareids.

The road from Washington to Alexandria was paved, and the one from Alexandria to the Hill was gravel. The bus ran twice a day; so during the war years—with air-raid drills and car-pooling—everyone learned to depend on and care for everyone else. They rode their car pools to work—Virginia would sit on Galbraith's boney knees—and argued politics and economics fiercely; and in the evenings and weekends the neighbors helped each other with household chores and cared for one anothers' children.

The Sevareids' nearest neighbors included the Douglass Caters, who moved in the 1950s; he was Washington editor of the *Reporter* magazine. And the next-door neighbors, with whom the Sevareids shared a driveway, were Philip and Adele Brown, who also lived in a house designed by Goodman. Over thirty years later at a dinner for the Caters and Browns at Eric's Georgetown home, they reminisced about the time Eric first met Mrs. Cater, then a striking redhead. Eric, attired in his riding outfit, had gone looking for his hunting dog and wandered onto the Cater property on the opposite hill. Libby Cater, he recalled in a toast, was "like a brook trout, she always lived in beautiful places." But the way he described his neighbor's wife matched how so many people, men and women, described him. "Everything about Eric reflected beauty," Cater said. His clothes always fit. He wore his riding clothes even though it appeared he was not going riding. But his costume reflected his romantic image of himself. Eric joined the Seminary Hill Association, a group meant to control the development of the area so as to protect its rural character, and on several occasions donned what Charles E. Beatley, Jr., later the local mayor, described as "his carpenter's outfit," to help nail the roof on Beatley's log cabin at the bottom of the hill.

Thus, in his new home on Valley Lane, Eric would seem to have achieved a harmonious balance between the two worlds he had always sought: Washington, the hub of political and journalistic activity viewed from the bricked terrace of a modish contemporary home; but a modern home ensconced in his rural past, where he could personally cut the meadow in front and clear the brush, and neighbors could look out for you—as they did in Velva, North Dakota.

Lois meanwhile, determined that the twins, whom she had not cared for personally since 1943, should get off to the right start in school, sought advice from Kathryn Stone, then vice president of the League of Women Voters, who had a reputation as an authority on education and had taught at Metairie Park Country Day School in New Orleans. It turned out they had met years before in Mount Vernon, Iowa, where Stone grew up, and they chatted for hours about Stone's "gleam in her eye," her dream for a new cooperative, ungraded, elementary school in the country, where learning would be fun, and where, in accordance with the latest theories of child development, each child could develop at his or her own pace.

The dream for the new school had begun with a group of parents at the Beverly Hills, Alexandria, community church who, appalled by the wretched state of overcrowded Virginia public schools, wanted to continue what they had begun at the church's preschool program. With the support of their pastor, Rev. William C. Basom, and his wife Ruth, they formed a working group and found a site, an old dairy farm, off Telegraph Road. By the fall of 1946, the Burgundy Farm Country Day School, with Lois as one of its founding directors, was ready to open.

From the founding beliefs and policies, to which Lois and Eric subscribed, we have some idea of Lois's, and to some extent Eric's, beliefs on elementary education:

> that spiritual growth must go on daily. That an intelligent and sensitive reaction to human existence requires more than mastery of material things and the world success of the individual. That it is a subtle, social reaching upward, which may be best cultivated together and whose potential for human happiness has scarcely been tapped.
>
> That good education is education that best helps the child to gradually take over responsibility for himself and develop a sense of responsibility for others . . .
>
> . . . that we must have teachers who respect children as individuals and feel that the essence of democratic living is the development of children through meeting problems real to them . . .
>
> . . . that children will learn to do many things with their hands . . .

Although Burgundy Farm was founded on "liberal Christian ideals," the Sevareids had no expressed religious convictions, and the school's only religious activity was a brief non-denominational "quiet time." Its deepest spiritual or religious principle, the Rev. Bason says today, was best expressed in a line that Eric borrowed from Norman Corwin's *In A Note of Triumph*, "Post proofs that brotherhood is not so wild a dream." From day to day the children learned to sing and dance, paint, and eat with good table manners, and develop their skills in conversation. And, according to school philosophy, their families had to pitch in.

In the summer before the opening, Lois threw herself into the grunge work. For days she scoured and scraped and polished an old stove that otherwise would have been thrown away. The minutes of the board meetings for 1946 and 1947 show her buying equipment, calculating the costs of lunches, editing a brochure, calling for more repairs to the house.

Kathryn Stone could soon tell that Lois, who had remarkable intelligence and managerial skills, knew very little about raising children. After all, Lois had been in Cairo while her mother reared her twins in Minneapolis. So Kathryn reentered her old friend's life on another level, as mentor as well as fellow board member. The boys loved the school. Peter, who went on to Harvard and Georgetown Law, recalls that he was dyslexic, he needed a lot of support and patience, a freedom to develop at his own pace. He doubts that any other school would have worked for him, although, he had trouble adapting to universities where learning was not necessarily considered fun. The Stones had a son Paul, the same age as the twins, and he and Peter became inseparable pals and stayed overnight at each other's homes.

Having established the household on Valley Lane, Lois took up another project: building a log cabin getaway for the family in Warrenton, Virginia, where she also took the Burgundy children for a holiday and taught them how to scramble eggs.

Eric is remembered as committing his personal time and energies to all these endeavors with a groan. According to Mrs. Stone, "He was not a very apt cooperator." Once he quipped wryly, "My only regret is that I have but one wife to give for Burgundy." But he did his share. For example, the board asked parents to help repair a culvert that had been washed away three times in the last seventeen years. So Eric Sevareid, with the other dads, got down in the ditch and dug. The year before he died, he told a Burgundy Farm newsletter (spring 1991), "I did a lot of work. It was probably good for me." When the school installed an out-door swimming pool, Eric was one of the parents to plunge in. "I can still remember him coming down to the pool in his swim suit," Ruth Basom recalls, "as handsome as all get-out."

In 1946 the founders sidestepped the issue of segregation. Eric re-called that "We knew we were going to have a desegretated school after three years, but we had to get established first." The founding documents don't mention desegregation; but after two or three years the children began asking why there were no colored children in the school, and parents began asking the same question. In 1950 Basom set up a sub-committee to study the issue "from all possible standpoints," and it soon became clear there was no way the school could remain true to its founding principles and remain all white. Four years before *Brown v. the Board of Education,* Burgundy Farm became the first integrated school in Virginia.

There was another aspect, however, to all the energy Lois was pouring into founding a school and building a house. Virginia Foster Durr tells a chilling story in her memoir:

> Eric Sevareid and his wife, Lois, lived on Seminary Hill. Poor Lois had a nervous breakdown, which created a good deal of excite-ment. She would go crazy and come running into your house, just as wild as she could be. She was not violent and dangerous. She was just mad. . . .

Lois's "nervous breakdown," which was a term used for many years to categorize a variety of symptoms and mental disorders, was later de-scribed as manic depression, or today, as bipolar syndrome, a mental illness characterized by wild mood swings, sometimes lasting weeks, months, or longer periods, in which the victim is for a while energetic, optimistic, extravagant, creative and hyperactive and then falls into terri-ble guilt, deep sadness, and helplessness.

In Lois's case it is difficult to pinpoint just when this illness developed.

Fred Manfred may have seen early symptoms as far back as Eric's college and newspaper days in Minneapolis, when he observed that in conversation Lois's words seemed to run ahead of her mind. Celia Brokaw Sevareid wonders whether Lois's almost compulsive laughter in the 1930s was a sign of her later problem. Her brother Eben suggests that her earlier medical history may have contributed to this collapse— the very difficult pregnancy, and the appendix operation she underwent two months before flying to Cairo, an ordeal for which she was not physically prepared. Joan Younger Dickinson, a journalist friend of the family from Paris days who stayed close to both Eric and Lois all their lives, believes the first attack, which she witnessed, was the episode in Sheean's apartment in 1945, when she fell into an almost catatonic state.

Rita Stearns, Eric's CBS secretary from 1946 to 1948, remembers Lois lying on the couch in her office, too depressed to function. Eben remembers seeing her in the depressed condition around 1948, sitting with a subdued stare, "a frightened lady." Nan (Scallon Taylor) Abell remembers meeting Lois on the street in Washington after not having seen her for years and finding her strangely "subdued." She just said, "Hello, Nan," with a coldness she had never shown before; she seemed to have retreated within herself.

Lois became increasingly difficult to live with. The malady became seasonal: depression in the fall and winter months, followed by elation, wild activity in the spring. Or sometimes the cycle would be daily—hyperactive in the morning, then gradually calming down between 5 and 9 P.M. when the medicine took effect. When she was up, she would play the piano; down, not a note. When she was manic she would be up all night, showering at 3 A.M., and sometimes her behavior would be so noisy or rowdy that some people who did not know she was ill—and there were many people in Eric's professional circle who did not grasp the nature of the illness for some time—thought her problem was alcohol. Also when she was high, she would spend a lot of money and expect her companions to do the same, which strained relations with friends and relatives who could not keep up with her and, one can imagine, aggravated Eric's already considerable anxiety, some would say neurosis, about having enough money for his needs.

The Seminary Hill folk, accustomed to well-served tea parties, learned something was wrong through her behavior when she was a hostess. An ash tray with an ash in it would be quickly spirited away to be emptied, but at a tea party she might fail to serve the tea, then conclude that, as the tea-less guests departed unfed, "Well, I guess they didn't want any tea." One day she set out to Washington carrying a shotgun in full view. She was taking it to Eric's office, she said, and had to be dissuaded from walking through the nation's capital with a shotgun in hand.

Her weight began to fluctuate dramatically, as much as sixty to eighty pounds. Part of it was directly due to her medication; part of it a sick woman's contempt for her body. A CBS newsman, who met Lois when Eric brought her to the set for the coverage of election night in 1952, remembers her as "beefy," looking like a "peasant woman." Only a dozen years before she was considered stunning, beautiful.

The remedies? Lois's mother came in from Minneapolis and lived with the family off and on for several years. She was a great help, by all accounts a wonderful grandmother. When Michael on his sled hit a car at the bottom of the steep hill from their house to Valley Lane, Grandmother Finger was there to deal with the crisis. When the boys reached high school age, their parents sent them to Episcopal High School, the boarding school. Although the school was only a few minutes away, it shielded them to some degree from their mother's illness during their most formative adolescent years. The boys often visited or had the support of other members of the extended family, like their Sevareid uncles John and Paul and Lois's brothers Eben and Sherman. For the troubling domestic crisis on Valley Lane was the focus now of not just a circle of Washington media and government coworkers but of a national network of Sevareids, Hougens, and Fingers committed to making the Sevareid-Finger marriage work.

Over the next decade, Lois was hospitalized again and again. The standard treatment in those days, mostly to relieve the effects of depression, was electroshock therapy; and Lois was subjected to shock treatments. She returned from each one saying her memory had been damaged, but they did not relieve her long-term pain. She researched her own malady and became convinced that it was hereditary, and that her father, who had died of a heart ailment, also suffered from depression. She managed to keep a sense of humor about her condition, refused to fall into self-pity, measured her moods, and knew when she was headed for trouble. Once on a walk with Joan Dickinson she said, "Oh dear, I'm going into my manic phase."

"How do you know?" Joan asked.

"Because my shoes don't match."

At the beginning, and through most of the 1950s, Eric reacted with great solicitude. His correspondence from the late 1940s through the early 1950s is filled with assurances to friends that Lois is in the hospital but we hope to have her home for Christmas, or that he has great faith she will pull through this. In October 1947 he writes to Burgundy Farm to excuse her "sudden departure from responsibilities." He puts her in the care of a Washington psychiatrist, Dr. Morris Kleinerman, who sees her three days a week. He plans skiing vacations with the family in New England, and in August 1948, while the boys are at Camp Timberlake in Vermont, took her to the Great Harbor Inn in Edgartown, Massachusetts, to golf, sail, and ride bikes.

Everyone who knew the Sevareids in those years has an opinion about what went wrong, and each analysis inevitably reflects the cultural and moral values of the analyst. Some of the Sevareids' contemporaries who are more sympathetic to Lois than to Eric are more likely to hold Eric strictly responsible for his behavior, to stress his obligation to his sick wife, rather than to look at his needs; and they ask how much Eric's wanderlust, his determination to promote his career, his tendency to see his wife as someone to take care of him rather than an individual with an identity and agenda of her own, contributed to Lois's fall.

Kathryn Stone defends Eric. She sees Lois as someone who, because of her long absense from America during the war, simply "couldn't make the transition from the stratosphere of internationalism" to the "family life of the '50s." Later Kathryn met the nurse who attended Lois in Arlington Hospital, who listened from the background to Eric and Lois talk, on the many nights when Eric came and lingered devotedly by her bedside. He was very loyal to her. He tried very hard to make it work.

But there was his career.

15

FINDING HIS VOICE

IT WAS THE LAST FRIDAY in March 1947; the time—5:59 P.M., in the CBS-WTOP studio in Washington; and as the engineers sat ready at the control panel, and the evening news program's new sponsor, the Metropolitan Life Insurance Company, sat listening in New York, Eric Sevareid—primed, well paid, and meticulously prepared—sat sweating before the microphone on the table before him. The second hand on the big studio clock clicked up to 6:00 P.M. The engineer signaled: You're on.

Silence. Sevareid froze. No words, no sounds could make their way from his brain to his mouth. He couldn't understand why. All he knew was that he couldn't talk. He sat there, struck dumb, for the whole fifteen minutes.

The episode was not totally unexpected, in that Sevareid's fear of the microphone was already well-known and much talked about among his peers; and they have kept talking about it after his death. For the first months in 1946, his WTOP staff had been holding their collective breath, praying that their boss would make it through his broadcasts. Yet, a fifteen-minute silence in radio is always unusual. Some have explained his nervousness in terms of the isolation, the hermetic atmosphere of the radio studio, the odd sensation of uttering well-chiseled thoughts into a machine with no realistic sense of the vast audience waiting for those thoughts to arrive. Or it could have been due to lack of training: unlike Murrow, Sevareid had never taken speech courses, never learned techniques of breath control—so all his life the engineers and other radio and TV reporters would watch him gasp and gulp his way through broadcasts, as he developed little defensive idiosyncrasies as the years went by, like the glass of warm water, always at his fingertips, as if that would relax his vocal cords or calm his jumpy nerves.

Or, of course, his inability to speak may have had deeper roots, in ambiguous feelings about his profession and his place in it, or in the tension looming up every day between his wife's condition and his need to advance his career.

Otherwise, his career was going very well. He was an administrator, appointed by Murrow, who was now vice president for news and public affairs. Murrow named him chief correspondent in D.C., director of all CBS news and local news; and he had a private office next to the newsroom where a staff of twelve worked from the AP and UP teletype machines.

He managed his staff gently, politely, and didn't play favorites in the office. Nor did he raise his voice, lose his temper, or curse. Though generally considered a dour Norwegian, he joked with his secretary, Rita Stearns, telling her he wanted to write a sexy historical novel with her as one of the characters. And he welcomed his secretary to Valley Lane, where she could see, with awe, his shelves and shelves of books—mostly history and military history, not much fiction—and get some sense of the sources of the wisdom he would tap daily into the typewriter on his desk.

He answered his mail well, dictating brief, polite replies to strangers who wrote asking personal and professional advice—like the college student with an interdisciplinary degree in American studies who wondered what he could do with that kind of a degree—always adding a turn of phrase which convinced the recipient, rightly, that he or she had received Eric Sevareid's personal attention.

He was also feeling the effects of fame. The *Saturday Review* (October 12, 1946) featured Elmer Davis's review of *Not So Wild a Dream* and put a powerful etching of Eric's handsome head, with brooding face and piercing eyes, on the cover. Now even more a celebrity than he had been in 1940, he got attention he had not expected. An advertising firm offered him $300 and a case of Calvert Reserve to pose for one of their full-page whiskey ads, very popular in the 1940s, featuring a "Man of Distinction," who drinks their product. He replied (April 29, 1947) "I don't want you to think I'm being stuffy about it, but what reserves of modesty and what sense of humor I have left is in an uproar about this. I just haven't got the guts to do it," and "my wife would just kid me out of the house if I accepted it." But when another advertiser offered him a free set of cookware if he would name his favorite hymn, to be performed on the ABC program, *Club Ties,* he replied (October 14, 1947),

"The only one I can remember as a favorite is 'Holy, Holy, Holy, Lord God Almighty,'" which he last sang in the Burma jungle in 1943.

More conscious of his image, he now ordered his suits custom-made from Richard Bennett, a New York tailor, and he checked his face often in the mirror, worried that perhaps his hair was beginning to thin.

When he saw his own face in the mirror he knew the public was beginning to look at him not just as a newsman, but as an "analyst"; but he doubted his ability. He took his own thoughts seriously, but he wasn't sure he always had something worth saying. For the time being, the question was half on the shelf: Metropolitan Life had made it very clear that they wanted straight news, no analysis; and Eric had been warned in a CBS memo (January 22, 1947) that if he made Metropolitan Life unhappy he would lose the show.

Nevertheless, analysis was in his bones; and, in the eyes of his public, he somehow kept saying very perceptive things. But his public, alas, was deeper than it was broad: according to the Hooper ratings, which measured an audience by phone calls, in New York he rated a 2.7, which was considerably lower than the news programs (WOR had 3.5) at the same time on the other three networks.

News analysis was becoming a self-conscious subprofession. In January 1947 the Association of Radio News Analysts, which Kaltenborn had pioneered since 1942, published a roster of thirty-nine members in New York and Washington—including Sevareid, Murrow, Collingwood, LeSueur, Kaltenborn, Shirer, Thomas, Davis, and others—with bylaws and a code of ethics which emphasized the proper distance between analysts and sponsors. It forbade analysts to read commercials and deplored the interruption of analysis by commercial announcements.

Because of his reluctance to think seriously about television, Eric Sevareid would not have sensed that the specialized tribe of radio commentators he was thinking of joining was both at its peak and on the way downhill. Indeed, he himself would be its last grand practitioner. The golden age of radio began around 1929 with *Amos n' Andy* and ended around 1948 when Milton Berle established himself on NBC television as the most important thing that happened every Sunday night. But insofar as radio listeners had a sacred fifteen minutes every evening or every week during which the house grew silent and only one voice was heard, that voice in the late 1940s probably belonged to a handful of men—Lowell Thomas, H. V. Kaltenborn, Elmer Davis, Fulton Lewis, Jr., Walter Winchell, or Drew Pearson.

The true extent of their influence is hard to measure but, like today's columnists and talk show hosts, they often set the agenda for the national discourse. It is fair to assume that these men did have strong followings because, however circumscribed their audiences, the public needed them. The late 1940s and 1950s were a time that people felt needed to be explained. The rise of commentators and syndicated columnists corresponded to the growth of government, with the New Deal in the 1930s and the national effort of the war. In short, the more complicated the news of the world became, the more the public needed experts—including opinionated self-described experts—to sort it all out.

Irving E. Fang, in *Those Radio Commentators* (1977) remarks that by 1947 the estimated number of radio commentators had risen from six in 1931 to six hundred, including all kinds of local reporters who tossed in their own opinions. A more conservative estimate would be to stick with the approximately sixty reporters, commentators, and analysts whom the networks employed at the end of the war and who would constitute their basic stable moving into the Cold War. Three typical commentators against whom a young Sevareid would be measured were Elmer Davis, Fulton Lewis, Jr., and, of course, H. V. Kaltenborn.

Meanwhile, Kaltenborn's Association of Radio News Analysts was really not satisfied with the networks' slippery distinction between *analysts* who give interpretation without taking positions; and *commentators*, who can say anything they please, and *newscasters*, who simply report. CBS staff chafed under Paul White's continuing insistence that the listener should have no idea where the analyst stood.

During the war Elmer Davis had left CBS to serve as director of the Office of War Information. In general he kept the respect of his former colleagues in the process, since he saw his role as promoting the flow of information rather that controlling it for propaganda. Back on the air, now on ABC, he established himself as a rational, folksy, plainspoken liberal. When Senator Joseph R. McCarthy first began his "anti-communist" attacks, Davis observed in a *Harper's* article, "I shall not speculate on his motives, being neither a psychologist nor an inspector of sewers."

On the right, Fulton Lewis, Jr., forged his identity by battling with Democratic administrations. When Hitler invaded Poland in 1939, Lewis had Lindbergh on his radio program predicting that the Third Reich could not be beaten. During the war he attacked government taxes and economic controls and wasteful government contracts. After the war, Lewis summed up his position, Fang writes, in these words: "Our country is locked in a death struggle between two irreconcilable forces— those who want to choke the breath out of our economic system by a liberty-throttling, private, initiative-killing government control, and those who are fighting tooth and nail to preserve the sacred principles of free enterprise that our Founding Fathers bequeathed to us. I'm in that fight.... I'm an American who can't sit by self-indulgently twiddling his thumbs while a bunch of drooly-mouthed fellow-traveling rats gnaw at the vitals of our government."

Kaltenborn, the original old lion, still winning awards in the late 1940s, was pushing seventy years. Although he called himself a liberal Democrat, he opposed FDR's third term and attacked labor for getting high wartime wages. Increasingly, pure opinion, often based on his feelings about personalities, replaced research and information. After 1948, he would be remembered above all, perhaps unfairly, for Harry Truman's hilarious imitation of Kaltenborn's clipped, confident delivery when he predicted Governor Thomas E. Dewey's victory on election night—in spite of all the evidence of Truman's two-million-vote lead.

But, as TV was gradually pushing radio out of the American consciousness, the voices of the commentators were fading into the night.

Thus, Sevareid's problem was to place himself, to find a niche that would use his talents and pay his salary. But when his arrangement with Metropolitan Life was ending its first contract year, CBS, nervous about the Hoopers, had Sevareid tack on an ingratiating little statement at the end of his broadcast. He explains that his method has been not to call attention to "so-called news beats" of his own; not to give personal comment; but to "winnow down, on the basis of the judgment his experience has given him, the avalanche of facts that each day sets in motion." He concludes:

> I have never mentioned my sponsors on the air; they have never asked me to. But I should like, tonight, to say that it is more than a

pleasure to speak the news on behalf of an organization such as Metropolitan Life, which fully agrees on the objective we seek, and which has never suggested that it be otherwise.

Yet the process he describes is subtler and more complex than his hearers may perceive. He implies that he is not Winchell or Kaltenborn, as if he is therefore "objective"; yet he selects the news items and rewrites them on the basis of his judgment. He knows his public is putting its mind in his hands, and the only test of his long-range integrity will be his ability to hold the public trust.

Meanwhile, Murrow, in his eighteen months as an executive, both made some remarkable innovations and cut some wounds that never healed. Of course Murrow's first love was always being a reporter, but he had taken the vice presidency because Paley had flattered him into believing he could play a role in the long-range direction of the network, that he would have a chance to continue what he had created during the war. For one thing, he wanted to hold the old war team together. When Howard K. Smith was tempted to take a job at *Life,* Murrow confronted him with, "You don't want to work for Luce," and Smith signed his CBS contract. A telling point—that postwar American journalism could go two ways: the *Time-Life* Luce style, where the whole publication was edited to reflect the publisher's vision of what was called the American Century, or the Murrow–CBS vision, in some ways as "subjective" as *Time*'s, but with the Paul White rules, including the golden rule that the listener, not the broadcaster, was to make the final judgment about his or her opinion on the news.

In 1946 Murrow introduced a media criticism show, *CBS Views the Press,* with Don Hollenbeck, and a popular historical drama, a predecessor of today's "docudrama," *CBS Is There,* in which CBS newsmen pretend to broadcast Napoleon's return from Elba or Julius Caesar's assassination, as if 1946's broadcast technology had been available in 1815 or the first century B.C. Today's reader too young to have heard those wonderful programs has missed the thrill of something like: "We are standing here just a few yards from where Napoleon has gotten out of his boat and he is headed this way . . . General! General! Over here! Could I ask you a few questions about your intentions in returning to

France?" And then the illusion of waiting to hear Napoleon himself speak—in English. When Norman Corwin was awarded a world trip by the Wendell Willkie-Freedom House Foundation for *On A Note of Triumph,* Paley and Murrow gave him equipment, including the first use of magnetic tape, to produce *One World Flight,* the most ambitious documentary of the decade.

But Murrow also had to do what executives don't like to do: fire people. Especially when the people are Paul White and Bill Shirer.

Paul White, of course, was a natural candidate for the job that Paley gave Murrow; but, in Paley's judgment, White was not as deep a thinker—also, word was that White was drinking too much. At the end of the war, White became, like the major in whom Eric had seen himself at the Rhine, one of those war casualties who had stayed "alive," but was psychologically dead. For a year the staff watched White, who had created CBS News, destroy himself with booze and pills. In April 1946, as CBS launched *Robert Trout with The News Till Now,* sponsored by Campbell Soup, with an enormous staff and a $65 million annual budget, what *Newsweek* called Murrow's "first brainchild," Murrow listened from his office as White came on the air obviously drunk. Accounts of what happened next vary, but according to some, Murrow came down to White's office and fired him on the spot. White went on to write a journalism text, *News on the Air,* and after he died in 1955 at age fifty-two, the Radio and Television News Directors Association created a Paul White Award, which they gave to Eric Sevareid when he retired.

Firing White was painful but unavoidable. The smoke that followed the firing of Shirer never blew away. At the bottom of the fight was a question Murrow and CBS, in spite of many explanations, never answered: the relationship between sponsors and the content of news and analysis programs. If a sponsor decided to drop a commentator, who had a particular time slot, the network could let the commentator go, or give him another time and keep him on at a much lower salary. In short, if the commentator, no matter how wise or talented, lacks corporate backing, he's out in the cold.

On March 10, 1947, Shirer learned that the J. B. Williams Company —soap and shaving cream—was dropping his Sunday afternoon news analysis, that Joseph C. Harsch would take his place, and that Shirer would get another slot. Shirer, convinced that the Williams Company objected to his liberal views, took his case to the public, and charged that a "soap company" was deciding what could be heard on the air. Liberal celebrities like Dorothy Parker and Gregory Peck protested and picketed CBS headquarters. At the Overseas Press Club luncheon in April, Shirer charged that CBS had cut him for his politics; when Murrow's time to speak came, he threw away his prepared talk and forcefully made the case that Shirer had been removed because the quality of his work had declined.

On the one hand, the dismissal freed Shirer to write a series of best-selling books, which included his 1,234-page *Rise and Fall of the Third Reich,* still one of the most absorbing one-volume histories of Hitler's catastrophic career, plus his three-volume memoir, *Twentieth Century Journey.* But unlike White, Shirer never got over his bitterness. He used both his memoirs and a 1954 novel, *Stranger Comes Home,* to portray himself as a reporter betrayed by an executive who fails to stand up for his liberal views.

Murrow's friends, on the other hand, stood by him, and have testified to a series of historians—from David Halberstam's *The Powers That Be,* to Edward Bliss, Jr.'s *Now the News* (1991)—that Shirer had simply slumped into sloppy work. He sat in his office pontificating and not doing the legwork that good journalism requires. Collingwood referred to him as a "stuck whistle." Sevareid told Bliss, "His commentaries were terrible; there wasn't a thing in them. Ed felt betrayed." And Eric, in the last years of his life, reacting to Shirer's version of his departure from CBS in the last volume of his memoirs, continued to angrily denigrate Shirer in interviews.

True, Bliss records, Shirer got the Peabody Award, radio's "Pulitzer," the year he was let go; but that was as much for his war reporting as for his recent work. Yet, as Joseph Persico points out in his Murrow biography, the sponsors indeed did have some control over who would read, write, or interpret the news. The sponsors could not pick a broadcaster whom CBS did not accept, but they could kill one whose ideas they did not like by dropping their sponsorship.

Alas, Murrow himself—the broadcaster rather than the executive—would soon be on both sides of the sponsor squeeze. In September 1947 when he gave up administration to return to the airwaves, he went along when the network bumped Robert Trout to give his slot to Murrow—

as Campbell Soup decreed. But in 1955, ALCOA (The Aluminum Company of America), after sponsoring his path-breaking *See It Now* for ten years, including more-or-less standing by him during the McCarthy controversy, didn't like Murrow's report on a small newspaper in Texas that stood up against a land scandal. He ended up sponsorless and—were it not for his status as a "legend"—as vulnerable as Shirer had been in 1946.

Eric would soon have his own sponsor problems.

Murrow's switch from administration to broadcasting in the fall of 1947 left Sevareid, who had taken the Washington bureau chief's job only to please Ed, out on a limb. Most of all, he was emotionally hurt. He had read about Murrow's return in *Variety;* his friend had not confided in him. "I was broken up," he said later. "I almost sat down and wept." Eric took a train to New York and the two friends sat and had a drink, and Ed apologized; but Eric always remembered that this strange, extraordinary man whom he adored had let him down.

Murrow's return also gave CBS an exceptionally strong evening lineup: Sevareid's Metropolitan Life news at 6 P.M.; Lowell Thomas, who had come back to CBS after years at NBC at 6:45; and Murrow at 7:45. All three covered the same stories, but each told a story from his own point of view. New York *Herald Tribune* radio critic John Crosby observed (October 1, 1947) that Thomas was less a newsman than a storyteller, who let his voice, from bass to tremolo, milk the humor, romance, and pathos from the event; Murrow, with his high intelligence and superb voice, was strongest of the three; Eric offered an excellent news review, but his material lacked polish. Once one of Eric's twins, thinking he would like to go into radio, said he wished he had Murrow's voice.

Eric replied, "So do I."

To one who reads Sevareid's news scripts today, it is clear that he had not yet found his literary voice, or the right job. He had not resolved the various tensions between print journalism and broadcasting, between reporting and analysis. And there are some indications of his unhappiness in a bizarre incident that for a while confused Eric's reputation in the profession.

Time (January 26, 1948) carried an odd news item, accompanied by a stern picture of Eric in its radio section:

> Lean, velvet-voiced Eric Sevareid quit as CBS's Washington bureau chief to give full time to newscasting, and tossed a few hard words over his shoulder. "Radio reporting is superficial [and] sloppy. The stream runs purer than in newspaper reporting but not so deep. Radio reporters . . . know that they won't be able to use more than a few lines in most stories [so] they quit digging. I think I'd be happier writing for print.

The picture caption: "I think I'd be happier. . ."

An angry Sevareid is a fierce animal. He threw his anger into damage control. He fired off a telegram to *Time:*

> I MUST PROTEST YOUR ARTICLE ABOUT ME IN THE RADIO SEC-
> TION OF TIME THIS WEEK. YOU QUOTE ME AS SEVERELY CRITICIZ-
> ING RADIO REPORTING AS SUPERFICIAL AND RADIO REPORTERS
> AS UNTHOROUGH. CLEARLY ANY RADIO JOURNALIST FEELING THE
> WAY YOU PICTURE ME AS FEELING OUGHT TO BE PUSHED OUT OF
> THE BUSINESS OR HE OUGHT TO HAVE ENOUGH INTEGRITY TO
> GET OUT VOLUNTARILY. OUT OF A TWO HOUR CONVERSATION
> WITH YOUR REPORTER IN WHICH I TRIED TO GIVE AN HONEST
> ESTIMATE OF WHAT IS FINE AND WHAT IS BAD ABOUT RADIO
> JOURNALISM YOU HAVE CHOSEN TO PRINT FOUR SENTENCES.
> THESE WARPED SENTENCES TAKEN ENTIRELY OUT OF CONTEXT
> HAVE RATHER CRUELLY MISREPRESENTED MY VIEWS AND HAVE
> DONE INJURY TO MY POSITION VIS A VIS MY PROFESSION AND MY
> COLLEAGUES IN RADIO FOR MOST OF WHOM I FEEL THE GREAT-
> EST RESPECT.

All day he had his secretary type letters explaining himself, including one to his brother Paul, also a newscaster in Minneapolis: "Anything you can do in Minneapolis to answer any gossip about this will be most appreciated. Mostly I wanted to assure you and the family that the story is wrong and I am not out of my mind as it would indicate."

For weeks Eric endured the jibes and taunts of his colleagues as he waited for his reply to appear. Finally *Time* printed a heavily edited version of his telegram and added its own snippy reply: "*Time* regrets that its snapshot of Newscaster Sevareid caught him in an expression that failed to do justice to his fine features.— Ed"

On February 7 CBS fought back in its *CBS Views the Press*: "Here's an example of the contempt which *Time* so often feels for its readers— brush 'em off with a wisecrack if they complain . . . Distortion by omission in an original story is bad enough; distortion by the same process in response to a call for fair play would seem to be compounding a journalistic felony to a truly amazing degree." Thirty years later, discussing the incident in an interview with NBC reporter Ray Scherer, Sevareid was still mad. He could hardly pronounce the name Henry Luce without a suppressed snarl.

In 1949 Eric, with Lois, made his first trip to Norway to discover a little more about his family roots and deepen the love relationship that was to bring him back with his family many times. He found and photographed the original Sevareid homestead, and met a number of people who said they were his relatives, only to find, after Lois checked the archives, that they had found the wrong homestead. He had once believed that "Sevareid" meant "isthmus," but Robert Ardrey mischievously wrote him a long linguistic analysis proving it meant "outhouse."

When they returned from their trip, Lois collapsed and was hospitalized again.

Back at work, Eric learned that if Norway loved him, Metropolitan Life did not—at least not as much as they would like to.

Because he admired Sevareid personally, Metropolitan Life vice president James L. Madden was reluctant to have his criticisms passed along; but CBS vice president and director of public affairs Davidson Taylor felt Eric had the disposition and stature to deal with the bad news. Metropolitan Life's new advertising manager wanted to drop Eric's broadcasts. There were lots of reasons. Eric was "high hat," and talked "over the heads" of Metropolitan Life policyholders. For two years the ratings had been flat. Not enough Sevareid listeners ordered Metropolitan Life booklets. Some letters say Sevareid is "too far left"—but that was *not* a consideration. Although Madden never listened to the broadcasts, he too thought they might be too "scholarly."

Taylor suggested that there might be things CBS could do to save the program, such as: get a new announcer with the ability to stimulate booklet requests; put Eric on the road giving well-promoted lectures in the sixteen major cities that broadcast his program. Frankly, Taylor told Sevareid, the CBS press relations people, "because of your dignity and the uncolored character of the broadcast," were having trouble publicizing him and felt he was taking a "rather negligent attitude" by not returning phone calls and conveying the attitude that publicity was not important. Taylor insisted that CBS would do everything possible to help; they would even send some 78 rpm recordings of Eric's broadasts to Madden's home so he could experience Eric's "warmth and directness." But the message was clear. His job was in danger.

A week later Eric and Madden had lunch. Eric agreed to hit the lecture trail immediately. Fudging the analysts' association code of ethics a bit, he suggested moving up the second commercial, then coming on at the end with a little story in the field of health or medicine, "often a story about a personal conquest of disease or disability"—apparently to subtly suggest that the listeners need life insurance. He would use a Washington rather than New York announcer to make the show more "intimate," and make the commercial copy more "optimistic," to go down better at the dinner hour. It didn't work. By March it was over. Eric had lost his sponsor.

Ironically, the separation turned out much to Eric's advantage. On April 1, 1950, CBS moved him to 11:00–11:15 P.M., when sixty rather than twenty-five stations would carry him, with a new format that devoted the last five minutes to analysis, giving him a chance to develop the "think pieces," he had been experimenting with for several years, but which now would define him to the American public. Eric called them commentaries, CBS called them analyses; but, because they are personal, not institutional, they should not be called editorials.

Heard then and read today, they were and remain remarkable documents. Many listeners could remember specific lines and phrases for forty years. According to Sevareid's friend Dan Rather, Eric told him that his short essays were modeled on those of the sixteenth-century founder of the essay form, the French philosopher Michel de Montaigne. There is a parallel in that both Sevareid's and Montaigne's works represent a lifetime of self-scrutiny, a continuing moral examination of one's ideas and values in light of an evolving social and political context.

On the other hand, as J. M. Cohen writes in his introduction to Montaigne's essays, Montaigne's "aim is to present a portrait of himself in a frame of timelessness, and Montaigne says of himself in "On

Presumption," "The world always looks outward, I turn my gaze inward; there I fix it, and there I keep it busy. Everyone looks before him; I look within." Yet there are intimations in the Frenchman of the Sevareid method. Montaigne takes pride in that his skill at introspection has given him a faculty "for sifting the truth," for taking these ideas that he has been born with and building on them by fortifying them with the "authority of others and the sound reasoning of the ancients."

One can also see the influence of Walter Lippmann's columns, which Sevareid had begun reading as a young man and to whom James Reston looked as a mentor, and maybe H. L. Mencken's *Prejudices*, which had an enormous influence on Sevareid's generation. But the form that Sevareid evolved was unique, largely because his pieces had to be read and heard clearly within five minutes—reduced later, in the *CBS Evening News with Walter Cronkite* years, to only four hundred words, about two and a half minutes. And, for the most part, each broadcast's commentary was inspired by a news item, and was written within that one day.

In the early years, Lois was a big help, in spite of her illness that came and went. He would start mulling over the topic in the late morning and keep working on it out loud at the dinner table, his conversation working in a circle, bringing the talk and the ideas around to his main question, testing his conclusions against Lois's mind, which, in the opinion of several who knew them both for many years, was at least the equal to his own.

He began his new job with a month-long tour through the heart of the country—Indiana, Illinois, Oklahoma, and Colorado—to break the intellectual isolation that inevitably endangers stay-at-home reporters. In Indiana he concluded that world, rather than merely local, problems had taken a permanent place in the subconscious of farmers, who feared, for example, that if a new Air Force Academy were built nearby, their farms and homes would become targets for Russian planes and atomic bombs. In Springfield, Illinois, he became one of the first commentators to call attention to the "chubby, warm-hearted man" in the governor's mansion. He finished his month on the road with his basic optimism intact; but with one important qualification:

> And yet, one senses the first, creeping inroads of the new atomic
> era upon the American mind. The first germs of knowledge are
> taking hold: that this country has lost its margin of absolute safety,

that it can be physically reached and hurt, that nobody's city is completely safe. This sense is bound to grow, working slow changes in our ways. Perhaps we are destined to the kind of twilight existence between safety and danger that Europeans have always known and adjusted to. It is, in a slightly sad and ironic sense, the measure of America's coming of age in this foreshortened world.

Also while he was in Springfield, he received word that for his 1949 Metropolitan Life broadcasts, "for the depth and clarity, perspicacity and lucidity of the reporting and interpretation," he would receive the Peabody Award.

16

ADLAI

IF THE INDIANA FARMER'S recognition that his land was a potential target for Russian planes bearing atomic bombs marks something
like another milestone in the weakening of midwestern isolationism, it
signals something else as well: the beginning of a national sense of extreme vulnerability—to be greatly increased in 1957 with the sight of
the Russian Sputnik coursing across the night sky and the realization
that the Soviets had developed an intercontinental ballistic missile. It was
a new age of anxiety, easily exploited by demagogues who could man-
ipulate that fear. It never occurred to the child Arnold Sevareid, when
he lived in that inland region, that explosives in the hands of foreigners
on the other side of the planet could turn the golden prairies black with
ashes. But now, as described by Godfrey Hodgson in *America in Our Time*
(1976), the world had entered a period in which four great facts dominated international politics: the atomic bomb; the rise of communism,
aggressively set in motion by Stalin before his death in 1953; the strength
of the United States; and the weakness of the other powers.

On one level, America's response to the Soviet threat was what was
known as the containment policy, the determination to resist Soviet en-
croachment in Greece, Turkey, Berlin, and Korea. The Truman doctrine
was to fortify the European economy with the Marshall Plan, and to
attempt to draw the line against the spread of communism by a commitment to intervene, through American economic or military aid, and
through mutual defense treaties like NATO, in those spots where "freedom" was threatened.

On another level, on the psychological level Richard Hofstadter described in *The Paranoid Style in American Politics,* a segment of America,
disappointed with its own failure to achieve the peace and prosperity
expected to follow victory in World War II, turned inward in its search
for someone to blame. There must be some conspiracy, it seemed, to deprive them of their rightful share of the American dream. In some ways

the cycle Eric had witnessed in Minneapolis in the 1930s, when the Silver Shirts were but a symptom of the deep current of fascism lurking in an "upwardly mobile" society where not everyone moved up, was coming around again.

America's response to the whole Chinese revolution, one of the great turning points of history, is but one indication of its psychic fragility. Perceived in the United States only as a defeat for Chiang, as an American "loss," for which American diplomats and journalists must have been responsible, it was but one of a series of events between 1948 and 1950 that culminate in that dark period of modern times characterized by what was called McCarthyism.

In 1948 the Russians blockaded access to Berlin and the United States flew supplies into West Berlin by airlift. In the spring of 1949, Mao Tse-tung became head of the Chinese People's Republic and that summer, in August, the Soviet Union successfully exploded an atomic bomb. In January, in New York, Alger Hiss, a Harvard Law School graduate, New-Dealer, and State Department official who had accompanied FDR to Yalta, was convicted of perjury. A former Communist and *Time* editor, Whittaker Chambers, who had shaped much of *Time*'s text on China, had accused Hiss of being a Communist spy, and California Senator Richard M. Nixon had championed Chambers' cause; and Hiss's conviction for perjury, though not, as widely charged, for treason, was widely interpreted as a vindication of Nixon and proof that Communists had penetrated the highest levels of government.

On January 21, having learned that Klaus Fuchs, who had worked on the development of the atomic bomb, had passed secrets to the Soviets, President Truman announced that the United States would build the hydrogen bomb, a more terrible weapon by many orders of magnitude. In his broadcast the next evening, Sevareid said that the public's "cool acceptance" of the decision was:

> a measure of what has happened since Hiroshima—the lessening fear of the divided atom as our minds became accustomed to the idea, a deep sense of futility in trying to reach understanding with the Russians; and, no doubt, after years of witnessing the most massive destruction of life this planet has known, a slow corroding of the human conscience.

On February 9, Senator Joseph R. McCarthy of Wisconsin, who had been looking for an issue to draw attention to himself, told a Republican women's club in West Virginia that he held in his hand a list of Communists in the State Department.

On June 24 the North Koreans invaded South Korea and took Seoul, the capital, within a week. Backed by a United Nations resolution, the United States sent troops and gained the offensive; but in November the Communist Chinese entered the war on the side of North Korea, and Truman wrote in his notebook, "It looks like World War III."

Against this background, McCarthy and his cohorts in politics and in the press played on fears that there was a Communist conspiracy to undermine the capitalist economic system, that Communists in education, the church, and the media were softening the country's morals, and that the conspirators had infiltrated the government on a grand scale. Since a number of early Soviet spies had been members of the American Communist Party or were consistently "liberal" in their politics, the McCarthy lists focused on all who espoused liberalism or supported attempts to "understand" Communism and the Soviet Union.

Eric Sevareid was "vulnerable" on several counts. Only because he had told the story in *Not So Wild a Dream*, it was public knowledge that he had been a student "radical," although his position in the protest against ROTC had been more pragmatic than ideological. He had established friendships with the diplomats who "lost" China, and he declined to forget those ties when his friends were under attack.

The networks immediately threw themselves into covering the Korean War. In 1948 all three networks had inaugurated fifteen-minute, daily, evening TV newscasts, starting in August with CBS's Douglas Edwards on *The CBS-TV News*. But because TV had not yet developed the logistics and technology to ship filmed reports back to the New York studios in time, it was again a radio correspondents' war.

Eleven days after the war broke out, Murrow was on his way to Korea. Bill Downs was there before him and warned him to go back, "It ain't our kind of war!" But Murrow's adrenaline was running again and he stayed. At first he supported the war and again made his way to the front, exposing himself to dangerous situations that frightened him more than anything had during World War II.

But the more he listened to the officers the more doubts he had about General MacArthur's strategy, calling for a major offensive that, according to Murrow's sources, the troops were not ready for. Although MacArthur's press guidelines forbade criticizing strategy, Murrow tried to tell the story anyway; CBS editors, backed by Paley, killed it. Murrow took this setback badly—he was not used to Paley telling him he was wrong—but he stayed on the case. In 1952, he returned to Korea at Christmastime, this time with cameras from his new TV news weekly *See It Now*, and combined traditional name-and-home-town holiday interviews with grim commentary on a frustrating war. At the end, Murrow told viewers how many of the soldiers interviewed had been killed since the film was made.

Sevareid, in commentaries that *Time* (August 28, 1950) called "hard-put to give both sides of every question in his allotted five minutes," generally supported the war. For him it was, like World War II, one where a clearly defined aggressor had crossed a line and could be stopped only by force. When the first casualties of the war began to come in, he delivered what he called the "Credo for the Era of the Cold War." It was the same piece that, slightly edited, he sent to the *Minnesota Daily* for its anniversary issue. It is a plea to adjust to a different kind of wartime, one that might last a generation, where we must "adjust our personal ambitions. We have a far higher calling than the accumulation of wealth and comfort." He accurately put his finger on the hallmark of the 1950s—abundance, the "affluent society"—and foresaw that the nation could not both seek its own comfort and deal with the other international and national social problems on the horizon.

In a June 1951 commentary, when the Senate was questioning the right wing's favorite target, Secretary of State Dean Acheson, on Far East policy, Sevareid reached back to his China experience and called for four more investigations: What happened to all the gold bullion we flew to China over the Hump? What happened to all the money private citizens sent for China relief? How much did the Chinese politicians keep for themselves and invest abroad? And exactly who constitutes the "China Lobby" and where do they get their money?

Of his many commentaries on the Korean War, two stand out. One, widely reprinted, was "Why Did They Fight?" broadcast on July 27, 1953, after the truce was signed. None of the usual motivations—loot, glory, religious zeal, protecting one's homeland, national passion—he said, applied; but the troops endured. Why? He replays his themes from World War II:

> The rest of it lies very deep in the heart and tissues of American life, and none among us can unravel all the threads of it. It has to do with their parents and their teachers and their ministers; it has to do with their 4-H clubs, their scout troops, their neighborhood centers; it has to do with their sense of belonging to a team, with the honor of upholding it, the shame of letting it down. But it also has to do with their implicit, unreasoned belief in their country, and their natural belief in themselves as individual men upon earth.

Sevareid does not quote de Tocqueville, but he describes the same phenomenon that the French traveler described in *Democracy in America*, based on his visit in the 1830s; he called it associationism, the tendency of Americans to be joiners, to take their identities from a network of voluntary societies, which supported the family and supplemented the political party. That these organizations, rather than a common vision of national purpose, carried a generation through a war, implies that at bottom the American character is nurtured more by local ties than a shared national spirit.

Sevareid's second commentary, was inspired by the great scandal of the war: some troops, as prisoners of war, gave in to their captors, submitted to what was sometimes called "brainwashing," but was, in most cases, a combination of those subtler forces that break already weak reeds. On December 15, Sevareid delivered an essay on those who did not fight as well as the others and asked himself why not. Twenty of the Americans in Communist tents at Panmunjom had decided to stay with their captors. Clearly they had not been corrupted intellectually by "egghead" college teachers nor were they spies nor reckless radicals. Nor racial minorities nor the Marxist "industrial proletariat." "These faces, by and large, are the faces of weak and irresolute young men." He risks a generalization:

> As I recollect, most of them come from small-town or rural regions of America; from farms or the lower middle class. And since

many of them were non-coms, they were not stupid, the outcasts of their primitive schooling. They had a certain sense of pride and personal aspiration; and they must have felt a frustration in their opportunities, for American small-town and rural life is not quite the happy fulfilling experience our folklore has pictured.

These were the people suspicious of strangers, the big city, the people who go for the Huey Longs and Father Coughlins and magical, simple solutions for their resentments. Eric does not mention McCarthy, but he is implying that the instinct that has led these confused boys to choose communism is the same one that snares folks at home into an anti-communist crusade. And one wonders whether Velva was listening that night. He had not been back since 1930, yet he must have sensed that if his father's bank failure had not liberated him from rural America, he could be in the same "tent" himself.

In the 1970s when the senior Eric Sevareid was at the peak of his popularity and received many more lecture invitations than he could accept and accepted more than he could individually prepare, he worked from a set of large-print notes called the standard speech, not so much an all-purpose creed, as a collection of the themes on which his audience expected him to touch. One was the presidency, and the kind of man, rather than a specific individual, who should occupy the office. One lines goes: "Let us have a man who seems honest, candid, who doesn't pretend to all the answers, whom we can trust *as a man*." The reporter Sevareid, who professionally is not supposed to identify with a candidate, felt he had met that man on his heartland tour in Springfield in 1950.

He had met Adlai Stevenson earlier, in the 1940s when Stevenson was working in the Navy Department early in the war, and had covered his election as governor of Illinois in 1948, and they became good friends. As governor, Stevenson was a quiet, hardworking reformer, who had almost overwhelmed the political machine by the great popular majority that swept him into office. During the 1950 visit Eric tried to get his friend to talk about the presidency, but Adlai put him off. In January 1952, Harry Truman called Stevenson to Blair House, where he was living while the White House was being renovated, and dumbfounded him by confiding that he did not plan to run again and wanted Stevenson to lead the country. It was the same week that, by sheer coincidence says Sevareid, Marquis Childs, Arthur Schlesinger, Jr., *Time* magazine, and Eric Sevareid had done articles or broadcasts suggesting that this heretofore unknown man from Illinois might—should—be the Democratic candidate.

Actually, many of them, like Sevareid, had been on Stevenson's mailing list, and they had been reading his speeches—like the one in 1950 when he worried that the Republican party, too long out of power, might resort to "epithets and witch hunts" to regain it. Perhaps here was the man to stand up against witch-hunters whom they had been looking for. And there was his speech at the Americans for Democratic Action's Roosevelt Day Dinner, where he said of FDR's place in history, "He knew that at the time he became president he was . . . the one man who could mediate between the old epoch that was dying and the new one coming to birth." Wasn't that what America needed again?

In March Adlai saw Truman again. Later, Eric met him at the Metropolitan Club and found him nervous, and even a little angry with Eric. "Since when are reporters trying to make presidents?" he blurted. "And that includes you too, Sevareid." Emotionally, Stevenson was having a difficult time. He was still affected by the unexpected breakup with his wife two years before, and now he could see either the challenge or temptation of the presidency looming ahead. In fact, he had left Truman with the impression that he had found his man.

The 1952 election was to be a watershed in several ways. It would mark the beginning of the Eisenhower era, when the country would turn for leadership to a man who, as William Manchester described him, "had no politics, no religion, no conspicuous guiding principles, and few known views on the great issues of his time." It was also the first television election. The first—although both candidates initially mistrusted the media—where the various "image industries" of public relations, advertising, and the media played a major role in presenting the candidate and his image to the voters, and thus in determining the election's outcome. Indeed, in those early days a few distinguished reporters doubled briefly as media advisers: CBS Paris correspondent David Schoenbrun tutored Eisenhower on how to deal with the TV camera, and even Murrow, who had never voted in his life but was enamored with Stevenson, rented a studio and tried fruitlessly to teach Adlai TV techniques.

As Sig Mickelson, who set up the CBS–TV coverage of the 1952 Republican and Democratic National Conventions in Chicago, describes that year in *From Whistle Stop to Sound Bite* (1989), "It was obvious as early as the winter of 1951 that the presidential election of 1952 would be an old-fashioned donneybrook." It was his job to help as many voters watch the donneybrook as possible.

Between January 1950 and 1951 the number of television sets in the country doubled from 3.2 million to 7.2 million, and it seemed reasonable to expect, considering the rate of sales, that the number would double again by the summer of 1952. Indeed, by spring 1952, an A. C. Nielsen Company survey, which had replaced the Hooper ratings, revealed that in the late evening more television sets than radios were turned on in America. The main reason was the marvelous list of popular shows and stars: Milton Berle, Sid Caesar and Imogene Coca, *I Love Lucy*, Dean Martin and Jerry Lewis, the *Ed Sullivan Show*, Jackie Gleason, and Arthur Godfrey.

And TV news, though still fighting with radio for budgets and resources, was coming into its own, as newsmen raised in radio were beginning to feel the tug in their own careers. Sevareid, already sounding nostalgic for past glories, told an interviewer when he got his Peabody Award that he was worried that TV's "frantic search for techniques" would lead to "scrappy" reporting that neglected "substance."

On Sunday afternoon November 18, 1951, Murrow and his new collaborator, Fred Friendly, with whom he had produced a recorded documentary of 1933–1945 called *I Can Hear It Now*, made television history with *See It Now*, a half-hour combination of documentary film and live reporting—indeed, several triumphs of "technique." Since the new coaxial cable had recently made it possible for the whole country to witness a scene at the same time, *See It Now* showed the Brooklyn Bridge and the Golden Gate on the same screen. And it brought in Eric Sevareid reporting from Washington. Now the cable, plus *See It Now* techniques, plus smaller, portable cameras, and the elaborate positioning of cameras around the Chicago ampitheater—which was chosen because the site would lend itself to better television—would enable, by Mickelson's early estimate, fifty million viewers in eighteen million homes to have a political-viewing experience like they had never had before. In fact, at peak periods, 60 percent of American homes were tuned in.

The conventions also marked the debut of Walter Cronkite as "anchorman," a term Mickelson coined. CBS originally hired Cronkite in 1950 to help cover the Korean War, but instead it used him in Washington on WTOP to fill in for Sevareid during his frequent minor illnesses, then put him on the 11 P.M. TV nightly news, the same time Eric was on radio. Mickelson saw in him a sturdy, dependable, professional quality—not a profound thinker like "Murrow's boys," but a journalist so well informed that coverage could center around him.

Sevareid arrived at the Democratic Convention privately convinced that the nomination was Stevenson's. Vice president Alben Barkley was too old, and Eric offended him by saying so on the air; Senator Estes Kefauver, who had gained a quick reputation as a crime fighter when his committee hearings on crime were televised, irritated Truman; patrician diplomat Averell Harriman had never run for office. Nevertheless, on Sunday night, as Averell, in his pajamas, sat up talking late with Eric and FDR's former secretary Grace Tully, the diplomat remained convinced that Truman would bless him at the last minute.

The next day, as Eric watched Adlai's welcoming address and heard the peals of applause well up spontaneously from the delegates, he became so convinced that they had caught the quality of the man, that they would draft him, he pleaded with Murrow to let him go on Murrow's 7:45 radio program and predict Adlai's nomination. Not even Truman, he thought, could stop him. Murrow agreed.

After the nomination Eric rode on Stevenson's train down to Springfield. He had young Peter, twelve, along, and Adlai sent his son John Fell, sixteen, to look after Peter, then took Peter back with him to stay at the governor's mansion while Eric stayed at the hotel with the press. With no sense of how to capitalize on publicity, Stevenson withdrew for over a day, while Peter slipped out from time to time to keep his father posted on the governor's plans, like Stevenson's decision to run his campaign from Springfield rather than from Washington. The next morning Adlai, Eric, and Peter had breakfast on the governor's veranda and Eric crossed the line between journalist and friend with friendly advice: address the American Legion Convention, postpone your vacation to Canada. Later at dinner Eric pressed him about where he had been for the last thirty-six hours. Adlai blushed, then finally confessed that the night before, unable to sleep, he had gone secretly after midnight to Lincoln's old house and sat there alone in the parlor thinking for hours.

Sevareid thought it was a wonderful campaign, with Stevenson's literary and witty speeches, but as soon as he saw Eisenhower's crowds, and once Eisenhower had said he would "go to Korea," Eric knew that Stevenson had no chance to win. Stevenson's entourage had urged him to make the same Korea promise earlier, but he thought it would be too manipulative, not right.

The month before the election, in a letter to Carl McGowan (October 2, 1952), Sevareid described Eisenhower more severely than in any of his commentaries. Ike was, in psychological terms, a "father image," who appealed to people's "prejudices, animosities, and ignorance," and "sense of weary perplexity." Without any real answers to problems, he *appeared* to have answers. Adlai, meanwhile, projected not an image of a father "but of the moral and intellectual proctor, the gad-fly called conscience." He had not excited the emotions, but had excited "the passions of the mind."

Right after the election, Sevareid wrote words of encouragement to Adlai: "No one has conducted a campaign so intelligent, so courageous and with such unswerving devotion to the simple cause of truth as you have done . . . There is no other effective national champion of civil liberties, of free speech, or the true American liberal movement and philosophy except yourself."

Eric and Adlai remained friends till Adlai's death in 1965. In the 1956 presidential campaign, Adlai even asked Eric to become his press officer. They saw one another or exchanged brief, admiring letters every few months, and although Eric would not claim they were intimates, they were certainly kindred spirits—both products of the Midwest, both having attached themselves to Lincoln as a lodestar. To an unusual degree, Stevenson was the vessel into whom others poured their hopes, not guessing that the vessel could contain just so much. Liberal intellectuals, impoverished by the absence of FDR—or, in Eric's case, Floyd Olson—looked to him to embody their ideals, yet, inevitably, expected more than he could honestly give.

During the 1956 campaign for the Democratic nomination one key issue was the implementation of the 1954 *Brown vs. Board of Education* Supreme Court decision ordering desegregation with "all deliberate speed." Stevenson, who certainly saw himself as a pro-civil rights liberal, opposed using federal troops to enforce integration or cutting off federal funds for education to areas that did not desegregate quickly enough. He considered his a moderate position, while AFL–CIO President George Meany and New York Senator Herbert Lehman were quite upset. But the *Washington Post*, Eleanor Roosevelt, and Eric Sevareid, also a moderate on civil rights, supported him. Sevareid thought Stevenson's position showed courage and common sense; children could not learn in an atmosphere of tension and potential violence. In two February 1956 commentaries he noted that the pace of integration was indeed slow; but, according to the way he read the American character, *Brown* marked the beginning of a process that would take generations to accomplish.

Sevareid was certainly a proponent of integration and sympathized profoundly with individual victims of racial injustice. In 1947, when a Negro man who worked for him was robbed in Washington D.C. and went to the police, the police treated the victim as if he were the criminal. In a letter describing the case to the *Washington Post* (July 7, 1947), Eric argued that crime in D.C. was probably much worse than statistics showed because the police disregarded Negroes. But his commentary on the *Brown* decision (May 19, 1954) emphasized sympathetic understanding for the South, which, he says, has replaced its old image of "an agrarian, torpid South, brooding in the weeds of its memories" with "an industrializing south, prosperous, electric with energy, new people, new ideas, developing a creative intellectual life perhaps more effectively than any part of the country."

Three years later, February 10, 1959, he described his home community of Alexandria's first day of school integration—including the new public school up the lane, now a paved street, where his boys used to ride their pony. He was pleased that, despite the tension, there had been no trouble. Then he reminisced, without naming the school, about Burgundy Farm Country Day School, which, he said, "at the start" the founders intended to integrate. He seemed to offer both local examples as models, as somehow evidence that the process was moving along, that a "community so imbued with and formed by the old and the past" could "confront the new and the present." It was also an example of his arguing from a small-town rural experience as if it were applicable to a larger, more complex society.

He stayed with the civil rights issues and continually adapted his ideas to events; but the same themes held. "No cause is now so fundamental to the health and integrity of this society as the Negro cause; of no other leaders are so much stamina and courage demanded as is now required of Negro leaders," he said in May 1963. If Negroes became more impatient in spite of progress, we should understand that it is the nature of revolution that the oppressed grow more eager when in sight of their goal. But gradualism remains a fact, a necessity. It took thirty years, he said, to end lynchings.

And, by 1963, if he still rejected military and economic force in compelling integration, he argued for moral and legal force. In a speech delivered at Freedom House award dinner, four days after President Kennedy's assassination, honoring Martin Luther King and Roy Wilkins, he also paid tribute to Joseph Cardinal Ritter, archbishop of St. Louis, who integrated his schools a year before *Brown* and considered segregation not just as a social wrong or immoral, but a *sin.* To the charge that you can't legislate changes in the human heart, Sevareid responded that you can; we have:

> Because laws, enforced, compel changes in human conduct. New conduct develops new habits, and new habits develop new attitudes, since man, to live within himself, must justify his conduct to himself. Action does change feelings, an old lesson of history, an old principle, I believe, of psychology.

The history of the civil rights movement after *Brown*—and its many martyrs—would demonstrate that resistance to desegregation in public accommodations, voting rights, transportation, and housing was deeper than Sevareid had imagined when he first spoke of the "new" South. He correctly foresaw that school desegregation would take a long time; he may not have foreseen that even after the constitutional remedies had been virtually exhausted, many areas of the North would remain in effect more segregated than the South and that inner-city northern public schools would be all-black hellholes characterized by drugs, knives, guns, and murders.

Stevenson's colleague and biographer, John Bartlow Martin, in *Adlai Stevenson and the World* (1977), regrets that Stevenson himself probably did not realize that he lacked "a strong emotional commitment to the civil rights cause." Robert Kennedy, by contrast, he says, felt the civil rights cause in his bones. "Stevenson mistrusted emotion, tried to keep it out of politics." So did Sevareid. But Sevareid was conscious of emotions, of passion, as a tremendous political force for both good and ill, and he read the civil rights movement with this in mind.

As the 1960 campaign approached, Adlai thought out loud with Eric about making a third run, but he settled for being John F. Kennedy's, and then Lyndon B. Johnson's ambassador to the United Nations, although he really wanted to be secretary of state. He admired Kennedy to a degree, but there was no way they could be friends; Stevenson was not comfortable with "tough" people, and JFK, of course, saw Adlai as "soft." Adlai once told Eric of Kennedy, "That young man in the White House, he never says please and he never says thank you." But he worked for Kennedy and Johnson, who sometimes offended him by using him dishonestly, by having their subordinates call him at the last minute with orders on how to mouth their policies on the Bay of Pigs, the U.S. invasion of the Dominican Republic, and Vietnam.

But the most dramatic and controversial hours of the Stevenson-Sevareid friendship were the last.

By July 1965 Stevenson was under pressure from his intellectual followers, whose ideals he had embodied in 1952 and 1956, to resign as U.S. ambassador to the United Nations in protest against Johnson's policies in both the Dominican Republic, where he had sent the marines to quell a rebellion, and Vietnam, where U.N. secretary U Thant was attempting to negotiate a settlement with Hanoi. Although Stevenson reportedly disapproved of the Dominican Republic intervention, biographer Martin, who was also a participant in the events, says there is no record of Stevenson's true position; furthermore, Stevenson had not yet thought out his own opinions on Vietnam. At least, according to Sevareid, Stevenson had not decided that the U.S. policy was unjust. Yet, Stevenson's followers presumed he agreed with them. Actually, his friend Sevareid, who went to the Dominican Republic to cover it for CBS, was convinced that Johnson's intervention was right: we were stopping, not starting, a war.

But Adlai, who worried a lot, had been reading Barbara Tuchman's *The Guns of August* and felt that once again, says Martin, "the world was caught up in an inexorable drift to war." At dinner he griped to David Schoenbrun that the Dominican Republic move was a "massive blunder," and Schoenbrun put his gripes on the air. In London on July 10,

Stevenson confided to William Benton that he planned to resign from the U.N., and Benton offered him $200,000 a year in salary and expenses to work for the Encyclopaedia Britannica—Benton had made a similar offer to Sevareid a few years before.

That Sunday night Adlai appeared on BBC-TV and resisted efforts to make him split with Johnson's Vietnam policy. After the show, Adlai took Eric over to the American embassy residence where he was staying, and that night, while Adlai was waiting for Kay Graham, who was also staying there, the two men fell into a conversation that, once disclosed, shook both Adlai's friends and the Johnson Administration.

With Sevareid, Stevenson poured out his complaints about the U.N. job, his frustrations with the Vietnam peace process—giving the impression that the Johnson administration was sabotaging rather than really seeking a settlement—and said he wanted to go back to Libertyville, Illinois, see the grandchildren, and "sit in the shade with a glass of wine and watch the people dance."

Eric felt he was looking at an exhausted man, too heavy, probably drinking too much but never drunk. He had not seen his friend in a while and was greatly shaken. Thirty-six hours later, Stevenson, on a walk with Marietta Tree, dropped dead with a heart attack on a London street. Sevareid almost immediately reported Stevenson's intention to resign in a radio broadcast; and, in a sensation-stirring article in *Look*, "The Last Hours of Adlai Stevenson," revealed much, though not all, of the rest of their conversation. The reaction, both positive and negative, was so strong that he found himself saying no to requests to reprint the article.

Eric's life became hell, as Stevenson colleagues denied he could have said what Sevareid reported, or said that Adlai was merely letting off steam, as he did with everybody, and that Eric Sevareid had mistaken it for an intimate conversation. Johnson defenders accused Sevareid of trying to embarrass the president. Martin's biography contends that Adlai was simply killing time waiting for Kay Graham to come by, while Graham, seeing the two men deep in talk, went to bed. The next day, Stevenson told Graham she should have rescued him from "that bore Sevareid"—certainly a quip meant to flatter Graham, not to reflect his feelings about Eric.

It is incredible that Sevareid could have misread either the content or the context of what Adlai told him that night, and his general practice was to go out of his way to avoid embarrassing presidents, simply because they were presidents. Eric had nothing to gain by reporting his encounter—other than the newsman's satisfaction in moving his audience closer to the truth. Personally, the encounter affected Eric profoundly, especially since at the time he was struggling with his own position on Vietnam.

In spite of the disappointments of Stevenson's two failed candidacies, and in spite of Lois's illness, which was not apparent to his CBS colleagues or even to the general community at Seminary Hill, on the surface the 1950s looked like good and prosperous years for Sevareid's career.

In 1952, his second book, *In One Ear*, a collection of 107 radio broadcasts from 1950 to 1952, made the best-seller lists and got flattering reviews. The *Christian Science Monitor* reviewer was amused at the number of times he fell back on "the equivalent of the traditional conversation with the taxi driver," but praised his "devastating" essays on McCarthy. Adlai dropped him a note (January 29, 1953): "This morning at breakfast Brooks Atkinson remarked that *In One Ear* was one of the best books he ever read."

In truth, the collection is a little gem of a book, dedicated to "my colleagues at CBS News," with the expected ongoing analyses of Korea, Truman, Eisenhower, Churchill—"a tiny, doll-like figure of a man" with the chubby, soft hands of a boy—and other leaders, but also touching reflections on Christmas and national holidays, and a powerful piece on how big-time college football both destroys those who play it and hurts those real students deprived of the scholarships that go to athletes. He remembers the Minnesota football stars of his youth:

> Most of them walked as gods, bathed in the blinding light of spurious fame. Football, their coaches always told them, would prepare them for the struggle of life. But sometimes we think many of them were not strengthened for life, but weakened. How many of those golden heroes slipped into the routine obscurity of average life to become perpetually dissatisfied, to spend their time daydreaming over their yellow clippings, living on memories, wishing life to be as bright and magical as it had been for them once?

Plans were moving along, he thought, for the Technicolor thriller, *Naga Headhunters,* to be produced by Twentieth Century Fox, starring Gregory Peck as Philip Adams. John Crosby, in the *Herald Tribune* (November 1, 1953), did a column on Sevareid's humor, with long quotes from his mockery of advertising, and its new "improved" products: "We absolutely refuse to buy, use or even mention any product that contains lanolin, chlorophyl, viratol, irridium, protopectins, or solinate, or any product that has been vitaminized, pressurized, homogenized or hammerized."

In the *Reporter* magazine, a prestigious liberal fortnightly founded in 1949 by Max Ascoli, which frequently printed Sevareid's broadcasts as columns, critic Marya Mannes wrote that "a network is known by the columnists it keeps"(August 4, 1953). She calls Sevareid "CBS's most distinguished ornament, a commentator of rare wisdom, courage, and compassion," and gives Paley credit for assembling a brilliant staff and giving them full trust and virtually complete freedom. "A CBS newscaster is expected to abide by his own conscience and code." If he violates this by injecting personal prejudice "he would be cut off in five minutes." Meanwhile, newspapers all over the country reprinted Sevareid's commentaries and congressmen frequently inserted them into the *Congressional Record.*

In January 1953 Sevareid began inching into television, repeating his nightly essay at 11:25 on WTOP-TV, complaining all the while about TV's reliance on pictures. The next month he began a half-hour Sunday afternoon educational TV program, *State of the Nation,* guiding viewers on a tour of a government agency, for example, the Treasury Department. Yet, in this transitional period, critics like the *New York Times'* Jack Gould were asking whether television news was using its talent well enough. The annual New Year's Day *Years of Crisis* roundtable discussion, when Murrow assembled correspondents from all over the world, demonstrated that CBS had powerful stars, allowed once a year to speak for themselves. But it was an indictment of the "journalistic inertia the rest of the year."

An exception to the inertia was Paley and Stanton's decision to work Sevareid more effectively into the TV schedule with the introduction on Sunday evenings in 1954 of *The American Week,* produced by Ernest Leiser, written by John Sharnik, and narrated by Sevareid, with his commentary at the end. Paley saw it as a low-budget *See It Now,* in a magazine format, each week touching on several topics, while Leiser leaned toward occasional in-depth treatment of particular issues. CBS was still small enough in the 1950s for executives and staff to work together closely. It had offices and studios in the Greybar Building at Grand Central Station, and later up in Liederkranz Hall on Fifty-seventh Street; and Paley and Stanton took a personal interest in putting the show together. They visited the new set, designed to resemble a film-editing studio with staff members, at Paley's insistence, wearing white smocks and white gloves to protect the film from their hands. At the time Leiser was hobbling around with a cast on his leg and had to be wheeled from the offices to the studio, and Eric was really wearing white gloves because he had developed shingles on his hands. But Eric's image was the centerpiece of the show, which opened with a close up of his hulking silhouette, as the camera zoomed in on his briefcase stamped, "ERIC SEVAREID, WASHINGTON, D.C."

Unfortunately, although it increased his fame, Eric's attitude toward the transition to television did not always endear him to his fellow workers. He told interviewers he would rather be writing books—including a novel—but the TV paycheck took care of grocery bills. Again, TV production is teamwork, while he was a loner who agonized over his scripts and was not always gracious when asked to edit them. He complained enough about "pictures" to make one wonder why he didn't get into another line of work. Meanwhile, the crew in New York worked all week on the show, waiting for the star who, the producer says, "didn't bust his ass," to arrive on Saturday afternoon. Whereupon he would disappear with one of the secretaries. Only forty-two, the star already walked like an old man, mumbled about his illnesses, and gave the impression to the younger staff that he was austere and diffident.

Actually, as he made clear in a long letter to a *Look* editor (May 24, 1955), he did appreciate the hard work of the whole team, he did enjoy television, he appreciated its power—"you feel like you're controlling the throttle of a locomotive"—but there was something in his bearing when he was around underlings—like crew members, photographers, or engineers—that made them think he would rather be talking to someone else. So, to deal with Sevareid's nervousness, which many labled hypochondria, before the show on Sunday Leiser would take him to the

Oak Room at the Plaza for lunch with a few scotches to calm him down.

The show was good. Its purpose was to give the events of the week a coherent pattern. In mid May 1954, for example, it looked at the *Brown* decision through the eyes of the Negroes in Washington who had pre-pared the case, through the eyes of whites and Negroes in the rural South, and at a school where desegregation had succeeded. Philip Ham-burger in the *New Yorker* (July 10, 1954) called Sevareid a "bright jewel," who thinks a problem through before he talks about it, who has a sense of history. The topics sometimes reflected Eric's life experiences—like Anglo-American relations and Chiang's Nationalist army training on For-mosa. Two outstanding programs—one dealing with atomic scientist J. Robert Oppenheimer's loss of his security clearance, and the other with race riots in the Trumbull Park housing development in Chicago—won the 1955 Sidney Hillman Foundation Award.

For Sevareid, things were going unmistakably well. To relax, he trav-eled frequently to Europe, skied and went trout fishing. On his forty-five-acre piece of land in the Blue Ridge hills of Warrenton, Virginia, where he and Lois had put up their log cabin with an outhouse in back, and stocked the lake with fish, he cleared brush and timber with the boys and liked to think of himself as an amateur farmer.

But in those years, like Adlai, he worried a lot. Not just about his ail-ments, his arthritis, and the shingles that hospitalized him. For one thing, CBS had been timid in resisting the red-baiting that was terrorizing much of the entertainment industry. In 1950 a New York publication called *Counterattack: The Newsletter of Facts on Communism*, published *Red Channels*, which purported to list 151 pro-communists in radio and tele-vision. It was, in effect, a black list, a largely successful attempt to deprive jobs from the accused. As Eric Barnouw makes clear in *Tube of Plenty,* the list was actually an honor roll of the true stars of the profession; at CBS it included Norman Corwin, William L. Shirer, and Howard K. Smith. CBS instituted an internal loyalty statement, which everyone, in-cluding Murrow and Sevareid, signed.

In October 1953 Alfred Sevareid died at seventy-one. At the time of his death he was vice president and secretary of the Federal Intermediate Credit Bank in St. Paul, and had sufficiently restored the family fortune to allow them to move into the same neighborhood with the Fingers and to leave Clara financially secure. His other two sons, Paul and John, were both army majors stationed in Japan. Eric's relationship with his father seems to have mellowed toward the end. They posed for pictures together in Minneapolis when *Not So Wild a Dream* appeared. He visited Lois and Eric at Valley Lane, and Adele Brown remembers driving with Lois and her father-in-law all the way to Florida and finding the older Sevareid a warm and lovely gentleman. After his death, Eric discovered that his father had carried a letter from him, in which Eric had tried to express his gratitude and affection, folded up tightly in his wallet.

At home he brooded.

Michael found him one day at the Warrentown cabin so dark and despondent that he was frightened of him. There is reason to believe he sought psychiatric help, at least to help him deal with Lois's illness. During Mental Health Week in May, 1954, he dedicated an analysis to the issue. Mental illness, he said, was "probably the worst destroyer of children, of marriages, of family life, of individual happiness than all the purely physical illnesses put together . . . this is the most baffling and heartbreaking of all illnesses to which the body and soul fall victim . . ." The bulk of his commentary was a plea for more federal funds for mental health research; but the underlying theme was his private agony. Yet the private agony was a reflection of what the country was going through.

One night in 1953 Eric drove his old friend Geoffrey Cox, who was stationed in Washington with the British foreign service, back to Valley Lane for dinner with his family. On the way, Eric confessed his darkest fear. He feared that Senator McCarthy would somehow find in the bowels of the State Department that report he had written on the corruption of the Chiang Kai-shek regime, and that, like so many others, he would be subpoenaed to appear before the McCarthy committee to explain it. He constantly, obsessively, turned over in his head the questions McCarthy might try to bludgeon him with and how he would try to answer. But he knew the logic or the truth of his answers would have no effect. He would be tainted. McCarthy would drive sponsors away from his evening program.

And here he was, said Cox, driving back to a remote and lonely house to a "mad wife" waiting for him, and warning his dinner guests that Lois had her "bouts" and he wasn't sure what she was likely to do.

In the Guild Lecture at the University of Minnesota, October 23, 1953, Sevareid read the passage from Ray Bradbury's story, "Farenheit 451," where "School is shortened, discipline relaxed, philosophies, histories, languages dropped, English and spelling gradually, gradually neglected . . . life is immediate, the job counts, pleasure lies all about after work . . ." and found it more frightening than Orwell's *1984,* because in Bradbury's story, we, not the state, had chosen the quick amusement, instant gratification that technology provided, treating it as more valuable than books or time to think. And this was around the time in which his friend Robert Ardrey's symbolic novel, *The Brotherhood of Fear* (1952), dedicated to Eric, warned about the danger that America would become a police state. Only two years later, Ardrey's play, *Sing Me No Lullaby* (1954), on "America's moral and political sickness" would fail to find an audience. In Sevareid's 1955 address accepting the 1954 Sidney Hillman Award, he told his audience he was "frightened to the marrow" at the way the attorney general, Herbert Brownell, by recklessly implying in a Chicago speech that Truman, as president, had abetted "treason," abused his power for political purposes.

The conventional wisdom is that the power of Joseph McCarthy was broken by two television events: the networks' decision to broadcast the McCarthy's committee hearings into alleged subversion of the military at Fort Monmouth, New Jersey; and the broadcast of Murrow's *See It Now,* on March 9, 1954, in which Murrow exposed McCarthy at his most thuggish, through skillfull film editing, and then concluded with a powerful Murrow-delivered editorial at the end.

That Senator McCarthy should have achieved national prominence in the first place is the result in large part to the laziness and pusillanimity of the press who, for a long while, printed accusations of subversion without evaluating them for truth. Eventually the establishment press, like the *Washington Post* and *Time* magazine investigated his charges and documented the senator's inability to back them up with facts. Meanwhile, it was up to the small, liberal, opinion magazines, like the *Reporter* and the Catholic *Commonweal,* and individual commentators—like Elmer Davis, Martin Agronsky, and Sevareid—to deal with the Wisconsin senator's accusations week after week.

Yet, Murrow's *See It Now* editorial, says Edwin R. Bayley in *Joseph McCarthy and the Press* (1981) was relatively mild. He says McCarthy exploited, did not create, the "situation of fear." "It was almost defensive, a justification for making such a program. It was not nearly as strong as the editorials that had appeared regularly in some newspapers for four years." Sevareid too felt that Murrow was late. His program came after the Army-McCarthy hearings had already damaged the demagogue's image.

From the very beginning, in 1950, Sevareid addressed the collection of symptoms that became known as McCarthyism. He expressed himself most vigorously in defense of the China diplomats like John Stewart Service, John Carter Vincent, and John Paton Davies who were accused of "losing" China. He also defended others like Owen Lattimore and Oppenheimer who he felt were falsely accused. At times he used humor to make his case. He compared Winnie the Pooh's tracking a "boogle" in a circle to McCarthy on the trail of a red. When McCarthy's aides, Roy Cohn and G. David Shine, gumshoed through Europe investigating American libraries abroad for pro-communist books, Sevareid simply ridiculed their expense accounts.

But his strongest condemnation came during the army hearings, January 10, 1954, in Sevareid's reaction to the moment when, in an act of desperation, McCarthy revealed that a young man on the staff of army counsel Joseph Welsh had a remote communist connection in his past. Welsh exploded with righteous indignation. Not till then had he guessed the depths to which McCarthy would stoop. "Have you no shame?" he cried, in words that rung across America. McCarthy, said Sevareid, had no sense that:

> the audience was crying shame upon him; he had no feeling that he had done anything morally wrong; clearly, his only feeling was that he had done something tactically wrong, that he had merely lost a point in that particular round; and what has long been clear to many observers here and what one may surmise became clear to thousands of others at that moment, is this: that those *were* his only feelings, because the capacity for other feelings is simply not there. He cannot help it. The personal tragedy of McCarthy is that the nerve or chord or cluster of cells that produce what men call conscience was not granted to him.

After McCarthy died in 1957, a friend remembers visiting the Sevareid home to be greeted by Lois calling out, "McCarthy's dead. Aren't you glad?" When Dean Acheson, who had every reason to be glad, said, "*De mortuis nisi bonum,*" Eric replied in a commentary that history could not adopt that pleasant rule of grace. "Nor may those who write and speak the first draft of history. They must, as they will, put it all down, the good and the ill." He concluded:

> Never once did he uncover a person in government proved to be a Communist. Yet millions believed with him that "Where there's smoke there's fire." And for a time the devil theory of politics was established—the theory that a few individuals in this vast government were responsible for giving whole nations over to the Red Army of Communist control.
>
> Washington respects power and power alone. When McCarthy had power, the highest officials attended his wedding. When his power was gone, though the human being was the same, he was cut dead socially. If history finds that McCarthy used his strength in a wrongful manner, it will find that the weakness of others was part of the fault.

If the McCarthy *See It Now* is remembered as a Murrow triumph, it also seems to mark the beginning of his gradual disaffection with CBS. To his "boys" he remained the revered teacher, though he drank and smoked more and started a flimsy celebrity interview show called *Person to Person.* But Paley was beginning to drift away from Murrow and from the tough journalism that *See It Now* represented. Cronkite, whom Murrow didn't like and thought "talked too much," along with NBC's team of Chet Huntley and David Brinkley, began to personify the new "comfortable" TV newsman. The networks were moving toward quiz shows, like CBS's *$64,000 Question,* positioned right before *See It Now* on Sunday. The Red Scare had not abated; both Murrow and Sevareid found their passports held up by the State Department.

The malaise became most evident in an incident in the summer and fall of 1956 that brought Sevareid to one of those professional and moral turning points that every man reasonably fears.

In July 1955 the U.S. Court of Appeals ruled that the right to travel is a natural right subject to reasonable regulation, but that the State

Department did not have full and free right to determine who could have a passport and who could not. Meanwhile, Murrow had been cultivating William Worthy, a quiet, young black journalist at the Baltimore *Afro-American*, and had helped him obtain a Nieman Fellowship at Harvard. As a stringer, Worthy had made a few broadcasts from Moscow for CBS, and in August 1956, although the State Department prohibited journalists from traveling in China, Worthy got in and took films and did shortwave broadcasts for CBS from Peking and Shanghai.

Undersecretary of State George Murphy, furious, got Paley on the phone, and when Worthy arrived home, the State Department denied renewal of his passport. Both Murrow and Sevareid jumped to his defense. Murrow, who called it a violation of free speech on the air, was reprimanded by CBS. Sevareid, who had rushed Worthy to a studio to debrief him, prepared a commentary for September 3. In it he argued that the government policy of barring journalists from any country made no sense, both because it was inconsistent and also inhibited our right and need to know. He made a carefully modulated argument that it was the "height of folly" to not get all the information on China we could. He ended: "What has been imposed here, as the *New York Times* suggests, is a form of peacetime government censorship on the free American press. Withholding a passport is censorship just as effective as wielding a blue pencil."

The commentary never aired. CBS killed it. His editor, John Day, asked for a commentary on another topic. Eric couldn't do it, so they put someone else on who flubbed, and listeners noticed. Sevareid, determined to get his piece out, passed it to a senator who put it in the *Congressional Record*. To Paley, this was insubordination. He called in Sevareid for a dressing down and barred Murrow, who wanted to accompany him, from the meeting.

"I'm going to have this out with the old man," Sevareid told Murrow.

But the old man was not about to yield. "You broke a commitment," he told Sevareid who, in Paley's mind, both had no right to leak a broadcast text, which belonged to CBS, and had violated the rule against editorializing in an analysis.

"There's no such thing as total neutrality," Sevareid replied. "What did you want me to say when Russia invaded Hungary? Was I to sound neutral? I couldn't. If I did, I wouldn't have an audience in two months. You can't be an intellectual eunuch."

The two men sat there across from one another. In a similar confrontation with Murrow over the fate of *See It Now*, Paley could sense the unspoken battle over whose network CBS really was. In the public mind, Murrow knew that *he* was CBS. But in 1956 Paley knew Sevareid could not make that claim. Paley had, as usual, the upper hand. The eunuch analogy was apt.

Despondent, Sevareid broke the silence, "Maybe I've been too long with CBS."

Paley just sat there silently looking at him—a signal that, yes, it was time for Eric Sevareid to resign. But he didn't. The two of them just sat there.

"I don't know why Paley didn't fire me," Sevareid told Sally Bedell Smith. But perhaps Paley realized he didn't have to fire him. He thought he had achieved his purpose.

"I rode along because of my nature," Sevareid said. "I was more interested in elucidating than in advocating." With a sick wife, two sons approaching college, and two homes, he was also more interested in earning a salary than in being unemployed. Besides, for all his aloofness, Sevareid had a very strong need to belong somewhere, if not to the Jacobins, then to Murrow's boys.

In fact, in the middle of his fight with Paley, Sevareid received a call at the Berkshire Hotel where he was staying in New York. It was Robert Kintner, president of NBC. "I know you're having trouble with Paley," he said, "and if you are leaving, I want you to come here. I want you to be the centerpiece of the news operation and I'll make you an officer in the company." When Eric got home to Valley Lane, he decided he couldn't move his family to New York. But that was a lame excuse. It is far more likely that he had long since defined "home" as CBS, unhappy home though it sometimes was.

The following February Sevareid lamented to his old friend Robert Sherrod, then managing editor of the *Saturday Evening Post*, that "I am in the unhappy position of having to decide whether I can go on in this line of work...." He asked, in a sad little joke, whether Sherrod needed an assistant copyboy. "I was a real good copyboy once, before I got uppity ideas."

17

DIVORCE

IT BEGAN as far back as 1950. Belen Marshall then was nineteen, living with her mother in New York, and she had just returned from a party in Connecticut where, she felt, too much drinking was going on, and she didn't want to stay. Then the phone rang. Her mother, a Cuban-born opera singer and voice teacher, was calling from another party in Manhattan. She was at the Chesters—Edmund Chester was CBS's director of news—and wanted Belen to come over and bring her guitar.

To the guests at the Chesters, it was easy to see why Carolina, Belen's mother, would want her to come over. She was a talented, attractive, cosmopolitan young woman. She had been born in Milan in 1931, where her mother sang at La Scala. After her Spanish father left while Belen was still an infant, her mother married again, but, Belen would say later, it had not been a good marriage. Now Belen clearly had the talent that would lead to her own career. She was also vivacious, and when she played and sang, everybody joined in.

Of course these were older people at the party, many of whom she did not know, so for a little while she withdrew by herself to a chair by the food table. And a tall, handsome man she had never seen before wandered over, picked up the carving knife and began to slice the turkey. "You know," he said, giving the young woman a glance, "This is not what I do for a living." Of course, she had no idea what he did for a living, or whether he was married; but, though he was just twice her age, he was a very attractive man.

The party was warming up again and the group was ready to sing. Did the tall man have any requests? Yes, he said, sing "Deep in the Heart of Texas."

It did not seem like the kind of song this serious-looking fellow would want to sing. But, as Belen would learn in the years ahead, this fellow occasionally did things that did not match his public image.

The stars at night
Are big and bright,
Clap! Clap! Clap! Clap!
Deep in the heart —
of Texas.

That night, when Belen and Carolina got home, her mother turned
to her and said, "I have met the man you are going to marry."

That was the beginning.

When Lois finally got the letter that contained the word "divorce," it
was the summer of 1959. She was stunned. She had not seen it coming.
True, she knew the marriage had problems and that her illness was only
one of those problems. Those close to him maintain that Eric was not
promiscuous, or a philanderer, or a "womanizer" who preys upon other
men's wives. But Eric's colleagues, and some of the other family members, knew that he was not the model of fidelity either. He was a difficult person—a "wanderer," said one of the family—and Lois must have
known of Belen's existence. But she had not foreseen this letter, post-
marked Spain, which caught up with her in Seattle, where she was
stopping off on the last leg of a round-the-world trip that had included
Moscow.

Meanwhile, Peter, who was in Philadelphia working as an intern for
the *Philadelphia Bulletin*, where family friend Bill Dickinson was editor,
got the word and called his brother Michael. From Chicago, where
Michael hoped to catch up with their mother, he was to bring her to
Philadelphia where she could stay with the Dickinsons and pull herself
together.

From Eric's point of view, this was an escape from an intolerable situation, from a long, drawn-out, debilitating existence that was sapping
his limited psychological strength and draining off energy he needed for
his work. Simply put, he was unhappy. Looking back over a series of
events during the previous year, it seems clear that this kind of break was
coming.

In June 1958 Lois suffered a heart attack, was hospitalized for several
weeks, and by the following November was still not sufficiently recovered to take a trip to the Warrenton cabin. Nevertheless, Eric still felt he

had to get away to Europe in July and August for a working vacation and he left alone. It was a decision that astonished their neighbor and Lois's close friend, Adele Brown, who saw it as a callous disregard for a vulnerable woman at a moment when she needed him.

Eric's complaints about his own health seemed to accelerate: he described himself in letters (May 23, 1958) as a "broken-down middle-aged man" with a bad back that pained him even when he sat erect, and as "feeling about eighty-five . . . down with a virus infection and creaking in every bone. (February 9, 1959). When Eric complained to CBS News president Sig Mickelson that he thought he was going stale and needed some kind of a break or a change, Mickelson mentioned that he would have an opening for a London correspondent, since Charles Collingwood would be coming home. Eric asked for it immediately. His first choice would have been Rome; but, whatever his criticisms of the British, their class system and the evidence of decline in their government, he did like London. He might even recapture the vitality of those days when he and Murrow first made their reputations.

There were other reasons why this seemed the right time to make his break. His father's estate was settled. His mother had just spent the previous winter in Washington, had survived six bad Washington snowstorms, and was now home in Minneapolis. His older brother Paul was also back in Minneapolis as a successful newscaster; and his younger brother John, who was in his second marriage, was running an army ordnance depot in New Jersey. Their sister Jeanne who, with her husband Colonel John Schmidt, had lived for three years in Tripoli, was now living in the Washington area. There was a good chance that the extended family, which was accustomed to giving him moral support, would continue to do so.

His two sons were in college, supposedly at an age when they might best endure the separation of their parents. Eric had the practice of intervening for them to get them summer jobs, and he had written to friends for advice on their college choices. In a letter to a professor friend at Washington and Lee University (January 29, 1958) he described Michael, who had worked as a laborer at friend Robert Craig's Aspen Institute for Humanistic Studies in Colorado in the summer of 1958, as "a quick-minded boy," who "simply hasn't learned systematic study, probably shying away from it because his brother is a good scholar." Mike had put all his energy into baseball—like Eric's father—

football, teen-age social life, and theater. Could Mike get into Washington and Lee? Is social life handy? "What about the supply of the opposite sex?" the father asks. Peter, on the other hand, though both had the same IQ, had been the valedictorian and ranked in the top fourth of his class. As it worked out, Mike went to Middlebury and Peter thought about Stanford, but at the last minute went to Harvard. At the moment Peter was laid up in his residence hall with a foot injury, but he would be all right.

In February 1959 Eric and Lois sold the home on Seminary Hill and moved into a smaller, two-story, redbrick house at 1610 Thirty-second Street in Georgetown. When the buyer, a medical doctor, came to inspect the Valley Lane home, he sensed the situation that had led to the decision to move. The place was not well-kept. Light bulbs lacked shades. Someone had painted the insides of the cupboards purple and the outsides of them green. Lois's hair was dissheveled and she was fat. It was obvious her life was coming apart at the very moment when her husband was reaching the height of his powers. Eric sent the new owner a long, meticulous directive on how to care for the house and grounds. While the fence *rails* were chestnut, the *posts* were locust; insist on *locust* when replacing them. Split the cost of maintaining the driveway with the Browns or help with the work. Watch the trees for heavy dead limbs which might fall on the house. The neighbors were "all fine people." Eric then sold the new occupant the old drapes he was leaving behind and accepted $300 for the piano. He also sold some other items, like the bikes, to the Caters. Shortly afterward, a leg fell off the piano.

The other incentive for making the break was the climate at CBS. Paley and some others, like, on occasion, Sig Mickelson, had grown weary of a certain attitude shared by Murrow, Sevareid, and Howard K. Smith: the commentators seemed to imagine that they had a special pipeline to inspired truth and that they, as superior beings, had an obligation, a right, to speak their wisdom regardless of the consequences. Paley's critics thought he was simply afraid of antagonizing Congress and the FCC; or, more likely, that Paley feared that Sevareid's continued criticisms of the Eisenhower administration would deprive Paley of a hoped-for appointment as an ambassador. To Paley's defenders, he was primarily concerned with keeping the loyalty of his affiliates. Commentary that was well received by sophisticated people in New York or

Washington did not always please the ears of station owners in other parts of the country; since the news was carried live, they resented having no say about what their audience would see and hear.

Meanwhile the death of a friend and mentor, a man of great wisdom and conscience, must have made Sevareid ponder the state of his own life. Elmer Davis died in June 1958 at the age of sixty-eight. In his CBS analysis Eric quoted a tribute he had delivered once to Davis at a public dinner:

> Elmer Davis is the whole man, the complete American. There is in the mind and spirit of this man a rare synthesis of the eternal and the contemporary. He was a boy in Indiana; and he was a scholar of the classics. And there is, therefore, in his precise and natural speech an effortless integration; an instinctive awareness of the tragedy of life, of the bleak glory of man's ancient pilgrimage, and yet through it all the warm and eager hope of the American dream.

Davis was dead and Murrow was in decline. In 1958, after a forty-five-minute face-off between Paley and Murrow and Friendly, Paley terminated *See It Now*. Tired of the constant gripes from senators who had power over the network's license, Paley told Murrow, "I don't want this constant stomach-ache every time you do a controversial subject."

"I'm afraid that's the price you have to be willing to pay. It goes with the job," Murrow made the mistake of replying. Paley, however, thought he would decide just what price he was willing to pay.

Murrow grew increasingly bitter and retaliated on October 15, in a speech at the meeting of the Radio and Television News Directors at the Sheraton-Blackstone Hotel in Chicago. This speech is his fundamental indictment of what television, in its search for ratings and profits, had become: purely an entertainment medium, when TV should be a medium of education.

> I am seized with an abiding fear regarding what these two instruments [radio and television] are doing to our society, our culture and our heritage. I invite your attention to the television schedules of all networks between the hours of 8 and 11 P.M. Eastern time ... Here you will find only fleeting and spasmotic reference to the fact that this nation is in mortal danger. There are, it is true, occasional

informative programs in that intellectual ghetto on Sunday afternoon. But during the daily peak viewing periods, television, in the
main, insulates us from the realities of the world in which we
live . . . I am frightened by the imbalance, the constant striving to
reach the largest possible audience for everything; by the absence
of a sustained study of the state of the nation . . . I would like television to produce some itching pills rather than this constant out-
pouring of tranquilizers.

Although Murrow delivered a scathing indictment, he did not propose any far-reaching structural changes. Commercial sponsors should
support higher quality public affairs programs, he proposed idealistically,
even though they did not necessarily draw large audiences. Public television has tried this with middling success.

The spring of 1959, the same time Eric was making his decision to
break away, Murrow decided that he and Janet would go to Europe
on sabbatical. When CBS announced in March that, beginning in June,
Eric Sevareid would take a leave of absence, then remain in London as a
roving European correspondent, those who had observed their parallel
careers had to ask if there was some special reason why both were leaving at the same time. Eric told the *New York Times* that there was no
connection between his decision and Murrow's announcement the
month before.

In 1957 Eric wrote a revealing little piece for the *Reader's Digest*
(April), "The Best Advice I Ever Had," in which he drew on his four
most significant life experiences to determine a moral or psychological
rule of behavior. When he and Walter Port were facing the last fearsome
450-mile leg of their journey into the wilderness in 1930, a Danish fur
trapper told them, "Just think about the next mile you have to go, not
about the ones after that, and I believe you can make it." "No advice has
ever meant more to me," Eric wrote. In the Burma jungle, wounded by
a boot nail in one foot and with blisters on both, and 140 miles to hobble to freedom, he convinced himself that he *could* hobble to the next
ridge or the next friendly village. In 1945, when he had to write a
quarter-million-word book, which became his "deepest source of professional pride," in six months, he convinced himself he could write
the next one paragraph. When he began writing daily for CBS, more

than two thousand scripts ago, he determined that he could write the next *one*.

By 1959 he either forgot the best advice he ever received or simply determined he could not live one more year with Lois. His May office correspondence is filled with references to his impending departure. One London letter writer presumes he is bringing Lois. Yet Mary Scammon remembers a Washington party at which friends were saying good-bye to Eric but not to Lois; friends knew she was not going with him. His decision is, in many ways, a touchstone of his life not just because the breakup of a marriage is, or can be, as traumatic as a death, but because of Sevareid's public reputation for wisdom, prudence, and integrity. This image would be enhanced a hundredfold with the stern visage familiar in the TV commentaries. Remember that he had written in 1945 that Murrow was great because he was what he seemed to be. Certainly, he too wanted to be what he seemed to be—a good man. Most people who knew him well agree that Eric was a man of great integrity. Frank Stanton said he never knew him to do anything dishonest or ignoble. But his leaving Lois raises some questions.

Those who went through it with them agree that living with Lois was extremely difficult. But some, particularly the women, suggest that Eric was not so easy to live with either. Because he was a child of the Depression, who never got over his father's bank failure, he was almost neurotic about money. Some say he was stingy. He had neither the ability nor inclination to do ordinary household chores; he could not cook for himself, he depended on women to take care of him. Lois, they suggest, was a professional woman who, married to someone else, could have had a career of her own; but married to him, ill or no, was forced to remain in his shadow. A few suggest that Eric's self-centeredness kept him from fully loving his sons; in letters to friends he reported on their status or progress, but he did not talk much about their accomplishments or "dote" on them the way other parents did with their children.

Eric lacked the basic ease, the ability to be honest and open with other people, which might have saved their relationship. One word for his retiring behavior is shyness; yet one man's shyness can be another man's rudeness. On social occasions like dinners and cocktail parties, incapable of "small talk," Eric would either disappear off in a corner and talk about world events with one person, or dominate a group, hold forth argumentatively as if the rest of the table were his radio audience. To people who saw him this way, his abandonment of a sick, forty-eight-year-old wife to flee with a twenty-eight-year-old woman was consistent with the self-centered behavior that had aggravated Lois's condition. As one CBS colleague put it, his decision was "utterly selfish."

Others, including members of both his own and Lois's family, describe Eric as a genuinely shy, private, but nevertheless thoughtful and generous man who did his best to deal with an impossible situation as long as he could. There is ample evidence in his correspondence of his consideration; he wrote beautiful notes to friends and relatives who suffered illness or family tragedies; he intervened to land old colleagues jobs, honors, or promotions. Although he would haggle for weeks with an air-conditioner repairman over a bill, he would also lend or give money to friends in need. When he and Lois visited Norway, they discussed inviting the daughter of a prominent Norwegian poet to come and live with them for a while. In New York in 1946 he met Katri Kirchner, whom he had known in Europe and in Rio; and she accompanied him on a little shopping expedition to help him buy a new hat. When he learned that she was in the midst of a divorce and she and her young son were having difficulty getting settled in America, he loaned her money and offered to take the son to live on Valley Lane and go to school with Peter and Michael, and later helped the boy get accepted at Phillips Andover.

Indeed, kindness and compassion are two of the words most often used to describe him. Virtues which, of course, can coexist with other human weaknesses. Sevareid's male colleagues, although they wondered about the wisdom of his new match—one quipped that he should marry her mother—in general declined to pass judgment. Howard K. Smith's analysis, for example, is that Eric was a man with a strong, natural need for affection, that he wasn't getting it, and had the right to a happier life. A woman friend of the family, worried about Lois's losing CBS's hospitalization insurance, suggested that Eric stay married to Lois but keep Belen as a mistress. Eric took umbrage at the thought. "But that would be immoral," he said indignantly. Finally, he told his friend, the CBS producer and writer Perry Wolff, "We have to protect the weak; but we can't allow the weak to destroy the strong."

In April 1959, Eric wrote to a friend, "I expect to enjoy Europe this next year, and I hope to travel as widely as I can. I am long, long overdue for a little mental stimulation, and that's about the only way I can get it." At the beginning of June he and Belen fled to Spain. There they linked up with Robert Ardrey and his wife at the Santa Clara Hotel in Torremolinos, a short drive from Malaga on the southern coast. They were looking forward to a wonderful new life. In July, William Benton, cruising north to Valencia, pulled his yacht into Malaga and welcomed the Ardreys and Sevareids aboard for an evening dinner cruise. Benton was wooing Eric to become editor of the Encyclopaedia Britannica. Ardrey and Benton were very taken with Belen. "She's a very, very attractive girl and I congratulate you," Benton wrote Sevareid (November 3). Eric did not want to run Britannica; he wanted to eat, sleep, and write magazine articles and fiction—but above all he wanted to calm his nerves.

In July, Ernest Hemingway and his entourage came to town. He stayed at the estate, called La Consula, of the wealthy American expatriate, Nathan (Bill) Davis, while he worked on an article for *Life,* which grew into the book, *The Dangerous Summer,* about a duel for supremacy between Spain's two greatest matadors. The brash, young Antonio Ordonez, whom Hemingway had befriended, was, city by city, overtaking the older Luis Miguel Dominguin, who had reigned since the death of Manolete in 1947, and who was also Ordonez' brother-in-law. The Malaga fights were to be the climax of their rivalry. That both matadors had recently been gored and would fight in spite of their barely healed wounds merely heightened expectations.

Hemingway, as his biographer Carlos Baker records the period, was not in a good mood. Preoccupied with the fact that he had just turned sixty, he longed for his lost youth, laced his language with more obscenities than ever, and seemed to treat his fourth wife Mary with more than his usual cruelty. He often spent days by the pool at Davis's estate, where Ordonez was recuperating, and sometimes in the evening after a fight he would take a horse-drawn carriage to the Miramar Hotel, where he would sit in the bar or on the terrace and look out over the sea.

There Eric could approach the Hemingways because both he and Mary Hemingway came from Minnesota, and at the Miramar they met and became occasional drinking companions. "Mary is gentle at all times and Ernest is gentle when he is not passionate about something,"

Eric wrote in *Esquire*, "and I fell in love with both." Sevareid's expertise in bullfighting was limited to his having read *Death in the Afternoon* and having seen a few fights in Mexico the previous December.

The day before the decisive fight, Eric—he never mentions Belen in his article—went out to La Consula and mixed with "Papa" Hemingway and his pals around the pool. The happy-go-lucky Ordonez, with an eight-inch wound from his thigh to his groin, would leap sideways into the air, bounce a tennis ball thrown by an American off his head in mid-air, and tumble into the pool. Eric's *Esquire* report, "Mano a Mano," on the contest, which he and Papa agreed had been the greatest bullfight in the history of the sport, was really Eric's attempt to do what Hemingway did better, but it is interesting that he tried it at all. His unique turn is his concluding distinction between the *great* athlete, Dominguin, who has earned his place by training and education, and the *master*, Ordonez, the natural, who "is in command of the bull because he is in command of himself. He knows himself." If Eric had applied the distinction to his own work, he probably would have identified with Dominguin—a man who had *learned* to do what he did.

Successful journalists in mid-life often dream of becoming "real" writers—which means that they imagine they should write fiction. Fiction, unlike their journalism, might last. And its form may allow them to say strongly felt things which the strictures of objective reporting and analysis smother. While in Spain, Sevareid wrote a short story, "The Meeting in Malaga," which has never reached the printed page. His agent Don Congdon had hopes for it, but the *New Yorker* and others turned it down. John Fischer, the editor of *Harper's*, was kind enough to explain in three letters to Congdon and Eric (December 17, 1959; March 11, 1960; April 20, 1960) why the story wasn't very good. It was "a little reminiscent of early Hemingway," with more Hemingway influence on the style than Eric realized. What bothered Fischer was "the attitude of the author towards his characters, and the characters toward the world—attitudes which in both cases seemed reminiscent both of Hemingway and other neo-Stoics." That Eric at this stage of his life was identifying with Hemingway, who was on the doorstep of a deep depression and in little more than a year would kill himself, is not a good sign. Fischer refers to a letter in which Eric complained about the new American tendency to "exalt the weak at the expense of the strong." On the surface, this may have been a reference to his hardening ideas in foreign policy, but there is also an echo of the sick (weak) wife who had been sapping his strength.

Meanwhile in Georgetown, Lois spent several days in a wooden chair staring blankly into a corner. For some weeks she moved in with Adele Brown who cared for her. When she learned Belen and Eric's planned address in London, in an angry, ironic gesture, she sent them a roomful of flowers. As they traveled in England and Europe, Eric sometimes introduced Belen as "Miss Sevareid," but Eric's journalism colleagues in London, while they found them a striking couple at informal gatherings, simply presumed they were lovers. When Sig Mickelson visited London that year, he was struck by how Eric, who had been so down when they last spoke, now seemed totally refreshed. It was as if he had recaptured his youth.

Lois and her lawyers fought the divorce hard. Much of the fight had to do with money. She had medical expenses, and there were symbolic issues that had to do with her self-esteem. She resented Eric assuming financial responsibility for the boys; she did not want a reduction in her living standard; she wanted a house for herself, which Eric might provide, and she didn't want to be converted into a dependent or a poor relation. Michael, who was more understanding of Eric's leaving than Peter, dropped out of Middlebury for a while, went to London to study drama, and lived with them. Peter also visited London, but he angered his father by apparently stopping his mother several times from accepting Eric's terms.

In July 1960 Eric wrote to Lois directly demanding a final settlement. In an October phone call and letter she so upset Eric that he wrote to Dr. Kleinerman, in near panic. She was now going right from the depression stage to the manic with no normal period in between. "I find myself haunted by fears for her," he wrote. "Has the divorce business undone everything? Do you have any feeling that she cannot regain a semi-normalcy such as she seemed to have in the last months I was living with her? . . . I find myself struggling with awful forebodings; how much is simply my long-conditioned imagination I cannot be sure." In November, Helga Sandburg Golby, Carl Sandburg's daughter, pleaded with Eric, as the stronger party, to please settle this business as soon as possible. But the struggle between them would continue for two more years.

Meanwhile, whatever his personal ups and downs, during these years Eric Sevareid produced some of his most significant commentaries and documentaries for *CBS Reports.* His fourth book, *This is Eric Sevareid* (1967), a collection of his commentaries, columns, and articles between his third book, *Small Sounds in the Night* (1956) and his return to Washington as national correspondent, shows him at the height of his powers.

Although he was out of the country during the Kennedy-Nixon campaign, he did return for election coverage; and he had been sharpening his intellectual pencil on that topic for some time. *Esquire* (November 1957) carried his long, very early "predictions" on the various candidates for both parties. His first prediction was that, "in this age of television and mass semi-literacy," personality alone would be the test. After pithy judgments on about twenty candidates—Kennedy has "Nixon's IBM calculator approach"; Kefauver is a self-absorbed, abstracted loner; Stassen is "cursed with total, Teutonic incapacity to sense other people's feelings"—his main point is that, because economic changes have blurred the distinctions between the two parties, and because southern white leaders have retreated into a blind, cannibalistic "frozen desert" resistance to civil rights, the national Democratic Party was losing its meaning—its soul.

In 1959 he published *Candidates 1960,* a collection of ten essays on the records and personalities of the candidates by Phil Potter, Mary McGrory, and other Washington political writers, with his own introduction. In it he stressed his favorite theme: the kind of man we need. He points out that television deceives: it made Kefauver look like a warm human being and Stevenson look uncomfortable with people, while exactly the reverse was true. The candidate's problem is that he must appear to be the universal man with whom every voter can identify, "yet one who is a little better than they." Eisenhower appeared warm, "yet possessed not a single truly intimate friend," not one "friend of the heart," as the French would put it.

With his penchant for categories and distinctions, Sevareid concludes with his rule of thumb about the political "men and boys": the boys want political power in order to *be* something; the men to *do* something.

He paints a grim picture of America—an old woman touching her beads, counting our "blessings" of "gross national product" and "block-long automobiles." He quotes Faulkner: "What happened to the American dream? We dozed and it abandoned us." He calls for bold leadership. The American people want to be "formed to the views, the faith, the vision of a great man. . . ."

His commentaries during the campaign show that neither candidate fulfilled his hopes. "These tidy, buttoned-down men are clothed in no myth or mystique," he wrote, "and where shall our mind's eye place them as it ranges back over the majestic skyline of American history and calls up the rugged and wind-blown captains who once led us?" They are the "first completely packaged products" of the managerial revolution. Neither has "acquired a true identity." In the past we identified our nominees by what they did, not by what they wear; now these men come in "washable, wrinkleproof Brooks Brothers garb." Finally, comparing the two, he concluded that Kennedy was the "stronger man, the kind of human being who can make a fateful decision and, like Harry Truman, sleep soundly in his bed."

Unlike many in the Washington press corps who were dazzled by what Teddy White later named Camelot, Sevareid, partly because he spent much of the Kennedy years in Europe, never got close to the Kennedy clan. When Kennedy was killed, Sevareid concluded that Kennedy's "intellectuality was perhaps the hallmark of his nature as President," but he was the rare man of action as well as contemplation. His confrontation with the Soviet Union over Cuba was "one of the boldest, most dangerous and most successful acts of statesmanship" in history. Throughout the weeks after the assassination, Sevareid returned continually to the shattered state of the country's soul.

He was in some ways like the priest or minister at the funeral for the father of a large family who has been killed in an accident caused by one of his children. He cannot deny the pain, which he knows his conregation feels, but his overriding goal is to assure his listeners that the family, the country, is not irreparably damaged, fundamentally offtrack.

If the most significant achievement of Eric Sevareid's life was his ability to explain to Americans day after day who they really were, where their country was, his November and December 1963 essays mark a high point, particularly the Christmas broadcast. Holidays—like July

Fourth, Memorial Day, and Christmas—frequently inspired his most eloquent paragraphs. This Christmas he warned that America now faces the trial of demonstrating to the world that it can come through this period calmly. "There is no certainty that we will surmount this trial. Deep strains of violence in our society and in the American nature have come to the surface in recent months. . . ." The events in Dallas—including the murder of Lee Harvey Oswald and the police and media's violation of Oswald's and Oswald-killer Jack Ruby's basic civil rights—reveal the venom in American society. But :

> Our period of mourning for the death of a good but mortal spirit is ending as the period of joy for the birth of the immortal spirit of goodness itself is beginning. It is as if we had need for the happening of a month ago to make us remember what we ought to be in this country, as well as for that of 2,000 years ago to make us remember what we ought to be in this life.
>
> This is the second time in one generation that such a concatenation of events has scraped the bones of our being. The first time was the December season of 1941, when we had to try to believe that all men are brothers and that love shall conquer hatred hard upon the stunning act of organized lunacy known as Pearl Harbor. Twice this American generation has been struck from behind and twice it has tried, in the name of Christ, if not to forget and immediately forgive, at least to save itself from the poison of hatred.
>
> We are an immature people in many minor ways; there are cancer spots of venom and panic in our system. Yet, when the major tests have come upon us the world has observed that we stand steady in our shoes. It is this steadiness that leaves room for goodness. In the American hierarchy of values it is not brilliance or strength or even success that crowns the structure, but goodness. This is the true secret of America, and if so many foreign observers miss it, it is not only because goodness does not make news, but because we do not know how to talk about it except now and then in mawkish embarrassment.

If the 1960 election and the tragedies of the next few years called forth some of Sevareid's most eloquent pieces, they also mark a shift in his thinking on international issues. Both while he was in London and after he and Belen returned to live and work in New York in September

1961, he continued to travel a great deal—to the Geneva and Paris summit meetings; to Lagos in 1959 to produce a CBS Report, *Nigeria: The Freedom Explosion*; to Brazil for another Report in November 1961; and back to Britain in March 1961 for the twentieth anniversary of the blitz. One of the effects of his travels was a general stiffening of his conviction that the Cold War was a real competition to be resolved by firmness and a show of strength, not by superficial gestures like the Peace Corps or various manifestations of good will.

He was also moving into a new relationship with CBS's corporate hierarchy. In 1961 when Frank Stanton reached into CBS's law firm to replace Sig Mickelson as president of CBS News with Richard S. Salant, Sevareid and Collingwood were among the first to head for Stanton's office to protest the appointment of a lawyer with no journalism experience as their boss. Actually, Salant had long exhibited at least enthusiasm for broadcasting, if he had not actually been a professional journalist.

As editor of the *Exonian* at Phillips Exeter he campaigned for the students' right to have radios in their rooms; at Harvard he took part in an experiment demonstrating that students studied better with low background noise; and as CBS attorney he convinced Murrow to give up his scheme to break Speaker Sam Rayburn's gag order on recording the House of Representatives by sneaking in a tape recorder and then testing the gag order in court. Salant proved an unusual combination of pragmatism and integrity; he appealed to the conscience as well as to the profit motive. And he came in with a particular desire to increase and improve public affairs programming. In Salant Sevareid would have a special friend and protector.

He would need one. Just before returning to the States in early 1961, he was once again on the verge of either quitting or forcing CBS to fire him; this time over Mickelson's insistence that he give up a syndicated column he had begun with the *New York Post*. Mickelson maintained that, although they had discussed it over dinner in London with a lot of distracting noise in the restaurant, he had never given Eric permission to do the column. Eric argued that he needed the money, that another idea —editing a private "prestige" newsletter for *Esquire*—hadn't worked, and that Mickelson had flatly said yes. Eric kept the column, until Stanton negotiated it away from him in 1966. But he was facing a period of rapid change at CBS headquarters.

In 1962 there was a major reshuffling of CBS jobs and faces. Walter Cronkite replaced Douglas Edwards as anchor of the *CBS Evening News*. Collingwood replaced Cronkite on *Eyewitness to History,* an ambitious Friday half-hour program dealing with the week's top story; and, for a while, Sevareid replaced Cronkite on the fifteen-minute *Sunday News Special.* But once again, news was not the best use of his talents. John Sack, who wrote most of the scripts, remembers that the rest of the staff would throw themselves into the hectic joy of beating NBC—for example, rushing the film of a Turkish airline crash from JFK airport to the studio by motorcade in time to develop it ninety seconds before air time, while Eric would read the news, including the baseball scores, in his stoic Norwegian way.

Eric felt more at home thinking and talking in terms of global movements; and as the 1950s moved into the 1960s the area of the most rapid and upredictable change was the Third World, the former French and British colonies of Africa and Asia and the developing countries of Latin America where, to the outside observer, chances of stability looked slim indeed. While Eric had a longtime hatred of colonialism, his impatience with some blustering new African leaders was also strong. In 1960 he offered them unsolicited advice on how to move from colonialism to democracy: Don't blame the whole white race for your problems; avoid self-pity; establish stability at home before pushing pan-Africanism. Visiting Brazil and Peru in 1961, in the aftermath of the Bay of Pigs, he concluded that the invasion itself was not wrong, it was just that we bungled it. He was ready to see our policy of intervention, including training men for guerrilla warfare, as part of our tradition of promoting freedom.

He was, in short, becoming more conservative. Or, as he makes the distinction in his introduction to *This Is Eric Sevareid,* a cultural conservative and a political liberal (That distinction would have a different meaning thirty years later). Perhaps influenced by Ardrey's *African Genesis,* as he said in his Christmas essay, "Take Heaven, Take Peace, Take Joy," he began to see human beings less as fallen angels than as risen apes— though risen to a considerable height. The decay of New York City gave him an increasingly grim view of urban life, and the liberal argument that poverty rather than Communist intervention was the sole cause of ·Latin America's problems actually made him angry.

In late June 1961 he poured out this anger in one of his weekly columns, shaking his liberal followers and amazing conservatives who had never suspected he was one of their own, "The showdown with the Communist world conspiracy is on," he wrote. Khrushchev's game was to isolate the United States, then impoverish it, then break its will. He derided the idea that there is any such thing as "world opinion," which America must be careful not to offend or that "neutral" nations were somehow "more high-minded and spiritual" than committed ones. The "gamesmen in the Kremlin," he said, must laugh when they hear ideas from American liberals—especially liberal social workers who do not grasp that illiteracy, low wages, concentrated land ownership and so on are not "social problems," but integral parts of a system of life and, therefore, enormously resistant to quick change by anything less than the "totalitarian discipline" which "the same liberals abhor."

The *New York Post* printed the column, but the editor, James Wechsler, called the piece "an attack on the liberal credo in foreign policy." "Sevareid argues the case with charateristic passion. But we find it no more persuasive on his typewriter than on William Buckley's." Buckley's *National Review* reprinted it with glee (July 1); and Richard Nixon sent him a letter of praise, with the hope they could get together and chat. Eric replied that the column had nothing to do with liberalism or conservatism as philosophies, only with "the iron facts" we have to face. Whatever his reputation as a liberal—a title he was glad to apply to himself—he was by nature a facer of facts, one who insisted on thinking through every new issue on a pragmatic basis. Remember that he opposed compulsory drill at the University of Minnesota not on pacifist grounds but because it was a waste of time: it was ineffective. Within a few years Vietnam would provide the outstanding test of that principle.

The *Post* column was a step in his growing conviction that America had to win a showdown with the Soviet Union. The confrontation came, in his judgment, over the Cuban missile crisis. There is a story among his colleagues that he was so convinced nuclear war was possible in October 1962 that he called "both his wives" to urge them to get out of the target area and head for the safety of the countryside.

On March 6, 1962, after Belen had changed her name to Sevareid, although they were not yet married, and a year after he and Belen had returned to live in New York, Eric wrote to his lawyer, William Rogers, attempting to bring about a little showdown of his own. He stressed that

Lois would never be in need as long as he was able to earn money, and that he was more concerned about Lois's security than Belen's, since Belen was young and healthy. But he did not want to lose control over his own finances. At the moment, however, he was living beyond his income, "There is no more blood in my turnip." If they did not settle soon, he'd have to cut Lois's current $250-a-week allowance or reduce payments to the boys at school. Indeed, that summer he complained strongly to Peter, who had dropped out of Harvard for a year, about the cost of his summer courses.

Finally, in August 1962, Lois was granted a divorce on the grounds of desertion. Eric would pay her a monthly alimony of $1,350 unless she remarried or his income dropped below $35,000 a year.

Now he had one more showdown to pull off. On February 1, 1963 he wrote Salant a long memo. He had reached the crossroads of his career, he said, and now had to decide what to do with the rest of his working life. He had been at CBS for twenty-three years and, although syndicates, lecture agencies, magazine and book publishers made daily demands on him, CBS had not made adequate use of his talents. They had promised him his own program when he returned from England, but they had not delivered. He was now making less money than when he had left Washington. Only that week another company had offered him a bigger salary to do no more than a five-minute TV broadcast five nights a week. He wants: an annual guarantee of $75,000 a year; from $700 to $3,000 for additional programs; $5,000 for the planned *Roots of Freedom* programs on Greece and Rome; return to Washington with a special title that demonstrates his preeminence.

Otherwise, he was ready to resign.

By the end of the month, Eric had what he wanted.

As if to reinforce CBS's wisdom in meeting Sevareid's demands, that spring the *Columbia Journalism Review* published the results of a survey which ranked Eric Sevareid highest among commentators for fairness and reliability—well above David Brinkley and Howard K. Smith, who had left CBS for ABC in 1961, after going beyond the Paley guidelines with his commentary on racism in Birmingham.

Eric and Belen married on February 26, 1963, in the Manhattan apartment of Theodore H. White, his friend from the China days, now renowned as the author of *The Making of the President, 1960*. Belen wore a long white wedding dress and Eric a pin-striped suit. She was quite tall; Eric did not have to bend far to kiss her and Teddy White had to reach up to give her a hug. In a photograph of their kiss one can see a reflection in the mirror of son Peter, lowering his eyes.

They had moved into the top two floors of a four-story brownstone walkup apartment on Eighty-third Street, and Belen enrolled in Hunter College to finish her degree. In April 1964, when Eric went west to receive the Teddy Roosevelt Rough Riders award from the North Dakota Press Association in Minot, he left Belen in Minneapolis with his brother Paul and his wife Beth so Belen could begin to know her new family. By then her own career as a singer and writer of Afro-Cuban songs had made progress, and some of her songs, like her 1953 "Luna Nel Rio," were hits in Italy and the Caribbean. She also was working as a translator of Italian poetry and fiction.

But her greatest joy, she told the family and the Minneapolis press, was the baby she was expecting in September.

At first Eric did not consider Belen's pregnancy good news. Partly he was terrified about how he, at his age of fifty-two, could adapt his life to another child. He told his old Velva confidant, Helen Kramer, that he was very ambivalent. At one moment he was frightened, at the next he thought that this too might make him young again. Helen told him he should hope for a girl, because he would need someone to take care of him. Eric liked the idea and started telling his CBS colleagues he wanted a girl. They named her Cristina because Belen wanted a name that sounded the same in English and Spanish. Despite Eric's objections, Belen, who had been raised a Catholic and gone to convent school, had their daughter baptized at the Church of Saint Ignatius Loyola on Park Avenue.

Lois moved to the country, to Flint Hill, Virginia, where she set about designing and building her own house, a modernistic, six-sided, glass-enclosed structure, where she kept a horse and dogs, and got a job as a local librarian in a nearby town. Thanks to lithium, her mood swings did level off; and although she suffered from diabetes, emphysema, hypertension, and extreme obesity as a side effect of the drugs, the later years of her life were relatively stable. She and Eric remained on good terms and talked from time to time on the phone.

In mid August 1970 she was taken to the George Washington University Hospital with high blood pressure and dizziness. Eric had often seen her in that condition and so at first did not worry much because the doctors said there was no sign of a stroke. Peter, who had married while in Georgetown Law School and gone to work in Nairobi, Kenya, had just come home. Michael had married a young Irish woman and was struggling with his acting career. Eric and the twins were all with Lois for her last three days and nights before she died at fifty-nine of a massive stroke on August 17, 1970. Adele Brown was notified as soon as Lois was hospitalized, but Lois passed away just before Adele arrived at her hospital room. Her Washington friends and neighbors gathered for church services in Flint Hill; she had asked to be cremated, and her ashes were scattered in the Virginia countryside where she had achieved a certain level of happiness in her final years.

Washington gossip has lingered for years that her death was a suicide. If this were true, it would reinforce the interpretation of her life that depicts her as a victim of an ambitious man's inability to be faithful. But there is no substantial evidence to support the theory. Both Mrs. Adele Brown and Michael maintain, correctly it seems, that she was too content to want to end her life. And although suicide is consistent with depression, it would not seem consistent with Lois's spirit.

In the Introduction to the 1976 edition of *Not So Wild a Dream*, Sevareid wrote passionately, but abstractly, about what happened to her and his decision to leave.

> Strength dwindled to a kind of mindless endurance. But I was not my father, after all. I became in my own way as ill as she, still functioning but with only the exposed tip of the mind. Professional skills masqueraded as creativity. A claustrophobia possessed me. I could find no door and the walls of my life were closing in. It was then that I learned the penalty of the loss of one's childhood religious faith. I tried to revive it and could not. I could believe only in miracles because nothing else was left. The fantasy grew in me that her last chance for health lay in my own departure as well as my own last chance to feel again, to see again with the poet's eye and perhaps, one day, to write something that would be more whole than the writer.

I never did, in spite of departure, of course, and of course she never found health. She endured her own far greater tragedy for a quarter century in all and then died with merciful speed.

However sincerely he might have meant that when he wrote it thirty-seven years later, saving Lois does not seem to have been the compelling motive in 1959. He also told a relative many years later that if he had understood the degree to which Lois's illness was genetically determined, and thus in no way her responsibility, he would not have left her. When Dan Rather, Eric's hunting companion and devoted disciple, was asked in 1994 how a man of Eric Sevareid's history, reputation, and integrity could justify leaving Lois for Belen, Rather answered: "He didn't justify it. It remained an object of excruciating guilt for him for all the rest of his life."

18

VIETNAM

WHEN AMERICANS REMEMBER the "sixties," it is likely that the images that leap to mind—the student slumped arrogantly behind the desk of the university president who has been driven by demonstrators from his office; naked youths frolicking in a pond at an upstate New York rock concert; a naked, running, wailing, little Vietnamese girl whose flesh has been seared off by napalm—represent events that spill over into the 1970s—a time of growing domestic anger and tensions over the character of American public life.

Rather than beginning with the election of John F. Kennedy and ending halfway through the first Nixon administration, the sixties, insofar as they represent a profound social upheaval and a collective reconsideration of what kind of a civilization America had become, began with the first Kennedy assassination—the event that precipitated our soul-searching—and ended, depending on how one wants to measure it, in two scenes. In 1974 ex-President Nixon's helicopter lifted him for the last time from the White House lawn and two marines rolled up the red carpet on which he had trod from the mansion to the helicopter steps; perhaps better, American helicopters evacuated Americans and Vietnamese personnel from the roof of the U.S. embassy in Saigon, as the North Vietnamese army prepared to enter the city on April 30, 1975.

Viewed in this way, the sixties were those years in which America lurched through an unprecedented series of violent episodes: race riots in Watts, Rochester, Newark, Detroit, Harlem, and Washington, D.C.; student demonstrations against school authorities and national policy at Berkeley, Columbia, Harvard, Yale, San Francisco State and many other universities all over the country; the assassinations of Martin Luther King, Malcolm X, and Robert Kennedy; the shooting by National Guardsmen of student protesters at Kent State; the "police riot" clubbing of the young people demonstrating against the Vietnam War at the

1968 Democratic National Convention in Chicago; the bloody repression of the Attica prison revolt in 1971. All these were signs of unprecedented stress on the value system of American society.

In Godfrey Hodgson's interpretation, the era's crisis stemmed from the tension between two national priorities that could not be satisfied at the same time: the "liberal consensus," which had dominated political and economic thought since World War II, held that a constantly expanding economy provided the means and will to create a "Great Society," to root out poverty, disease, illiteracy, and racial hatred; the same consensus also held that internationally America had to resist communism wherever it showed a sign of expansion—in Latin America, in Africa and Laos, and increasingly in Vietnam. In a meeting with Ambassador Henry Cabot Lodge, right after the Kennedy assassination, Lyndon B. Johnson insisted, "I am not going to lose Vietnam. I am not going to be the President who saw Southeast Asia go the way China went."

It was on the rock of Vietnam that the two imperatives of American society crashed and foundered. Beginning the day after LBJ's reelection in 1964, America's internal destiny was both determined and framed by its commitment to achieving its will in Southeast Asia. To those who came to oppose this commitment, the violence that American armed forces visited upon the villages of Vietnam was only an extension of the pattern of racial and labor violence laid out in American history and inherent in the American character: the Mexican War, Wounded Knee, the Ku Klux Klan, the Pullman Strike, the Ludlow Massacre, and a whole series of ghetto explosions. It was the confrontation with violence, especially as portrayed on television—the civilian casualties, the My Lai massacre during the Tet offensive, and the Nixon-Kissinger Christmas bombing of Hanoi—which made the war's moral issues inescapable. They echoed the question asked when Kennedy was killed: What kind of a people are we?

Of course the sixties were more than race riots, assassinations, and the Vietnam War. They saw the development of a counterculture, a demographic revolution in which a critical mass, if not the majority, of the younger generation in colleges and universities rejected the authority of those institutions that had normally given society its basic structures—the government, the business community, the family, the churches, and because of their collaboration with the government's "oppressive" structures, the universities themselves.

From the dominant culture of materialism, greed, and oppression, as they saw it, young people found an escape in music—the Beatles, Bob Dylan, and the Rolling Stones. While the music too had its ugly underside of drugs and violence: the August 1969 rainy romp of the Woodstock Festival of Life was followed by the sickening 1970 Rolling Stones concert at Altamont where the Hell's Angels beat a young black man to death with a pool cue while Mick Jagger sang a few feet away and hordes of young people went wild on LSD.

At its worst, the counterculture expressed itself in what Todd Gitlin, in his history, *The Sixties* (1987), called the culture of death. On March 6, 1970, in a townhouse on Eleventh Street in New York, Diana Oughton, a Bryn Mawr graduate and a member of a radical offshoot of the SDS called the Weathermen, connected the wrong wires in the process of making pipe bombs "for a guerrilla action," and blew up the house, killing herself and two others. The home contained enough dynamite to blow up a city block.

In one sense this was the logical culmination of the amoral anarchy that inspired a fringe group of revolutionary ideologues, a symbol of an undercurrent of madness in a broad and complex movement that for the most part had been impelled not by violence but by ideals basic to the American character. Gitlin lists five areas—social equality, wide-open "life styles," the limitation of national violence, care of the earth, and democratic activity—where the social activists of these years achieved redemptive social change in America.

At the end of 1963, Eric Sevareid moved back to Washington to begin a new job providing analysis at the end of *The CBS Evening News with Walter Cronkite.* For the next fourteen years he would have about two and a half minutes a night—about 400 to 800 words—to explain America to itself during a succession of crises we have come to call "the sixties." Crises that broke the back of the national complacency at what Henry Luce of *Time* magazine once called "the American Century."

America was also being explained to its people by a media industry that itself, in response to the new demands of its material, was in a period of rapid transformation. In print journalism, a number of "alternative" or "underground" magazines and weekly newspapers—like New York's *Village Voice,* founded in 1955; and *I. F. Stone's Weekly* (1953), a one-man muckraking newsletter, and *Rolling Stone*, a rock music magazine that caught the iconoclastic political sensibility of the new generation with the drug-and-booze-sotted prose of "Gonzo journalist" Hunter Thompson—greatly increased their circulation and influence. And established magazines like *Esquire* and *Harper's* gave their pages to the "new journalism," a nonfiction prose enriched by fiction-writing techniques.

Television's immediate response, with CBS, thanks to Salant's initiative, in the lead, was to double the traditional fifteen-minute news broadcast into a half hour, thus allowing for more features and for commentary. On Labor Day 1963 Walter Cronkite—who may have lacked the cerebral depth and Murrow lineage of Collingwood and Sevareid, but who embodied the kind of trust with the public that CBS wanted to establish—opened the new series. In a videotaped interview with Cronkite from Hyannisport, during that first broadcast, President Kennedy used CBS to pass the word to Vietnam President Ngo Dinh Diem that he was dissatisfied with Diem's conduct of the war against the communist Vietcong in Vietnam. Few viewers realized they were witnessing a prelude to a coup that would leave Diem dead and, in many minds, Kennedy responsible.

But the long-range importance of that broadcast was that it both set a new level of competition among the three major networks—NBC and ABC soon followed by expanding to a half hour as well—and altered the daily routine of millions of Americans. It meant that the popular understanding of some of the most controversial episodes in American history would be mediated through television, that a much deeper significance than Cronkite ever intended would be gradually attached to Walter Cronkite's trademark sign-off every night of "That's the way it is." For an increasing number of Americans, particularly the more sober, educated viewers who were attracted by CBS's sober, Murrow tradition, the eye of the CBS logo was the eye through which they viewed and interpreted reality. In time, this was not just good journalism, it was good business. By 1967, CBS pulled ahead of NBC in the ratings.

It also meant that, in a way not foreseen, television, carrying the press's traditional agenda-setting function to a new level, affected, changed, recreated reality. Viewers, whether or not they would articulate the concept, sensed this and apparently concluded that CBS, perhaps like the *New York Times,* could be trusted to convey the news without imposing its own personality between the event and the viewer. Later, of course, following the shocks of Nixon's resignation and the American pullout from Vietnam, the trust would be turned inside out. The public would come to blame the press as if it had caused what it had reported.

Paley, while he enjoyed CBS's reputation for high-mindedness, cared most about ratings. Six months into the half-hour format, frustrated that CBS still lagged behind Huntley-Brinkley, Paley forced Stanton to fire Salant and replace him with Fred Friendly. In the ratings war the networks experimented with various combinations of anchormen and analysts on both the evening news and—in 1964, 1968, and 1972—the Democratic and Republican National Conventions. When Cronkite seemed to be fumbling as anchor of the 1964 Republican Convention, Paley intervened again and ordered him replaced for the Democratic Convention by a team of Roger Mudd and Robert Trout, who did no better. Cronkite was soon back anchoring conventions and, in an assignment he particularly seemed to relish, the space program.

In 1966, when Friendly resigned—publicly to protest CBS's refusal to give more live airtime to diplomat George Kennan's congressional testimony on Vietnam, but privately because he resented the appointment of another vice president, Jack Schneider, between himself and Stanton/Paley—Stanton, Cronkite and Sevareid joined forces to bring about Salant's return. Together, in the sixties, these men nurtured what might be called "Murrow's nephews." The deep, breathless, occasionally purple prose of Winston Burdett still emanated from Rome; Richard C. Hottelet was at the United Nations, Charles Collingwood reported from all over the globe; and Daniel Schorr was in Russia.

Marvin Kalb was Murrow's last hire, but the next generation knew Murrow more as icon than as personal mentor. Harry Reasoner, Peter Kalischer, Mike Wallace, Morley Safer, Don Webster, Jack Laurence, Charles Kuralt, Dan Rather, Roger Mudd, Bernard Kalb, Bob Schieffer, Robert Pierpoint, Fred Graham and others—reporting from Selma, Saigon, and Capitol Hill, and in their annual "Year of Crisis" roundtables—all helped fix CBS in the public consciousness. And some of them, as young Sevareid had done twenty-five years before, were making their impact, and their careers, by reporting from the battlefields.

Imagine the map of Washington as a clock with the White House more or less the center. The lush, tree-lined suburban enclave of Chevy Chase would be at about eleven o'clock. On Bradley Lane, a few blocks in from Wisconsin Avenue, directly across from the green expanse of the Chevy Chase Country Club golf course, the largest house in the neighborhood is a hulking, gray stone rectangular structure with a green tile roof, set back about forty yards from a low stone wall half protecting it from the sidewalk. There are a few big trees in front, and a curved driveway leads up to and away from the front door. It is a few blocks from where Eric, Lois, and the boys had lived briefly in the 1940s, and retains just a hint of the bucolic isolation of Valley Lane. Eric insisted that Cristina, born in September, had to grow up with trees. There was a front lawn for Eric to mow, but no brush to hack and clear.

The Sevareids settled in at the end of 1963 and began a decade in which the appearance of Eric's face three or four times a week on *CBS Evening News* would make him one of the most famous and revered public persons in the world, but which became, within a few years, the most painful and troubled period of his life.

Belen made a major project out of redecorating the house, establishing the imprint of her taste and personality. Geoffrey Cox recalls visiting Bradley Lane and observing the new decor, "very feminine decorations and lots of soft furniture . . . not at all Eric's kind of setting, with Eric's study, with a kind of log cabin atmosphere, stuck off in the corner." And Belen, a woman raised in a Cuban and Italian culture that traditionally cut off one's property from the view of the neighbors and passersby, had a high wooden fence built to enclose the backyard and screen off the outside world.

There Eric Sevareid entered into a working routine that he maintained until he retired in 1977, interrupted only to travel on assignment or for his speaking engagements, fishing trips, and vacations.

He rose at 8 A.M. and first of all did his bit with the car pool in driving Tina to school—at the beginning to West Chevy Chase Elementary School, then Holton Arms on River Road, and finally to the Madeira School, a boarding school that allowed her to come home on weekends. After breakfast he read the *New York Times* and *Washington Post,* and then drove his dark blue Volvo to CBS's new office building, a bland, redbrick construction at 2020 M Street in midtown Washington. He would arrive around 10 A.M. There, in his relatively large corner office, clustered with the executives but in view of the newsroom, with its window overlooking M Street, its gray couch along one wall and his bookshelves along the other, he sat and stared at his gray manual Royal typewriter.

A major challenge was his correspondence, which he answered, usually after lunch, not by dictation but by typing out a rough draft, rarely going beyond a few carefully chiseled sentences, on yellow or gray paper and passing it to his secretary to be retyped. Everyone, it seems, wrote to him. And just about everyone, unless the writer questioned his integrity, received a kind, gracious reply. To distant relatives and long-ago Velva neighbors he wrote, "Of course I remember you. Your house was just . . ." He wrote many tender, eloquent sympathy notes, without falling into a bland formulaic expression of an oft-repeated emotion. He occasionally told suffering friends that he would pray for them. And of course senators, Supreme Court justices, and presidents reacted constantly to his programs, usually with praise. One White House note (May 11, 1965) signed simply LBJ, said the "Sevareid touch was both visible and aromatic . . . Incisive, to-the-point, good." But when insulted, which was rare, Eric's replies to critics betrayed a fierceness that seldom surfaced in his public prose.

His one task was to decide what he would write about for that evening's commentary. Strictly speaking—and Walter Cronkite would emphasize this—it was not a commentary but an *analysis.* An editorial proposes a line of action; an analysis selects a news item from the disparate events of the day, dissects it into its parts, and puts it in a broader perspective; a commentary gives the journalist's personal opinion. Cronkite, who would often introduce Sevareid with a formula like, "Here is Eric Sevareid with some thoughts on . . ." feels that only rarely did Sevareid cross the line between analysis and commentary, although the producers and Paley probably believed he crossed it too often. Yet, much of Sevareid's attraction for the viewers was not his dispassionate analysis but, like the attraction of Walter Lippmann and James Reston, the experience of watching a good mind come to a conclusion, a clear opinion that will help move a public trying to make up its mind.

Over the years, although few people would suggest topics to him, and although he was not obliged to write about that day's events, he did talk out his pieces with several people. Bill Small, who had replaced David Schoenbrun as Washington bureau chief in 1963, provided firm leadership for eleven years, during what everyone acknowledges as the Washington bureau's golden age. Small sent Roger Mudd to Capitol Hill, Dan Rather to the White House, and Marvin Kalb to the State Department, and he brought Daniel Schorr, John Hart and Fred Graham to his team as well. Small created an atmosphere where talent could thrive and enabled a group of big egos to operate together in relative harmony. He also helped Eric talk out his ideas at lunch.

But Eric's creative process was complex, and a number of people had some influence, usually oblique, on what he said. For about six years, Sandy Socolow, *CBS Evening News* producer in New York, talked with Sevareid daily on his topics; as did Ed Fouhy, producer in the Washington bureau from 1969 to 1975. Sevareid also made phone calls and picked the brains of local experts, without allowing himself to become the mouthpiece of any particular government figure, as did his friend Scotty Reston during the Nixon years when he sometimes wrote columns easily traceable to Kissinger's voice on the other end of the phone.

Occasionally Sevareid would leave the office and move his tall, brooding figure up and down the hall, not greeting the staff members who passed him, but rather just exuding the air of a somber, lonely figure bearing the cares of the world on his shoulders. Those who knew Murrow remembered that Murrow had emanated some of the same portentousness and they concluded that Eric had probably consciously or unconsciously adopted Murrow's mannerisms.

Yet Eric retained a frivolous streak that could throw colleagues off guard. Daniel Schorr returned from Moscow in 1966 and married for the first time at fifty. One day in 1967, hearing that Dan's wife was pregnant, Eric dropped into his office, loomed over his desk and offered some ponderous advice. "You better hope it's a girl. If it's a boy, when he is ten years old and you want to take him to play baseball in the park, you'll be sixty-one. So you better hope it's a girl." If this was an example of Eric's humor, Dan missed it. Nor did it occur to him that Eric's comments probably reflected his own concern over what kind of a parent he would be for Tina.

The Schorrs had a son, and Dan did take him to play baseball in the park.

For heavier sessions, Eric dropped in on Marvin Kalb, the young Harvard doctoral candidate hired by Murrow as a specialist, and who thus, though the "kid" among the senior correspondents, had their respect. When Eric returned to Washington in 1963, Kalb had just come back from a stint as Moscow diplomatic correspondent. With him Eric had a chance to talk things through with an intellectual trained in Russian history, about which he himself had read comparatively little.

Eric would sit across from Kalb's desk wordless for several minutes, then light a cigarette, inhale, blow out the smoke and suck it in again, then say, slowly, "I've been thinking about Vietnam today, but from a different point of view. . . ." Or he would ask, diffidently, "Is it your understanding that? . . ." Kalb knew Eric was test-marketing that evening's analysis. Until after the Tet offensive in January 1968, they differed on the war—Kalb the pragmatist who thought we should look out for our interests, while Sevareid, increasingly, the moralist, the old-fashioned patriot, was upset by his country's behavior.

Eric relied heavily on his secretaries—Marion Freedman Goldin from 1963 to 1969, Suzanne Stamps from 1969 to 1974—for feedback and research. The Barnard College- and Harvard-educated Goldin, who had heard of Eric's reputation as an aloof, egocentric whiner, found him extremely gracious and solicitous and relished the job. Developing the skills that later made her a leading investigative reporter on CBS's *60 Minutes* and ABC's *20/20*, she plunged into the excitement of dealing with so many issues and personalities, from Vietnam to the colorful longshoreman-philosopher, Eric Hoffer, for whose famous interview she drew up a five-page, single-spaced briefing paper. About twice a week Eric and Marion had lunch at the Knife and Fork, a little restaurant with red leatherette banquettes near the office, to talk about work. Four years later she would carry the spirit of this apprenticeship into a whole series of *60 Minutes* investigative pieces on Watergate.

His relationship with Suzanne Stamps, partly because she was in her early twenties and perceived as a representative of the generation that occasionally got Eric riled up, was exceptional. She had been raised in New Orleans, a society both intolerant in its smug self-satisfaction and tolerant in its acceptance of different lifestyles and points of view. Now, just a year or so out of Tulane, she was at the center of the media world, which her friends at home blamed for the confusion and political division that had beset the country.

Sometimes Eric ate lunch as he worked at his desk, but the regular Sevareid lunches with his professional colleagues were a central part of his work and social life. Sometimes he would go to the Metropolitain

Club, where he also liked to swim to ease the pain of his arthritis, with "best friend" Scotty Reston. Often, with any number of the Washington correspondents, or Small, or with Bill Leonard—who was responsible for election coverage, conventions and documentaries, and to whom Eric became particularly close in the later years—he would settle in at Le Provençal or the Rive Gauche, or a place around the corner from CBS, and chat and gossip for over an hour.

Ironically, for a man whose profession is to communicate, in private conversation Sevareid was a terrible mumbler. His mother Clara had been very soft spoken, and her family would have to lean forward to hear her, which had the effect of capturing the attention of her audience quite decisively. Once at Valley Lane Eric corrected his son Michael for mumbling, and Michael responded, "Well, *you* mumble, Dad." Eric got annoyed, and Lois chimed in, "Well, you *do* mumble, dear."

He kept doing it, and it got worse as he went on—although he seems to have done it more with friends than those he didn't know well. His voice would rise and fall, and a syllable would pop out—"And if mmm-mmm the PRESident mmmmmmmm"—as the guests would lean forward, straining for familiar words or sounds, watching the movements of his lips and eyes and brow for some other signal of his mood, his thought. Depending on the mood and the company, the conversation focused on heavy analysis of international affairs or basic griping about CBS, or about his ailments or arthritis, for which he began wearing leather wrist cuffs to strengthen his arms and copper bracelets, suspecting they would not reduce his pain but determined to try something. Kalb characterized Eric's griping as "kvetching," and when his pals would call him a hypochondriac he would break into a broad smile and say, "Well, hypochondriacs can be sick too."

Sometimes he was in no hurry to get back to the office. The glum-faced commentator had retained a taste for the low life, the fascination with seedy bars in the worst ports that he had manifested in his wartime travels. Eric and Ed Fouhy one day stopped in after lunch at a dump near CBS called The Black Sheep, and within a few minutes Eric was deep into a session with a couple of the pub's denizens on his "topic." He would not ask his companions directly what they thought, but somehow, as he had often done at Valley Lane with Lois, the topic would just come up. Occasionally after lunch or in the evening he would induce his colleagues to stop by a topless bar or a "strip joint," apparently never intimidated by the fear of what being spotted there would do to his TV image. One evening Cronkite delighted him by leading him to a Fourteenth Street strip show himself; if by chance they were observed, it was more likely that Walter would have to shoulder the embarrassment.

Back at the office after lunch, he closed the door and stared at the typewriter again. Or, because he often did not sleep well at night, he would stretch his long frame out on the gray couch for a quick nap, usually between writing and delivering his product. Some coworkers, who did not think four hundred words needed a lot of agonizing, considered him lazy; and he unknowlingly reinforced this impression when he skipped work for real and imaginary illnesses.

But he was not just writing four hundred words. These had to be his four hundred best words. Words that would last. He once told novelist Kurt Vonnegut that he felt he was writing the Gettysburg Address every day. And, when he was older, Arthur Burck asked him on a visit to Palm Beach how he felt, and Eric responded with an exhausted sigh, "Arthur, do you have any idea what it is like trying to be profound for two minutes every day?"

So he smoked steadily, developing an elaborate method of inhaling in which he would take an enormous pull on the cigarette, blow out a big cloud in a burst in front of his face, then inhale the smoke again through his nose and blow it out again. Once he began to type, though, the text had been thoroughly thought out, so his manuscripts show few signs of major rewriting, other than crossing out a paragraph probably to save a few seconds; but he did mark and underline words for emphasis as he read them.

Next he had to clear the script with Bill Small. Small recalls saying no to only one script, an attack on the planned Hirshhorn Museum, which opened its doors in 1974. The mining mogul Joseph H. Hirshhorn had given his art collection to the government, and President Johnson had accepted it for a museum to be built on the Mall. Sevareid saw Hirshhorn as a shady businessman who was trying to buy immortality by naming a monument for himself on America's sacred ground. Small saw the analysis as a personal attack on an individual whom Eric didn't like. Anyway, since the audio had been recorded, the piece did go out on radio. Eric told Paley's biographer, Sally Bedell Smith, of two other suppressed commentaries—one on Clare Booth Luce, which Ernest Leiser did not think was well written; and one kidding the president of Pepsi Cola for selling it in Romania, which Friendly killed—but Eric did not consider three nos an unreasonable limitation in thirteen years.

While the Cronkite-Sevareid relationship was cordial and respectful, despite their different temperaments, they never grew close because of Eric's continued physical isolation from the day-long process of putting the program together. Cronkite worked at his managing editor's desk in New York, the same desk from which he would broadcast that night, in constant interaction with his crew. Eric worked in Washington, independent of most of the production process, taping his analysis to be fed to New York around 4:30 in the afternoon, less than two hours before airtime.

Finally, the script would be retyped in large type for the teleprompter. Then a makeup artist would apply her art to the handsome Nordic head. When he was ready, he started down the hall toward the studio. If another correspondent happened to be sitting under the lights when "God," as they joshingly referred to him, was on the way, he or she was hustled out of the chair well before Eric arrived. The stage manager simply uttered, "Sevareid's coming," as a signal that people should move. The atmosphere would change.

In spite of all his years under lights and in front of a microphone, Sevareid did not handle the nightly two-minute taping sessions smoothly. He would hold his hand up over his eyes so often to shield his eyes from the lights that he looked as if he was saluting, and he tended to complain about the way he was produced, how he looked. Eventually a producer devised a way of lowering the lights so they would soften Eric's features and help the softer image blend with his soft voice. Nevertheless, he compared the process to being nibbled to death by ducks; and there is a story, most likely an exaggeration, that he once asked what the little red light was on the TV camera.

Although Sevareid long complained that TV sacrificed words to images, it was often his image as well as his words that conveyed his authority. Viewers, who at the end of his analysis had only a sketchy idea of what he meant, were somehow convinced he had said something profound extraordinarily well and that the large screen-filling head from which the words emanated belonged to a very wise and good man.

Even when he was not as brilliant as he had been the night before, his last words seemed the perfect final punctuation to the *Evening News*, the appropriate penultimate moment to Cronkite's "That's the way it is."

The ordeal of taping completed, Eric would drag himself upstairs to his office, wash off the makeup and retreat to his office for another cigarette. Suzanne Stamps, also a smoker, would join him for a cigarette as he unwound, in relaxed bull sessions about "everything." Sometimes their conversations would take the form of a postgraduate history education which she, as an English major, had failed to pick up. Eric would tease her, "Do you think history began in 1945 when you were born?" This was a very serious man, she realized, but one who had aptly described himself in his *Look* article on Adlai Stevenson as a man with a heart of mush. A man described as no good at one-on-one relationships who taught her both modern history and how to appreciate pizza with anchovies. Who could send hundreds of dollars to an old newspaper friend who was broke, but snap at a woman hotel employee who mishandled his coat; fly over battlefields in Vietnam, but cringe in panic from a fan who approached him on the street.

Back in Chevy Chase, the Sevareids usually had dinner at home, cooked by a Chilean woman, Maria, who lived in a basement apartment with her two daughters; and after dinner Eric withdrew to his second floor study to read and work. As he had at Valley Lane, he found time on weekends to enter into the spirit of the neighborhood. On Sunday morning he liked to don his battered work clothing and go over to a local diner, Robert's on Wisconsin Avenue in Bethesda, where he enjoyed fitting in with the local plumbers and painters who hung out there as he ate breakfast and read the morning paper. In his later years on Bradley Lane, an interracial family moved in on East Avenue, adjacent to his back yard, and there were rumors of a petition against this first black family in the neighborhood. The Sevareids invited them to tea, served outdoors so neighbors might see that he supported them.

And he always made time for Tina, helping her with homework. He was no good at math, but his help on history sometimes took the form of a twenty-minute discourse, filled with stories about Lincoln, Churchill, and George Marshall—stories that Tina could repeat in class and the other students would ask, How did you know that? On Saturdays he drove her to riding lessons in Rock Creek Park. When she asked him how he got his arthritis, he replied that he got it from playing ping-pong with Gregory Peck. Tina knew he was kidding, but it thrilled her to have a Dad who knew Gregory Peck.

To those who defended both the ends and the means of the Vietnam War, American policy was modeled on the Munich analogy. The men and women of vision in the late 1930s were those who saw that Hitler's assault on Czechoslovakia was an assault on all Western civilization. In the same way, North Vietnam's "aggression" against the South, like North Korea's invasion of South Korea, was interpreted as the first step in a communist effort to conquer all Southeast Asia.

Those who opposed the war insisted that 1939 Europe offered no parallel to 1960s Vietnam, but argued instead that the men and women of vision were those who saw *early on* that American policy was both politically and morally wrong. Politically wrong in that its stated goals— a "free" and "democratic" South Vietnam allied with American aims for the region—were unattainable; and morally wrong in that our manner of conducting the war—destroying the countryside and killing and maiming thousands of innocent civilians—created an evil disproportionate to any good we might achieve and violated principles of decency and justice that should be basic to the American character.

Seeing the evil early meant knowing the war was wrong before the trauma of the 1968 Tet offensive—and the public reaction that perceived Tet as an American defeat—forced both the mainstream news media, like *Newsweek* and Walter Cronkite, and public opinion in their wake to acknowledge that the policy was failing and that it would be wiser to extricate ourselves from the Vietnam quagmire than to plunge in deeper in pursuit of "victory."

Eric Sevareid was no early prophet on Vietnam. He shared many of the assumptions of the Cold War, and he tended to support Lyndon Johnson's policies. But between his first commentaries in January 1964 and the end of the war, his writings and private statements on the war moved from detached analysis to passionate criticism.

The evolution of his thinking was helped a great deal by the presence of one of CBS's great producers of the sixties, Leslie Midgley, a veteran journalist from the New York *Herald Tribune* and *Look* magazine, who came to CBS in the late 1950s, not even owning a TV set, to work on Eric Sevareid's short-lived Sunday program. He stayed to produce special reports on the Hungarian revolt, the Suez crisis, the Kennedy assassination, the Warren Report, and the *CBS Evening News with Walter Cronkite*. An admirer of Salant, he almost quit when Friendly replaced him; but Friendly pleaded with him to stay, promising he could do "anything" he wanted.

Midgley wanted to go to Vietnam. He took Charles Collingwood with him, and came back with a classic *CBS Reports* that made clear that the war was not being won and there was no guarantee it could be, that America was headed for years of casualties and economic sacrifice. Midgley did sixteen more reports on Vietnam in 1964, and Collingwood went back in the fall with Peter Kalischer and Bernard Kalb to do another special, *Vietnam—How We Got In—Can We Get Out?*

Images of the war were beginning to accumulate in the public's mind. One of the most enduring was in Morley Safer's report of a U.S. marine setting fire to Vietnamese thatched huts with his Zippo lighter at Cam Ne on August 2, 1965. When Friendly and Leiser viewed the film in New York, they foresaw its impact, and ran it on Cronkite's show. Johnson administration officials questioned Safer's loyalty to America and demanded that he be dismissed, but CBS stood by him. Yet it would be a mistake to remember the media's role as one of opposition to the war. For the most part, until 1968, the mainstream media shared the administration's goals. Only gradually did they question first the effectiveness of the means used, and then their morality.

It took a while for Sevareid to warm up to the topic. He talked about the Beatles, whose arrival in New York he compared to an outbreak of teenage German measles (February 10, 1964); about Jack Ruby, whose Dallas trial for the murder of Lee Harvey Oswald seemed to fascinate him like the Weidman trial in 1937 Versailles; about Muhammad Ali, whom he found undereducated and humorless, but far from a bum, with the instincts of a gentleman (March 26, 1964); and the new cars, whose names—Star Fire, Malibu, Valiant, Mustang—bespoke youth, ardor, excitement, and whose expanding list of accessories suggested that the cars will become all accessories and no car, "as cigarettes tend to become all filter and no tobacco" (September 24, 1964). But in the same spirit of Collingwood's tough questioning, on April 23, 1965, Sevareid listed the credits and debits of the war: at the end of the tenth week of bombing inside North Vietnam, protests against the policy were mounting abroad and at home. "The war is not out of hand; but tomorrow's events remain unpredictable. The situation is described as one of fluid stalemate."

From the start, the CBS-Cronkite-Sevareid formula was working. Hal Humphrey wrote in the June 28, 1964, *Los Angeles Times*, "The brightest and wittiest commentary available over TV comes in those two-minute capsules written and delivered by Eric Sevareid during Walter Cronkite's week night CBS News . . . You never will hear Eric calling a close election a 'nip-and-tuck affair.' On the night of California's recent primary, Eric said in his TV comment, 'Rockefeller and Goldwater came to the finish line last night at the Los Angeles airport, both exhibiting smiles, but in their teeth, not their hearts.'" Interviewed about his success, Eric told Humphrey, "I'm not a flashy guy. I grow on you, or don't. Either way, it takes a while."

On April 27, 1965, Edward R. Murrow died of cancer at fifty-six at his New York State Quaker Hill home. He had left CBS, disillusioned by his diminished influence, to head the United States Information Service in the Kennedy administration. But years of abusing his heath and chain-smoking brought him down. He lost a lung and a tumor attacked his brain. In his last years he tried to put his life in order, inviting Bill Shirer to his home for a reconciliation; but Shirer stayed cool. Eric had seen Ed for the last time when Janet drove him hundreds of miles into western Pennsylvania to attend the wedding of Eric's son Peter. The trip was clearly a valiant effort on Ed's part.

Murrow was cremated and his ashes were scattered over his farm. Sevareid said in one of his most brilliant broadcasts:

> There are some of us here, and I am one, who owe their professional life to this man. There are many, working here and in other networks and stations, who owe to Ed Murrow their love of their work, their standards, and sense of responsibility. He was a shooting star; we will live in his afterglow a very long time . . . He was an artist, passionately alive, living each day as if it were his last, absorbing and radiating the glories and miseries of his generation; the men, the machines, the battles, the beauties. The poetry of America was in his bones. He believed in his family, his friends, his work and his country. Himself, he often doubted.

Next to his own land, he loved England the most. I will presume to use the words of England's greatest poet about another brave and brooding figure who also died too young—"Now cracks a noble heart. Good night, sweet prince."

If Sevareid's opposition to Vietnam came slowly, it was partly because he liked to support soldiers in their mission, however ambiguous the mission became. On Armed Forces Day, May 14, 1965, he delivered virtually word for word the same tribute he had offered their "elder brothers" in Korea. He did not yet sense how inappropriate the same sentiments would become. Furthermore, he followed the rules of CBS news analysis—he was not supposed to tell people what to think.

And when he let his viewers know where he stood, as he did in May 1965 when he donned his old war correspondent's togs to cover the United States' Marines' expedition to put down a rebellion in the Dominican Republic, he turned out to be an interventionist.

Johnson had dispatched twenty thousand troops on April 28, after the American ambassador had warned that American lives were in danger. But the president's decision to break into prime-time TV to blurt out a confused justification of the intervention and his later implausible exaggeration of the communist role in the fighting, exacerbated Johnson's already bad relations with the press and started digging the credibility gap that would yawn wider as he tried to justify his policies in Vietnam.

But for a few days, May 20–24, Eric was back in his old element. "I'm speaking from a balcony of the Ambassador Hotel; down below, by the swimming pool, over by the polo grounds, American soldiers are dug in with their big guns."(May 20) American forces, he said, were a third force trying to bring about a political settlement between the junta—whose leader General Embert told Johnson's emissaries that once he runs the country he'll get the lazy peasants out working at dawn and keep them in the fields till nightfall—and the rebels holed up in the central city. Eric concluded, May 24, not convinced of all the administration's rationale, but persuaded that "we did prevent a bloodbath a lot worse than the very bad one that did occur in that perpetually unhappy land."

Today, that land remains almost as unhappy as its island-sharing neighbor Haiti. The rebellion had been an attempt to restore the elected president, Juan Bosch, whom the junta had overthrown. The subsequent U.S.-arranged, CIA-managed election installed as president a crony of the assassinated dictator Rafael Trujillo, Joaquin Balaguer, who shared U.S. opposition to communism, and who remains in power today.

Meanwhile, each month Vietnam entered more and more often into Sevareid's analyses. It was becoming—like the economy, racial violence, presidential politics, the short wars in the Middle East, and the energy debate—one of those inescapable issues—soon to be joined by student protests and Watergate—that established the character of the sixties.

Of the events that moved Sevareid's voice toward strong feeling on the war, the first was the death on July 14, 1965, of Adlai Stevenson. In his broadcast that night from London, he told the story of their late night conversation and interpreted Stevenson's personal dilemma: Washington had thought in terms of American power in the world; while Stevenson, as ambassador to the only world forum mankind possesses, "had to think and to talk always in terms of the world community," of the moral authority that had to come into being if peace were to be kept. Eric himself thought in terms of American power, since no effective world authority existed. But soon his normally pragmatic emphasis would begin to shift.

In his *Look* article on Stevenson's last days (November 30, 1965), Eric repeated the story of the late-night revelations, adding details about their disagreement over the execution—if not the main thrust—of the Santo Domingo decision, and the more startling news on UN Secretary-General U Thant's two 1964 attempts, both rebuffed by the Johnson administration, to negotiate a Vietnam cease-fire. As soon as he read the article, Walter Lippmann sent Eric a note: "you have done a very great service to Adlai and his friends by making such a wholly credible record."

Lippmann, whom Eric had interviewed for a CBS Special Report in February, was one of those who, in his insistence that this was indeed a civil war, had fueled his doubts. So Eric, laid up in the hospital for a week in February for routine tests and the usual minor ailments, spent every minute reading about Vietnam. He devoured everything he could, especially history, but still he had to go there to see for himself.

For a month, from April 25 to May 25, 1966, now fifty-four, he reported from Saigon, Bangkok, and the front lines; but the lead sentence of his first report set the theme for what would follow: "This is a most inglorious war, the heroes are those soldiers, American and Vietnamese, who actually fight and actually die; and the poor, who endure." John Sack, who was on leave from CBS to write *M,* an in-depth study of one infantry company that he had followed through training, for *Esquire,* had dinner alone one night with Eric in Saigon. At that stage Sack, who had lived with his troops for months, was confident that, more than most correspondents, he knew what was going on in the troops' minds, and he was struck by the fact that Sevareid, widely viewed as a pontificator, had actually come to learn, to listen.

"What this great man was doing," Sack said, "was really wonderful. There's a rule that all journalists should have: that every journalist knows nothing. Homer Bigart used to call it 'portable ignorance.' Eric Sevareid lived this. Good journalists go in naked. You would think all reporters would do that, but they don't." Sack told Sevareid that American troops hated the Vietnamese, that they joked about putting all the Vietnamese on barges and atom-bombing them; that the lowest estimate on civilian casualties was that we killed six civilians for every Vietcong we killed; and that more than half of our troops were killed by "friendly fire."

Eric listened carefully; some of this would influence his analyses, some would not. His reports, like his wartime broadcasts from Washington and Europe, were often summary appraisals of the general situation—casualties, desertions, infiltration up and down—plus atmosphere. Bangkok: "Nightfall dilutes the crashing heat; but the fragrance of the night-blooming jasmine is overcome by the gaseous fumes of auto traffic, well on its way to throttling this city, too." And, as in Naples and Rome, Saigon's seedy side and the impact of GIs on the local economy are indices of a deeper social problem: "If the bar girls and taxi drivers rise to the top of the economic heap, only a Solomon could be sure that is worse than the absentee landlords, racketeers and corrupt generals who have always been at the top." He found that these American troops were not the "boys" he had known in World War II but mostly professionals; most of the officers and noncoms, he thought, were enjoying the war. He wrote home to his secretary, Marion Goldin, "That's why we have wars." But the South Vietnamese army reminded him of Chiang's Nationalist troops in the latter stages of World War II. The vast military structures concealed a political anarchy.

Sevareid's month in Saigon, as Dan Rather remembers it, was also a key moment in the development of the friendship of the two men—the depth of which some Rather-watchers question, but which still seems to have been genuinely close at one time.

After a few wines with dinner at the Saigon's Caravelle Hotel, the 155 mm howitzers booming in the background, Eric assumed the role of mentor and counseled the young correspondent, who had been poorly educated at Sam Houston State College, that if he wanted to become a truly great journalist he should take a year off and read all those great books he had failed to read growing up in Texas. Rather remembers the suggestion as something like the Nieman Fellowships that grant journalists a sabbatical to study at Harvard. He should read Machiavelli, Montaigne, Henry James, Thomas Jefferson, Aristotle, Plato, and Herodotus. Rather said Eric emphasized Herodotus because it shed light on the Vietnam War. Rather, of course, after discussing the idea with his wife, decided he could not spare the time away from work, but determined to read the recommended books on his own.

What follows is a little story about an older and younger man drawn to one another because of genuine admiration and because each offered something the other did not have. And who squabbled over a minor point. Unfortunately for Rather, Sevareid denied the "book list" story several times, most pointedly in Peter J. Boyer's book, *Who Killed CBS?* (1988). In his own defense, Rather maintains that when Boyer interviewed Eric he was going through a difficult period, including a squabble with CBS over money, and that it was Rather's including Herodotus on Eric's list that angered him.

Boyer and other Rather critics refer to the episode as an example of Rather's tendency to embellish reality, to create a myth about himself that would cast him in the Murrow tradition, of which Sevareid was the last exemplar. Yet, the Rather version is credible. Sevareid eventually made Rather one of his hunting and fishing companions, and a man is unlikely to fish with someone he doesn't respect. It is also believable that Eric, who had adored Murrow and who, as one woman said, "was quite willing to be adored," would take under his wing an obviously ambitious young man as the "journalist-son he never had."

It's also true that Sevareid complained about CBS salaries in the 1980s—particularly Rather's; he resented the millions of dollars paid to anchors while he himself had worked so long for comparatively so little. Finally, a reference to Herodotus would offend him because it was not Herodotus, author of *The Persian Wars*, but the other fifth-century Greek historian, Thucydides, whose work, *The Peloponnesian War*, on the wars between Athens and Sparta, was believed to shed light on Vietnam. Rather's gaffe made Eric look as if he didn't know his Greeks.

Rather's other Sevareid-in-Vietnam memory was more pertinent to his mission. When they met outside Hue, Eric gave Dan his assessment of the whole situation. "I don't like it," he said. "I don't like it partly because I don't believe anyone has thought it through."

Eric went home, thought it through, and presented his conclusions on June 21, 1966, in a half-hour special report, *Vietnam: Eric Sevareid's Personal Report*. It was an extraordinary performance, one that today's emphasis on visual appeal would not allow an analyst to attempt. He simply sat at a wooden desk, with no props other than a map on the wall, and talked for thirty minutes.

He was not an expert on Asia or war, Eric said, but he knew something about truth. "It is the reporter's business to tell appearance from reality, rhetoric from fact." He takes on the domino theory right away and concludes that this conflict is more like World War I than World War II; that our presence, already palpable in Laos, Thailand, and Cambodia, is more likely to spread the war than contain it. This was a civil war that we were transforming into an international conflict. He praised our marines who work as social workers among the refugees, but pointed out that we have created the refugees, fleeing the terror of our napalm and our high explosives. Casualties, especially among newly arrived "green" troops, were high; one green company recently lost 130 killed or wounded out of 170.

We were not losing nor about to lose the war, he said; but the process of winning, of establishing democracy in a society that was not a nation, could open a Pandora's box of new problems. It would drag us more deeply into politics we could not control. But the deepest forces moving Asia were not politics but the scientific-industrial revolution. "Asians have discovered the great secret, so long hidden from their hope: that man is not born to short life of pain and work and poverty." If this war leads not to a better life but a bigger war, he concluded, "all this will be lost, and that would break history's heart."

From then on, Sevareid's Vietnam analyses became more frequent and more morally sensitive. "It is no answer to say that the Vietcong have murdered more civilians by knife and rope than we have killed by bombing. Our human values are not Asiatic values; we have to live by our own mores, not theirs." (December 29, 1966) In one of his most acclaimed speeches, "Politics and the Press," to the Massachusetts State Legislature, January 24, 1967, he warned that the real credibility gap was not only between journalists and the truth but between our national leadership and the truth.

He warned against the Vietnam/Hitler Germany analogies. And questioned whether the United States could or should "try to renovate the economies, the institutions, the ways of life of distant and alien societies." Even Archimedes knew that he was in and of the world, that there was no place on which he could "stand" and, with levers and screws, "move" the world. As John Adams said, "Power always thinks it has a great soul." "If our country is indeed the last, best hope of man, it is imperative that somehow, some way, America prove to be the exception, in the long litany of power misused." In February, 1966, after his own first trip to Vietnam, Hedley Donovan had written, to Luce's satisfaction, "Vietnam: The War Is Worth Winning" for a special issue of *Life*. After Eric's talk, Donovan, then *Time* editor, wrote him his reaction, "I think these are some of the wisest words ever written on the subject." By early 1968, *Life* was calling for a negotiated peace.

When CBS's Don Webster reported that American troops had cut off the ears of dead enemy soldiers, Sevareid interpreted this not as evidence of this war's immorality but as a phenomenon of war itself. Strongly influenced by his understanding of France's failure in Indochina, he told the story of the French officer who had tortured prisoners to extract information that would save other lives. The officer concluded: "I know I had no choice, but I also know I am morally destroyed"(October 9, 1967). Sevareid wrote to Bill Moyers that he hates to talk about Vietnam on the air "because it is no joy to sound critical so much. But the thing obsesses me somewhat, too"(November 22, 1967).

But as Sevareid's opposition to the war evolved according to his own lights, he angered and bewildered many of the liberals who had revered him and who opposed the war but who squirmed during his repeated condemnations of the student demonstrators. Sevareid the antiwar demonstrator of 1935 might have recognized himself in the college radicals of the sixties. But he refused. He stated his objections succinctly December 5, 1966.

> Unless my history is off, the first real, nationwide student protest movement was that of the thirties, when the economy had broken down and fascism and war were rising in the world. We had our parades, demonstrations and mass meetings. But my own memory is devoid of actions that forcibly prevented the physical functioning of the university administration, faculty or facilities. . . . It takes generations to build a university's quality. It takes very little time to tear it down."

Two articles for *Look*—"Dissent or Destruction," September 5, 1967, and "The American Dream," July 9, 1968—summed up with extraordinary precision his interpretation of the sixties and his hopes, some of which now seem naive, for America's future. "Dissent or Destruction" was widely interpreted as an assault on the young. Rather, it was a courageously frank list of what he saw as the fallacies, the untruths, in the arguments (shouts, screams) of both the radical students and the Johnson administration. His starting point was that this college generation, far from being oppressed, were the most privileged generation this country has ever known. Confronted with those who depict the downtrodden as victims of a cigar-smoking "power Elite," he quotes Sheridan Whiteside, the curmudgeonly character in *The Man Who Came to Dinner*, who said, in one of the play's great laugh lines, "I may vomit."

Swinging in the rhetorical cannons of repetition and parallelism, Eric organizes the article with a list of "It is outrageous and unsupportable for . . ." to desecrate the flag, to terrorize cities as blacks did in Newark and Detroit, to become indignant about civilian casualties without condemning Vietcong murders, to chant, "Hey, hey, LBJ, how many kids did you kill today?"

But, on the other side, it is also unreasonable to: charge protesters with "letting the boys down," when actually they are trying to save the boys' lives; to draft protesters as punishment for protesting.

He resents the youth cult, which was not generated by the young but by older people concerned with youth, psychologists, and advertising writers who knew young people had money, "by publishers of girlie magazines who realized the old moral barriers were giving way." He quotes Eric Hoffer, Jacques Maritain and Edmund Burke to lend authority to his thesis that the real leaders of the next generation were not the Stokely Carmichaels, but those with *gravitas*, those committed for the long haul.

His "American Dream" essay, packaged with a gorgeous layout of pastoral sunsets of cornfields, sums up the dream as well as any historian: "It was rebirth, the eternal, haunting craving of men to be born again, the yearning for the second chance. The New World was the second chance." "Vietnam was not typical; it was a mistake, now recognized as such by most serious thinkers in this country."

Perhaps he displays his hopes more than his wisdom when he says:

> By the year 2000, we will look back upon these present years not only as one of America's periodic convulsions but as a rather backward period. By then, the typical American family will have an income of around $20,000 a year or more; the typical American adult will have at least two years of college, with far broader intellectual and aesthetic horizons. By then, the old urban centers will have been rebuilt, and many millions will live in satellite "new cities," part-urban, part-rural. The incurable diseases like cancer and arthritis will be under far better control.

Alas, his salary prediction was rendered moot by the inflation of the 1970s, the "new cities" concept was inspired by city planners like Lewis Mumford and Jane Jacobs whose ideas did not win out, the old urban centers are emptier than ever, aesthetic horizons have been debased by television. Arthritis kept Eric in pain until cancer killed him.

Reaction to both articles was strong. Letters to *Look* on "Dissent" reminded Sevareid that Johnson was responsible for the deaths of children every day, that he himself had revealed in the Stevenson article that Johnson shunned negotiations, and that young protesters read not Marx but Sartre and were thus unmoved by the so-called intrinsic values that Eric evoked. In personal letters, Ann Landers, the advice columnist, wrote "I have fallen in love with you all over again," and left the red imprint of her lips upon the page. (September 22, 1967); her sister, Abigail Van Buren, who writes "Dear Abby," chimed in, "Just keep educating the people, Sweetheart. We need you" (September 24, 1967). But Chaplain

W. Morrison, a history professor at Youngstown University in Ohio, wrote to criticize Sevareid's censure of Martin Luther King for exaggerating civilian casualties (King estimated one million), and his failure to contradict the Johnson administration on several points, accusing him of repeating the administration's propaganda. He concluded, in words that must have seemed right to him when he typed them, "Ed Murrow would be appalled if he could see what has become of his finest protégé"(September 2, 1967).

Eric burned up his keyboard: "I do not normally reply to insulting letters especially when they are based on ignorance; but since you carry the formal credentials of a person dedicated to the distinctions between truth and appearance, I think you should have this reply.... Your outrageous letter happens to arrive just after I have been privately hammered by both the secretary of state and the president in an effort to make me change my negative views about the Vietnam War.... If your normal methods of research and reasoning are of the level suggested by your letter to me then the greatest service you can do for American education is to cease teaching immediately."

When an old colleague from the *Minnesota Daily*, Jane Loevinger (now Mrs. S. I. Weissman) complained to Salant about Sevareid's apparent sympathy for Humphrey over Gene McCarthy, Eric denounced her for going over his head. She accepted the rebuke, but came back with hard words: "The complaint against the deterioration in the quality of your reporting and commentary is not a private quirk of mine. I have heard it from many sides. An astute young political science professor regards your recent article in *Look* magazine [American Dream] as a particularly bad example. You are putting makeup on the face of the American tragedy."

Yet, whatever his philosophical and emotional distance from the young, Sevareid the reporter responded quickly to the abuse of the state's power. At the Democratic National Convention in Chicago in August 1968, an event that was for many American liberals the moment when they first began to look upon the American power structure as fascist, Sevareid and Roger Mudd, along with millions of Americans fixed to their TVs, watched, on Wednesday evening, August 28, the Chicago police, taking their cue from Mayor Richard Daley, beat and tear-gas hundreds of student demonstrators outside the Conrad Hilton Hotel.

From his anchor booth suspended over the convention hall, Walter Cronkite turned to Sevareid and Mudd for their reflections. Sevareid had long complained that he didn't like to give spontaneous analyses, but:

> Sevareid: Well, Walter, just about everything that needs saying has been said except one thing, that this is the most disgraceful night in the history of American political conventions, and I don't mean what happened in this hall but what happened in downtown Chicago. . . .
>
> Mudd: . . . I suppose the only explanation, and I can't read a policeman's mind, is that when so many men are prepared for a confrontation and are drilled to be ready for everything, that when the time comes, even approaching a confrontation, they regard it as their moment to go into action.
>
> Sevareid: Well, I have personally never seen such cold ferocity by policemen on young men and women. Whatever they've done, they haven't done much more than demonstrate. Why it is necessary, in order to put a boy or a girl into a paddy wagon, to beat them over the heads and kidneys and whatnot is beyond me. I've never been so shaken by anything in a long time. I saw some of this very close at hand yesterday.

A year later, in October 1969, he gave three commentaries on the great antiwar moratorium staged at campuses all over the country, and interpreted the protests as consistent with those against the Filipino War at the turn of the century and the Korean War at its later stage, wars waged not by the will of the people but by the government's decision. Sevareid continued to censure student violence for the next several years, as long as the papers reported a speaker shouted down here, a window broken there. Yet when public reaction to the United States invasion of Laos (February 10, 1971) was mild, he paid tribute to the students who had carried the main burden of opposition to the war.

> But vast yearning can start the hard workers on the road to changes. The student movement of recent years has produced no new overall ideology for America to live by—ideologies flourish poorly in American soil—but to some degree this movement has

changed the public climate, helped resurrect values and dreams about the good life, some so old they seem very new, and thrown up some potential leaders of thought and action.

Depressed students who think they have accomplished nothing are pretty surely wrong. They have played a part in turning around the war policy, in opening up the racial walls, in the new preoccupation by the powers that be with consumer rights and the salvaging of our physical sources of life.

The difficulty is that student accomplishments are not subject to anything like precise measurement, which is also true of the lifework of millions of adults. But if American life in the '70s becomes increasingly humane and rational, many students of the '60s will have their place in the remembered role of honor.

The assassinations of Martin Luther King and Robert Kennedy both evoked those tributes that the commentator exists to deliver and engaged the question of America's heart. Was there something in the American nature that doomed these men or were chance or broader or deeper causes responsible? Sevareid's coverage of King had been both admiring and critical. Just as he could consider the Negro revolution, when it began, the closest thing to a true people's revolt we have had in America, but still castigate ghetto rioters who were really no more than hoodlums, he could both praise and admonish King or any Negro leader depending on the issue before him.

When King won the Nobel Peace Prize, Sevareid called him not just a Negro thinking about the future of Negroes but, perhaps even more, an American thinking about the future of his country (December 10, 1964). When King's march on Montgomery in March 1965 took on a discordant note of triumph, Eric warned that this did not fit in with Lincoln's principle, "with malice toward none" (March 25, 1965). When King attempted to transfer the nonviolent principles he had emphasized in the civil rights movement into moral opposition to the Vietnam War, Sevareid's put-down was blunt. Again, he slapped his opponent with the yardstick of history: "that great men, almost without exception, have one and only one great mission to accomplish in life. And that when they attempt a second career, in a second momentous direction, they fail and damage their original meaning and authority" (September 5, 1965).

It had the tone of: How dare a religious leader, untrained in politics, open his mouth on this one! Yet Sevareid did not share what many consider King's insight: that violence abroad and injustice at home were intimately connected. To Sevareid, the civil rights movement was a revolution that had lost its way; school desegregation had stalled, and Negro leadership had passed into the hands of black racists. (Later, when Ralph Abernathy said there was a white conspiracy to destroy blacks, Eric said Abernathy's neurosis reminded him of the Silver Shirts (January 7, 1970). Vietnam was not a product of American culture but an aberration, a failure in logic. Something that just hadn't been thought through. Thus, the martyred King is not a victim of American society but its fullest expression.

> Almost surely he was the most important American of his time, white or black. He, more than any other man, wielded the cutting edge of history for this time and place.

> He preached love, so hate, of course, destroyed him, as it destroyed 2,000 years ago the man whose gospel he followed, as it destroyed 20 years ago in India the man whose strategies he adopted. Saints are usually killed by their own people; Dr. King was not.

> He was not an American Negro, he was a Negro American. As Dr. Abernathy once said of King, he seeks to save the nation and its soul, not just the Negro. King grasped the white man by his shoulder, forced him to turn around and look long and hard upon his fellow black American. To some the sight was frightening; to many others the landscape of our lives looked richer and full of much greater promise.

> There are those who proclaimed that white society killed Dr. King. Democracy cannot function under such a theory. To blame everyone is to blame no one. Only the Hitlers of this world, and their spiritual kin, like young Mr. Carmichael, believe in mass guilt and in genocide as justice.

> There are those who proclaim that this is a sick society. It is a society containing many sick individuals, white and black, including the moral invalid who fired the shot last night.

> It is doubtful if this nation has ever before gone into officially proclaimed mourning, its flags everywhere at half staff, over the

death of a private citizen—and this man was the descendant of slaves. This is not the reaction of a sick society, but of a fundamentally healthy society trying desperately to cleanse itself of the one, chronic, persistent poison in its body.

So the label of his life must not be a long day's journey into night; it must be a long night's journey into day. (April 5, 1968).

Then, when the smoke of burning buildings broke the Washington skyline and blacks rioted for three days, Sevareid did draw a connection between the war abroad and the one at home. The war must end. The racial issue was "the central and supreme task for this American generation," and "there is not time, organized will and attention or resources enough to conduct the two crusades simultaneously and effectively" (April 8, 1968).

Two months later, as Senator Robert F. Kennedy, shot in the head right after winning the California Democratic primary, lingered and then died, Sevareid, in two commentaries the same day (June 5), still resisted calling America sick. Yes, there was a long tradition of public violence in the American story. Yes, our literature and films make heroes of burglars and brutes. Modern philosophy fosters contempt for authority and encourages in the young a concept of freedom without restraints. Yes, the Kennedys are a star-crossed family. But is ours a star-crossed nation? Perhaps we can learn from these tragedies. "These events may well herald the ultimate end of the age of permissiveness, of organized leniency, of the equation of freedom with personal and political license." He thought the renewed interest in gun control would have results.

The case of Lieutenant William Calley, who in March 1968, during the Tet offensive, murdered women and children at My Lai, returned Sevareid to his standard response, that war brutalizes some young men and enobles others. But this crime edged him into some exceptionally blunt rhetoric on the moral impact of all wars:

> Vietnam is not new to our moral experience, just the worst such episode . . . It was World War II which institutionalized and rationalized mass murder of the innocent. The aerial bomb returned warfare to the frightfulness of antiquity—whole cities put to the flame and the sword. And coarsened the conscience of man.
>
> Whole villages, scores of them, have been put to the flame in Vietnam, Laos, Cambodia. By the touch of the bomb-release

button; by a jerk on the cord of the artillery piece. From a sanitizing distance.

Calley was the end product of the process. He did it point blank, looking his victims in their pleading eyes.

But the Calley case is just the beginning of another process, the searching out of the full truth of what we have done to Asians, and to ourselves. (March 29, 1971)

But how was the stepped-up coverage of Vietnam succeeding where it counted, in the hinterlands, with the viewers and station owners outside the New York–Washington corridor, who ultimately decide whether the network succeeds? Paley, a Republican, regularly complained that Cronkite and Sevareid were moving beyond what their viewers could accept; but he seldom interfered.

In 1970, to face this issue imaginatively, Salant, Manning, and Leonard decided to move the Cronkite show to Los Angeles and broadcast the *Evening News* from the annual convention for the affiliates of all the networks at the Century Plaza Hotel. For months the station owners, who were mostly conservatives, had been complaining that CBS News was run by a bunch of left-wingers who were "persecuting" Nixon.

The day of their broadcast, Friday, May 8, was four days after the National Guard had killed four students at Ohio's Kent State University and the U.S. "incursion" into Cambodia, which had brought on nationwide student protests, was still in progress. Les Midgley, who was running the show, had to use satellite film that he had not seen of soldiers on their way to battle who had little notion of why the battle was necessary. Also, Eric had been criticizing this invasion since it was launched the week before.

After the show, in a question and answer session, the station owners lambasted the TV reports as proof of the liberalism they had complained about, and Leonard and Midgley had reason to wonder whether the show had been a good idea.

Then something interesting happened. That night, when Eric, who had spent much of the day on a guided tour-bus ride of the movie stars' homes, arrived for the final banquet, Dinah Shore came rushing up to him and made a big fuss. After cocktails, as dinner progressed, each of the network stars on the dais was introduced, with much fanfare, for a round of applause. The longest and loudest applause was first for Cronkite, and then for Eric Sevareid. The same men called ultra-liberals at the afternoon's session were the heroes of the evening. One of the differences was that station owners had brought their families to the dinner. Whatever the politics of the affiliates, with their families present they acknowledged Walter and Eric for the professionals—and the stars— they were.

19

NIXON

PRESIDENT NIXON got some depressing news on the morning of February 21, 1971, as his blue-and-white *Air Force One,* renamed *The Spirit of '76,* broke through the smog from a million coal-burning chimneys and hovered over Peking ready to land in the country that he himself, for most of his political career, had helped to distort and demonize in the American public mind. This was the country that Democrats had "lost." Was he here to win it back? The puzzling news was something he could do nothing about: there were no crowds waiting to cheer as he got off the plane.

His hosts had decided to set the tone of this visit to fit their design, rather than the domestic agenda of a president anxious to project himself as a world statesman. The *Evening News* would have no pictures of China's millions cheering wildly as Nixon rode triumphant through their midst.

But it was an extraordinary week: a secret meeting with Chairman Mao in his old, yellow-roofed residence surrounded by chrysanthemums in the southwest corner of the Forbidden City; a jubilant banquet in the Great Hall of the People; a parade of athletes and a thrilling table-tennis exhibition—symbolic of the Chinese-American ping-pong diplomacy—in the Capital Stadium; a twenty-minute, cold and sunny excursion to the Great Wall; and fifteen hours of very secret formal discussions—all to be explained by National Security Adviser Henry Kissinger only after they were over.

For one of the four hundred Americans in Nixon's entourage, this was a return to the scene of one of the most formative experiences in his life. Fifteen years ago he had lived in fear that what he had written in 1944 about the corruption of this country's leadership would be unearthed and used to discredit him. Today the Nixon people were not comfortable with his presence; but his prestige was too great for them to confront him directly.

But, as the press landed in Shanghai the day before the Nixon party came into Peking, the city made the country look new to this reporter, and made him feel old. He was only fifty-nine, but was acting older. The events of the totally orchestrated week clicked along with Haldemanian efficiency, and Eric, who had become fussier with age, required enough baby-sitting to keep him on schedule. News director Gordon Manning wanted a commentary almost immediately, and Eric had to stand out in the snow, struggling with a teleprompter, requiring so many retakes that the viewer could detect the lighter and heavier snowfalls within the two-minute televised report.

As in 1943, Eric had his old friend Teddy White on hand, returning to the land where both had made their reputations. As he did in 1943, he warmed up for his reports by sitting long in front of his typewriter, knocking out his hour-by-hour observations.

> What is "maoist man"? French revolution was to produce new kind of human being . . . also was to be "soviet man" . . . basic nature of man changeable only in evolutionary sense, but his behavior toward others can be conditioned, at least for a time . . . Chinese are not Russians, not same tragic view of life, not dour, but bouncy, cheerful despite their endless tragedies . . . deep sense of cultural superiority . . . why could they take nationalism and industrialization from the west but not Christianity and democracy . . . partly because the first two help people feel powerful, second do not . . . they must reduce the birth rate or they cannot succeed . . . the great plain of Peking could be Dakota . . . fertile, flat . . . last night and this morning Peking had kind of ghostly air . . . the silent bicycles . . . the fog, partly smog, coal burning city . . . more variety of dress than expected . . . leaders are liquidated frequently: just disappear . . . Nixon—born into circumstances less affluent than either chou or mao . . . Most revolutions led by middle class intellectuals . . .

Since the Nixon–Chou En Lai conversations were secret, there was no hard news, and the correspondents had to hustle for feature stories. Sevareid visited Peking University and was appalled to find not a real university but a kind of inferior junior college where nobody flunked and students learned from each other. He could not resist: "the extreme extension of what so many young Americans want in their colleges." He compares this to his own university days: "We were taught to believe that life is a search for truth that never ends. They claim they have arrived. Soviet Russia is a freer place for the life of the mind" (February 23). Another day he admired the silent bicycles and warned that once they put motors on the bikes China would slide into pollution, noise, and a greasy garage at every corner. Later, back at the White House, when the Nixon cabinet sat back and evaluated the China trip, Nixon couldn't help adding that "the most naive comment" of the week "was Eric Sevareid's that there was more freedom in Moscow. I have been there and there is no more freedom in Moscow than in Peking" (Safire, 415).

As Robert J. Donovan and Ray Sherer spell out in *Unsilent Revolution: Television News and American Public Life, 1948–1991* (1992), the antagonism between Nixon and the press ran deep. Much of it went back to his career as senator and vice president and his failed race for governor in California. And much of it was due to his manner, his coarseness, his suspiciousness and personal insecurity, his tendency to lump all reporters together as a bad lot, and inevitably his continued sponsorship of a Vietnam policy that many journalists were convinced was bankrupt.

But Nixon won the 1968 election against Humphrey largely through his controlled use of the media, by isolating himself from tough questions and orchestrating televised sessions with "average citizens." From the beginning of his administration he and his staff viewed their relationship with the press as a battle, categorized individual correspondents as friends or enemies, and looked for ways to punish those who offended them.

Meanwhile, starting with his November 13, 1969, Des Moines speech against the media, written by Pat Buchanan, Vice President Spiro T. Agnew delivered a series of attacks on the press designed to both discredit the leading anchormen and commentators as "elitist" and to intimidate the media, by threatening to use of the power of the Federal Communications Commission, into granting more favorable coverage.

Nevertheless, many leading correspondents admired Nixon's abilities, and even those who did not trust him managed to cover him as fairly as possible. Just before the 1968 election, anticipating Nixon's victory, Eric wrote to Ardrey, "I can't bear the thought of four years working here with Nixon in charge," But his CBS analyses of Nixon from the 1960 campaign through his pre-Watergate years are largely devoid of the "bias" the Nixon White House attributed to the press. Indeed, on January 18, 1969, Nixon wrote to Sevareid thanking him and CBS for their campaign coverage. "In an election as close as this one, I, personally, am convinced that one of the major factors which could have tipped the scales in my favor was the balanced coverage I received from the electronics [sic] media."

On October 2, 1969, Haldeman sent speech writer William Safire a memo noting that on September 30 Eric Sevareid had said that few seemed aware of Nixon's political philosophy, his vision of America. The President wanted his PR staff to work on his philosophy.

Twice—July 1, 1970, and January 4, 1971—Nixon sat for hour-long conversations with the leading correspondents—ABC's Howard K. Smith, NBC's John Chancellor, PBS's Nancy Dickinson (in 1971), and Sevareid; and viewers who expected to see the stars "take on" Nixon were disappointed. In 1970 CBS-WTOP's Washington media critic Edwin Diamond said the commentators had become old Washington hands, abstracted from hard questions. "Sevareid appeared as if he was listening to some after-dinner talk. But he did ask the toughest question about sending U.S. troops back into Cambodia. The failure was in follow through." In 1971 the questioning was no tougher, although Eric did get Nixon to admit he should not have rebroadcast one of his more partisan speeches the night before the 1970 elections. But Sevareid did not think it was up to reporters to ask questions which were "hard" or "soft"—only substantive.

The euphoria—or the Nixon media triumph—of the China trip did not last long. By late 1972, following the two exceptionally long and detailed reports on Watergate on Cronkite's *Evening News*, CBS was once again seen as an enemy camp. One by one the events of 1973 forced Nixon back into the public consciousness not as the "New" Nixon he seemed to have created from his own ashes, but as the "Tricky Dick" his critics had always portrayed.

Ironically, one Nixon-Agnew victory in their ongoing battle with the networks was won with Eric Sevareid's assistance. For years the White House had been carping about "instant analysis," those sessions after a presidential address, when the correspondents would immediately take it apart, measure it for consistency and hidden meanings. In fact, most analysis was not "instant" at all, since the reporters had had a day to study advance copies of a speech. But the analysis—for example when Marvin Kalb contradicted Nixon's interpretation of a Ho Chi Minh letter on negotiations in 1969—inevitably weakened the impact the president tried to achieve. But Eric always wanted leisure to ruminate over a text. In May 1973, Eric sent Paley a private memo arguing against the practice, on the grounds that it was bad journalism to interpret Nixon's ambiguities under pressure. Paley agreed. The Washington correspondents objected strongly, and the two Kalbs, Mudd, and George Herman—though not Dan Rather—sent Paley a letter of protest. Five months later, when Averell Harriman told Paley he no longer watched CBS because it had gotten dull, instant analysis was restored, but it never regained the vigor it had displayed before Sevareid complained.

The seven indicted Watergate agents of the Committee for the Reelection of the President came to trial. The Senate opened televised hearings that the networks carried for 37 days. The Nixon recordings of all conversations in the Oval Office were discovered and, after a court fight, released, in part, to the Senate. Nixon accepted the resignations of his key aids, H. R. (Bob) Haldeman and John Ehrlichman, and tried to explain himself in a TV address. He toured the South seeking support, addressing an Orlando, Florida, meeting of the Managing Editors of the Associated press, by saying, "People have a right to know whether or not their president is a crook. Well, I am not a crook."

On April 29, 1974, on TV, Nixon released parts of the transcripts of the Oval Office tapes to the public. Reading them, establishment columnist Joseph Alsop, usually an administration supporter, said their language might have emanated from the "back room of a second-rate advertising agency in a suburb of hell." In June Nixon traveled abroad again, to the Middle East and Moscow. For the last week of July, 90 million Americans watched the hearings of the House Judiciary Committee leading to its July 30 vote for three-count impeachment. On August 5, one of the Oval Office tapes that Nixon had attempted to withhold, finally surrendered to Judge John J. Sirica, revealed that Nixon had ordered a cover-up of the Watergate break-in, an act of obstruction of justice, on June 27, 1972, only six days after the crime.

In an argument with Teddy White, who tended to sympathize with the politicians he wrote about, including Nixon, Eric began pounding on the table. "You're a damn fool . . . You just don't understand the evil in the man. He is evil! Evil! Evil!" A rare explosion from a man who was often angry but usually almost excessively sensitive to moral ambiguity.

Once, trying to delve into the mysterious Nixon psyche, Eric speculated that the roots of Nixon's mania might lie in his impoverished early childhood, in his relationship with his mother. "I know the kind of woman who would never show warmth—only expectations," Eric said. Was he saying that in Nixon he recognized something of his own experience, his own dark side, offering a clue to his own driven rise from small-town poverty to Washington power? Whatever his speculations on the state of Nixon's soul, Sevareid held them back till the end. At this stage of his career, indeed approaching its twilight, Eric Sevareid was very conscious of both his power and his responsibility. He knew that 20 million Americans watched him every night, many of them waiting for him to tell them what to think. His job was not to get Nixon out of office but to help his listeners understand, if Nixon had to go, why.

In mid April, as the public awaited further grand-jury indictments of White-House-connected individuals, Sevareid said, "Whatever the names, we are reaching the climax of one of the most destructive political scandals in recent times." As the moral authority of the executive branch eroded it was becoming increasingly paralyzed. "There is really no way out, except the truth" (April 13, 1973).

When Nixon accepted the resignations of Haldeman, Ehrlichman, and Attorney General Richard Kleindienst and installed Elliot Richardson as his third attorney general—the first two driven out in disgrace —Sevareid wondered whether Richardson had the inner strength to pursue the investigation (April 30, 1973). Yet an anecdote Sevareid used in a May 10 broadcast best portrays his feelings about the change in the moral tone of domestic policies. In the early fifties, he said, Senator Bob Taft accidentally left some confidential Republican election strategy papers on a chair in Harry Truman's cabinet meeting room. When the president's counsel, Charles Murphy, discovered the papers and realized what they were, he neither read them nor mentioned it to Truman, but immediately sealed them and sent them back to Taft. Last year, during the 1972 campaign, Sevareid concluded, the opposition's mail was not only read: it was stolen and it was fabricated. When Agnew accepted a plea bargain for taking bribes in his White House office, Sevareid used simple rhetoric on his old nemesis to witty effect.

> So Mr. Agnew, apostle of law and order, who used to preach against permissive judges, was treated permissively in the name of the general good.
>
> Mr. Agnew preached the old fashioned virtues and practices old fashioned vices.

When Nixon, in what has become known as the "Saturday Night Massacre," through Alexander Haig, ordered Richardson to fire special prosecutor Archibald Cox, Richardson refused to do so and then himself resigned. And his successor, William Ruckelshaus, resigned as well. Sevareid weighed in on Monday night, October 22, with one of his most powerful denunciations.

> A century ago Clemenceau, the great World War I French leader, was a journalist covering the impeachment effort against President Andrew Johnson. He wrote that the congress progressively shackled the president, filed a claw, drew a tooth ... but then, he wrote, Samson summons all his strength and bursts his bonds with a mighty effort.
>
> That is what Mr. Nixon tried to do this weekend. The last mighty effort of the original Sampson, of course, brought the whole temple down upon himself and everyone else.

On January 24, 1974, when Nixon aide Egil Krogh went to jail for six months, Sevareid reflected on these second-level young men, educated in the law but, sucked into the insecurity at the top, broke the law in service of their chief. They had learned the Bill of Rights but missed its spirit; they had read the Constitution backwards and used it to rationalize a police state. When Nixon made available the "private Nixon," the transcripts of many—but not all—of the Oval Office tapes, Sevareid moved more deeply into personal moral condemnation.

These pages constitute a moral indictment without known precedent in the story of American government. There is no talk in these endless conversations about the welfare of the American people, their faith in their leaders, the nation's reputation in the world, no awareness of what Jefferson was talking about when he invoked a "decent respect for the opinions of mankind." There are minimal references to truth; but innumerable conjectures about the most saleable publicity techniques for defending themselves.

These are men whose minds are irrevocably fixed in the "We or They" view of life and politics; men holding the supreme power in the land, talking like besieged conspirators, men unforgetting, unforgiving, constantly calculating how they can "get" their opponents and critics.

They are not interested in destroying their opponent's arguments: but in destroying their opponents, personally. Mr. Nixon himself talks of using the FBI and other agencies to do this. From these pages rises the rancid odor of hatred. (May 1, 1974)

That night Paley suddenly called up Eric at home. Eric's immediate thought was that maybe he was once again on the brink of losing his job. But, no, Paley didn't want to chew him out; he had watched Eric's commentary and just wanted to talk. For years Paley, as a Republican, had had some commitment to Nixon, and now he was gradually realizing he had been wrong.

Finally, on August 8, he began his commentary: "These are with no serious doubt the last hours of the thirty-seventh presidency of the United States. . . . Resignation, with dignity, is the only safe and civilized way remaining to transfer the power." And as Richard Nixon's presidency came to an end, Eric Sevareid completed what some CBS colleagues consider his finest hour, even at a time when many thought his powers were beginning to wane.

20

BELEN

JUST AS McCARTHYISM engulfed him when the collapse of his first marriage made him most vulnerable, Vietnam and Watergate made their demands during a decade when the failure of his second marriage was sucking him into confusion and sadness.

Eric wrote to Shirley Clurman, wife of *Time* writer Richard Clurman, February 1, 1967, "We are great these days. Belen is making all the society columns, here and in Boston, just because she opened her ruby lips at a couple of parties and sang some songs. She is really fabulous and has now decided she wants to go back to professional singing. So various arrangements will be in the works if we can arrange them." But there is the familiar ring of the independent, ambitious wife and the husband who needs a woman to care for him.

Perhaps the first sign was the fence. Belen had been raised in a culture where good families screened out both strangers and their neighbors. Eric had been raised in Velva where even today few fences mark the line between one family's turf and its neighbor's.

Belen was young and liked to have fun. She liked parties, singing, and dancing. But she did not drive, and was thus, in a sense, a semiprisoner on Bradley Lane. For the most part, Eric shunned the usual Washington social whirl of cocktail parties and embassy receptions, and for a while they entertained visitors like Justice William O. Douglas and Eric and Adlai's mutual friend Marietta Tree though, according to Belen, the Restons kept their distance out of respect for Lois, whom Belen had replaced. Belen, meanwhile, a musician and an entertainer, was apolitical, knew nothing about the congressmen and diplomats whose names studded conversations with Eric's distinguished guests. Eric, it seemed, didn't know how to have fun. He was witty and could be funny, and could suddenly discard his Norwegian frozen face and spontaneously decorate their apartment, as he did once at Christmas in Italy, or walk on his hands, as he did at a Manhattan party with Teddy White, and he could write witty analyses about advertising or technology. And he could relax at his cabin or trout fishing. But he didn't really know how to have fun.

Belen did. Yet in the world of CBS executives and producers she did not always come across well. One referred to her bluntly as a "pain in the ass." Another mentioned how at a cocktail party she would laugh at your funny story and then rest her head on your shoulder as if she was flirting. She began to drink heavily and hang out with a younger crowd. One day she appeared at Eric's office, apparently under the influence, with a young man in tow. She often complained that Eric did not give her enough money, even for carfare to get her from one part of New York or Washington to the other. It did not take long for the pattern to make itself known, and inevitably a moment arrived when Eric realized he had made a terrible mistake. More than once he even called up Lois and weeping, poured out his troubles to the wife he had left. And he told friends he worried about Tina's safety when Belen was drinking and not responsible for what she might do.

At the same time, it was clear to some of Eric's colleagues and to members of his own family that a good bit of the responsibility for the failure of his second marriage, like the first, was Eric's. He brought Belen into a city where she had no roots and no support. In 1959 he could defy convention by sweeping her away to Malaga, London, and Paris; in the sixties he could continue their travels during vacation time—they bought a condominium in Acapulco—but his day-to-day life was to retire to his study and read up on Vietnam, Cambodia, the energy crisis, the Middle East, and Nixon. It was small wonder that Belen grew restless in the role of caged wife.

And though he could talk to twenty million fellow Americans every night, he could not talk to Belen. She tried to get him to talk out their problems, but he clammed up. Though they did not formally divorce until 1973, she spent longer and longer periods away, with her mother in New York, in Italy, in Argentina, where she tried to rebuild her singing career. When she finally moved out of the house on Bradley Lane, returning to Italy, she left Tina with Eric, because she was convinced her daughter had a brighter future as the daughter of Eric Sevareid than with her.

Today, still an elegant and beautiful woman, Belen lives on New York's East Side, works as a court clerk, and describes herself as a recovering alcoholic. After many years she is just beginning to once again pick up her guitar.

There were other tensions in his career. In 1967 Larry Erickson, chairman of the North Dakota Democratic and Non-Partisan League Party, decided that the senior senator from North Dakota was, at the age of seventy, vulnerable and he asked Eric Sevareid to run for the Senate against him in 1968. This was not a passing flight of fancy but a real invitation, and Eric took the proposal seriously enough to discuss it with North Dakota's Democratic governor, William L. Guy, who cautioned that a Sevareid candidacy could be challenged in the courts on residency qualifications. But this flirtation with a different kind of political power was another of Sevareid's half-attempts to break away from CBS.

In October 19 59 Eric's mother died in a Minneapolis nursing home. In 1970 he worried about his sons and their futures. Both he and Lois were helping to support Michael and his wife Jackie, as Michael, who had been with the Guthrie Theater in Minneapolis and moved to Hollywood, struggled to get a firm footing in his acting career. And Peter, in Kenya, teaching administrative law in Nairobi and helping Kenya establish its own legal system, was looking for a job teaching adminstrative law somewhere back home, worried that, since he had not been Law Review and Georgetown was not then a leading school, it would be tough to get what he wanted. He was even willing to teach history in a prep school.

Then Lois died, reviving all the guilt and doubts Eric had felt about leaving her.

In the spring of 1971 Eric wrote another plaintive Dear Dick letter to Salant asking for the whole summer off. His doctor had told him he was showing increasing signs of nervous exhaustion and should take this break lest something worse happen by fall or winter. Salant was torn between his affection for Eric and the needs of CBS. By putting Eric on almost every night he had established that CBS was not afraid of ideas and that Sevareid's unillustrated thoughts were clearly worth more than pictures. To go three months without Sevareid analyses would imply that his analyses could be done without. Eric replied with a long whine about his arthritis, his loss of sleep, how hard he works, how little help he has compared with "the phalanx of helpers and protectors that Murrow used to have," the smallness of his office and the greatness of his piles of letters to be answered. He concluded: "Since you know that I love you, consider this a family spat"(May 18, 1971).

Between May and August 1972 he commiserated with Robert Ardrey, who was living in Rome, and fighting charges that his anthropological ideas were "reactionary." Ardrey saw the two of them as men of great reputation with declining energies, driven by a Protestant need to do good to others, particualarly the young. Maybe they should become college professors. Referring possibly to Eric's divorce, Ardrey wrote: "I bleed for you in your present situation, one so irrational and so far beyond your own control. You've got a precious asset that you didn't used to have, the affection and loyalty of your sons."

His other asset, Eric was quick to tell people, was his delightful little daughter.

In May 1973, on a plane flight from Washington to New York, Eric fell ill and checked into Booth Memorial Hospital in Flushing, Queens, complaining of abdominal pains. What he feared to be a heart attack turned out to be gastric upset. Three weeks later he had his gall bladder removed.

He didn't like giving up his weekly syndicated column in 1966. He had decided at the age of six that he wanted to be a print journalist and never really changed his mind. From London he had tried to set up a regular relationship with *Esquire*. Before moving to Washington with the *CBS Evening News* slot, he had once again considered leaving television, this time to be the editor of the *Saturday Evening Post*. In the sixties *Look* published some of his best material. Ironically, the more he published the more it became clear that he should write another book, a sequel to *Not So Wild a Dream*, but he had neither the time nor the emotional energy to approach it. Besides, he feared that the poetry had gone out of him.

Maybe in retirement.

Some of his public controversies lapped over into private quarrels. A January 5, 1967, commentary, one of several on Dallas's handling of the Jack Ruby trial described the city as "at the adolescent, awkward age. It grew up too quickly. It is a metropolis in body, but not yet in spirit." The Dallas station KVIL snapped back that Sevareid had "whipped the people on TV until they bled. Then Eric Sevareid whipped Dallas for bleeding." Sevareid's remarks had also offended Cronkite who, in a rare intervention, harrumphed, cleared his throat, and tacked on a note of editorial disagreement after Eric's sign-off. "And we might add, Eric, that's true of a lot of towns."

Eric was furious. "It puts me in a demeaned and humiliating position. Actually last night's exercise, in view of the substance of what I said, also hurt you, at least in my own opinion," he wrote in a private memo to Walter the next day. "I have never claimed that everything and anything I write must always be used, as is. But to use it and then knock it down on the air, and particularly without any notice given to me that this is going to be done—this is insupportable." Cronkite flew to Washington and made amends. He did not do that again, and their relationship remained one of mutual respect—though there is good evidence that tension bubbled beneath the surface of their comradeship, particularly during the national conventions.

After the 1976 conventions, Eric's last before retirement, he wrote a sad letter to Teddy White, who it seems had lost his job as a CBS convention analyst because Eric brought Bill Moyers on as a partner. Eric apologized mournfully, lamented what he imagined was their lost friendship, and fell into some heavy moaning: "given the actual outcome of the convention coverage by CBS, I now wonder if there is anything left there to be loyal to. Moyers and I were destroyed by Cronkite and the Cronkite system. It was particularly humiliating for Moyers since this was to be his inaugural flight with CBS. For me, it was a repetition of '68 when Cronkite got his revenge for his failure in '64, a time when the entire bulk of the press praise went to me. You escaped a totally miserable experience last week." Teddy responded graciously, "I'm not mad. Honest, I'm not. You and I are both too old and too poor to afford to lose a friend—especially a friendship that's lasted for thirty years. Friends are all that's left after the money and the energy has been spent" (July 26, 1976).

There were other tiffs. In January 1974 Bill Small moved to New York as vice president, with the hope of replacing Salant some day as president of CBS News. Sevareid, in one of his occasional behind-the-scenes interventions in CBS internal politics, had recommended Small to Paley; and later, when Eric, after watching Small in action in New York, withdrew his sponsorship, Small stormed into Eric's office feeling angry and betrayed.

Eric and Daniel Schorr had not been close friends, but there had at least been mutual respect between them. When Schorr came to Washington from Europe in 1953, Eric and Lois had entertained him at Valley Lane; and while Schorr was Moscow correspondent they would meet annually for the year-end roundups, usually followed by a highly convivial dinner with Paley and all the correspondents. At one of these gatherings, in the early 1960s, when Eric was moving into his more "conservative" phase, and Paley's wine had helped raise the heat of their political arguments, Dan said, "Eric, you really are a fascist." Eric blew up. No matter how mad he got, he never raised his voice; but his brow knit, he bit his lip, and his eyes narrowed. He poured out a furious "How dare you . . ." reply, filled with rage, but still in perfect sentences.

They worked well enough together in the Washington bureau after Dan returned from Moscow in 1966; but uneasiness developed when Dan, assigned to Watergate as an investgative reporter, became progressively more irritated by Eric's remarks denigrating investigative reporters as a group. Dan in those years was very aggressive, and his face appeared on screen more often than any other CBS correspondent's—except Sevareid.

The tension between them exploded when Schorr, in an answer to a student's question after a talk at Duke University, January 17, 1975, voiced his suspicion that the CBS hierarachy, and CBS president Arthur Taylor in particular, had passsed the word to its correspondents and commentators to go easy on Nixon after the broadcast of his resignation speech—not to be "vindictive." Schorr makes a case based on circumstantial evidence to support his idea: Taylor had come to Washington that day and gone to discuss coverage of the impeachment hearings at the White House, and found that Nixon was about to resign. Taylor feared Nixon might attack the media, and denounce CBS in particular in his resignation speech and, Schorr surmises, got the newsmen to go soft in exchange for peace with the soon to be former president. Schorr believes this was the reason Salant canceled a Nixon political obituary that Schorr and Fred Graham had prepared. Taylor denies any such deal, and Sandy Socolow, who was present, calls Schorr's story, "out-of-sight bullshit." If there was any restraint, he says, it was self-imposed.

Except for Roger Mudd's, the commentary was soft. Dan Rather called this Nixon's "finest hour . . . a touch of class, a touch of majesty." Eric called Nixon's speech "as effective and magnanimous a speech" as Nixon had ever given and used the resignation to comment on the coming 1976 bicentennial of the Declaration of Independence. We could not have entered into the true spirit of our forefathers if we had continued as a nation to go on this way.

After Schorr's charges were published in early 1975, Sevareid denounced him and demanded an apology in a public letter to *New York* magazine. Once again, Eric took Schorr's remarks as an assault on his personal integrity. Schorr issued a clarification, not an apology. On April 2, Eric sent him a memo again demanding a public apology and retraction, and reminded Schorr that he had previously impugned the integrity of the people he worked with. "My friendship is not easily given or easily withdrawn. But the price of trying to be your friend has proved to be too high." They never spoke again.

Eric also took public lumps from a few unexpected quarters. In 1971 Philip Roth published a short satirical novel, *Our Gang: Starring Tricky and His Friends*, a very funny fantasy on the Nixon administration, in which President Trick E. Dixon is assassinated and a media character with a familiar name broadcasts the funeral.

> Good evening. This is Erect Severehead with a cogent news analysis from the nation's capital . . . A hushed hush pervades the corridors of power. Great men whisper whispers while a stunned capital waits. Even the cherry blossoms along the Potomac seem to sense the magnitude. And magnitude there is. Yet magnitude there has been before, and the nation has survived. A mood of cautious optimism surged forward just at dusk. Then set the age-old sun behind these edifices of reason, and gloom once more descended. Yet gloom there has been, and in the end the nation has survived . . .

And Sevareid survived the parody. Though when a style reaches the stage where parody comes easily, it's a sign the style is beginning to rust. Av Westin's book *Newswatch: How TV Decides the News* (1982) claims that in Eric's last years at CBS, "When Sevareid was on the money, it was recognized that he had no equal." A prime example was his Monday night commentary on the Saturday Night Massacre, for which everyone at CBS waited impatiently all weekend. "But those who were keeping score felt that the quality of Sevareid's commentaries was deteriorating from one good one in three to one in twelve."

Reading through them all today, one is struck by the recurrence of stock phrases, aphorisms—like the American religion is education, or John Adams' "power always thinks it has a great soul"—which the writer might or might not realize he used some months before. On the other hand, all writers who write frequently are bound to repeat themselves. How many intelligent people have more than a basic stockpile of really good ideas which can be recycled for changing circumstances? Yet, Eric's later pieces, though shorter, are often less dense, less compact, less pointed than the best radio essays he did before television days. And, except for a convoluted piece on the college craze of "streaking," and another on Henry Kissinger's second marriage (an odd topic)—the seriousness of the sixties' life and death and morality issues drained off much of his humor.

Two very admiring but frank articles—William Holland's "The Brooding Optimist," in the *Washington Star Sunday Magazine* (June 15, 1969) and Phil Hilts' "Eric Sevareid Suffers Elegantly," in the *Washington Post's Potomac Magazine* (December 14, 1975)—finally gave some sustained acknowledgment to his enormous influence and his melancholy complexity.

A portrait far crueler in spirit was Barney Collier's interview in *Hope and Fear in Washington: (The Early Seventies) The Story of the Washington Press Corps* (1975), a collection of irreverent encounters with people like Bill Small, Rather, Mudd, and Eric, whom he mocks. When they meet in Eric's office—after Collier was kept waiting while Eric napped—they share a macabre conversation about suicide. "He looked at me tragically, and said slowly, in a voice of doom, 'Two of my best friends . . . have died of shotgun blasts.'" The "best friends" turn out to be *Washington Post* publisher Phil Graham and Ernest Hemingway. Graham was a manic depressive, and his suicide coincided with Lois's illness and the breakup of their marriage.

Why Eric would bring Graham's death into the 1975 interview is not clear. And if Hemingway was one of Eric's "best friends," it is news to Hemingway's many biographers who never mention Sevareid. "They were two men I respected most of my life," he said. By now Belen has moved to Italy and Eric refers only obliquely to her "problem." Collier provides a vignette of life at Bradley Lane. Tina flirts with daddy, climbs all over him, and hugs and kisses him. At night, too scared to sleep alone, she sleeps in Eric's room "until her fears of what Eric calls 'her mother leaving' have gone away." Eric tries to make clear to Collier in a vague mumbled sentence that whatever he writes must be respectful of Tina.

But the tone of the Collier chapter was a sign to a new generation of readers and viewers that the private life of a public person—including this most private of persons—is no longer as private as it used to be. He had become one of the best known and most admired men in America and it is not too strong a term to say that he had helped nurse his beloved country through the third crisis—after the Depression and World War II—of his lifetime. Now the commentator who was being referred to only half jokingly as "God" was taking on an unaccustomed air of vulnerability.

21

PEACE

THE WEATHER was terrible that day—as if the gods knew that an era was ending and wanted to sympathize with humanity for its loss—at least that portion of humanity that regularly watched the last minutes of *CBS Evening News*.

So in Washington, on Thursday, November 10, 1977, the heavens wept and it rained heavily throughout the day. But for a moment the rain eased while the big limousine drove up to the Sevareid house on Bradley Lane, picked up Eric and Tina, now thirteen, and drove them both back to Washington, to Lafayette Square, across from the White House, to the Stephen Decatur House. There in a big plastic tent set up in the bricked courtyard, several hundred people had gathered to celebrate Eric Sevareid's retirement.

Retirement at sixty-five was the CBS rule—a rule applicable to everyone except the man who made it, William Paley, who was hanging on for as long as possible. Eric thought it was a bad rule, but he told interviewers that he was ready to go. He had lost much of his fire; as always, he looked and seemed older than he was. Though he was tired, he had nevertheless made lots of plans for keeping busy—*Between the Wars*, a documentary series on the great events of Sevareid's youth, and especially what he hoped would be a series of programs on *Not So Wild a Dream*. He would write articles and spend more time hunting and fishing and traveling with his daughter. He would take her to Norway to give her a sense of where she had come from. Though he remained, as always, very anxious about money, CBS was retaining him with the vague title of consultant, with an office and a secretary, and a good stipend. Nevertheless he worried too about how long that would continue.

The CBS executives and *Evening News* staff flew down from New York, their plane buffeted by the storm over the capital. Bill Small, though irked by their recent quarrel, was on board. Of course Walter

Cronkite was there, with Dan Rather, Roger Mudd, Bruce Morton, and Fred Graham; and Howard K. Smith came over from ABC and David Brinkley from NBC.

From the original Velva Sevareid family, the survivors—his sister Jeanne Schmidt, now a widow who was living in Virginia, and younger brother John. With both parents and older brother Paul now gone, John and Tharsella, his second wife, were Eric's main family support. They had taken in Tina during the divorce to shelter her from what Eric feared might be the "ugly" details of the hearing; and when Eric visited them in Radford, Virginia, they bought him privacy by throwing a neighborhood cocktail party—which he hated but went along with—on the first night of his stay, with the understanding that the neighbors would leave him alone for the rest of the visit.

But here was a lavish cocktail party Eric could not hate. William O. Douglas was there, in a wheelchair, with his young wife Cathy. Eric had interviewed the unconventional Douglas a few years before for a series of "conversations" with eminent citizens; and, in a rare personal aside, Eric had mentioned public criticism of Douglas's many marriages and the age gap with the latest spouse. But then he added, for Douglas, that this was none of the public's business.

Chief Justice Warren Burger was there too, and Eric's fellow Minnesotan Vice President Walter Mondale. The other Minnesotan, Hubert Humphrey, had called from his hospital bed declaring that he would make it even if he had to drag the doctors with him. But the doctors prevailed.

As the rainwater flowed harmlessly under the tent flaps, Salant presented Eric with a new fishing rod, and Paley, declaring Eric "a legend in his own time," handed him an old 1890s Blickensderfer typewriter. Eric quipped that his critics complained that he wrote as if he lived in the 1890s.

In a mellow mood, Eric joked about his perpetual scowl when he looked into the camera. It was a "family thing," he said, inherited from "generations of ancestors peering through the mists of Norway." Then he turned to Tina. Thirteen years ago, he said, he had named her Cristina Belen, only to realize afterward that he had given her the initials, CBS. So, he had started his career with one CBS and was ending it with another. And he couldn't think of a nicer way to do it.

Two weeks later, on November 18, 19, 20, he concluded his career officially with three farewell commentaries, the last of which was taped the previous Sunday to avoid the emotionalism of the last day, and widely reprinted in papers across the country, with excerpts carried that same evening on ABC and NBC.

Anyone who had read him or listened to him over the years quickly realized that here was a marvelous distillation of everything he had been trying to say. The first traced the influence of television on political and cultural life: the mass media have increased our awareness of violence and our indignation about it; but pictures tend to overwhelm words, and "no one can take a picture of an idea." The second traced his relationship with his generation, and called for a heightened sense of individual responsibility and self-denial.

> People need three things: security, identity and stimulation. Most now have security, and we see the drive for identity as people pull apart into groups and cults and causes; for stimulation as they flee in a thousand ways from boredom. This is now accompanied by the convenient conviction that something called society is responsible for one's ills, and that society's handy personification—government—can remove them. It can and must try for those truly victimized. But most of us are victims of ourselves. Democracy is not a free ride. It demands more of each of us than any other arrangement. There can be no rights and privileges without responsibilities. My forebears here were at ease with the word "duty." They knew that self-denial was not just a puritanical test of character, but a social necessity, so that others, too, might have elbow room in which to live.

The third repeated his romantic view of CBS's early days, and combined his gratitude to his colleagues and listeners with his own journalistic creed. It deserves to be pasted on the inside front cover of every journalism student's notebook.

> We were like a young band of brothers in those early radio days with Murrow. If my affections are not easily given, neither are they easily withdrawn. I have remained through it all with CBS News, and if it is regarded as old-fashioned to feel loyalty to an organization, so be it.

Mine has been here an unelected, unlicensed, uncodified office and function. The rules are self-imposed. These were a few: Not to underestimate the intelligence of the audience and not to overestimate its information. To elucidate, when one can, more than to advocate. To remember always that the public is only people, and people are only persons, no two alike. To retain the courage of one's doubts as well as one's convictions, in this world of dangerously passionate certainties....

In the end, of course, it is not one's employers or colleagues that sustain one quite so much as the listening public when it be so minded. I have found that it applies only one consistent test: not agreement with one on substance, but the perception of honesty and fair intent. There is in the American people a tough, undiminished instinct for what is fair. Rightly or wrongly, I have the feeling I have passed that test. I shall wear this like a medal. Millions have listened, intently and indifferently, in agreement and in powerful disagreement. Tens of thousands have written their thoughts to me. I will feel, always, that I stand in their midst. This was Eric Sevareid in Washington. Thank you and good-bye.

The careful listener could not miss the almost jarring note in Sevareid's use of the word "was." He had been something permanent and present in their lives. Yet it was a brave statement that he knew this phase of his life was really finished.

In his last years Sevareid had become passionately outspoken in his loyalty to CBS. Between 1975 and his death he beat the same drums —critics would say, he played the same violins—in interviews (e.g., *Broadcasting* magazine, September 12, 1977, and September 14, 1987) and lectures, which had become his main medium. On one level, he was press-bashing—needling TV critics, who had always irked him, for superficial criticism. On another, he was sticking up for the institution that had made him. In a talk at the Washington Journalism Center, June 3, 1976, he lashed out at critics of television and professional television critics. He even claimed that television stimulated conversation, increased the habit of reading, and improved the general level of diction.

He complained that critics deplore the low level of TV material but ignored the high-level series of conversations with George Kennan, John McCloy and others he had presented the previous season. He was angry at the myths irresponsible book writers had spread about CBS: that Friendly, Shirer, and Murrow had been fired or driven out; that the corporation was de-emphasizing news and public affairs; that Paley cared about nothing but money.

The main danger to the press was not monopoly, he said, but fragmentation, a new tower of Babel as national magazines and networks died and small magazines and TV channels proliferated. Communications, he said, was the principal cement that held society together. Without it, anarchy. Although he supported the big-network system as a source of national unity, he had long argued, he said often, for greater diversity in broadcast opinions. He opposed the FCC Fairness Doctrine, which required stations to give time to opposing points of view because as he saw it, it was a government restriction on free expression; but, for twenty years he had advocated the full-hour news program with a variety of commentators, which would allow the public to talk back—so he would not have to be *the* commentator every night.

Anyway, he wanted to get all this out before he left. And he would have many occasions to repeat these ideas as long as anyone would listen.

Perhaps in 1976 the full impact of watching TV all day on children and students was less evident than it is today. Anyone who cares about precision in the language could write a book on how TV announcers do violence to language and pass along their unique bloodied syntax—like "impact" as a verb, the grammatically indistinguishable "who" and "whom," and "media" as a singular noun—to the viewing population. Indeed, Edwin Newman, who once wrote for Sevareid, did, in *Strictly Speaking*. Anyone who has taught high school or college for the past twenty years knows that the superficial junk of TV sitcoms, MTV, and late-night talk shows has preempted any leisure time that students might otherwise give to reading.

Perhaps Sevareid could not foresee how all-absorbing the medium would become. More likely, except for Tina, he lacked the prolonged exposure to young people that might teach him how their minds worked. Sometimes he would learn something by listening to students on campus visits; at other times he would inexplicably clam up during a class discussion or, as in a 1973 visit to Georgetown, refuse to answer questions. When he imagined that TV stimulated conversation, he could not have imagined animated college students chattering about *Leave It To Beaver* or a soap opera they'd watched in the afternoon when they could have been in the library, or even jogging.

In response to the retirement announcement, about four hundred letters poured into Sevareid's office—many from people like Alf Landon, Matthew Ridgeway, Harold Stassen, and the same people who had filled the tent at Decatur House. But the majority came from the ordinary listeners in whose midst he had stood. Mr. and Mrs. William and Agnes Muehlhause of Baltimore wrote: "Your deep insight that Americans—and all others—need to be maladjusted to the war system, to the inequities of a crippling economic order, to the wrongs of race prejudice, and to the vulgarities of popular morals, has helped us to give ourselves to a cause which we cannot always expect to see finished" (November 29, 1977). Some regret his apparent growing conservatism; many mention the influence of *Not So Wild a Dream*; but consistent themes are gratitude for his emphasis on justice, for his ability to rebuke where necessary, but still to inspire hope.

One of the over four hundred Americans to write to him on retirement was a Franciscan Brother, Michael Genencser, O.F., from Oldenburg, Indiana (July 22, 1977). He explained that his religious community, like millions of Americans, relaxed every night by listening to *CBS Evening News*. He said: "Your 'voice of America,' can be used as an effective instrument of justice and equality for all. May it be a beacon for all those to follow amidst the cloud of prejudice and hatred. As the psalmist states, 'My song is about kindness and justice.'" He thanks Eric Sevareid for what he has given to America, and ends with an Old Testament blessing: "May the Lord look kindly on you and give you peace."

He gave a series of "farewell" interviews—to Walter Cronkite for CBS Radio, to the *Washington Post* and *Washington Star*, and *Broadcasting* magazine, and a special one-hour "conversation" on December 13, produced by Perry Wolff, with Charles Kuralt, an early admirer of *Not So Wild a Dream*, for CBS-TV. Much of what he said was familiar to those who already knew his story; yet there were new emphases that pop from a man who feels a new freedom to say things about his life and ideas that he could only imply in dispassionate analyses for the evening news.

The idea of journalistic objectivity, he said, was a myth, a disastrous notion. A good goal—but not an attainable one. On some complex issues, there are a dozen "sides," on some—like Hitler and McCarthy—only one. Ideologues, including many columnists, were like a "stuck whistle." The good columnists, like Lippmann and his "old and dear friend Scotty Reston," were not predictable. What is happening to the homely virtue of self-reliance? People like the Santa Barbara California citizens who are repeatedly wiped out by fires should not look to the federal government to save them from catastrophes. "In my father's time, it wouldn't have occurred to people." This applies to the black revolution. "You can't go on and on and on just blaming society. Poor me."

Yes, he was a protester in his youth. "I hope had I been a college kid in the sixties I would of had enough guts to have protested the Vietnam War." But he would not have broken the law.

> I look at society differently now. The young tend to look at it as architecture, a structure. Well, let's tear it down and build a new one. I don't. To me it's a—it's living vegetation. It's like a vast coral reef, built up over centuries. There are billions of little passages and safety chambers all developed out of some need or desire. Now you can rechannel and you can enlarge this. You can renovate and repair but you cannot tear that thing down without death everywhere. You can't do it.

Yes, the McCarthy era took its toll on him. He had his phone number taken out of the book because he got threatening calls at night. Nixon, comparatively, was less a threat. "His trouble never lay in the press. It lay in the facts." He had given Nixon the benefit of the doubt and hoped he would do well. But Nixon was a strange man. He would phone Eric with "stroking calls." Lyndon Johnson also called to flatter and chew him out; one time Johnson gave him a twenty-minute lecture on the budget at a party.

Murrow had a little Hemingway in him—took a big drink of whiskey before entering the studio—fighting himself. Then he would work himself into exhaustion. And yes, Murrow was late taking on McCarthy, after people like Elmer Davis and Raymond Swing and Martin Agron-sky had already shown real courage.

Anything he would change? Maybe his private life. But publicly, he was glad he'd stayed with CBS. "We started, just a few of us, and there was a high romance about it. There was a certain rapture about it that I never quite got over. . . ."

The fellow-pundit reactions to his retirement were, for the most part, rhapsodic. James Reston, in his *New York Times* column (November 27), said that Sevareid had brought this era the three essentials of a great re-porter: a good pair of legs, a sense of history and, though he looked excessively gloomy on the tube, a sense of humor. He quoted Eric's trib-ute at a dinner honoring Elmer Davis and applied it to Eric himself; and, furthermore, he had "the novelist's gift of catching the echoes or inward mutterings of the age, and maybe he will now take time to prove it." Eric's favorite tribute, the one he put aside in a packet for his grandchil-dren, was an affectionate piece that Charles Collingwood published in a short-lived New York tabloid, the *Trib* (January 9, 1968). In the "band of brothers" days, Collingwood said, there were no personal rivalries, "grasping for airtime at the expense of others, or competition for higher salaries—all of which have come to characterize a later generation of broadcasters." To those who thought Eric a dull stick, he replied: "I can assure you he is a very human person. He has, for instance, as sharp an eye for a well-turned ankle as he does for a well-turned phrase." A southern columnist, Jerry E. Brown of the Vinton, Virginia, *Messenger* (December 7, 1977) thanked him for being the "moral referee" on inte-gration, the "kindly man in a salt-and-pepper tweed coat who kept the righteous indignation of the country in check while necessary events took their course."

One of the most perceptive was Tom Shales in the *Washington Post* (November 30, 1977). The "venerable prune face," he said, presented a "one-man coalition of enlightened common sense . . . the Great Opin-ion—an ultimate, melting-pot statement of opinion produced from remnants of all available viewpoints." Eric's departure was a "tacit victory for the forces of fractionalism and specialization in broadcasting and American life generally."

The cartoonists could not overlook his farewell. A *New Yorker* couple (December 17, 1977) sit in the glow of their TV tube: says the female spouse, "Eric Sevareid has retired, but I like to think that somewhere out there, on his own time, he's still commenting on the crucial issues of the day." And in "Doonesbury," a parody of Philip Roth's parody, as Eric delivers his "swan song"—"Men come and go. And so, if we are to heed the historians, do reputations. In this respect, these are times like all others—in the slag that is corporate policy, reverence for sagacity clearly has its limits. Never mind that one man's retirement age is another's intellectual apogee!"—till Walter yanks him off.

One writer glad to see him go was Gloria Emerson, who had covered the Vietnam War for the *New York Times*. In a tough piece in *New York* magazine (December 5, 1977), "Why I Won't Miss Eric Sevareid," she criticized him for, in recent years, sounding like a head of state, a slightly soured professor, for sending forth "a river of mush." His most memorable trait, she said, was "the manner in which he could blunt and make boring the most unforgettable moments of our lives." For example, in 1975, when Iranian dissidents in the United States demonstrated against the visit of the shah of Iran, Sevareid said nothing about the history of our poisonous bond with Iran," but settled for a metaphor comparing monarchies and democracies to a sailing ship and a raft. But she admired *Not So Wild a Dream*, especially the passage when he described the party in Delhi where the "fat and powerful men gathered to congratulate one another upon their fat and their power."

Two criticisms stick. First, his vision locked in an America symbolized by Velva, he cannot find room in his heart for the rebellious generation. Second, "He was a brilliant war correspondent; his energy and courage never failed. Perhaps a reporter who has done his best work in a war never leaves the war—in Mr. Sevareid's case, he seemed pinned forever in the forties."

Geoffrey Cox, who was one of Eric's best friends during that period and stayed close to him till his death, lends indirect support to that theory. Eric was at the height of his powers, Cox says, during World War II; and, in a sense, paradoxical as it might seem, that was the happiest time of his life. Then all his faculties were challenged to their fullest, even though they were challenged amid the stench of corpses and the folly of military commanders—as they were when Cox met him between the Italian and southern France campaigns. Yet, James Reston feels that Eric was at his best in Washington, "in the early days before his wife died";

and Robert Craig, who met Eric in the 1950s when his relationship with Lois was falling apart, feels Eric was happiest, most at peace, in retirement, when he had settled down, could do more fishing, more seminars with businessmen—and had a new wife.

Meanwhile, the question in media circles was, now that Sevareid was gone, who would take his place? In the *Wall Street Journal,* Vermont Royster pointed out that CBS had given him "as many farewell appearances as Sarah Bernhardt," and that a visitor from Mars might wonder what the fuss was all about. But the fuss was because he had used his position of influence so carefully, he knew the uniqueness of his role and felt its responsibility. The media (CBS) should not replace him, said Royster, but find a way to offer a broader diversity of opinion.

In May 1977 the *New York Times* reported that Salant had offered the job to Bill Moyers. But Moyers was upset because CBS was cutting back on its commitment to documentaries—he had been promised he could do twelve *CBS Reports* and had got only nine or ten a year; and now they wanted him to break the hour-long format into a "mixed" format of short pieces, more like *60 Minutes.* The real impact of the documentary, he felt, came from its hour-long length. He was being asked to throw himself into the ratings war. Something he wasn't ready to do. Moyers did do some *Evening News* commentaries, as did Rod MacLeish, who happened to look and sound a bit like Eric—with his own carefully crafted prose, but short on Eric's metaphorical twists and turns. According to one rumor, CBS also tried to lure anchorman John Chancellor as a commentator from NBC; but there was little in Chancellor's record, distinguished as it was, that would make his prose or insight a match for Sevareid's.

With Sevareid's retirement, commentary died, for seven reasons. First, largely because *60 Minutes* had proven that news could also be financially profitable as well as the foundation of the network's prestige, management now evaluated the content and ratings of news programs in terms of the "bottom line," so commentary would have to be somehow profitable.

Second, thanks to new technology, like satellite disks, which could bring in correspondents live from all over the world, competition for air time among ambitious young reporters was fiercer than ever. Producers were less willing to give two minutes to ideas.

Third, commentary had come into vogue during the New Deal, when the complexities of the new big government demanded "expert" columnists to interpret what was happening. Columnists like Lippmann, Reston, and Joseph Alsop gained clout because of their close contact with decision makers. Now cabinet secretaries and presidents explain their policies directly on MTV and talk shows.

Fourth, in journalism in general, with the explosion of information and thus more need for context and interpretation, the line between reporting and interpretation was growing fuzzy again. If the magazine writer or reporter on the scene could interpret the event, there was less need for a generalist analyst to sort out the meaning at the end of the program.

Fifth, Public Television and the Cable News Network developed new TV formats—like the *MacNeil-Lehrer News Hour, Washington Week in Review, The McLaughlin Group, The Capitol Hill Gang,* and *Crossfire.* Some of these featured experienced correspondents or columnists or academic experts sitting around a table, like the old CBS year-end specials. There the similarity ends. In the December 15, 1965, *Where We Stand in Vietnam,* Sevareid, Collingwood, Kalischer, Reasoner, Mudd, Safer, and British journalist James Cameron were all journalists, not professors, made experts by their experience. Today, "pundits" are often former political operatives who either chat seriously or yell at one another; and this is called "analysis."

Sometimes it is mainly an attempt at "balance," weighing the five sides of every question to the point where any point is lost. Often it is a highly stylized clash of personalities, a shouting match as an entertainment form. Meanwhile, talk and call-in show hosts, hired for their ideology and personality rather than any training or competence, have become opinion-mongers. In short, analysis died because the word lost its meaning. The quiet Sevareid, had he continued, would have been shouted down.

Sixth, the picture people won out over the word people. The new style and technology that made commercials and MTV "hot," split-second images of well-muscled, beer-guzzling volleyball players and skinny rock stars flashing before the eye long enough to make their impact but too fast to be examined, carried over to news and the new documentaries. Neither viewers nor producers had the concentration to watch someone talking for two minutes without pictures to catch their attention. Programs are produced to gratify the "channel surfer," the couch potato with the remote control who will zap the "boring" half-second into "history."

Seventh, Sevareid was not replaced because he was irreplaceable. No one else could do what he did as well as he, so no one tried. National Public Radio has a stable of several dozen essayists—housewives, novelists, professors—all over the country who offer short, witty or touching mood pieces on an irregular basis. And Rod MacLeish and Daniel Schorr do well-crafted radio analyses in the Sevareid tradition once or twice a week. But Sevareid was unique in that he spoke to the whole country in a way that no NPR commentator can ever be expected to do, and in that few contemporary journalists—and even fewer broadcast journalists—are likely to have his education. The major newspapers today hire young men and women with master's and doctoral degrees; but few journalists in their late twenties combine a university education, the voracious reading of history and literature undistracted by time-consuming television and popular music, and the experience of surviving a major war. When eulogists said of Murrow and Sevareid, "We shall not see his like again," they were not just using a figure of speech.

An excellent example of what we may never see again—a fair taste of Sevareid's best work in the last ten years of his career—is the series of documentaries he made under the general title of *Conversations with Eric Sevareid* and those he did on the American Revolution, produced by his friend Perry Wolff.

Of the three basic forms of TV news—the stand-up report from the scene of the news story; the "talking head" giving news or analysis from the studio; and the researched documentary—the documentary is often the most powerful. Like a nonfiction book, it combines history, the social sciences, and the producer-director's art to achieve a unified impact, and they often—like Murrow's "Harvest of Shame" (1960) on the plight of migrant workers—educate the public on a social crisis. The premise of *Conversations* was that viewers could be both educated and entertained by watching two intelligent people—Eric Sevareid plus one of thirteen notable Americans," like Walter Lippmann, Eric Hoffer, and so on—talk for an hour.

The selection of the persons, as well as the interviewer's manner, reveals much about Sevareid's values. He chose older men and women who were "just below the surface of the news," whom he respected and who trusted him, who would offer vision and experience that would teach the younger generation. He also chose persons who were important to him personally. Lippmann had long been an intellectual mentor to both Reston and him. Marietta Tree, was with Stevenson when he died. Supreme Court Justice William O. Douglas was a friend. Anne Morrow Lindbergh recalled the days in which both she and her husband, Charles, opposed America's participation in World War II and shared some of his own obsession with personal privacy. So these sessions, though they did not skirt controversies, like Douglas's extra-court activities for a private foundation, were by no means "investigative" journalism.

Conservative *Washington Star* columnist James J. Kilpatrick was disrespectful enough to point out after the Douglas interview that reporters with harder noses than Sevareid's would have mentioned that Albert B. Parvin, whose foundation would train Third World leaders, gave Douglas $12,000 a year to be president, and also gave mobster Meyer Lansky $200,000 to help him buy a Las Vegas casino-hotel. Douglas also wrote for *Playboy* magazine, to "reach eighteen million youngsters." Sevareid should have asked, according to Kilpatrick, whether Douglas was selling his respectability (September 18, 1972).

Nevertheless, Eric had certainly chosen these people because he knew they were going to say things he wanted said. Daniel Patrick Moynihan, for example, told how black urban rioters quieted down after he, as Nixon's representative, told mayors that if they could not control their cities they wouldn't get federal aid. And the banker John J. McCloy, prince of the establishment that he denied existed, evoked memories of an era when public servants had integrity and really "great men" like Henry Stimson and George Marshall and the two Roosevelts set the tone.

The proper response to the series was often what Eric intended—awe. The day after Eric Hoffer appeared, his books sold out in bookstores across the country. And many considered the last of the series with Anne Morrow Lindbergh, which CBS kept on the shelf till Eric lobbied Paley to have it aired, a worthy conclusion to Eric's lifework.

The basic production method, which Perry Wolff adapted just for Sevareid, was to film as much as three or four hours of conversation with three cameras and edit it down to one hour. A standard documen-tary might take nine months to do, with six weeks for shooting and sixteen for editing, with countless interruptions to adjust lighting and for other changes. But Eric demanded that each show be filmed at one sitting, lest any interruptions break his train of thought. The result some-times was a certain visual rigidity, with Eric sitting motionless, hands folded in front of him, in a dark suit, only the lower lip and jaw mobile in the long, gray head. At other times, warm and more youthful-looking in his turtleneck shirt and tweed sport coat, he would stroll along a Cambridge Street or across a lawn with the wise man and talk as if they were old friends—as they often were.

Lippmann's first of a series of TV appearances was in a 1960 inter-view with Howard K. Smith, the last with Sevareid in 1965. The first session, says Eric Alterman in *Sound and Fury: The Washington Punditocracy and the Collapse of American Politics* (1992), broke an old barrier. Never before had TV given an hour to the views of someone who was not a politician or an entertainer. It also gave TV new prestige—and a new sense of its power to shape the American political dialogue. The Sevareid dialogue, more a straight questioning than an interchange of ideas, re-turned often to standard Sevareid themes: the disquieting involvement in Vietnam's "civil war"; the "deep crisis" in Great Britain; the greatness of the recently buried Churchill; and the far-sightedness of de Gaulle.

Clearly Sevareid's fascination with Hoffer, author of *The True Believer* and *The Passionate State of Mind,* whose discussions were broadcast Sep-tember 19, 1967, and January 28, 1969, was twofold. Hoffer was a "popular" philosopher with a certain disdain for academic intellectuals; and he was a laborer, he did things with his hands— a trait Eric admired as much as he admired courage or beauty. Read today, if some of what Hoffer says seems exaggerated, offensive, or outrageous, it may be be-cause he did exaggerate, or because contemporary sensibilities wince at straight talk. Some black spokesmen called him a racist. But that term is often carelessly used. Hoffer was certainly making points that some crit-ics of intellectuals and of the Negro revolution were glad to hear.

Intellectuals, as a type, he said, were more corrupted by power than any other human type, and intellectuals hated Johnson, whom Hoffer considered the greatest president of the century, because "they can't stand the common American." The Negro revolution was a fraud, simply the tool of the Negro middle class to achieve its desires. "Vietnam is going to do for the Negro what Israel has done for the Jews"—generate a spreading pride in Negro soldiers' accomplishments. California State College should be turned over to the students, who will turn it into an "animal kingdom" and eat one another. The only honest Negro leader is Roy Wilkins. Eldridge Cleaver is a "sewer rat." We are not a sick society. The trouble with historian Arthur Schlesinger, who called us the most frightening people on earth, "is that he lived with Schlesingers all his life."

The April 6, 1971, "A Conversation with Lord North," followed a year later by "The Last King of America," a conversation with George III, were part of CBS's and Sevareid's celebration of the 1976 bicentennial of the American Revolution. In a sense, their format went back to the venerable *CBS Was There*, in which modern technology returned its reporters and viewers to a historic moment. But this time there was no script. Sevareid and actor Peter Ustinov mastered their material independently; then Ustinov fell totally into the character of North, the prime minister, and the "mad" king, and improvised his sputtering, narrow-minded—though often clever—denunciations of Colonial drunkards, ragamuffins, and rabble whom Americans have come to consider as their sacred founders. Occasionally Ustinov lets himself have almost too much fun, as when he rants that John Hancock "has no *insurance*"; and, in an amusing moment of contemporary relevance, he invents the "domino" theory," explaining the new game to Sevareid to illustrate colonial policy: "let the American colonies go . . . then the Indies, then Ireland, then Scotland, and then . . ." According to Wolff, the patriotic Eric, though usually impassive on camera, was becoming so agitated at Ustinov's arguments that he felt that someone had to stick up for America.

One of the researchers on the 1971 Lord North program was Suzanne St. Pierre. In July 1979, in her family home in Worcester, Massachusetts, she married Eric Sevareid. She was forty-two, divorced, and now a Washington producer for *60 Minutes*. For a while they lived on Bradley Lane in Chevy Chase, which was again redecorated; but in 1985 they bought Dan Rather's old, white, shingled row house on Thirty-third Street in Georgetown, just four blocks down from Georgetown University. Though the house, which they remodeled stem to stern, looks small from the front, it is deep, and there is a little fountain in the backyard. This was the house, said Rather, that Sevareid loved the most.

He professed to enjoy retirement. He traveled to Tokyo, Hawaii, Alaska, Berlin, France, England, and throughout the United States, and wrote to Philip Dunne, son of Peter Finley Dunne, that he had "discovered only late in life that a happy marriage just doesn't make one happy and comfortable—it provides a *freedom,* which includes the freedom to be brave; and it does not all stop there because as Churchill said, borrowing from Aristotle, courage is the prime virtue because it makes the other virtues possible."

Indeed, Eric's letters during these years are those of a generally contented and happy man. He worried about his family, about the ups and downs of Michael's career in Hollywood, and wrote to Norman Corwin, who had become a professor, asking him to advise Michael about the possibilities of a teaching career (September 8, 1986). He fretted about Tina's reluctance to go to college—although he himself had not gone immediately to college after high school. Tina had done well at Madeira school, which gained some notoriety when its headmistress, Jean Harris, murdered her lover, the renowned diet doctor, Dr. Tarnower. (In 1986 Eric, convinced that Harris had suffered a mental breakdown, wrote to New York Governor Mario Cuomo adding his name to those asking clemency for Harris).

Frightened by the onset of emphysema, Eric gave up smoking in 1978 and put on some weight. A 1983 sinus operation cleared up an infection that had been poisoning him with headaches, toothaches, and throat-aches for a year or more. His arthritis, which had plagued him for twenty years, was getting him in his hips and neck; he now wore a back brace for support and he described himself as partly crippled, but not deformed. He was determined to avoid a wheelchair. With his cane, he walked slowly through the beautiful Georgetown neighborhood, by Walter Lippmann's old home a few blocks away, by Georgetown University and the old Visitation Convent and School. If recognized on the street, he would respond cordially to a hello, but not invite conversation.

The deaths of friends weighed heavily on him over the years and intensified his loneliness and sense of his own mortality—Murrow, Stevenson, H.V. Kaltenborn, Lippmann, Humphrey, Collingwood, and as he learned in 1980, of Philip Adams, who had rescued him in Burma long ago. In 1986 his brother John died in his sleep of cancer at seventy-one, with Eric and Jeanne standing by. All his life John had shared the

Sevareid family male trait of not being able to display emotions. Once when Tharsella, his second wife, had pointed out that he never told her he loved her, he replied, "How can you say that? I married you." It was like him to die quietly in the night, sooner than the doctor predicted, so as not to inconvenience anyone.

Eric answered letters from young students. Depending on their requests and partly on whether he knew their families already, he told one to do her own research on Richard Nixon, gave another a one-page life story, and wrote a full critique of a young man's descriptive essay, "My Oak":

> Your imagery is vivid, but in this case too vivid, or rather, it is too rich. You should not strive for a bright color with every sentence stroke. . . . You use "which" where "that" is not only more correct but helps the flow of the sentence. You see, you must "sound" each sentence, if only silently, in your mind. There must be rhythm.

He added, "I can't think in my life I've done more than a half-dozen really well enough to be proud of. Don't stop trying. Writing with imagination is the hardest work there is; that's why it's worth it; and you have the spark. This little essay is far more ambitious and better done than anything I wrote at your age" (November 20, 1970).

In spite of his fabled impatience with young demonstrators, he could be very patient with and open to the young, indeed to almost anyone in the profession whom he could help. In May 1990, CNN reporter Tom Farmer (30), asked Eric for an interview on the Bush-Gorbachev summit and was frankly astonished when Eric quickly agreed. He went looking for Eric at the CBS 2020 M Street address, only to find that his retirement office was not there in the middle of things, but down the street, a world away from the working bureau. He found Eric waiting in a small windowless office, "dressed in tweeds and waistcoat like my grandfather in his Sunday best."

Eric could not have been more gracious and receptive. He took Tom's questions seriously and, when they were finished taping, said modestly, "I hope there is something there you can use."

Tom did not have the heart to tell him that whatever he said would be snipped up and inserted into the packages of correspondents like

Charles Bierbauer and Ralph Begleiter. He had a college-age intern with him who was not really sure who Eric Sevareid was; but he left her in Eric's office quizzing him about his life and times, Eric answering the most naive questions in earnest.

Farmer was appalled that one of the great voices of the twentieth century was "grudgingly housed in a crappy office well removed from the action." He would always remember "that angular dignified figure proudly inhabiting that backwater of an office, perhaps still waiting for the phone to ring, for New York to order up some perspective. Or, more likely, knowing that they didn't want him anymore" (June 8, 1993).

Eric complained that Sue was gone so often working on her *60 Minutes* stories, but he was proud of her best programs and her prizes; and, she brought a level of relative tranquility into his life that he had not known for many years. In a December 18, 1988, letter to Dunne, in which he complained about a lot of other things—London is getting tawdry, style is vanishing everywhere, "only in Claridges's and Maxim's was a necktie required . . . slobs slowly taking over"—he confessed: "Friends seem to vanish every day; I am so lucky to have a relatively young and totally loving wife, so I am going to escape loneliness at least. Otherwise, my carcass contains about every annoying ailment old age can provide."

Meanwhile, as he saw it, he had to earn a living. Ever since he turned down the "Man of Distinction" whiskey ad in the 1950s he had struggled with the issue of commercial endorsements. One time he agreed to narrate a film for the tobacco industry, until he read the script and found it required him to end the film by smoking on camera and praising the product. He agreed to take part in an airline ad, then cancelled when he didn't like it. Now, in retirement, he was offered a deal to do testimonials for an investment house—three weeks' work a year for three years for a million dollars. He consulted friends and family and lay awake nights asking himself whether he should leave his children "a name with no tarnish on it, or a name with a little bit of tarnish and some sustenance." Finally he just felt in his gut that he shouldn't do it.

Now, in a sense, he was very busy, but not busy doing what he did best. He narrated the PBS television documentary series *Between the Wars* and *Enterprise*. These films are now in hundreds of university libraries, and future generations of college students will know Sevareid's voice—the way they know Walter Winchell's voice from *The Untouchables*—but, since he didn't write these programs, they won't know his ideas.

His agent signed him up for all kinds of voice-overs and personal appearances. He showed up in feature films like *The Right Stuff* and *The Jigsaw Man*. He presented awards and he received them. In 1980, hired by the public relations firm of Carl Byoir & Associates, he flew to Berlin, largely because he wanted to see the city where he had covered the Berlin airlift, once more. There he made a series of ninety-second spots on Berlin's cultural attractions for U.S. stations, publicizing a cultural festival celebrating the relationship between Berlin and its sister city, Los Angeles, on L.A.'s 200th birthday. During the four-day shoot, he ducked into East Berlin for a quick evening tour, and then, trench coat collar turned up, walked the foggy streets of West Berlin communing with the old ghosts he had not faced in years.

He participated, at Bob Craig's request, in the October 1989 Ceres Williamsburg Conference on new technologies and the future of food and nutrition, and participants, some of the leading scholars in the field, found him an inspiring presence and wise moderator of their discussions. He also narrated the video corporate report on the meeting.

Worthy causes. He was working, picking up big fees, but still not doing what he did best.

In 1985, CBS gathered its old veteran Murrow's Boys in London to celebrate the fortieth anniversary of V-E Day with a special broadcast. As William L. Shirer records the reunion in the last volume of his memoirs, *Twentieth Century Journey*, there was some amusing competition for control of the microphone between Walter Cronkite and Dan Rather, who had replaced Cronkite in 1981, and a cordial but sad reunion between Eric, Collingwood, and himself, who dined together after not seeing one another in years, talking about old ties.

Sad, Shirer felt, because Eric seemed at loose ends. He had not found enough work to make him happy, and he had not done as much writing as he had hoped. Sad, because Collingwood, though he still had a job, had been shunted aside in favor of younger talent. Sad because Collingwood disclosed at the end, "Bill, I've got cancer." He was taking chemotherapy, but died a few months later—with Eric at his bedside at the end. That same year, Eric's own physical exam revealed no sign of cancer, yet.

Then in January 1991, J. J. Yore, an editor at NPR's radio program of business news, *Marketplace*, wrote and told Eric that when he was a kid in Washington D. C., "there was one TV journalist who made everyone in our family put down their scotch . . . and pay attention." He even remembered a particular essay on urban riots and the consumer society's display of wealth. That made him think Eric Sevareid would be a good commentator for *Marketplace*.

Eric accepted and began a well-publicized series of two-minute bimonthly pieces, although he had wanted more time. These programs, unfortunately, did not break new ground. They were good, but anyone who had listened to Sevareid for years had heard them before— Gertrude Stein on "publicity saints," Eric Hoffer, college athletes, Walter Lippmann, his boyhood experiences riding the rails, stealing watermelons in Velva. His final illness and hospitalization cut them short.

Of course, he "should" have written another book, the second volume of his autobiography, and publishers urged him to do so. But he seemed to lack both the energy and the desire. He told *New York Times* correspondent Nan Robertson (June 19, 1979) that to write a book he would have to withdraw from people, "sink into" himself for two or three years. That was too big a risk. Although he did not say so, in no way would he have been able to write about himself and Belen. Meanwhile, so much of his energies in the last years seemed tied up in the past, trying to come to terms with it, making sure the record was straight.

In 1986, when he read Richard Critchfield's *Those Days*, his family memoir about growing up in a small town in North Dakota, with a traditional mother and a doctor father, who was both secretly alcoholic and sexually involved with a younger woman, Eric was so moved he called Critchfield and, in tears, told him he recognized his own family. Daniel Patrick Moynihan had also read the book, and at a little party at the Moynihan home, he and Eric stood staring into the fire and reminisced about their own childhoods: both had hopped freight cars as part of growing up, Eric in the Depression, Moynihan a decade later.

In 1990, when Ed Apfel wrote the Emmy Award PBS documentary, *Edward R. Murrow: This Reporter*, Sevareid was very grumpy about participating. He wanted the questions in advance and studio lighting that wouldn't make his "eyes disappear." He got neither, but came anyway.

He arrived on time, wrists bandaged, leaning on a cane, and glowering. But he came prepared, loaded with notes, his memory sharp and detailed. Apfel had been warned that Eric would not play the role of Murrow's acolyte; but Eric made it clear he "worshipped" the man. He also returned to a subject that marked his letters and other interviews: his anger at Shirer for attacking Murrow, in the latest volume of his autobiography, once again for "firing" him. In material that never made it into the final version, Sevareid also attacked George Bush for invading Panama and the press for taking so long to count the hundreds of innocent civilian dead.

Indeed, true to the hope expressed in a *New Yorker* cartoon, Eric Sevareid kept commenting "on his own time," in interviews and letters, on the news of the day. He remained a "pessimist about tomorrow and an optimist about the day after." Again and again he supported that optimism by referring to Jacques Maritain, who claimed that Americans had learned to "keep their souls apart" from the depersonalizing forces of material progress (*US News and World Report,* December 26, 1977). By 1985, because he liked the young politicians and students he met on a recent trip, he finally overcame his profound distrust of the German people expressed so vividly in *Not So Wild a Dream* (*US News and World Report,* May 6, 1985).

What worried him most was the fragmentation of American society. It used to be that everyone who came here came to be Americans, to acquire and contribute to a distinctive American personality. Now ethnic groups were becoming not a means of preserving a distinctive culture, but economic demand groups, devices for getting things from the government. He told the *Ripon Forum* (November 1983) that unchecked immigration from Latin America was making the American Southwest the "dumping ground for all the region's poor." "I have an intuition that English-Spanish bilingualism will prove to be a greater strain on national unity than black-white biracialism. Language is so fundamental; it's more fundamental than skin color. Dr. Johnson, you know, once said that language is the nerve of the nation."

During the 1988 presidential campaign he told Dunne that George Bush seemed a "flimsy man who has run along the boundary, at least, of dishonor with his campaign tactics, 'the patriotism thing.'" During the gulf war he protested the restrictions on correspondents and told Dan

Rather, in Dan's last visit to the Georgetown house, that maybe he'd like to go to the Persian Gulf.

Yet, though his interviews may seem cranky, most of his complaints were based not on an old man's irritation with a changed world, but on a coherent vision that he had reworked but kept rationally consistent all his life. One of his last addresses was to the American Association of Retired Persons in 1991. He told "his" generation that we are the same person at eighty-five as we are at twenty-five, that history belongs to the young, how America survives crime, pollution, and economic crisis will depend on each individual's inner character, our willingness to assume personal responsibility for our world.

More and more, with the end of his days in sight, he reached back to first principles. He had also learned how to pray again.

Two books that he urged friends to read were Norman MacLean's *A River Runs Through It* (1976) and Evan S. Connell's *Son of the Morning Star: Custer and the Little Big Horn* (1984). On one level, of course, he would love MacLean because it describes fly-fishing, the effort to out-smart the brown trout, with affectionate detail. But it's also the story of a family "where there is no clear line between religion and fly-fishing," where two brothers love one another but don't communicate well, where one keeps trying to help the other and never succeeds. In a key scene, the father, a Presbyterian minister, reads the Bible on a fishing trip and meditates on the first line of John's gospel, intended to echo the first line of the creation narrative, "In the beginning was the word." In the order of creation, he determined, the word came before water. The book concludes: "Eventually, all things merge into one, and a river runs through it. The river was cut by the world's great flood and rocks are timeless raindrops. Under the rocks are the words, and some of the words are theirs.

"I am haunted by waters."

In September 1990, while fishing with Bob Craig in the Big Horn River in Montana, Eric visited the Custer battlefield and moved among the white stones marking the spot where each soldier's naked, gleaming white, mutilated corpse had been found. The last, tightest group of stones was not quite at the top of the hill overlooking the Little Big Horn River. It all looks much as it did in 1876. Eric loved the west and all its myths, but he did not like the new myths which romanticized the

Indians—some of his ancestors had been killed by Indians on the North Dakota frontier. And he was, in his last years, continually preoccupied by the history of human conflict, barbarism, the problem of evil. He confided to Craig, "I've spent all of my life trying to understand how and why men do these things, and I never seem to have any real answers. I think we'd better go fishing."

His last published comment on the news was a letter to the *New York Times* (March 15, 1991) protesting the government's restraints on war correspondents in the Persian Gulf. Since modern military leadership had put an end to the correspondents' role, he said, we would have no more Murrows or Ernie Pyles. "I would settle for that only if future American wars were equally unlikely, which is doubtful."

At the end of 1991, Eric Sevareid began to die. Geoffrey Cox observed that cancer has a way of subconsciously letting one know it's coming. Eric had stomach cancer and two thirds of the stomach was removed. Then he had radiation and lost a lot of weight. He was hospitalized again with pneumonia, then returned home. Yet now, when he was really sick, he would talk to friends on the phone and make no mention of his illness. To his great joy, Tina graduated from Hood College with a degree in accounting and, in spite of his weakness, he made it to the graduation and watched her receive her degree.

When Michael saw him struggling in considerable pain to get up and get out of bed, he said to him, "My God, you're tough." And Eric looked at him and said, "You really think so?" He seemed to doubt his own strength.

The last time Michael watched him climb the stairs of the Georgetown house, step by step, emaciated but still a big man, he wondered how he would ever catch his father if he fell. But he made it to the top.

Eric died on Thursday, July 9, 1992, at 3:45 A.M. His body was cremated, and some of his ashes were scattered over Norway.

When the widow, Suzanne St. Pierre, discovered to her surprise that he had left his estate not directly to her but rather in trust, so that Belen, the sons and daughter, and grandchildren would also be well provided for, so the grandchildren could go to college, she sued to break the will. Yet, reflecting on his life, it is clear why he would dispose of his estate in this way. He never got over his father's period of poverty, his own struggle to work his way through college, his worries over Lois and the cost of her illness. For years he had contributed to the support of Lois's family as well as his own. In 1960, he kept Lois in his will because he felt Belen was healthy and talented and could support herself. Very possibly he was confident that Suzanne, to whom he left about a third of his estate, had independent means. Yet, the harmony and peace that had united the family during his dying was now disrupted by the dispute over the will.

And what of Eric Sevareid's other legacy? Would his journalistic ideals survive?

Richard Salant died of heart failure at seventy-eight, February 16, 1993, while giving a talk on news coverage to a group of elderly people in Connecticut.

The internal wars at CBS, about which Eric, although he complained in private, said little in public, erupted in the public press again. CBS News' ratings, at their peak in 1976, when sixteen percent of households with TVs watched CBS, had declined steadily to ten percent in 1992. Walter Cronkite told the *American Journalism Review* (May 1994) that the cuts in news bureaus' budgets, particularly foreign bureaus, had been an "amputation," and that the great percentage of the public who could not or would not read was growing, and becoming "suckers for a demagogue." Jon Katz, in an unfriendly article on Dan Rather in *Rolling Stone* (October 14, 1993), said Rather—as well as Stringer, the *60 Minutes* people, and even Cronkite, who sat on the board of directors—had acquiesced in the dismantling, which began in 1986, of everything that had distinguished CBS News.

At the September 1993 Radio and Television News Directors Association Convention, which Janet Murrow attended for the unveiling of the U.S. postal stamp honoring Ed, Dan Rather, as if anticipating Katz's attack, gave a speech in which he recalled Murrow's 1958 address to the same group. He donned Murrow's spiritual trenchcoat to deliver a scathing criticism of television news. He drew a picture very contrary to the rosy defense in Eric's 1976 Journalism Center address; it was of an industry, he said, ruled by commercialism, fluff, and fear.

William L. Shirer finished his last book, on Tolstoy's last years, and died at the end of the year.

In early 1994 Walter Port died. Eric had lost contact with him after their 1980 return to Hudson Bay and in 1985 didn't even know if Walt was still alive.

"What mattered . . . was his example," Russell Baker said in his *New York Times* column. "He showed it was possible in the news business to be decent and still be successful." In the 1950s the governor of Minnesota had named a lake after Eric Sevareid, and Eric, honored so early in his career, wondered what the name of the lake would mean to anyone years after he was gone.

If a historian walks by the lake when someone from Mars asks that question, he or she, warming to the question, will probably say three things. First, he embodied best and longest the Murrow-Stanton-Salant tradition: that news broadcasting has a noble purpose: to educate and inform more than to entertain and make money. Second, that Sevareid was a master of the language that rose to the occasion. He wrote better than Walter Lippmann; no one in the profession expressed either lofty or witty thoughts so well.

Finally, the historian will get to Sevareid's most important contribution—the real reason lakes are named after him and books are written by and about him: he spoke for all America. He was America, at its best, speaking to itself. He did it during times of national crisis, when the country was divided and angry and in danger of uncivil war. Again and again, in ways hard to measure, his words pulled us back from the brink. His faith in us was what we needed then. He retired just in time, because he was out of step with the popular culture, and he would not have had the resources or the support to roll back the tide of fads and ideas—for example, the glorification of ethnicity for its own sake over national unity—dominating popular discourse. But while his audience was there, he spoke for the nobler instincts of the American center better than anyone else explaining America to America.

The paradox of his life was that he really did not belong in broadcasting, and much of his obvious unhappiness must have come from his knowing that. His heart was always in writing; yet, because of his personal family problems and other emotional and financial insecurities, he could not break from CBS and the security and sense of belonging it gave.

If Eric Sevareid's importance to journalism history and his public legacy are clear, the private Sevareid remains in death still very much the private man he insisted on being during his life. Those fishing and hunting trips with Dan Rather were often characterized by long periods of silence. The word that James Reston, to whom he bequeathed a book of speeches by his beloved Lincoln, used again and again to describe Eric was quiet. Quiet. "A quiet man in a noisy generation." Yes he was a "gloomy gus," naturally sensitive, and cautious; but he was not a "journalist" in the sense that many journalists are "loud." And Eric's quiet, direct, deliberate thoughtfulness, said Reston, is very rare.

The anecdotes his colleagues tell about him are few, mostly centered on his alleged parsimony and health complaints. But respect for his intellectual depth and the crafted beauty of his prose is nearly universal. Few seemed to know him well, but some who did sensed in him a feeling of incompleteness, as if he believed toward the end that he had somehow failed to achieve all he should have. The occasional hints of jealousy of Murrow, complaints about Cronkite's dominance, and of envy of Rather's salary suggest that he himself felt he should have inherited the Murrow mantle. He did inherit the special relationship with Paley; but in that culture, the top meant being anchor. He knew there was discussion of making him anchor, just as he knew that he was, by style and temperament, unsuited for it. But few men can be passed over without inner grievance.

Asked to identity Eric's major fault, Larry LeSueur responded that, "Well, he was self-centered." Then he added, "But, we're all self-centered." Some of the women in his life seemed to know him better— both more critically and more sympathetically—than his male colleagues, many of whom knew nothing about his wives and children. In the 1940s, Gitta Sereny knew his strengths and weaknesses. A weakness was his inability to love "damaged people," he was more a "giver" than a "taker," and after Murrow died and he himself became more famous, he took himself very seriously and lost something in the process. But, she wrote, "I think that Eric always was and remained a moral man, and to me the real, 'classic' America was and is moral. He was 'clean'—it was unimaginable that he could do anything corrupt—in that sense, he was untouchable. And I think his audience knew this—and loved him for it! . . . I think being American was Eric's greatest gift, or achievement.

He loved and understood his country. And because he had this other extraordinary gift of writing absolutely beautifully, indeed almost poetically, the spoken word—for himself to speak—he was able to communicate that love and that understanding . . ." (March 29, 1994).

Eric's sister-in-law, Celia Brokaw Sevareid, John's first wife, suggests that Eric was very much like his maternal grandfather, a preacher and writer, "whose journalistic career so absorbed him that his wives and children were subordinated to the great ideal. In the earlier day, the religious profession was where prestige and renown were won, and collections of sermons were best-selling books." Clerics were idolized by crowds of women, and crowds were swayed by the preacher's voice and "show business" skill. That young Arnold Eric Sevareid once thought of becoming a preacher, as he confided to his son Peter, makes sense. What better way to both use his talents and protect his ideas? As Celia sums him up, "He was a perfectly delightful friend when I knew him. That was very long ago, and to me he is as he was"(November 16, 1993).

What drove him? Part of the answer stands on an isolated hilltop, an hour and a half west of Washington, about eight miles outside Warrenton, Virginia, in rolling hills of horse farms and dark, deep woods, where, if you are not from there you will have very little sense of just where you are. The visitor takes a dirt road and climbs the hill into the trees, wondering if he's lost, struck again by the feeling of self-inflicted loneliness that pervaded Alexandria's Seminary Hill.

Finally, the trees open and the road leads into an immense, long, rectangular clearing spread across the hilltop, interrupted by big, freestanding trees. At the end of the clearing, under rough stone markers, rests the original farm family that first tilled this soil. The "farm" is forty-four acres, and right in the middle of the clearing's near end stands a log-and-shingle cabin—the kind of dwelling Abraham Lincoln's father or Thoreau would have built if they had had a little more money. A tall chimney runs up the side. There's running water for the kitchen sink, but not for regular indoor plumbing. A neat, little outhouse sits a few yards away. Below, out of sight, stocked with bass and bream, lies a pond with a rickety dock, where Eric would fish, laughing with little children, or with an old friend, in silence.

It is a representation of the primitive America he loved. It is also open space. Like the open space he saw from the hills around Velva. Seeing all that space, said Richard Critchfied, can give a prairie small-town child the feeling of omnipotence, the sense that there are no limits to what he can do with his life. If he breaks away from the small town—seizes what the railroad symbolizes—he carries that sense of infinite possibility with him always. If he does not break away, the town will kill his spirit. Add to that drive the high expectations of a mother who knows the world is bigger than Velva, and the strong sense of entitlement—that he was meant for a writing career—begun in Velva and nourished at Central High School and at the university. Add a strong wife who supports him. And the decision to go to Europe in 1937. Add the bitterness and sadness of failed marriages that, with Norwegian guilt, he did not know how to discuss. Add to all this a brilliant, independent intellect—the mind suspicious of easy answers and ideologies, primarily rationalistic, yet open to the promptings of the spirit, and educated by the heart. And there is Eric Sevareid.

ACKNOWLEDGMENTS

I wrote this book on sabbatical from Loyola University in New Orleans. I thank Loyola's faculty, administration, and students for this freedom and pray that this work may in some way enrich their lives as it has mine.

I am extremely grateful to the staffs of these institutions who assisted me so generously: the Library of Congress, both the manuscript and photo divisions; the Loyola University Library, New Orleans; Georgetown University Library; the University of Minnesota Library Archives; the Minnesota Historical Society, St. Paul; the Minneapolis *Star Tribune*; the Minneapolis Public Library; the New York Public Library; the Museum of Television and Radio in New York; the Vanderbilt University Television News Archive; the Oral History Office of the Columbia University Library.

I was welcomed in my travels by Saint Cecilia's Roman Catholic Parish and the citizens and officials of Velva; at the Jesuit Novitiate in St. Paul, Minnesota, where I got the lead that brought me to Walter Port, and where Richard Burbach, S.J., said, "Eric Sevareid spoke to us about the meaning of the great moments of our history. In the scriptural sense, in the sense of Jesus in the gospel, he spoke as one who had authority. His integrity shone through." In my further travels I was lodged at St. Peter's College in Jersey City, Jogues' Retreat in Cornwall, New York, St. Ann's Jesuit Parish in West Palm Beach, and the Weston Jesuit Community in Cambridge, Mass.

For most of the year, I lived at Georgetown University and did much of the writing at the Jesuit house at Centreville, Maryland. I will be forever grateful to my fellow Jesuits of the midnight seminar—Bill McFadden, S.J, Jim Walsh, S.J., Jim Reddington, S.J., and Otto Hentz, S.J.—who occasionally asked me "how Eric was coming," and listened indulgently when I told them, even when they had not asked.

During the year I also participated in a discussion group of biographers, psychiatrists, and psychologists—including William Lanouette,

Floyd Galler, John Langan, S.J., Bud Pray, Stan Goldberg, Curtis Bryant, S.J., Charles Tartaglia, and William Richardson, S.J.—who gave me encouragement and fresh insights into my topic.

But I must single out four people whose names leap to the forefront: William Lanouette, who meticulously reviewed the whole manuscript and valiantly cheered me on; Ed Bliss, who gave me my first leads, on whose book I leaned, and who also read the whole manuscript; Perry Wolff, who gave trust, advice, and, with his wife Tuuliekki, gave hospitality as well; and Celia Sevareid, who opened up the family history and transmitted much of her love of Eric to me.

Several other friends have been kind enough to read various chapters and offer advice, nearly all of which I have tried to follow: Joan Dickinson, Larry Padberg, David Danahar, R. Emmett Curran, S.J., John Paton Davies, Daniel Degnan, S.J., Douglass Cater, Robert Burke, S.J., Bob Keck, S.J., John Eddy, S.J., Thomas Stahel, S.J. Among the readers are former and present students. I owe them special thanks. I write in part to make myself more worthy to teach them; now their perspective has enriched these pages: René Sanchez, Mike Wilson, Jim O'Neill, Peter Reichard, Jennifer Johnson, and Chris Bonura.

I thank my editor, Thomas Powers, who grasped the idea of this book from the start and, through encouragement and criticism, brought out the best in me and in my subject.

The following talked with me about Eric Sevareid: (Where persons have changed their names in marriage, I have tried to include the name which would help the reader identify the source and her relationship to the subject. Several of those interviewed have died during the year of my research; I have marked them with a †) Nan Scallon Abell, Ed Apfel, John Armstrong, Judy Anderson, Rev. William Bason, Charles E. Beatley, Jr., John Bessor, Ed Bliss, Adele and Philip Stoddard Brown, Arthur and Rutilia Burck, Francelia Butler, Douglas Cater, Sir Geoffrey Cox, Robert W. Craig, Richard Critchfield†, Walter Cronkite, William Crawford, John Paton Davies, Michael Deaver, Rita Stearns Delmont, Joseph T. Dembo, Joan Dickinson, Sherman Finger, Sherman Finger III, Eben Finger, Jane Hougen Fast, Edward M. Fouhy, Gerald E. Gaull, M.D., Marion Freedman Goldin, Nancy Bean White Hector, Richard C. Hottelet, Alice Hougen, Lee Hougen, Jack Jackson, Irene Jaskokoski, Marvin Kalb, Thomas King, S.J., Al Kosek, Helen Kramer, Earl Larson, John

Lawler, Ernest Leiser, Bill Leonard†, Larry LeSueur, Margaret Loberg, Lee Loevinger, Dottie Lynch, Frederick Manfred†, Gordon Manning, Robert Manning, Abigail McCarthy, Sig Mickelson, Edmund Morris, Janet Murrow, Connie Newson, Newbold Noyes, Janet Olson, Mrs. Jefferson Patterson (Mary Marvin Breckinridge), Michael Port, Walter Port†, Martin Quigley, Dan Rather, Suzanne Stamps Rheinstein, James Reston, Michael Russo, John Sack, John Sample, Richard and Mary Scammon, Jeanne Sevareid Schmidt, Daniel Schorr, Celia B. Sevareid, Jack Schneider, Elizabeth L. Sevareid, Michael Sevareid, Belen Marshall Sevareid, Tharsella Sevareid, Cristina Sevareid Kennedy, William J. Small, Howard K. and Benedicte Smith, Sally Bedell Smith, Sandy Socolow, Ray Scherer, Ann Sperber†, Frank Stanton, Jerry and Lisa Stewart, Emerson Stone, Robert Syme, M.D., Kathryn Stone, Arthur Taylor, Joseph and Shirley Wershba, J. Russell Wiggins, Perry Wolff.

In response to notices in the *New York Times Book Review*, the *Washington Post Book World*, and word of mouth, a good many have written to me about their experiences with or ideas about Sevareid. The overwhelming number of responses were prompted by the *New York Times* note. John Ayres Armstrong, Ed Apfel, Emil Antonucci, Michael Avallone, Ruth Cates Baird, Steve Barnes, Mrs. Gerald (Katri Kirchner) Blake, Benson A. Bowditch, Andrea Cohen Bresnick, Edith Bard Blum, Mimi Thompson Breed, Edward C. Brown, Arthur Burck, Alice B. Colonna, Stuart D. Cowan, Robert W. Craig, Richard Critchfield, Gwen Davis, Joseph T. Dembo, John DeMetropolis, Joan Dickinson, William D. Dinges, Frank A. Dolan, Martin K. Doudna, George Doyle, Jed Duvall, Murray Elwood, Tom Farmer, Judith A. Fieldstone, Robert Freund, Janet Sussman Gartner, James Nelson Goodsell, Jeff Gralnick, Richard J. Graving, Mora Gregg, Ann Guscio, Paul H. Hamre, Michael A. Hanu, William F. Herrick, Arthur R. Haskins, Sr., Robert Henkel, James N. Holsen, Margo Howard, Helen Johns, Christina D. Koetel, John D. Knowlton, Elaine M. Kunz, Susan H. Llewellyn, Ronald J. LeFrancois, Eileen C. Lord, John A. Mann, Robert Alexander Marshall, Ronald A. May, Harold Mayfield, Remy McBurney, Jerome L. McLaughlin, John A. Middleton, Pat Munroe, William M. Murphy, Ruth C. Plymat, Gregory Resch, Irene C. Richard, Earl M. Richardson, Karen Ragatz Roberts, S. J. Ronnie, Jan Saenger, Wallace Salshutz, Don Sandstrom, Geraldine Schofield, William P. Schrandt, Pat Schroth, Gitta Sereny, Celia

Brokaw Sevareid, Robert Sherrod†, Jennifer A. Sternaman, Beth Zimmerschied Sweeney, Clem Taylor, Joe Tiernan, John Robert Tucker, Lewis Turco, Kurt Vonnegut.

NOTES AND SOURCES

Abbreviations:

LC   Arnold Eric Sevareid Collection, in the Library of Congress
ES   Eric Sevareid
NSWD *Not So Wild a Dream*
RAS   Raymond A. Schroth, S.J.
MHS   Minnesota Historical Society

INTRODUCTION

The events described on this "typical" news day are from the *New York Times* and *Washington Post* for October 19–21, 1970. I viewed this and other *CBS Evening News* programs on tapes on loan from the Vanderbilt University Television News Archive in Nashville, Tennessee. Murrow's joke about Sevareid's (hereafter ES) appearance is from an interview with Joseph Wershba. All of the interviews were conducted between August 1993 and July 1994, and the notes and summaries of the interviews, in my papers, will be available to scholars through the Loyola University Library.

In these notes, I will not refer to a book if the reference is already in the text. The publishing information on the book is in the selected bibliography. Any additional references to a book in the notes will be simply to the author. All the scripts and letters referred to, unless otherwise indicated, are in LC.

The descriptions of the memorial service at the National Press Club come from the text, audiotape, and videotape of the service, from my later visit to the club, and letters from and interviews with those who attended, including Ed Bliss, Larry LeSueur, Emerson Stone, Robert Craig, Ernest Leiser, Lee Hougen, Bill Leonard, Dottie Lynch, Dan Rather, Tina Sevareid Kennedy, Michael Sevareid, and J. J. Yore.

Richard Salant's remarks at the New Canaan Library, September 20, 1992, are in the files of the New Canaan Library Association. The Stringer quotes and the description of the Charles Collingwood memorial are in Peter Boyle, *Who Killed CBS.* For more on the problems of CBS during the 1980s, see: Boyer; David Halberstam, "The Power that Was," *Fame* magazine; and Ken Auletta, *Three Blind Mice: How the TV Networks Lost Their Way.* In interviews, Sandy Socolow and Ernest Leiser were helpful on this period.

The account of William Paley's memorial service is in Sally Bedell Smith's *In All His Glory.*

The manuscripts of ES radio and television commentaries are in the Arnold Eric Sevareid Collection at the Library of Congress (hereafter LC). The collection seems to contain nearly everything ES said on the air or wrote for publication, or said in a lecture. There are more than twenty thousand documents, including correspondence, though very little family or personal material, in 95 boxes, plus many more files of commentaries and letters after 1959 which, as this is written, are still being catalogued.

The texts of his best radio commentaries, columns, and magazine articles from the 1940s through 1967 are in *In One Ear, Small Sounds in the Night,* and *This Is Eric Sevareid.* Wherever possible, I will refer to the broadcast by its date, so its text can be traced through LC, Vanderbilt, or CBS archives; or, if it has been reprinted, I will refer to the book title.

An indispensable source in studying ES's commentaries is Sister M. Camille D'Arienzo, R.S.M.'s "Eric Sevareid Analyzes the News," her 1973 Ph.D. dissertation in speech at the University of Michigan. Sister D'Arienzo sampled 164 transcripts between 1969 and 1973 and interviewed ES in depth. My selection of significant broadcasts during this period has been guided by her research.

The other indispensable resource is Judy Anderson's "Take Heaven, Take Peace, Take Joy," an annotated bibliography of 145 ES articles and interviews. Ms. Anderson is at Delmar College, in Corpus Christi, Texas.

I based the Bob Craig material here and in later chapters on an interview with Craig, Craig's memorial talk, and the Craig-ES correspondence in LC. Bill Leonard's career is well portrayed in his own memoir, *In the Storm of the Eye: A Lifetime at CBS,* and in the several CBS histories that appeared around the same time. These pages are based on our interview and the text of his talk. The story of the D-day anniversary broadcast comes from an interview with Shirley Wershba, who was present.

Chapter One: VELVA

My description of Velva and Minot comes from my three-day visit there in October, 1993, and interviews with Velva citizens, particularly Helen Kramer, who remained ES's friend till his death, and Margaret Loberg. I am especially indebted to Jack Jackson, editor of the *Valley Star*, published in Velva, and its centennial issue (June 30, 1993), the main source for Velva history, along with ES's *Not So Wild a Dream* (hereafter *NSWD*) and the files of the old *Velva Journal*. Also helpful were the brochures of the Velva Community Development Corporation and the Velva Association of Commerce, and the ongoing correspondence between Velva citizens and ES in LC.

See Larry Woidwode, *Beyond the Bedroom Wall: A Family Portrait*. The "Velva future" is, of course, ES. The quotes describing the town, unless otherwise indicated, are from *NSWD*. The story of the wandering five-year-old is from an undated, unidentified clipping in the LC. Internal evidence suggests it is from the Minneapolis Central High School student newspaper, circa 1932.

The family history of the Sevareids and Hougens is thoroughly documented in "European Centennial of Jens Johannessen and Christine Olsdater Hougen, 1857–1957," compiled by their grandchildren, celebration at Story City, Iowa, Sunday, June 30, 1957. This includes a family tree tracing ES's relatives from the seventeenth century; and it was updated for a 1982 Hougen reunion. I also relied on standard biographical dictionaries and clippings files in the Minnesota Historical Society (MHS) in St. Paul, the Minneapolis Public Library, and the Minneapolis *Star Tribune*, which faithfully recorded the careers, marriages, divorces of ES and his brothers, Paul and John. The *Minneapolis Journal* is on microfilm at the MHS and many clippings from that paper are in the LC files. Also, Helen Kramer has recollections of early Sevareid family history. Duane W. Fenstermann, archivist of the Luther College Library, Decorah, Iowa, sent me material on Alfred Sevareid and Clara Hougen and on ES's relationship with Luther College.

Chapter 2: THE CANOE TRIP

The descriptions and history of Minneapolis are from my own visit, *Minnesota: A State Guide;* Joseph Stipanovich, *City of Lakes: An Illustrated History of Minneapolis;* Robert T. Smith, *Minneapolis-St. Paul: The Cities, Their People;* Hedley Donovan, *Right Places, Right Times: Forty Years in Journalism Not Counting My Paper Route;* and Carl Solberg, *Hubert Humphrey: A Biography.* The ES-Jack Dempsey story is in "Advice to Young Men," *Saturday Evening Post,* May 10, 1959. Walter Port told me ES didn't raise his hand in school when he knew the answer. Other details on Port at Central High School are from *Central High News* clippings, courtesy of Michael Port. Alice Hougen gave me insights on ES as a young man as he planned the trip.

This book's account of the canoe trip relies on ES's *NSWD; Canoeing with the Cree;* the ES-Port accounts in the *Minneapolis Star,* June 25 to October 13; and the original notebooks from the trip, in LC. For background, see Percy Knauth, *The North Woods;* Calvin Rutstrum, *North American Canoe Country;* Ernest C. Oberholtzer, review of *Canoeing with the Cree, Minnesota History,* (fall, 1968); and ES, "Return to God's Country," *Audubon,* September 1981.

Chapter 3: WEST BY RAIL

ES describes the University of Minnesota in "The University of Minnesota," *The Lincoln-Mercury Times* (November–December 1950), and *NSWD.* Also see "The University of Minnesota," (university pamphlet, 1935), James Gray, *The University of Minnesota, 1851–1951;* various issues of the *Minnesota Daily* and the yearbook, the *Gopher.* The description of America during the Depression is drawn partly from William Manchester, *The Glory and the Dream.*

Chapter 4: UNIVERSITY YEARS

Along with the Donovan, Solberg, *NSWD,* and Gray, other sources on the University of Minnesota in the 1930s include George H. Mayer, *The Political Career of Floyd B. Olson* and Dan Cohen, *Undefeated: The Life of Hubert H. Humphrey,* which includes the Humphrey-Lippincott encounter.

Arthur Schlesinger, Jr., describes Laski's American influence in his review of Isaac Kramnick and Barry Sheerman, *Harold Laski: A Life on the
Left* (New York: Viking, 1993) in *The Washington Monthly*, November,
1993. The Laski papers, according to Kramnick and Sheerman, note
Laski's influence on ES. For background on the truckers' strike, see Solberg and Lois Quam and Peter J. Rachleff, "Keeping Minneapolis an
Open-Shop Town: The Citizens' Alliance in the 1930s," *Minnesota History* (fall 1986). My account is also based on the *Minneapolis Star* from
May through August 1934. George W. Garlid, "The Antiwar Dilemma of
the Farmer-Labor Party," *Minnesota History* (winter 1967), gives the
larger political context of the student demonstrations. ES describes the
antidrill campaign in the *Areopagus, The Cornell Journal of Opinion* (November 1934). Lee Loevinger's talk is in LC. For ES university years, I
interviewed Jeanne Sevareid Schmidt, Richard Scammon, Celia Brokaw
Sevareid, Mrs. Richard G. Abell (Nan Scallon), Earl Larson, Lee Loevinger, Arthur Burck, Al Kosek, Martin Quigley, John Lawler, Sherman
Finger, and Eben Finger.

Chapter 5: MARRIAGE

The information on Lois Finger and her parents and family comes from
interviews with Lois's brothers Sherman and Eben and, briefly, the
younger Sherman's son, Sherman III, plus stories from the *Minneapolis
Star,* the *Minneapolis Journal,* and clippings in the files of the *Minneapolis
Star Tribune.* The *Minnesota Daily* has stories on Finger's coaching career.
Descriptions of the Finger home and the university neighborhood are
based on my visit to Minneapolis and St. Paul. Also helpful in interviews
on this period were Celia B. Sevareid, Mrs. Richard G. Abell (Nan Scallon), Lee Loevinger, Richard Scammon, and Frederick Manfred. The
details of campus life are from either interviews, *NSWD,* or the *Minnesota Daily* and university yearbook, the *Gopher.* ES's academic transcript and Silver (January 5, 1956) and Frienrich (April 21, 1936) letters
are in LC. ES's brief version of the convention is in *NSWD* and the text
of the MacFadden speech is in LC. On the Dupont scholarship, see LC:
ES to Ralph Casey, March 29, 1955; Casey to ES, April 3, 1955; and ES
to Casey, April 8, 1955.

Chapter 6: FIRED

On the early days of the newspaper guild, see Michael Emery and Edwin Emery, *The Press and America* and *NSWD*. For Minneapolis newspapers, see George S. Hage, *Newspapers in Minnesota Frontier, 1848–1860*. Hage, an ES contemporary as a student, was on the *Daily* staff and a University of Minnesota professor until his death in 1994.

The *Minneapolis Journal* Silver Shirt articles were republished in a pamphlet, *A Reporter Tells the Truth about the Silver Shirts: An Expose of Un-American Activities in Minneapolis* (undated, in the Minnesota Public Library), along with letters and editorials from the *Minneapolis Star*, August 2, 1938; the *Minneapolis Journal*, August 17, 1948; and the *Minneapolis Tribune*, August 5, 1938. For historical background and William Dudley Pelley; see Leo P. Ribuffo, *The Old Christian Right: The Protestant Far Right from the Great Depression to the Cold War*.

For the influence of fascism on American politics, see Manchester. Frederick Manfred's recollections of ES are from my interview. Manfred, who corresponded with ES for years, died of lymphoma, September 7, 1994, at eighty-two.

Chapter 7: PARIS

The Murrow-Sevareid dinner story is told many times: in *NSWD*; in Ann Sperber, *Murrow: His Life and Times;* in Joseph E. Persico, *Edward R. Murrow: An American Original;* and in numerous published ES interviews and tapes. ES's reflections on the British are in *NSWD*, and also throughout Richard Critchfield, *An American Looks at Britain*.

I am grateful to Robert Alexander Marshall, former managing editor of the *Minnesota Daily*, who commissioned ES's dispatches, called my attention to them, and shared his analysis of them with me (Marshall to RAS, July 15, 1993). For the history of the Paris edition of the New York *Herald Tribune*, see Richard Kluger, *The Paper: The Life and Death of the New York Herald Tribune*; Al Laney, *Paris Herald: The Incredible Newspaper;* and Bruce Singer, *100 Years of the Paris Trib, from the Archives of the International Herald Tribune*. ES reminisced about those days in "I Remember, I Remember, (Those Americans in Paris)," an undated ms, probably 1940s, in LC.

Francelia Butler's reminiscences were published in the *International Herald Tribune*, October 3–4, 1987, and developed in an interview with me. The Ernst Adam and Karli Frucht episodes are in *NSWD*, and there are several letters from Frucht in LC. On ES's intervention for Frucht and Adam, see LC: Sumner Welles to ES, January 4, 1941; A. M. Warner, State Department, to ES, February 15, 1941; Malvinia C. Thompson to ES, March 6, 1941.

Francis Grierson's *Famous French Crimes* devotes a chapter to the Weidmann case. My account is based primarily on ES's almost daily reports from March 6 to June 18, 1939.

Chapter 8: FLIGHT

Tille Olson's reflection on the 1930s is in *Newsweek*, January 3, 1994. The history of early broadcasting is based on Edward Bliss, Jr.'s encyclopedic *Now The News: The Story of Broadcast Journalism;* Sally Bedell Smith, *In All His Glory: The Life and Times of William S. Paley*; the Sperber and Persico biographies of Murrow; Manchester; and David Halberstam, *The Powers That Be*. The brief biographical sketches of the journalists hired by Murrow can be found in *The Biographical Dictionary of American Journalism*, Bliss, Sperber, and Persico.

ES told the story of his CBS hiring several times: in *NSWD* and in interviews. The Charnley meeting is in William Hollman, "This is Eric Sevareid in Paris," *UP/Date* (summer 1980), University of Minnesota. On ES's response to the Poland invasion, ES told the story to Gordon Manning, who told me. The account of ES's movements during the fall of France is based on *NSWD*, interviews with Mrs. Jefferson Patterson (Mary Marvin Breckinridge), Joan Younger Dickinson, Larry LeSueur, and Francelia Butler. A recording of ES's broadcast of the Paris bombing is in the Museum of Television and Radio in New York. The *Herald Tribune*'s Walter Kerr in this chapter is Walter B. Kerr, not to be confused with Walter F. Kerr, drama critic for the *Herald Tribune*, and later the *New York Times*. The *Herald Tribune*'s account of Paris's last days of freedom is in Kluger and Singer's histories. ES tells versions of the Bordeaux broadcast in *NSWD* and "A Warning to Young Men," *Saturday Evening Post*, May 10, 1959. ES tells the Bunau-Varilla story in "The Man Who Invented Panama," *American Heritage*, August, 1963.

For general background and strategy of World War II, I used J. F. C. Fuller, *The Second World War, 1939–1945*, Robert Leckie, *Delivered from Evil: The Saga of World War II*, 1987, and standard reference works. ES describes the Lisbon interlude in "Lisbon—Escape Hatch of Europe," *The Living Age*, January, 1941.

ES describes the birth of his sons in *NSWD*. Joan Dickinson, Larry LeSueur, Lois's brothers Sherman and Eben have added information on the birth and return to New York. The details of the crossing and arrival are in Lois's *Minneapolis Star Journal*, June 11, 1940, report.

Chapter 9: LONDON

Some of the insights on Murrow's relationship with his staff come from conversations with Stanley Cloud and Lynn Olson, authors of *Murrow's Boys*. The description of ES's life in London comes from *NSWD*, Sperber and Persico, Smith's *Paley*, Larry LeSueur's script in LC, my interview with LeSueur, and the extensive interviews with the participants in R. Franklin Smith, *Edward R. Murrow, The War Years*. The status of the Murrow-Laski friendship is in Persico, who interviewed ES. The ES "world opinion" column, frequently reprinted, was in the *Reporter* (July 6, 1961) and in *This Is Eric Sevareid*.

Chapter 10: HOME

The Paley meeting and Winchell encounter are in *NSWD*. The ES draft cards are in LC. The script of the Election Day broadcast, as well as the other broadcasts referred to, are in LC. On Washington, see *Washington: City and Capital;* Volkmar Kurt Wentzel, *Washington by Night;* and Scott Hart, *Washington at War, 1941–1945*. On the proposed play, see ES to Robert E. Sherwood, February 19, 1941, and Robert Ardrey to ES, April 3, 1941, in LC. On the film script, see ES to Helen Meinardi, April 4, 1941, in LC. On Paul White, see Paul White to ES, July 7, 1941; ES to White, undated ms; and White to ES, July 15, 1941, in LC. On the Ardrey play, see ES to drama editor, October 19, 1954, in LC.

On the Louisiana war games, see *NSWD*, scripts in LC, and Robert Sherrod to RAS, June 14, 1993. Sherrod, a distinguished historian of World War I, died in February 1994. For the Rio conference, see ES,

"Where Do We Go from Rio?" *Saturday Evening Post*, March 28, 1942; *NSWD;* and scripts in LC.

Chapter 11: BURMA

The material on the Burma-China adventure comes from *NSWD*, the ES Associated Press story, "Head Hunters Save Downed Fliers," *New York Times*, August 1943; ES notes and diaries in LC; broadcast scripts and other memorabilia in LC; letters from William Schrandt to RAS, June 11 and September 14, 1993; and an interview with John Paton Davies, who was kind enough to read this chapter. That ES once considered the ministry is in a letter from Peter Sevareid to ES, undated, while Peter was at Harvard, in LC. On the Nagas, see Asoso Yonuo, *The Rising Nagas* and Julain Jacobs, *The Nagas.* On Stilwell, see Barbara Tuchman, *Stilwell and the American Experience in China, 1911–1945.* The ES Davies commentary, frequently reprinted, is in *Small Sounds in the Night.*

Chapter 12: CLIMAX

For the changes in CBS during the war, see Bliss, Sperber, Persico, and Smith. On UNRRA, see George Woodbridge, *UNRRA: The History of the United Nations Relief and Rehabilitation Administration.* On the Italian campaign, David Nichols, ed., *Ernie's War: The Best of Ernie Pyle's World War II Dispatches* and Martin Blumenson, *Mark Clark.* The ES-Gertrude Stein meeting is based on both *NSWD* and James R. Mellow, *Charmed Circle: Gertrude Stein and Company.* The text of "Only the Solder Knows the War" is in *NSWD.* The narrative of ES activities comes from *NSWD*, his notes and scripts in LC, and interviews with Sir Geoffrey Cox, Newbold Noyes, Larry LeSueur, Richard C. Hottelet, and Joan Dickinson.

Chapter 13: THE DREAM

Michael Sevareid described life at Carmel in an interview. Richard Critchfield shared his insights on ES in an interview, as well as in his several books. LC contains many letters, reviews and clippings on *NSWD*. And many of the letters to RAS about ES describe the impact of *NSWD* on its first readers. Samuyelk W. Stein to *Author Meets the*

Critics, November 2, 1946, LC. Feike Feikema to ES, December 3, 1946, LC. Reston to ES cable in LC. On Lois's health, interview with Joan Dickinson. On the Gitta Sereny relationship, Gitta Sereny to RAS, March 24, 1994. For Howard K. Smith's German experience see *Last Train from Berlin* and Bliss. For Norman Corwin, see *Current Biography* and Smith's Paley biography. Corwin and ES remained friends and corresponded occasionally for many years.

Chapter 14: VALLEY LANE

The description of Alexandria and the Seminary Hill neighborhood and home, the relationships between the Sevareids and their neighbors, and Lois's health is based on my visits, Virginia Foster Durr's *Outside the Magic Circle,* and interviews with Adele and Philip Stoddard Brown, Richard and Mary Scammon, Michael Sevareid, Tharsella Sevareid, Eben Finger, Nan Scallon Abell, Sherman Finger, Robert Syme, Jr., M.D., Elizabeth L. Sevareid, Kathryn Stone, Charles E. Beatley, Jr., Lee Hougen, Douglass Cater, Sir Geoffrey Cox, Joan Dickinson, Jane Fast, Rita Stearns Delmont, and Howard K. and Benedicte Smith. For the story of the founding of Burgundy Farm Country Day School, I am grateful to Ruth Woods, archivist, Kathryn Stone, and Rev. William Bason.

Chapter 15: FINDING HIS VOICE

The story of ES's loss of voice is in ES to Harry Harding, April, 1, 1947, LC. On the office at WTOP, Rita Stearns Delmont interview. On the Calvert ad, ES to William Cole, April 29, 1947. The relationship with Metropolitan Life is in a series of letters in LC: Davidson Taylor to ES, September 1, 1949; ES to James L. Madden, September 15, 1949; James L. Madden to ES, March 29, 1950; Madden to Marquis Childs, May 11, 1950. The descriptions of the various commentators is drawn largely from Fang and from personal memory.

Chapter 16: ADLAI

ES commentaries on the Korean War, Adlai Stevenson, the civil rights movement after the *Brown* decision, and McCarthy are reprinted in *In One Ear* and *Small Sounds in the Night.* The CBS history during this period is largely from Bliss, Halberstam, Sperber, and Persico. The ES-Adlai Stevenson correspondence is in the Princeton University Library, with copies in the LC. The Columbia University Oral History Project interview, conducted by Kenneth Davis, December 12, 1967, with ES on Stevenson is in the Oral History Research Office at Columbia University Library in New York. Interviews: Ernest Leiser, Dan Rather, Michael Sevareid, Sir Geoffrey Cox, Douglas Cater, Bill Leonard, Joseph Wershba, William Crawford, Ray Scherer, and John Bessor.

Chapter 17: DIVORCE

The description of the relationship between Belen Marshall and ES and of the divorce from Lois is based on interviews with Belen Sevareid, Jeanne Sevareid Schmidt, Michael Sevareid, Tharsella Sevareid, Eben Finger, Sherman Finger, Elizabeth L. Sevareid, Joan Dickinson, Bill Leonard, Perry Wolff, James Reston, Dan Rather, Sir Geoffrey Cox, Douglas Cater, William J. Small, Larry LeSueur, Ernest Leiser, James Reston, Emerson Stone, Sig Mickelson, Robert Manning, Howard K. and Benedicte Smith, Robert Craig, Nancy Bean White Hector, Adele and Philip Stoddard Brown, Helen Kramer, Richard and Mary Scammon, Robert Syme, Jr., M.D., Kathryn Stone, Jane Fast, and Lee Hougen.

The "Mano a Mano" article, originally written for *Esquire,* is in *This Is Eric Sevareid.* The columns concerning JFK, and ES's more conservative foreign policy views are also in *This Is Eric Sevareid.*

Letters in LC on Lois's health include: ES to Alice Drechsler, June 26, 1958; ES to Ralph Casey, June 27, 1958; ES to Tom Frost, November 12, 1958. On the trip to Spain: William Benton to ES, April 21, 1959; ES to Robert Craig, April 10, 1959; ES to Edward L. Cushman, April 17, 1959. On Belen, William Benton to ES, November 3, 1959. On the divorce settlement: ES to William D. Rogers, July 25, 1960; William D. Rogers to ES, November 26, 1960; ES to Dr. Morris Kleinerman, October 6, 1960; ES to Helen Sandburg Golby, November 4, 1960.

On the dispute over ES's column: Sig Mickelson to ES, Jan 6, 1961; ES memo, undated; ES to Nate Bienstock, January 20, 1960; ES to Mickelson, Jan 9, 1960. Interview with Mickelson.

On the contract negotiations: Richard Salant to ES, February 1, 1963; ES to Salant, February 11, 1963; ES to Bienstock, February 27, 1963.

On Lois's death: ES to Pat and Andrea Flynn, undated.

Chapter 18: VIETNAM

The introductory material on the sixties draws on Godfrey Hodgson's *America in Our Time*, Todd Gitlin's *The Sixties*, I. F. Stone's *In A Time of Torment*, Halberstam, Manchester, and personal participation in some of the events described, such as civil rights and peace marches, and the Democratic Convention in Chicago in 1968. My description of the Bradley Lane house is based on my visit to the site and interviews with those who lived in or visited the home. I have reconstructed ES's day through interviews of those who lived and worked with him: Belen Sevareid, Tina Sevareid, Michael Sevareid, Marvin Kalb, Sandy Socolow, Daniel Schorr, Suzanne Stamps Rheinstien, Edward M. Fouhy, Marion Freedman Goldin, William J. Small, Emerson Stone, Joseph Wershba, William Crawford, Jack Schneider, Walter Cronkite, Sig Mickelson, Frank Stanton, and Gordon Manning. Among letters: Jeff Duval to RAS, June 14, 1993; Kurt Vonnegut to RAS, April 6, 1994; Judith A. Fieldstone to RAS, on life in Chevy Chase, October 4, 1993.

The development of CBS's Vietnam coverage is from Leslie Midgley's *How Many Words Do You Want?*, Halberstam, Bliss, Manchester, Knightley, and the films of the various CBS Vietnam specials available in the Museum of Television and Radio in New York. As previously indicated, Sister Camille D'Arienzo's University of Michigan Ph.D. thesis, "Eric Sevareid Analyzes The News," is particularly strong on this period. Interviews on Vietnam and the China trips: Dan Rather, John Sack, Abigail McCarthy, Marvin Kalb, Suzanne Stamps Rheinstein, Edward M. Fouhy, Marion Freedman Goldin.

Chapter 19: NIXON

The description of Nixon's arrival in China is based on *The President's Trip to China*, with an introduction by *Baltimore Sun* correspondent and former Jacobin, Philip Potter; plus ES's notes and scripts of his broadcasts. The most helpful book on the Nixon period, particularly on Vietnam and Watergate, is Robert J. Donovan and Ray Scherer, *Unsilent Revolution*. Also, of course, Halberstam, Bliss, Hodgson, and Gitlin. The Safire memo to Halberstam is in William Safire, *Before the Fall: An Inside View of the Pre-Watergate White House*. The Teddy White-ES discussion of

Nixon as "evil" is in Philip Hilts, "Eric Sevareid Suffers Elegantly," *Potomac* magazine, December 14, 1975. Paley's late-night call to ES at home is in the transcript of ES's interview with Sall Bedell Smith.

Chapter 20: BELEN

On the North Dakota Senate race: ES to Larry Erickson, May 3, 1967; Erickson to ES, April 27, 1967 and April 25, 1967. On letters for Michael: ES to Sam Goldwyn, Jr., January 16, 1969; ES to Rosten, May 20, 1969; ES to Desmond Fry, May 18, 1970; ES to Michael, October 29, 1969. On Peter: Peter Sevareid to ES, May 31, 1970; Peter to ES, February 3, 1971. The ES-Cronkite memo on the Dallas broadcast is in LC, as are the ES-Teddy White letters over the convention coverage. The account of the Daniel Schorr–Nixon resignation controversy is based on viewing tapes of the broadcast, on Scherer and other publications, and on interviews with the participants: Schorr, Arthur Taylor, and Sandy Socolow.

Chapter 21: PEACE

The scene at the Decatur House is based on newspaper clippings and interviews with Jeanne Schmidt, Tina Sevareid, William Crawford, and other participants. Among the principal interviews that ES gave after retirement are: the "CBS News Special: A Conversation with Eric Sevareid," with Charles Kuralt, produced by Perry Wolff, December 13, 1977; "Eric Sevareid: He Was There," *Broadcasting,* September 12, 1977; "Eric Sevareid on Change in America," with Ned Scharff, in the *Washington Star,* November 27, 1977; *Ripon Forum,* November, 1983; "CBS, The First 60 Years," *Broadcasting,* December 14, 1987; a documentary on the twenty-fifth anniversary of Murrow's death, "A Man of Words, A Man of Truth," by Michael A. Hanu, for the Voice of America in 1990; and "Edward R. Murrow: This Reporter," the 1991 Emmy Award documentary for the *American Masters* series on Public Television, by Ed Apfel. I am very grateful for taped interviews on this period sent to me by Ray Scherer, Edward C. Brown, and Andrea Bresnick. On ES's trip to Berlin, Robert Henkel to RAS, June 7, 1993.

The picture of ES in these years comes from interviews with Bill Leonard, Larry LeSueur, Ed Bliss, Mrs. Jefferson Patterson, Robert Craig,

Edward M. Fouhy, Perry Wolff, Sir Geoffrey Cox, Dan Rather, Joan Dickinson, Michael Sevareid, Tina Sevareid, Richard Critchfield, Gerald E. Gaull, and others, many letters in the LC files on day-to-day matters, and other letters: Tom Farmer to RAS, June 8, 1993; Ed Apfel to RAS, June 7, 1993.

The description of the Warrenton cabin is based on my experience.

SELECTED BIBLIOGRAPHY

Alterman, Eric. *Sound and Fury.* New York: Harper's, 1992.

Ardrey, Robert. *The Brotherhood of Fear.* New York: Random House, 1952.

————. *Thunder Rock.* New York: Dramatists' Play Service, 1950.

Auletta, Ken. *Three Blind Mice: How the TV Networks Lost Their Way.* New York: Random House, 1991.

Baker, Carlos. *Ernest Hemingway: A Life Story.* New York: Charles Scribner's Sons, 1969.

Barnouw, Erik. *The Golden Web: A History of Broadcasting in the United States.* vol. 2, *1930–1953.* New York: Oxford University Press, 1968.

————. *The Image Empire, A History of Broadcasting in the United States.* vol. 3, *from 1953.* New York: Oxford University Press, 1970.

————. *Tube of Plenty: The Evolution of American Television.* New York: Oxford University Press, 1975.

Bayley, Edwin R. *Joe McCarthy and the Press.* Madison: University of Wisconsin Press, 1981.

Bliss, Edward, Jr. *Now The News: The History of Broadcast Journalism.* New York: Columbia University Press, 1991.

Blumenson, Martin. *Mark Clark.* New York: Congdon and Weed, 1984.

Boettcher, Thomas D. *Vietnam: The Valor and the Sorrow.* Boston: Little Brown, 1985.

Boyer, Peter J. *Who Killed CBS?: The Undoing of America's Number One News Network.* New York: Random House, 1988.

Burlingame, Roger. *Don't Let Them Scare You: The Life and Times of Elmer Davis.* Westport, Conn.: Greenwood, 1974.

Cohen, Dan. *Undefeated: The Life of Hubert H. Humphrey.* Minneapolis: Lerner, 1978.

Collier, Barney. *Hope and Fear in Washington (The Early Seventies): The Story of the Washington Press Corps.* New York: Dial, 1975.

Cook, Fred J. *The Nightmare Decade.* New York: Random House, 1971.

Critchfield, Richard. *An American Looks at Britain.* New York: Anchor, 1990.

————. *Trees, Why Do You Wait?* Washington: Island, 1991.

————. *Those Days: An American Album.* New York: Anchor, 1986.

D'Arienzo, R.S.M., Sister M. Camille. "Eric Sevareid Analyzes the News," University of Michigan, Ph. D. dissertation. Ann Arbor, Michigan, 1974.

Donovan, Hedley. *Right Places, Right Times: Forty Years in Journalism Not Counting My Paper Route.* New York: Henry Holt, 1989.

Donovan, Robert J. and Scherer, Ray. *Unsilent Revolution.* Washington: Woodrow Wilson International Center for Scholars and Cambridge University Press, 1992.

Doudna, Martin K. *Concerned About the Planet: The Reporter Magazine and American Liberalism, 1949–1969.* Westport, Conn.: Greenwood, 1977.

Durr, Virginia Foster. *Outside the Magic Circle: The Autobiography of Virginia Foster Durr.* University of Alabama Press, 1985.

Emery, Edwin and Michael Emery. *The Press and America: An Interpretive History of the Mass Media.* Englewood Cliffs, N.J.: Prentice Hall, 1988.

Fang, Irving E. *Those Radio Commentators!* Ames, Iowa: Iowa State University Press, 1977.

Fuller, J. F. C. *The Second World War, 1939–1945.* 1948. Reprint, New York: Da Capo, 1993.

Gates, Gary Paul. *Air Time: The Inside Story of CBS News.* New York: Harper & Row, 1978.

Gitlin, Todd. *The Sixties: Years of Hope, Days of Rage.* New York: Bantam, 1993.

Gray, James. *The University of Minnesota, 1851–1951.* Minneapolis: University of Minnesota Press, 1951.

Grierson, Francis. *Famous French Crimes.* London: Frederick Muller, 1959.

Gunther, John. *Inside Latin America.* New York: Harper and Brothers, 1941.

Hage, George. *Newspapers on the Minnesota Frontier, 1849–1860.* St. Paul: Minnesota Historical Society, 1967.

Halberstam, David. *The Powers That Be.* New York: Alfred A. Knopf, 1979.

Hart, Scott. *Washington at War, 1941–1945.* Englewood Cliffs: Prentice-Hall, 1970.

Hodgson, Godfrey. *America in Our Time.* New York: Vintage, 1976.

Jacobs, Julian. *The Nagas.* London: Thames and Hudson, 1990.

Keogh, James. *President Nixon and the Press.* New York: Funk and Wagnalls, 1972.

Kluger, Richard. *The Paper: The Life and Death of the New York Herald Tribune.* New York: Alfred A. Knopf, 1986.

Knauth, Percy. *The North Woods.* New York: Time-Life, 1972.

Knightley, Phillip. *The First Casualty.* New York: Harcourt Brace Jovanovich, 1975.

Laney, Al. *Paris Herald: The Incredible Newspaper.* New York: Greenwood, 1968.

Leckie, Robert. *Delivered from Evil: The Saga of World War II.* New York: Harper and Row, 1987.

Leonard, Bill. *In the Storm of the Eye: A Lifetime at CBS.* New York: G. P. Putman's Sons, 1987.

LeSueur, Larry. *Twelve Months that Changed the World.* New York: Alfred A. Knopf, 1943.

Manchester, William. *The Glory and the Dream: A Narrative History of America, 1932–1972.* New York: Bantam, 1973.

Manfred, Frederick. *Dinkytown.* Minneapolis: Dinkytown Antiquarian Bookstore, 1984.

Martin, John Barlow. *Adlai Stevenson of Illinois.* New York: Doubleday, 1976.

Matusow, Barbara. *The Evening Stars.* Boston: Houghton Mifflin, 1983.

Mayer, George H. *The Political Career of Floyd B. Olson.* Minneapolis: University of Minnesota Press, 1951.

McCabe, Peter. *Bad News at Black Rock: The Sell-Out of CBS News.* New York: Arbor House, 1987.

McKerns, Joseph P., ed. *Biographical Dictionary of American Journalism.* New York: Greenwood, 1989.

Mellow, James R. *Charmed Circle: Gertrude Stein and Company.* New York: Praeger, 1974.

Metz, Robert. *CBS: Reflections in a Bloodshot Eye.* New York: Playboy Press, 1975.

Mickelson, Sig. *From Whistle Stop to Sound Bite.* New York: Praeger, 1989.

Midgley, Leslie. *How Many Words Do You Want?* New York: Birch Lane Press, 1989.

Minnesota: A State Guide. Works Progress Administration. New York: Viking, 1937.

The New Yorker Book of War Pieces. New York: Schocken, 1947.

Nichols, David. *Ernie's War: The Best of Ernie Pyle's World War II Dispatches.* New York: Random House, 1986.

Norris, Kathleen. *Dakota: A Spiritual Geography.* New York: Ticknor and Fields, 1993.

Persico, Joseph E. *Edward R. Murrow: An American Original.* New York: Laurel, 1988.

Postman, Neil. *Amusing Ourselves to Death.* New York: Penguin, 1985.

Potter, Philip, and others. *The President's Trip to China.* New York: Bantam, 1973.

Rather, Dan, with Mickey Herskowitz. *The Camera Never Blinks.* New York: William Morrow, 1977.

Ribuffo, Leo P. *The Old Christian Right: The Protestant Far Right from the Great Depression to the Cold War.* Philadelphia: Temple University Press, 1983.

Rivers, William L. *The Opinionmakers.* Boston: Beacon, 1967.

Russo, Michael A. "CBS and the American Political Experience: A History of CBS News Special Events and Election Units, 1952–1968." Ph.D. dissertation, New York University, 1983.

Rutstrum, Calvin. *North American Canoe Country.* New York: Macmillan, 1964.

Safire, William. *Before the Fall.* New York: Doubleday, 1975

Schell, Jonathan. *The Real War.* New York: Pantheon, 1968.

Schoenbrun, David. *America Inside Out: At Home and Abroad from Roosevelt to Reagan.* New York: McGraw Hill, 1984.

Schorr, Daniel. *Clearing the Air.* Boston: Houghton Mifflin, 1977.

Schudson, Michael. *Watergate in American Memory.* New York: Basic Books, 1992.

Sevareid, Eric. *Canoeing with the Cree.* 1935. Reprint, St. Paul: Minnesota Historical Society, 1968.

———. *Not So Wild a Dream.* 1946. 2nd ed. New York: Atheneum, 1976.

———. *In One Ear.* New York: Alfred A. Knopf, 1952.

———. *Small Sounds in the Night.* New York: Alfred A. Knopf, 1956.

———, ed. *Candidates 1960.* New York: Basic Books, 1959.

———. *This Is Eric Sevareid.* New York: McGraw Hill, 1967.

———, ed. *Conversations with Eric Sevareid: Interviews with Notable Americans.* Washington: Public Affairs Press, 1976.

Sheean, Vincent. *Personal History.* 1935. 2nd ed. Boston: Houghton Mifflin, 1968.

———. *Between the Thunder and the Sun.* New York: Random House, 1943.

Shirer, William L. *Twentieth Century Journey.* Vol. 2, *The Nightmare Years.* Boston: Little, Brown, 1984.

———. *Twentieth Century Journey.* Vol. 3, *A Native's Return.* Boston: Little, Brown, 1990.

Smith, R. Franklin. *Edward R. Murrow: The War Years.* Kalamazoo, Mich.: New Issues Press, 1978.

Smith, Sally Bedell. *In All His Glory.* New York: Simon and Schuster, 1990.

Smith, Howard K. *Last Train from Berlin.* New York: Alfred A. Knopf, 1942.

Snyder, Louis L. and Richard B. Morris. *The Treasury of Great Reporting.* New York: Simon and Schuster, 1962.

Solberg, Carl. *Hubert Humphrey: A Biography.* New York: W. W. Norton, 1984.

Sperber, A. M. *Murrow: His Life and Times.* New York: Freundlich, 1986.

Steel, Ronald. *Walter Lippmann and the American Century.* Boston: Little Brown and Co., 1980.

Steffens, Lincoln. *The Autobiography of Lincoln Steffens.* 2 vols. New York: Harcourt, Brace, and World, 1931.

Stipanovich, Joseph. *City of Lakes: An Illustrated History of Minneapolis.* Woodland Hills, Cal.: Windsor, 1982.

Tuchman, Barbara. *Stilwell and the American Experience in China, 1911–1945.* New York, Macmillan, 1971.

Washington: City and Capital. Federal Writers' Project, Works Progress Administration. Washington: Government Printing Office, 1937.

Weisberger, Bernard. *The District of Columbia: The Seat of Government.* New York: Time-Life, 1970.

Westin, Av. *Newswatch: How TV Decides the News.* New York: Simon and Schuster, 1982.

White, Theodore H. *In Search of History.* New York: Warner, 1978.

Woiwode, Larry. *Beyond the Bedroom Wall: A Family Album.* New York: Farrar, Straus, Giroux, 1975.

Woodbridge, George. *UNRRA: The History of the United Nations Relief and Rehabilitation Administration.* Vol. 1. New York: Columbia University Press, 1950.

Yonuo, Asoso. *The Rising Nagas.* Delhi: Vivek, 1974.

INDEX

Abell, Nan (Scallon Taylor), 86, 107, 287
Abernathy, Ralph, 378
Acheson, Sec. of State Dean, 308, 326
Adam, Ernst, 121, 179, 192
Adams, Philip, 216, 217, 218, 232, 320, 416
Agnew, Vice Pres. Spiro T., xiv, xv, xvi, 385, 389; "instant analysis" condemned by, 167; Sevareid's analysis of, xvi–xvii
Agronsky, Martin, 324, 408
Alexander, Field Marshal Viscount, 242, 251, 252
Algiers: Allied command in, 240–241; Allied landing in, 202
Allen, Jay, 98, 111
Almazon, Gen. Juan Andreu, 186
Alsop, Joseph, 387, 411
American Experience, The (documentary), 19, 268
American Week, The, 320–321
Analysis: on *CBS Evening News,* 353, 356, 357, 361–363, 393–394; *vs.* editorial, 357; "instant," 167, 386–387; late-night radio, 230–231; new definition of, 411
Analyst: *vs.* commentator, 294; Sevareid as, 293, 302, 357
Apfel, Ed, 420, 421
Ardrey, Robert, 191, 194, 301, 324, 386, 337, 344, 394
Areopagus, Cornell University, 62
Arnold, Thurmond, 283
Association of News Analysts, 182
Association of Radio News Analysts, 293, 294
Atkinson, Brooks, 223, 225, 319
Atomic bomb, 306
Attica prison revolt, 352
Audience analysis, science of, 133
Audubon magazine, 29, 39, 41

Author Meets the Critic, 268
Awards: Dupont, 95; Paul White, 297; Peabody, 304, 312; Sidney Hillman Foundation, 322, 324; Teddy Roosevelt Rough Riders, 347

Bagdolio, Field Marshall Pietro, 242, 262
Baillie, Hugh, 138, 253
Baker, Russell, 425
Baltimore Sun, 58, 196
Basom, Rev. William C., 284, 285, 286
Bayley, Edwin R., 325
Bazelton, David T., 270
BBC, 240; Broadcasting House, 164; early broadcasting of, 110; E. Murrow's relationship with, 163
Bech, Dr. Joseph, 144, 179
Beebe, "Aunt Jessey", 15, 16, 17
Believe It or Not, Ripley's, 147
Bennett, James Gordon, Jr., 115, 117
Benton, William, 318, 337
Berens, Chief, 34, 40
Berlin: blockade of, 306; last visit to, 419
Between the Wars (documentary), 401, 418
Bigart, Homer, 240, 253, 369
Black Panther Party, xiii, xv
Bloomquist, Helen, 13, 14
Blumenson, Martin, 245
Bolitho, William, 123
Bosch, Juan, 368
Bourke-White, Margaret, 240
Boyer, Peter J., xviii, 370
Brandeis, Justice Louis, 58
Breckinridge, Mary Marvin, xxvi, 146, 151–152, 154, 185
Brinkley, David, 326, 355, 346, 402
Britain, Battle of, 161, 174; broadcasting of, 166–167, 168; Buckingham Palace, 177

Broadcasting industry, 130; congressional regulation of, 133; rivalry with newspapers, 135

Broadcasting magazine, 404, 406

Bromfield, Louis, 119

Brooklyn Eagle, 131, 240

Brown, Adele, 283, 323, 331, 339, 348

Brown, Jerry E., 408

Brown, Philip, 283

Brown vs. Board of Education Supreme Court decision, 314–315

Buchenwald, 172

Buckley, William, 345

Bullitt, Amb. William C., 118, 146, 154, 230

Bunau-Varilla, Philippe, 147–148

Burck, Arthur, 80, 81, 88, 249–250, 361

Burdett, Winston, 239, 355

Burgundy Farm Country Day School, 284–285, 286, 288, 289, 315

Burke, Edmund, 374

Burma: Allied invasion of, 229; Japanese invasion of, 200; march through jungle of, 217–218; Naga tribe of, 213, 217, 218–219, 231–233; plane crash in, 205–206, 211, 212; rescue from, 219–220; travel to, 208; village sojourn in, 212–217

Butchart, Ralph, 36, 40

Butler, Francelia McWilliams, 117, 120

Butler, Jerome, 117, 153

Butler, Nicholas Murray, 102

Calley, Lt. William L., Jr., xiii, 379

Camacho, Pres. Avila, 185, 186, 187

Cambodia, U.S. "incursion" into, 380

Cambrai, France, 150, 151

Candidates 1960 (Sevareid), 340

Canoeing with the Cree (Sevareid), 12, 25–40, 47, 51, 141

Cardenas, Pres. Gen. Lazaro, xiii, 186

Carmichael, Stokely, 374, 378

Carter, Boake, 134

Casablanca Conference, 242

Casey, Ralph D., 76, 77, 95

Cater, Douglass, 283

Cater, Libby, 283

CBS (Columbia Broadcasting System), 109, 135, 156, 203, 238, 255, 321, 356–357, 403; affiliates of, 380–381;

evening lineup of, 299; and firing of W. Shirer, 298; first job with, 139; guidelines of, 134; internal wars at, 424; last years at, 397–398; London bureau of, 251; long relationship with, 343; loyalty to, 328, 403–404, 408; major changes at, 344; Murrow's departure from, 173; negotiations with, 334, 346, 370, 394; neutrality guidelines of, 136; postwar change in, 272; programming policy of, 132; rivalry with NBC, 132, 134, 137; F. Stanton at, 133; and transatlantic broadcasting, 129–130; war correspondents of, 240; wartime broadcasting of, 136–137, 142, 154; wartime principles of, 140–141

CBS Evening News, xx, 64, 78, 167, 344, 358, 394, 406; analysis on, 353, 356, 357, 361–406; retirement from, 401

CBS News, xxi, 297, 380, 395; beginnings of, 131; ratings for, 424

CBS Reports, 340, 365, 410

CBS Views the Press, 296, 301

Censors: in early World War II, 144–145; and fall of Paris, 155

Censorship: and autobiography, 270; of China story, 228; of French press, 156; peacetime government, 327; and war reporting, 166, 201

Chaffee, Roger B., xxi

Chancellor, John, 386, 410

Charnley, Mitchell, 95, 138–139

Chennault, Col. Claire L., 206, 220, 227, 229

Chiang Kai-shek, Generalissimo, 222, 229

Chiang Kai-shek, Madame, 205, 206, 207, 211, 220, 225, 228

Chicago Tribune, 129, 145, 271, 275; Paris edition of, 136

Childs, Marquis, xvi, 311

China: Chungking broadcasts, 220–221; Communist victory in, 206, 230, 306; last trip to, 383–385; Nixon's visit to, 383–385, 386; return from, 276

China policy, essay on, 228–229

Chou En Lai, 384

Christian Science Monitor, 319

Churchill, Pamela, 262, 273

Churchill, Winston, 129, 163, 166, 176, 216, 227, 246, 252, 262, 264, 270, 273, 363, 414

Church of the Air, 134
Citizen's Alliance, 24; and *Minneapolis Journal,* 98; and trucker's strike, 72–73
Civil rights movement, 315–316, 340, 377
Clark, Gen. Mark, 195, 202, 242, 244, 248, 250
Clurman, Richard and Shirley, 391
Coffman, Lotus Delta, 44, 53, 59–60, 62, 64, 67, 68, 76, 79, 80, 81, 90
Cold War, 343, 364
Collier, Barney, 398–399
Collier's magazine, 15, 17, 257
Collingwood, Charles, xix, 165, 172–173, 239, 273, 293, 298, 331, 343, 344, 354, 355, 365, 408, 416, 419
Columbia Journalism Review, 346
Commentaries: demise of, 410–412; farewell, 403; popularity of, 320; suppressed, 362
Commonweal magazine, 324
Communism: democracy and, 114; during 1930s, 100; in postwar Europe, 262; postwar scare, 306. *See also* McCarthyism
Congdon, Don, 338
Conger, George P., 65, 66
Conversations with Eric Sevareid (Sevareid), 412–414
Cooper, Duff, 163, 177
Corwin, Norman, 278–279, 285, 297, 322, 416
Costello, Bill, 58
Coughlin, Father Charles, 90, 99, 102, 134, 310
Coventry, bombing of, 178
Cox, Archibald, 389
Cox, Geoffrey, 143–144, 237, 252, 323, 356, 409, 423
Craig, Robert, xxiii, xxiv, 331, 410, 419, 422, 423
Critchfield, Richard, 267, 420, 428
Croce, Benedetto, 247–248
Cronkite, Walter, xiii, xiv, xix, xx, 240, 326, 344, 354, 355, 357, 361, 364, 402, 419, 424, 426; debut of, 313; Sevareid's relationship with, 362, 395
Crosby, John, 299, 320
Cuban missile crisis, 341, 345
Culhane, David, xiii

Daladier, Edouard, 126, 148
Darlan, Adm. Francois, 157, 159, 189, 201, 202, 239, 241, 244
Davies, John Paton, 205, 211, 212, 213, 215, 218, 219, 221, 226, 230–231, 232, 264, 325
Davis, Elmer, 137, 151, 154, 197, 268, 292, 293, 294, 324, 333, 408
Davis, Richard Harding, 103, 115, 158, 194, 269, 270, 274
Day, John, 327
Dayton Daily News, 185
De Gaulle, Gen. Charles, 159, 241, 254, 258–259, 414
DeKoven, Jean, 122
Delta Phi Lambda, 47
Dempsey, Jack, 23, 34
Depauw University, 68
Depression, Great, 62; media and, 57, 129; school years during, 43, 44; travel during, 48–49
Determan, Anna, 70
Diamond, Edwin, 386
Dickinson, Joan Younger, 287
Dickinson, Nancy, 386
Diem, Pres. Ngo Dinh, 354
Dominguin, Luis Miguel, 337
Dominican Republic, intervention in, 317, 367
Donovan, Hedley, 21, 23, 24, 43, 44, 54–55, 62, 63, 67, 75, 77, 372
Douglas, Justice William O., 283, 391, 402, 413
Downs, Bill, 240, 262
Dreschler, Alice Fitzgerald, 50
Dreyfus, Capt. Alfred, 147
Dryer, Sherman, 58, 63, 92, 101
Dulles, Sec. of State John Foster, 231
Dunkirk, British Expeditionary Force trapped at, 152, 154, 169
Dunne brothers, 106, 72, 73, 74
Dunne, Peter Finley, 270, 416
Dunne, Philip, 416, 418, 412
Dunne, Ray, 73
Durr, Clifford, 282
Durr, Virginia Foster, 282, 286

Economics, London School of, 163
Eddy, Nelson, 89, 130, 132

Eden, Anthony, 163
Edwards, Douglas, xx, 307, 344
Edwards, India, 173
Edward VIII, abdication of, 109
Ehrlichman, John, 387, 388
Eisenhower, Col. Dwight D., 195–196,
    202, 235–236, 239, 252, 254, 273, 340;
    Crusade in Europe of, 269; media advisor
    for, 311; presidential campaign of, 314;
    on war correspondents, 238
Emerson, Gloria, 409
England, impression of, 111–112. *See also*
    Britian; London
Enterprise, 418
Erickson, Larry, 393
"Eric Sevareid Suffers Elegantly" (Hilts), 398
Espionage Act of 1917, 101
Esquire magazine, 338, 343, 354, 369, 394
Ethics: media, 171; of wartime journalism,
    140–141; *See also* Values
Ethnocentricity, 114
Everett, Willie, 34
Eyewitness to History, 344

Fairness Doctrine, FCC, 134, 405
Fang, Irving E., 294, 295
Farmer, Tom, 417–418
Farmer-Labor Party, 60, 61, 65, 69
Fascism, 24, 74, 89, 141; American, 102,
    201; art and, 256; democracy and, 114;
    as evil, 277; in Germany, 99; homegrown,
    90; in India, 210; Kuomintang govern-
    ment, 222; in Latin America, 187; of
    prewar Europe, 120; in Spain, 98, 100,
    102; and World War II, 180
Felix, Lt. Charles, 212, 213, 215, 233
Fell, John, 313
Fifth Army, 244: broadcast from, 246–247,
    248; and fall of Rome, 250
Fischer, John, 338
Fish, Congr. Hamilton, Jr., 102
Fitzgerald, F. Scott, 256
Flickinger, Lt. Col. Don D., 213, 215,
    216, 219–220
Fortune magazine, 264
Fouhy, Ed, 358, 360
France: capitulation of, 157, 162–163; and
    declaration of war, 142–143; detention

camps of, 145; landing in southern,
    252–253; liberation of, 258; public
    execution in, 127; Sevareid's flight from,
    157–159; troops of, 145–146; war plan of,
    143. *See also* Paris
Francis, Bill, 5, 10, 14, 15, 16, 17, 20, 45, 49
Franco, Generalissimo Francisco, 98, 100,
    102, 126
Free French, 159, 240
Free speech, 193
French resistance, 255
Friendly, Fred, 312, 355, 362, 365, 405
Fromson, Murray, xiii
Frucht, Karli, 121, 145, 150, 179, 192
Frye, W. Hamilton, 90

Galbraith, John Kenneth, 283
Gandhi, Mahatma, 210
Garlid, George W., 65
Gass, William, 269, 271
Gelhorn, Martha, 257
Genencser, Bro. Michael, 406
Gerasi, Frank, 257
Gibbons, Floyd, 129, 131, 158
Giraud, Gen. Henri, 202, 241
Golby, Helga Sandburg, 339–340
Goldberg, Justice Arthur, xiv, xv
Goldin, Marion Freedman, 359, 369
Gopher (yearbook), 45
Graham, Fred, 355, 358, 396, 402
Graham, Phil, 398
Grandin, Thomas, 138, 139, 142, 146, 155
Griffith, Major, 83
Grissom, Virgil I. "Gus", xxi
Gronvold, Dr. Frederick, 32
Growe, Joan, 95
Guild shops, 97
Guinazu, Amb. Ruiz, 198

Hage, George S., 46
Haig, Alexander, 389
Haiti, 367
Haldeman, H.R. (Bob), 384, 386, 387, 388
Halliburton, Richard, 269, 274
Handler, Meyer, 156
Hanoi, bombing of, 352
Harper's magazine, 188, 294, 338, 354
Harriman, Averell, 387

Harris, Jeanne, 416
Harsch, Joseph C., 297
Hart, John, 358
"Harvest of Shame" (Murrow), 412
Health, Sevareid's, 313, 321, 331, 368, 393; arthritis, 360, 364, 374; emphysema, 416; gall bladder surgery, 394; treatment for cancer, 423
Hemingway, Ernest, 55, 136, 171, 256, 258, 270, 274, 275, 337–338, 398, 407
Hemingway, Mary, 337
Hepburn, Katherine, 102–104
Herald, Paris, 114–115, 117–118, 124, 138, 155, 189
Herald Tribune, New York, 299, 320, 364
Herman, George, 387
Herodotus, 370, 371
Hess, Rudolph, 122
Hester, General, 195
Hills, Laurence, 115–116
Hilts, Phil, 398
Hirshhorn, Joseph H., 361
Hodgson, Godfrey, 305, 352
Hoffer, Eric, 359, 374, 412, 413, 414–415, 420
Holland, William, 398
Hollenbeck, Don, 296
Holmes, Justice Oliver Wendell, 58
Hoover, Pres. Herbert, 50, 92, 99
Hopkins, Harry, 72, 207
Hottelet, Richard C., 240, 355
Hougen, Lt. Col. John (uncle), 243
Hughes, Sen. Harold, xxii
Humphrey, Hal, 366
Humphrey, Hubert H., 43, 44, 54, 57, 58, 61, 72, 94, 375, 385, 402, 416
Huntley-Brinkley, news program, 326, 355
Hydrogen bomb, reaction to, 306

I. F. Stone's Weekly, 353–354
Information, explosion of, 411
In One Ear (Sevareid), 319
"Instant analysis," 167, 386–387
Iran, shah of, 409
Isolationism, 94, 193, 305
Italian campaign, 236, 242–244; Allied Headquarters for, 244–245; Anzio, 246–247; fall of Rome, 250; meaning

of, 251–252; success of, 251; and Yugoslav partisans, 245–246

Jackson, Jack, 19
Jacobin Club, 55–59, 78, 81, 105, 107, 179
Jardin, Renée, 125, 126
"Jingo Day," 69
Johnson, Pres. Lyndon B., xiii, 317, 318, 352, 361; relationship with press, 367–368; Sevareid's relationship with, 407; Vietnam policy of, 364
Johnson, Thrine Kristine (grandmother), 4
Jones, Pvt. Alfred, 34
Jones, Carl W., 46, 55
Jones, Herschel V., 46
Journalism: broadcast, 137, 165–167; "Chicago School" of, 131; graduate courses in, 79, 90, 91; "investigative", 413; moral dilemmas in, 106; "new", 354; principles of, 165–174, print *vs.* broadcast, 139. *See also* Broadcasting
Journalist: as hero, 270; as reformer, 274; as world citizen, 274

Kalb, Bernard, 355, 365, 387
Kalb, Marvin, 355, 358–359, 360, 387
Kalischer, Peter, 355, 365
Kaltenborn, Hans Von (H.V.), 131, 134, 137, 139, 154, 181, 293, 294, 295, 416
Kaplan, Sheldon, 68, 70
Kefauver, Sen. Estes, 313, 340
Kellogg, Sec. of State Frank B., 55, 60
Kemp, Betty, 34–35, 40
Kennan, George, 355, 405
Kennedy, Pres. John F., 316, 317, 340–342, 351
Kennedy, Amb. Joseph P., 163, 179
Kennedy, Sen. Robert, 316, 351, 377, 379
Kent State University, shooting at, xiii, 351, 380
Kerr, Walter F., 118, 144, 152, 154, 156, 194
Kilpatrick, James, 413
King, Martin Luther, Jr., 316, 351, 375, 377–379
Kintner, Robert, 328
Kirchner, Katri, 336
Kissinger, Henry, xx, 358, 383, 398
Klauber, Edward, 131, 134, 140

Kleinerman, Dr. Morris, 289, 339
Knickerbocker, H.R., 240
Knightley, Phillip, 177, 238
Korean War, 376; commentaries on,
    308–309; network coverage of, 307
Kosek, Al, 58, 70, 75, 76, 77, 78–80, 81, 88
Kramer, Helen, 12–13, 16, 347
Kramer, John, 13, 15
Kuomintang government, 222, 223
Kupka, Emma, 39
Kuralt, Charles, 355, 406
Kwoh Li, Lt. Col., 218, 227

Landers, Anne, 374
Larson, Earl, 57, 75, 80
Laski, Harold, 57, 58, 59, 97, 163–164, 227
Latin America, 185–186; developing
    countries of, 344; column on, 170
Laurence, Jack, 355
Laval, Pierre, 157
Lee, Capt. Duncan, 211, 213, 215
Lehman, Sen. Herbert, 315
Leiser, Ernest, 320–322, 362, 365
Leonard, Bill, xxiv, 360, 380
LeSueur, Larry, xix, xx, xxvi, 149, 171,
    175, 181, 202, 262, 269, 271, 275, 293,
    426; as CBS Russian correspondent,
    239; diary format of, 271
Le Temps, 148
Lewis, Fulton, Jr., 294, 295
Lewis, Sinclair, 89, 98
Life magazine, 206, 230, 296, 337, 372
Lindbergh, Charles Augustus, 60, 73, 136,
    193
Lindsay, Mayor John, xiv, xx
Lippincott, Benjamin E., 58–60, 76,
    88–89, 163, 227
Lippmann, Walter, xvii, 58, 97, 98, 116,
    120, 274, 303, 357, 368, 407, 411, 412,
    413, 414, 416, 420
Lisbon Clipper (Sevareid), 192
Loevinger, Jane, 375
Loevinger, Lee, 57, 66, 67, 71, 75, 76,
    77, 80, 86, 92, 93, 94, 110
London, 110; American correspondents
    in, 161; blitz of, 131, 161, 166–168, 189;
    bombing of, 189; last broadcast from, 178;
    major bombing of 175–177, Murrow's

offices in, 170–171; postblitz broadcasts
    from, 263; principles of journalism
    established in, 165–174
Long, Sen. Huey P., 89, 98, 99, 102, 310
Look magazine, 318, 321, 363, 364–365,
    368, 373, 394
Los Angeles Times, 366
Lowell, Thomas, 131
Luce, Clare Booth, 216, 362
Luce, Henry, 21, 206, 230, 259, 301, 353
Lutheran Church, 8, 14, 19, 23, 213–214

MacArthur, Charles, 220
MacArthur, Gen. Douglas, 308
MacFadden, Bernarr, 92, 93
MacLean, Norman, 422
MacLeish, Archibald, 196
MacLeish, Rod, 410, 412
Madden, James L., 301
Maginot line, 143, 145–146, 156
Mailer, Norman, 74, 270, 275
Manchester, William, 48, 102, 311
Manfred, Frederick, 60, 87, 104–105,
    106, 190, 269, 286–287
Manning, Gordon, 380, 384
Mao Tse-tung, 206, 383
Maquis, 255, 257, 272
Marketplace, 420
Marshall, Belen, 329–330, 337, 339,
    346–347. See also Sevareid, Belen
Marshall, Gen. George C., 196, 207,
    224, 230, 363, 413
Martin, Eben Wever, 84
Martin, Frank, 219
Martin, Lois, 84
Mauldin, Bill, 171, 240, 253
McCarthy, Sen. Joseph R., 102, 230,
    240, 294, 307, 323, 407; commentary on,
    325–326; fall of, 324
McCarthyism, 268, 306, 325, 391
McCloy, John J., 405, 413
McCracken, Paul, xiv–xv
McGowan, Carl, 314
McKelway, St. Clair, 219, 220
McKnight, G.W., 6
Meany, George, 315
Media: and American public, 129; and
    national purpose, 193; nature of, 405;

Nixon's control of, 385; and Vietnam policy, 364–365; war and, 116–117. *See also* Newspapers; Radio; Television

Media advisers, 311

Meinardi, Helen, 192

Memorial service, xviii–xxv

Messenger, Vinton, VA, 408

Metropolitan Life, 293, 295–296, 301

Metropolitan Life news, 299, 301–302

Mexico, CBS assignment in, 185–187

Mickelson, Sig, 312, 331, 332, 339, 343

Middleton, Drew, 238

Midgley, Leslie, 364, 380

Minneapolis Central High School, 23–24

Minneapolis Journal, 51, 57, 72, 81, 141; creative tension at, 105–106; K. Hepburn articles in, 103; F. Manfred at, 104; Sevareid as reporter on, 45–46; Sevareid fired by, 106; Silver Shirts articles, 98–102; workplace atmosphere, 97

Minneapolis, MN: 21–24, 72, 98

Minneapolis Star, 29, 30, 33, 34, 35, 45, 46, 63, 74, 98, 106

Minneapolis Star Journal, 98, 150–151

Minnesota, University of, 43, 44, 45; campaign against compulsory military drill at, 65–70; L.D. Coffman's tenure at, 53–54, 59–60, 62, 67, 68, 79, 80, 81; coursework at, 91; freshman year at, 47; graduation from, 90; Guild Lecture at, 324; Jacobin Club at, 56–59, 78, 81, 105, 107; last quarter at, 89; life at, 61–62; B.E. Lippincott at, 59–60; mock political convention at, 92–94; peace movement at, 65–66; student elections at, 85; student unrest at, 53; ties to, 94–96; and trucker's strike, 73

Minnesota Daily, 43, 44, 45, 46, 54, 58, 61–62, 75, 88, 91, 111, 112, 196, 375; anniversary issue of, 308; and campaign against military drill, 68–70; competition for editorship, 76–81; fiftieth anniversary issue of, 81–82; last article for, 120; and pacifist movement, 66. 67; rejection by, 79–82; Sevareid's work for, 65

Minnesota History, 65, 72

Moratorium, antiwar, 376

Morley, Christopher, 44, 76

Moro-Giafferi, M. de, 123, 126

Morrill Land Grant Act (1862), 68

Morrison, W., 375

Morton, Bruce, 402

Mountbatten, Lord Adm. Louis, 225, 229

Moyers, Bill, xx, 372, 395, 410

Moynihan, Daniel Patrick, 413, 420

Mudd, Roger, 94, 355, 358, 375, 387, 397, 402

Muehlhause, Mr. and Mrs. William, 406

Mumford, Lewis, 374

Munich crisis, radio coverage of, 137

Murphy, Charles, 389

Murrow, Edward R., 58, 61, 109, 127, 131, 136, 137, 157, 291, 293, 370, 404, 407, 416, 426; and advertising policy, 135; Allied policy and, 239; background of, 112–113; during Battle of Britain, 162; bomber riding of, 238; broadcasting style of, 165–166; as CBS vice president, 292, 296; character of, 164, 335; crisis point in life of, 261–262; death of, 366–367; on democracy, 168–170; eulogy of, 366–367; fame of, 196; health of, 146–147; job offer from, 138–139; on E. Klauber, 134; and Korean War, 307–308; London offices of, 170–171; mannerisms, 358; marriage of, 113, 114, 263; as media adviser to A. Stevenson, 311; moral standards of, 173; negotiations with CBS, 334; and Paley's leadership at CBS, 130, 333; and Pearl Harbor attack, 196; personality of, 113, 139; principles of, 165–174; return to broadcasting, 298–299; Sevareid as replacement for, 263; E. Sevareid on, 173–174; on Sevareid's enlisting, 203–204; as Sevareid's mentor, 162; television productions of, 296–297; testimony to, 412; and use of television, 334

Murrow, Janet Huntington Brewster, 109, 113, 114, 146, 196, 262, 263, 273, 334, 366, 424

"Murrow's boys," xviii, 162, 165, 181, 273, 313, 326, 328, 419

"Murrow's nephews," 355

Murrow's principles, 165–174

Mussolini, 242, 247

Mydans, Carl, 240, 249–250

My Lai massacre, xiii, 352, 379

Nagas (Burmese tribe), 213, 217, 218–219, 227, 231–233
Naples, broadcast from, 243
National Press Club: memorial service at, xviii–xx, xxiii–xxv; Sevareid's description of, xix
National Public Radio (NPR), 412, 420
National Review, 345
NBC (National Broadcasting Company), 181; early war coverage of, 136–137; rivalry with CBS, 132, 134, 137; and transatlantic broadcasting, 129–130; wartime principles of, 140–141
Neveu, Lt. Harry, 212
New Deal, 99, 188, 411
"New Journalism," 354
Newman, Edwin, 405
News: international, 131; television vs. newspaper coverage, xiv
Newspaper Guild, 97
Newspapers: effect of war on, 130; Minneapolis, 46, 98; *vs.* news broadcasters, 135. *See also* Press
New York City, 344; exploration of, 182; merger of newspapers in, 115, 116; return to, 181–182; Sevareid on, 110
New York Daily News, 202, 275
New Yorker, The, 238, 322, 338, 408, 421
New York Herald Tribune, 116, 144
New York Post, 109, conservatism in, 345; syndicated column for, 343
New York Times, xiii, xiv, 48, 104, 127, 134, 193, 204, 222, 223, 320, 327, 334, 354, 408, 409, 410, 420, 425; D. Rather's op-ed protest in, xviii; last letter to, 423; on S. Agnew, xvi
New York World, 134, 231
Nicholson, Dean E.E., 56, 67, 69, 77, 89, 92, 90
Nigeria: The Freedom Explosion, 343
Nixon, Pres. Richard M., xiii–xiv, xv, xvi, xx, 306, 345, 351; CBS analyses of, 386; in China, 383; condemnation of, 389; relations with the press, 385; resignation of, 355; "Saturday Night Massacre" and, 389; Sevareid's relationship with, 407; and Vietnam War, xxii; and Watergate, 387
Normandy, landing at, 251

North Africa, Allied invasion of, 201, 239
Not So Wild a Dream (Sevareid), 11, 12, 15, 19, 24, 25, 28, 29, 33, 35, 37, 38, 41, 45, 64, 71, 74, 81, 86, 98, 101, 103, 110, 121, 127, 143, 147, 158, 162, 173, 184, 187, 198, 208, 209, 210, 217, 225, 233, 253, 260, 266–270, 323, 348, 406; review of, 271, 279, 292; sequel to, 394, 420; writing of, 275–276
Noyes, Newbold, 86, 171, 253
Nye, Sen. Gerald P., 55, 75, 193

Oberholtzer, Ernest C., 25, 26, 27
"Objectivity:" journalistic, 407; and media ethics, 171; standards of, 131
Olson, Gov. Floyd B., 56, 60, 61, 69, 73, 76, 92, 93, 101, 272, 314
Olympic Games, 84, 85
Operation Anvil, 252
Oswald, Lee Harvey, 342, 365
Oswalt, Sgt. Walter, 212, 216
Overseas Press Club, 298
Oxford movement, 55, 66, 67, 75, 195

Paley, Dorothy, 134, 153, 273
Paley, William, xviii, xx, xxi, 129, 130, 181, 262, 272–273, 274, 320, 390, 401; advertising policy of, 135; and *The American Week,* 321; background of, 132; and censorship issues, 327–328; E.R. Murrow and, 296; guidelines of, 346; and instant analysis, 387; ratings and, 355; recording policy of, 167; special relationship with, 426
Pan American Conference, Third, 197–199
Paris, 114, 151; Allied headquarters in, 261; American hangouts in, 118; Bastille Day parade (1939), 142; bombing of, xvi, 153–154; and declaration of war, 142–143; fall of, 152, 155–156; flight from, 150–152; *Herald* offices in, 114–116, 117–118; last broadcast from, 155; liberation of, 254; refugee populations in, 120, 121, 151; Weidmann trial, 123–127
Parker, Dorothy, 298
Parvin, Albert B., 413
Patterson, Jefferson, 152, 192
Patterson, Mrs. Jefferson, xxvi, 185. *See also* Breckinridge, Mary Martin

Paul VI, xx
Peace movement, of 1930s, 55, 67
Pearl Harbor, 342; attack on, 196; losses at, 199–200; Sevareid on, 197
Peck, Gregory, 298, 320, 364
Pegler, Westbrook, 76, 98, 118
Pelley, William Dudley, 99, 100, 101, 201
Pelley's Weekly, 101
Perry, Lt. Col. William, 257
Persico, Joseph, 165, 298
Personal History (Sheean), 207, 269, 270, 275
Pétain, Marshall, 156, 157, 158, 159, 201, 222, 256
Pierpont, Robert, 355
Pius XII, 124, 250
Plymat, William, 75, 77, 88, 95
Poland, invasion of, 140, 141, 295
Port, Walter, 27, 28, 334, 425; later years, 38–39; reunion with, 39–41
Portugal, during World War I, 178–179
Potomac Magazine, Washington Post's, 398
Potter, Phil, 58, 62, 69, 196, 340
Press: "alternative", 353–354; and Pres. Lyndon B. Johnson, 367; McCarthyism and, 324; Minneapolis, 60; and Pres. R. Nixon, 385; Winston Churchill and, 163. *See also* Newspapers
Priestley, J.B., 168
Propaganda: German, 156; and Office of War Information, 294; wartime, 273
Public Broadcasting System, 268
Public opinion, American, 182; China in, 208, 222; and Madame Chiang Kai-shek, 206; and victory in Europe, 259–260; and Vietnam policy, 364–365
"Pundit, The," E. Sevareid as, xxvi
Pyle, Ernie, 166, 238, 240, 243, 246, 247, 259, 423

Quigley, Martin, 58, 63

Race riots, 322, 351, 379
Radio: 197, 230–231, 278, 293, 424; FDR's mastery of, 135; golden age of, 293; Munich crisis covered on, 137; news on, 165–167; programming for, 130; and rising popularity of television, 295; spread of, 130

Rather, Dan, xviii, 302, 355, 358, 370, 371, 387, 397, 402, 415, 419, 421–422, 424; hunting and fishing trips with, 426; at memorial service, xx, xxiii
Ratings, 293, 312; CBS News, 424; news programs in, 354–355; Sevareid's, 301.
Ravenholt, Albert, 219
Reader's Digest, 222, 228, 334
Reasoner, Harry, xx, 355
Red-baiting, 322
Red Scare, 80, 326
Religion, Sevareid on, 214, 234
Reporter magazine, 283, 320, 324
Republican Convention, 1964, 355
Reston, James "Scotty", xvi, xxiii, 177, 190, 264, 270, 271–272, 273, 303, 357, 360, 391, 407, 408, 409, 411, 426
Retirement, Sevareids, 18, 356; announcement of, 406; celebration of, 401–402; 159; plans for, 394; reactions to, 408; travel during, 416
Reynaud, Paul, 148–149, 155, 156, 158
Ribuffo, Leo P., 99
Ritter, Joseph Cardinal, 316
Robertson, Ben, 168, 175
Robertson, Nan, 420
Robertson, William C., 117–118
Robert Trout with The News Till Now, 297
Romer, Harry, 183
Roosevelt, Eleanor, 72, 121, 192, 196, 223, 315
Roosevelt, Pres. Franklin Delano, 55, 74, 92, 93, 99, 101, 102, 161, 185, 189, 413; China policy of, 229; death of, 272, and invitation to Burma, 207; isolationists and, 193; Pearl Harbor invasion and, 196; press conference of, 202; Sevareid's admiration for, 202
Roosevelt, Pres. Theodore, 28, 47, 146, 147, 413
ROTC (Reserve Officers Training Corps), at Univ. of Minnesota, 66, 68, 70, 183, 195, 307
Roundtable discussions, Murrow's, 262
Royal Canadian Mounties, 34, 40
Royster, Vermont, 410
Ruby, Jack, 342, 365, 394
Rutstrum, Calvin, 26

Sack, John, 344, 369
Saerchinger, Cesar, 109
Safer, Morley, 355, 365
Safire, William, 386
Sage, Robert, 117
Saigon, reporting from, 368–370
Saint-Exupéry, Antoine de, 152, 157
Salant, Richard, xvii–xviii, 343, 346, 354, 355, 365, 375, 380, 393, 395, 410, 424
Sans Souci, 29, 31, 34
Sarnoff, David, 132
Saturday Evening Post, 103, 195, 198, 328, 394
Saturday Review, 268, 292
Scallon, Nan, 86, 107, 287
Scammon, Mary, 335
Scammon, Richard, 57, 58–59, 66, 67, 68, 69, 70, 75, 81, 92, 94, 97
Scherer, Ray, xix, 301
Schieffer, Bob, 355
Schlesinger, Arthur Jr., 58, 311, 415
Schmaltz, John, 257
Schmidt, Jeanne (Sevareid), 402
Schmidt, Col. John, 331
Schneider, Jack, 355
Schoenbrun, David, 311, 317, 357
Schorr, Daniel, 355, 358, 396, 397, 412
Schrandt, William, 212–213, 218
See It Now (Murrow), xv, 299, 308, 312, 326, 328; on McCarthy's committee hearings, 324, 328; termination of, 333
Sereny, Gitta, 274, 426
Service, John Stewart, 230, 325
Sevareid, Alfred Eric (father), 3–4, 5, 11, 74–75, 87, 182, 322–323
Sevareid, Belen Marshall (wife), 345, 356, 423; later years, 393; and marriage breakup, 391–392, 399
Sevareid, Clara Pauline Elizabeth Hougen (mother), 4, 9–10, 323, 331, 360, 393, 428
Sevareid, Cristina (daughter), 19, 347, 356, 358, 363, 392, 394, 399, 401, 402, 416, 423
Sevareid, Eric: birth of, 8; conservatism of, 256, 344–345, 406; as cub reporter, 46–47; delivery, of 299, 302, 310; divorces of, 330–333, 346, 391–392; early years of, xv, 2–3, 6–7, 8–10, 13; education of, 23–24, 43–47, 59, 65; and fear of microphone, 166, 291–292; humor of 63,

320, 325, 325; image of, 174; as journalist-in-training, 50; legacy of, xix, 425; anxiety about money, 137, 287–288, 335, 401; name change, 119; personality of, 113, 214, 258; personal morality of, 173; respect for, xviii; work patterns of, 64–65
Sevareid, Jeanne (sister), 8, 121, 138, 331, 416
Sevareid, John (brother), 8, 101, 288, 323, 331, 402, 416
Sevareid, Lois Finger (wife), 84–88, 101–102, 105, 106–107, 137, 138, 148, 303, 326, 360; divorce, 330, 335, 346; flight from Paris, 152–153; health of, 273, 286–289, 330; later years, 347–348, 393; in Paris, 120; pregnancy of, 149; and twins' education, 285; UNRRA job of, 237, 241
Sevareid, Michael (son), xxv, 149, 152–153, 237, 267, 272, 284, 285, 288, 289, 323, 330, 331, 339, 348, 360, 393, 416, 423
Sevareid, Paul (brother), 8, 101, 288, 300, 323, 331, 347
Sevareid, Peter (son), 149, 152–153, 237, 267, 284, 285, 289, 313, 330, 332, 339, 346, 347, 348, 366, 393, 427
Sheean, Vincent "Jimmy", 164–165, 168, 175, 207, 222, 265, 269, 270, 273, 276, 277, 278, 287
Shepley, James, 219
Sheriff, R. C., 110
Sherrod, Robert, 194–195, 328
Sherwood, Robert E., 190, 191, 272
Shirer, William L., xx, 135, 136, 138, 146, 154, 269, 271, 293, 298, 322, 366, 404, 419, 421, 424; firing of, 297–298
Sieburg, Friedrich, 179
Sigma Delta Chi, 98
Silver Shirts, 180, 201, 306, 378; composition of, 99–100; reaction to articles on, 101–102; Sevareid's discovery of, 100; stories on, 100–101
$64,000 Question, CBS's, 326
60 Minutes, CBS's, 359, 410, 415, 424
Skinner, Mary P., 77
Ski-U-Mah, 54, 57, 76
Small Sounds of the Night (Sevareid), 340
Small, William, 357–358, 360, 361, 395–396, 401
Smith, Gerald L. K., 99

Smith, Howard K., xiv, xx, 239, 275, 269, 277, 296, 322, 336, 346, 386, 402, 414
Smith, R. Franklin (Bob), 165, 171, 172, 173
Smith, Sally Bedell, 133, 273, 328, 361
Socolow, Sandy, 358, 396
Southeast Asia, 352
Spanish Civil War, 116, 117, 126, 131
Sperber, Ann M., 147, 165, 166
Sponsors: and McCarthyism, 323; Metropolitan Life, 295; and program content, 297–299
Sputnik, Russian, 305
St. Paul Daily News, 72–73
Stamps, Suzanne, 359, 363
Stanley, Mike, xiii
Stanton, Frank, xviii, xx, xxi, 131, 133, 273, 343, 355
Stanton, Ruth, 133
Stanton, William, 211, 218, 320
Stassen, Harold E., 43, 44, 94, 340, 406
State of the Nation, 320
Stearns, Rita, 91, 287, 292
Steffens, Lincoln, 269, 274, 275, 277
Stein, Gertrude, 76, 119, 136, 256–258, 260, 274, 420
Stein, Samuel W., 268
Stevenson, Adlai, III, xvi, 363, 368, 413, 416; campaign of, 314; friendship with, 314; nomination of, 313; as potential presidential candidate, 310; and segregation, 314–315; Sevareid's article on, 318–319; as United Nations ambassador, 317; and Vietnam policy, 317–318
Steward, Prof. T.E., 77
Stewart, Jerry and Lisa, 19, 20
Stilwell, Maj. Gen. Joseph "Vinegar Joe", 200, 205, 207, 211, 220, 224, 227, 229
Stone, Emerson, xvii
Stone, Kathryn, 284, 285, 289
Stone, Paul, 285
Stringer, Howard, xviii, 424
Student demonstrators, 71, 76, 351; defense of, 376–377; Sevareid's views on, 373
Style, Sevareid's, 138, 169; broadcasting, 291; descriptive powers, 141; insights into, 208–209; prose, 154; rhetoric, 193; use of living metaphor, 248, 276
Sunday News Special, 344

Sunday Tribune, Minneapolis, 268
Sun Yat-sen, Madame, 222–223
Swope, Herbert Bayard, 231

Taft, Sen. Bob, 388
"Talking heads," 412
Taylor, Arthur, 396
Taylor, Davidson, 301, 302
Taylor, Edmond, 155, 157
Television: attitudes toward, 113; early, 110; increasing popularity of, 295, 312; McCarthy's committee hearings on, 324; E. R. Murrow's views of, 111, 333–334; national conventions on, 312–313; news mediated through, 354; reality and, 354–355; support of, 404–405; transition to, 321
Tet offensive, 352, 359, 364, 379
"Think pieces," 302
This is Eric Sevareid (Sevareid), 340, 344
Thomas, Lowell, 135, 294, 299
Thomas, Norman, 93, 99
Thompson, Dorothy, 44, 99, 116
Thompson, Frederick, 121
Thompson, Hunter, 354
Time magazine, 194, 206, 224, 229, 259, 264, 300–301, 306, 308, 311, 324, 353, 372, 391
Toklas, Alice B., 256
"Town Meeting of the Air," 194
Tree, Marietta, 318, 391, 413
Tribune, Minneapolis, 46
Trout, Robert, 136, 298, 355
Trucker's strike, Minneapolis, 53, 72–74
Truman, Pres. Harry, 230, 306, 307, 310, 311, 324, 341, 388
Tuchman, Barbara W., 230, 317
Twain, Mark, 28, 115, 208, 269
20/20, ABC's, 359
Tydings, Sen. Joseph, xvi

Un-American Activities Committee, House, 101
Unions: and Citizen's Alliance, 72–73; and trucker's strike, 73
United Nations: Cairo office of, 241; establishment of, 272; Korea resolution of, 307
United Nations Relief and Rehabilitation Administration (UNRRA), 237, 273

United Press (UP), 137, 165, 239
Universities: antiwar movement during
   1930s at, 66–67; and counterculture, 352
Ustinov, Peter, xxiv, 415

Values: American, 7, 267, 342, 352, 366,
   372, 425; celebrity, 60; education as, 43;
   fairness, 81; idealism and isolationism, 94;
   preparedness and perserverance, 38;
   Sevareid's, 413; wartime, 277; and
   wilderness adventure, 26
Van Buren, Abigail, 374
Vargas, Pres. Getulio, 198
Variety, 299
V-E day: celebration of, 419; commentary
   on, xxv
Velva Journal, xix, 5, 10, 13, 16, 18, 19,
   20, 45, 49, 78
Velva Valley Star, 19
Velva, ND: description of, 1–2, 3, 8–9;
   early years in, 2–3, 6–7; history of, 5, 12;
   population of, 5–6; Sevareid's return to,
   13–15, 18–19, 39, 264; Sevareid's view
   of, 12, 16–17; as spiritual center,
   275–276, 278
Vietnam: Eric Sevareid's Personal Report,
   371
*Vietnam—How We Got In-Can We Get
   Out?,* 365
Vietnam policy, 316, 318, 364
Vietnam War, xvii, 173, 268, 371;
   American pullout from, 355; commen-
   tary on, xxii–xxiii; evolving opposition
   to, 372–374, 376–377; issues raised by,
   352; Sevareid on, 359, 366–367, 368–372,
   407; stepped-up coverage of, 380
Village Voice, 353
Ville de Liege, 157–159, 189
Vogue magazine, 228
Von Braun, Werhner, 214
Vonnegut, Kurt, 361

Wallace, Vice Pres. Henry, 186
Wallace, Mike, xiii, 355
Waller, George Platt, 144
Wanger, Walter, 194
War: 204, 209; broadcast journalism during,
   165–167; and class differences, 177; corre-

spondents in, 151; declaration of, 141; and
   ethics of journalism, 140–141; "glory" of,
   246; newspapers and, 130; Sevareid's views
   on, 64, 144, 379–380
Washington Bureau, CBS, 203, 299
Washington, D.C.: city of, 187; news desk in,
   187; riots in, 379; Sevareid's view of, 188
Washington Post, xiii, xiv, xvi, 315, 324, 398,
   406, 408
Washington Star, 86, 171, 406, 413
Watergate caper, xvii, 359, 268, 386
Webster, Don, 355, 372
Weidmann, Eugen, 123–127
Weidman trial, 365
Welsh, Joseph, 325
Westin, Av, 397
Wheeler, Sen. Burton, 193, 194
White, Paul, 131, 135, 136, 137, 140, 141,
   148, 151, 193, 245, 249, 257, 294, 296, 297
White, Theodore H. "Teddy", 224, 229,
   270, 341, 346, 384, 388, 392, 395
White, William Allen, 115, 148, 149
Whiteside, Sheridan, 373
"Why I Won't Miss Eric Sevareid" (Emer-
   son), 409
Wilkins, Roy, 316, 415
Willkie, Wendell, 220, 222
Winchell, Walter, 27, 135, 182, 295
Wire services, 135
Wolff, Perry, 336, 406, 412
Woodbridge, George, 241
Woollcott, Alexander, 45, 169
Words Without Music (Corwin), 278
World is Round, The (Stein), 119
World War I, 60, 65–66, 68
World War II, 50, 70, 141, 409. *See also*
   specific events
Worthy, William, 327
Writing, vs. broadcasting, 425
WTOP, 189, 291

"Year of Crisis" roundtables, 355
Years of Crisis, New Year's Day, 320
Yore, J.J., 420
"You Can Go home Again" (Sevareid), 15
Younger, Joan, 153